THE FAKE BOOK OF EVERYBODY'S FAVORITE SONGS

WHAT IS A FAKE BOOK?

When a musician is asked to play a song he's never played before, he "fakes" it. One of the most valuable possessions any musician can have is a **fake book** which contains the melodies, lyrics and chords for hundreds and hundreds of songs. With the access to the melody, lyrics and chords, the musician can improvise his own arrangement of a song.

CRESCENT BOOKS
New York

ALPHABETICAL LISTING

Editor's Note to Guitarists: If there is no X or O over a string in a chord diagram, the string(s) should not be played.

A

10 A-Hunting We Will Go
10 A-Tisket, A-Tasket
28 Aba Daba Honeymoon, The
10 Abide With Me
11 Ach, Du Lieber Augustin
29 Adios Muchachos
12 After The Ball
13 Ah! Sweet Mystery Of Life
14 Air *(On The G String)*
30 Alexander's Ragtime Band
15 All God's Children Got Shoes
15 All My Trials
16 All Through The Night
16 Aloha Oe
14 Alouette
15 Alphabet Song, The
37 Also Sprach Zarathustra
17 Amazing Grace
17 America *(My Country, 'Tis Of Thee)*
18 America, The Beautiful
23 American Cadets March
18 American Patrol, The
28 Anchors Aweigh
11 Andante Cantabile *(Tchaikovsky)*
19 Angels We Have Heard On High
19 Animal Fair
20 Annabel Lee
22 Annie Laurie
21 Anvil Chorus
23 Arkansas Traveler
22 As With Gladness Men Of Old
20 Assembly/Reveille
24 Au Clair De La Lune
24 Auld Lang Syne
25 Aura Lee
25 Ave Maria *(Bach/Gounod)*
26 Ave Maria *(Schubert)*
27 Away In A Manger *(W.J. Kirkpatrick)*
27 Away In A Manger *(James R. Murray)*
27 Away In A Manger *(Spillman)*

B

38 Baa! Baa! Black Sheep
38 Banana Boat Song, The
38 Band Played On, The
39 Banks Of The Ohio
39 Barbara Allen
40 Barbara Polka
41 Barber Of Seville Overture, The
40 Barcarolle
42 Barnyard Song, The *(I Had A Rooster)*
42 Battle Cry Of Freedom, The
43 Battle Hymn Of The Republic, The
48 Be Kind To Your Web-Footed Friends
31 Be My Little Baby Bumblebee
48 Bear Went Over The Mountain, The
43 Beautiful Brown Eyes
44 Beautiful Dreamer
48 Beautiful Isle Of Somewhere
45 Beautiful Savior
33 Because
46 Beethoven's Fifth Symphony *(1st Movement Theme)*
44 Behold The Savior Of Mankind
45 Believe Me If All Those Endearing Young Charms
46 Bicycle Built For Two, A *(Daisy Bell)*
49 Big Rock Candy Mountain, The
52 Bill Bailey, Won't You Please Come Home?
32 Billboard March, The
50 Billy Boy
51 Bingo
34 Bird In A Gilded Cage, A
44 Birthday Song, The
49 Black Is The Color
53 Blessed Assurance
50 Blest Be The Tie That Binds
52 Blood On The Saddle
51 Blow The Man Down
53 Blue Bells Of Scotland, The
55 Blue Danube Waltz
54 Bluetail Fly
54 Boar's Head Carol, The
56 Boll Weevil, The
35 Boola! Boola!
55 Bowery, The
57 Brahms' Lullaby
56 Bridal Chorus *(From "Lohengrin")*
58 Bring A Torch, Jeannette, Isabella
57 Bringing In The Sheaves
58 Buckeye Jim
59 Buffalo Gals
59 Bury Me Not On The Lone Prairie
36 By The Beautiful Sea
36 By The Light Of The Silvery Moon

C

60 Caissons Go Rolling Along, The
60 Campbells Are Coming, The
63 Camptown Races
62 Can Can
61 Cantabile
61 Capriccio Italien Theme
65 Careless Love
65 Carnival Of Venice
64 Carol Of The Bells
64 Carry Me Back To Old Virginny
66 Chiapanecas
77 Chinatown, My Chinatown
66 Chopin Ballade No. 1
77 Chopsticks
67 Christ The Lord Is Ris'n Today
65 Christ Was Born On Christmas Day
67 Church In The Wildwood, The
68 Cielito Lindo
68 Ciribiribin
69 Clair De Lune
71 Clarinet Polka
69 Clementine
70 Cockles And Mussels *(Molly Malone)*
72 Columbia, The Gem Of The Ocean
70 Come Back To Sorrento
79 Come, Josephine In My Flying Machine
73 Come To The Sea
73 Come, Thou Almighty King
73 Comin' Through The Rye
78 Concerto Theme *(Rachmaninoff) - (Concerto No. 2, 1st Movement)*
78 Concerto Theme *(Rachmaninoff) - (Concerto No. 2, 3rd Movement)*
72 Country Gardens
74 Coventry Carol, The
74 Crawdad Song, The
75 Cripple Creek
75 Crown Him With Many Crowns
76 Cruel War Is Raging, The
77 Cuddle Up A Little Closer, Lovey Mine

D

82 Dance Of The Hours
80 Dance Of The Sugar-Plum Fairy
76 Danny Boy
83 Danube Waves
83 Dark Eyes
81 Deck The Hall
80 Deep River
81 Desperado, The
84 Did You Ever See A Lassie?
84 Dixie
85 Dog-gone Blues
86 Down By The Old Mill Stream
86 Down By The Riverside
84 Down By The Station
87 Down In The Valley
79 Down The Field
87 Drink To Me Only With Thine Eyes
85 Drunken Sailor, The
88 Dry Bones
89 Du, Du Liegst Mir Im Herzen

E

88 Eency, Weency Spider
90 Eine Kleine Nachtmusik *(Opening Theme)*
89 El Capitan
91 Elegie
93 Emilia Polka
92 Emperor Waltz
90 Entertainer, The
91 Erie Canal, The
94 Ev'ry Time I Feel The Spirit
94 Ezekiel Saw The Wheel

F

95 Faith Of Our Fathers
95 Fantasie Impromptu *(Chopin)*
98 Far Above Cayuga's Waters
96 Farmer In The Dell, The
105 Fascination
95 Fight Ye Bulldogs
105 Finlandia
99 First Noel, The
97 Fledermaus Waltz
97 Flow Gently, Sweet Afton
98 Foggy, Foggy Dew, The
96 For He's A Jolly Good Fellow
104 Forty-Five Minutes From Broadway
100 Frankie And Johnny
96 Freight Train
101 Frère Jacques
103 Friendly Beasts, The
99 Froggie Went A-Courtin'
102 Funeral March Of A Marionette
102 Funeral March
101 Funiculi, Funicula
103 Für Elise

G

107 Gavotte
111 Girl I Left Behind, The
108 Git Along Home, Cindy
109 Git Along, Little Dogies
108 Give Me That Old Time Religion
106 Give My Regards To Broadway
110 Gladiator March
106 Glow Worm
111 Go In And Out The Window
109 Go Tell Aunt Rhody
110 Go, Tell It On The Mountain
107 God Of Our Fathers
111 God Rest Ye Merry, Gentlemen
114 God Save Our King *(Queen)*
112 Gold And Silver Waltz
115 Goober Peas
113 Good Christian Men, Rejoice
116 Good King Wenceslas
114 Good Night Ladies
114 Goodbye Girls, I'm Through
116 Goodbye, Old Paint
105 Goodbye, My Lady Love
117 Grandfather's Clock
115 Green Grass Grew All Around, The
118 Green Grow The Lilacs
119 Greensleeves
117 Grey And Gold Waltz
118 Grieg Piano Concerto *(Theme)*
119 Gypsy Love Song
120 Gypsy Rondo

H

120 Habañera *(From "Carmen")*
121 Hail, Columbia
123 Hail To The Chief
124 Hail! Hail! The Gang's All Here
122 Hallelujah Chorus
123 Hand Me Down My Walking Cane
124 Happy Farmer, The
126 Hark! The Herald Angels Sing
136 Harrigan
125 Hatikvah
125 Hava Nagilah
126 He's Got The Whole World In His Hands
126 Hear Them Bells
124 Hearts And Flowers
127 Helena Polka
137 Hello! My Baby
128 Here We Come A-Caroling
127 Hey, Diddle, Diddle
127 Hey, Ho! Nobody Home
129 Hickory, Dickory, Dock
128 High School Cadets
129 Holly And The Ivy, The
130 Holy God, We Praise Thy Name
131 Holy, Holy, Holy
130 Home On The Range
132 Home Sweet Home
131 Honey, Won't You Come Back To Me?
132 Hopak
129 Hot Cross Buns
133 Hot Time In The Old Town Tonight, A
133 House Of The Rising Sun
131 How Dry I Am!
134 Humoresque
134 Humpty Dumpty
134 Hungarian Dance No. 5
135 Hush, Little Baby

I

135 I Am The Captain Of The Pinafore
144 I Gave My Love A Cherry *(The Riddle Song)*
144 I Heard The Bells On Christmas Day
137 I Love You Truly
145 I Love You With All My Heart
145 I Saw Three Ships
136 I Want A Girl
146 I Wish I Were Single Again
138 I Wonder Who's Kissing Her Now
146 I'll Take You Home Again, Kathleen
147 I've Been Working On The Railroad
138 I've Got Rings On My Fingers
148 Ich Liebe Dich *(I Love Thee)*
139 Ida, Sweet As Apple Cider
140 If I Had My Way
145 If You're Happy *(And You Know It)*
149 Il Bacio *(The Kiss)*
140 In My Merry Oldsmobile
148 In Old New York
150 In The Evening By The Moonlight
141 In The Gloaming
151 In The Good Old Summertime
150 In The Hall Of The Mountain King
142 In The Shade Of The Old Apple Tree
152 In The Sweet Bye And Bye
154 Invitation To The Dance
151 Irish Washerwoman
152 It Ain't Gonna Rain No Mo'
152 It Came Upon The Midnight Clear
156 It's A Long, Long Way To Tipperary
153 It's Raining, It's Pouring
153 Italian Street Song

J

157 Jack And Jill
157 Jeanie With The Light Brown Hair
158 Jenny Lind Polka
156 Jesu, Joy Of Man's Desiring
158 Jesus Loves Me!
160 Jingle Bells
160 John Brown's Body
161 John Henry
159 John Jacob Jingleheimer Schmidt
159 John Peel
161 Johnny Has Gone For A Soldier
142 Jolly Coppersmith
163 Jolly Old St. Nicholas
164 Joshua Fought The Battle Of Jericho
162 Joy ToThe World
162 Juanita
164 Julida Polka
163 Just A Closer Walk With Thee
165 Just A Song At Twilight

K

181 Keep The Homefires Burning
165 Kerry Dance, The
166 King Cotton
167 Kookaburra
163 Kum-Bah-Yah

L

167 La Cucaracha
167 La Donna e Mobile
168 La Golondrina
168 La Marseillaise
169 La Paloma
182 La Sorella
170 Largo *(From The "New World Symphony")*
171 Las Mañanitas
170 Lavender's Blue
171 Lazy Mary, Will You Get Up?
170 Let Me Call You Sweetheart
171 Let Us Break Bread Together
172 Liberty Bell, The
174 Liebestraum
173 Light Cavalry Overture
172 Listen To The Mocking Bird
175 Little Annie Rooney
174 Little Bit Of Heaven, A
175 Little Bo Peep
175 Little Boy Blue
177 Little Brown Jug
176 Little Buttercup, *(I'm Called)*
176 Little Jack Horner
177 Little Miss Muffet
177 Little Tommy Tucker
178 Lo, How A Rose E're Blooming
178 Loch Lomond
178 London Bridge
179 Lonesome Road
179 Lonesome Valley
179 Long, Long Ago
180 Looby Loo
180 Love's Old Sweet Song

M

188 Mademoiselle From Armentiers
187 Man On The Flying Trapeze, The
188 Man Without A Woman, A
192 Maori Farewell Song
189 Maple Leaf Rag
190 March Of The Toys
191 March Slav *(Tchaikovsky)*
191 Marche Militaire
190 Marianne
192 Marine's Hymn
194 Martha Polka
195 Mary Had A Little Lamb
181 Mary's A Grand Old Name
181 Matilda
192 Mattinata
195 Mazel Tov
194 Meditation *(From "Thais")*
182 Meet Me In St. Louis, Louis
196 Meet Me Tonight In Dreamland
197 Melody In A
197 Melody In F
198 Melody Of Love
196 Merrily We Roll Along
184 Merry Widow Waltz
198 Mexican Hat Dance
196 Michael Finnegan
199 Michael, Row The Boat Ashore
193 Midnight Special
193 Mighty Fortress Is Our God, A
199 Mighty Lak' A Rose
199 M-I-N-E
183 Minuet In G
200 Missouri Waltz, The
201 Moment Musicale *(Schubert)*
185 Moonlight Bay
201 Moonlight Sonata *(1st Movement)*
202 Morning
202 Mulberry Bush, The
203 Musetta's Waltz
206 My Bonnie
206 My Gal Sal
185 My Heart At Thy Sweet Voice
184 My Hero
186 My Melancholy Baby
204 My Old Kentucky Home
204 My Wild Irish Rose

N

207 National Emblem
219 Nearer My God To Thee
208 'Neath The Old Chestnut Tree
208 Nine Hundred Miles
209 Nobody Knows The Trouble I've Seen
210 Nocturne *(Chopin)*
207 Noel! Noel!
205 Norwegian Dance
211 Now Thank We All Our God
210 Now The Day Is Over

O

211 O Canada!
213 O Christmas Tree
212 O Come, All Ye Faithful
212 O Come, Little Children
214 O Come, O Come Emmanuel
212 O Holy Night
214 O Little Town Of Bethlehem
214 O Sanctissima
215 O Sole Mio
216 Oats, Peas, Beans And Barley Grow
215 Oberek
215 Ode To Joy
217 Oh, Dear! What Can The Matter Be?
216 Oh Marie
218 Oh, Promise Me
217 Oh, Susanna
218 Oh, Them Golden Slippers
216 Oh Where, Oh Where Has My Little Dog Gone?
232 Oh! You Beautiful Doll
220 Old Chisholm Trail, The
221 Old Dan Tucker
222 Old Folks At Home
209 Old Gray Mare, The
220 Old Joe Clark
221 Old King Cole
223 Old MacDonald Had A Farm
223 Old Oaken Bucket
232 On A Sunday Afternoon
224 On The Banks Of The Wabash
224 On Top Of Old Smoky
225 On Wisconsin!
225 Once In Royal David's City
226 Onward Christian Soldiers
228 Orange Marmalade Rag
228 Our Director March
226 Over The River And Through The Woods
227 Over The Waves

P

227 Pat-A-Pan
230 Peg O' My Heart
233 Peter And The Wolf
229 Pizzicato Polka
230 Play A Simple Melody
236 Poet And Peasant Overture
235 Polly Wolly Doodle
237 Polonaise, Opus. 53 *(Chopin)*
234 Polovetzian Dance
235 Pomp And Circumstance
238 Pop! Goes The Weasel
237 Praise God From Whom All Blessings Flow
239 Prayer Of Thanksgiving
238 Prelude *(From "Carmen")*
233 Put On Your Old Grey Bonnet
231 Put Your Arms Around Me, Honey

R

234 Ragtime Cowboy Joe
240 Rain-Rain Polka *(Prsi-Prsi)*
239 Red Raven Polka
240 Red River Valley
248 Red Wing
241 Reuben And Rachel
241 Reverie
242 Ride Of The Valkyries
243 Ring The Banjo
248 Roamin' In The Gloamin'
242 Rock Island Line, The
244 Rock Of Ages

243 Rock-A-Bye, Baby
244 Romance *(Rubenstein)*
245 Romeo And Juliet
250 Rondeau *(Mouret)*
250 Rosalie Schottische
245 Rose Of Tralee, The
246 Roses From The South
249 Row, Row, Row
247 Row, Row, Row Your Boat

S

251 Sailing, Sailing
252 Sailor's Hornpipe
251 Salty Dog
252 Santa Lucia
249 Scarborough Fair
253 Schnitzelbank
263 School Days
251 Scotland The Brave *(Tunes Of Glory)*
256 Semper Fidelis
254 Serenade *(Drigo)*
254 Serenade *(Schubert)*
255 Serenade *(Toselli)*
255 Shall We Gather At The River
257 She Is More To Be Pitied Than Censured
257 She Wore A Yellow Ribbon
258 She'll Be Comin' 'Round The Mountain
258 Shenandoah
276 Shine On Harvest Moon
275 Shoo, Fly, Don't Bother Me
259 Shortnin' Bread
260 Sidewalks Of New York, The
260 Silent Night
259 Silver Threads Among The Gold
261 Simple Simon
273 Sing A Song Of Sixpence
262 Sing We Now Of Christmas
261 Skaters, The
262 Skip To My Lou
262 Sleep Holy Babe
264 Sleeping Beauty Waltz *(Tchaikovsky)*
265 Sometimes I Feel Like A Motherless Child
264 Song Of India
265 Song Of The Volga Boatman
266 Sound Off
266 Spring Song *(Mendelssohn)*
267 St. James Infirmary
276 St. Louis Blues
268 Star Spangled Banner, The
268 Stars And Stripes Forever
270 Streets Of Laredo, The
270 Surprise Symphony *(Theme)*
271 Swan Lake *(Theme)*
278 Swan, The
279 Sweet Adeline
271 Sweet And Low
274 Sweet Betsy From Pike
272 Sweet Genevieve
278 Sweet Rosie O'Grady
280 Sweetheart Of Sigma Chi, The
272 Sweethearts
273 Swing Low, Sweet Chariot

T

287 Ta-Ra-Ra Boom-Der-É
282 Take Me Out To The Ball Game
290 Tales From The Vienna Woods
279 Tango *(Albeniz)*
274 Taps
288 Tarantella
287 Tchaikovsky Piano Concerto *(1st Movement)*
289 Tchaikovsky Symphony No. 6 *(1st Movement)*
289 Tell Me Why
288 Ten Little Indians
292 Tenting Tonight
280 That's A Plenty
275 That's Why I Do Like I Do
294 There Is A Tavern In The Town
291 There Was An Old Woman Who Lived In A Shoe
282 There's A Long, Long Trail
283 They Didn't Believe Me
292 This Old Man
293 This Train
295 Three Blind Mice
295 Thunder And Blazes
296 Thunderer
298 Tinker Polka
298 Tit-Willow
299 To A Wild Rose
283 Too-Ra-Loo-Ra-Loo-Ral *(That's An Irish Lullaby)*
297 Toreador Song *(Bizet)*
302 Tourelay, Tourelay
300 Toyland
286 Trail Of The Lonesome Pine, The
297 Tramp! Tramp! Tramp!
300 Traumerei
302 Triumphal March *(From "Aida")*
301 Trumpet Tune
304 Trumpet Voluntary
301 Turkey In The Straw
304 Turkish March
284 12th Street Rag
305 Twelve Days Of Christmas, The
303 Twinkle, Twinkle, Little Star
306 Two Guitars

U

306 Under The Double Eagle
308 Unfinished Symphony, The *(Theme)*
309 University Of Michigan Song
307 Up On The Housetop

V

310 Valse Bleue
308 Venetian Boat Song
309 Vienna Life
312 Vilia
310 Vive L'Amour

W

311 Wabash Cannon Ball, The
312 Wait Till The Sun Shines, Nellie
313 Wait For The Wagon
330 Waiting For The Robert E. Lee
313 Waltz *(Brahms)*
314 Waltz *(Chopin)*
314 Waltz Of The Flowers
332 Washington And Lee Swing
316 Washington Post March
316 Wayfaring Stranger
315 We Three Kings Of Orient Are
318 We Wish You A Merry Christmas
318 Wearing Of The Green, The
317 Wedding March
319 Were You There?
320 What A Friend We Have In Jesus
321 What Child Is This?
321 When Irish Eyes Are Smiling
320 When Johnny Comes Marching Home
322 When The Saints Go Marching In
324 When You And I Were Young, Maggie
322 When You Were Sweet Sixteen
331 When You Wore A Tulip
324 When You're Away
326 While Shepherds Watched Their Flocks
325 While Strolling Through The Park One Day
323 Whispering Hope
332 Whistler And His Dog, The
325 White Coral Bells
327 Who Threw The Overalls In Mrs. Murphy's Chowder
326 Will The Circle Be Unbroken
328 William Tell Overture
327 Worried Man Blues

Y

329 Yankee Doodle
334 Yankee Doodle Boy, The
336 Yellow Rose Of Texas, The
335 You Are My True Love
333 You Made Me Love You
335 You Tell Me Your Dream
334 You're A Grand Old Flag

Z

335 Zum Gali Gali

CLASSIFIED LISTING

Children's Songs

10 A-Hunting We Will Go
10 A-Tisket, A-Tasket
15 All God's Children Got Shoes
14 Alouette
15 Alphabet Song
19 Animal Fair
24 Au Clair De La Lune
38 Baa! Baa! Black Sheep
42 Barnyard Song, The (I Had A Rooster)
48 Be Kind To Your Web-Footed Friends
48 Bear Went Over The Mountain, The
50 Billy Boy
51 Bingo
51 Blow The Man Down
57 Brahms' Lullaby
63 Camptown Races
77 Chopsticks
72 Country Gardens
84 Did You Ever See A Lassie?
84 Down By The Station
88 Eency, Weency Spider
96 Farmer In The Dell, The
101 Frère Jacques
108 Git Along Home, Cindy
111 Go In And Out The Window
109 Go Tell Aunt Rhody
117 Grandfather's Clock
115 Green Grass Grew All Around, The
127 Hey, Diddle, Diddle
127 Hey, Ho! Nobody Home
129 Hickory, Dickory, Dock
129 Hot Cross Buns
134 Humpty Dumpty
135 Hush, Little Baby
147 I've Been Working On The Railroad
145 If You're Happy (And You Know It)
152 It Ain't Gonna Rain No Mo'
153 It's Raining, It's Pouring
157 Jack And Jill
159 John Jacob Jingleheimer Schmidt
167 Kookaburra
171 Lazy Mary, Will You Get Up?
175 Little Bo Peep
175 Little Boy Blue
176 Little Jack Horner
177 Little Miss Muffet
177 Little Tommy Tucker
178 London Bridge
180 Looby Lou
195 Mary Had A Little Lamb
196 Merrily We Roll Along
196 Michael Finnegan
202 Mulberry Bush, The
216 Oats, Peas, Beans And Barley Grow
216 Oh Where, Oh Where Has My Little Dog Gone?
209 Old Gray Mare, The
221 Old King Cole
223 Old MacDonald Had A Farm
226 Over The River And Through The Woods
233 Peter And The Wolf
235 Polly Wolly Doodle
238 Pop! Goes The Weasel
241 Reuben And Rachel
243 Rock-A-Bye, Baby
247 Row, Row, Row Your Boat
251 Sailing, Sailing
259 Shortnin' Bread
261 Simple Simon
273 Sing A Song Of Sixpence
262 Skip To My Lou
288 Ten Little Indians
291 There Was An Old Woman Who Lived In A Shoe
292 This Old Man
295 Three Blind Mice
302 Tourelay, Tourelay
303 Twinkle, Twinkle Little Star
325 White Coral Bells

Christmas Carols

16 All Through The Night
19 Angels We Have Heard On High
22 As With Gladness Men Of Old
27 Away In A Manger (W.J. Kirkpatrick)
27 Away In A Manger (Murray)
27 Away In A Manger (Spillman)
54 Boar's Head Carol, The
58 Bring A Torch, Jeannette, Isabella
64 Carol Of The Bells
65 Christ Was Born On Christmas Day
74 Coventry Carol, The
80 Dance Of The Sugar-Plum Fairy
81 Deck The Hall
99 First Noel, The
103 Friendly Beasts, The
110 Go, Tell It On The Mountain
111 God Rest Ye Merry, Gentlemen
113 Good Christian Men, Rejoice
116 Good King Wenceslas
126 Hark! The Herald Angels Sing
128 Here We Come A-Caroling
129 Holly And The Ivy, The
144 I Heard The Bells On Christmas Day
145 I Saw Three Ships
152 It Came Upon The Midnight Clear
160 Jingle Bells
163 Jolly Old St. Nicholas
162 Joy To The World
178 Lo, How A Rose E're Blooming
190 March Of The Toys
207 Noel! Noel!
213 O Christmas Tree
212 O Come, Al l Ye Faithful
212 O Come, Little Children
214 O Come, O Come Emmanuel
212 O Holy Night
214 O Little Town Of Bethlehem
214 O Sanctissima
225 Once In Royal David's City
227 Pat-A-Pan
260 Silent Night
262 Sing We Now Of Christmas
262 Sleep Holy Babe
305 Twelve Days Of Christmas, The
307 Up On The Housetop
315 We Three Kings Of Orient Are
318 We Wish You A Merry Christmas
321 What Child Is This?
326 While Shepherds Watched Their Flocks

Classics

14 Air (On The G String)
37 Also Sprach Zarathustra
11 Andante Cantabile (Tchaikovsky)
21 Anvil Chorus (from "Il Trovatore")
25 Ave Maria (Bach/Gounod)
26 Ave Maria (Schubert)
41 Barber Of Seville Overture, The
40 Barcarolle (From "Tales of Hoffman")
46 Beethoven's 5th Symphony (1st Movement Theme)
55 Blue Danube Waltz
57 Brahms' Lullaby
56 Bridal Chorus (From "Lohengrin")
62 Can Can
61 Cantabile
61 Capriccio Italien (Theme)
66 Chopin Ballade No. 1
69 Clair De Lune
78 Concerto Theme (Rachmaninoff) (Concerto No. 2, 1st Movement)
78 Concerto Theme (Rachmaninoff) (Concerto No. 2, 3rd Movement)
82 Dance Of The Hours
80 Dance Of The Sugar-Plum Fairy
83 Danube Waves
90 Eine Kleine Nachtmusik (Opening Theme)
91 Elegie
95 Fantaisie-Impromptu (Chopin)
105 Finlandia
102 Funeral March Of A Marionette
102 Funeral March
103 Für Elise
107 Gavotte
112 Gold And Silver Waltz
118 Grieg Piano Concerto (Theme)
120 Gypsy Rondo
122 Hallelujah Chorus
124 Happy Farmer, The
132 Hopak
134 Humoresque
134 Hungarian Dance No. 5
135 I Am The Captain Of The Pinafore
148 Ich Liebe Dich (I Love Thee)
148 Il Bacio (The Kiss)
150 In The Hall Of The Mountain King
154 Invitation To The Dance
156 Jesu, Joy Of Man's Desiring
167 La Donna è Mobile (From "Rigoletto")
170 Largo (From "The New World Symphony")
174 Liebestraum
173 Light Cavalry Overture
176 Little Buttercup, (I'm Called)
191 March Slav (Tchaikovsky)
191 Marche Militaire
192 Mattinata
194 Meditation (From "Thais")
197 Melody In F
184 Merry Widow Waltz
183 Minuet in G (Padrewski)
201 Moment Musicale (Schubert)
201 Moonlight Sonata (1st Movement)
202 Morning (From "Peer Gynt")
203 Musetta's Waltz (From "La Boheme")
185 My Heart At Thy Sweet Voice
210 Nocturne (Chopin)
205 Norwegian Dance
215 Ode To Joy
233 Peter And The Wolf
229 Pizzicato Polka
236 Poet And Peasant Overture
237 Polonaise, Opus. 53 (Chopin)
234 Polovetzian Dance
238 Prelude (From "Carmen")
241 Reverie
242 Ride Of The Valkyries
244 Romance (Rubenstein)
245 Romeo And Juliet (Tchaikovsky)
250 Rondeau (Mouret)
254 Serenade (Drigo)
254 Serenade (Schubert)
255 Serenade (Toselli)
261 Skaters, The
264 Sleeping Beauty Waltz (Tchaikovsky)
264 Song Of India
266 Spring Song (Mendelssohn)
270 Surprise Symphony (Theme)
271 Swan Lake *(Theme)*
278 Swan, The
290 Tales From The Vienna Woods
279 Tango (Albeniz)
287 Tchaikovsky Piano Concerto (1st Movement)
289 Tchaikovsky Symphony No. 6 (1st Movement)
298 Tit-Willow
299 To A Wild Rose
297 Toreador Song (Bizet)
300 Traumerei
302 Triumphal March (From "Aida")
301 Trumpet Tune

304 Trumpet Voluntary
304 Turkish March
306 Two Guitars
308 Unfinished Symphony, The (Theme)
310 Valse Bleue
308 Venetian Boat Song
309 Vienna Life
313 Waltz (Brahms)
314 Waltz (Chopin)
314 Waltz Of The Flowers (Tchaikovsky)
317 Wedding March
328 William Tell Overture

Country/Bluegrass

23 Arkansas Traveler
25 Aura Lee
43 Beautiful Brown Eyes
59 Bury Me Not On The Lone Prairie
65 Careless Love
75 Cripple Creek
87 Down In The Valley
109 Git Along, Little Dogies
116 Goodbye, Old Paint
117 Grandfather's Clock
130 Home On The Range
152 In The Sweet Bye And Bye
220 Old Chisholm Trail, The
221 Old Joe Clark
224 On Top Of Old Smoky
240 Red River Valley
248 Red Wing
242 Rock Island Line, The
251 Salty Dog
301 Turkey In The Straw
326 Will The Circle Be Unbroken

Folk Songs

15 All My Trials
16 All Through The Night
14 Alouette
17 Amazing Grace
20 Annabel Lee
22 Annie Laurie
23 Arkansas Traveler
24 Auld Lang Syne
25 Aura Lee
38 Banana Boat Song, The
39 Banks Of The Ohio
39 Barbara Allen
43 Beautiful Brown Eyes
45 Believe Me If All Those Endearing Young Charms
49 Big Rock Candy Mountain, The
49 Black Is The Color
52 Blood On The Saddle
51 Blow The Man Down
53 Blue Bells Of Scotland
54 Bluetail Fly
56 Boll Weevil, The
58 Buckeye Jim
59 Buffalo Gals
59 Bury Me Not On The Lone Prairie
65 Careless Love
69 Clementine
74 Crawdad Song, The
75 Cripple Creek
76 Cruel War Is Raging, The
84 Dixie
87 Down In The Valley
87 Drink To Me Only With Thine Eyes
85 Drunken Sailor, The
91 Erie Canal, The
97 Flow Gently, Sweet Afton
98 Foggy, Foggy Dew, The
100 Frankie And Johnny
96 Freight Train
99 Froggie Went A-Courtin'
96 Girl I Left Behind, The
108 Git Along Home, Cindy
109 Git Along, Little Dogies
115 Goober Peas
116 Goodbye, Old Paint
118 Green Grow The Lilacs
119 Greensleeves
126 Hear Them Bells
132 Home Sweet Home
133 House Of The Rising Sun
144 I Gave My Love A Cherry (The Riddle Song)
147 I've Been Working On The Railroad
160 John Brown's Body
161 John Henry
161 Johnny Has Gone For A Soldier
170 Lavender's Blue
177 Little Brown Jug
179 Lonesome Road
190 Marianne
181 Matilda
199 Michael, Row The Boat Ashore
193 Midnight Special
206 My Bonnie
208 Nine Hundred Miles
218 Oh, Them Golden Slippers
220 Old Chisholm Trail, The
221 Old Dan Tucker
220 Old Joe Clark
224 On Top Of Old Smoky
240 Red River Valley
242 Rock Island Line, The
245 Rose Of Tralee, The
252 Sailors Hornpipe
251 Salty Dog
249 Scarborough Fair
257 She Wore A Yellow Ribbon
258 She'll Be Comin' 'Round The Mountain
258 Shenandoah
275 Shoo, Fly, Don't Bother Me
259 Shortnin' Bread
262 Skip To My Lou
265 Sometimes I Feel Like A Motherless Child
267 St. James Infirmary
270 Streets Of Laredo, The
271 Sweet And Low
274 Sweet Betsy From Pike
293 This Train
301 Turkey In The Straw
312 Vilia
313 Wait For The Wagon
316 Wayfaring Stranger
320 When Johnny Comes Marching Home
327 Worried Man Blues
329 Yankee Doodle
336 Yellow Rose Of Texas, The

From the Musical Stage

13 Ah! Sweet Mystery Of Life
119 Gypsy Love Song
120 Habañera (From "Carmen")
135 I Am The Captain Of The Pinafore
148 In Old New York
153 Italian Street Song
167 La Donna è Mobile (From "Rigoletto")
176 Little Buttercup, (I'm Called)
194 Meditation (From "Thais")
184 Merry Widow Waltz
203 Musetta's Waltz (From "La Boheme")
238 Prelude (From "Carmen")
242 Ride Of The Valkyries
298 Tit-Willow
297 Toreador Song (Bizet)
302 Triumphal March (From "Aida")
330 Waiting For The Robert E. Lee

Inspirational

10 Abide With Me
15 All God's Children Got Shoes
15 All My Trials
17 Amazing Grace
43 Battle Hymn Of The Republic, The
48 Beautiful Isle Of Somewhere
45 Beautiful Savior
44 Behold The Savior Of Mankind
53 Blessed Assurance
50 Blest Be The Tie That Binds
57 Bringing In The Sheaves
67 Christ The Lord Is Ris'n Today
67 Church In The Wildwood, The
73 Come, Thou Almighty King
75 Crown Him With Many Crowns
80 Deep River
88 Dry Bones
94 Ev'ry Time I Feel The Spirit
94 Ezekiel Saw The Wheel
95 Faith Of Our Fathers
108 Give Me That Old Time Religion
107 God Of Our Fathers
122 Hallelujah Chorus (From "Messiah")
126 He's Got The Whole World In His Hands
130 Holy God, We Praise Thy Name
131 Holy, Holy, Holy
152 In The Sweet Bye And Bye
158 Jesus Loves Me!
164 Joshua Fought The Battle Of Jericho
163 Just A Closer Walk With Thee
163 Kum-Bah-Yah
171 Let Us Break Bread Together
179 Lonesome Valley
199 Michael, Row The Boat Ashore
193 Mighty Fortress Is Our God, A
219 Nearer My God To Thee
209 Nobody Knows The Trouble I've Seen
211 Now Thank We All Our God
210 Now The Day Is Over
218 Oh, Promise Me
226 Onward Christian Soldiers
237 Praise God From Whom All Blessings Flow
239 Prayer Of Thanksgiving
244 Rock Of Ages
255 Shall We Gather At The River
273 Swing Low, Sweet Chariot
319 Were You There?
320 What A Friend We Have In Jesus
322 When The Saints Go Marching In
326 Will The Circle Be Unbroken

International Favorites

11 Ach, Du Lieber Augustin
29 Adios Muchachos
14 Alouette
22 Annie Laurie
24 Au Clair De La Lune
24 Auld Lang Syne
40 Barbara Polka
53 Blue Bells Of Scotland, The
55 Blue Danube Waltz
60 Campbells Are Coming, The
62 Can Can
61 Capriccio Italien (Theme)
65 Carnival Of Venice
66 Chiapanecas
68 Cielito Lindo
68 Ciribiribin
71 Clarinet Polka
70 Cockles And Mussels (Molly Malone)
70 Come Back To Sorrento
73 Come To The Sea

73 Comin' Through The Rye
72 Country Gardens
83 Dark Eyes
89 Du, Du Liegst Mir Im Herzen
93 Emilia Polka
105 Finlandia
101 Frère Jacques
101 Funiculi, Funicula
114 God Save Our King (Queen)
125 Hatikvah
125 Hava Nagilah
127 Helena Polka
151 Irish Washerwoman
153 Italian Street Song
158 Jenny Lind Polka
159 John Peel
162 Juanita
164 Julida Polka
165 Kerry Dance, The
167 La Cucaracha
168 La Golondrina
168 La Marseillaise
169 La Paloma
171 Las Mañanitas
178 Loch Lomond
192 Maori Farewell Song
194 Martha Polka
195 Mazel Tov
198 Mexican Hat Dance
205 Norwegian Dance
211 O Canada!
215 O Sole Mio
215 Oberek
216 Oh Marie
229 Pizzicato Polka
240 Rain-Rain Polka (Prsi-Prsi)
239 Red Raven Polka
250 Rosalie Schottische
252 Santa Lucia
253 Schnitzelbank
265 Song Of The Volga Boatman
288 Tarantella
298 Tinker Polka
306 Two Guitars
310 Vive L'Amour
318 Wearing Of The Green, The
335 Zum Gali Gali

Marches

23 American Cadets March
18 American Patrol, The
28 Anchors Aweigh
48 Be Kind To Your Web-Footed Friends
32 Billboard March, The
35 Boola! Boola!
60 Caissons Go Rolling Along, The
72 Columbia, The Gem Of The Ocean
79 Down The Field
89 El Capitan
95 Fight Ye Bulldogs
105 Finlandia
110 Gladiator March
123 Hail To The Chief
128 High School Cadets
156 It's A Long, Long Way To Tipperary
142 Jollly Coppersmith
166 King Cotton
168 La Marseillaise
182 La Sorella
172 Liberty Bell, The
191 March Slav (Tchaikovsky)
191 Marche Militaire
192 Marine's Hymn
207 National Emblem
225 On Wisconsin!
228 Our Director March
235 Pomp And Circumstance
250 Rondeau (Mouret)
251 Scotland The Brave (Tunes Of Glory)
256 Semper Fidelis
266 Sound Off
268 Stars And Stripes Forever
295 Thunder And Blazes
296 Thunderer
297 Tramp! Tramp! Tramp!
304 Turkish March
306 Under The Double Eagle
309 University Of Michigan Song
332 Washington And Lee Swing
316 Washington Post March
320 When Johnny Comes Marching Home
322 When The Saints Go Marching In
329 Yankee Doodle
336 Yellow Rose Of Texas, The
334 You're A Grand Old Flag

Patriotic

17 America (My Country, 'Tis Of Thee)
18 America, The Beautiful
28 Anchors Aweigh
20 Assembly/Reveille
43 Battle Hymn Of The Republic, The
60 Caissons Go Rolling Along, The
72 Columbia, The Gem Of The Ocean
121 Hail, Columbia
123 Hail To The Chief
172 Liberty Bell, The
192 Marine's Hymn
256 Semper Fidelis
268 Star Spangled Banner, The
268 Stars And Stripes Forever
274 Taps
329 Yankee Doodle
334 You're A Grand Old Flag

Sentimental

12 After The Ball
22 Annie Laurie
25 Aura Lee
39 Banks Of The Ohio
39 Barbara Allen
44 Beautiful Dreamer
33 Because
45 Believe Me If All Those Endearing Young Charms
59 Bury Me Not On The Lone Prairie
85 Dog-gone Blues
97 Flow Gently, Sweet Afton
105 Goodbye, My Lady Love
117 Grandfather's Clock
118 Green Grow The Lilacs
119 Greensleeves
119 Gypsy Love Song
124 Hearts And Flowers
132 Home Sweet Home
131 Honey, Won't You Come Back To Me?
144 I Gave My Love A Cherry (The Riddle Song)
137 I Love You Truly
145 I Love You With All My Heart
146 I'll Take You Home Again, Kathleen
148 Ich Liebe Dich (I Love Thee)
141 In The Gloaming
157 Jeanie With The Light Brown Hair
161 Johnny Has Gone For A Soldier
165 Just A Song At Twilight
179 Long, Long Ago
180 Love's Old Sweet Song
208 'Neath The Old Chestnut Tree
218 Oh, Promise Me
299 To A Wild Rose

Singalongs

28 Aba Daba Honeymoon, The
12 After The Ball
30 Alexander's Ragtime Band
24 Auld Lang Syne
38 Band Played On, The
48 Be Kind To Your Web-Footed Friends
31 Be My Little Baby Bumblebee
46 Bicycle Built For Two, A (Daisy Bell)
52 Bill Bailey, Won't You Please Come Home?
34 Bird In A Gilded Cage, A
55 Bowery, The
36 By The Beautiful Sea
36 By The Light Of The Silvery Moon
63 Camptown Races
64 Carry Me Back To Old Virginny
77 Chinatown, My Chinatown
79 Come, Josephine In My Flying Machine
81 Desperado, The
84 Dixie
86 Down By The Old Mill Stream
86 Down By The Riverside
87 Drink To Me Only With Thine Eyes
105 Fascination
96 For He's A Jolly Good Fellow
104 Forty-Five Minutes From Broadway
106 Give My Regards To Broadway
114 Good Night Ladies
114 Goodbye Girls, I'm Through
105 Goodbye, My Lady Love
115 Green Grass Grew All Around, The
124 Hail! Hail! The Gang's All Here
123 Hand Me Down My Walking Cane
136 Harrigan
137 Hello! My Baby
130 Home On The Range
131 How Dry I Am!
137 I Love You Truly
136 I Want A Girl
146 I Wish I Were Single Again
138 I Wonder Who's Kissing Her Now
146 I'll Take You Home Again, Kathleen
138 I've Got Rings On My Fingers
139 Ida, Sweet As Apple Cider
140 If I Had My Way
140 In My Merry Oldsmobile
148 In Old New York
150 In The Evening By The Moonlight
151 In The Good Old Summertime
142 In The Shade Of The Old Apple Tree
156 It's A Long, Long Way To Tipperary
157 Jeanie With The Light Brown Hair
160 John Peel
165 Just A Song At Twilight
181 Keep The Homefires Burning
170 Let Me Call You Sweetheart
175 Little Annie Rooney
177 Little Brown Jug
180 Love's Old Sweet Song
198 Mademoiselle From Armentiers
187 Man On The Flying Trapeze, The
188 Man Without A Woman, A
190 Marianne
181 Mary's A Grand Old Name
182 Meet Me In St. Louis, Louis
196 Meet Me Tonight In Dreamland
196 Merrily We Roll Along
199 M-I-N-E
200 Missouri Waltz, The
185 Moonlight Bay
206 My Bonnie
206 My Gal Sal
184 My Hero
186 My Melancholy Baby
204 My Wild Irish Rose
217 Oh, Susanna
232 Oh! You Beautiful Doll
222 Old Folks At Home

209 Old Gray Mare, The
223 Old Oaken Bucket
232 On A Sunday Afternoon
224 On The Banks Of The Wabash
230 Peg O' My Heart
230 Play A Simple Melody
233 Put On Your Old Grey Bonnet
231 Put Your Arms Around Me, Honey
234 Ragtime Cowboy Joe
248 Roamin' In The Gloamin
249 Row, Row, Row
253 Schnitzelbank
263 School Days
257 She Is More To Be Pitied Than Censured
257 She Wore A Yellow Ribbon
276 Shine On Harvest Moon
260 Sidewalks Of New York, The
259 Silver Threads Among The Gold
279 Sweet Adeline
272 Sweet Genevieve
278 Sweet Rosie O'Grady
280 Sweetheart Of Sigma Chi, The
287 Ta-Ra-Ra Boom-Der-É
282 Take Me Out To The Ball Game
292 Tenting Tonight
294 There Is A Tavern In The Town
282 There's A Long, Long Trail
283 They Didn't Believe Me
283 Too-Ra-Loo-Ra-Loo-Ral, That's An Irish Lullaby
286 Trail Of The Lonesome Pine, The
284 12th Street Rag
310 Vive L'Amour
311 Wabash Cannon Ball, The
312 Wait Till The Sun Shines, Nellie
330 Waiting For The Robert E. Lee
332 Washington And Lee Swing
321 When Irish Eyes Are Smiling
324 When You And I Were Young Maggie
322 When You Were Sweet Sixteen
331 When You Wore A Tulip And I Wore A Big Red Rose
324 When You're Away
325 While Strolling Through The Park One Day
323 Whispering Hope
327 WhoThrew The Overalls In Mrs. Murphy's Chowder
334 Yankee Doodle Boy, The
333 You Made Me Love You
335 You Tell Me Your Dream

Special Occasions

24 Auld Lang Syne
25 Ave Maria (Bach/Gounod)
26 Ave Maria (Schubert)
33 Because
44 Birthday Song, The
56 Bridal Chorus (From "Lohengrin")
83 Danube Waves
125 Hava Nagilah
137 I Love You Truly
218 Oh, Promise Me
226 Over The River And Through The Woods
235 Pomp And Circumstance
301 Trumpet Tune
304 Trumpet Voluntary
317 Wedding March
335 You Are My True Love

Standards

28 Aba Daba Honeymoon, The
12 After The Ball
30 Alexander's Ragtime Band
16 Aloha Oe
24 Auld Lang Syne
38 Band Played On, The
31 Be My Little Baby Bumblebee
33 Because
46 Bicycle Built For Two, A (Daisy Bell)
52 Bill Bailey, Won't You Please Come Home?
34 Bird In A Gilded Cage, A
55 Bowery, The
36 By The Beautiful Sea
36 By The Light Of The Silvery Moon
64 Carry Me Back To Old Virginny
77 Chinatown, My Chinatown
79 Come, Josephine In My Flying Machine
77 Cuddle Up A Little Closer, Lovey Mine
76 Danny Boy
81 Desperado, The
86 Down By The Old Mill Stream
86 Down By The Riverside
90 Entertainer, The
98 Far Above Cayuga's Waters
105 Fascination
104 Forty-Five Minutes From Broadway
106 Give My Regards To Broadway
106 Glow Worm
114 Goodbye Girls, I'm Through
136 Harrigan
137 Hello! My Baby
133 Hot Time In The Old Town Tonight, A
136 I Want A Girl
138 I Wonder Who's Kissing Her Now
139 Ida, Sweet As Apple Cider
138 I've Got Rings On My Fingers
140 If I Had My Way
140 In My Merry Oldsmobile
148 In Old New York
150 In The Evening By The Moonlight
141 In The Gloaming
151 In The Good Old Summertime
142 In The Shade Of The Old Apple Tree
181 Keep The Homefires Burning
170 Let Me Call You Sweetheart
172 Listen To The Mocking Bird
175 Little Annie Rooney
174 Little Bit Of Heaven, A
179 Long, Long Ago
180 Love's Old Sweet Song
188 Mademoiselle From Armentiers
187 Man On The Flying Trapeze, The
188 Man Without A Woman, A
189 Maple Leaf Rag
181 Mary's A Grand Old Name
182 Meet Me In St. Louis, Louis
196 Meet Me Tonight In Dreamland
197 Melody In A
199 Mighty Lak' A Rose
199 M-I-N-E
200 Missouri Waltz, The
185 Moonlight Bay
206 My Gal Sal
184 My Hero
186 My Melancholy Baby
204 My Old Kentucky Home
204 My Wild Irish Rose
217 Oh, Susanna
232 Oh! You Beautiful Doll
222 Old Folks At Home
223 Old Oaken Bucket
232 On A Sunday Afternoon
224 On The Banks Of The Wabash
228 Orange Marmalade Rag
230 Peg O' My Heart
230 Play A Simple Melody
233 Put On Your Old Grey Bonnet
231 Put Your Arms Around Me, Honey
234 Ragtime Cowboy Joe
248 Red Wing
243 Ring The Banjo
248 Roamin' In The Gloamin'
249 Row, Row, Row
263 School Days
257 She Is More To Be Pitied Than Censured
276 Shine On Harvest Moon
260 Sidewalks Of New York, The
259 Silver Thread Among The Gold
276 St. Louis Blues
279 Sweet Adeline
272 Sweet Genevieve
278 Sweet Rosie O'Grady
280 Sweetheart Of Sigma Chi, The
272 Sweethearts
287 Ta-Ra-Ra Boom-Der-É
282 Take Me Out To The Ball Game
289 Tell Me Why
292 Tenting Tonight
280 That's A Plenty
275 That's Why I Do Like I Do
282 There's A Long, Long Trail
283 They Didn't Believe Me
283 Too-Ra-Loo-Ra-Loo-Ral (That's An Irish Lullaby)
300 Toyland
286 Trail Of The Lonesome Pine, The
284 12th Street Rag
311 Wabash Cannon Ball, The
330 Waiting For The Robert E. Lee
332 Washington And Lee Swing
321 When Irish Eyes Are Smiling
324 When You And I Were Young, Maggie
322 When You Were Sixteen
331 When You Wore A Tulip
324 When You're Away
325 While Strolling Through The Park One Day
323 Whispering Hope
332 Whistler And His Dog, The
327 Who Threw The Overalls In Mrs. Murphy's Chowder
333 You Made Me Love You
335 You Tell Me Your Dream

Waltzes

11 Ach, Du Lieber Augustin
12 After The Ball
55 Blue Danube Waltz
68 Cielito Lindo
79 Come, Josephine In My Flying Machine
92 Emperor Waltz
105 Fascination
97 Fledermaus Waltz
104 Forty-Five Minutes From Broadway
112 Gold And Silver Waltz
118 Green Grow The Lilacs
117 Grey And Gold Waltz
137 I Love You Truly
138 I Wonder Who's Kissing Her Now
149 Il Bacio (The Kiss)
140 In My Merry Oldsmobile
151 In The Good Old Summertime
168 La Golondrina
198 Melody Of Love
184 Merry Widow Waltz
200 Missouri Waltz, The
184 My Hero
216 Oh Marie
232 On A Sunday Afternoon
227 Over The Waves
246 Roses From The South
252 Santa Lucia
278 Sweet Rosie O'Grady
272 Sweethearts
290 Tales From The Vienna Woods
289 Tell Me Why
310 Valse Bleue
309 Vienna Life
313 Waltz (Brahms)
314 Waltz (Chopin)
314 Waltz Of The Flowers (Tchaikovsky)

A-HUNTING WE WILL GO

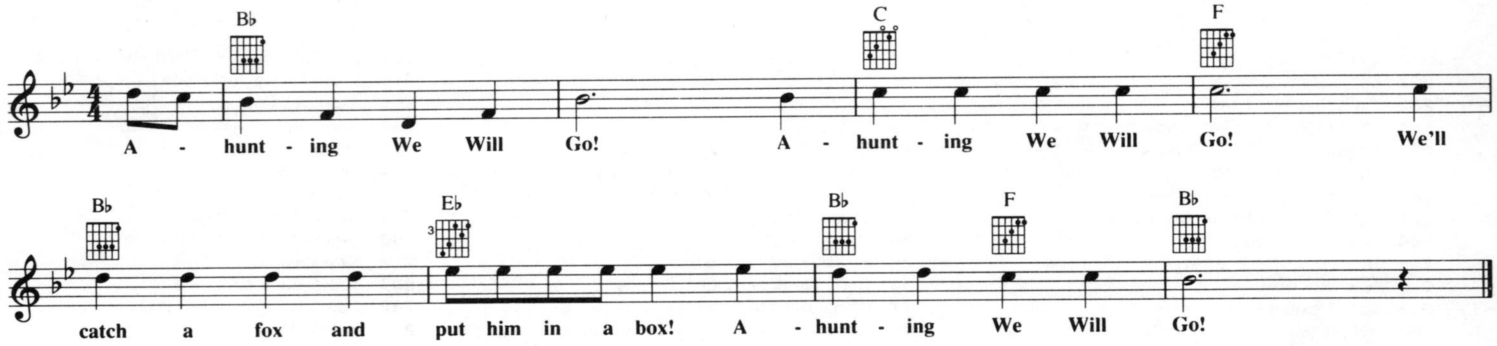
B♭ C F
A - hunt - ing We Will Go! A - hunt - ing We Will Go! We'll
B♭ E♭ B♭ F B♭
catch a fox and put him in a box! A - hunt - ing We Will Go!

A-TISKET, A-TASKET

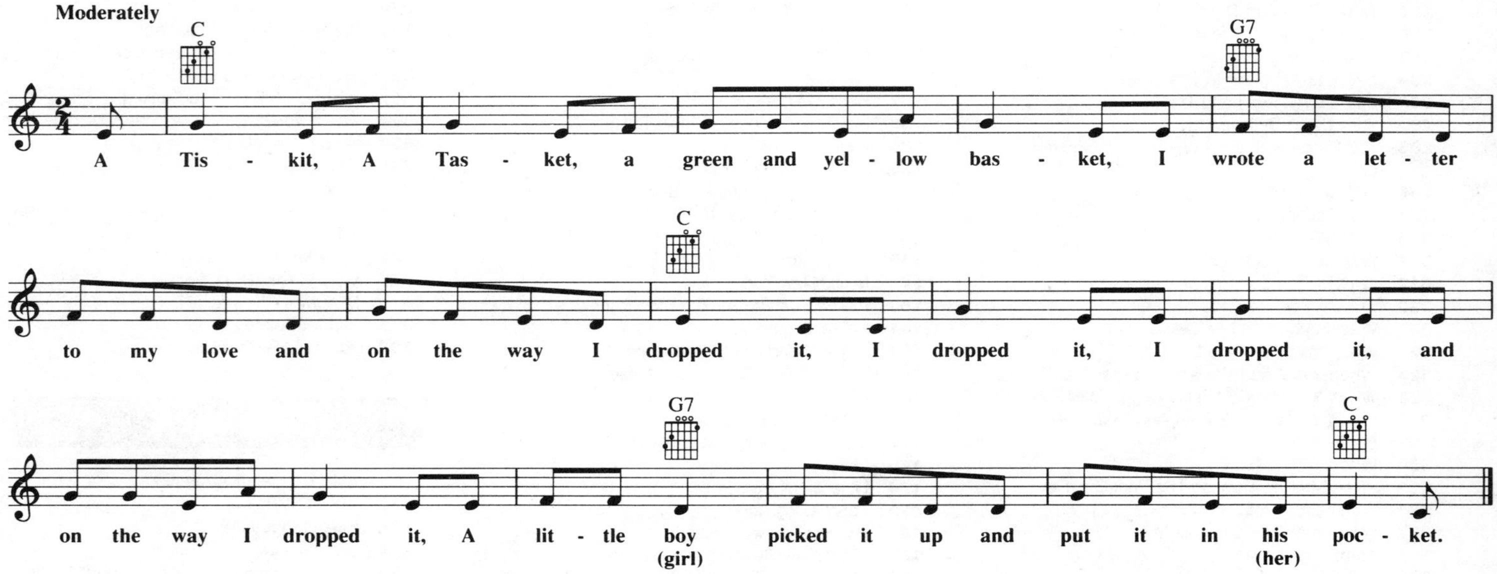
Moderately
C G7
A Tis - kit, A Tas - ket, a green and yel - low bas - ket, I wrote a let - ter
C
to my love and on the way I dropped it, I dropped it, I dropped it, and
G7 C
on the way I dropped it, A lit - tle boy picked it up and put it in his poc - ket.
(girl) (her)

ABIDE WITH ME

Words by Henry F. Lyte; Music by William H. Monk

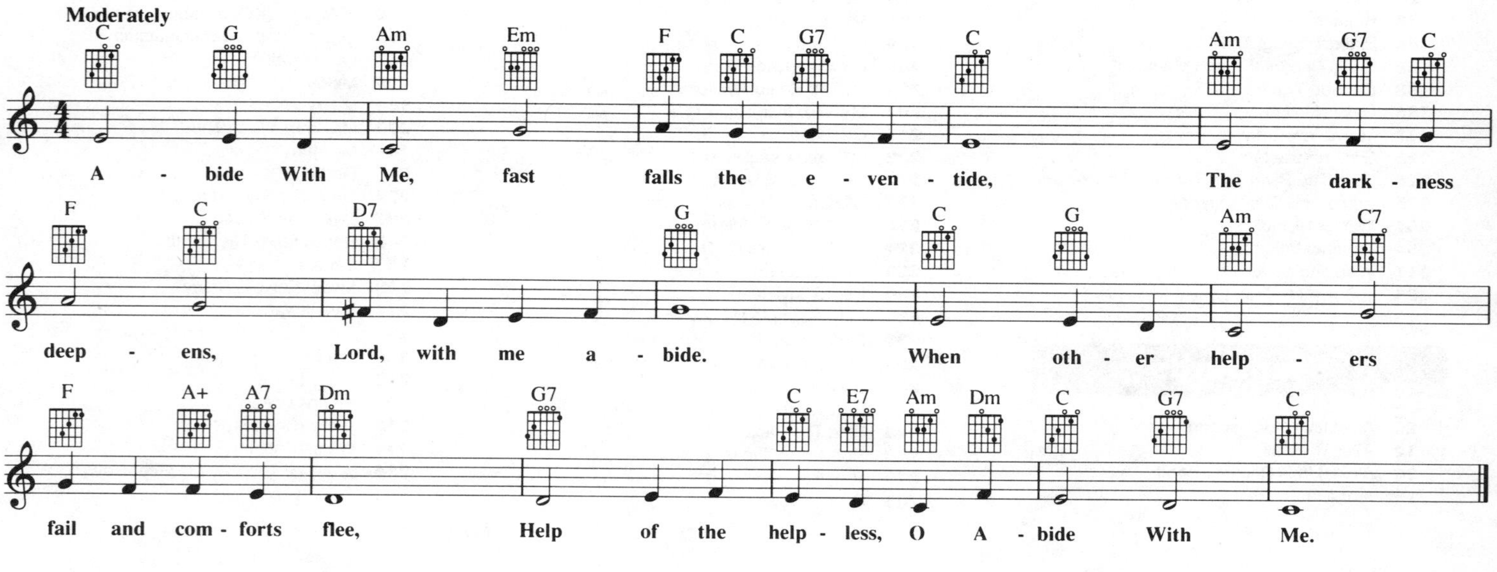
Moderately
C G Am Em F C G7 C Am G7 C
A - bide With Me, fast falls the e - ven - tide, The dark - ness
F C D7 G C G Am C7
deep - ens, Lord, with me a - bide. When oth - er help - ers
F A+ A7 Dm G7 C E7 Am Dm C G7 C
fail and com - forts flee, Help of the help - less, O A - bide With Me.

ACH, DU LIEBER AUGUSTIN

Moderately
F C7 F
Ach, Du Lie - ber Au - gus - tin, Au - gus - tin, Au - gus - tin,
C7 F
Ach, Du Lie - ber Au - gus - tin, al - les ist weg:
C7 F C7 F
Bock ist weg, stock ist weg, Auch ich bin in dem dreck
C7 F
Ach, Du Lie - ber Au - gus - tin, al - les ist weg.

ANDANTE CANTABILE
(Tchaikovsky)

P.I. Tchaikovsky

Slowly
Gm7 C7 F B♭ C7 F C7
F Dm E7 Am Cm D7 Gm C7 F Dm F G7 C7
F Cm D7 Gm C7 F Dm F G7 C7 F

AFTER THE BALL

Words and Music by Charles K. Harris

Fast Waltz
G D7 Am
1. A lit - tle maid - en climbed an old man's knee, Begged for a
2. "Bright lights were flash - ing in the grand ball - room, Soft - ly the
3. (See additional lyrics)
D7 G
sto - ry, "Do, un - cle, please! Why are you sin - gle;
mu - sic, play - ing sweet tunes, There came my sweet - heart,
E7 Am C G A7 D7
why live a - lone? Have you no ba - bies, have you no
my love, my own, "I wish some wa - ter; leave me a -
G Em Am B7 C G
home?" "I had a sweet - heart, years, years a - go;
lone." When I re - turned, dear, there stood a man,
C G A A7 D7 G
Where she is now, pet, you will soon know. List to the
Kiss - ing my sweet - heart, as lov - ers can. Down fell the
E7 Am C G
sto - ry, I'll tell it all, I be - lieved her faith - less,
glass, pet, bro - ken that's all, Just as my heart was,
A7 D7 G Chorus G C G
Af - ter The Ball."
Af - ter The Ball."
Af - ter The Ball is o - ver, Af - ter the
D7 Am E7 Am D7
break of morn, Af - ter the danc - ers' leav - ing; Af - ter the stars are

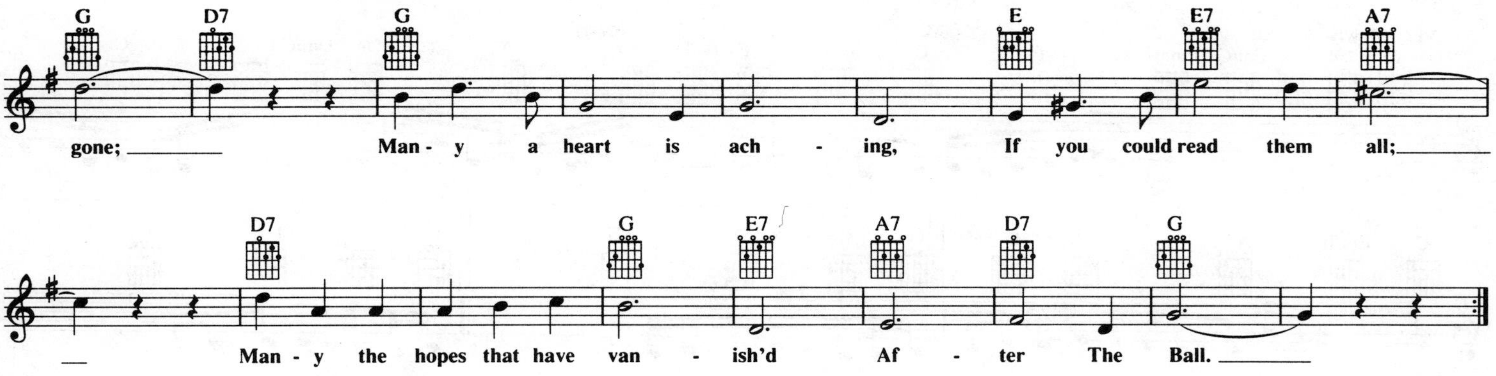
G D7 G E E7 A7
gone; Man-y a heart is ach-ing, If you could read them all;
D7 G E7 A7 D7 G
Man-y the hopes that have van-ish'd Af-ter The Ball.

Additional Lyrics

3. Long years have passed, child. I've never wed,
True to my lost love, though she is dead.
She tried to tell me, tried to explain;
I would not listen, pleadings were vain.
One day a letter came from that man;
He was her brother, the letter ran.
That's why I'm lonely, no home at all;
I broke her heart After The Ball.

AH! SWEET MYSTERY OF LIFE

Lyric by Rida Johnson Young
Music by Victor Herbert

Flowing
B♭ Cm7 F7
Ah! Sweet Mys-ter-y Of Life, at last I've found thee, Ah! I know at last the sec-ret of it
B♭ B♭m F/C C C7
all; All the long-ing, seek-ing, striv-ing, wait-ing, yearn-ing, The burn-ing hopes, the joy and i-dle tears that
F7 B♭ Cm7
fall! For 'tis love, and love a-lone, the world is seek-ing; And 'tis
love, and love a-lone, the world is seek-ing; For 'tis
F7 B♭ G7
love, and love a-lone, that can re-pay! 'Tis the an-swer, 'tis the end and all of
love, and love a-lone, that can re-pay! 'Tis the an-swer, 'tis the end and all of
Cm E♭m B♭/F Cm/E♭ Dm 1 B♭ 2 B♭
liv-ing, For it is love a-lone that rules for aye! For 'tis
liv-ing, For it is love a-lone that rules for aye!

AIR
(On The G String)

J.S. Bach

ALOUETTE

ALL GOD'S CHILDREN GOT SHOES

Lively
G6 C6 D7 G D9 G D7 G G6 C6 D9 G D7 G D9 G6
1. I got a shoe, you got a shoe, All God's Child - ren Got Shoes. When I get to heav - en gon - na
2. I got a robe, you got a robe, All God's child - ren got robes. When I get to heav - en gon - na
3. I got a harp, you got a harp, All God's child - ren got harps. When I get to heav - en gon - na
put on my shoes, I'm gon - na tromp all o - ver God's heav-en, heav-en, heav-en. Ev - 'ry - bod - y talk - in' 'bout
put on my robe, I'm gon - na shout all o - ver God's heav-en, heav-en, heav-en. Ev - 'ry - bod - y talk - in' 'bout
play on my harp, I'm gon - na play all o - ver God's heav-en, heav-en, heav-en. Ev - 'ry - bod - y talk - in' 'bout
heav - en ain't a - go - in' there, Heav - en, heav - en, gon - na tromp all o - ver God's heav - en.
heav - en ain't a - go - in' there, Heav - en, heav - en, gon - na shout all o - ver God's heav - en.
heav - en ain't a - go - in' there, Heav - en, heav - en, gon - na play all o - ver God's heav - en.

ALL MY TRIALS

Freely, with intensity
C Gm C Em F Dm C Am Dm G7 C C7 F Dm C Am Dm G7 C
1. Hush, lit - tle ba - by, don't you cry, You know your ma - ma was born to die.
2. If re-ligion was a thing that money could buy, The rich would live and the poor would die.
3. I had a lit - tle book that was given to me, And ev'ry page spelled lib - er - ty.
All my tri - als, Lord, Soon be o - ver.
Refain:
Too late, my broth-ers, Too late, but nev - er mind.
All my tri - als, Lord, Soon be o - ver.

THE ALPHABET SONG

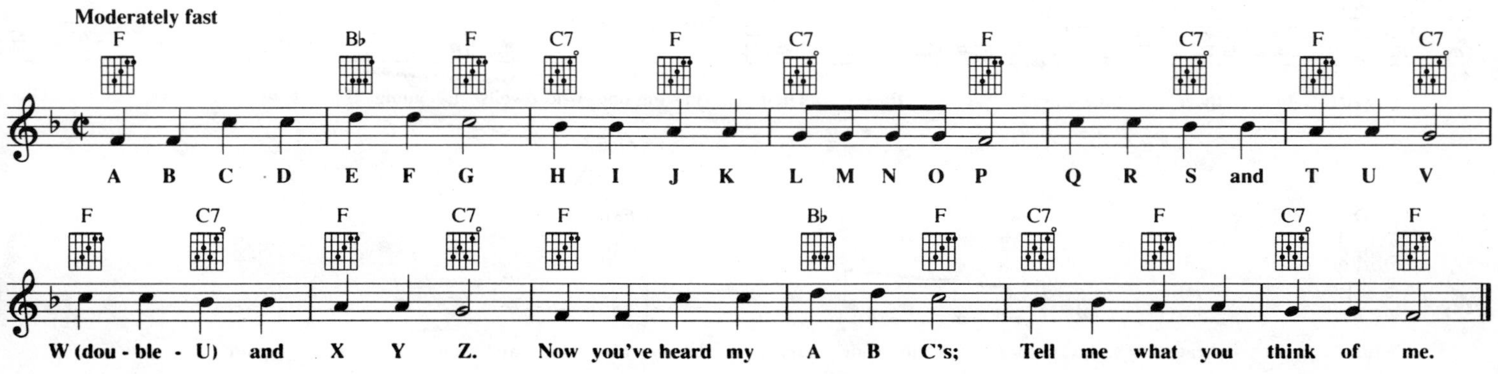
Moderately fast
F B♭ F C7 F C7 F C7 F C7 F C7 F C7 F B♭ F C7 F C7 F
A B C D E F G H I J K L M N O P Q R S and T U V
W (dou - ble - U) and X Y Z. Now you've heard my A B C's; Tell me what you think of me.

ALL THROUGH THE NIGHT

Moderately
F Bb F G C F Bb C7 F Bb F
Sleep, my Child and peace at - tend Thee, All Through The Night; Guard - ian an - gels
While the moon her watch is keep - ing, All Through The Night; While the wear - y
You, my God, a Babe of won - der, All Through The Night; Dreams you dream can't
G C F Bb C7 F Gm F Gm Am Bb Am Gm F Gm F C7 Dm
God will send Thee, All Through The Night. Soft the drow - sy hours are creep - ing, Hill and vale in
world is sleep - ing, All Through The Night, Through your dreams you're swift - ly steal - ing, Vis - ions of de -
break from thun - der, All Through The Night. Chil - dren's dreams can not be brok - en; Life is but a
F C7 Dm C F Bb F G C F Bb C7 1,2 F 3 F
slum - ber sleep - ing, God His lov - ing vig - il keep - ing, All Through The Night.
light re - veal - ing. Christ - mas time is so ap - peal - ing, All Through The Night.
love - ly tok - en. Christ - mas should be soft - ly spok - en All Through The Night.

ALOHA OE

Words and Music by Queen Liliuokalani

Slowly
Ab Db Ab Eb7
Proud - ly swept the rain cloud by the cliff As on it glid - ed through the trees. Still
Ab Db Ab Db Eb7 Ab
fol - low - ing with grief the li - ko, The a - mi - mi - le - mua of the vale. Fare -
Db Ab Eb7 Ab
well to thee, fare - well to thee, Thou charm - ing one who dwells a - mong the bow - ers. One
Db Ab Eb7 Ab
fond em - brace be - fore I now de - part, Un - til we meet a - gain.

AMAZING GRACE

Moderately
G D7 Em C G
1. A - maz - ing Grace! How sweet the sound That saved a
2 - 5. (See additional lyrics)
D7 G C
wretch like me! I once was lost but now am
G Em G D7 1-4 G 5 G
found; Was blind, but now I see. 'Twas me.

Additional Lyrics

2. 'Twas grace that taught my heart to fear,
And grace my fears relieved;
How precious did that grace appear
The hour I first believed.

3. Thro' many dangers, toils and snares,
I have already come;
'Tis grace hath bro't me safe thus far,
And grace will lead me home.

4. How sweet the name of Jesus sounds
In a believer's ear.
It soothes his sorrows, heals his wounds,
And drives away his fear.

5. Must Jesus bear the cross alone
And all the world go free?
No, there's a cross for ev'ry one
And there's a cross for me.

AMERICA
(My Country, 'Tis Of Thee)

Lyrics by Samuel F. Smith
Music by Henry Carey

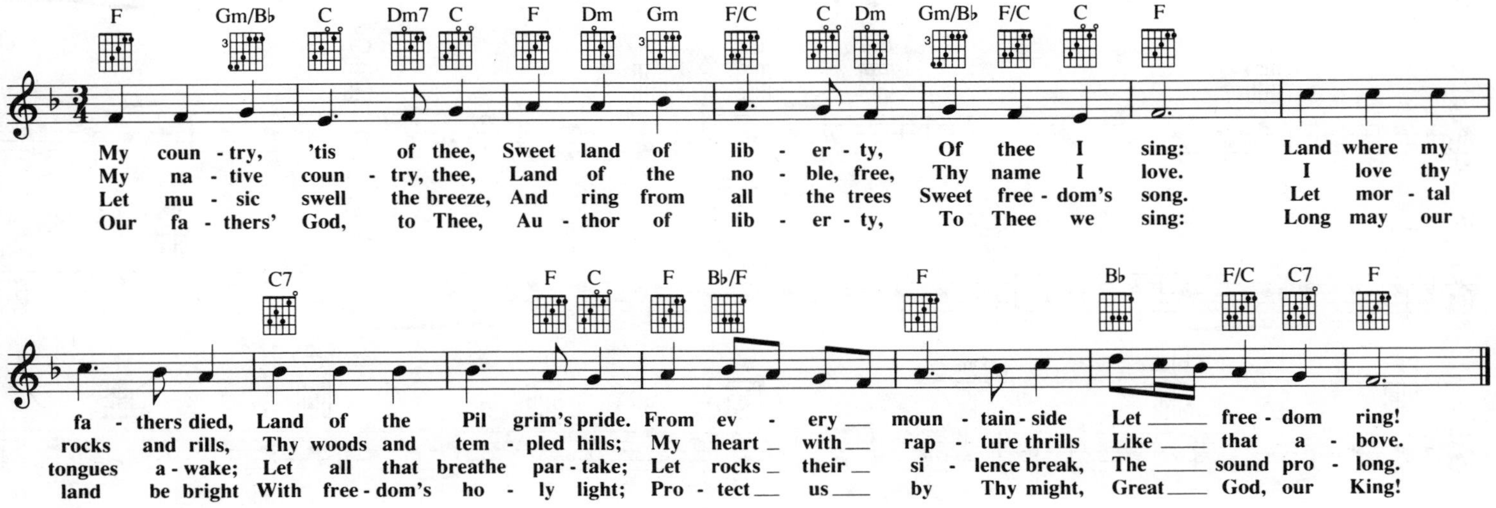
F Gm/B♭ C Dm7 C F Dm Gm F/C C Dm Gm/B♭ F/C C F
My coun - try, 'tis of thee, Sweet land of lib - er - ty, Of thee I sing: Land where my
My na - tive coun - try, thee, Land of the no - ble, free, Thy name I love. I love thy
Let mu - sic swell the breeze, And ring from all the trees Sweet free - dom's song. Let mor - tal
Our fa - thers' God, to Thee, Au - thor of lib - er - ty, To Thee we sing: Long may our
C7 F C F B♭/F F B♭ F/C C7 F
fa - thers died, Land of the Pil grim's pride. From ev - ery moun - tain - side Let free - dom ring!
rocks and rills, Thy woods and tem - pled hills; My heart with rap - ture thrills Like that a - bove.
tongues a - wake; Let all that breathe par - take; Let rocks their si - lence break, The sound pro - long.
land be bright With free - dom's ho - ly light; Pro - tect us by Thy might, Great God, our King!

AMERICA, THE BEAUTIFUL

Lyrics by Katherine Lee Bates
Music by Samuel A. Ward

Bb Bdim7 F7 Bb F+ Bb Bbm6
O beau - ti - ful for spa - cious skies, For am - ber waves of grain, For pur - ple moun - tain
O beau - ti - ful for pil - grim feet, Whose stern, im - pas - sioned stress A thor - ough - fare for
O beau - ti - ful for he - roes proved In lib - er - at - ing strife, Who more than self their
O beau - ti - ful for pa - triot dream That sees be - yond the years Thine al - a - bas - ter
F Ddim7 F C7 F7 Bb F7
maj - es - ties A - bove the fruit - ed plain! A - mer - i - ca! A - mer - i - ca! God
free - dom beat A - cross the wil - der - ness! A - mer - i - ca! A - mer - i - ca! God
coun - try loved, And mer - cy more than life! A - mer - i - ca! A - mer - i - ca! May
cit - ies gleam, Un - dimmed by hu - man tears! A - mer - i - ca! A - mer - i - ca! God
Bb C7 Eb Bb Eb Edim7 Bb/F F7 Bb
shed His grace on thee, And crown thy good with broth - er - hood, From sea to shin - ing sea.
mend thine ev - ery flaw, Con - firm thy soul in self con - trol, Thy lib - er - ty in law.
God thy gold re - fine, 'Til all suc - cess be no - ble - ness, And ev - ery gain di - vine.
shed His grace on thee, And crown thy good with broth - er - hood, From sea to shin - ing sea.

THE AMERICAN PATROL

F. W. Meacham

Moderately
F C7
F G7 C F
Bb Gm C7 F C7
F C7 F Bb
F C#dim7 Dm Bb F C7 F

ANGELS WE HAVE HEARD ON HIGH

F Am Csus C F C F C C7 F Am
1. An - gels We Have Heard On High Sweet - ly sing - ing o'er the plains, And the moun - tains
2. Shep - herds, why this ju - bi - lee? Why your joy - ous strains pro - long? What the glad - some
3 - 4. (See additional lyrics)
Csus C F C F C C7 F D Gm C
in re - ply Ech - o - ing their joy - ous strains.
ti - dings be Which in - spire your heaven - ly song?
Refrain
Glo - -
F B♭ C C7 F C F B♭ F C F D
- - ri - a in ex - cel - sis De - - o, Glo -
Gm C F B♭ C C7 F C F B♭ F C7 F
- - - ri - a. in ex - cel - sis De - o.

Additional Lyrics

3. Come to Bethlehem and see
Him whose birth the angels sing;
Come, adore on bended knee
Christ the Lord, the newborn King.
(Refrain)

4. See within a manger laid
Jesus, Lord of heaven and earth!
Mary, Joseph, lend your aid,
with us sing our Savior's birth.
(Refrain)

ANIMAL FAIR

Moderately
A E7
I went to the An - i - mal Fair, The birds and beasts were there, The
A
big ba - boon, by the light of the moon Was comb - ing his au - burn hair. The
E7
mon - key, he got drunk, And sat on the el - e - phant's trunk, The el - e - phant sneezed, And
A
fell on his knees, And what be - came of the monk, the monk, the monk, the monk?

ANNABEL LEE

Flowing
C F C Am Dm F G7
It was man - y and man - y a year a - go, In a king - dom by the
I was a child and she was a child, In this king - dom by the
this is the rea - son that long, long a - go, In this king - dom by the
love, it was strong - er by far than the love of the ones who were old - er than
moon nev - er beams with - out bring - ing me dreams In this king - dom by the
C F C Am Dm
sea, That a maid - en there lived whom you may know by name, by the name of
sea, But we loved with a love that was great - er than love, So loved I and my
sea, There a - rose a strong wind blow - ing out of a cloud, Chilled and killed my dear
we, Of the man - y far old - er and wis - er than we, Of those old - er and
sea, And the stars nev - er rise but I feel the bright eyes Of the beau - ti - ful
G9 C Fm C
An - na - bel Lee. And this maid - en lived with no oth - er thought Than to
An - na - bel Lee. With a love so strong that the an - gels watched, E - ven
An - na - bel Lee. And her high - born kins - men, they quick - ly came, And they
wis - er than we. Ah but neith - er an - gel in sky a - bove, Nor the
An - na - bel Lee. Thru the night I lie by my dear - est one, By the
Fm B♭7 E♭ G7 C F C
love and be loved by me. Oh this maid - en she lived with no oth - er
cov - et - ed her and me. With a love so strong that the an - gels
bore her a - way from me. And they sealed her re - mains in a se - pul - cher
de - mons be - neath the sea, Could sev - er my soul from the soul of my
side of my bride to be, Though she lies in her se - pul - cher si - lent and
Am Dm 1-4 G7 C 5 G7 C
thought Than to love and be loved by me! For
watched E - ven cov - et - ed her and me! And
deep, In this king - dom by the sea! But our
love Of my beau - ti - ful Ann' - bel Lee! And the
cold Oh my beau - ti - ful An - na - bel Lee!

ASSEMBLY/REVEILLE

(ASSEMBLY)
C
(REVEILLE)
G
D7
G
D7
G

ANVIL CHORUS

Giuseppe Verdi

ANNIE LAURIE

By William Douglas and Lady John Scott

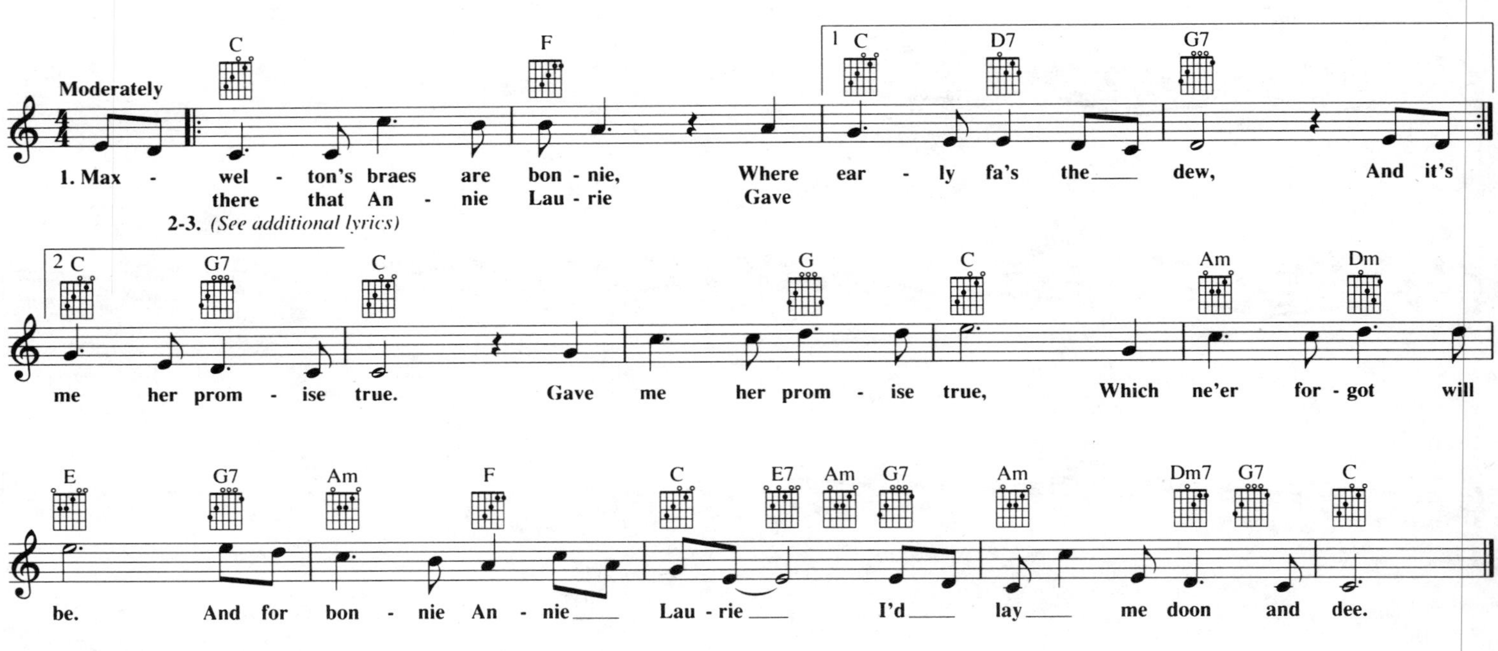
Moderately
C F C D7 G7
1. Max - wel - ton's braes are bon - nie, Where ear - ly fa's the___ dew, And it's
there that An - nie Lau - rie Gave
2-3. (See additional lyrics)
C G7 C G C Am Dm
me her prom - ise true. Gave me her prom - ise true, Which ne'er for - got will
E G7 Am F C E7 Am G7 Am Dm7 G7 C
be. And for bon - nie An - nie___ Lau - rie___ I'd___ lay___ me doon and dee.

Additional Lyrics

2. Her brow is like the snawdrift,
Her neck is like the swan,
Her face it is the fairest
That e'er the sun shone on,
That e'er the sun shone on,
An' dark blue is her ee . . .

3. Like dew on the gowan lying
Is the fa' o' her fairy feet;
An' like winds in summer sighing,
Her voice is low an' sweet,
Her voice is low an' sweet,
An' she's a' the world to me . . .

AS WITH GLADNESS MEN OF OLD

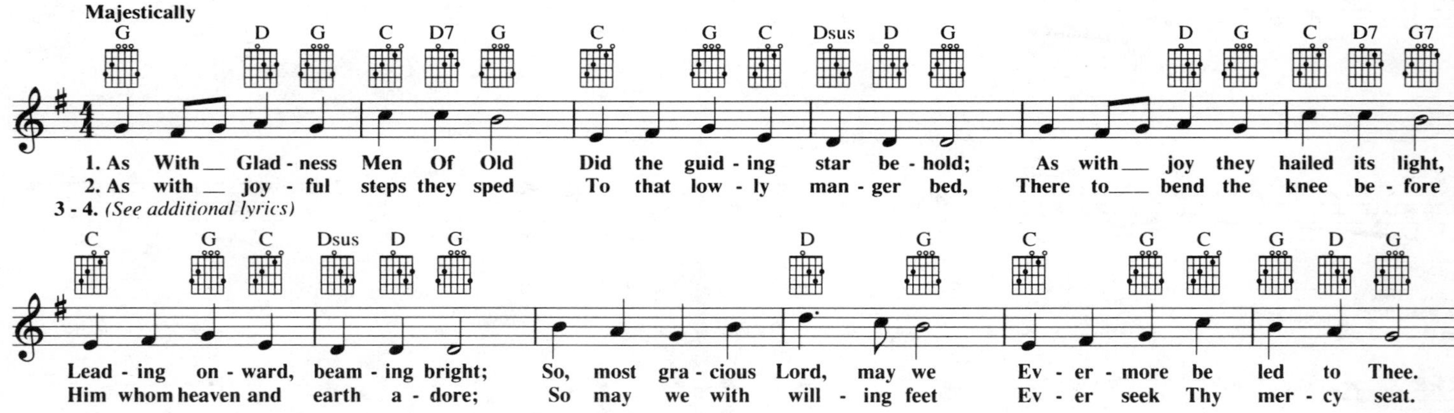
Majestically
G D G C D7 G C G C Dsus D G D G C D7 G7
1. As With___ Glad - ness Men Of Old Did the guid - ing star be - hold; As with___ joy they hailed its light,
2. As with___ joy - ful steps they sped To that low - ly man - ger bed, There to___ bend the knee be - fore
3 - 4. (See additional lyrics)
C G C Dsus D G D G C G C G D G
Lead - ing on - ward, beam - ing bright; So, most gra - cious Lord, may we Ev - er - more be led to Thee.
Him whom heaven and earth a - dore; So may we with will - ing feet Ev - er seek Thy mer - cy seat.

Additional Lyrics

3. As they offered gifts most rare
At that manger rude and bare,
So may we with holy joy,
Pure and free from sin's alloy,
All our costliest treasures bring.
Christ, to thee, our heavenly King.

4. Holy Jesus, every day
Keep us in the narrow way;
And, when earthly things are past,
Bring our ransomed souls at last
Where they need no star to guide,
Where no clouds Thy glory hide.

ARKANSAS TRAVELER

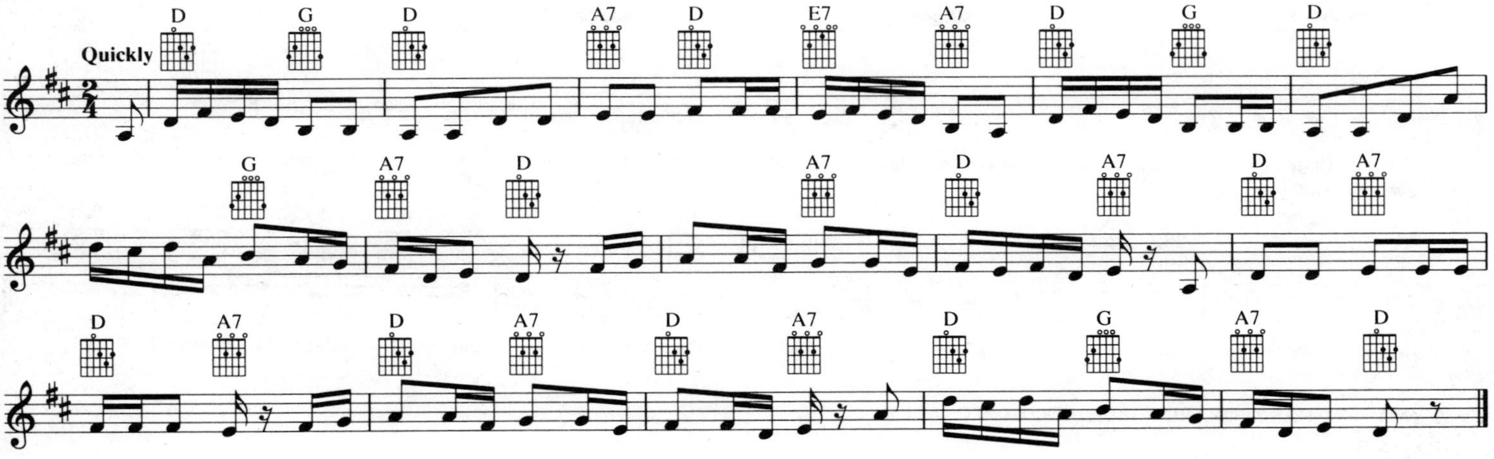

AMERICAN CADETS MARCH

AU CLAIR DE LA LUNE

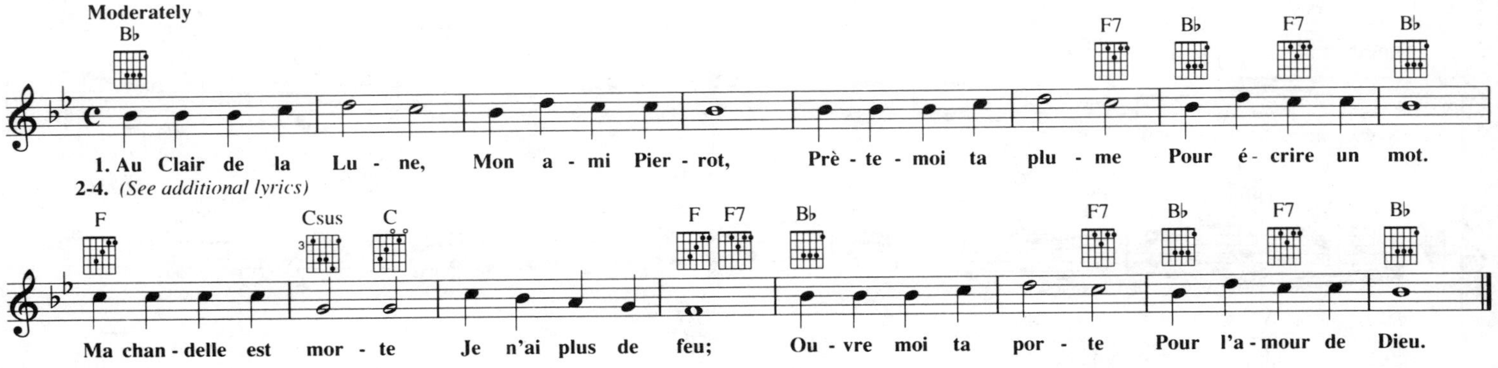
Moderately
B♭ F7 B♭ F7 B♭
1. Au Clair de la Lu - ne, Mon a - mi Pier - rot, Prè - te - moi ta plu - me Pour é - crire un mot.
2-4. *(See additional lyrics)*
F Csus C F F7 B♭ F7 B♭ F7 B♭
Ma chan - delle est mor - te Je n'ai plus de feu; Ou - vre moi ta por - te Pour l'a - mour de Dieu.

Additional Lyrics

2. Au Clair De La Lune Pierrot répondit,
"Je n'ai pas de plume, je suis dans mon lit.
Va chez la voisine, je crois qu'elle y est.
Car dans sa cuisine on bat le briquet."

3. Au clair De La Lune s'en fût Arlequin,
Frapper chez la brune, ell' répond soudain:
"Qui frapp' de la sorte?" Il dit à son tour:
"Ouvrez votre porte, pour le dieu d'amour!"

4. Au Clair De La Lune, on n'y voit qu'un peu.
On chercha la plume, on chercha du feu.
En cherchant d'la sorte, je n'sais c'qu'on trouva;
Mais je sais qu'la porte sur eux se ferma.

Singable Translation

1. "At thy door I'm knocking, by the pale moonlight,
Lend a pen, I pray thee, I've a word to write;
Guttered is my candle, my fire burns no more;
For the love of heaven, open up the door!"

2. Pierrot cried in answer by the pale moonlight,
"In my bed I'm lying, late and chill the night;
Yonder at my neighbor's, someone is astir;
Fire is freshly kindled, get a light from her."

3. To the neighbor's house then, by the pale moonlight,
Goes our gentle Lubin to beg a pen to write;
"Who knocks there so softly?" calls a voice above.
"Open wide your door now for the God of Love!"

4. Seek they pen and candle by the pale moonlight,
They can see so little since dark is now the night;
What they find while seeking, that is not revealed;
All behind her door is carefully concealed.

AULD LANG SYNE

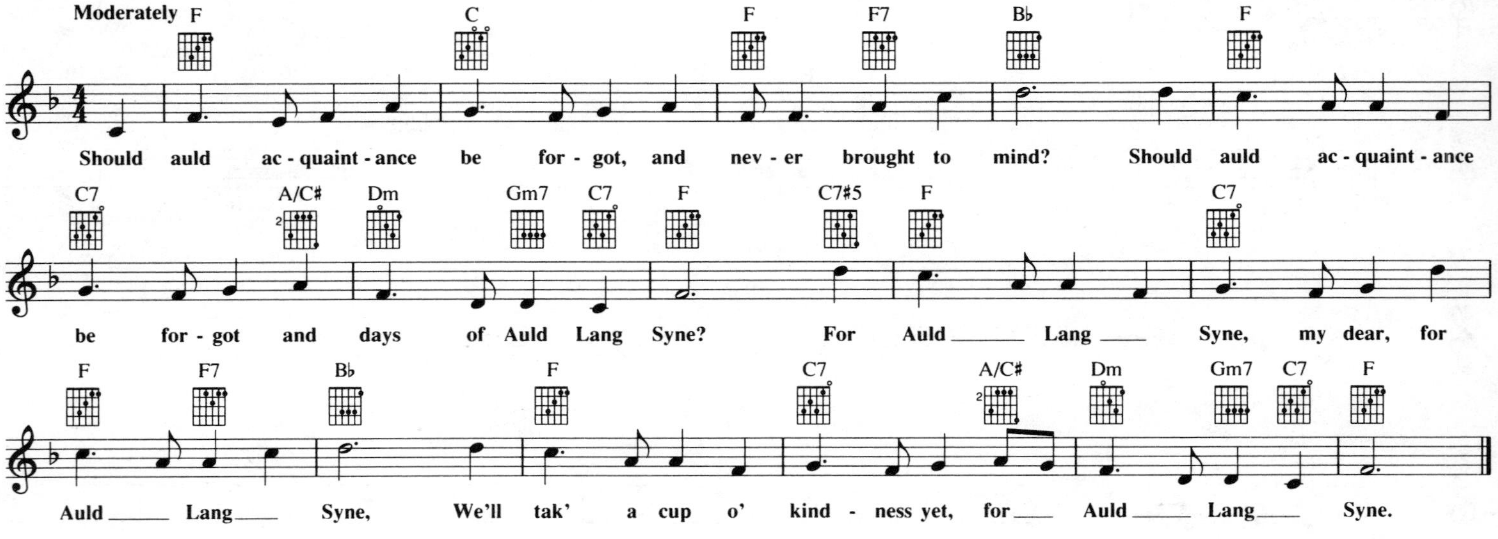
Moderately
F C F F7 B♭ F
Should auld ac - quaint - ance be for - got, and nev - er brought to mind? Should auld ac - quaint - ance
C7 A/C♯ Dm Gm7 C7 F C7♯5 F C7
be for - got and days of Auld Lang Syne? For Auld ___ Lang ___ Syne, my dear, for
F F7 B♭ F C7 A/C♯ Dm Gm7 C7 F
Auld ___ Lang ___ Syne, We'll tak' a cup o' kind - ness yet, for ___ Auld ___ Lang ___ Syne.

AURA LEE

By W.W. Fosdick and George R. Poulton

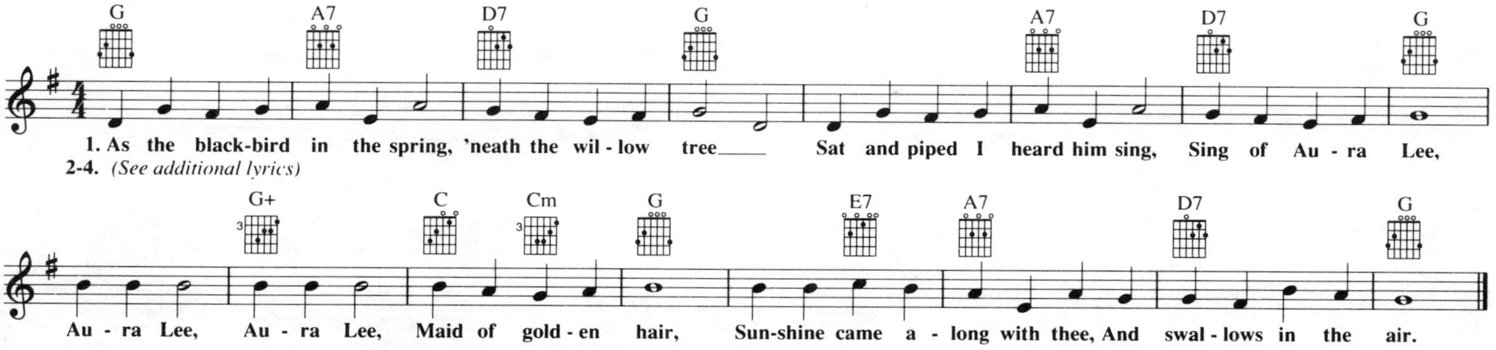
G A7 D7 G A7 D7 G
1. As the black-bird in the spring, 'neath the wil - low tree Sat and piped I heard him sing, Sing of Au - ra Lee,
2-4. (See additional lyrics)
G+ C Cm G E7 A7 D7 G
Au - ra Lee, Au - ra Lee, Maid of gold - en hair, Sun-shine came a - long with thee, And swal - lows in the air.

Additional Lyrics

2. In thy blush the rose was born;
Music when you spake.
Through thine azure eyes the moon
Sparkling seemed to break.
Aura Lee, Aura Lee,
Birds of crimson wing
Never song have sung to me
As in that bright, sweet spring.

3. Aura Lee, the bird may flee,
The willow's golden hair
Swing through winter fitfully,
On the stormy air.
Yet if thy blue eyes I see,
Gloom will soon depart.
For to me, sweet Aura Lee
Is sunshine through the heart.

4. When the mistletoe was green
'Midst the winter's snows,
Sunshine in thy face was seen,
Kissing lips of rose.
Aura Lee, Aura Lee,
Take my golden ring.
Love and light return with thee,
And swallows with the spring.

AVE MARIA
(Bach/Gounod)

J.S. Bach
Charles Gounod

Reverently
F Gm C7 F Dm G7 C F
A - ve, Ma - ri - a! Gra - ti - a ple - na. Do - mi - nus Te - cum
Dm G7 C Cdim Gm C7 F
be - ne - dic - ta tu in mu - li - e - ri - bus et be - ne - dic - tus
B♭ Gm C7 F F7 B♭ Ddim
fruc - tus ven tris tu - i Je - sus. Sanc - ta Ma - ri - a Sanc - ta Ma -
Fm B♭m C7 F Gm C7 Ddim
ri - a Ma - ri - a, O - ra - pro no - bis, no - bis pec - ca - to - ri - bus nunc et in
F Gm C7 F F7 B♭ C7 F
Ho - ra, in ho - ra mor - tis nos - trae. A - men. A - men.

AVE MARIA
(Schubert)

Music by Franz Schubert

Very slowly
F F7 B♭/F
Edim/F F Dm F/C C7
A - ve, Ma - ri -
A - ve, Ma - ri -
Dm Gm/B♭ C7 F F+
a! Gra - ti - a ple - na. Ma - ri - a
a! Ma - ter De - i. O - ra pro
Dm/F Bdim/E E7 Edim Dm
gra - ti - a ple - na, Ma - ri - a, gra - ti - a ple - na, A -
no - bis pec - ca - to - ri - bus, O - ra, o - ra pro no - bis. O -
C/E D/A C/G G7 C C7
ve, A - ve! Do - mi - nus Do - mi - nus te - cum. Ben - e - dic - ta -
ra, O - ra pro no - bis, pec - ta - to - ri - bus. Nunc et in
F/C C7 Dm
tu in mu - li - e - ri - bus. Et ben - e - dic - tus, et
ho - ra mor - tis. In ho - ra - mor - tis nos - trae, In
C A Gm Ddim C
ben - e - dic - tus fruc - tus ven - tris, ven - tris, tu - i, Je - sus.
ho - ra - mor - tis, mor - tis nos - trae, in ho - ra mor - tis nos - trae.
C7 F Dm F/C C7 F
A - ve, Ma - ri - a!
A - ve, Ma - ri - a!
F7 B♭/F Edim/F F
2nd time to Coda
CODA
F

AWAY IN A MANGER
(Spillman)

Music by Jonathan E. Spillman

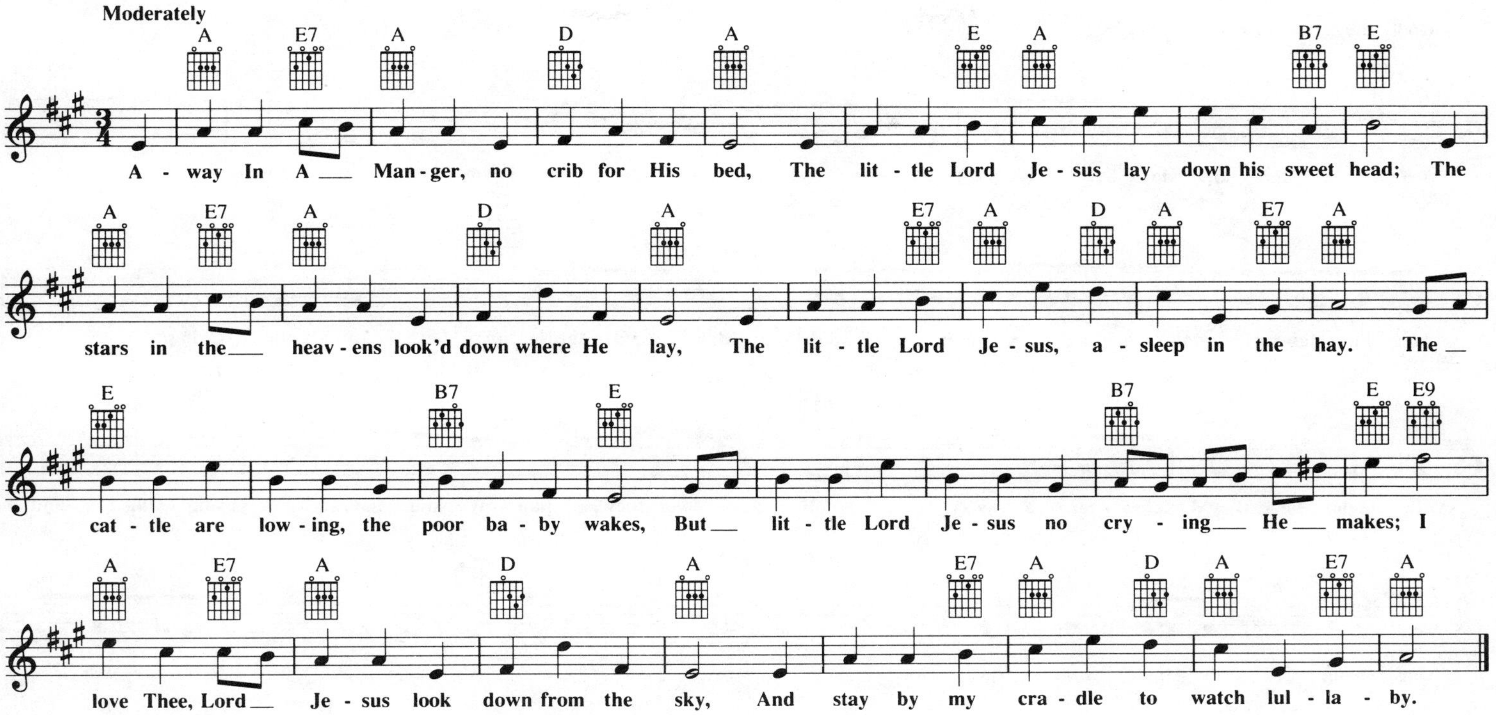
Moderately
A - way In A ___ Man - ger, no crib for His bed, The lit - tle Lord Je - sus lay down his sweet head; The
stars in the ___ heav - ens look'd down where He lay, The lit - tle Lord Je - sus, a - sleep in the hay. The ___
cat - tle are low - ing, the poor ba - by wakes, But ___ lit - tle Lord Je - sus no cry - ing ___ He ___ makes; I
love Thee, Lord ___ Je - sus look down from the sky, And stay by my cra - dle to watch lul - la - by.

AWAY IN A MANGER
(James R. Murray)

Music by James R. Murray

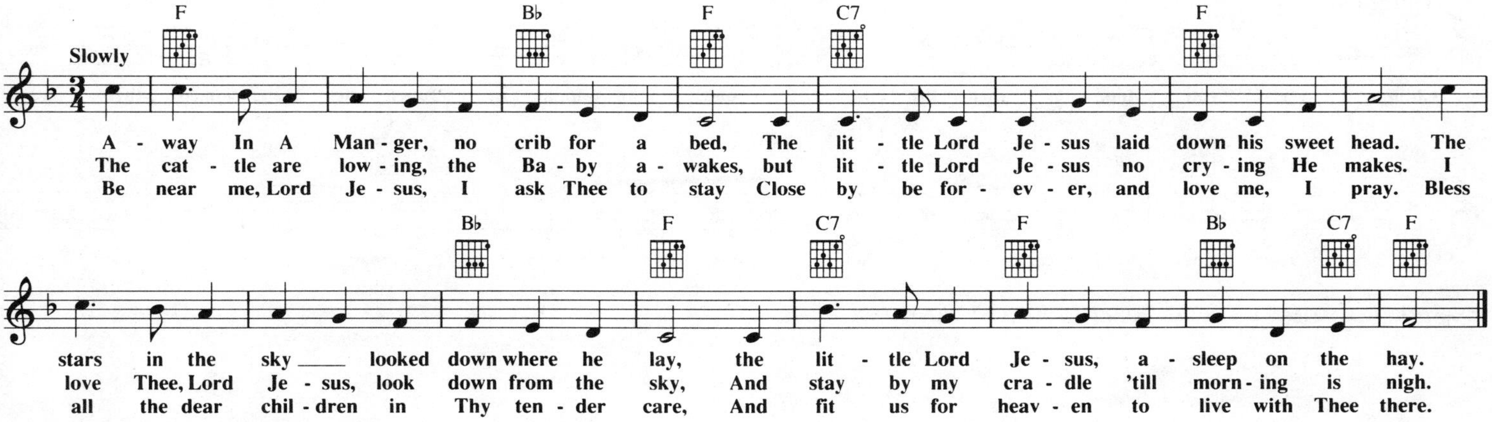
Slowly
A - way In A Man - ger, no crib for a bed, The lit - tle Lord Je - sus laid down his sweet head. The
The cat - tle are low - ing, the Ba - by a - wakes, but lit - tle Lord Je - sus no cry - ing He makes. I
Be near me, Lord Je - sus, I ask Thee to stay Close by be for - ev - er, and love me, I pray. Bless
stars in the sky ___ looked down where he lay, the lit - tle Lord Je - sus, a - sleep on the hay.
love Thee, Lord Je - sus, look down from the sky, And stay by my cra - dle 'till morn - ing is nigh.
all the dear chil - dren in Thy ten - der care, And fit us for heav - en to live with Thee there.

AWAY IN A MANGER
(W.J. Kirkpatrick)

Music by W.J. Kirkpatrick

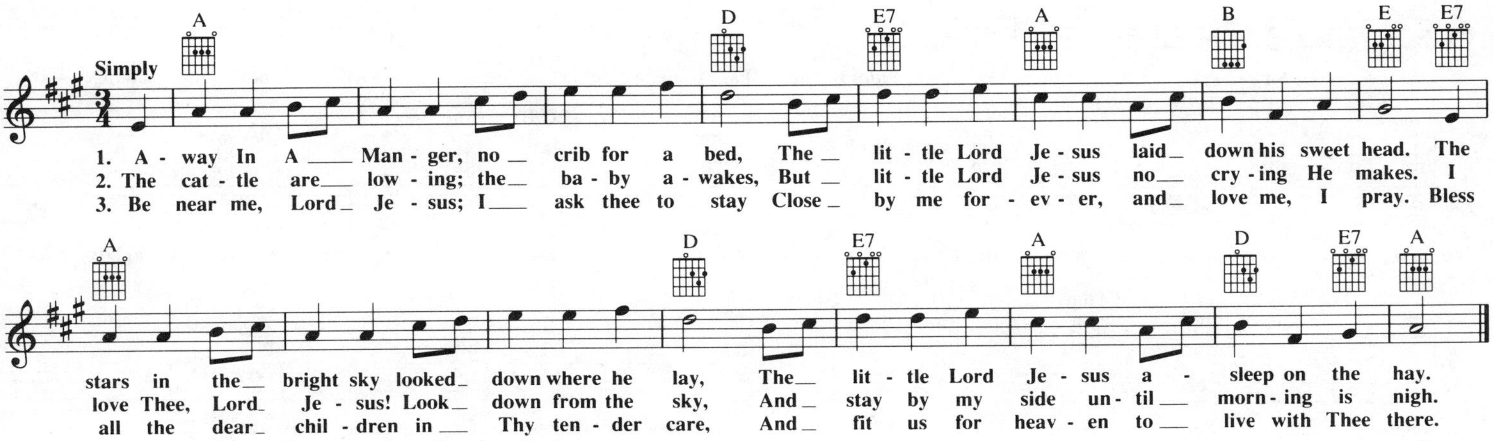
Simply
1. A - way In A ___ Man - ger, no ___ crib for a bed, The ___ lit - tle Lord Je - sus laid ___ down his sweet head. The
2. The cat - tle are ___ low - ing; the ___ ba - by a - wakes, But ___ lit - tle Lord Je - sus no ___ cry - ing He makes. I
3. Be near me, Lord ___ Je - sus; I ___ ask thee to stay Close ___ by me for - ev - er, and ___ love me, I pray. Bless
stars in the ___ bright sky looked ___ down where he lay, The ___ lit - tle Lord Je - sus a - sleep on the hay.
love Thee, Lord ___ Je - sus! Look ___ down from the sky, And ___ stay by my side un - til ___ morn - ing is nigh.
all the dear ___ chil - dren in ___ Thy ten - der care, And ___ fit us for heav - en to ___ live with Thee there.

THE ABA DABA HONEYMOON

Words and Music by Arthur Fields and Walter Donovan

Moderately
"Ab - a, dab - a, da - ba, da - ba, dab - a, dab - a, dab," said the Chim - pie to the Monk,
"bab - a, dab - a, dab - a, dab - a, dab - a, dab - a, dab," said the Mon - key to the Chimp.
All night long they'd chat - ter a - way, all day long they're hap - py and gay, swing - ing and
sing - ing in their hun - key, ton - key way. "Ab - a, dab - a, dab - a, dab - a,
dab - a, dab - a, dab," means "Monk, I love but you," "bab - a, dab - a, dab," in mon - key talk means
"Chimp, I love you too," then the big ba - boon, one night in June, he mar - ried them, and
ver - y soon they went up - on their ab - a, dab - a hon - ey - moon.

ANCHORS AWEIGH

Words and Music by Capt. Alfred H. Miles (Ret.), and Chas. A. Zimmerman

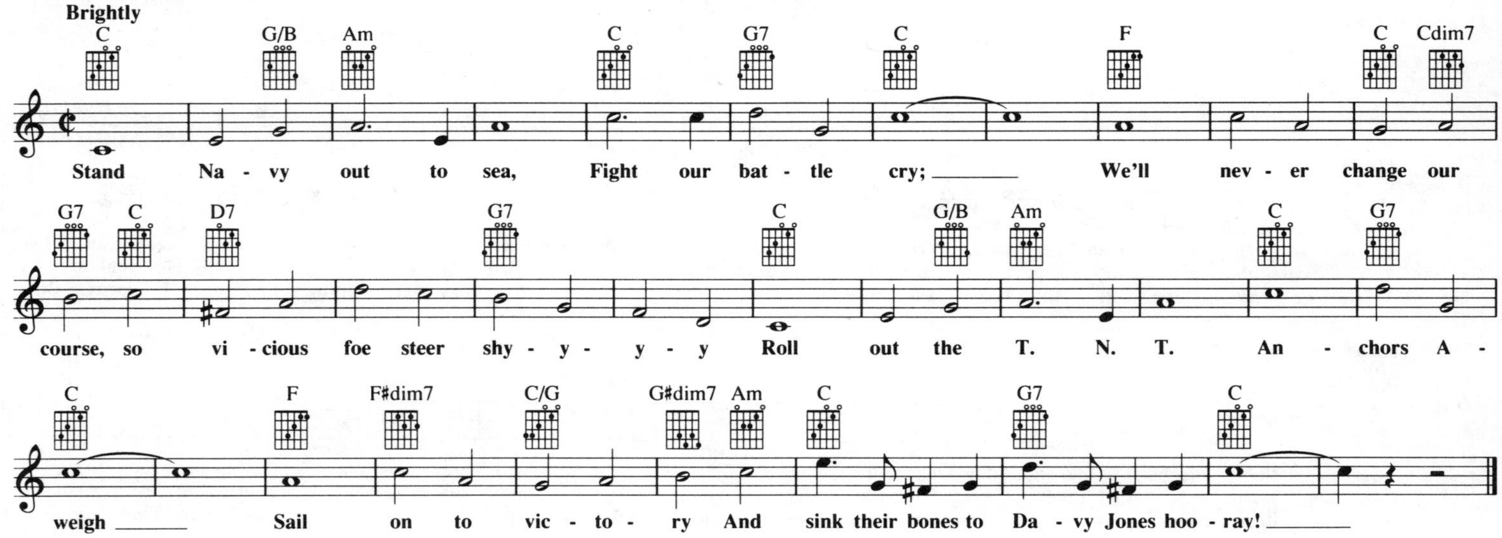
Brightly
Stand Na - vy out to sea, Fight our bat - tle cry; We'll nev - er change our
course, so vi - cious foe steer shy - y - y - y Roll out the T. N. T. An - chors A -
weigh Sail on to vic - to - ry And sink their bones to Da - vy Jones hoo - ray!

ADIOS MUCHACHOS

Julio Sanders

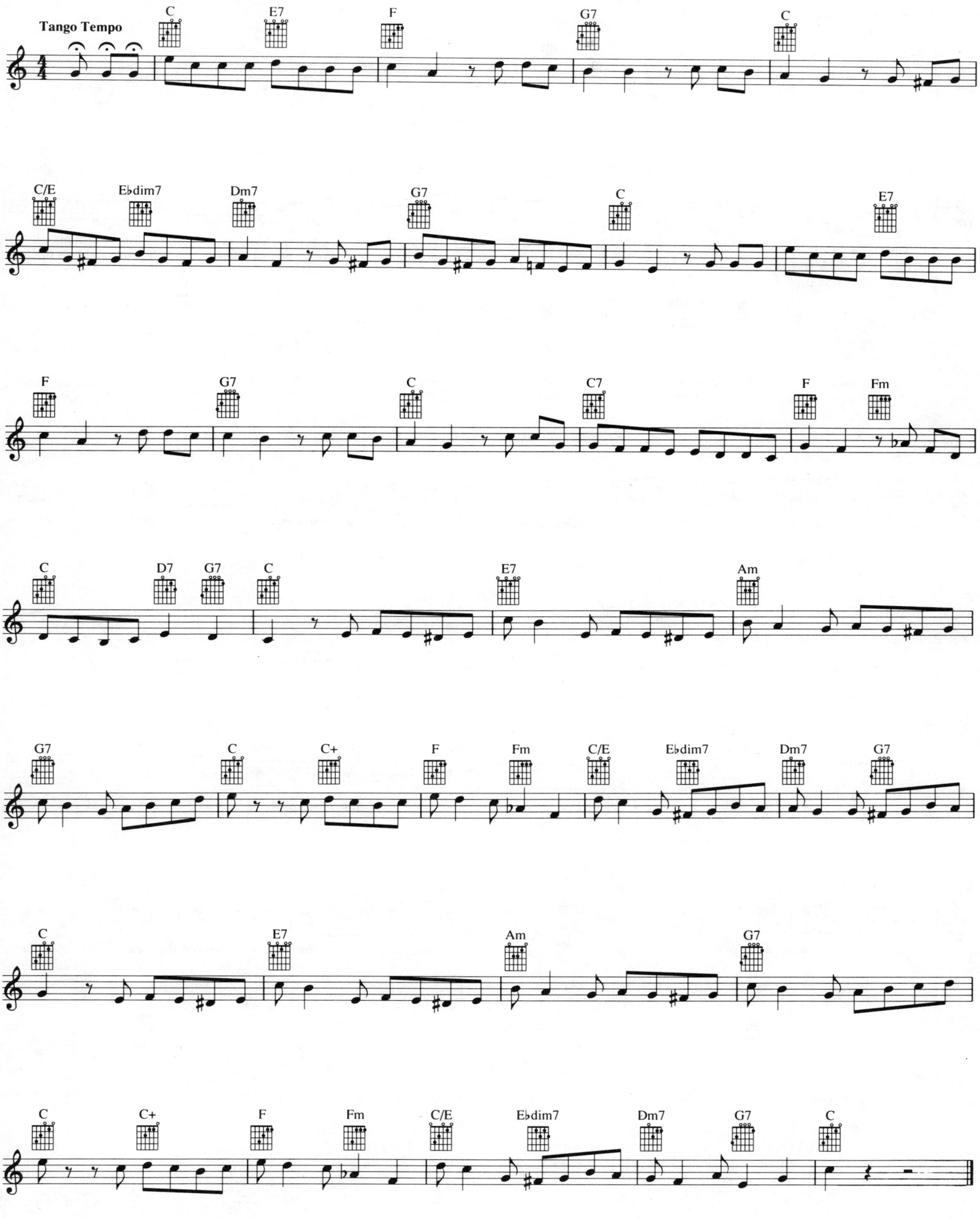

ALEXANDER'S RAGTIME BAND

By Irving Berlin

Moderately
C C7 F Dm7 G7 C
Oh, ma hon - ey, Oh, ma hon - ey, Bet - ter hur - ry and let's me - an - der, Ain't you go - in'
Oh, ma hon - ey, Oh, ma hon - ey, There's a fid - dle with notes that screech - es, Like a chick-en,
D7 G7 C C7
Ain't you go - in, To the lead - er man, rag - ged me - ter man? Oh, ma hon - ey, Oh, ma hon - ey,
Like a chick-en, And the clar - in - et is a col - ored pet, Come and lis - ten, Come and lis - ten,
F Dm7 G7 C C7 F Cdim C G7 C C7
Let me take you to Al - ex - an - der's grand - stand, brass band, Ain't you com-ing a - long?
To a class - i - cal band what's peach - es, come now, some - how, Bet - ter hur - ry a - long.
Come on and
F C7 F Bb
hear, Come on and hear Al - ex - an - der's Rag - time Band, Come on and hear, Come on and hear, It's the
F
best band in the land, They can play a bu - gle call like you nev - er heard be - fore, So nat - ur - al that you
C Cdim G7 C C7 F
want to go to war; That's just the best - est band what am, hon - ey lamb, Come on a - long, Come on a -
C7 F Bb
long, Let me take you by the hand, Up to the man, Up to the man who's the lead - er of the
F7 Bb Fdim F
band, And if you care to hear the Swan - nee Riv - er played in rag - time, Come on and hear, Come on and
Fdim C7 1 F Cdim C7 2 F
hear Al - ex - an - der's Rag - time Band. Come on and Band.

BE MY LITTLE BABY BUMBLEBEE

Lyric by Stanley Murphy
Music by Henry I. Marshall

Moderately
E7 A7
Be My Lit - tle Ba - by Bum - ble Bee, (buzz a - round, buzz a - round, keep a buzz - in 'round,)
D7 G D7
Bring home all the hon - ey, love, ___ to me, (lit - tle bee, lit - tle bee, lit - tle bee.)
E7 A7
Let me spend the hap - py hours __ Ro - ving with you 'mongst the flow'rs and when we get where
D7 G#dim D7 E7
no one else can see, (cud - dle up, cud - dle up, cud - dle up.) Be My Lit - tle
A7 D7
Ba - by Bum - ble Bee, (buzz a - round, buzz a - round, keep a buzz - in 'round,) We'll be just as
C7 B7 B7♭5 E7
hap - py as can be, (you and me, you and me, you and me,) Hon - ey keep a
A7
buzz - in' please, __ I've got a doz - en cou - sin bees, __ But I
G Em A7 D7 G Cm G
want you ___ to be my ba - by bum - ble bee. ___

THE BILLBOARD MARCH

John N. Klohr

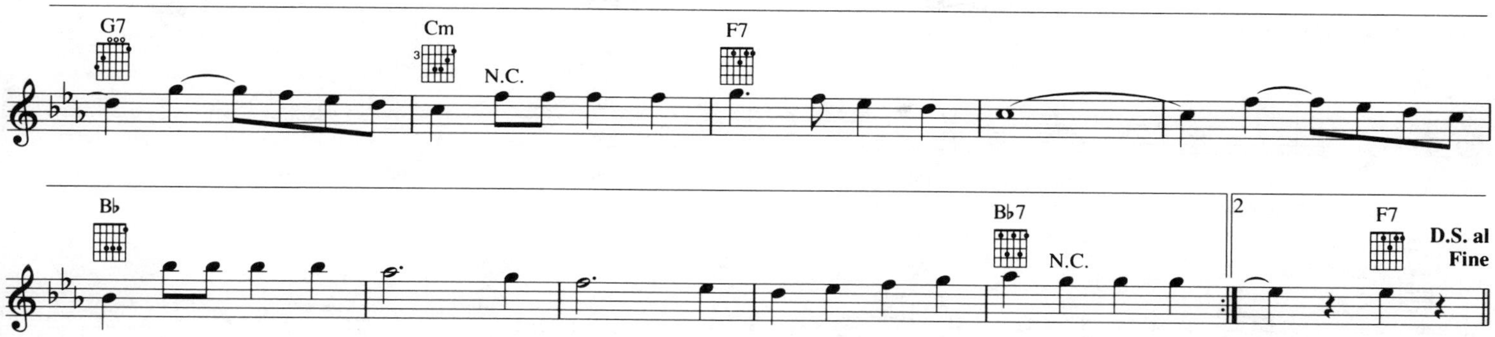
G7 Cm N.C. F7
Bb Bb7 N.C. 2 F7 D.S. al Fine

Words by Edward Teschemacher
Music by Guy d'Hardelot

BECAUSE

Slowly
Be - cause you come to me with naught save love, And hold my hand and lift mine eyes a - bove, A wi - der world of hope and joy I see, Be - cause you come to me.
cause God made thee mine I'll cher - ish thee Thru light and dark - ness thru all time to be, And pray His love may make our love di - vine, Be - cause God made thee mine.
Instrumental
To Coda
Be - cause you speak to me in ac - cents sweet, I fiind the ros - es wak - ing 'round my feet, And I am led through tears and joy to thee, Be - cause you speak to me
Instrumental
D.S. al Coda
Be -
CODA
Bb Dm Cm6 F7 G Cm Cm7 Eb6/9 Bb7 Eb Edim Bb/F C7 Fm D7 Gm Gb+ Ebm/Gb Cm7/F Dm/F

A BIRD IN A GILDED CAGE

Arthur J. Lamb and Harry von Tilzer

Moderately
C Dm G7 C C7 F Bdim Am D7 E7 A7 F#dim
The ball - room was filled with fash - ion's throng, It shone with a thou - sand lights, And there was a wom - an who passed a - long, The fair - est of all the sights, A girl to her lov - er then soft - ly sighed, "There's rich - es at her com - mand;" "But she mar - ried for wealth, not for love," he cried, Though she lives in a man - sion grand.
I stood in a church - yard just at eve, When sun - set a - dorned the west, And looked at the peo - ple who'd come to grieve, For loved ones now laid at rest, A tall mar - ble mon - u - ment marked the grave, Of one who'd been fash - ion's queen, And I thought she is hap - pi - er here at rest, Than to have peo - ple say when seen.
She's on - ly A Bird In A Gild - ed Cage, A beau - ti - ful sight to see, You may think she's hap - py and free from care, She's not, though she seems to be. 'Tis sad when you think of her

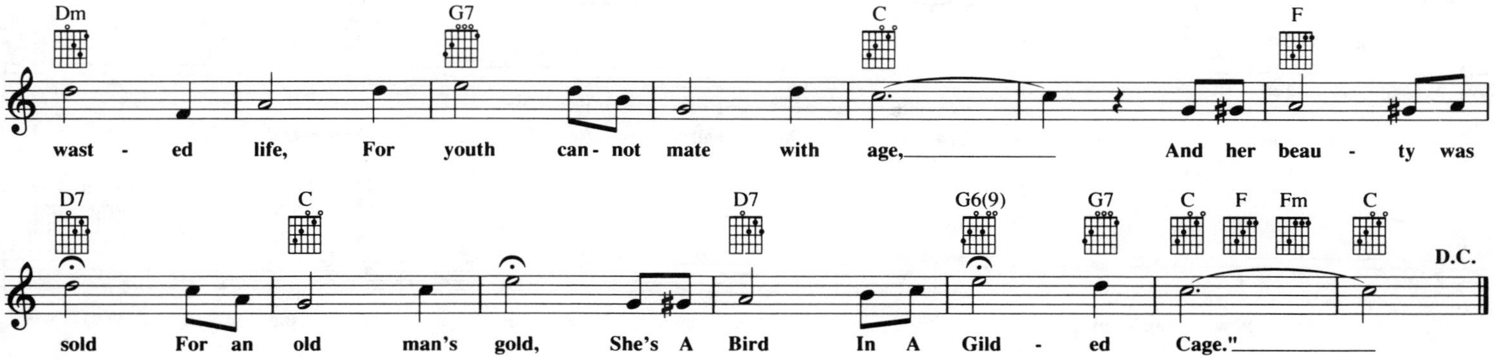
Dm G7 C F
wast - ed life, For youth can- not mate with age, And her beau - ty was
D7 C D7 G6(9) G7 C F Fm C
D.C.
sold For an old man's gold, She's A Bird In A Gild - ed Cage."

A.M. Hirsch

BOOLA! BOOLA!

March Tempo
N.C.
Fine
Trio
N.C.
D.S. al Fine

BY THE BEAUTIFUL SEA

Words by Harold R. Atteridge
Music by Harry Carroll

Bright Tempo
Bb7 Bb+ Eb
By the sea, by the sea By The Beau - ti - ful Sea You and I, you and
Bb7 Bbdim Bb7 Bbdim Bb7
I Oh how hap - py we'll be When each wave comes a - roll - ing in We will
Bbdim Bb7 A Bb Eb N.C. Bb7
duck or swim And we'll float and fool a - round the wa - ter O - ver and
Bb+ Eb
un - der and then up for air Pa is rich, Ma is rich so now what do we care?
Bb Eb7 Ab Ab6 Ebdim Gm Gm7 C9 C7 F7
I love to be be - side your side, Be - side the sea, be - side the sea - side
Bb7 1 Eb Bbdim Bb7 2 Eb
By The Beau - ti - ful Sea. By the Sea.

BY THE LIGHT OF THE SILVERY MOON

Lyric by Ed Madden
Music by Gus Edwards

Moderately
C D7
By The Light Of The Sil - ver - y Moon. I want to
G7 C Gdim G7 C
spoon, To my hon - ey I'll croon love's tune, Hon - ey moon
F A7 Dm A Dm C D7 Fm
keep a shin - ing in June, Your sil - v'ry beams will bring love
Am E7b5 A A7 D7 C G7 C F C
dreams We'll be cud - dling soon, By the sil - ver - y moon.

ALSO SPRACH ZARATHUSTRA

R. Strauss

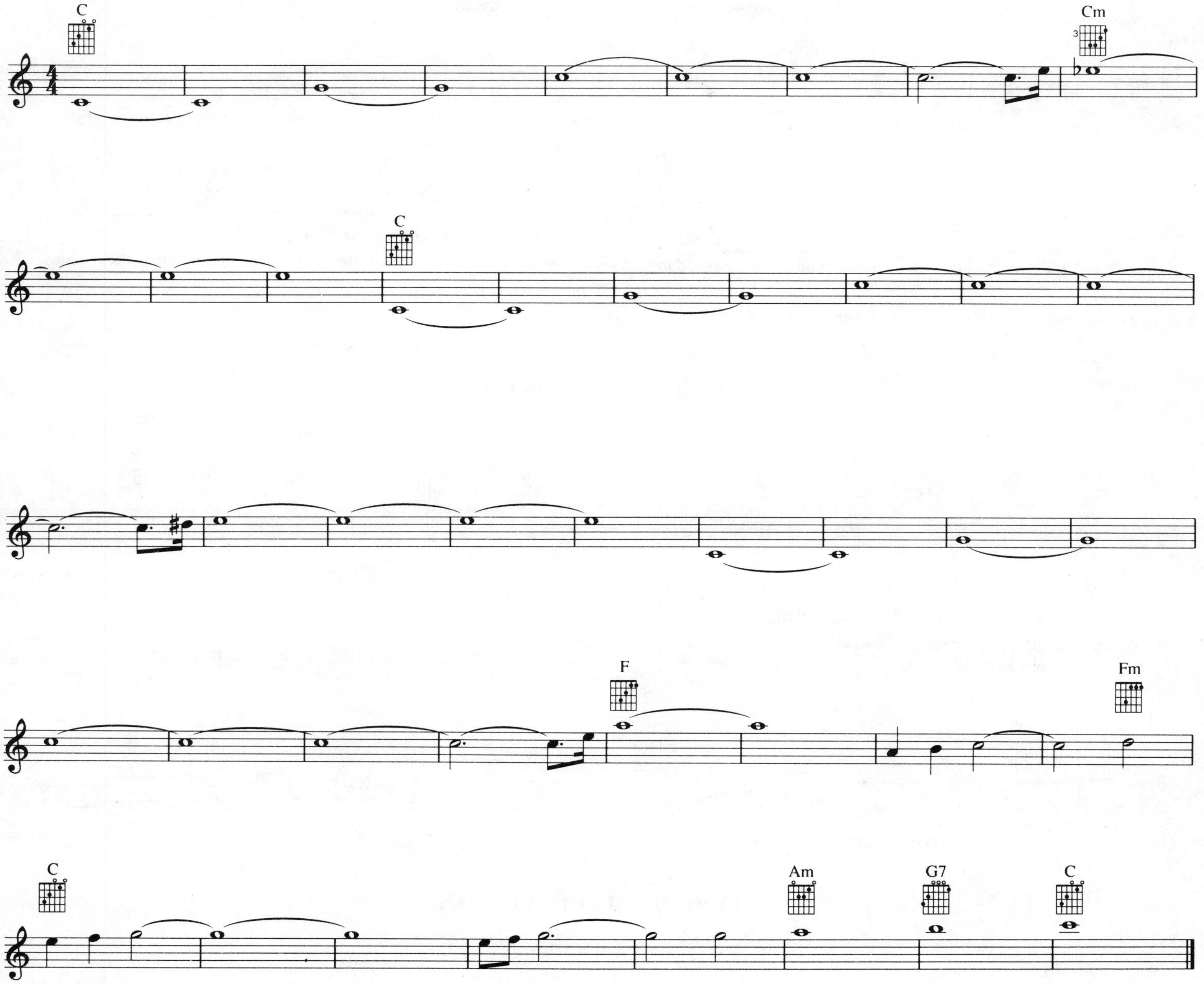

BAA! BAA! BLACK SHEEP

Brightly
Baa! Baa! Black Sheep have you an - y wool! Yes, Sir, Yes, Sir, Three bags full.
One for my mas - ter and one for my dame, But none for the lit - tle boy that cries in the lane.

THE BANANA BOAT SONG

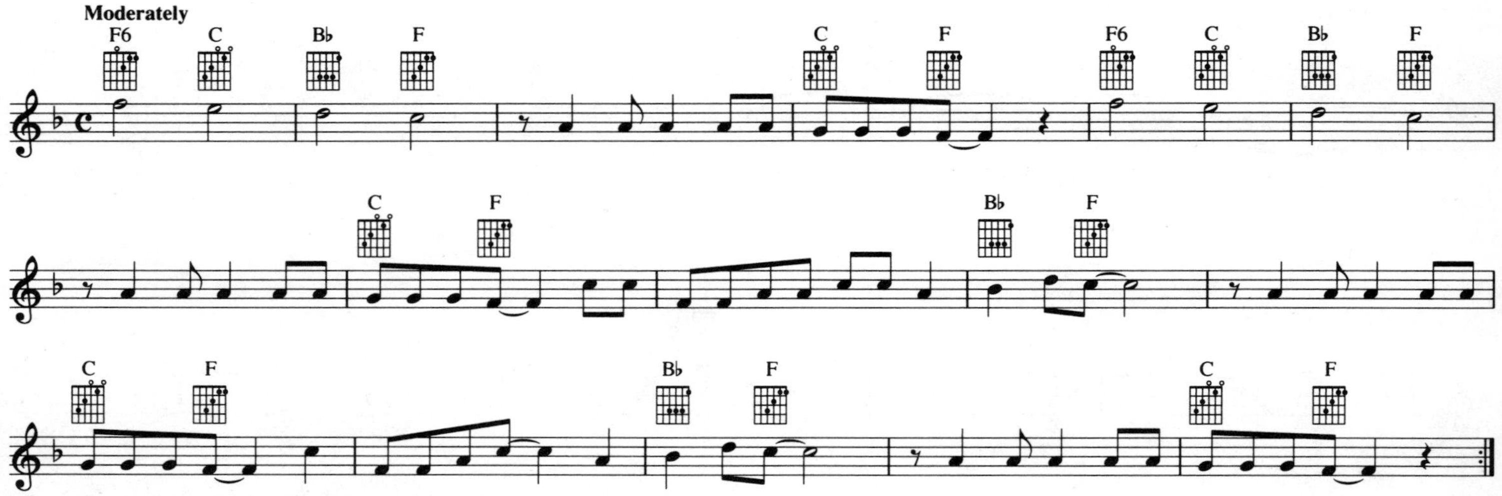
Moderately

THE BAND PLAYED ON

By John E. Palmer

Moderately
Cas - ey would waltz with a straw - ber - ry blonde, And The Band Played On, He'd glide 'cross the
floor with the girl he a - dor'd and The Band Played On. But his brain was so load - ed it
near - ly ex - plod - ed. The poor girl would shake with a - larm. He'd ne'er leave the girl with the
straw - ber - ry curls, And The Band Played On. On.

BANKS OF THE OHIO

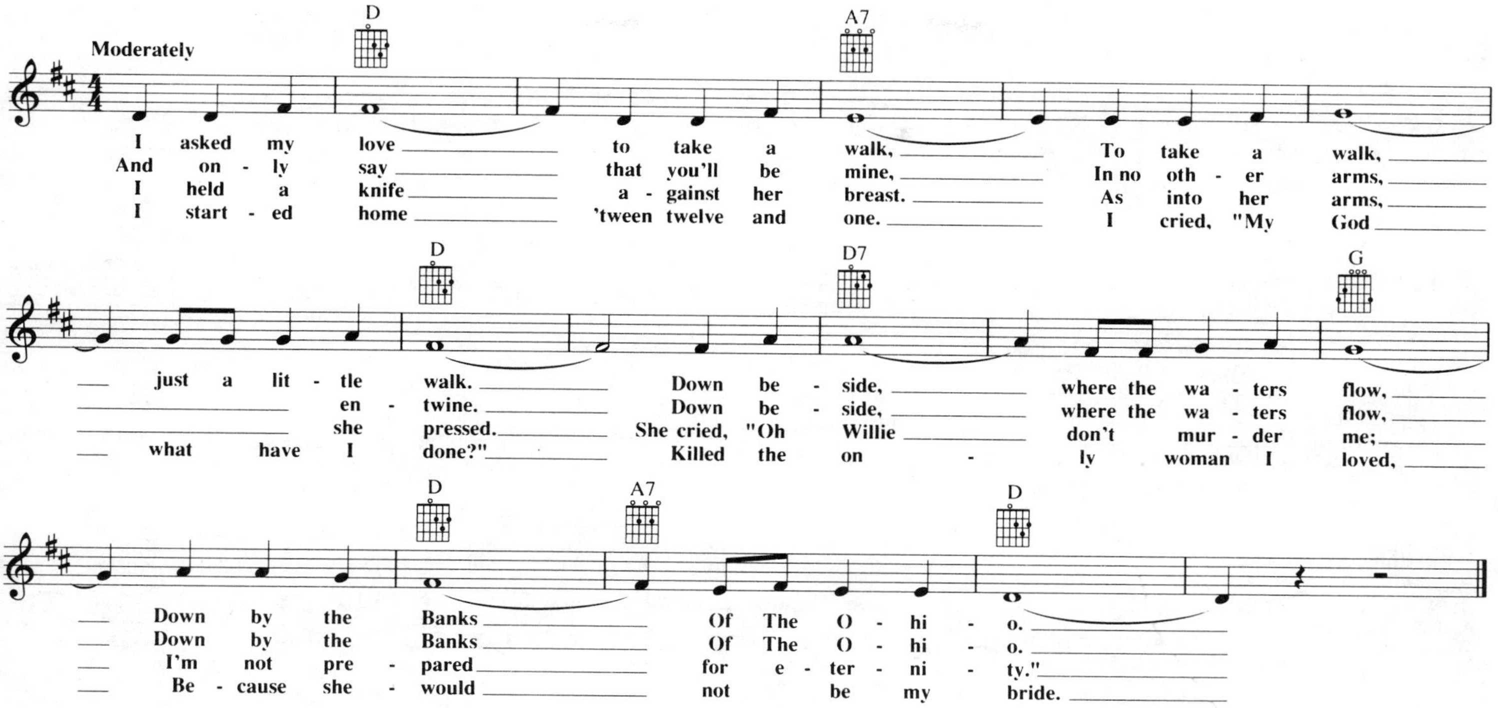
Moderately
D A7 D D7 G D A7 D
I asked my love to take a walk, To take a walk, just a lit-tle walk. Down be-side, where the wa-ters flow, Down by the Banks Of The O-hi-o.
And on-ly say that you'll be mine, In no oth-er arms, en-twine. Down be-side, where the wa-ters flow, Down by the Banks Of The O-hi-o.
I held a knife a-gainst her breast. As into her arms, she pressed. She cried, "Oh Willie don't mur-der me; I'm not pre-pared for e-ter-ni-ty."
I start-ed home 'tween twelve and one. I cried, "My God what have I done?" Killed the on-ly woman I loved, Be-cause she would not be my bride.

BARBARA ALLEN

Slowly
C Am Em F C F G7 C
1. In Scar-let Town, where I was born, There was a fair maid dwell-in' Made ev-'ry youth cry well-a-day! Her name was Bar-b'ra Al-len.
2. All in the mer-ry month of May, When green buds they were swell-in' Sweet Wil-liam on his death-bed lay, For love of Bar-b'ra Al-len.
3 - 9. (See additional lyrics)

Additional Lyrics

3. He sent his servant to the town,
He sent him to her dwelling,
Sayin', "Master's sick, he's very sick,
For the love of Barbara Allen."

4. Then slowly, slowly she got up,
And slowly she came nigh to him;
And all she said when she got there,
"Young man, I think you're dyin'."

5. When he was dead and in his grave,
Her heart was filled with sorrow,
"Oh mother dear, go make my bed,
For I shall die tomorrow."

6. And as she on her death-bed lay,
Begged to be buried by him,
And she repented of the day
That she did e'er deny him.

7. "Farewell, farewell, ye maidens all,
And shun the fault I fell in;
So now rake warning by the fall
Of cruel Barbara Allen."

8. They buried her in the churchyard,
And William's buried by her.
A red rose grew from William's breast,
And from her feet there grew a briar.

9. They grew as high as the church top,
They could not grow any higher;
There they tied in a lover's knot,
For all true lovers to admire.

BARBARA POLKA

BARCAROLLE

Jacques Offenbach

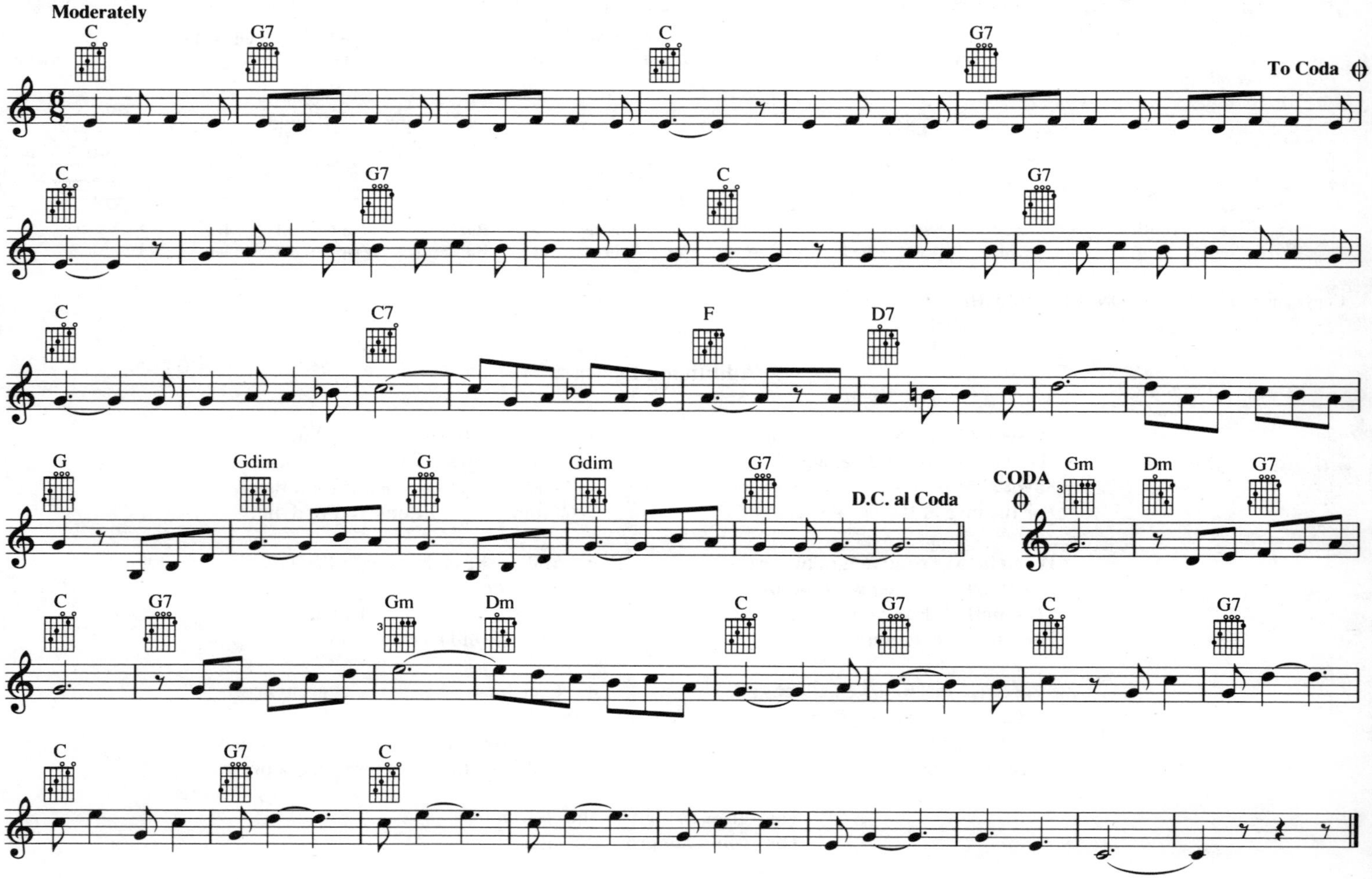

THE BARBER OF SEVILLE OVERTURE

Gioacchino Rossini

THE BARNYARD SONG
(I Had A Rooster)

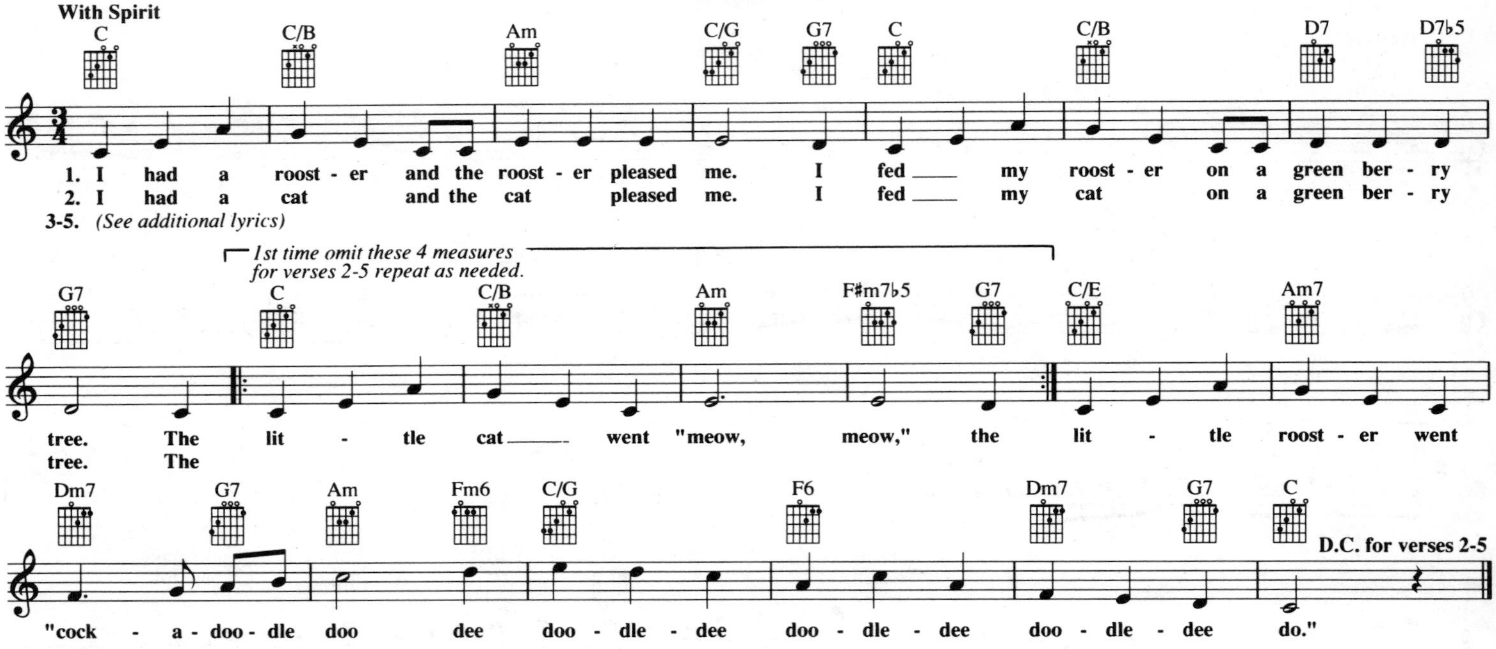
With Spirit
C C/B Am C/G G7 C C/B D7 D7♭5
1. I had a roost - er and the roost - er pleased me. I fed ___ my roost - er on a green ber - ry
2. I had a cat and the cat pleased me. I fed ___ my cat on a green ber - ry
3-5. (See additional lyrics)
1st time omit these 4 measures for verses 2-5 repeat as needed.
G7 C C/B Am F#m7♭5 G7 C/E Am7
tree. The lit - tle cat ___ went "meow, meow," the lit - tle roost - er went
tree. The
Dm7 G7 Am Fm6 C/G F6 Dm7 G7 C
"cock - a - doo - dle doo dee doo - dle - dee doo - dle - dee doo - dle - dee do."
D.C. for verses 2-5

Additional Lyrics

3. I had a pig and the pig pleased me.
   I fed my pig on a green berry tree.
   The little pig went "oink oink."
   The little cat went "meow meow."
   Chorus:

4. I had a cow and the cow pleased me.
   I fed my cow on a green berry tree.
   The little cow went "moo moo."
   The little pig went "oink oink."
   The little cat went "meow meow."
   Chorus:

5. I had a baby and the baby pleased me.
   I fed my baby on a green berry tree.
   The little baby went "waah waah."
   The little cow went "moo moo."
   The little pig went "oink oink."
   The little cat went "meow meow."
   Chorus:

THE BATTLE CRY OF FREEDOM

George F. Root

With spirit
C F C G7
Yes, we'll ral - ly 'round the flag boys, we'll ral - ly once a - gain, Shout - ing The Bat - tle Cry Of Free - dom; We will
We are spring - ing to the call of our broth - ers gone be - fore, Shout - ing The Bat - tle Cry Of Free - dom; And we'll
C F C G7 C
ral - ly from the hill - side, we'll gath - er from the plain, Shout - ing The Bat - tle Cry Of Free - dom. The
fill the va - cant ranks with a mil - lion free - men more, Shout - ing The Bat - tle Cry Of Free - dom.
G7
Un - ion for - ev - er, hur - rah, boys, hur - rah! Down with the trai - tor, Up with the star; While we
C F C G7 C
ral - ly 'round the flag, boys, ral - ly once a - gain, Shout - ing The Bat - tle Cry Of Free - dom.

THE BATTLE HYMN OF THE REPUBLIC

Lyrics by Julia Ward Howe
Music by William Steffe

Majestically
G C G D7 G C G D7 G
Mine eyes have seen the glo - ry of the com - ing of the Lord; He is tram - pling out the vin - tage where the grapes of wrath are stored; He hath loosed the fate - ful light - ning of His ter - ri - ble swift sword; His truth is march - ing on.
I have seen Him in the watch - fires of a hun - dred cir - cling camps, They have build - ed Him an al - tar in the eve - ning dews and damps; I can read His right - eous sen - tence by the dim and flar - ing lamps, His day is march - ing on.
He has sound - ed forth the trum - pet that shall nev - er call re - treat, He is sift - ing out the hearts of men be - fore His judg - ment seat, Oh, be swift, my soul, to an - swer Him, be ju - bi - lant, my feet, Our God is march - ing on.
Refrain:
C G
Glo - ry, glo - ry hal - le lu - jah! Glo - ry, glo - ry hal - le - lu - jah!
C Am G D7 G
Glo - ry, glo - ry hal - le - lu - jah! His truth is march - ing on.

BEAUTIFUL BROWN EYES

Moderately
F Bb F C7
Refrain: Beau - ti - ful, Beau - ti - ful Brown Eyes, Beau - ti - ful, Beau - ti - ful Brown Eyes,
(See additional lyrics)
F Bb C7 F
Beau - ti - ful, Beau - ti - ful Brown Eyes, I'll nev - er love blue eyes a - gain.

Additional Lyrics

1. Willie, my darling, I love you,
Love you with all of my heart;
Tomorrow we were to be married,
But liquor has kept us apart.
Refrain

2. I staggered into the barroom,
I fell down on the floor,
And the very last words that I uttered,
"I'll never get drunk any more."
Refrain

3. Seven long years I've been married,
I wish I was single again,
A woman don't know half her troubles
Until she has married a man.
Refrain

Steven Foster

BEAUTIFUL DREAMER

Sweetly
C Dm G7
Beau - ti - ful Dream - er, wake un - to me, Star - light and dew - drops are
Sounds of the rude world heard in the day, Lulled by the moon - light have
Gone are the cares of life's bus - y throng, Beau - ti - ful Dream - er a -
To Coda
1 C 2 C G7
wait - ing for thee.
all passed a way. Beau - ti - ful Dream -
wake un - to
C Am D7 G7
D.C. al Coda
er, queen of my song, List while I woo thee with soft mel - o - dy.
CODA C E7 Am F C G7 C
me. Beau - ti - ful Dream - er, a - wake un - to me.

BEHOLD THE SAVIOR OF MANKIND

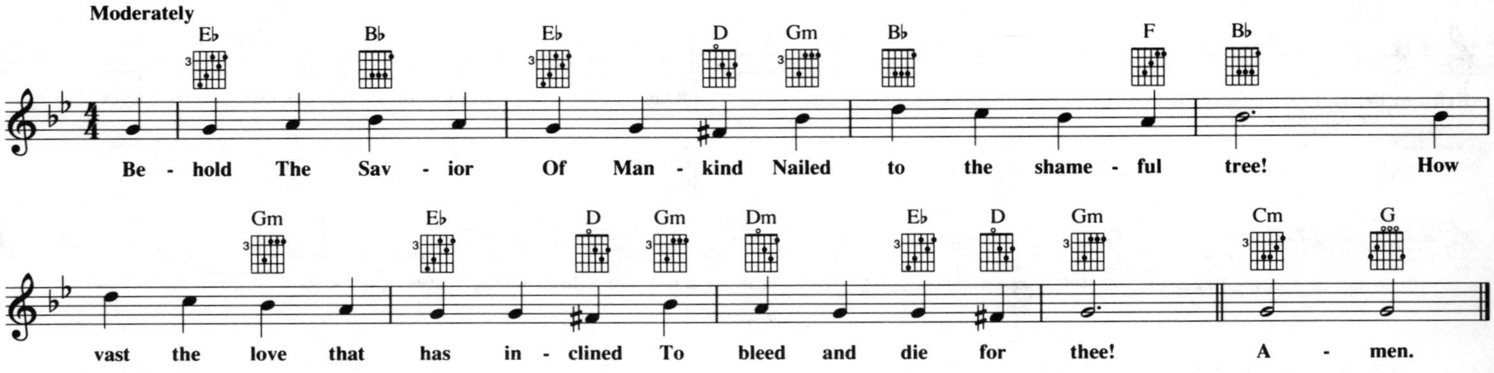
Moderately
Eb Bb Eb D Gm Bb F Bb
Be - hold The Sav - ior Of Man - kind Nailed to the shame - ful tree! How
Gm Eb D Gm Dm Eb D Gm Cm G
vast the love that has in - clined To bleed and die for thee! A - men.

THE BIRTHDAY SONG

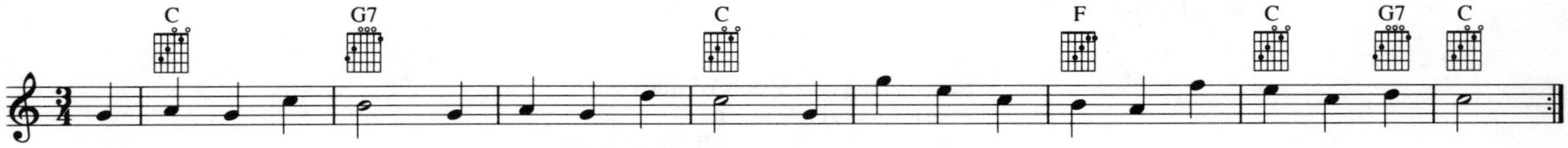
C G7 C F C G7 C

BEAUTIFUL SAVIOR

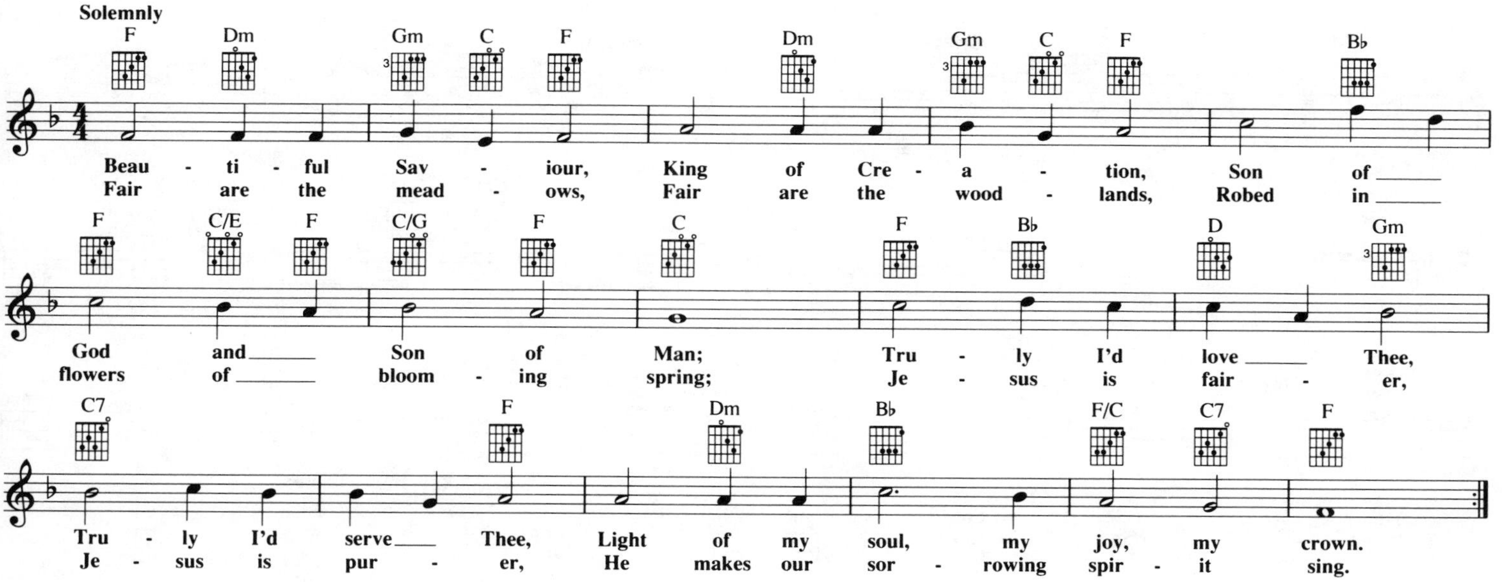
Solemnly
F Dm Gm C F Dm Gm C F B♭
Beau - ti - ful Sav - iour, King of Cre - a - tion, Son of
Fair are the mead - ows, Fair are the wood - lands, Robed in
F C/E F C/G F C F B♭ D Gm
God and Son of Man; Tru - ly I'd love Thee,
flowers of bloom - ing spring; Je - sus is fair - er,
C7 F Dm B♭ F/C C7 F
Tru - ly I'd serve Thee, Light of my soul, my joy, my crown.
Je - sus is pur - er, He makes our sor - rowing spir - it sing.

BELIEVE ME IF ALL THOSE ENDEARING YOUNG CHARMS

Slowly, with a deep feeling
D G D A7
Be - lieve Me, If All Those En - dear - ing Young Charms which I gaze on so fond - ly to -
D G D A7
day, Were to change by to - mor - row and flee from my arms, Like fai - ry gifts fad - ing a -
D G
way. Thou wouldś't still be a - dored as this mo - ment thou art: Let thy
D A7 D
love - li - ness fade as it will, And a - round the dear ru - in, each
G D A7 D
wish of my heart, Would en - twine it - self ver - dant - ly still.

BEETHOVEN'S FIFTH SYMPHONY
(1st Movement Theme)

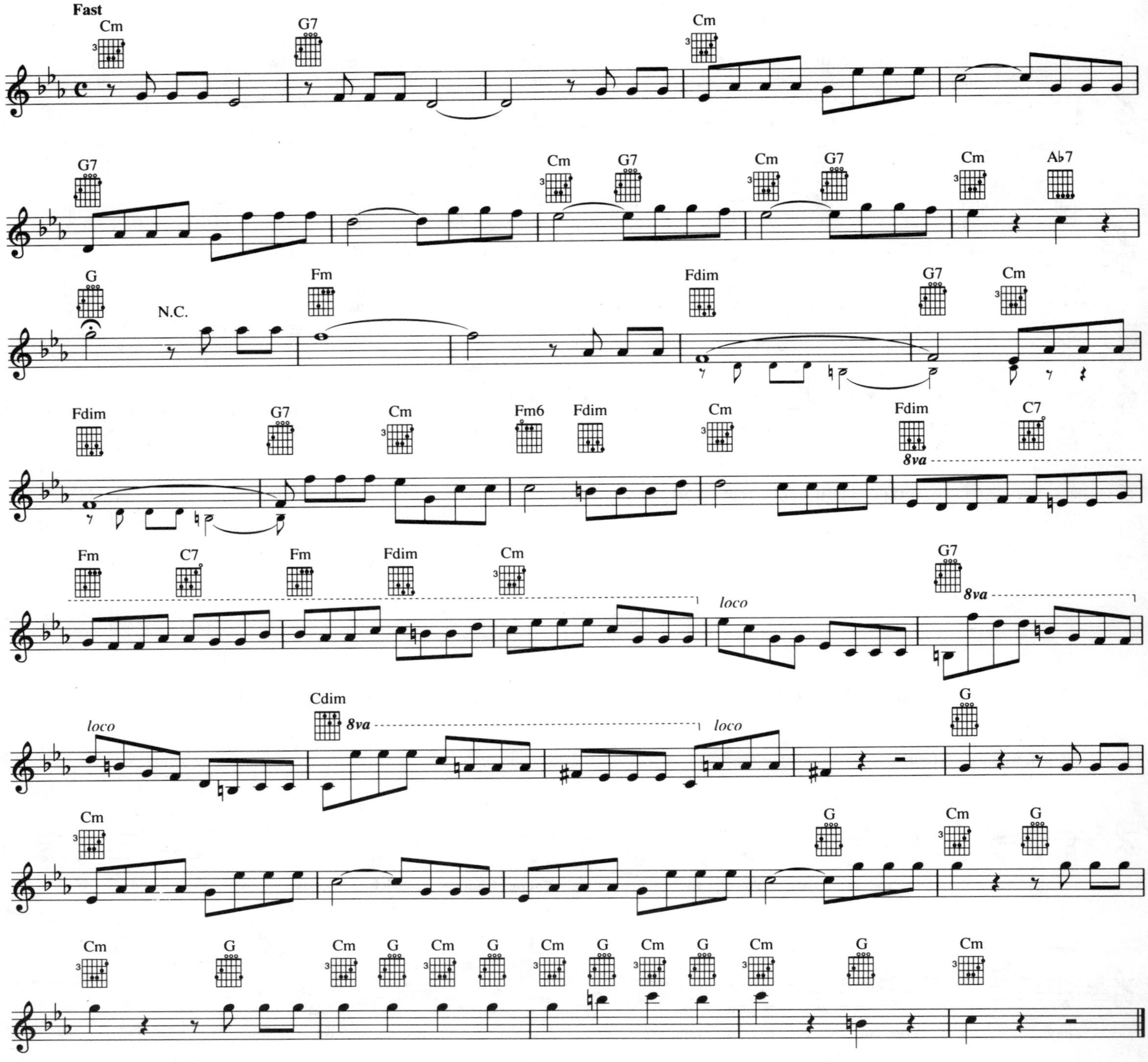

A BICYCLE BUILT FOR TWO
(Daisy Bell)

Words and Music by Harry Dacre

F C C7 F Dm A7
Plant - ed by Dai - sy Bell! Wheth - er she loves me or
I and my Dai - sy Bell! When the road's dark we can
Dm Gm B♭7 A7
loves me not, Some - times it's hard to tell;
both de - spise P'lice - men and "lamps" as well;
Dm A7 Dm G7
Yet I am long - ing to share the lot Of beau - ti - ful Dai - sy
There are "bright lights" in the daz - zling eyes Of beau - ti - ful Dai - sy
C C7 F
Bell!
Bell!
Dai - sy, Dai - sy,
B♭ F C7 F
Give me your an - swer, do! I'm half cra - zy,
G7 C7 D Gm C
All for the love of you! It won't be a styl - ish
C7 F C F B♭ F C7
mar - riage, I can't af - ford a car - riage, But
F F♯dim7 C7 F F♯dim7 C F Dm7 Gm7 C7 F
you'll look sweet On the seat of A Bi - cy - cle Built For Two!

Additional Lyrics

3. I will stand by you in "wheel" or woe,
   Daisy, Daisy!
   You'll be the belle which I'll ring, you know!
   Sweet little Daisy Bell!
   You'll take the "lead" in each "trip" we take,
   Then, if I don't do well,
   I will permit you to use the brake,
   My beautiful Daisy Bell!

BE KIND TO YOUR WEB-FOOTED FRIENDS

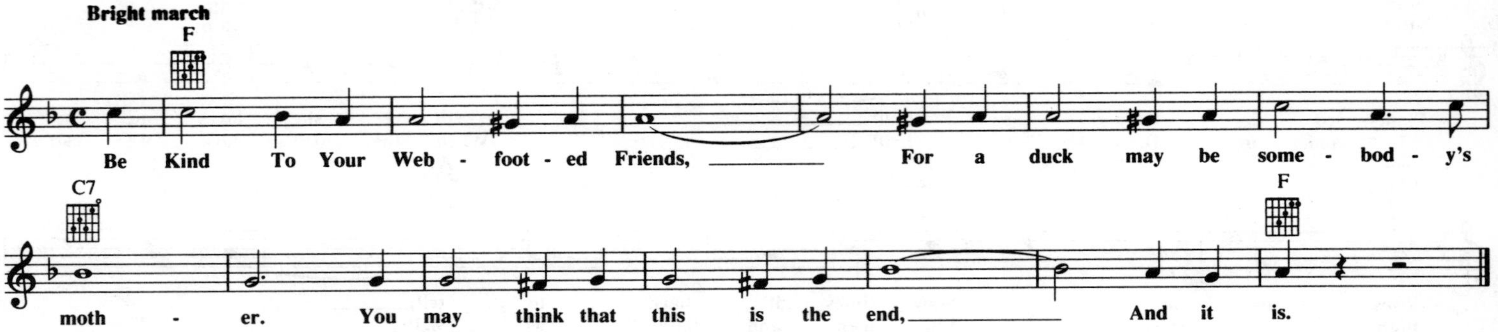
Bright march
F
C7
Be Kind To Your Web - foot - ed Friends, For a duck may be some - bod - y's moth - er. You may think that this is the end, And it is.

THE BEAR WENT OVER THE MOUNTAIN

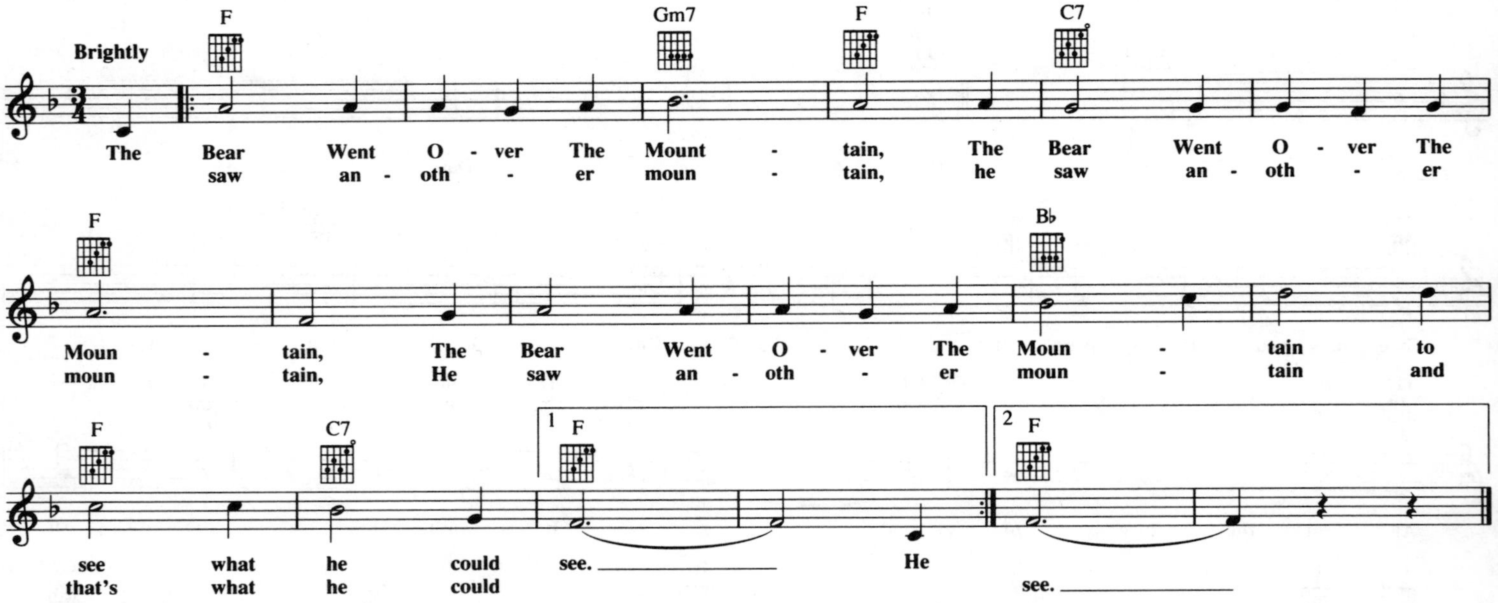
Brightly
F Gm7 F C7 F Bb F C7 F F
The Bear Went O - ver The Mount - tain, The Bear Went O - ver The Moun - tain, The Bear Went O - ver The Moun - tain to see what he could see. He
saw an - oth - er moun - tain, he saw an - oth - er moun - tain, He saw an - oth - er moun - tain and that's what he could see.

Words by Jessie Brown Pounds
Music by J.S. Fearis

BEAUTIFUL ISLE OF SOMEWHERE

Slowly, in two
Ab Ebsus Eb Eb7 Ab Eb/Bb Bb7 Eb Eb7 Ab Fm Bb7 Eb Eb7 Ab Eb Ab7 Db Ab/Eb Eb7 Ab
Some - where the sun is shin - ing, Some - where the song - birds dwell; Hush, then thy sad re - pin - ing; God lives, and all is well.
Some - where the day is long - er, Some - where the task is done; Some-where the heart is strong - er, Some - where the guer - don won.
Some - where the load is lift - ed, Close by an o - pen gate; Some-where the clouds are rift - ed, Some - where the an - gels wait.
Some - where, Some - where, Beau - ti - ful Isle Of Some - where! Land of the true, where we live a - new, Beau - ti - ful Isle Of Some - where!
rit.

THE BIG ROCK CANDY MOUNTAIN

Moderately
C G7 C G7 C G7
To Coda
On a sum - mer day in the month of May, A burly bum came
shad - y lane, thru the sug - ar cane He was look - ing for his
bum can stay for man - y'a day and he won't need an - y
1 C 2 C G7 C
hik - ing Down a lik - ing As he roamed a - long he sang a song of the
G7 C D.S. al Coda CODA C G7
land of milk and hon - ey, Where a mon - ey. Oh! the
C C7 F C
buzz - in' of the bees in the cig - ar - ette trees, Near the So - da Wa - ter foun - tain, At the
G7 C G7 C
lem - on - ade springs Where the blue - bird sings, In The Big Rock Can - dy Moun - tain.

BLACK IS THE COLOR

Freely
Em D Em
Black, black, Black Is The Col - or of my true love's hair. Those
How I love my love and well she knows, I
Am
lips are like some ros - y fair; The pur - est eyes and the
love the grass where - on she goes: When she on earth no
Em Am
neat - est hands, I love the grass where - on she stands.
more I see, My life will quick - ly o - ver be.

BILLY BOY

Moderately
C G7 C F#dim C G7 C
1. Oh where have you been, Billy Boy, Billy Boy, Oh where have you been, charming Billy? I have been to seek a wife, she's the joy of my life. She's a young thing and cannot leave her mother.
2. Did she bid you come in, Billy Boy, Billy Boy, Did she bid you come in, charming Billy? Yes, she bade me to come in, let me kiss her on the chin.
3 - 7. (See additional lyrics)

Additional Lyrics

3. Did she set for you a chair, Billy Boy, Billy Boy,
Did she set for you a chair, charming Billy?
Yes, she set for me a chair,
And the bottom wasn't there,
She's a young thing and cannot leave her mother.

4. Can she bake a cherry pie, Billy Boy, Billy Boy,
Can she bake a cherry pie, charming Billy?
She can bake a cherry pie,
Quick as a cat can wink her eye,
She's a young thing and cannot leave her mother.

5. How old is she, Billy Boy, Billy Boy,
How old is she, charming Billy?
She's three times six and four times seven,
Twenty-eight and eleven,
She's a young thing and cannot leave her mother.

6. Can she sing a pretty song, Billy Boy, Billy Boy,
Can she sing a pretty song, charming Billy?
She can sing a pretty song,
But she gets the words all wrong,
She's a mother and cannot leave her young thing.

7. Are her eyes very bright, Billy Boy, Billy Boy,
Are her eyes very bright, charming Billy?
Yes, her eyes are very bright
But unfortunately lack sight
And she can't describe me to her mother.

BLEST BE THE TIE THAT BINDS

Words by John Fawcett
Music by Hans Georg Nageli

Moderately
G D7 G C G D D7 G D7 G C G D7 G D7 G
Blest Be The Tie That Binds Our hearts in Chris - tian love. The fel - low - ship of kin - dred minds Is like to that a - bove.

BINGO

NOTE: Each time a letter of BINGO is deleted in the lyric, clap your hands in place of singing the letter.

Moderately
G C D G D
There was a farm - er had a dog and Bin - go was his
G Em Am D G
name - o. B - I - N - G - O, B - I - N - G - O,
_ - _ - N - G - O, _ - _ - N - G - O,
_ - _ - _ - _ - O, _ - _ - _ - _ - O,
C Am D7 C/G G
B - I - N - G - O
_ - _ - N - G - O
_ - _ - _ - _ - O
and Bin - go was his name - o. There
C D G D G
was a farm - er had a dog and Bin - go was his name - o.
Em Am D G C
_ - I - N - G - O, _ - I - N - G - O, _ - I -
_ - _ - G - O, _ - _ - G - O, _ - _ -
_ - _ - _ - _ _ - _ - _ - _ _ - _ -
Am D7 1, 2 G 3 G
N - G - O
_ - G - O
_ - _ - _
and Bin - go was his name There name - o.

BLOW THE MAN DOWN

Fast Waltz
C
Oh, Blow The Man Down, bul - lies, Blow The Man Down. To me way,
C#dim7 Dm G7
hey, Blow The Man Down. Oh___ Blow The Man Down, bul - lies, Blow him a -
C
way, Give me some time to Blow The Man Down.

BILL BAILEY, WON'T YOU PLEASE COME HOME?

Words and Music by Hughie Cannon

Brightly
G C#dim G G#dim
Won't you come home, Bill Bai - ley, won't you come home? She moans the whole day
D7
long; I'll do the cook - ing, dar - ling I'll pay the rent, I know I've
D9#5 G C#dim G
done you wrong. "Mem- ber that rain - y eve that I drove you out, With
G7 C E7/B Am G7#5 C C#dim G
noth - in' but a fine tooth comb? I know I'm to blame, well, ain't that a
E7 A7 D9 D7 1 G A7 D7 2 G
shame? Bill Bai - ley, Won't You Please Come Home? Home?

BLOOD ON THE SADDLE

Slowly
G C G
1. There was Blood On The Sad - dle, And blood on the ground;
2, 3. (See additional lyrics)
D7 G
And a great big pud - dle of blood all a - round.

Additional Lyrics

2. The cowboy lay in it,
All covered with gore,
And he won't go riding
No broncos no more.

3. Oh, pity the cowboy,
All bloody and red,
For his bronco fell on him
And mashed in his head.

BLESSED ASSURANCE

Lyrics by Fanny Crosby, Van Alstyne
Music by Phoebe P. Knapp

Lively
Bless-ed As - sur - ance Je - sus is mine___ Oh, what a fore - taste of glo - ry di - vine.___ Heir of sal -
Per - fect sub - mis - sion all is at rest___ I in my Sav - ior am hap - py and blest.___ Watch-ing and
va - tion pur-chase of God___ Born of His Spir - it washed in His blood.___
wait - ing look - ing a - bove___ Filled with His good - ness lost in His love.___
This is my
sto - ry this is my song___ Prais-ing my Sav - ior all the day long___ This is my
sto - ry this is my song___ Prais - ing my Sav - ior all the day long.___

THE BLUE BELLS OF SCOTLAND

Moderately
1. "Oh where, tell me, where is your___ High - land lad - die
2-5. (See additional lyrics)
gone?" "He's gone wi' stream - ing ban - ners where___ no - ble deeds are
done; And it's oh, in my heart, I___ wish him safe at home."

Additional Lyrics

2. "Oh what, lassie, what does your Highland laddie wear?"
(repeat)
"A scarlet coat and bonnet wi' bonnie yellow hair,
And there's nane in the world can wi' my love compare."

3. "Oh where, tell me, does your Highland laddie dwell?"
(repeat)
"He dwells in merry Scotland at the sign of the Blue Bell,
And it's oh! in my heart that I love my laddie well."

4. "Suppose, just suppose, that your Highland lad should die?"
(repeat)
"The bagpipes should play o'er him, and I'd lay me down and cry;
But it's oh! in my heart that I wish he may not die."

5. "Oh what will you claim for your constancy to him?"
(repeat)
"I'll claim a priest to wed us, and a clerk to say amen!
And I'll ne'er part from my bonnie Highland man."

BLUETAIL FLY

Freely
Verse:
Dm Bb F C7
1. When I was young I used to wait on Mas - ter and hand him his plate, And
2. And when he'd ride in the af - ter - noon, I'd fol - low after with a hick - o - ry broom; The
3 - 5. (See additional lyrics)
Dm Bb C7 F
a tempo
pass the bot - tle when he got dry, And brush a - way the Blue - tail Fly!
po - ny be - ing ver - y shy, When bit - ten by the Blue - tail Fly!
Refrain:
C7 F
Jim - my crack corn, and I don't care, Jim - my crack corn, and I don't care,
F7 Bb C7 F
Jim - my crack corn, and I don't care, My Mas - ter's gone a - way.

Additional Lyrics

3. One day while riding round the farm,
The flies so numerous they did swarm;
One changed to bite him on the thigh,
The devil take the Bluetail Fly!
Refrain

4. The pony run, he jump, he kick.
He threw my Master in the ditch;
He died and the jury wondered why,
The verdict was the Bluetail Fly!
Refrain

5. They laid him under a 'simmon tree,
His epitaph is there to see:
"Beneath this stone Jim forced to lie,
A victim of the Bluetail Fly!"
Refrain

THE BOAR'S HEAD CAROL

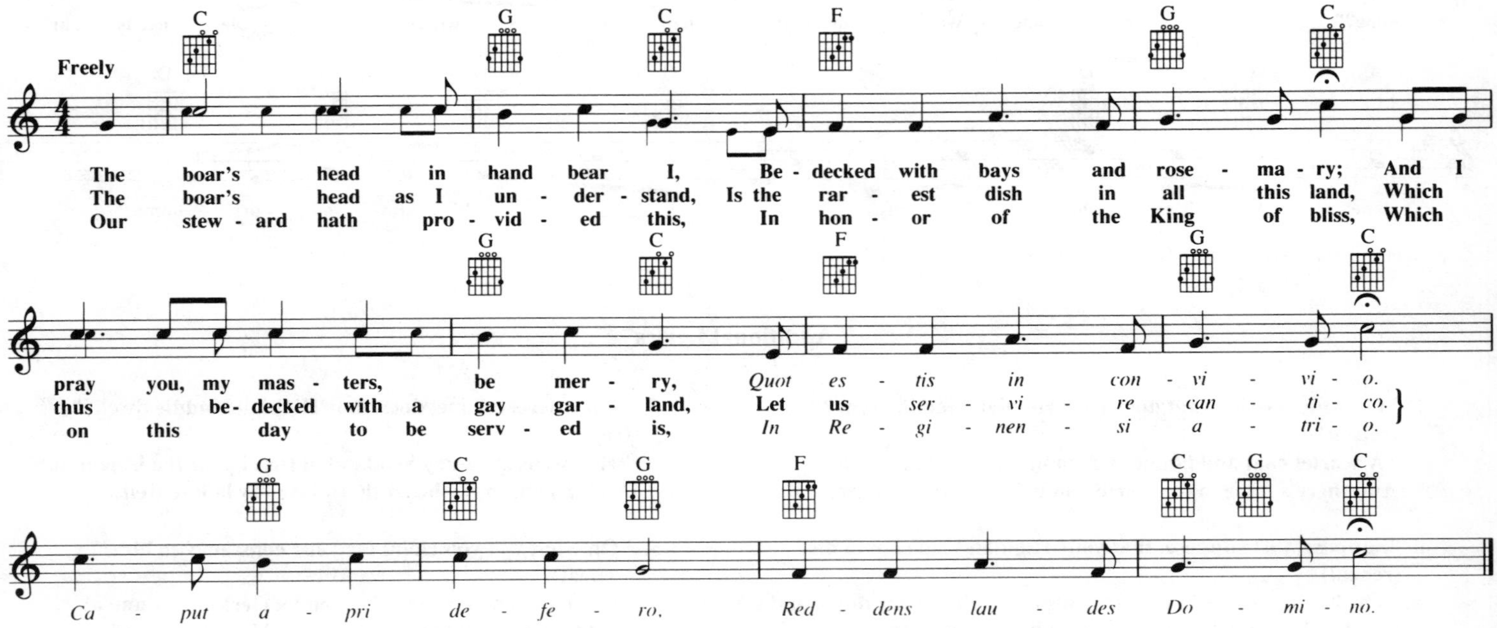
Freely
C G C F G C
The boar's head in hand bear I, Be - decked with bays and rose - ma - ry; And I
The boar's head as I un - der - stand, Is the rar - est dish in all this land, Which
Our stew - ard hath pro - vid - ed this, In hon - or of the King of bliss, Which
G C F G C
pray you, my mas - ters, be mer - ry, Quot es - tis in con - vi - vi - o.
thus be - decked with a gay gar - land, Let us ser - vi - re can - ti - co.
on this day to be serv - ed is, In Re - gi - nen - si a - tri - o.
G C G F C G C
Ca - put a - pri de - fe - ro, Red - dens lau - des Do - mi - no.

BLUE DANUBE WALTZ

Johann Strauss

THE BOWERY

Words by Charles H. Hoyt
Music by Percy Gaunt

THE BOLL WEEVIL

BRIDAL CHORUS
(From "LOHENGRIN")

Richard Wagner

Johannes Brahms

BRAHMS' LULLABY

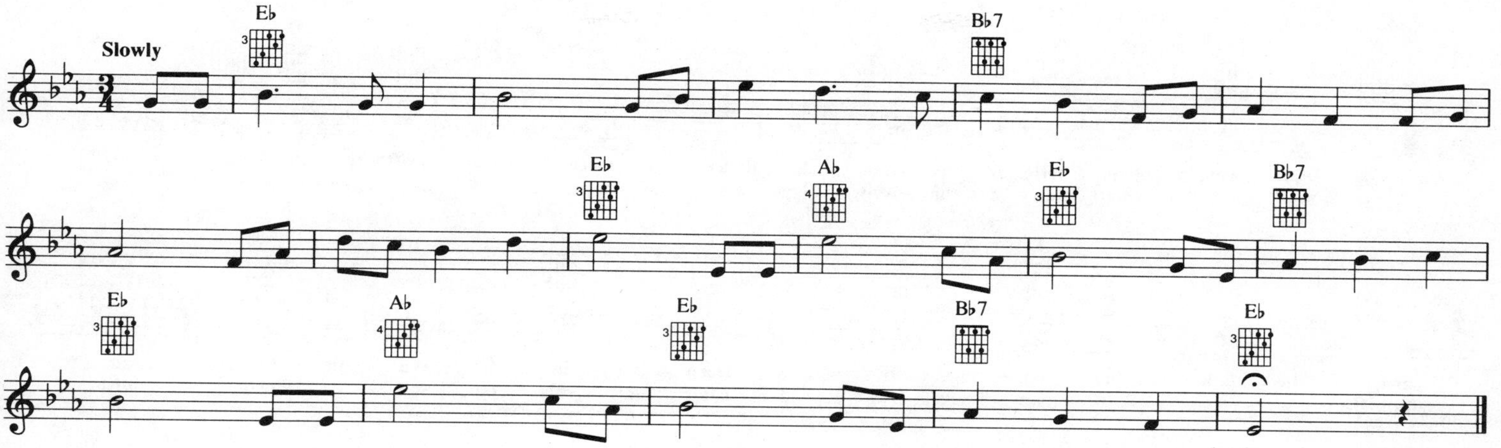
Slowly
E♭ B♭7
E♭ A♭ E♭ B♭7
E♭ A♭ E♭ B♭7 E♭

BRINGING IN THE SHEAVES

Lyrics by Knowles Shaw
Music by George A. Minor

Happily, in moderate time
B♭ E♭ B♭
Sow - ing in the morn - ing, sow - ing seeds of kind - ness, Sow - ing in the noon - tide
Sow - ing in the sun - shine, sow - ing in the shad - ows, Fear - ing nei - ther clouds nor
Go - ing forth with weep - ing, sow - ing for the Mas - ter, Tho' the loss sus - tained our
F B♭ E♭
and the dew - y eve, Wait - ing for the har - vest and the time of reap - ing,
win - ter's chill - ing breeze, By and by the har - vest and the la - bor end - ed,
spir - it of - ten grieves, When our weep - ing's o - ver he will bid us wel - come,
B♭ F7 B♭ B♭ E♭ B♭
We shall come re - joic - ing, Bring - ing In The Sheaves. Bring - ing In The Sheaves, Bring - ing In The Sheaves,
C7 F F7 B♭ E♭ B♭
We shall come re - joic - ing, Bring - ing In The Sheaves. Bring - ing In The Sheaves, Bring - ing In The Sheaves,
1, 2 F7 B♭ 3 F7 B♭ F7 B♭ E♭ B♭
We shall come re - joic - ing, Bring - ing In The Sheaves. Bring - ing In The Sheaves.

BRING A TORCH, JEANNETTE, ISABELLA

Moderately slow
G Em Am D G Em C D G
Bring A Torch, Jean - nette, Is - a - bel - la, Bring a torch, come swift - ly and run. Christ is
Has - ten now, good folk of the vil - lage, Has - ten now, the Christ Child to see. You will
D C G D Em D
born, tell the folk of the vil - lage, Je - sus is sleep - ing in His cra - dle, Ah, ah,
find Him a - sleep in a man - ger, Qui - et - ly come and whis - per soft - ly, Hush, hush,
G D Em D G D7 G
Beau - ti - ful is the Moth - er, Ah, ah, Beau - ti - ful is her Son.
Peace - ful - ly now He slum - bers, Hush, hush, Peace - ful - ly now He sleeps.

BUCKEYE JIM

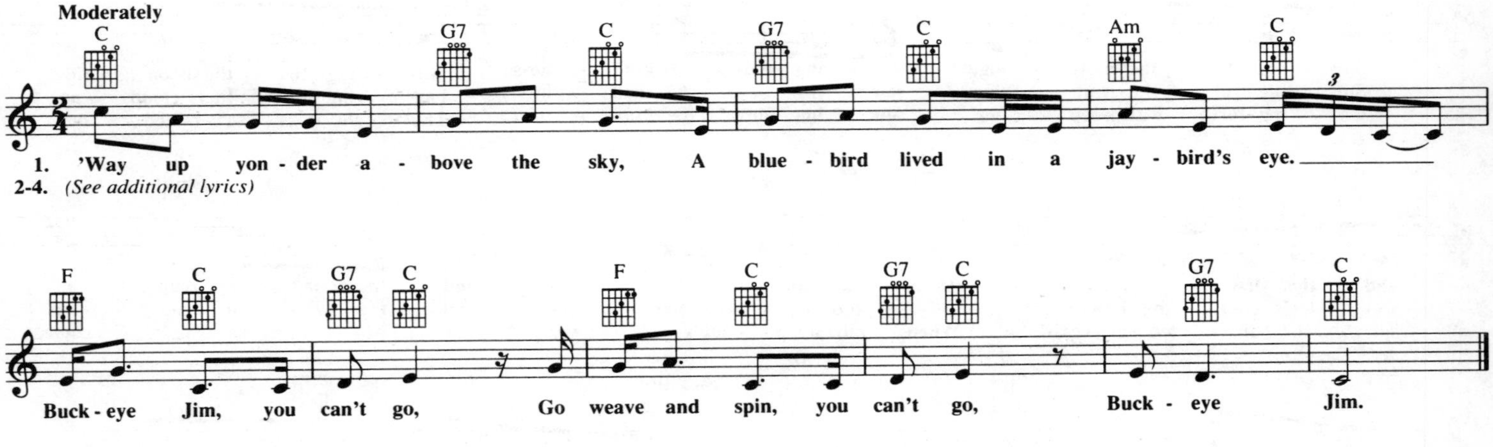
Moderately
C G7 C G7 C Am C
1. 'Way up yon - der a - bove the sky, A blue - bird lived in a jay - bird's eye.
2-4. (See additional lyrics)
F C G7 C F C G7 C G7 C
Buck - eye Jim, you can't go, Go weave and spin, you can't go, Buck - eye Jim.

Additional Lyrics

2. 'Way up yonder above the moon,
   A blue-jay nests in a silver spoon.

3. 'Way down yonder in a wooden trough,
   An old *wo*-man died of the whoopin' cough.

4. 'Way down yonder on a hollow log,
   A red bird danced with a green bullfrog.

BUFFALO GALS

Brightly
C
G7
C
1. As I was walk - ing down the street, down the street, down the street, A pret - ty lit - tle girl I
2-3. (See additional lyrics)
G7
C
Chorus:
G7
chanced to meet, and we danced by the light of the moon. Buf - fa - lo Gals won't you come out to - night, come out to - night
Dm7
C
G7
C
come out to - night? Buf - fa - lo Gals won't you come out to - night, and dance by the light of the moon?

Additional Lyrics

2. I asked her if she'd stop and talk, stop and talk, stop and talk,
Her feet took up the whole sidewalk, and left no room for me.

3. I asked her if she'd be my wife, be my wife, be my wife,
Then I'd be happy all my life, if she'd marry me.

BURY ME NOT ON THE LONE PRAIRIE

Slowly
F
C7
1. "Oh, Bu - ry Me Not On The Lone Prai - rie," These words came low
2. "Oh, Bu - ry Me Not On The Lone Prai - rie," Where the wild coy - otes
3-6. (See additional lyrics)
F
and___ mourn - ful - ly From the pal - lid lips of a youth who
will___ howl o'er me, In a nar - row grave, just___ six by
C7
F
lay On his dy - ing bed at the close of day.
three. Oh, Bu - ry Me Not On The Lone Prai - rie."

Additional Lyrics

3. "I've always wished to be laid when I died
In the little churchyard on the green hillside;
By my father's grave there let mine be,
And Bury Me Not On The Lone Prairie."

4. "Oh, bury me not"– and his voice failed there,
But we took no heed of his dying prayer.
In a narrow grave, just six by three,
We buried him on the lone prairie.

5. And the cowboys now, as they roam the plain,
(For they marked the spot where his bones were lain)
Fling a handful of roses over the grave,
With a prayer to Him who his soul will save.

6. "Oh, Bury Me Not On The Lone Prairie,
Where the wolves can howl and growl o'er me.
Fling a handful of roses over my grave,
With a prayer to Him who my soul will save."

THE CAISSONS GO ROLLING ALONG

Words and Music by Edmund L. Gruber

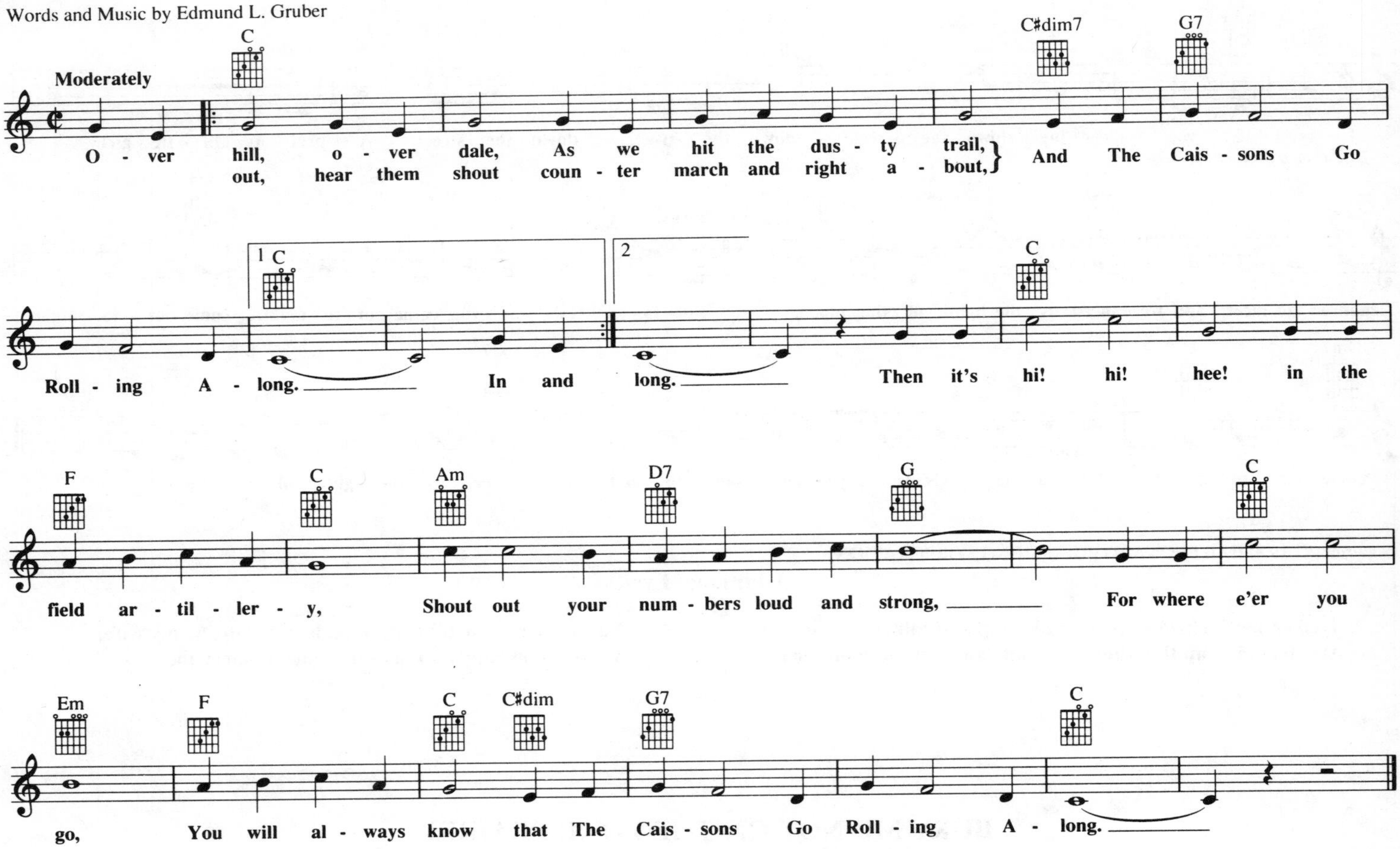
Moderately
C
C#dim7
G7
O - ver hill, o - ver dale, As we hit the dus - ty trail, } And The Cais - sons Go
out, hear them shout coun - ter march and right a - bout,
1 C
2
C
Roll - ing A - long. In and long. Then it's hi! hi! hee! in the
F
C
Am
D7
G
C
field ar - til - ler - y, Shout out your num - bers loud and strong, For where e'er you
Em
F
C
C#dim
G7
C
go, You will al - ways know that The Cais - sons Go Roll - ing A - long.

THE CAMPBELLS ARE COMING

Rhythmically
C
G7
C
F
C
C
F
C
F
1 C
2 C

CANTABILE

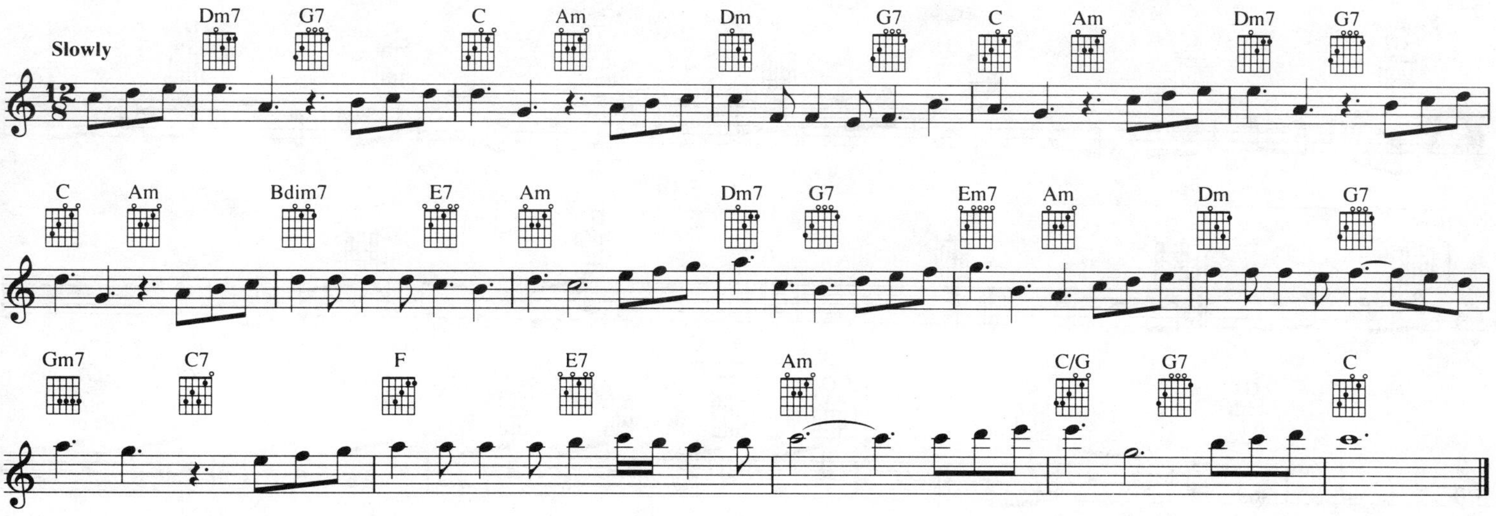
Slowly
Dm7 G7 C Am Dm G7 C Am Dm7 G7
C Am Bdim7 E7 Am Dm7 G7 Em7 Am Dm G7
Gm7 C7 F E7 Am C/G G7 C

CAPRICCIO ITALIEN THEME

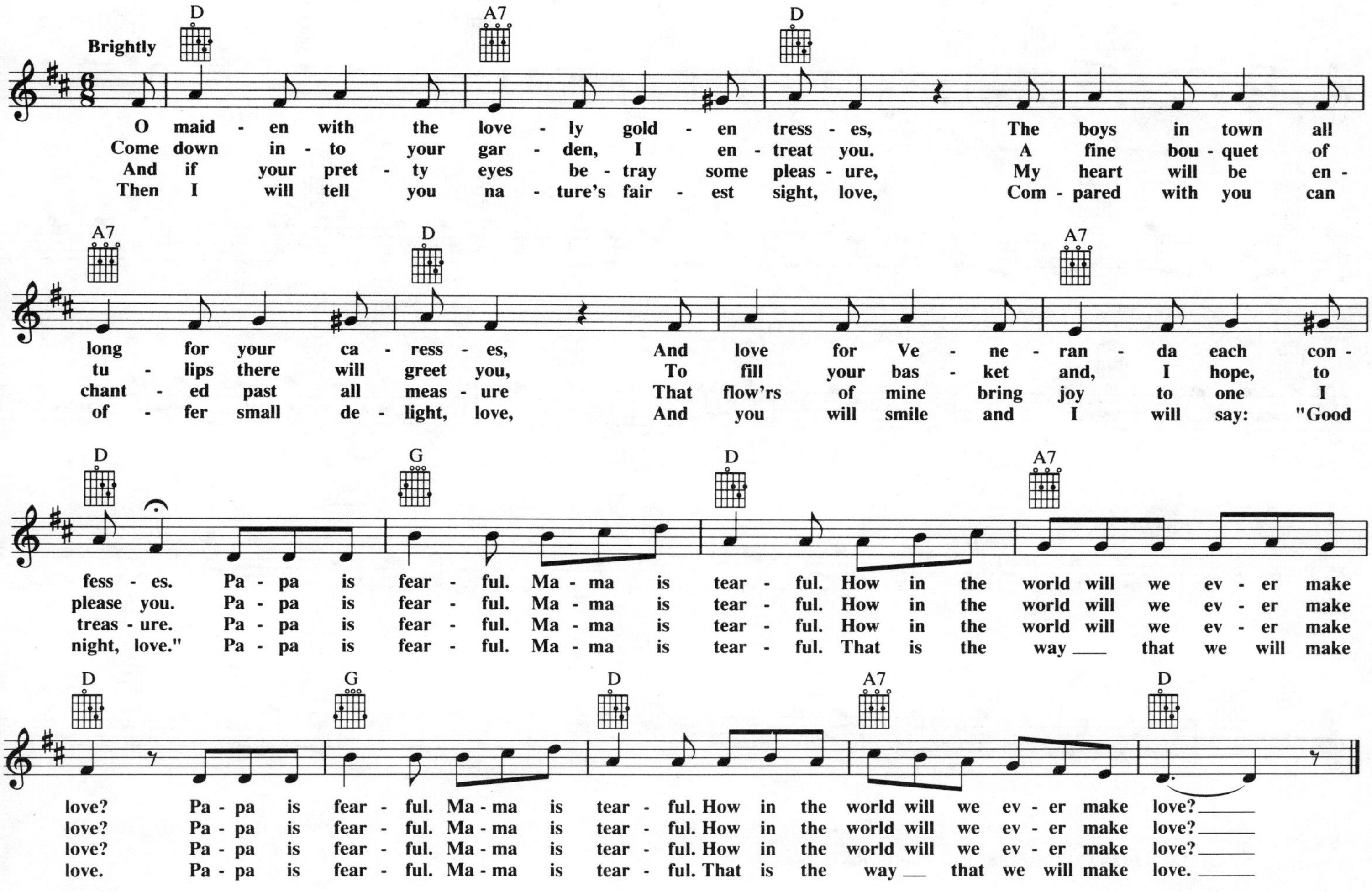
Brightly
D A7 D
O maid - en with the love - ly gold - en tress - es, The boys in town all
Come down in - to your gar - den, I en - treat you. A fine bou - quet of
And if your pret - ty eyes be - tray some pleas - ure, My heart will be en -
Then I will tell you na - ture's fair - est sight, love, Com - pared with you can
A7 D A7
long for your ca - ress - es, And love for Ve - ne - ran - da each con -
tu - lips there will greet you, To fill your bas - ket and, I hope, to
chant - ed past all meas - ure That flow'rs of mine bring joy to one I
of - fer small de - light, love, And you will smile and I will say: "Good
D G D A7
fess - es. Pa - pa is fear - ful. Ma - ma is tear - ful. How in the world will we ev - er make
please you. Pa - pa is fear - ful. Ma - ma is tear - ful. How in the world will we ev - er make
treas - ure. Pa - pa is fear - ful. Ma - ma is tear - ful. How in the world will we ev - er make
night, love." Pa - pa is fear - ful. Ma - ma is tear - ful. That is the way that we will make
D G D A7 D
love? Pa - pa is fear - ful. Ma - ma is tear - ful. How in the world will we ev - er make love?
love? Pa - pa is fear - ful. Ma - ma is tear - ful. How in the world will we ev - er make love?
love? Pa - pa is fear - ful. Ma - ma is tear - ful. How in the world will we ev - er make love?
love. Pa - pa is fear - ful. Ma - ma is tear - ful. That is the way that we will make love.

CAN CAN

Jacques Offenbach

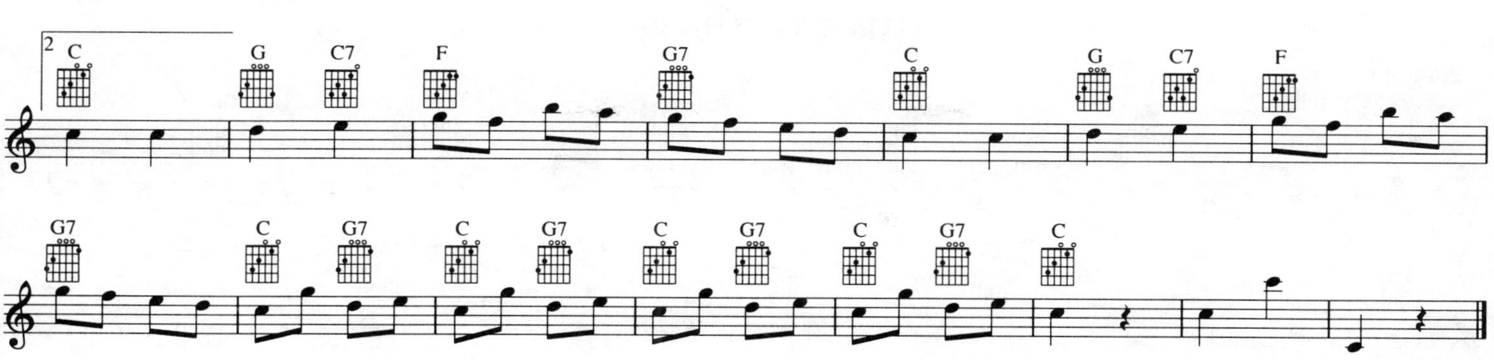
2
C G C7 F G7 C G C7 F
G7 C G7 C G7 C G7 C G7 C

CAMPTOWN RACES

By Stephen Foster

Fast, at a gallop
C G7
1. Camp - town la - dies sing this song, Doo - dah, doo - dah.
2-4. (See additional lyrics)
C G7 C
Camp - town race - track five miles long, Oh doo - dah - day.
G7
Come down there with my hat caved in, Doo - dah, doo - dah,
C G7 C
Go back home with my pock - et full of tin, Oh doo - dah - day.
Chorus
C F C
Goin' to run all night, Goin' to run all day, I
G7 C
bet my mon - ey on the bob - tail nag, Some - bod - y bet on the bay.

Additional Lyrics

2. The long-tail filly and the big black hoss . . .
   They fly the track and they both cut across . . .
   The blind hoss sticken in a big mud hole . . .
   Can't touch bottom with a ten-foot pole . . .
   Chorus

3. Old muley cow come onto the track . . .
   The bobtail fling her over his back . . .
   Then fly along like a railroad car . . .
   Running a race with a shooting star . . .
   Chorus

4. See them flying on a ten-mile heat . . .
   'Round the race track, then repeat . . .
   I win my money on the bobtail nag . . .
   I keep my money in an old towbag . . .
   Chorus

CAROL OF THE BELLS

P. Leontovich

Exuberantly
Gm
Gm7/F
E♭
Gm/D
Gm
Gm7/F
E♭
Gm/D
E♭
Gm7
Cm7
Gm
E♭6
Gm
E♭6
Gm
Gm6
Gm7
Gm6
Cm
Gm
Cm
Gm
D
D7
Gm
D
D7
Gm
Gm7
Cm
Gm7
Cm7
Gm

CARRY ME BACK TO OLD VIRGINNY

Words and Music by James A. Bland

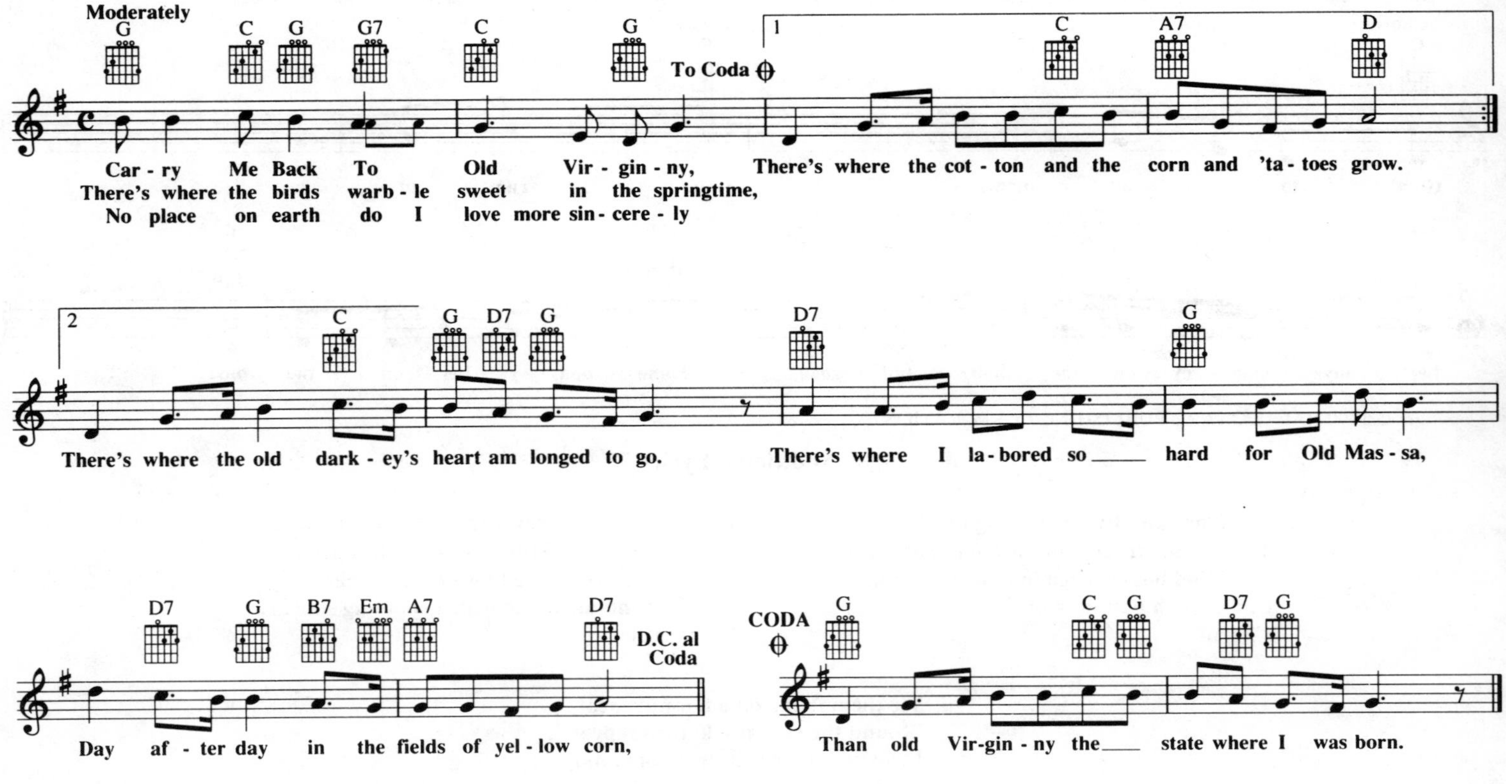
Moderately
G
C
G
G7
C
G
To Coda
1
C
A7
D
Car - ry Me Back To Old Vir - gin - ny, There's where the cot - ton and the corn and 'ta - toes grow.
There's where the birds warb - le sweet in the springtime,
No place on earth do I love more sin - cere - ly
2
C
G
D7
G
D7
G
There's where the old dark - ey's heart am longed to go. There's where I la - bored so ___ hard for Old Mas - sa,
D7
G
B7
Em
A7
D7
D.C. al Coda
Day af - ter day in the fields of yel - low corn,
CODA
G
C
G
D7
G
Than old Vir - gin - ny the ___ state where I was born.

CARELESS LOVE

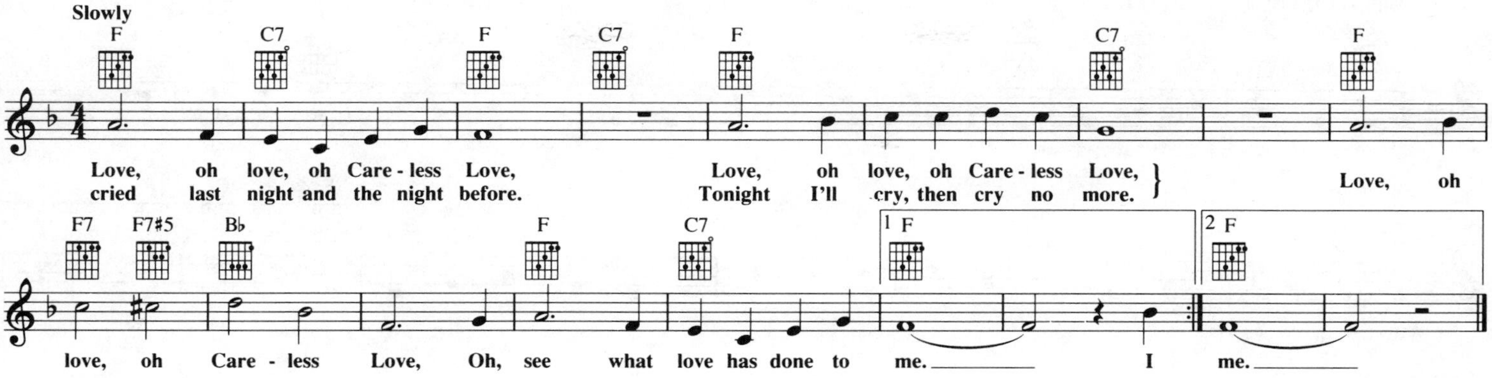
Slowly
F C7 F C7 F C7 F
Love, oh love, oh Care - less Love, Love, oh love, oh Care - less Love,
cried last night and the night before. Tonight I'll cry, then cry no more.
Love, oh
F7 F7#5 B♭ F C7 1 F 2 F
love, oh Care - less Love, Oh, see what love has done to me. I me.

Julius Benedict

CARNIVAL OF VENICE

Moderately
C G7 C
G7 C
G7 C
G7 C

CHRIST WAS BORN ON CHRISTMAS DAY

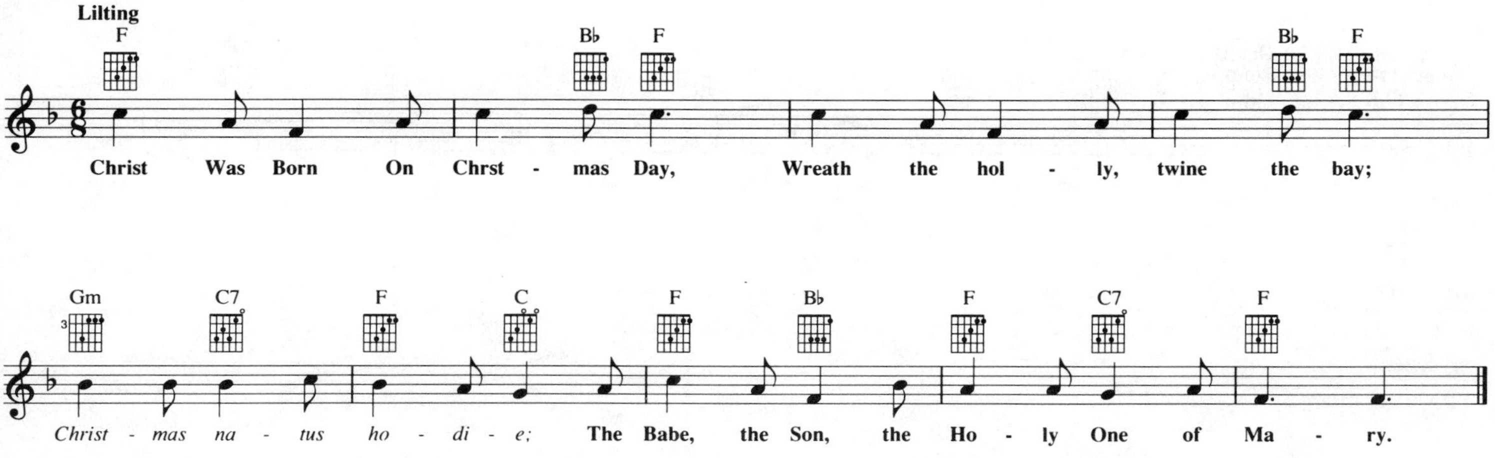
Lilting
F B♭ F B♭ F
Christ Was Born On Chrst - mas Day, Wreath the hol - ly, twine the bay;
Gm C7 F C F B♭ F C7 F
Christ - mas na - tus ho - di - e; The Babe, the Son, the Ho - ly One of Ma - ry.

CHIAPANECAS

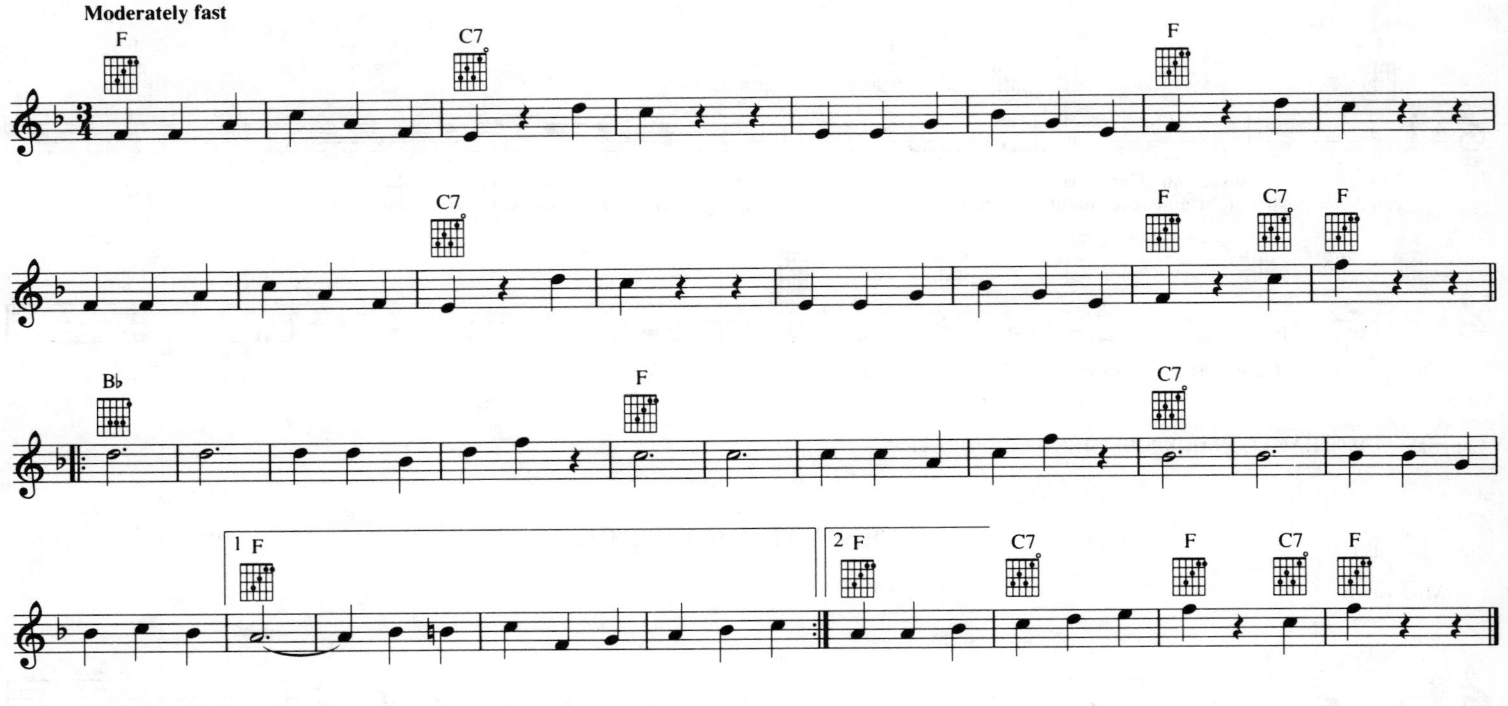

CHOPIN BALLADE NO. 1

CHRIST THE LORD IS RIS'N TODAY

C G/B F/A C Dm7 G7 C F/A
Christ The Lord Is Ris'n To - day, Al - le - lu - ia! Our tri - umph - ant
Hymns of praise then let us sing, Un - to Christ, our
But the pains which He en - dured, Our sal - va - tion
Dm7 G C Dm7 G7 C G C G7 C G D7/A
ho ly day, Al - le - lu - ia. Who died once up - on the Cross, Al - le -
heav'n - ly King, Who en - dured the Cross and grave,
have pro - cured, Now a - bove the sky He's King,
G/D D7 G C F/A F F/C C Dm7 C/G G7 C
lu - ia. Suf - fer to re - deem our loss. Al - le - lu - ia.
Sin - ners to re - deem and save.
Where the an - gels ev - er sing.

THE CHURCH IN THE WILDWOOD

By Wm. S. Pitts

Moderately
B♭ F7 B♭ E♭
1. There's a church in the val - ley by the wild - wood, No love - li - er spot in the dale; No place is so dear to my
2. Oh come to The Church In The Wild - wood, to the tress where the wild flow - ers bloom; Where the part - ing hymn will be
3. (See additional lyrics)
B♭ F7 B♭ E♭ B♭ F
child - hood As the lit - tle brown church in the vale. Oh, come, come, come, come, Come to The Church In The Wild - wood, Oh,
chant - ed We will weep by the side of the tomb.
B♭ E♭ B♭ F7 B♭
come to the church in the vale. No spot is so dear to my child - hood As the lit - tle brown church in the vale.

Additional Lyrics

3. From the church in the valley by the wildwood,
When day fades away into night;
I would fain from this spot of my childhood
Wing my way to the mansions of light.

CIELITO LINDO

By C. Fernandez

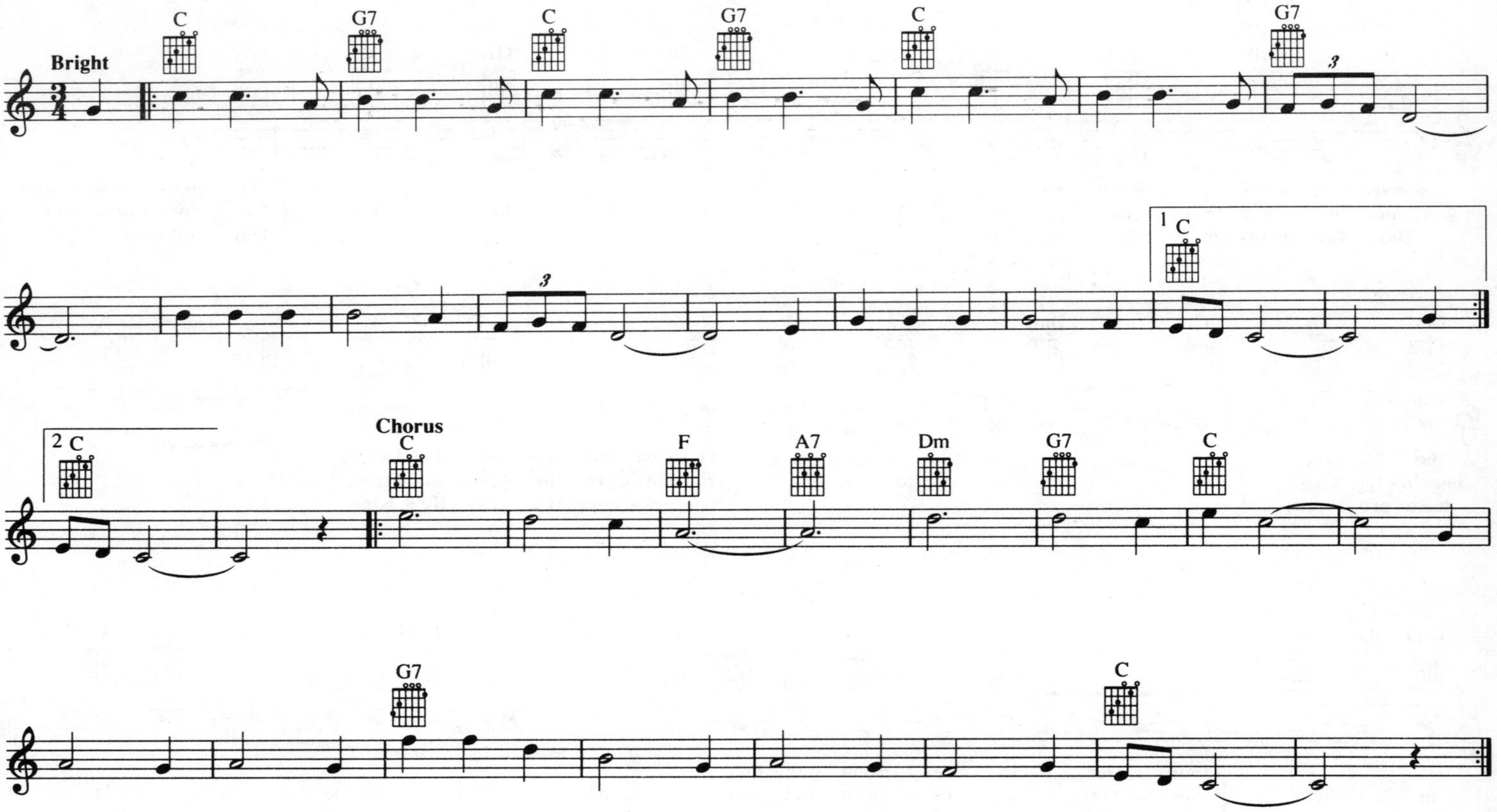

CIRIBIRIBIN

Music by A. Pestalozza

CLAIR DE LUNE

Claude Debussy

Slowly
C/E Fm C/E Dm F/C G/B
Am7 E7/G# C/G Dm/F C/E G7 C F
C/E F C7/G F Dm
G7
A♭dim7 Dm7/A Bm7♭5 F/C
Dm7 C/E Am7♭5 G7sus/D G7 C

CLEMENTINE

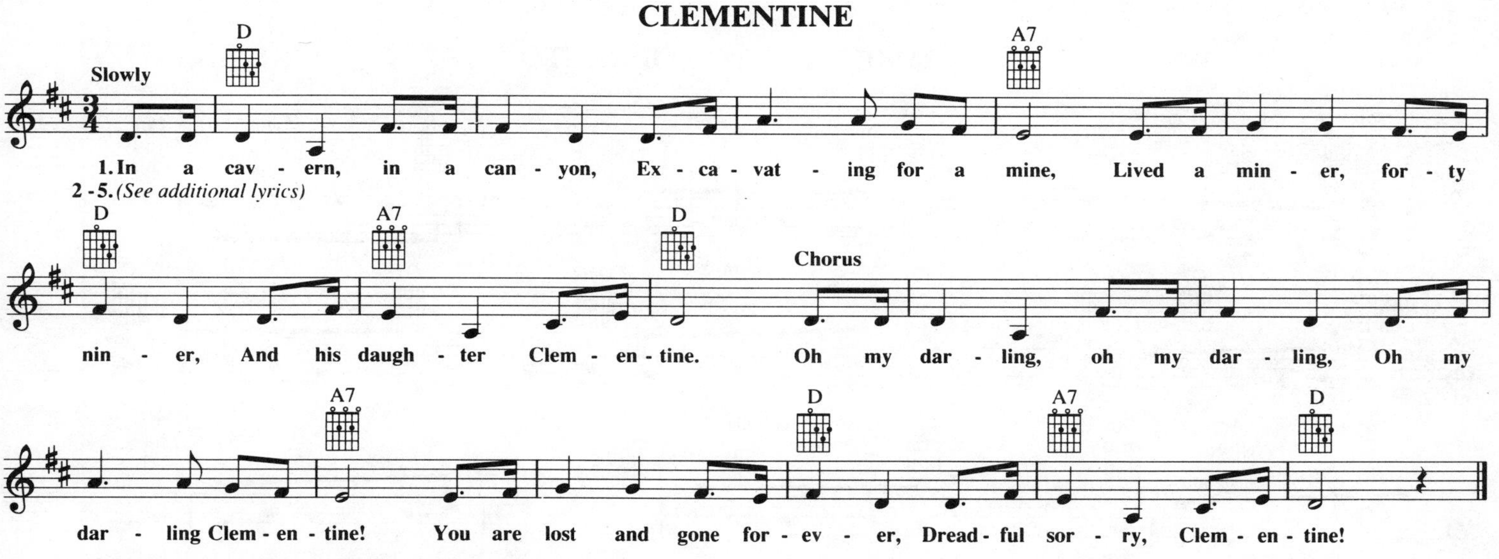
Slowly
D A7
1. In a cav - ern, in a can - yon, Ex - ca - vat - ing for a mine, Lived a min - er, for - ty
2 - 5. (See additional lyrics)
D A7 D
Chorus
nin - er, And his daugh - ter Clem - en - tine. Oh my dar - ling, oh my dar - ling, Oh my
A7 D A7 D
dar - ling Clem - en - tine! You are lost and gone for - ev - er, Dread - ful sor - ry, Clem - en - tine!

Additional Lyrics

2. Light she was and, like a fairy,
And her shoes were number nine,
Herring boxes, without topses,
Sandals were for Clementine.
Chorus

3. Drove she ducklings to the water,
Every morning just at nine,
Stubbed her toe upon a splinter,
Fell into the foaming brine.
Chorus

4. Ruby lips above the water
Blowing bubbles soft and fine,
But alas I was no swimmer,
So I lost my Clementine.
Chorus

5. There's a churchyard, on the hillside,
Where the flowers grow and twine,
There grow roses, 'mongst the posies,
Fertilized by Clementine.
Chorus

COCKLES AND MUSSELS
(Molly Malone)

Gently
F Dm Gm/B♭ C7 F Dm Gm/B♭ C7 F Dm7 Gm/B♭ C7
In Dub - lin's fair cit - y, Where girls are so pret - ty, 'Twas there I first met with sweet Mol - ly Ma - lone. She drove a wheel - bar - row Through streets broad and nar - row,
She was a fish - mon - ger, But sure 'twas no won - der, For so were her moth - er and fa - ther be - fore. They drove their wheel - bar - rows Through streets broad and nar - row,
She died of a fe - ver, And noth - ing could save her, And that was the end of sweet Mol - ly Ma - lone. Her ghost wheels a bar - row Through streets broad and nar - row,
Cry - ing,
F Dm7 Gm/B♭ C7 F Dm Gm/B♭ C7 F Dm7 Gm/B♭ C7 F
"Cock - les And Mus - sels, a - live, a - live - o. A - live, a - live - o, A - live, a - live - o." Cry - ing, "Cock - les And Mus - sels, A - live, a - live - o."

COME BACK TO SORRENTO

By Ernesto Di Curtis

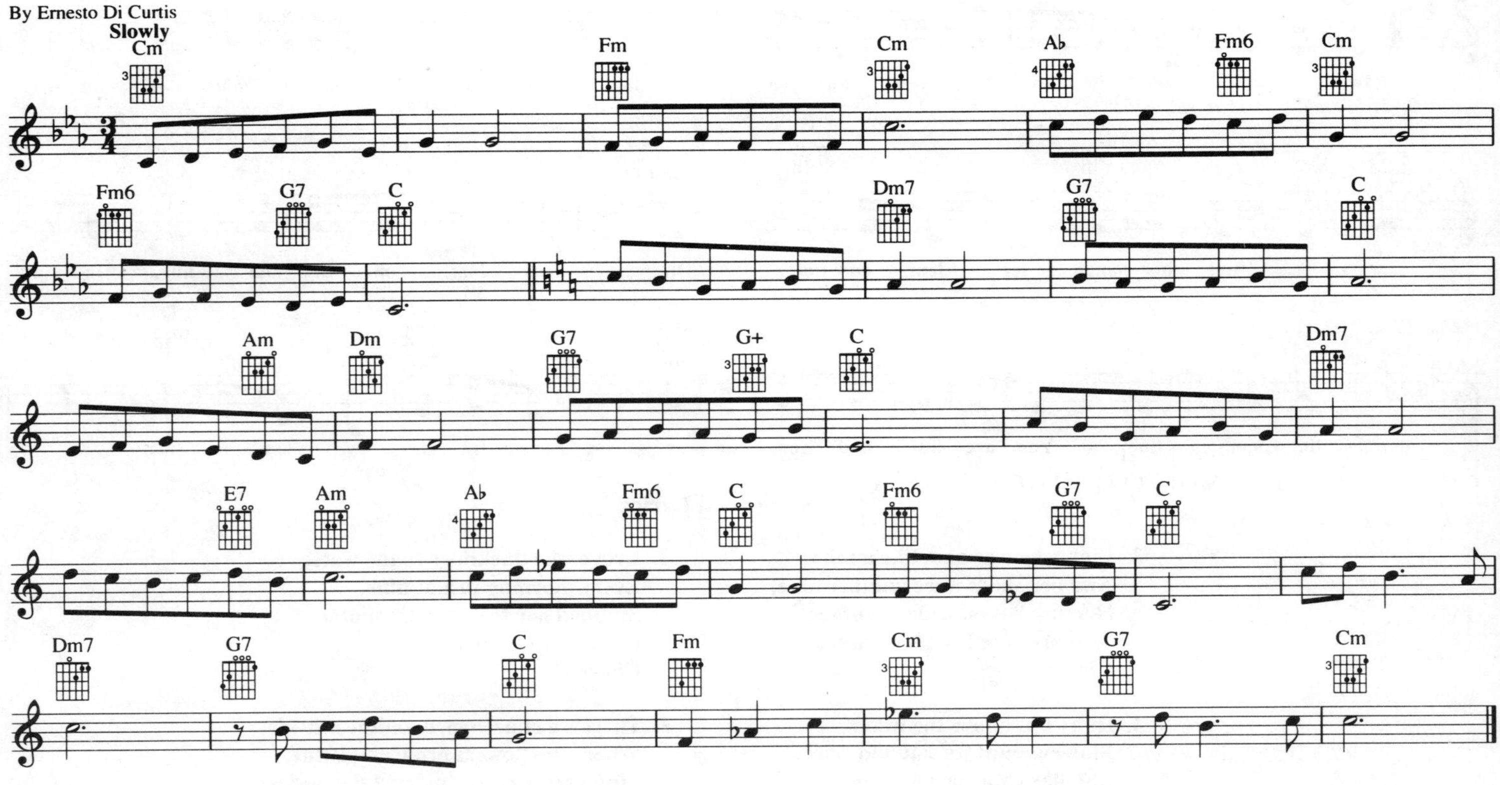
Slowly
Cm Fm Cm A♭ Fm6 Cm
Fm6 G7 C Dm7 G7 C
Am Dm G7 G+ C Dm7
E7 Am A♭ Fm6 C Fm6 G7 C
Dm7 G7 C Fm Cm G7 Cm

CLARINET POLKA

COLUMBIA, THE GEM OF THE OCEAN

Words by David T. Shaw
Music by Thomas Becket

Moderately
O Co - lum - bia, The Gem Of The O - cean, The home of the brave and the
free, the shrine of each pa - triot's de - vo - tion, A world of - fers hom - age to
thee. Thy man - dates make he - roes as - sem - ble, When Lib - er - ty's form stands in
view; Thy ban - ners make tyr - an - ny trem - ble When borne by the red, white and
Fine
blue. When borne by the red, white and blue, When blue; Thy
D.S. al Fine

COUNTRY GARDENS

Moderately

COME TO THE SEA

Slowly
Eb Bb7 Eb Ab Eb
Come, Come To The Sea, Come, come love to me,
Ab Bb7 Ab Eb Bb7 Eb
Let us go drift - ing on sil - ver - y dreams For - ev - er and aye.

COME, THOU ALMIGHTY KING

Felice Giardini

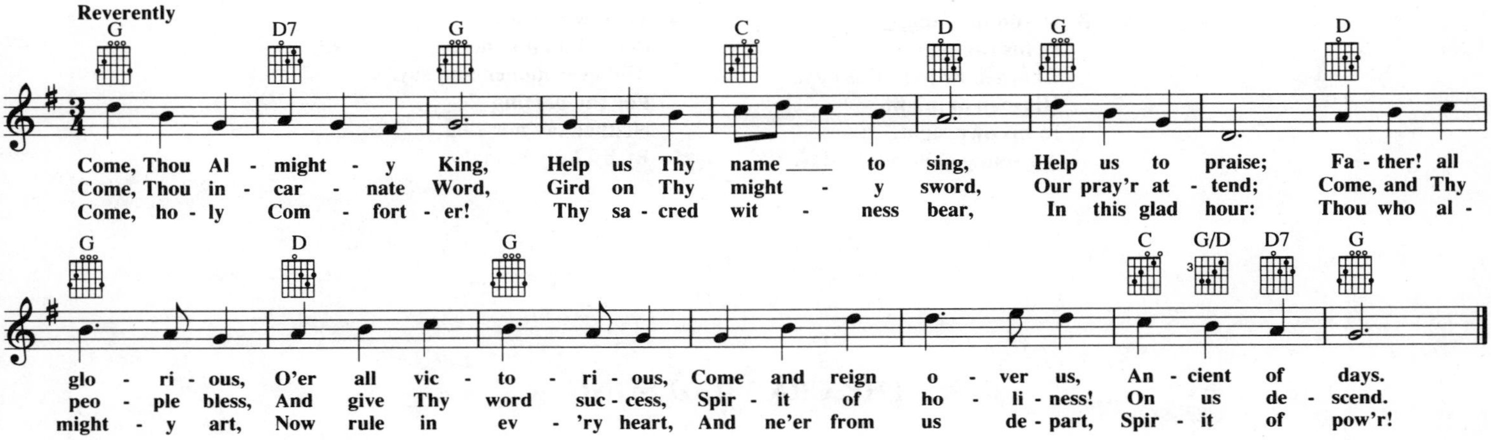
Reverently
G D7 G C D G D
Come, Thou Al - might - y King, Help us Thy name to sing, Help us to praise; Fa - ther! all
Come, Thou in - car - nate Word, Gird on Thy might - y sword, Our pray'r at - tend; Come, and Thy
Come, ho - ly Com - fort - er! Thy sa - cred wit - ness bear, In this glad hour: Thou who al -
G D G C G/D D7 G
glo - ri - ous, O'er all vic - to - ri - ous, Come and reign o - ver us, An - cient of days.
peo - ple bless, And give Thy word suc - cess, Spir - it of ho - li - ness! On us de - scend.
might - y art, Now rule in ev - 'ry heart, And ne'er from us de - part, Spir - it of pow'r!

COMIN' THROUGH THE RYE

Stately
F
If a bod - y meet a bod - y Com - in' Through The Rye. If a bod - y
If a bod - y meet a bod - y Com - in' frae the town. If a bod - y
Fsus
kiss a bod - y, Need a bod - y cry.
greet a bod - y, Need a bod - y frown.
Ev - 'ry las - sie has her lad - die;
F Bb F/C C7 F/C C7 F/C C7 F
Nane, and say, ha'e I. Yet a' the lads they smile on me When Com - in' Through The Rye.

THE COVENTRY CAROL

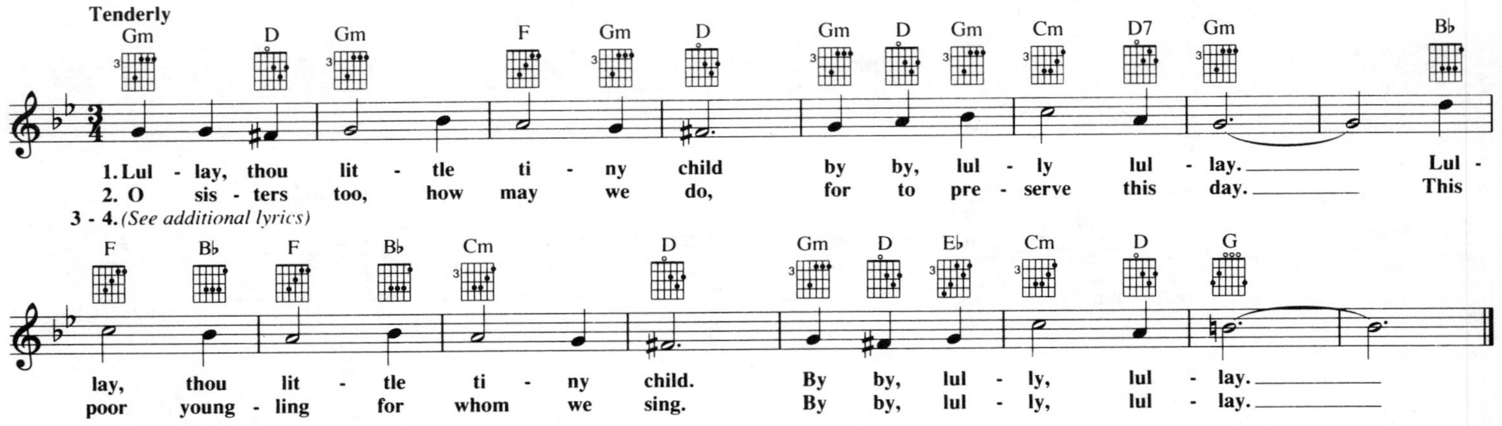
Tenderly
Gm D Gm F Gm D Gm D Gm Cm D7 Gm B♭
1. Lul - lay, thou lit - tle ti - ny child by by, lul - ly lul - lay. Lul -
2. O sis - ters too, how may we do, for to pre - serve this day. This
3 - 4. (See additional lyrics)
F B♭ F B♭ Cm D Gm D E♭ Cm D G
lay, thou lit - tle ti - ny child. By by, lul - ly, lul - lay.
poor young - ling for whom we sing. By by, lul - ly, lul - lay.

Additional Lyrics

**3. Herod the king,
In his raging,
Charged he hath this day.
His men of might,
In his own sight,
All young children to slay.**

**4. Then woe is me,
Poor child for thee!
And ever mourn and say,
For thy parting
Neither say nor sing
By by, lully lullay!**

THE CRAWDAD SONG

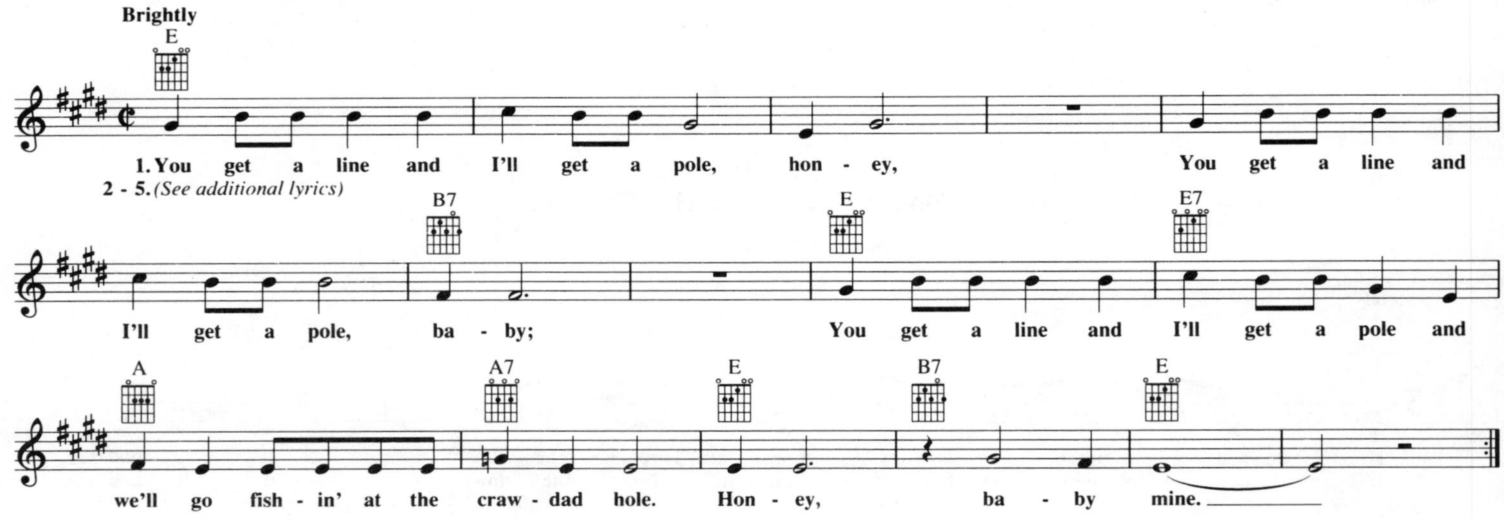
Brightly
E
1. You get a line and I'll get a pole, hon - ey, You get a line and
2 - 5. (See additional lyrics)
B7 E E7
I'll get a pole, ba - by; You get a line and I'll get a pole and
A A7 E B7 E
we'll go fish - in' at the craw - dad hole. Hon - ey, ba - by mine.

Additional Lyrics

**2. Get up old man, you slept too late, honey, (twice)
Get up old man, you slept too late,
Last piece of crawdad's on your plate,
Honey, sugar baby mine.**

**3. Get up old woman, you slept too late, honey, (twice)
Get up old woman, you slept too late,
Crawdad man done passed your gate,
Honey, sugar baby mine.**

**4. What you gonna do when the lake goes dry, (twice)
What you gonna do when the lake goes dry,
Sit on the bank and watch the crawdads die,
Honey, sugar baby mine.**

**5. What you gonna do when the crawdads die, honey? (twice)
What you gonna do when the crawdads die,
Sit on the bank until I cry,
Honey, sugar baby mine.**

CRIPPLE CREEK

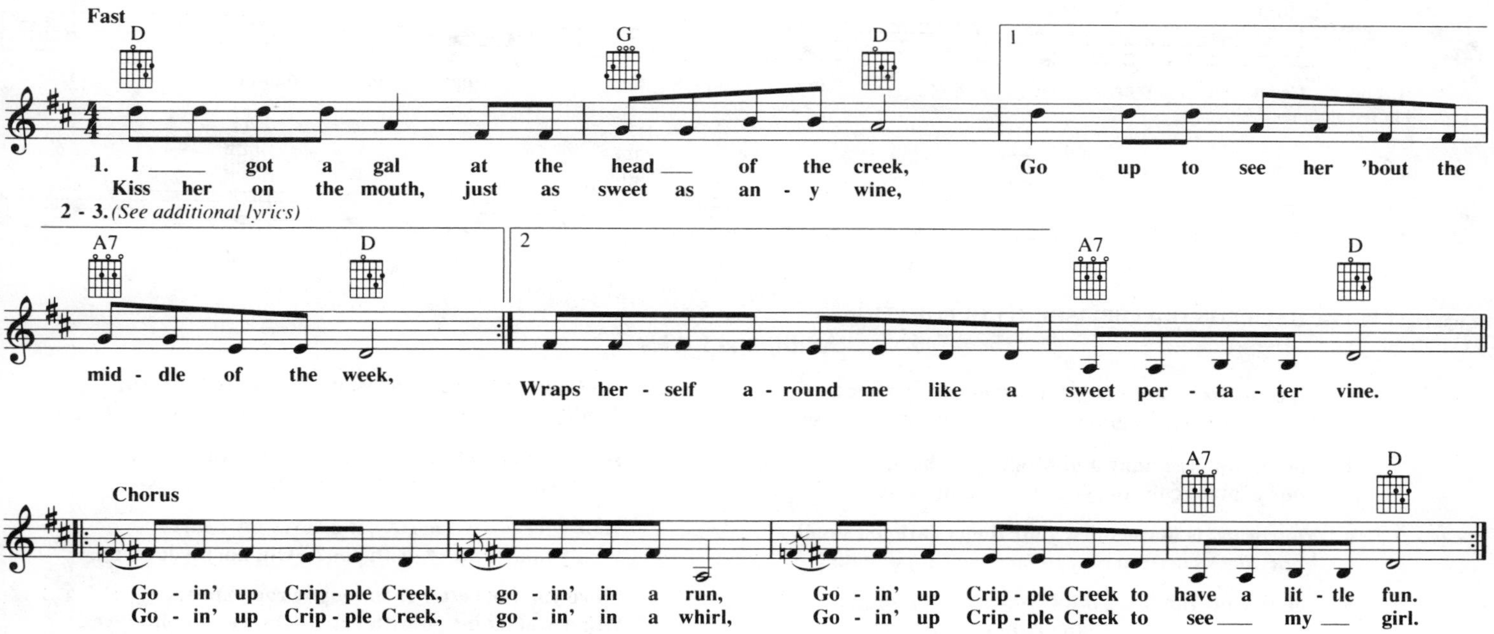
Fast
D G D A7 D A7 D
1. I ___ got a gal at the head ___ of the creek, Go up to see her 'bout the mid - dle of the week,
Kiss her on the mouth, just as sweet as an - y wine, Wraps her - self a - round me like a sweet per - ta - ter vine.
2 - 3. (See additional lyrics)
Chorus
A7 D
Go - in' up Crip - ple Creek, go - in' in a run, Go - in' up Crip - ple Creek to have a lit - tle fun.
Go - in' up Crip - ple Creek, go - in' in a whirl, Go - in' up Crip - ple Creek to see ___ my ___ girl.

Additional Lyrics

2. Girls on the Cripple Creek 'bout half grown,
Jump on a boy like a dog on a bone.
Roll my britches up to my knees,
I'll wade old Cripple Creek when I please.

3. Cripple Creek's wide and Cripple Creek's deep,
I'll wade old Cripple Creek afore I sleep,
Roads are rocky and the hillside's muddy
And I'm so drunk that I can't stand study.*

*steady

CROWN HIM WITH MANY CROWNS

M. Bridges

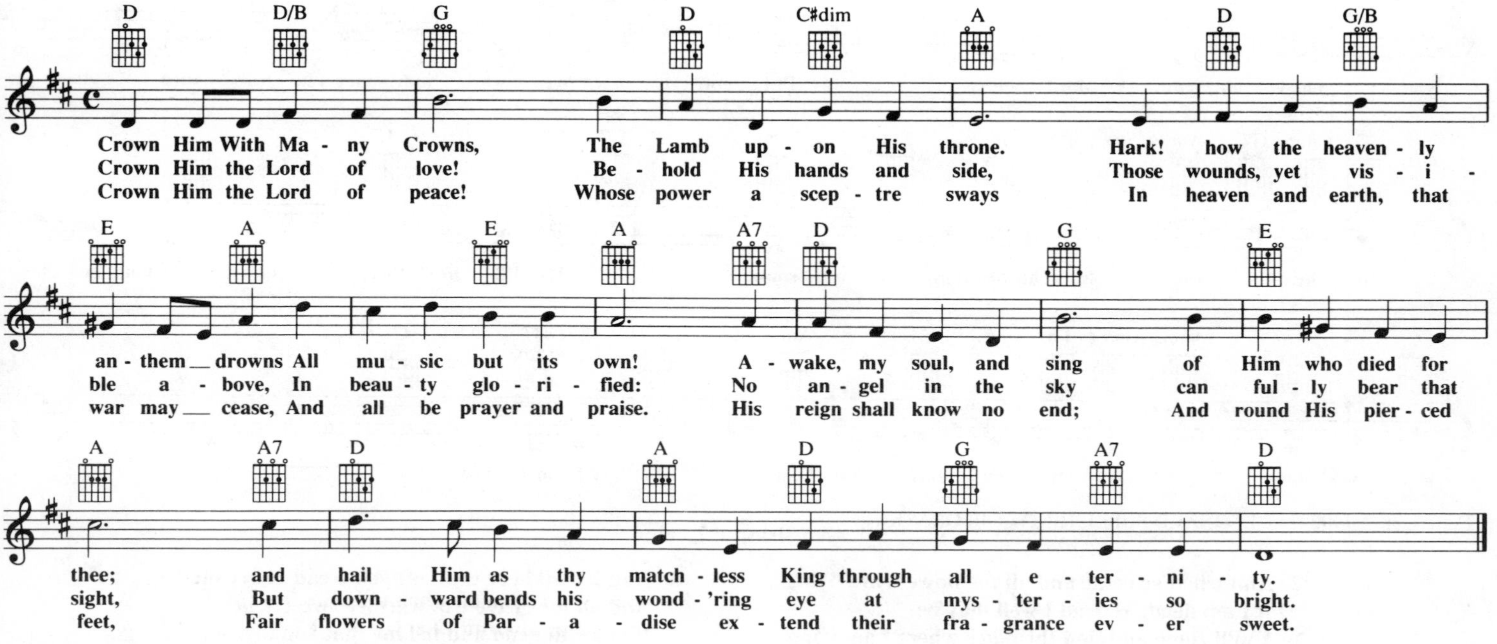
D D/B G D C#dim A D G/B
Crown Him With Ma - ny Crowns, The Lamb up - on His throne. Hark! how the heaven - ly
Crown Him the Lord of love! Be - hold His hands and side, Those wounds, yet vis - i -
Crown Him the Lord of peace! Whose power a scep - tre sways In heaven and earth, that
E A E A A7 D G E
an - them ___ drowns All mu - sic but its own! A - wake, my soul, and sing of Him who died for
ble a - bove, In beau - ty glo - ri - fied: No an - gel in the sky can ful - ly bear that
war may ___ cease, And all be prayer and praise. His reign shall know no end; And round His pier - ced
A A7 D A D G A7 D
thee; and hail Him as thy match - less King through all e - ter - ni - ty.
sight, But down - ward bends his wond - 'ring eye at mys - ter - ies so bright.
feet, Fair flowers of Par - a - dise ex - tend their fra - grance ev - er sweet.

THE CRUEL WAR IS RAGING

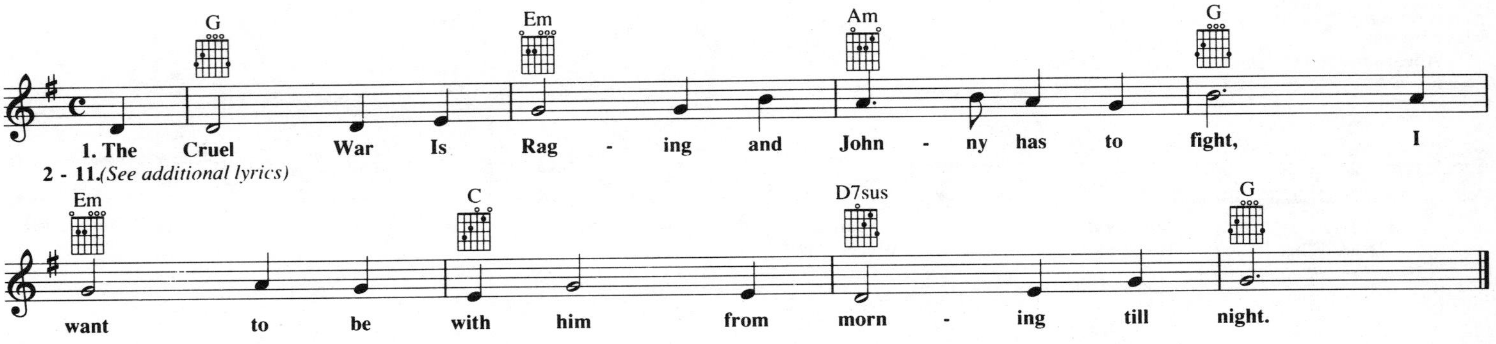
G Em Am G
1. The Cruel War Is Rag - ing and John - ny has to fight, I
2 - 11.(See additional lyrics)
Em C D7sus G
want to be with him from morn - ing till night.

Additional Lyrics

2. I'll go to your captain, get down upon my knees,
Ten thousand gold guineas I'd give for your release.

3. Ten thousand gold guineas, it grieves my heart so;
Won't you let me go with you? - Oh, no, my love, no.

4. Tomorrow is Sunday and Monday is the day
Your captain calls for you, and you must obey.

5. Your captain calls for you, it grieves my heart so,
Won't you let me go with you? - Oh, no, my love, no.

6. Your waist is too slender, your fingers are too small,
Your cheeks are too rosy to face the cannonball.

7. Your cheeks are too rosy, it grieves my heart so,
Won't you let me go with you? - Oh, no, my love, no.

8. Johnny, oh Johnny, I think you are unkind,
I love you far better than all other mankind.

9. I love you far better than tongue can express,
Won't you let me go with you? - Oh, yes, my love, yes.

10. I'll pull back my hair, men's clothes I'll put on,
I'll pass for your comrade as we march along.

11. I'll pass for your comrade and none will ever guess,
Won't you let me go with you? - Yes, my love, yes.

DANNY BOY

Melody Traditional
Lyrics by Fred Weatherly

Slowly
C C7 F Dm G7 C
1. Oh Dan - ny Boy the pipes the pipes are call - ing from glen to glen and
2. (See additional lyrics)
Am Dm G7 C C7 F
down the moun - tain side The sum - mer's gone and all the ros - es fall - ing 'tis you, 'tis
C Dm G7 C Cdim G7 C Em C
you must go and I must bide. But come ye back when Sum - mer's in the mea - dow,
C Cdim G7 Am F Em Dm G7 C7 F
or when the val - ley's hushed and white with snow. 'Tis I'll be there in sun - shine or in
C Am Am/G Am/F# Fm C/E Am Dm7 G7 C
sha - dow Oh Dan - ny Boy, Oh Dan - ny Boy I love you so.

Additional Lyrics

2. And when ye come and all the flowers are dying
If I am dead, as dead I well may be
You'll come and find the place where I am lying
And kneel and say an Ave there for me.

3. And I shall hear tho' soft you tread above me
And all my grave will warmer sweeter be
If you will bend and tell me that you love me
Then I shall sleep in peace until you come to me.

CHINATOWN, MY CHINATOWN

Words by William Jerome,
Music by Jean Schwartz

Allegro Moderato
C G7 Am E7 Am
Chi - na - town, My Chi - na - town, Where the lights are low, Hearts that know no oth - er land,
D7 G7 C C G7 C7 C+ F
Drift - ing to and fro, Dream - y, dream - y Chi - na - town, Al - mond eyes of brown,
Fm6 C Gm6 A7 D7 Dm7 G7 1 C C♯dim7 Dm Gm6 G7 2 C
Hearts seem light and life seems bright in dream - y Chi - na - town town.

CHOPSTICKS

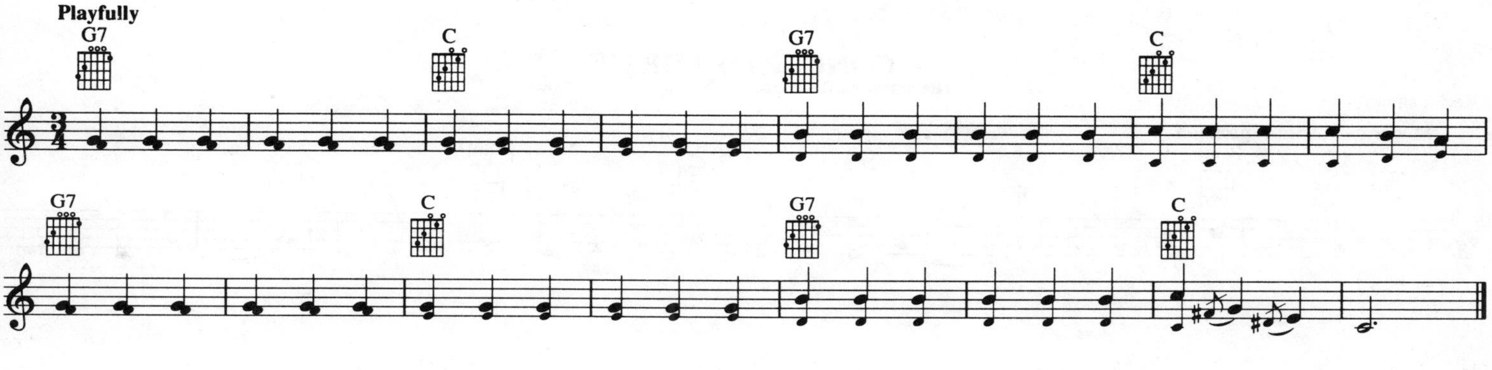
Playfully
G7 C G7 C
G7 C G7 C

CUDDLE UP A LITTLE CLOSER, LOVEY MINE

Words by Otto Hauerbach
Music by Karl Hoschna

Slowly
C C/E E♭dim7 G7
Cud - dle Up A Lit - tle Clos - er, Lov - ey Mine, Cud - dle up and
G7♯5 C A7 D7 G7
be my lit - tle cling - ing vine. Like to feel your cheek so ro - sy, Like to make you com - fy,
G♯dim7 Am D7 E♭dim7 C/E D7 G7 C
co - zy, 'Cause I love from head to toe - sy, Lov - ey mine.

CONCERTO THEME

(Rachmaninoff) - (Concerto No. 2, 1st Movement)

Rachmaninoff

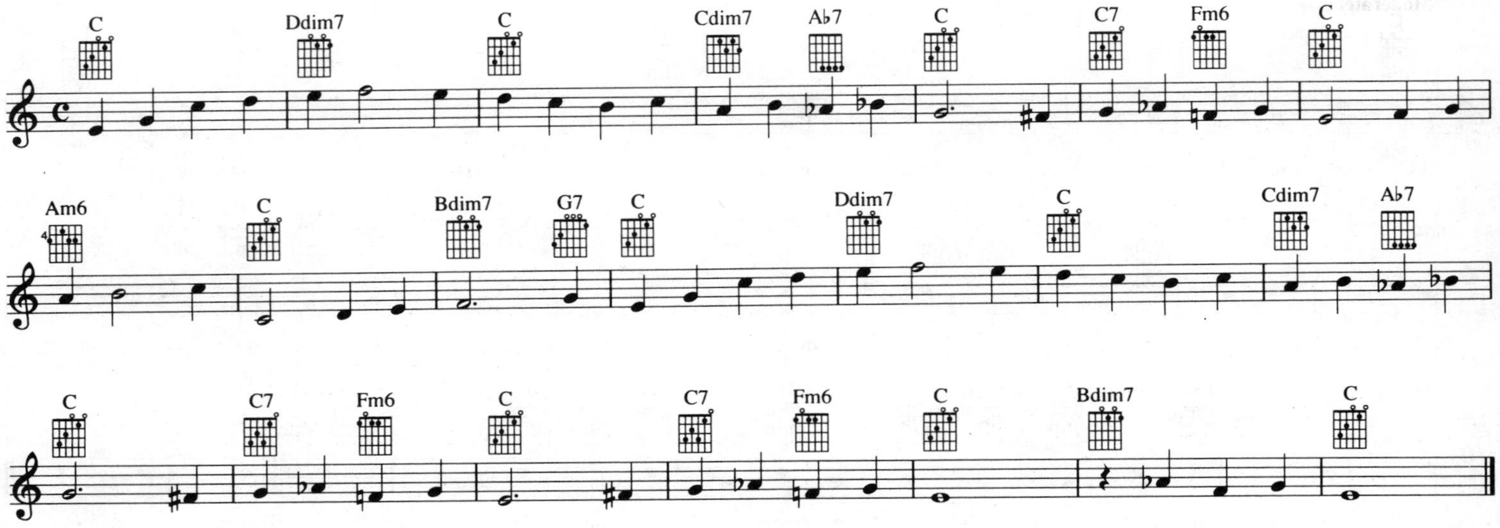

CONCERTO THEME

(Rachmaninoff) - (Concerto No. 2, 3rd Movement)

Rachmaninoff

Moderately, with expression

COME, JOSEPHINE IN MY FLYING MACHINE

Words by Alfred Bryan
Music by Fred Fisher

Moderately

C G7
Come Jo - se - phine In My Fly - ing Ma - chine, Go - ing up she goes! up she goes!
Gdim7 G7 C
Ba - lance your - self like a bird on a beam, in the air she goes! there she goes!
Cdim7 G7 C Cdim7 G7
Up, up, a lit - tle bit high - er, Oh! my! the moon is on fire.
C G7 C G7 C
Come Jo - se - phine In My Fly - ing Ma - chine, Go - ing up, all on, "Good - bye!"

DOWN THE FIELD

Words by C. W. O'Connor
Music by Stanleigh P. Friedman

March tempo

B♭ F7 B♭ E♭ B♭ E♭ B♭ E♭
March, march on Down The Field, fight - ing for E - li, Break thru the crim - son
D7 Gm C7 F7 B♭ F7
line, their strength to de - fy, We'll give a long cheer for E - li's men, we're
B♭ E♭ C7 B♭ G7 C7 F7 B♭
here to win a - gain, Har - vard's team can fight to the end, but Yale will win.

DANCE OF THE SUGAR-PLUM FAIRY

Peter Tchaikovsky

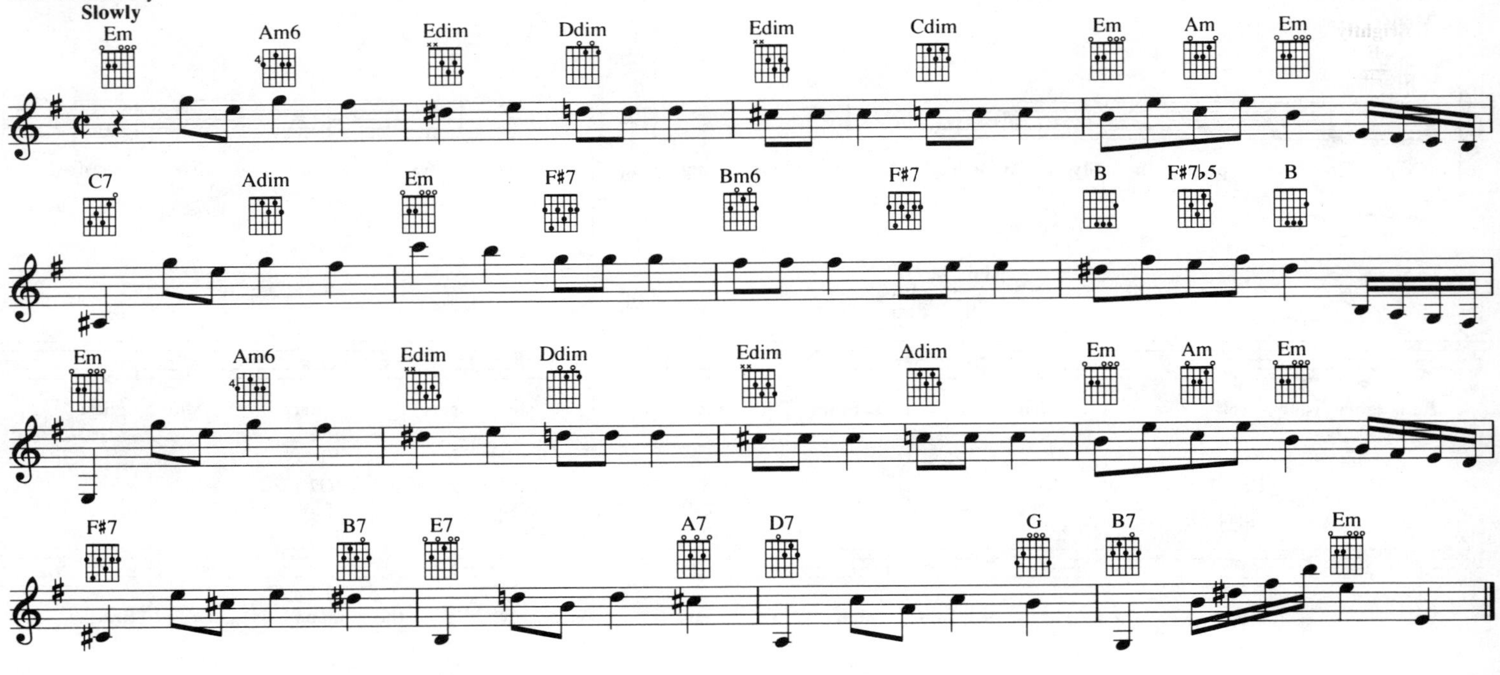
Slowly
Em Am6 Edim Ddim Edim Cdim Em Am Em
C7 Adim Em F#7 Bm6 F#7 B F#7♭5 B
Em Am6 Edim Ddim Edim Adim Em Am Em
F#7 B7 E7 A7 D7 G B7 Em

DEEP RIVER

Slowly
F B♭ Gm7 F Dm Am C7sus F F7 B♭ Bdim7
Deep River, my home is over Jordan. Deep River, Lord, I
F Bdim7 Gm7 C7 F N.C.
Faster
Dm A7 Dm A7 Dm
want to cross over into campground. Oh, don't you want to go to that Gospel feast, That promised land where
go into heav'n and take my seat. I'll cast my crown at
when I get to heav'n I'll walk all about. There's no one there to
A7♯5 Dm C7 F Bdim7 Gm7 C7 F C7
CHORUS - Slowly
F B♭ Gm7 F Dm
all is peace? Lord, I want to cross over into campground. Oh,
Jesus' feet. Lord, I want to cross over into campground. Oh,
turn me out. Lord, I want to cross over into campground. Oh,
Deep River, my home is over
Am C7sus F F7 B♭ Bdim7 F Bdim7 Gm7 C7 1-2 F 3 F
Jordan. Deep River, Lord, I want to cross over into campground. I'll Oh, campground.

DECK THE HALL

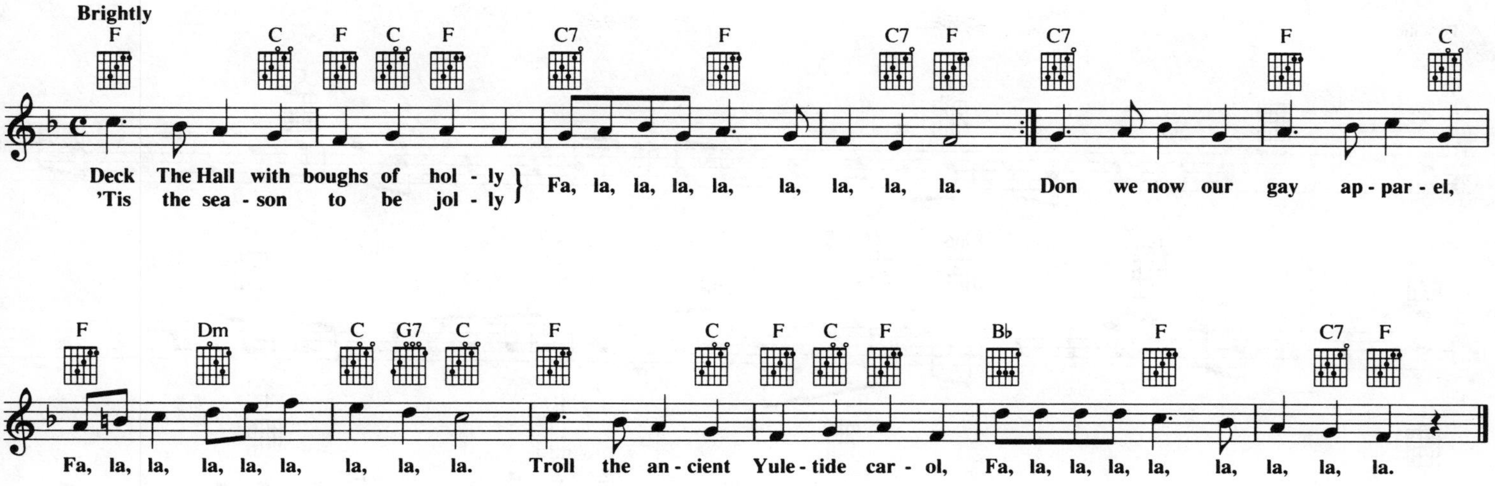
Brightly
F C F C F C7 F C7 F C7 F C
Deck The Hall with boughs of hol - ly
'Tis the sea - son to be jol - ly
Fa, la, la, la, la, la, la, la, la. Don we now our gay ap - par - el,
F Dm C G7 C F C F C F B♭ F C7 F
Fa, la, la, la, la, la, la, la, la. Troll the an - cient Yule - tide car - ol, Fa, la, la, la, la, la, la, la, la.

THE DESPERADO

C G7
1. He was a des - pe - ra - do from the wild and wool - ly west, He came in to Chi - ca - go just to give the west a
2 - 3. (See additional lyrics)
C F C G7
rest. He wore a big som - brer - o and a gun be - neath his vest, And ev - 'ry - where he went he gave his war
C G7
Chorus
whoop. He was a big brave man and a des - pe - ra - do, From Crip - ple Creek way down in Col - o - ra - do, and he
C F C G7 C
walked a - round like a big tor - na - do, And ev - 'ry - where he went he gave his war whoop.

Additional Lyrics

2. He went to Coney Island just to take in all the sights,
He saw the hootchie-kootchie and the girls dressed up in tights,
He got so darned excited that he shot out all the lights,
And everywhere he went he gave his war whoop.
Chorus

3. A great big fat policeman was a-walking down his beat,
He saw the desperado come a-walking down the street.
He grabbed him by the whiskers, and he grabbed him by the seat,
And threw him where he couldn't give his war whoop.
Chorus

DANCE OF THE HOURS

A. Ponchielli

DANUBE WAVES

By Ion Ivanovici

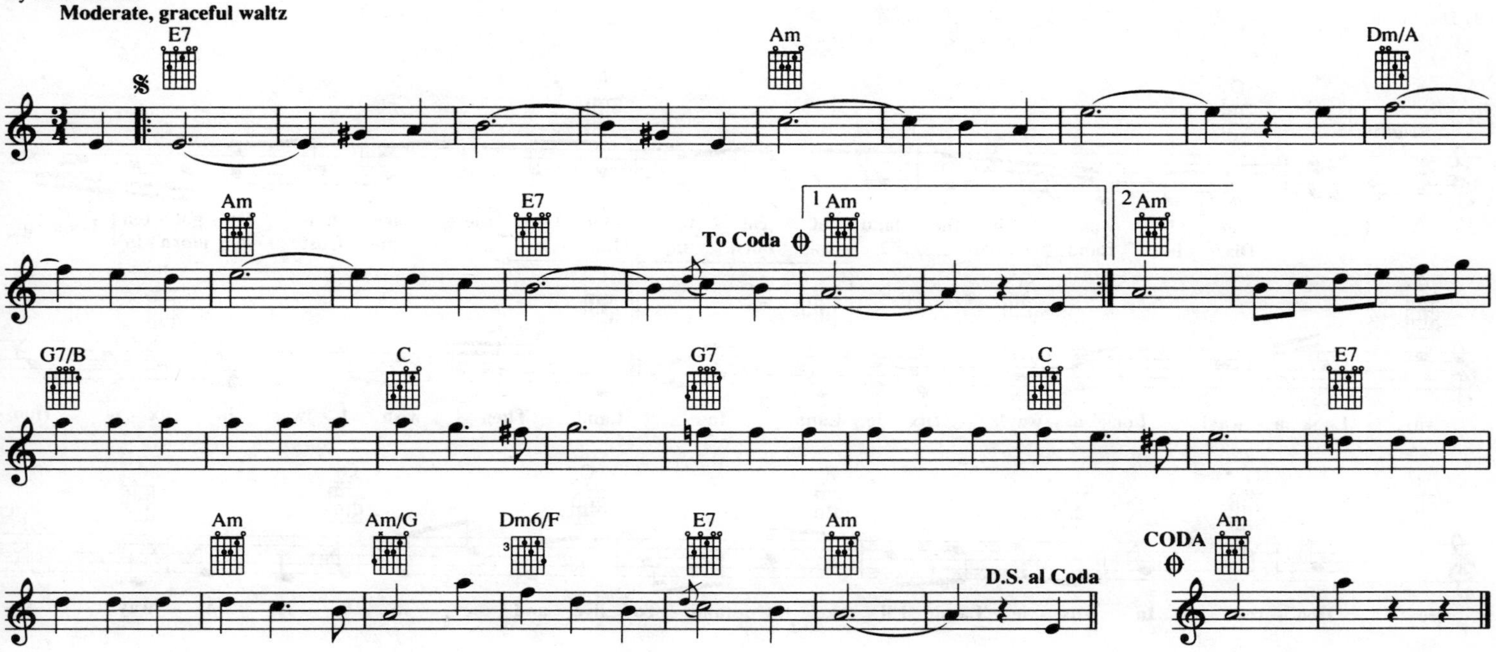

DARK EYES

DID YOU EVER SEE A LASSIE?

Moderately
F C7 F C7
Did You E - ver See A Las - sie, a las - sie, a las - sie, Did You E - ver See A Lass - sie go this way and
F C7 F C7 F C7 F
that? Go this way and that way, go this way and that way, Did You E - ver See A Las - sie go this way and that?

DIXIE

By Dan Emmett

Brightly
C F
I ___ wish I was ___ in the land of cot - ton, Old times there are not for - got - ten
Dix - ie Land ___ where ___ I was born in, Ear - ly on one frost - ty morn - in'
Look a -
C G7 1 C 2 C F
way! Look a - way! Look a - way! Dix - ie Land. In ___ Land. Then I wish I was in Dix - ie Hoo -
D7 G7 C F C G7 C
ray! Hoo - ray! In Dix - ie Land, I'll take my stand To live and die in Dix - ie; A - way, A -
C G7 C
way, A - way down South in Dix - ie, A - way, A - way, A - way down South in Dix - ie.

DOWN BY THE STATION

Lively
D A7 D A7 D
Down By The Sta - tion ear - ly in the morn - ing, See the lit - tle puf - fer - bil - lies all in a row.
A7 D A7 D
See the en - gine driv - er pull the lit - tle han dle. Choo! Choo! Toot! Toot! Off they go!

DOG-GONE BLUES

C6 Cm6 G6 E7 A7
Dog - gone Blues. _ Yes, I'm sing - ing those Dog - gone Blues. _ Life is bring - ing me all bad news_ and
D7 G Em E♭7 D7 C6 Cm6
bro - ken dreams. _ E - ven the milk - man brought me sour_ cream._ Dog - gone Blues. _ What on earth am I
G6 E7 A7 D7 G6 C7 G6
gon - na do?_ I feel so bad and I'm so con - fused._ I can't lose those Dog-gone _ Blues. _______

THE DRUNKEN SAILOR

With spirit
Dm C
1. What shall we do with The Drunk - en Sail - or? What shall we do with The Drunk - en Sail - or?
2. Put him in the long boat till he's so - ber, Put him in the long boat till he's so - ber,
3 - 5. (See additional lyrics)
Dm Am C Dm
What shall we do with The Drunk - en Sail - or?
Put him in the long boat till he's so - ber,
Ear - lye in the morn - ing.
Chorus
Hoo - ray and up she ris - es,
C Dm Am C Dm
Hoo - ray and up she ris - es, Hoo - ray and up she ris - es, Ear - lye in the morn - ing.

Additional Lyrics

3. Pull out the plug and wet him all over,
Pull out the plug and wet him all over,
Pull out the plug and wet him all over,
Earlye in the morning.
Chorus

4. Tie him to the top mast when she's under,
Tie him to the top mast when she's under,
Tie him to the top mast when she's under,
Earlye in the morning.
Chorus

5. Put him in the scuppers with the hosepipe on him,
Put him in the scuppers with the hosepipe on him,
Put him in the scuppers with the hosepipe on him,
Earlye in the morning.
Chorus

DOWN BY THE OLD MILL STREAM

Music by Tell Taylor

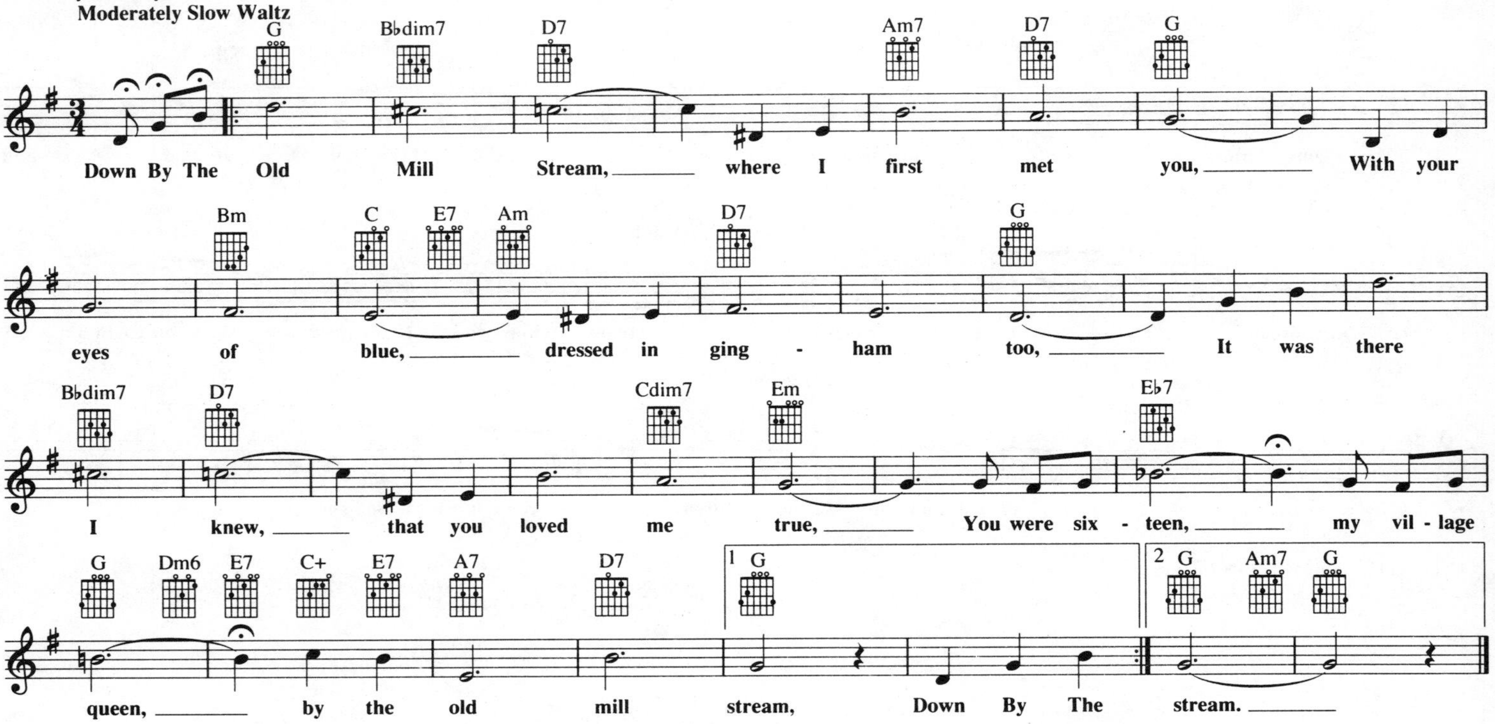
Moderately Slow Waltz
G Bbdim7 D7 Am7 D7 G
Down By The Old Mill Stream, where I first met you, With your
Bm C E7 Am D7 G
eyes of blue, dressed in ging - ham too, It was there
Bbdim7 D7 Cdim7 Em Eb7
I knew, that you loved me true, You were six - teen, my vil - lage
G Dm6 E7 C+ E7 A7 D7 1 G 2 G Am7 G
queen, by the old mill stream, Down By The stream.

DOWN BY THE RIVERSIDE

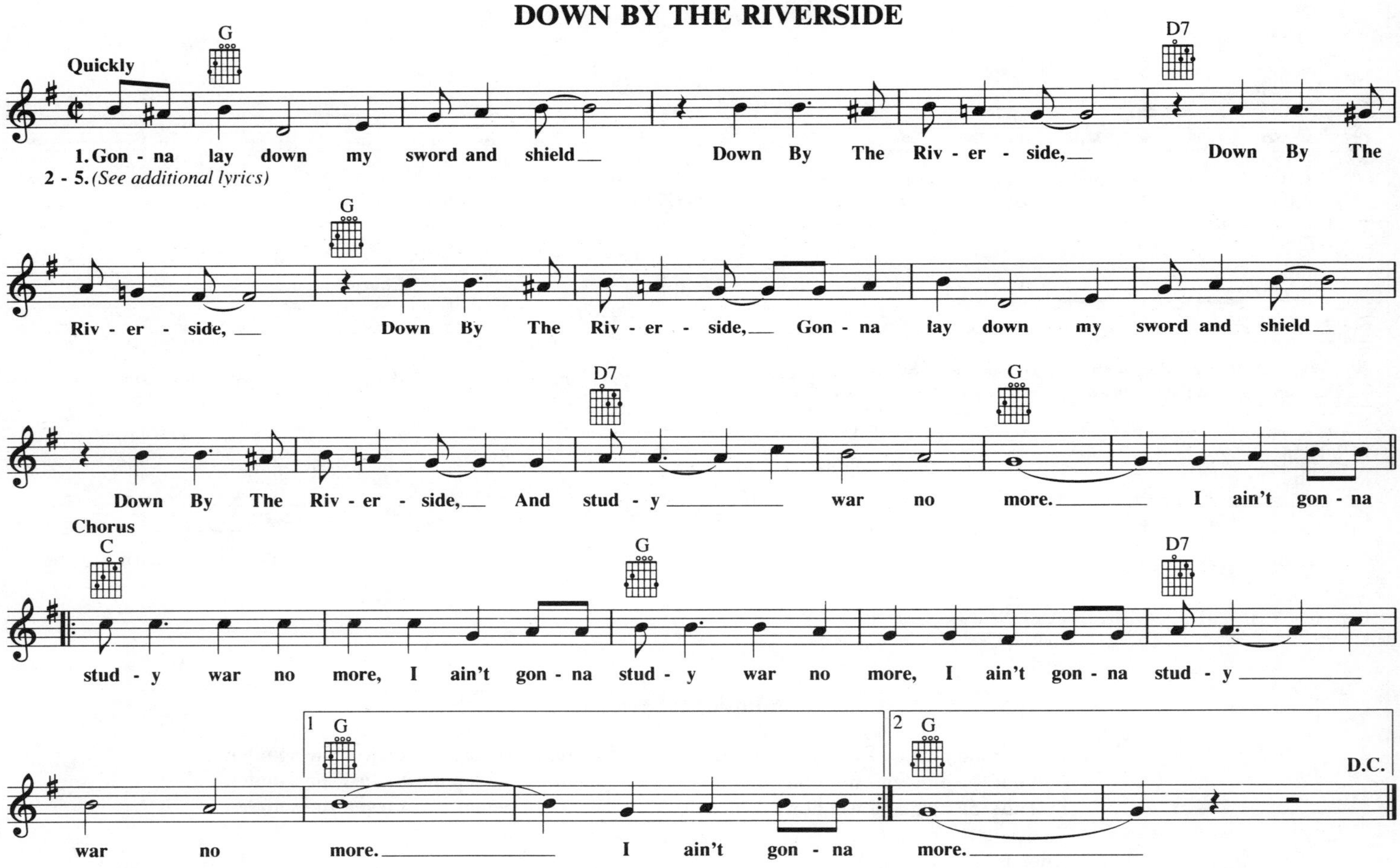
Quickly
G D7
1. Gon - na lay down my sword and shield Down By The Riv - er - side, Down By The
2 - 5. (See additional lyrics)
G
Riv - er - side, Down By The Riv - er - side, Gon - na lay down my sword and shield
D7 G
Down By The Riv - er - side, And stud - y war no more. I ain't gon - na
Chorus
C G D7
stud - y war no more, I ain't gon - na stud - y war no more, I ain't gon - na stud - y
1 G 2 G
war no more. I ain't gon - na more.
D.C.

Additional Lyrics

2. I'm gonna join hands with everyone,
Down By The Riverside, Down By The Riverside,
Down By The Riverside,
I'm gonna join hands with everyone,
Down By The Riverside,
And study war no more.

3. I'm gonna put on my long white robe . . .

4. I'm gonna walk with the Prince of Peace . .

DOWN IN THE VALLEY

D
A7
1. Down In The Val - ley, Val - ley so low,
2 - 5. (See additional lyrics)
D
Hang your head o - ver, Hear the wind blow.

Additional Lyrics

2. Roses love sunshine, violets love dew
Angels in heaven, know I love you.
Know I love you dear, know I love you.
Angels in heaven, know I love you.

3. If you don't love me, love whom you please
Throw your arms round me, give my heart ease.
Give my heart ease love, give my heart ease.
Throw your arms round me, give my heart ease.

4. Build me a castle forty feet high
So I can see him as he rides by
As he rides by love, as he rides by
So I can see him as he rides by.

5. Write me a letter, send it by mail
Send it in care of Birmingham jail.
Birmingham jail love, Birmingham jail
Send it in care of Birmingham jail.

DRINK TO ME ONLY WITH THINE EYES

C G7 C Dm C G7 C
1. Drimk To Me On - ly With Thine Eyes, And I will pledge with mine;
2 - 3. (See additional lyrics)
G7 C Dm C G7 C
Or leave a kiss with - in the cup and I'll not ask for wine. The
F C G7
thirst that from the soul doth rise, Doth ask a drink di - vine,
C G7 C Dm C G7 C
But might I of Jove's nec - tar sip, I would not ask for wine.

Additional Lyrics

2. I sent thee late a rosy wreath,
Not so much honoring thee,
As giving it a hope that there
It could not withered be.

3. But thou thereon didst only breathe,
And sent'st it back to me,
Since when it grows and smells, I swear,
Not of itself, but thee.

DRY BONES

Rhythmically
E - ze - kiel cried, "Them Dry Bones!" E - ze - kiel cried, "Them Dry Bones!" Oh, hear the word of the Lord! The
foot bone con-nect - ed to the leg bone, the leg bone con-nect - ed to the knee bone, The knee bone con-nect - ed to the
thigh bone, The thigh bone con-nect - ed to the back bone, The back bone con-nect - ed to the neck bone, The
neck bone con-nect - ed to the head bone, Oh, hear the word of the Lord! Them bones, them bones gon - na
walk a - roun', them bones, them bones gon - na walk a - roun', Oh, hear the word of the Lord! The
head bone con-nect - ed to the neck bone, the neck bone con-nect - ed to the back bone, The back bone con-nect - ed to the
thigh bone, The thigh bone con-nect - ed to the knee bone, The knee bone con-nect - ed to the leg bone, The
leg bone con-nect - ed to the foot bone, Oh, hear the word of the Lord!

EENCY, WEENCY SPIDER

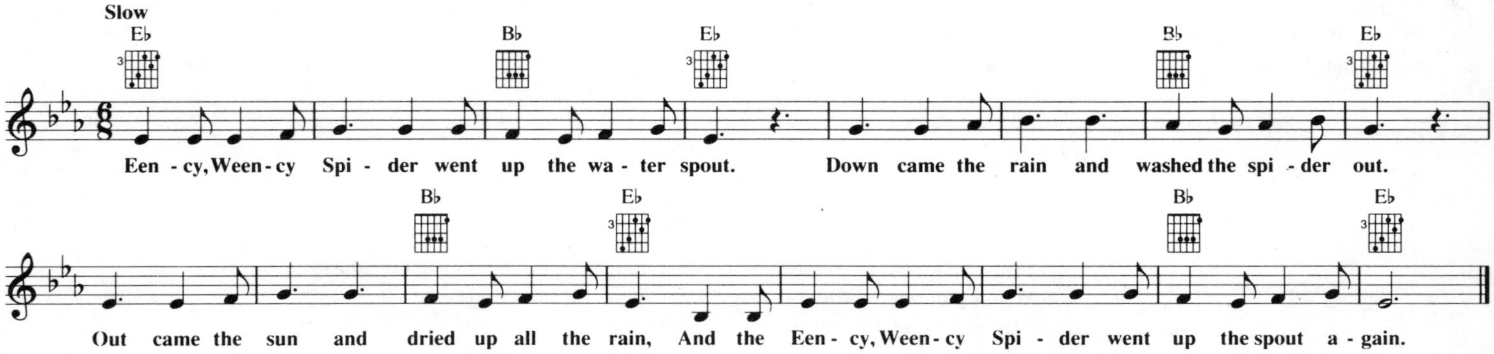
Slow
Een - cy, Ween - cy Spi - der went up the wa - ter spout. Down came the rain and washed the spi - der out.
Out came the sun and dried up all the rain, And the Een - cy, Ween - cy Spi - der went up the spout a - gain.

DU, DU LIEGST MIR IM HERZEN

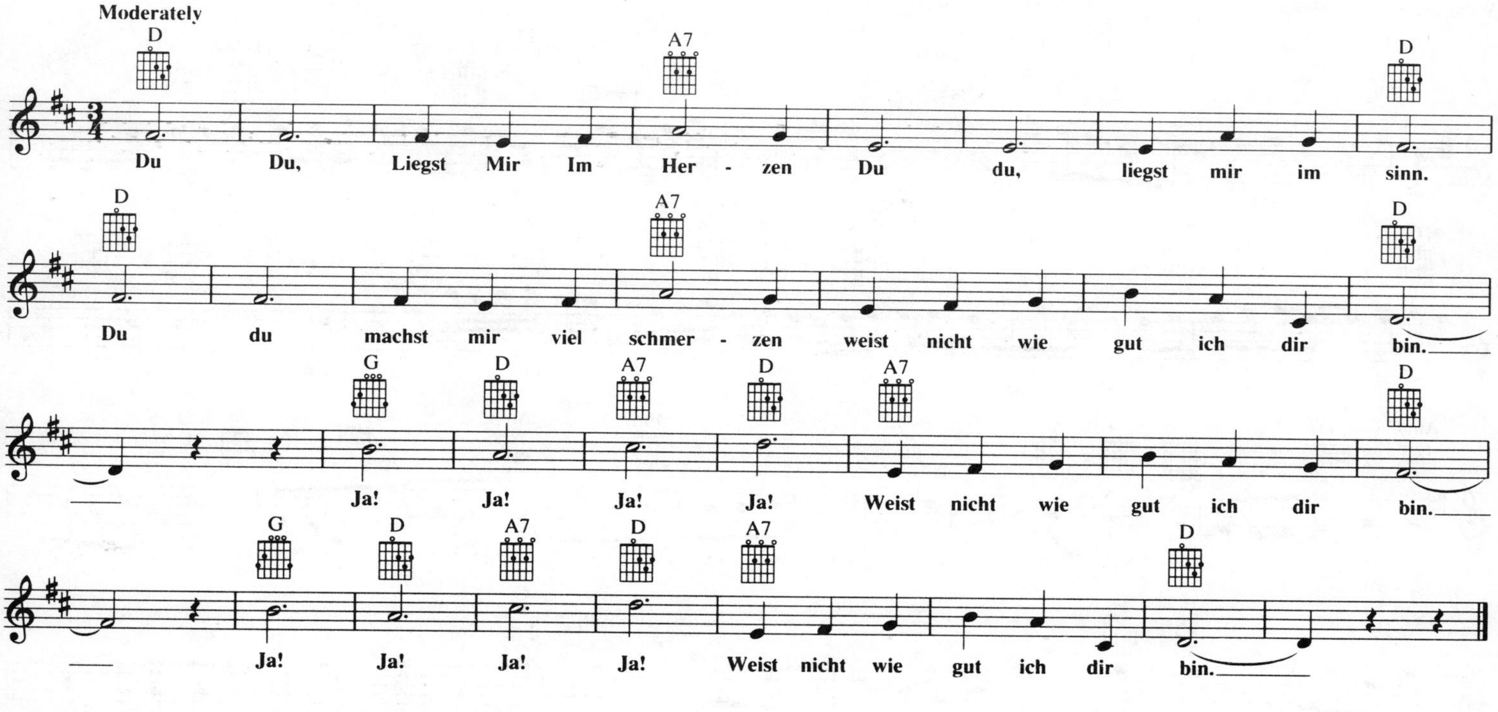
Moderately
Du Du, Liegst Mir Im Her - zen Du du, liegst mir im sinn.
Du du machst mir viel schmer - zen weist nicht wie gut ich dir bin.
Ja! Ja! Ja! Ja! Weist nicht wie gut ich dir bin.
Ja! Ja! Ja! Ja! Weist nicht wie gut ich dir bin.

EL CAPITAN

John Philip Sousa

Brightly

EINE KLEINE NACHTMUSIK
(Opening Theme)

Wolfgang Amadeus Mozart

THE ENTERTAINER

Scott Joplin

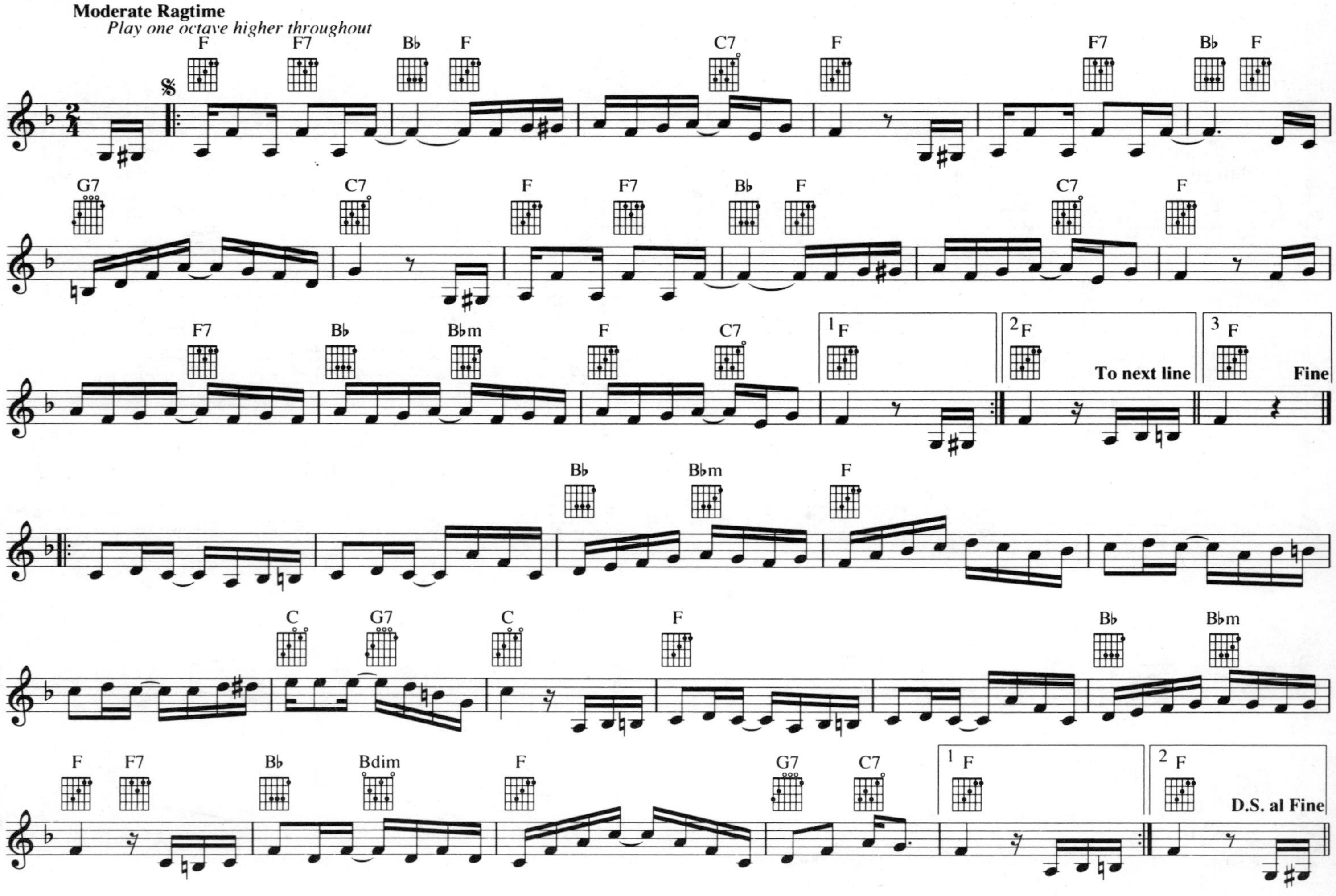

ELEGIE

Jules Massenet

Slowly
Em Am6 B7 Em
Am6 B7 Em A7 G D7 G D7 G D7
B7 Em B7 Em Am6 B7
E7 Am B7 Em

THE ERIE CANAL

Moderately
Dm Gm A Dm A7 Dm
I've got a mule, her name is Sal, Fif-teen miles on The E-rie Can-al. She's a good old work-er and a
We'd bet-ter get a-long our way 'Cause you bet your life I nev-er
Gm A Dm A7 Dm F Am C7
good old pal, Fif-teen miles on The E-rie Can-al. We've hauled some barg-es in our day,
part with Sal, Get up there, mule, here comes a lock,
F Gm7 A Dm Gm A Dm
filled with lum-ber, coal and hay, And we know ev-'ry inch of the way From Al-ba-ny to
we'll make Rome 'bout six o'-clock. One more trip and back we'll go, Right back home to
A7 Dm C7 F C7 F Dm Gm7 C7 F
Buf-fa-lo.
Buf-fa-lo. Low bridge ev-'ry-bod-y down! Low bridge, for we're go-ing thru a town; And you'll
C7 F C7 F Gm7 F C7 F
al-ways know your neigh-bor, you'll al-ways know your pal, If you've ev-er nav-ig-at-ed on The E-rie Can-al.

EMPEROR WALTZ

Johann Strauss

EMILIA POLKA

EV'RY TIME I FEEL THE SPIRIT

Moderately, very steady
G7 D G7 D A7 D G7
Ev - 'ry Time I ___ Feel The Spir - it, ___ Mov - in' in my heart, __ I will pray. ___ Ev - 'ry Time I ___ Feel The
D G7 D A7 D A7
Fine
Verse
Spir - it, ___ Mov-in' in my heart, __ I will pray. ___ Up - on the moun - tain __ when my Lord spoke, __ Out of his mouth came _ fire and
Oh, I have sor - rows _ and I have woe, ___ And I have heart-ache _ here be -
D A7 1 D 2 D
D.S. al Fine
smoke. _ Look'd all a - round me, __ It look'd so fine, ___ 'Till I asked my Lord __ if all were mine. ___ Ev - 'ry
low; ___ But while God leads me, __ I'll nev - er fear, ___ For I am shel - tered __ by His care. ___ Ev - 'ry

EZEKIEL SAW THE WHEEL

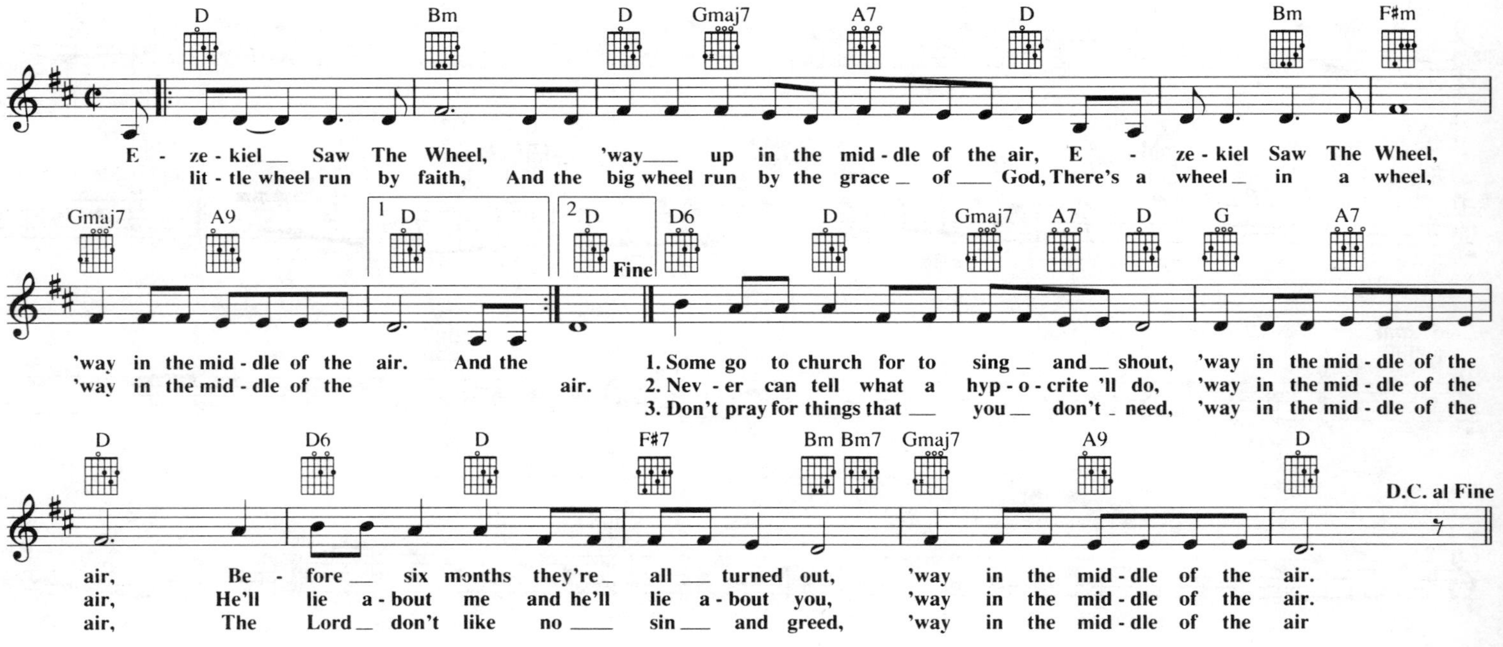
D Bm D Gmaj7 A7 D Bm F#m
E - ze - kiel __ Saw The Wheel, 'way ___ up in the mid - dle of the air, E - ze - kiel Saw The Wheel,
lit - tle wheel run by faith, And the big wheel run by the grace _ of ___ God, There's a wheel _ in a wheel,
Gmaj7 A9 1 D 2 D D6 D Gmaj7 A7 D G A7
Fine
'way in the mid - dle of the air. And the air.
'way in the mid - dle of the
1. Some go to church for to sing _ and _ shout, 'way in the mid - dle of the
2. Nev - er can tell what a hyp - o - crite 'll do, 'way in the mid - dle of the
3. Don't pray for things that ___ you __ don't _ need, 'way in the mid - dle of the
D D6 D F#7 Bm Bm7 Gmaj7 A9 D
D.C. al Fine
air, Be - fore __ six months they're _ all __ turned out, 'way in the mid - dle of the air.
air, He'll lie a - bout me and he'll lie a - bout you, 'way in the mid - dle of the air.
air, The Lord _ don't like no ___ sin __ and greed, 'way in the mid - dle of the air

Additional Lyrics

4. There's one thing sure that you can't do,
'way in the middle of the air,
You can't serve God and Satan, too,
'way in the middle of the air.
Chorus

5. One of these days about twelve o'clock,
'way in the middle of the air,
This old world's gonna reel and rock,
'way in the middle of the air.
Chorus

FAITH OF OUR FATHERS

Words and Music by Fredrick W. Faber
Henry F. Hemy and J. G. Walton

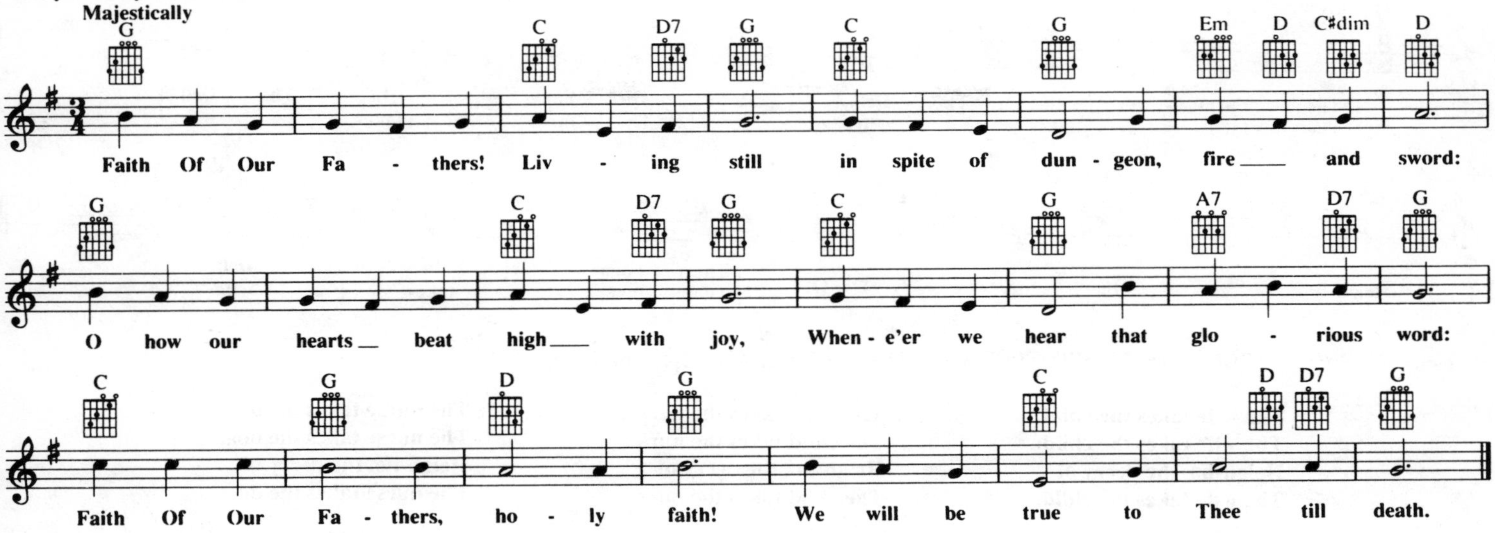
Majestically
G C D7 G C G Em D C#dim D
Faith Of Our Fa - thers! Liv - ing still in spite of dun - geon, fire and sword:
G C D7 G C G A7 D7 G
O how our hearts beat high with joy, When - e'er we hear that glo - rious word:
C G D G C D D7 G
Faith Of Our Fa - thers, ho - ly faith! We will be true to Thee till death.

FANTASIE IMPROMPTU
(Chopin)

Frederic Chopin

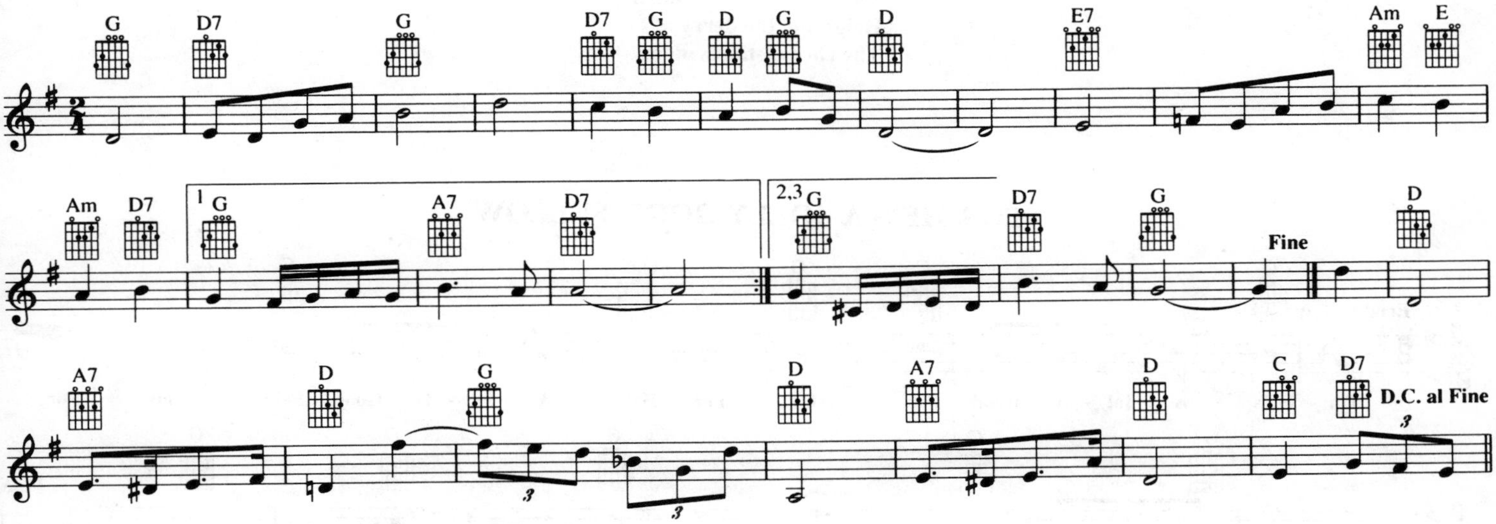
G D7 G D7 G D G D E7 Am E
Am D7 G A7 D7 G D7 G D
Fine
A7 D G D A7 D C D7
D.C. al Fine

FIGHT YE BULLDOGS

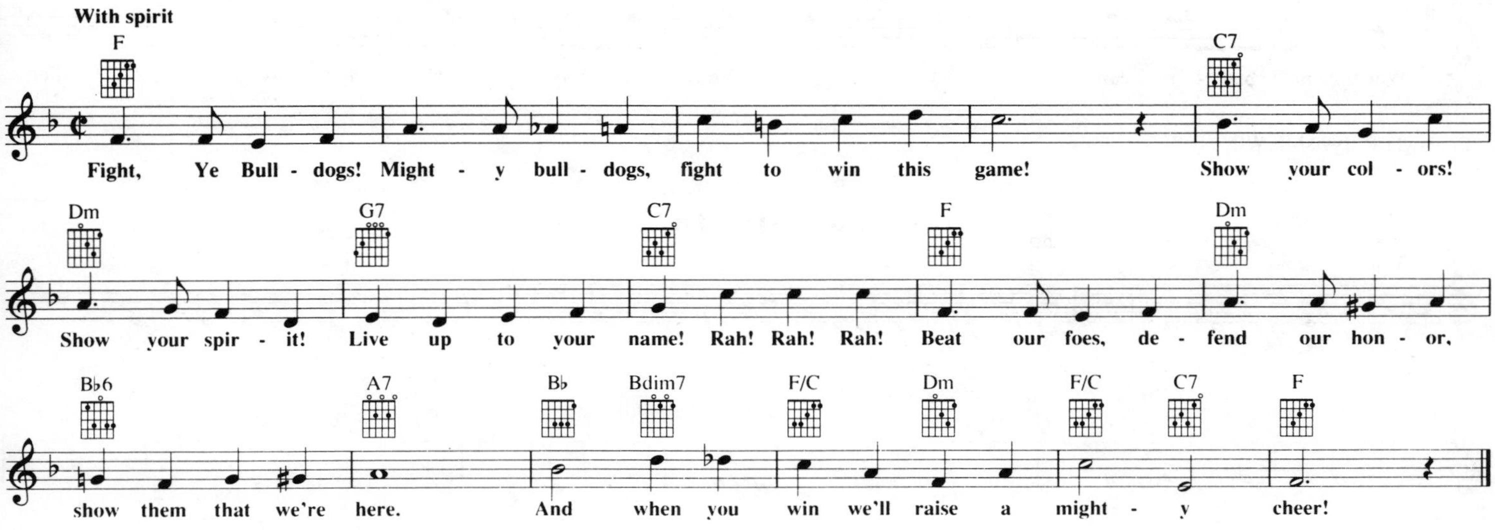
With spirit
F C7
Fight, Ye Bull - dogs! Might - y bull - dogs, fight to win this game! Show your col - ors!
Dm G7 C7 F Dm
Show your spir - it! Live up to your name! Rah! Rah! Rah! Beat our foes, de - fend our hon - or,
Bb6 A7 Bb Bdim7 F/C Dm F/C C7 F
show them that we're here. And when you win we'll raise a might - y cheer!

THE FARMER IN THE DELL

Quickly
E♭
B♭
1. The Farm - er In The Dell, The Farm - er In The Dell,
2. The farm - er takes a wife, The farm - er takes a wife,
3. (See additional lyrics)
Heigh - ho, the der - ry O! The Farm - er In The Dell.
The farm - er takes a wife.

Additional Lyrics

3. The wife takes the child,
The wife takes the child,
Heigh-ho, the derry o!
The wife takes the child.

4. The child takes the nurse,
The child takes the nurse,
Heigh-ho, the derry o!
The child takes the nurse.

5. The nurse takes the dog,
The nurse takes the dog,
Heigh-ho, the derry o!
The nurse takes the dog.

6. The dog takes the cat,
The dog takes the cat,
Heigh-ho, the derry o!
The dog takes the cat.

7. The cat takes the rat,
The cat takes the rat,
Heigh-ho, the derry o!
The cat takes the rat.

8. The rat takes the cheese,
The rat takes the cheese,
Heigh-ho, the derry o!
The rat takes the cheese.

9. The cheese stands alone,
The cheese stands alone,
Heigh-ho, the derry o!
The cheese stands alone.

FOR HE'S A JOLLY GOOD FELLOW

Brightly
G C G D7 G
For He's A Jol - ly Good Fel - low, For He's A Jol - ly Good Fel - low, For
G7 C G D7 G
Fine
He's A Jol - ly Good Fel - low, Which no - bod - y can de - ny,
G C G C G
D.S. al Fine
Which no - bod - y can de - ny, Which no - bod - y can de - ny. For

FREIGHT TRAIN

C G7 C
E7 F C F G7 C

FLEDERMAUS WALTZ

Johann Strauss

Waltz tempo
G
G#dim7
D7/A
D7
G
Am6
D7
G
B
F#7
B
N.C.
G
Am
G
D7
G
Am
G
D7
G

FLOW GENTLY, SWEET AFTON

Music by Alexander Hume
Words by Robert Burns

Gently
D
G
D
A7
1. Flow Gent - ly, Sweet__ Af - ton, a - mong thy green braes; Flow gent - ly, I'll sing thee a song in thy praise; My
2 - 3. (See additional lyrics)
D
G
D
A
D
D7
G
A7
D
Mar - y's a - sleep by thy mur - mur - ing stream, Flow Gent - ly, Sweet Af - ton, dis - turb not her dream. Thou _
A7
E7
A
E7
A
A7
stock dove, whose ech - o re - sounds from the hill, Ye__ mild whis - tling black - birds in yon,__ thorn - y___ dell, Thou
D
G
D
A
D
D7
G
A7
D
green crest - ed___ lap - wing, thy scream - ing for - bear. I charge you, dis - turb not my slum - ber - ing fair.

Additional Lyrics

2. How lofty sweet Afton, thy neighboring hills,
Far marked with the courses of clear winding rills.
There daily I wander as morn rises high,
My flocks and my Mary's sweet cot in my eye.
How pleasant thy banks and green valleys below,
Where wild in the woodlands the primroses blow.
There oft as mild evening creeps over the lea,
The sweet-scented birk shades my Mary and me.

3. Thy crystal stream Afton, how lovely it glides,
And winds by the cot where my Mary resides.
How wanton thy waters her snowy feet lave,
As gath'ring sweet flow'rets, she stems thy clear wave.
Flow Gently, Sweet Afton, among thy green braes,
Flow gently, sweet river, the theme of my lays.
My Mary's asleep by the murmuring stream,
Flow Gently, Sweet Afton, disturb not her dreams.

FAR ABOVE CAYUGA'S WATERS

Lyrics by A.C. Weekes and W. M. Smith
Music by H. S. Thompson

Moderately
Far A - bove Cay - u - ga's Wa - ters, With its waves of blue;
Far a - bove the bus - y hum - ming of the bustl - ing town.
Stands our no - ble Al - ma Ma - ter, Glo - ri - ous to view.
Reared a - gainst the arch of Heav - en looks she proud - ly down.
Raise the cho - rus, speed it on - ward, Loud her prais - es tell;
Hail to thee, our Al - ma Ma - ter! Hail! All hail! Cor - nell!

THE FOGGY, FOGGY DEW

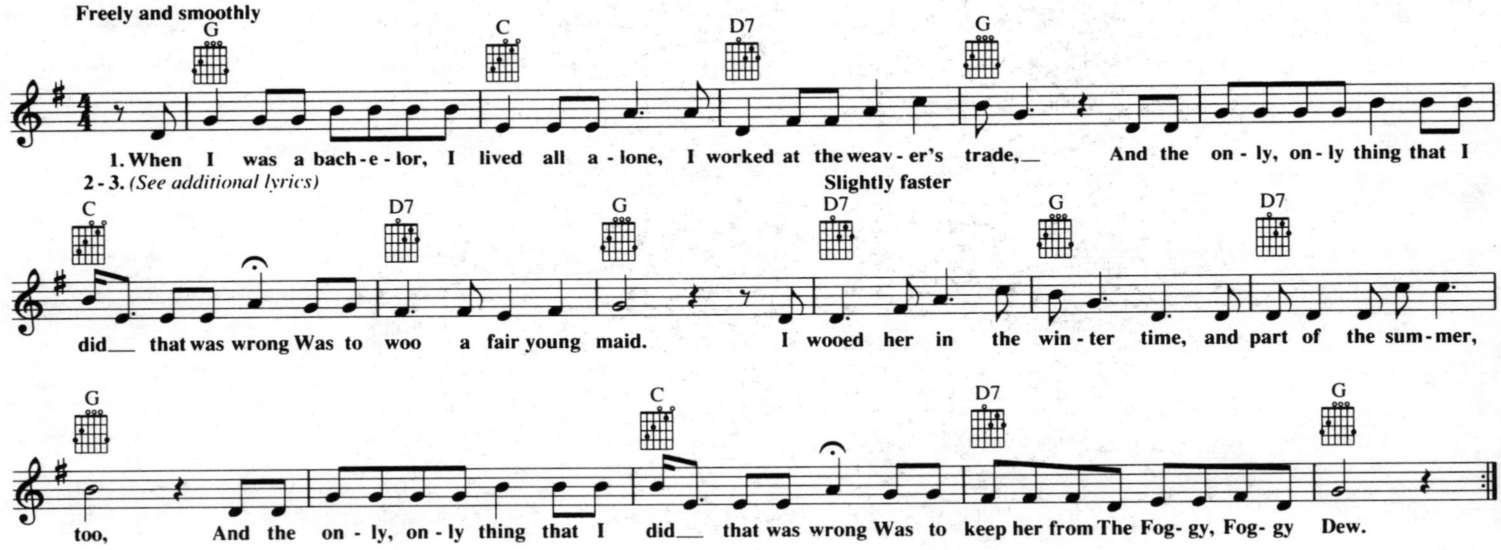
Freely and smoothly
1. When I was a bach - e - lor, I lived all a - lone, I worked at the weav - er's trade, And the on - ly, on - ly thing that I did that was wrong Was to woo a fair young maid.
2 - 3. (See additional lyrics)
Slightly faster
I wooed her in the win - ter time, and part of the sum - mer, too, And the on - ly, on - ly thing that I did that was wrong Was to keep her from The Fog - gy, Fog - gy Dew.

Additional Lyrics

2. One night she came to my bedside,
When I was fast asleep,
She flung her arms around my neck
And then began to weep.
She wept, she cried, she tore her hair,
Ah me, what could I do?
So all night long I held her in my arms,
Just to keep her from the foggy, foggy dew.

3. Still I am a bachelor, I live with my son,
We work at the weaver's trade.
And every time I look into his eyes
He reminds me of that fair young maid.
He reminds me of the winter time,
And part of the summer, too,
And of the many, many times I held her in my arms,
Just to keep her from the foggy, foggy dew.

THE FIRST NOEL

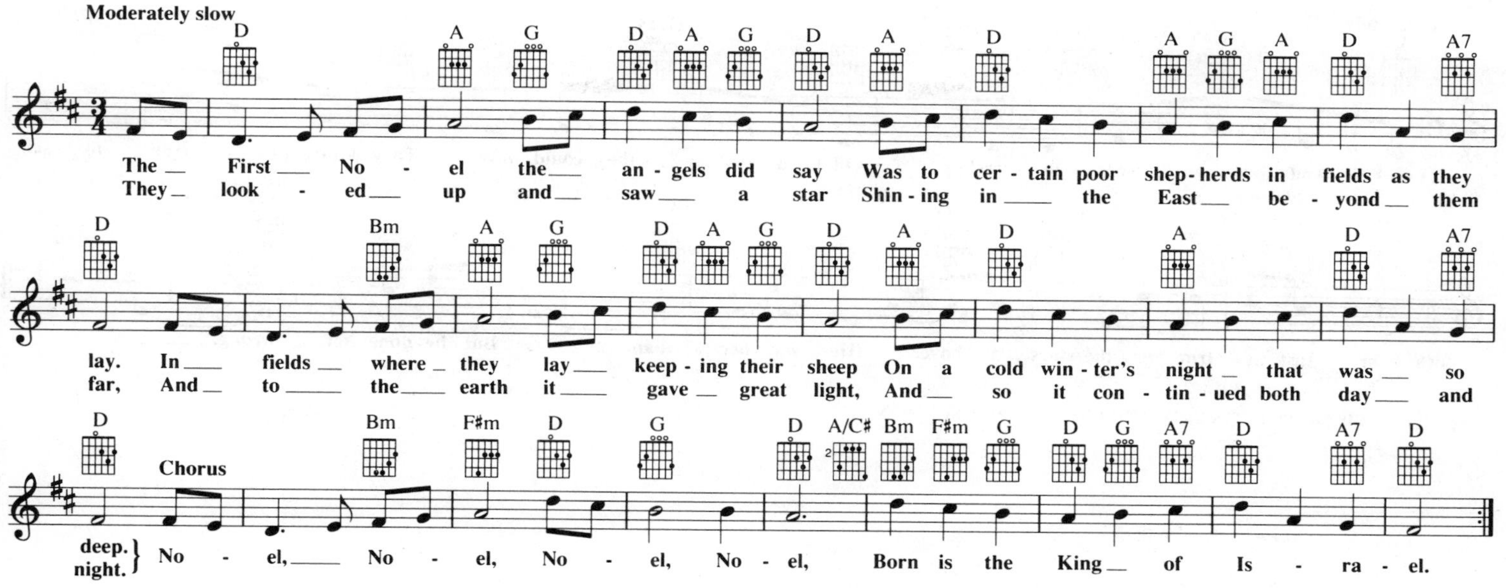
Moderately slow
D A G D A G D A D A G A D A7
The First No - el the an - gels did say Was to cer - tain poor shep - herds in fields as they
They look - ed up and saw a star Shin - ing in the East be - yond them
D Bm A G D A G D A D A D A7
lay. In fields where they lay keep - ing their sheep On a cold win - ter's night that was so
far, And to the earth it gave great light, And so it con - tin - ued both day and
D Bm F#m D G D A/C# Bm F#m G D G A7 D A7 D
Chorus
deep. night. No - el, No - el, No - el, No - el, Born is the King of Is - ra - el.

FROGGIE WENT A-COURTIN'

E
1. Frog - gie Went A - court - in' and he did ride, A huh, a huh Frog - gie Went A - court - in' and
2 - 15. (See additional lyrics)
A B7 E
he did ride, A sword and pis - tol by his side, A huh, a huh.

Additional Lyrics

2. Well, he rode down to Miss Mouses's door, a-huh, a-huh,
Well, he rode down to Miss Mouses's door,
Where he had ofter been before, a-huh, a-huh.

3. He took Miss Mousie on his knee, a-huh, a-huh,
He took Miss Mousie on his knee,
Said, "Miss Mousie will you marry me?" A-huh, a-huh.

4. "I'll have to ask my Uncle Rat, etc.
See what he will say to that.", etc.

5. "Without my Uncle Rat's consent,
I would not marry the President."

6. Well, Uncle Rat laughed and shook his fat sides,
To think his niece would be a bride.

7. Well, Uncle Rat rode off to town
To buy his niece a wedding gown.

8. "Where will the wedding supper be?"
"Way down yonder in a hollow tree."

9. "What will the wedding supper be?"
"A fried mosquito and a roasted flea."

10. First to come in were two little ants,
Fixing around to have a dance.

11. Next to come in was a bumble bee,
Bouncing a fiddle on his knee.

12. Next to come in was a fat sassy lad,
Thinks himself as big as his dad.

13. Thinks himself a man indeed,
Because he chews the tobacco weed.

14. And next to come in was a big tomcat,
He swallowed the frog and the mouse and the rat.

15. Next to come in was a big old snake,
He chased the party into the lake.

FRANKIE AND JOHNNY

Moderately
C
G7♯5
C
G7♯5
C
G7♯5
C
C7
F
1. Frank - ie And John - nie were lov - ers! Oh, Lord - y how — they could love! They swore to be true — to each
2-13. (See additional lyrics)
F♯dim7
C/G
G7
C
oth - er, Just as true as the stars a - bove, — He was her man, ——— But he done her wrong. ———

Additional Lyrics

2. Frankie she was a good woman
As everybody know,
Spent a hundred dollars
Just to buy her man some clothes.
He was her man, but he was doing her wrong.

3. Frankie went down to the corner
Just for a bucket of beer,
Said: "Mr. bartender
Has my loving Johnny been here?
"He was my man, but he's a-doing me wrong."

4. "Now I don't want ot tell you no stories
And I don't want to tell you no lies
I was your man about an hour ago
With a gal named Nellie Bligh
He was your man, but he's a-doing you wrong."

5. Frankie she went down to the hotel
Didn't go there for fun,
Underneath her kimona
She carried a forty-four gun.
He was her man, but he was doing her wrong.

6. Frankie looked over the transom
To see what she could spy,
There sat Johnny on the sofa
Just loving up Nellie Bligh.
He was her man, but he was doing her wrong.

7. Frankie got down from that high stool
She didn't want to see no more;
Rooty-toot-toot three times she shot
Right through that hardwood door.
He was her man, but he was doing her wrong.

8. Now the first time that Frankie shot Johnny
He let out an awful yell,
Second time she shot him
There was a new man's face in hell.
He was her man, but he was doing her wrong.

9. "Oh roll me over easy
Roll me over slow
Roll me over on the right side
For the left side hurts me so."
He was her man, but he was doing her wrong.

10. Sixteen rubber-tired carriages
Sixteen rubber-tired hacks
They take poor Johnny to the graveyard
They ain't gonna bring him back.
He was her man, but he was doing her wrong.

11. Frankie looked out of the jailhouse
To see what she could see,
All she could hear was a two-string bow
Crying nearer my God to thee.
He was her man, but he was doing her wrong.

12. Frankie she said to the sheriff
"What do you reckon they'll do?"
Sheriff he said "Frankie,
"It's the electric chair for you."
He was her man, but he was doing her wrong.

13. This story has no moral
This story has no end
This story only goes to show
That there ain't no good in men!
He was her man, but he was doing her wrong.

FRÈRE JACQUES

D
Frè - re Jac - ques, Frè - re Jac - ques, Dor - mez vous, dor - mez vous?
Are you sleep - ing, are you sleep - ing, Broth - er John, broth - er John?
Son - nez les ma - ti - nes, son - nez les ma - ti - nes
Morn - ing bells are ring - ing, morn - ing bells are ring - ing
Ding, ding, dong, ding, ding, dong.

FUNICULI, FUNICULA

Happily
C G7 C G7 C
G7 C G7 C
Em B7 Em B7 Em B7 Em B7 Em
G D7 G D7 G D7 G D7 G
G7 C
E7/B Am E7/G# Am F C G7 C

FUNERAL MARCH

Frédéric Chopin

FUNERAL MARCH OF A MARIONETTE

Charles Gounod

THE FRIENDLY BEASTS

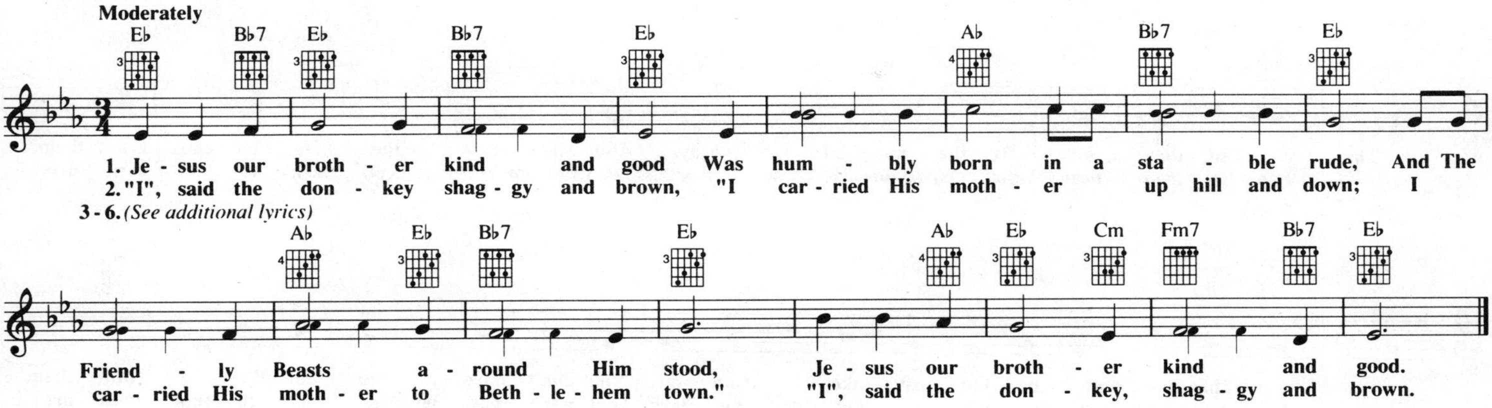
Moderately
Eb Bb7 Eb Bb7 Eb Ab Bb7 Eb
1. Je - sus our broth - er kind and good Was hum - bly born in a sta - ble rude, And The
2. "I", said the don - key shag - gy and brown, "I car - ried His moth - er up hill and down; I
3 - 6. (See additional lyrics)
Ab Eb Bb7 Eb Ab Eb Cm Fm7 Bb7 Eb
Friend - ly Beasts a - round Him stood, Je - sus our broth - er kind and good.
car - ried His moth - er to Beth - le - hem town." "I", said the don - key, shag - gy and brown.

Additional Lyrics

3. "I," said the cow all white and red,
"I gave Him my manger for His bed;
I gave Him my hay to pillow His head."
"I," said the cow all white and red.

4. "I," said the sheep with the curly horn,
"I gave Him my wool for His blanket warm;
He wore my coat on Christmas morn."
"I," said the sheep with curly horn.

5. "I," said the dove from the rafters high,
"I cooed Him to sleep that He would not cry;
We cooed Him to sleep, my mate and I."
"I," said the dove from the rafters high.

6. Thus every beast by some good spell,
In the stable dark was glad to tell
Of the gift he gave Emanuel,
The gift he gave Emanuel.

FÜR ELISE

Ludwig Van Beethoven

Brightly
N.C. Am E Am N.C.
Am E 1 Am N.C. 2 Am C G/B
Am E N.C. Am E
Am N.C. Am E 1 Am 2 Am

FORTY-FIVE MINUTES FROM BROADWAY

George M. Cohan

Brightly
The West, so they say, is the home of the jay, And Mis - sou - ri's the state that can grind them.
bun - co men hear that their game is so near, They'll be swarm - ing here thick - er than bees are;
This may all be, but just take it from me, You don't have to go out West to find them.
In Bar - num's best days, why he nev - er saw jays, That were eas - ier to get to than these are.
If you want to see the real jay del - e - ga - tion, The place where the real ru - bens dwell,
You tell them old jokes and they laugh till they sick - en; There's gig - gles and grins here to let.
Just hop on a train at the Grand Cen - tral Sta - tion, Get off when they shout, "New Ro - chelle!
I told them that one a - bout "Why does a chick - en," The ru - bens are all laugh - ing yet.
On - ly For - ty - five Min - utes From Broad - way, think of the chang - es it brings; For the
On - ly For - ty - five Min - utes From Broad - way, not a ca - fé in the town; Oh! the
short time it takes, what a dif - f'rence it makes In the ways of the peo - ple and things.
place is a bird, no one here ev - er heard of Del - mon - i - co, Rec - tor, or Browne. With a
Oh! what a fine bunch of ru - bens, Oh! what a jay at - mos - phere; They have whis - kers like
ten dol - lar bill you're a spend - thrift, if you o - pen a bot - tle of beer You're a sport, so they
hay, and im - ag - ine Broad - way on - ly for - ty - five min - utes from here. When the
say, and im - ag - ine Broad - way on - ly for - ty - five min - utes from here.

FASCINATION

F. D. Marchetti

FINLANDIA

J. Sibelius

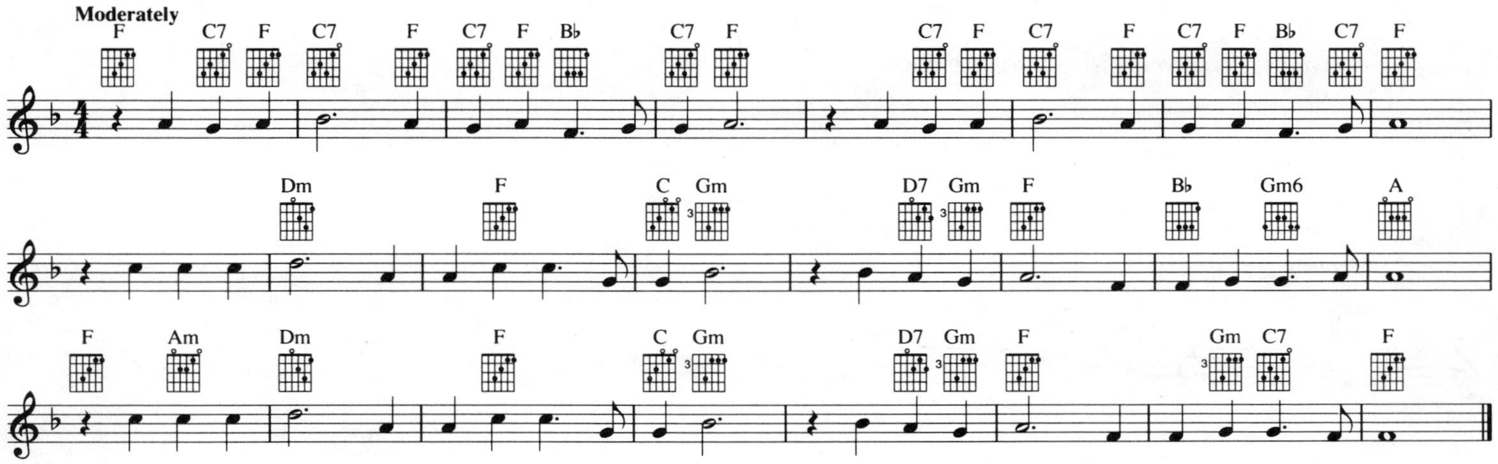

GOODBYE, MY LADY LOVE

Joseph E. Howard

GIVE MY REGARDS TO BROADWAY

George M. Cohan

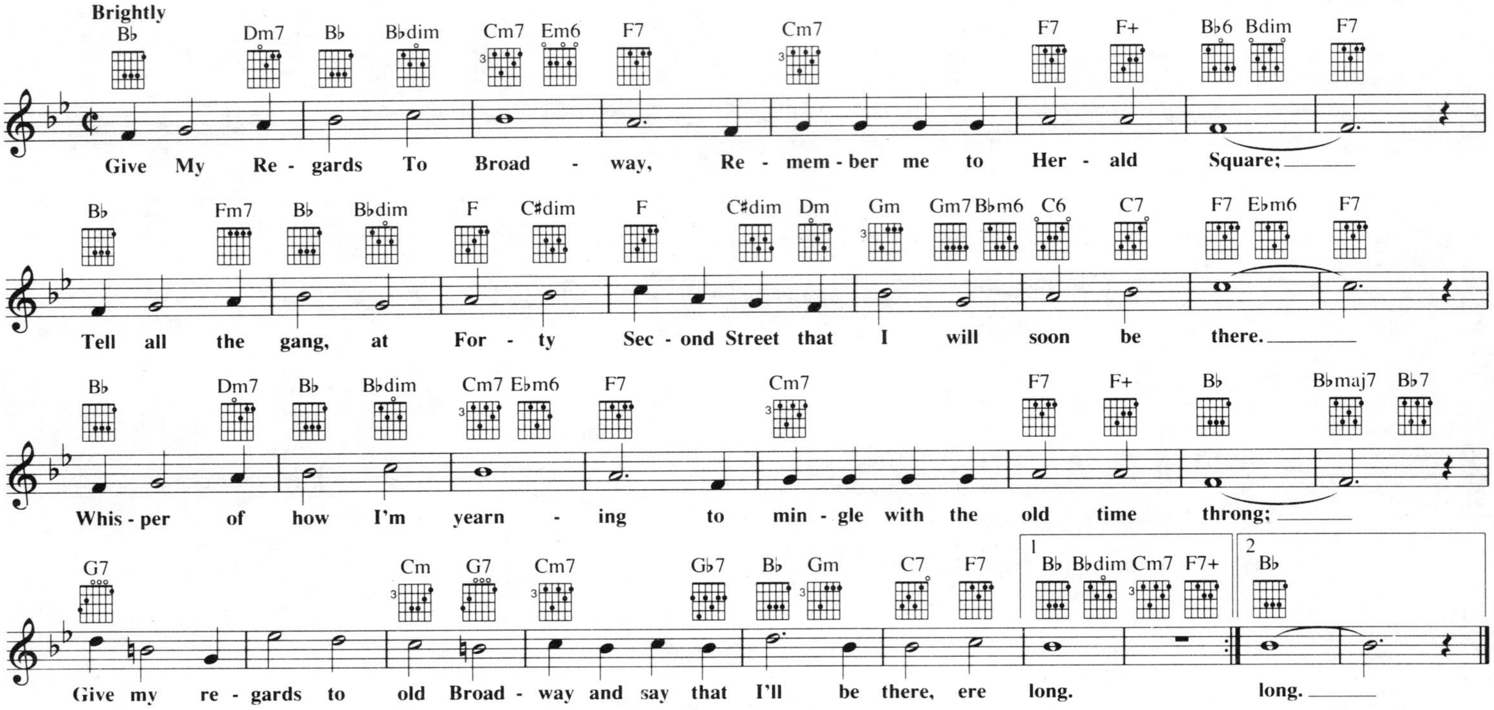

GLOW WORM

Paul Lincke

GAVOTTE

Francois J. Gossec

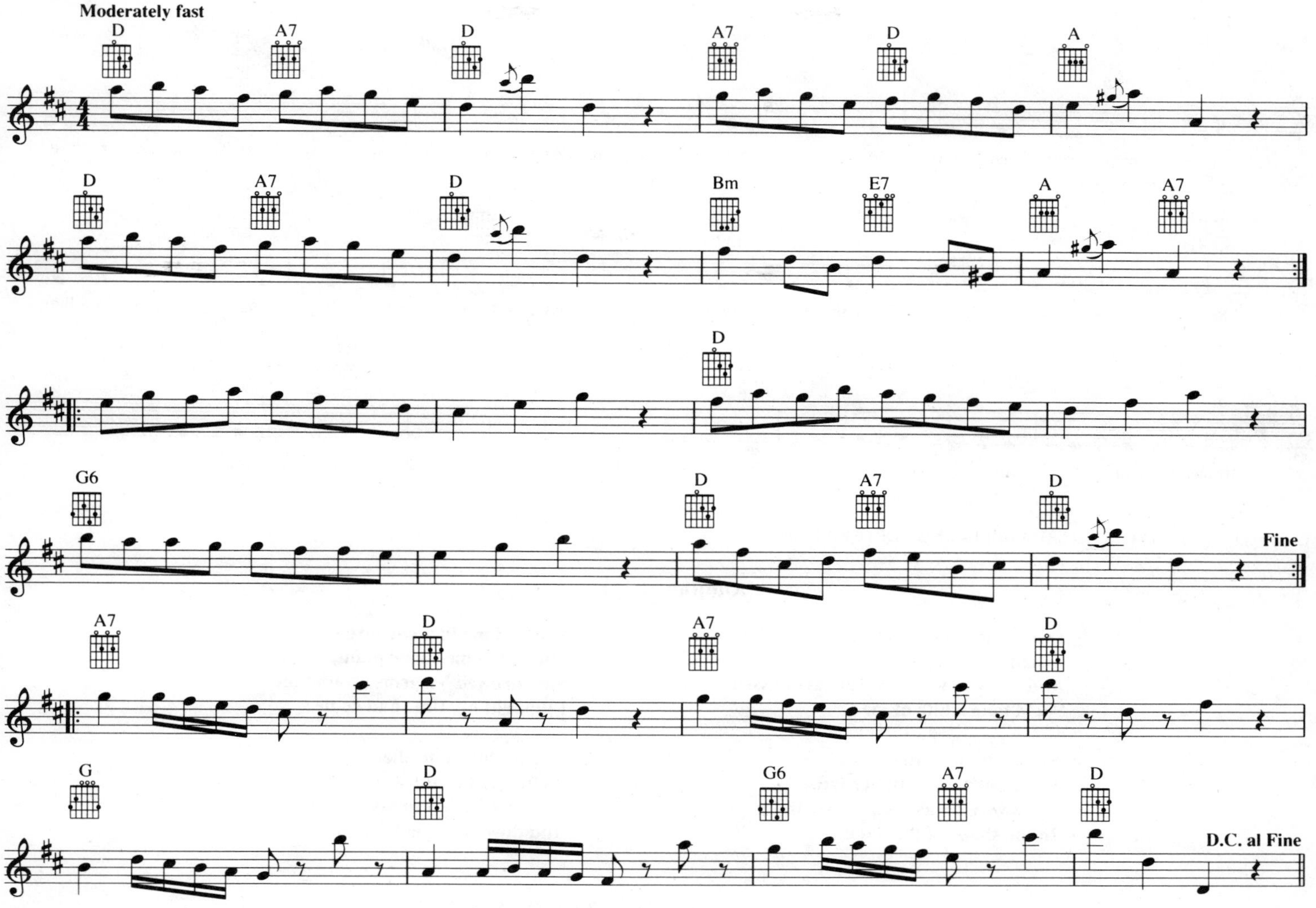
Moderately fast
D A7 D A7 D A
D A7 D Bm E7 A A7
D
G6 D A7 D
Fine
A7 D A7 D
G D G6 A7 D
D.C. al Fine

GOD OF OUR FATHERS

Daniel C. Roberts
George Warren

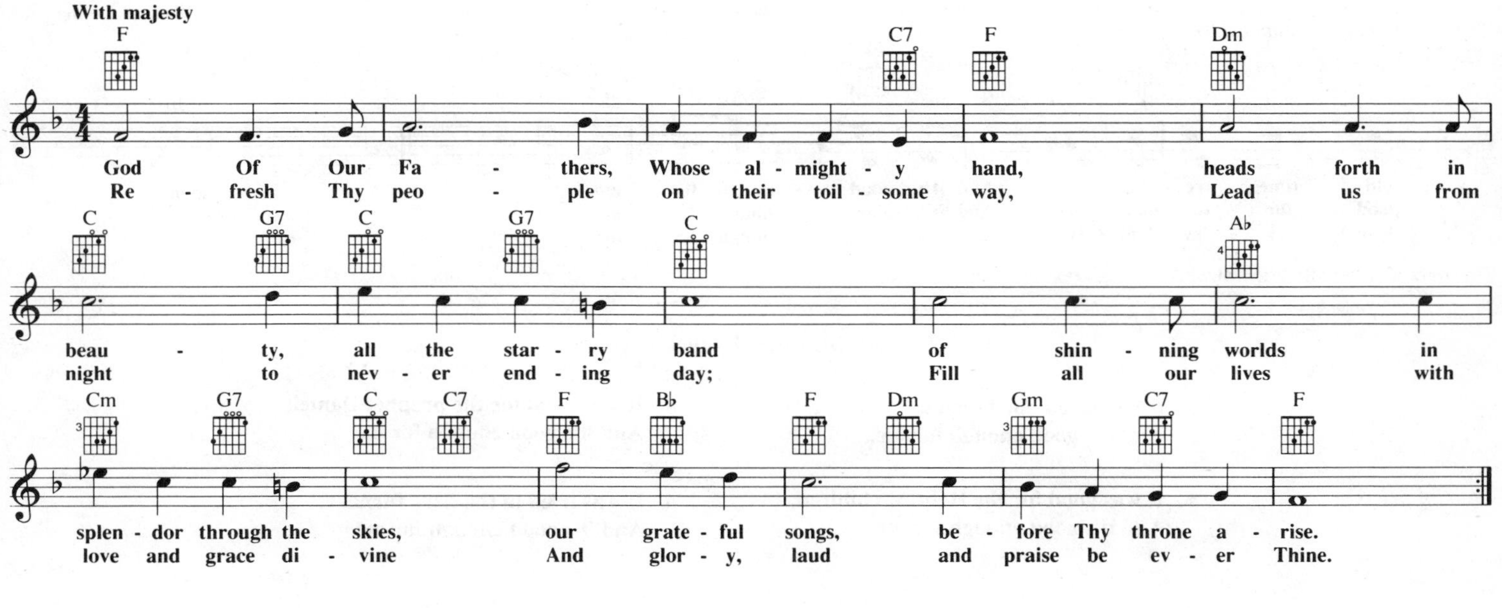
With majesty
F C7 F Dm
God Of Our Fa - thers, Whose al - might - y hand, heads forth in
Re - fresh Thy peo - ple on their toil - some way, Lead us from
C G7 C G7 C A♭
beau - ty, all the star - ry band of shin - ning worlds in
night to nev - er end - ing day; Fill all our lives with
Cm G7 C C7 F B♭ F Dm Gm C7 F
splen - dor through the skies, our grate - ful songs, be - fore Thy throne a - rise.
love and grace di - vine And glor - y, laud and praise be ev - er Thine.

GIT ALONG HOME, CINDY

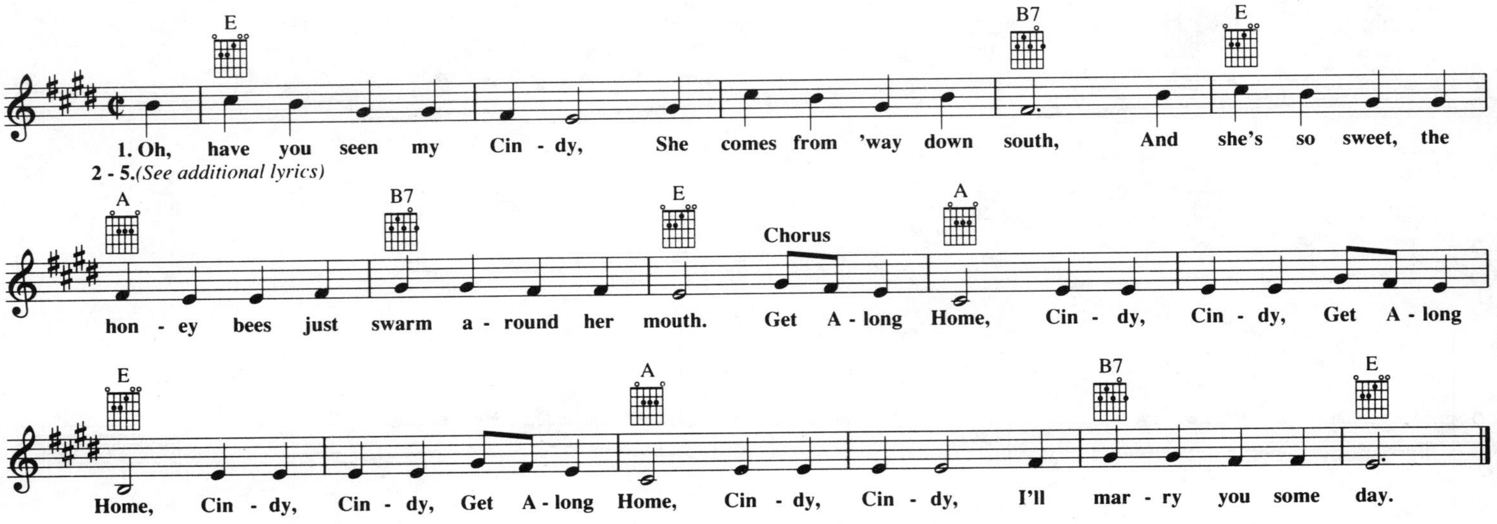
E
B7
E
1. Oh, have you seen my Cin - dy, She comes from 'way down south, And she's so sweet, the
2 - 5.(See additional lyrics)
A
B7
E
Chorus
A
hon - ey bees just swarm a - round her mouth. Get A - long Home, Cin - dy, Cin - dy, Get A - long
E
A
B7
E
Home, Cin - dy, Cin - dy, Get A - long Home, Cin - dy, Cin - dy, I'll mar - ry you some day.

Additional Lyrics

2. I wish I was an apple,
A-hangin' in a tree,
And ev'ry time my sweetheart passed,
She'd take a bite of me.

3. She told me that she loved me,
She called me sugar plum,
She throwed 'er arms around me,
I thought my time had come.

4. She took me to the parlor,
She cooled me with her fan.
She swore I was the purtiest thing
In the shape of mortal man.

5. I wish I had a needle,
As fine as I could sew;
I'd sew the girls to my coat tail,
And down the road I'd go.

GIVE ME THAT OLD TIME RELIGION

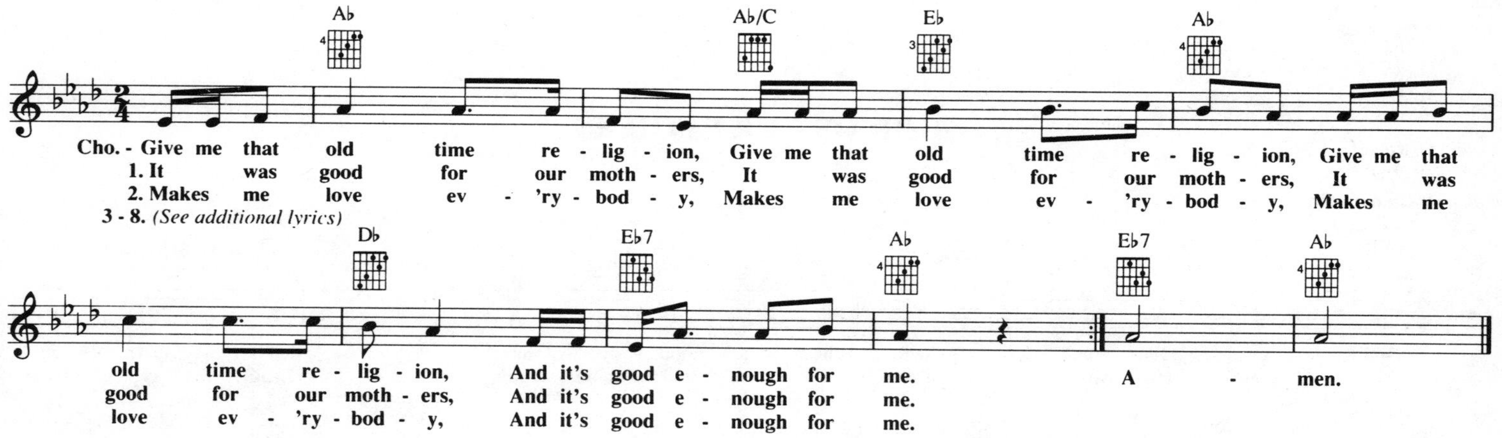
A♭
A♭/C
E♭
A♭
Cho. - Give me that old time re - lig - ion, Give me that old time re - lig - ion, Give me that
1. It was good for our moth - ers, It was good for our moth - ers, It was
2. Makes me love ev - 'ry - bod - y, Makes me love ev - 'ry - bod - y, Makes me
3 - 8. (See additional lyrics)
D♭
E♭7
A♭
E♭7
A♭
old time re - lig - ion, And it's good e - nough for me. A - men.
good for our moth - ers, And it's good e - nough for me.
love ev - 'ry - bod - y, And it's good e - nough for me.

Additional Lyrics

3. It has saved our fathers,
And it's good enough for me.

4. It was good for the prophet Daniel,
And it's good enough for me.

5. It was good for the Hebrew children,
And it's good enough for me.

6. It was tried in the fiery furnace,
And it's good enough for me.

7. It was good for Paul and Silas,
And it's good enough for me.

8. It will do when I am dying,
And it's good enough for me.

GIT ALONG, LITTLE DOGIES

Moderately
C F G7 C F G7 C
1. As I was a - walk - in' one morn - ing for pleas - ure, I spied a cow - punch - er a - stroll - in' a - long. His
2 - 7. (See additional lyrics)
F G7 C F G7 C
hat was throwed back and his spurs were a - jin - glin', And as he ap - proached he was sing - ing this song.
Chorus
Whoop - ee
C7 F C7 F
ti - yi - yo, Git A - long Lit - tle Do - gies, It's your mis - for - tune, and none of my own, Whoop-ee
C G7 C F G7 C
ti - yi - yo, Git A - long Lit - tle Do - gies, you know that Wy - o - ming will be your new home.

Additional Lyrics

2. Early in the springtime we'll round up the dogies,
Slap on their brands and bob off their tails;
Round up our horses, load up the chuck wagon,
Then throw those dogies upon the trail.

3. It's whooping and yelling and driving the dogies,
Oh, how I wish you would go on,
It's whooping and punching and go on, little dogies,
For you know Wyoming will be your new home.

4. Some of the boys goes up the trail for pleasure,
But that's where they git it most awfully wrong;
For you haven't any idea the trouble they give us,
When we go driving them dogies along.

5. When the night comes on and we hold them on the bed-ground,
These little dogies that roll on so slow;
Roll up the herd and cut out the strays,
And roll the little dogies that never rolled before.

6. Your mother she was raised way down in Texas,
Where the jimson weed and sandburs grow;
Now we'll fill you up on prickly pear and cholla,
Till you are ready for the trail to Idaho.

7. Oh, you'll be soup for Uncle Sam's Injuns,
"It's beef, heap beef," I hear them cry.
Git along, git along, git along, little dogies,
You're going to be beef steers by and by.

GO TELL AUNT RHODY

Slowly
G D7 G C D7 G
1. Go Tell Aunt Rho - dy, Go Tell Aunt Rho - dy, Go Tell Aunt Rho - dy the old grey goose is dead.
2-5. (See additional lyrics)

Additional Lyrics

2. The one she was saving, *(three times)*
To make a feather bed.

3. The gander is weeping, *(three times)*
Because his wife is dead.

4. The goslings are crying, *(three times)*
Because their mama's dead.

5. She died in the water, *(three times)*
With her heels above her head.

GLADIATOR MARCH

John Philip Sousa

Brightly
Gm A7 Dm Eb E A
Dm Gm A7 Dm Bb7
A
1 N.C.
2 N.C.
C7 F
C7 F Ddim F C7
F C7 F7
1
2
Bb F7 Bbdim Bb
Eb Ebm Bb F7 Bb

GO, TELL IT ON THE MOUNTAIN

Moderately
G D7 G
While shep - herds kept their watch - ing O'er si - lent flocks by night, Be - hold through - out the
shep - herds feared and trem - bled When lo! a - bove the earth rang out the an - gel
A7 D7 G C G D7
heav - ens There shone a ho - ly light.
cho - rus that hailed our Sav - ior's birth.
Go, Tell It On The Moun - tain O - ver the hills and
G C G Am G/D D7
1 G
2 G
ev - 'ry - where, Go, Tell It On The Moun - tain that Je - sus Christ is born. The born.

GO IN AND OUT THE WINDOW

Brightly
F C7 F
Go In And Out The Win - dow, Go In And Out The Win - dow, Go
forth and choose your part - ner, Go forth and choose your part - ner, Go
C7 1 F 2 F
In And Out The Win - dow, As we have done be - fore. Go
forth and choose your part - ner, As we have done be - fore.

THE GIRL I LEFT BEHIND

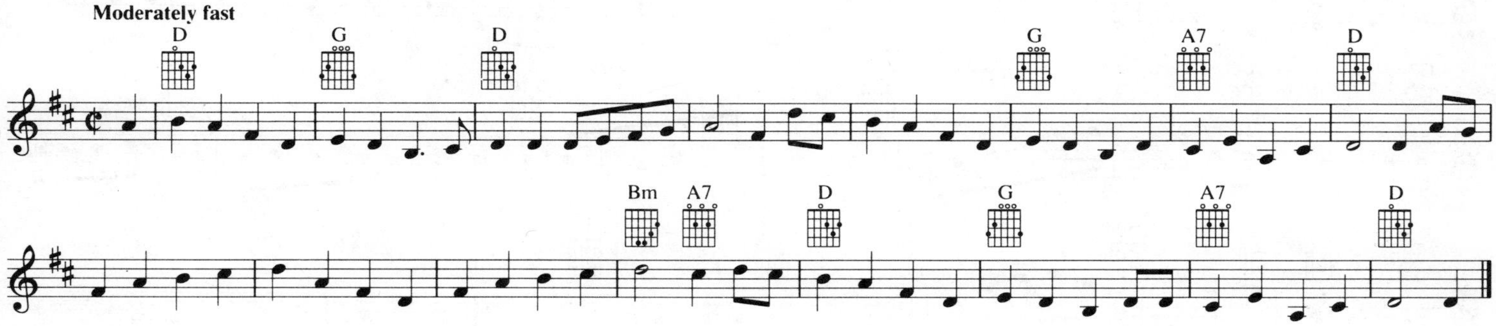
Moderately fast
D G D G A7 D
Bm A7 D G A7 D

GOD REST YE MERRY, GENTLEMEN

Brightly
Em B7 Em C G C B7 Em B7 Em B7
God Rest Ye Mer - ry Gen - tle - men, let noth - ing you dis - may. Re - mem - ber Christ our
In Beth - le - hem, in Jew - ry. This bless - ed Babe was born. And laid with - in a
From God our Heav'n - ly Fa ther, a bless - ed An - gel came; And un - to cer - tain
Em C G C B7 Em B7 Am G Am G B7
Sa - vi - our was born on Christ - mas Day. To save us all from Sa - tan's pow'r. When
man - ger, up on this bless - ed morn; That which His Moth - er Ma - ry, did
Shep - herds, brought ti - dings of the same; How that in Beth - le - hem was born the
Em A7 D7 G C G Am B7 Em A7
we were gone a - stray;
noth - ing take in scorn. } O ti - dings of com - fort and joy, com - fort and
Son of God by Name.
D G Em Am B7 Em
joy. O ti - dings of com - fort and joy.

GOLD AND SILVER WALTZ

Franz Lehar

C Cdim7 C E7 F Dm7 C
G7 C G7 Dm G7 C
G D7
G
B7 C E7 Am
E7 Am Gdim7 G D7 G

GOOD CHRISTIAN MEN, REJOICE

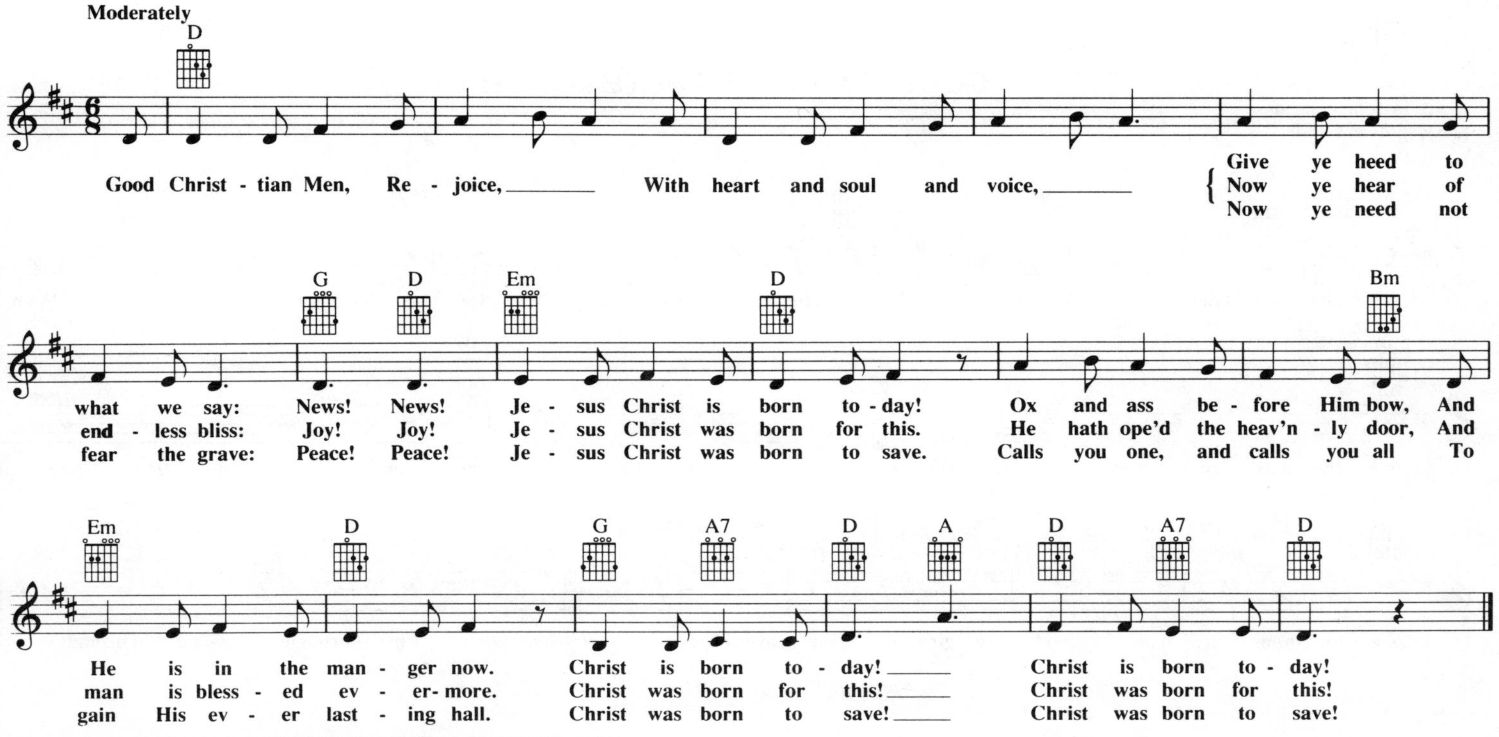
Moderately
D
Good Christ - tian Men, Re - joice, With heart and soul and voice,
Give ye heed to what we say: News! News! Je - sus Christ is born to - day!
Now ye hear of end - less bliss: Joy! Joy! Je - sus Christ was born for this.
Now ye need not fear the grave: Peace! Peace! Je - sus Christ was born to save.
G D Em D Bm
Ox and ass be - fore Him bow, And He is in the man - ger now. Christ is born to - day! Christ is born to - day!
He hath ope'd the heav'n - ly door, And man is bless - ed ev - er - more. Christ was born for this! Christ was born for this!
Calls you one, and calls you all To gain His ev - er last - ing hall. Christ was born to save! Christ was born to save!
Em D G A7 D A D A7 D

GOD SAVE OUR KING (QUEEN)

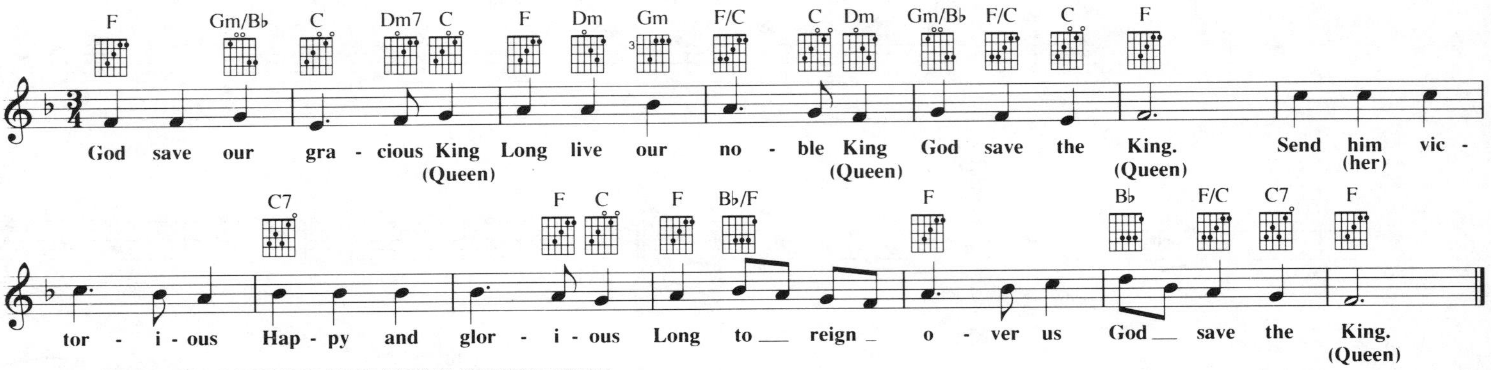
F Gm/B♭ C Dm7 C F Dm Gm F/C C Dm Gm/B♭ F/C C F
God save our gra - cious King (Queen) Long live our no - ble King (Queen) God save the King. (Queen) Send him (her) vic -
C7 F C F B♭/F F B♭ F/C C7 F
tor - i - ous Hap - py and glor - i - ous Long to reign o - ver us God save the King. (Queen)

GOOD NIGHT LADIES

Brightly
B♭ F7
Good Night, La - dies, Good Night, La - dies!
B♭ B♭7 E♭ B♭ F7 B♭
Good Night La - dies, We're going to leave you now.
F B♭ F F7 B♭
Mer - ri - ly we roll a - long, roll a - long, roll a - long, Mer - ri - ly we roll a - long, O'er the deep blue sea.

GOODBYE GIRLS, I'M THROUGH

Words by John Golden
Music by Ivan Caryll

Moderato
B♭ Gm B♭ F Cm
Good - bye Girls, I'm Through. Each girl that I have met I say good - bye to you With -
B♭ Gm B♭ E♭
out the least re - gret I've done with all flir - ta - tion You've no more fas - ci - na - tion There's but
Edim7 B♭ G7 C7 F 1 B♭ 2 B♭
one to whom I'm true good - bye girls, (good - bye boy) Good - bye Girls I'm Through Good- Through.

GOOBER PEAS

Moderately
G C G C D
1. Sit - ting by the road - side on a sum-mer day, Chat - ting with my mess - mates, pass - ing time a - way,
2-4. (See additional lyrics)
G C G C G D7 G
Ly - ing in the shad - ow un - der-neath the trees, Good-ness, how de - li - cious, eat - ing Goo - ber Peas!
C D7 G C G D7 G
Peas! peas! peas! peas! eat - ing Goo - ber Peas! Good-ness how de - li - cious, eat - ing Goo - ber Peas!

Additional Lyrics

2. When a horseman passes, the soldiers have a rule,
To cry out at their loudest, "Mister, here's your mule!"
But another pleasure enchantinger than these,
Is wearing out your grinders, eating Goober Peas!

3. Just before the battle the Gen'ral hears a row,
He says, "The Yanks are coming, I hear their rifles now."
He turns around in wonder, and what do you think he sees?
The Georgia Militia - eating Goober Peas!

4. I think my song has lasted almost long enough,
The subject's interesting, but rhymes are mighty rough,
I wish this war was over, when free from rags and fleas,
We'd kiss our wives and sweethearts and gobble Goober Peas!

THE GREEN GRASS GREW ALL AROUND

Lively
G C G D G
Once there was a tree, was the pret - ti - est lit - tle tree, and the tree grew in the ground.
C G D G
And on that tree there grew a limb,
And on that limb there grew a branch,
And on that branch there grew a leaf,
and The Green Grass Grew All A - round. And the
D G
tree in the ground,
and the limb on the tree,
and the branch on the limb,
and the leaf on the branch,
and The Green Grass Grew All A - round.
D G C G D 1 G 2 G
Oh, The Green Grass Grew All A - round, all a - round, and The Green Grass Grew All A - round. round.

GOOD KING WENCESLAS

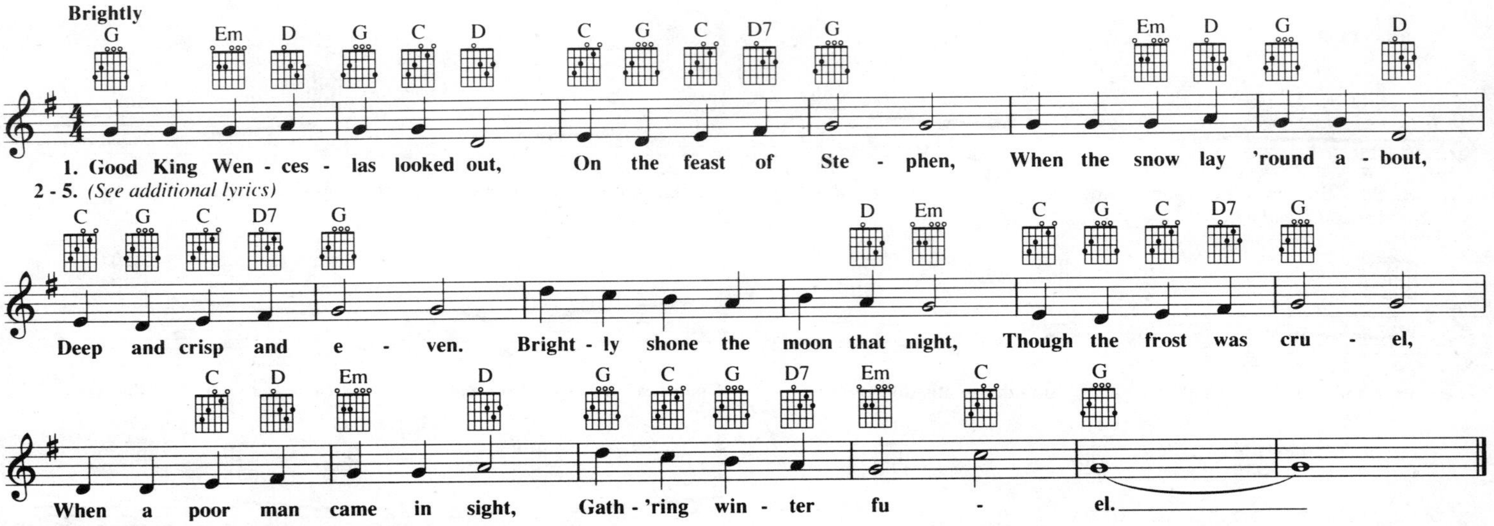
Brightly
G Em D G C D C G C D7 G Em D G D
1. Good King Wen - ces - las looked out, On the feast of Ste - phen, When the snow lay 'round a - bout,
2 - 5. (See additional lyrics)
C G C D7 G D Em C G C D7 G
Deep and crisp and e - ven. Bright - ly shone the moon that night, Though the frost was cru - el,
C D Em D G C G D7 Em C G
When a poor man came in sight, Gath - 'ring win - ter fu - el.

Additional Lyrics

2. "Hither page, and stand by me,
If thou know'st it, telling,
Yonder peasant, who is he?
Where and what his dwelling?"
"Sire, he lives a good league hence,
Underneath the mountain;
Right against the forest fence,
By Saint Agnes' fountain."

3. "Bring me flesh, and bring me wine,
Bring me pine-logs hither;
Thou and I will see him dine,
When we bear them thither."
Page and monarch forth they went,
Forth they went together;
Through the rude winds wild lament:
And the bitter weather.

4. "Sire, the night is darker now,
And the wind blows stronger;
Fails my heart, I know not how,
I can go not longer."
"Mark my footsteps, my good page,
Tread thou in them boldly:
Thou shalt find the winter's rage
Freeze thy blood less coldly."

5. In his master's steps he trod,
Where the snow lay dinted;
Heat was in the very sod
Which the saint had printed.
Therefore, Christain men, be sure
Wealth or rank possessing,
Ye who now will bless the poor,
Shall yourselves find blessing.

GOODBYE, OLD PAINT

Gently and flowing
B♭ F B♭ E♭
Good - bye, Old Paint, I'm a - leav - in' Chey - enne.
1. I'm a - leav - in' Chey -
2. My foot in the
3. Old Paint's a good
B♭ E♭6 F E♭6 B♭ F B♭
enne, I'm off to Mon - tan', Good - Bye, Old Paint, I'm a leav - in' Chey - enne.
stir-rup, my po - ny won't stand, Good - Bye, Old Paint, I'm a leav - in' Chey - enne.
po-ny, he pac - es when he can, Good - bye lit-tle An-nie, I'm off to Mon - tan'.

GRANDFATHER'S CLOCK

Henry C. Work

Moderately slow
G D7 G C G/D D7 G D
1. My grand - fath - er's clock was too large for the shelf so it stood nine - ty years on the floor. It was
tall - er by half than the old man him - self tho' it weighed not a pen-ny-weight
2- 4. (See additional lyrics)
G Em A7 D7 G Em
more. It was bought on the morn of the day that he was born and was al - ways his trea - sure and
A7 D7 G D7 G C G D7
pride; But it stopped short nev - er to go a - gain when the old man
G
died. Nine - ty years with - out slum-ber - ing, tick, tock, tick, tock, his life sec-onds num-ber - ing, tick, tock, tick, tock. It
D7 G C G/D D7 G
stopped short nev - er to go a - gain when the old man died.

Additional Lyrics

2. In watching its pendulum swing to and fro,
   Many hours had he spent while a boy;
   And in childhood and manhood the clock
   seemed to know,
   And to share both his grief and his joy.
   For it struck twenty-four when he entered
   at the door,
   With a blooming and beautiful bride.

3. My grandfather said that of those he could hire,
   Not a servant so faithful he found;
   For it wasted no time, and had but one desire,
   At the close of each week to be wound.
   And it kept in its place, not a frown upon its face,
   And its hands never hung by its side.

4. It rang an alarm in the dead of the night,
   An alarm that for years had been dumb;
   And we knew that his spirit was pluming
   its flight,
   That his hour of departure had come.
   Still the clock kept the time, with a soft and
   muffled chime,
   As we silently stood by his side.

GREY AND GOLD WALTZ

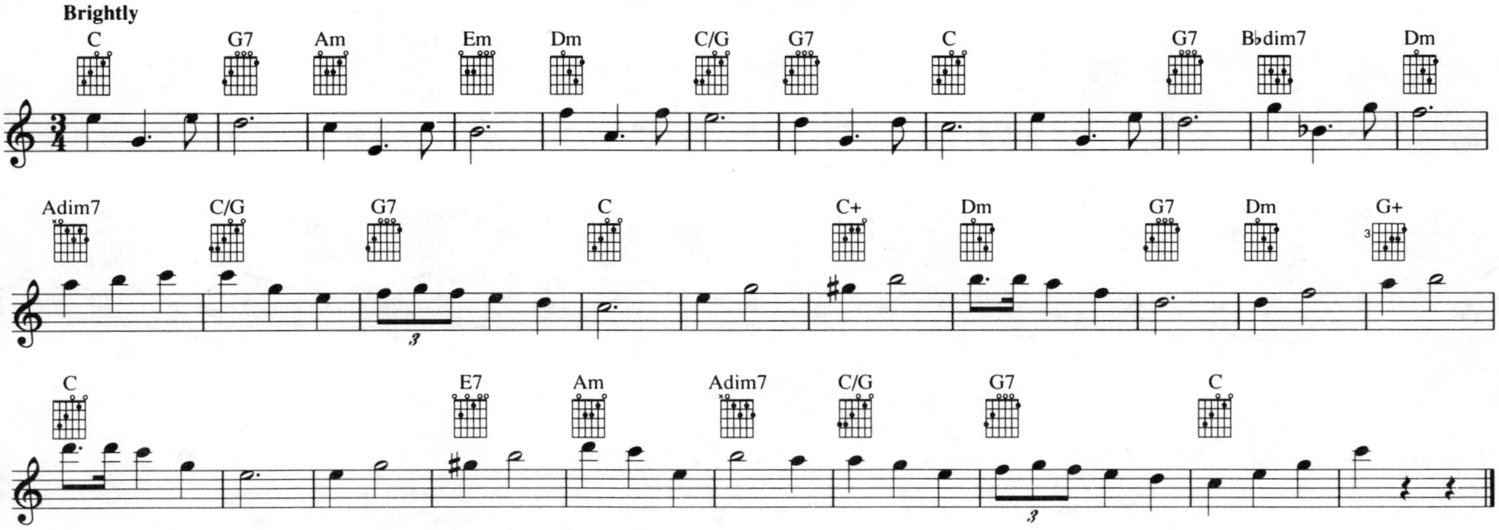
Brightly
C G7 Am Em Dm C/G G7 C G7 B♭dim7 Dm
Adim7 C/G G7 C C+ Dm G7 Dm G+
C E7 Am Adim7 C/G G7 C

GREEN GROW THE LILACS

Tenderly

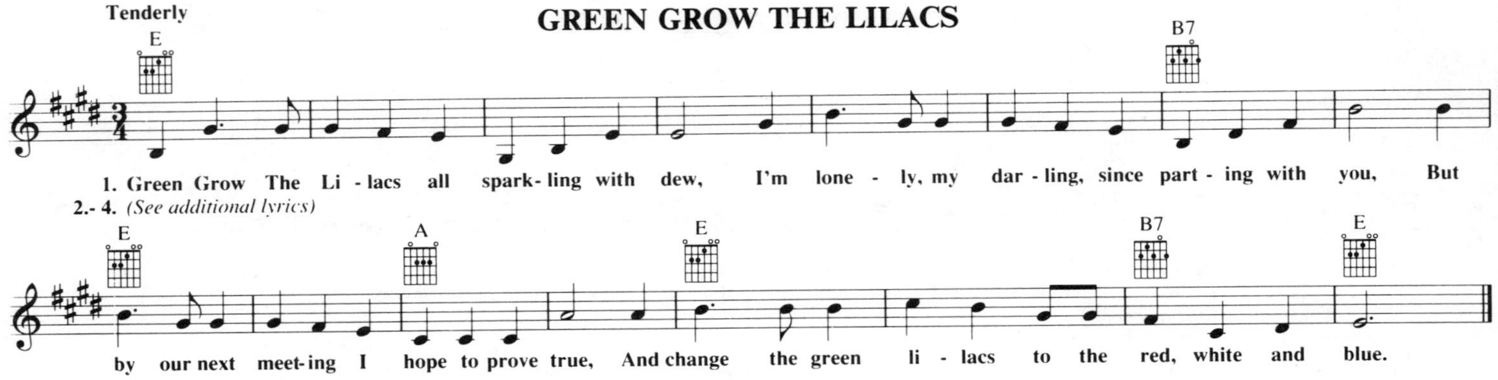

Additional Lyrics

2. I used to have a sweetheart, but now I have none,
Since she's gone and left me, I care not for one.
Since she's gone and left me, contented I'll be,
For she loves another one better than me.

3. I passed my love's window, both early and late,
The look that she gave me, it made my heart ache.
Oh, the look that she gave me was painful to see,
For she loves another one better than me.

4. I wrote my love letters in rosy red lines,
She sent me an answer all twisted in twines,
Saying, "Keep your love letters and don't waste your time,
Just you write to your love and I'll write to mine."

GRIEG PIANO CONCERTO
(Theme)

Edvard Grieg

Moderately

GREENSLEEVES

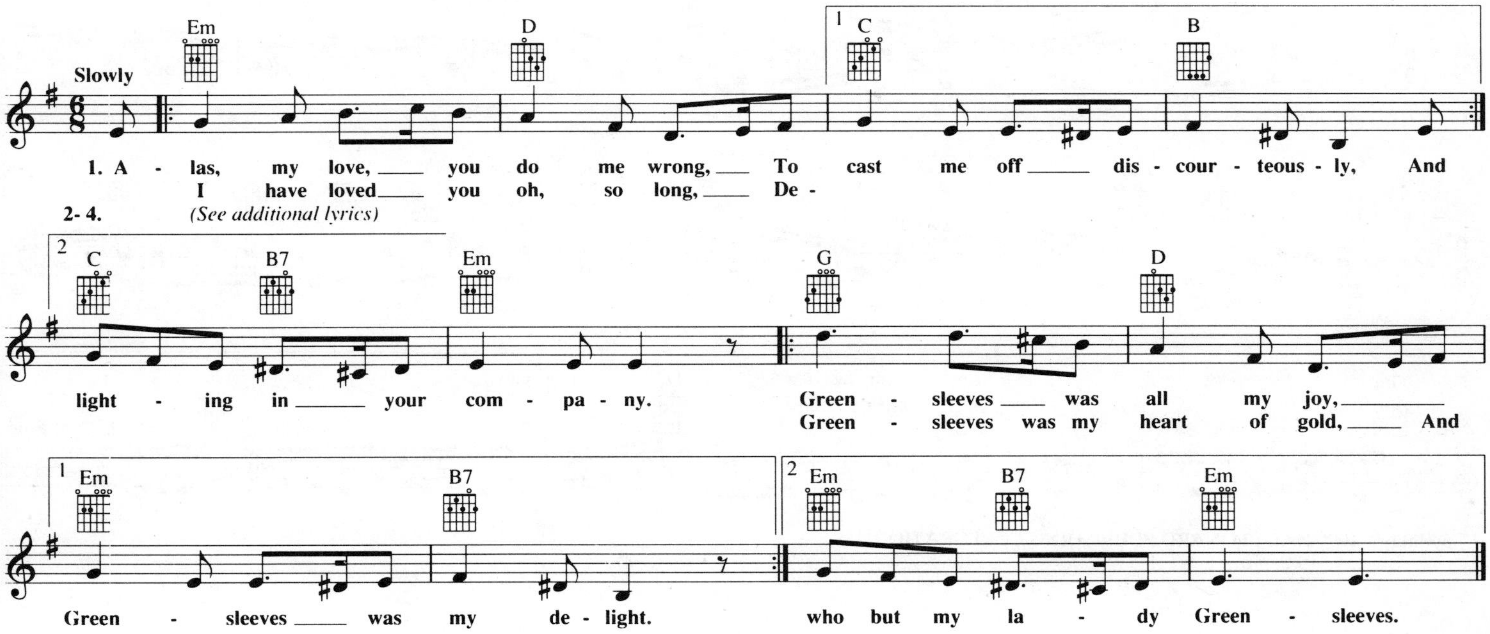
Slowly
Em
D
C
B
B7
G
1. A - las, my love, you do me wrong, To cast me off dis - cour - teous - ly, And
I have loved you oh, so long, De -
2- 4. (See additional lyrics)
light - ing in your com - pa - ny.
Green - sleeves was all my joy,
Green - sleeves was my heart of gold, And
Green - sleeves was my de - light.
who but my la - dy Green - sleeves.

Additional Lyrics

2. I have been ready at your hand,
To grant whatever you would crave;
I have both wagered life and land,
Your love and good-will for to have.
If you intend thus to disdain,
It does the more enrapture me,
And even so, I still remain
A lover in captivity.

3. My men were clothed all in green,
And they did ever wait on thee;
All this was gallant to be seen;
And yet thou wouldst not love me.
Thou couldst desire no earthly thing
But still thou hadst it readily.
Thy music still to play and sing;
And yet thou wouldst not love me.

4. Well, I will pray to God on high,
That thou my constancy mayst see,
And that yet once before I die,
Thou wilt vouchsafe to love me.
Ah, Greensleeves, now farewell, adieu,
To God I pray to prosper thee,
For I am still thy lover true,
Come once again and love me.

GYPSY LOVE SONG

Harry B. Smith
Victor Herbert

Moderately
C
C7
F
D7
G7
To Coda
Slum - ber on, my lit - tle gyp - sy sweet - heart, Dream of the field and the
Can you hear me, hear me in that dream - land,
Can you hear the song that tells you,
grove.
Where your fan - cies rove?
B7
E7
Bm7♭5
A7
Em7
Am7♭5
Slum - ber on, my lit - tle gyp - sy sweet - heart, Wild lit - tle wood - land
Dm7
D.C. al Coda
dove.
CODA
A♭7
All my heart's true love?

GYPSY RONDO

Joseph Haydn

HABAÑERA
(From "CARMEN")

Georges Bizet

HAIL, COLUMBIA

Words by Joseph Hopkinson
Music by Philip Phile

March
1. Hail, Col - um - bia, hap - py land, Hail, ye he - roes, heav'n born band, Who fought and bled in
2. Im - mor - tal pa - triots, rise once more, De - fend your rights, de - fend your shore, Let no rude foe with
3-4. (See additional lyrics)
Free - dom's_ cause, Who fought and bled in Free - dom's_ cause, And when the storm of war__ was__ gone, En -
im - pi - ous hand, Let no rude foe with im - pi - ous hand, In - vade the shrine where sa - cred_ lies Of
joy'd___ the____ peace your va - lor won. Let in - de - pen - dence be__ our_ boast, Ev - er mind - ful
toil ____ and____ blood the well - earned prize, While of - f'ring peace, sin - cere_ and_ just, In heav'n we place a
what it cost, Ev - er__ grate - ful for__ the__ prize, Let its al - tar reach the skies.
man - ly trust, That truth and_ jus - tice may_ pre - vail, And ev - 'ry scheme of bond - age fail.
Chorus
Firm, u - nit - ed let___ us___ be, Ral - 'ying round our lib - er - ty,
As a band of___ broth - ers____ join'd, Peace______ and_______ safe - ty we shall find.

Additional Lyrics

3. Sound, sound the trump of fame,
Let Washington's great fame
Ring through the world with loud applause,
Ring through the world with loud applause,
Let ev'ry chime to freedom dear,
Listen with a joyful ear,
With equal skill, with God-like pow'r
He governs in the fearful hour
Of horrid war, or guides with ease
The happier time of honest peace.
Chorus

4. Beloved the chief who now commands,
Once more to serve his country stands,
The rock on which the storm will beat,
The rock on which the storm will beat.
But arm'd in virtue firm and true,
His hopes are fixed on Heav'n and you,
When hope was sinking in dismay,
When glooms obscured Columbia's day,
His steady mind from changes free
Resolv'd on Death or Liberty.
Chorus

HALLELUJAH CHORUS

G. F. Handel

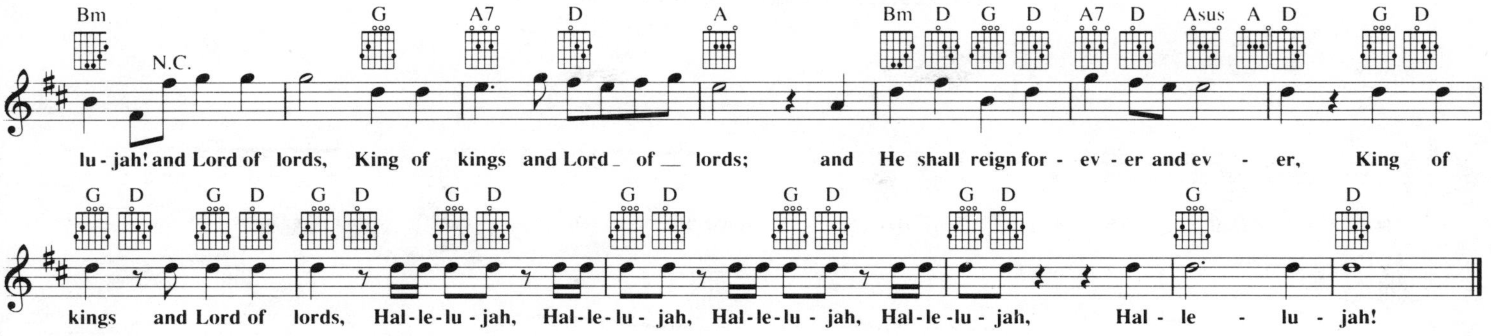
Bm N.C. G A7 D A Bm D G D A7 D Asus A D G D
lu-jah! and Lord of lords, King of kings and Lord of lords; and He shall reign for-ev-er and ev-er, King of
G D G D G D G D G D G D G D G D
kings and Lord of lords, Hal-le-lu-jah, Hal-le-lu-jah, Hal-le-lu-jah, Hal-le-lu-jah, Hal-le-lu-jah!

HAIL TO THE CHIEF

James Sanderson

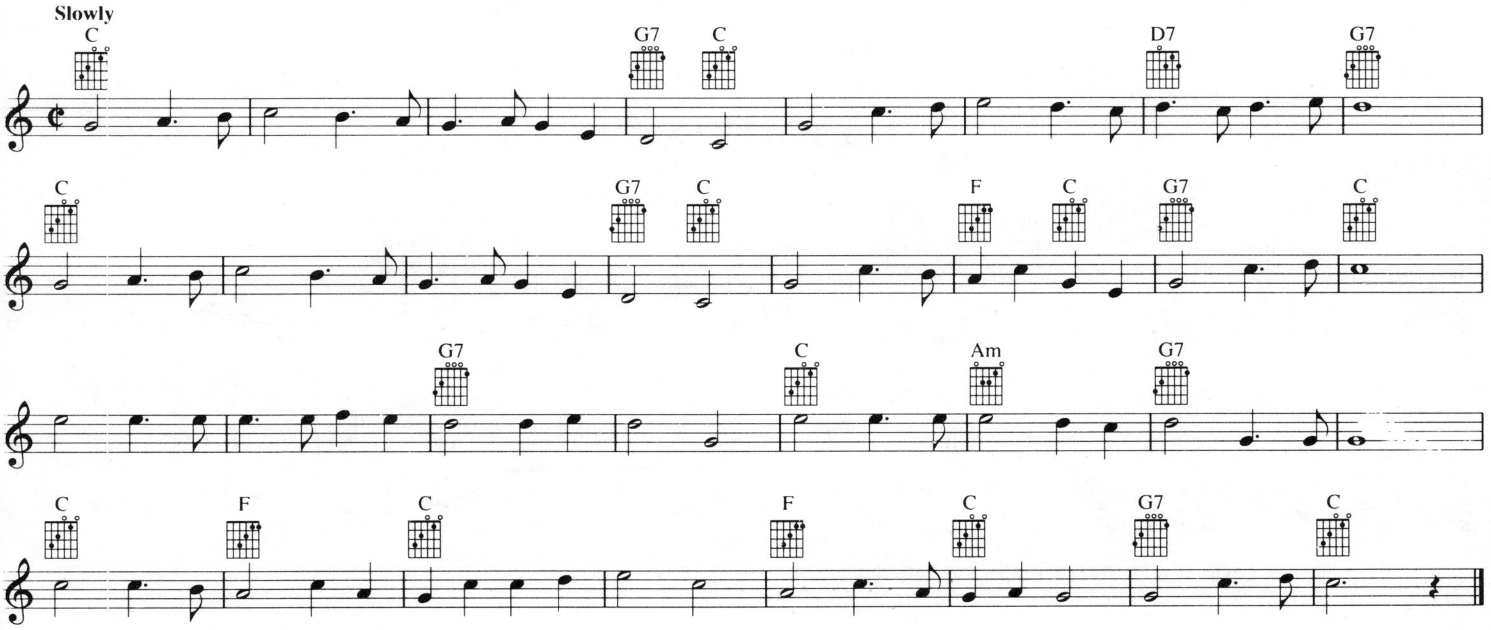
Slowly
C G7 C D7 G7
C G7 C F C G7 C
G7 C Am G7
C F C F C G7 C

HAND ME DOWN MY WALKING CANE

James A. Bland

Moderately
G D7 G D7
Hand Me Down My Walk-ing Cane, Hand Me Down My Walk-ing
down my bot-tle of corn, Hand me down my bot-tle of
G C G C
Cane, Oh, Hand Me Down My Walk-ing Cane, I'm a goin' to leave on that
corn, Oh, hand me down my bot-tle of corn, I'm a goin' to leave Drunk as
D7 G D7 G 1 2
mid-night train, 'Cause all of my sins are tak-en a-way. Hand me
sure as you're born, 'Cause all of my sins are tak-en a-way.

HAIL! HAIL! THE GANG'S ALL HERE

THE HAPPY FARMER

Robert Schumann

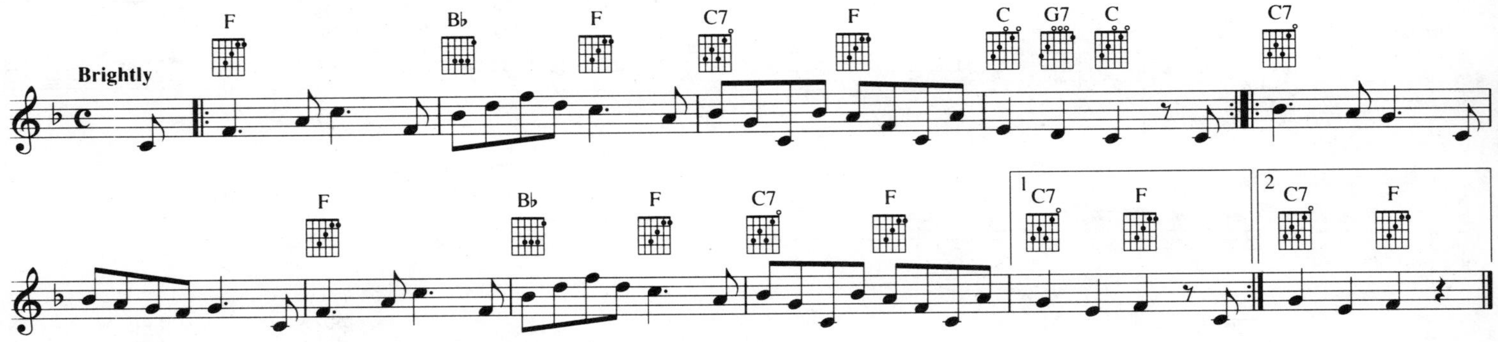

HEARTS AND FLOWERS

Theo. M. Tobani

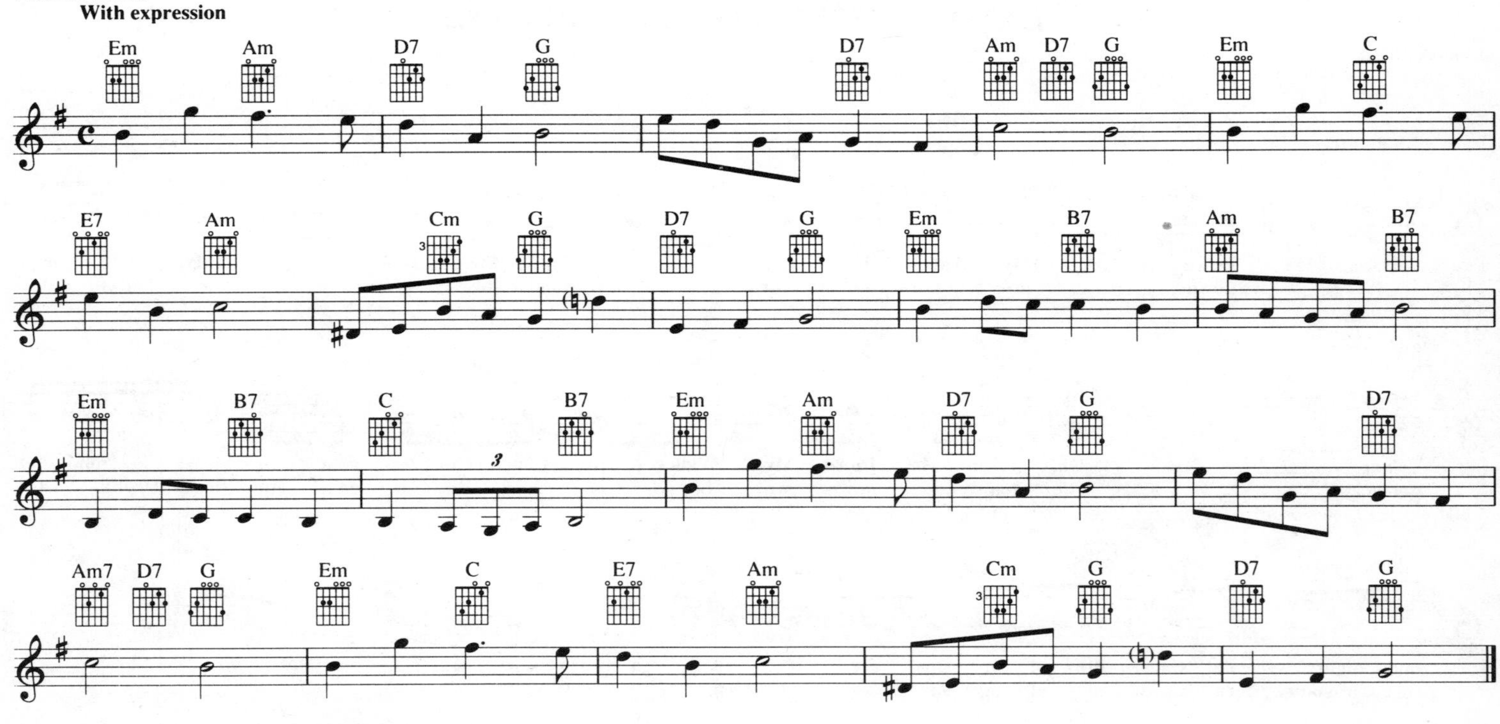

HATIKVAH

Slowly
Dm Gm Dm Gm Dm E7 A7 Dm
Kol — od ba - le - vav p'nee - mah ne - fesh y' - hu - dee ho - mee - yah Ul -
Bb F F#dim7 Gm Dm Gm Dm E7 A7 Dm
fa - a - tey - miz - rach ka - dee - mah a - yin l' - tzi - yon tso - fee - yah.
Bb Gm C F Bb Gm C F
Od lo av - dah tik - va - te - nu Ha - tik - vah shnot al - pa - yim
A7 Dm C F Gm Dm E7 A7 1 Dm 2 Dm
li - yot am chuf - shee bar - tse - nu Er - ets tzi - yon v' - yru - sha - la — yim. yim.

HAVA NAGILAH

Getting faster throughout
B7 Em B7
Ha - va Na - gi - la Ha - va Na - gi - la Ha - va Na - gi - la v' - nis — m' - cha, Ha - va Na - gi - la
Em B7 Am
Ha - va Na - gi - la Ha - va Na - gi - la v' - nis — m' - cha. Ha - va n' - ra - n' - na, ha - va n' - ra - n' - na,
B7 Am
ha - va n' - ra - n' - na, v' - nis — m' - cha. Ha - va n' - ra - n' - na, ha - va n' - ra - n' - na, ha - va n' - ra - n' - na,
B7 Em
v' - nis — m' - cha. U - ru u - ru a - chim, u - ru a - chim b' - lev sa - me - ach, u - ru a - chim b' - lev sa - me - ach,
Am B7 Em
u - ru a - chim b' - lev sa - me - ach, u - ru a - chim b' - lev sa - me - ach, u - ru a - chim, u - ru a - chim, b'lev sa - me - ach.

HARK! THE HERALD ANGELS SING

Words by Charles Wesley
Music by Felix Mendelssohn-Bartholdy

Brightly
G D7 G C G D7 G
Hark! The Her - ald An - gels Sing, "Glo - ry to the new - born King! Peace on earth and
A7 D A7 D A7 D G D7 G D
mer - cy mild, God and sin - ners re - con - ciled." Joy - ful all ye na - tions rise
G D7 G D C Am E7 Am D7 G
Join the tri - umph of the skies; With an - gel - ic host pro - claim "Christ is born in
D7 G C Am E7 Am D7 G D7 G
Beth - le - hem." Hark! The Her - ald An - gels Sing, "Glo - ry to the new - born King!"

HE'S GOT THE WHOLE WORLD IN HIS HANDS

Brightly
C G7 C
He's Got The Whole World In His Hands, He's Got The Whole World In His Hands, He's Got The
G7 G9 C
Whole World In His Hands, He's Got The Whole World In His Hands.

HEAR THEM BELLS

Brightly
G D7 G Am7
Hear Them Bells! Mer - ry Christ - mas bells! They are ring - ing out the
D7 G D7
e - vil of the sword; Hear Them Bells! Mer - ry
G Am7 D7 G
Christ - mas bells! They are ring - ing in the glo - ry of the Lord!

HELENA POLKA

Lively
To Coda
D.C. al Coda
CODA

HEY, DIDDLE, DIDDLE

Moderately
Hey, Did - dle, Did - dle, the cat and the fid - dle, The cow jumped o - ver the moon. The
lit - tle dog laughed to see such sport, And the dish ran a - way with the spoon.

HEY, HO! NOBODY HOME

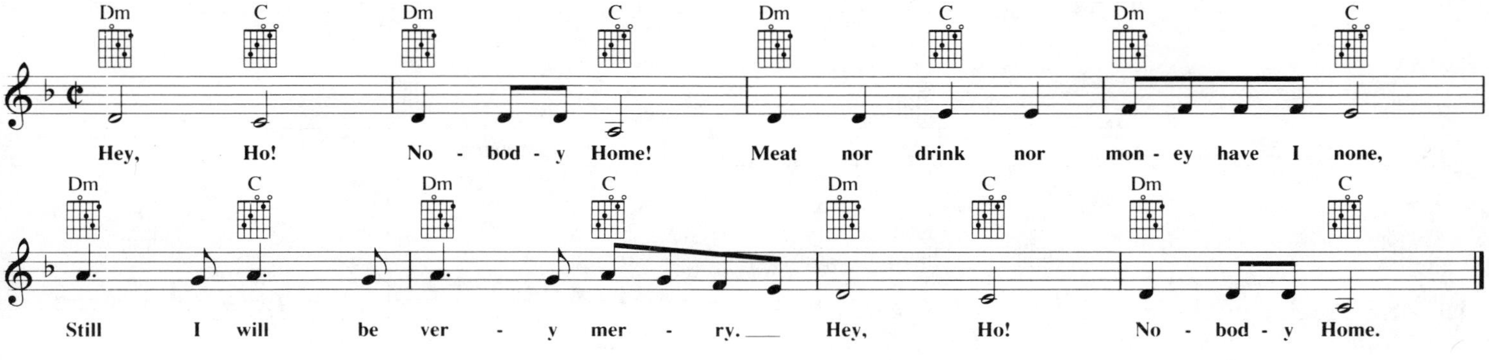
Hey, Ho! No - bod - y Home! Meat nor drink nor mon - ey have I none,
Still I will be ver - y mer - ry. Hey, Ho! No - bod - y Home.

HERE WE COME A-CAROLING

Brightly
D G D Em A7 D G D G D B7 Em A7 D G D B7 Em A7 D
Here We Come A-car-ol-ing a-mong the leaves so green; Here we come a wan-d'ring so
fair to be seen: Love and joy come to you, and to you glad Christ-mas, too, and God
bless you and send you a Hap-py New Year, and God send you a Hap-py New Year.

HIGH SCHOOL CADETS

John Philip Sousa

Brightly
F C7 F Dm Gm Dm G7 C C C7 F C7 F C7 F Dm D♭7 F C7 F F

HICKORY, DICKORY, DOCK

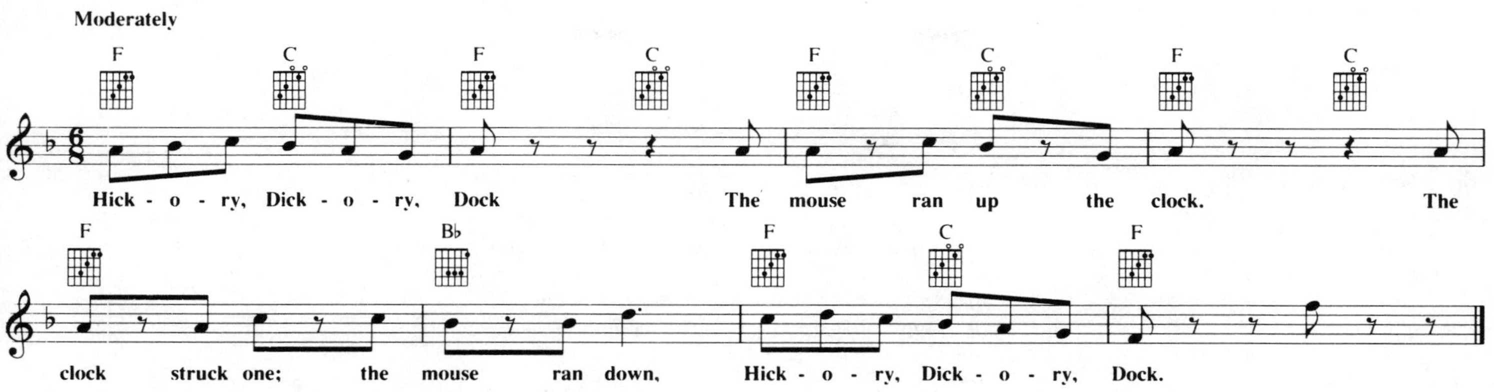
Moderately
F C F C F C F C
Hick - o - ry, Dick - o - ry, Dock The mouse ran up the clock. The
F B♭ F C F
clock struck one; the mouse ran down, Hick - o - ry, Dick - o - ry, Dock.

THE HOLLY AND THE IVY

Slowly
G C G C D G
1,6. The Hol - ly And The I - vy, when they are both full grown, Of all the trees that are
2. The hol - ly bears a blos - som, as white as the li - ly flower, and Ma - ry bore sweet
3. The hol - ly bears a ber - ry, as red as a - ny blood, and Ma - ry bore sweet
4- 5. (See additional lyrics)
C G Em C D G C G C G C
in the wood, the hol - ly bears the crown.
Je - sus Christ, to be our sweet Sa - vior.
Je - sus Christ, to do poor sin - ners good.
The ris - ing of the sun and the run - ning of the
D G C G Em C D G
deer, the play - ing of the mer - ry or - gan, sweet sing - ing in the choir.

Additional Lyrics

4. The holly bears a prickle,
As sharp as any thorn
And Mary bore sweet Jesus Christ
On Christmas Day in the morn.
(Refrain)

5. The holly bears a bark,
As bitter as any gall,
And Mary bore sweet Jesus Christ
For to redeem us all.
(Refrain)

HOT CROSS BUNS

Moderately
D A7 D A7 D A7 D A7 D
Hot Cross Buns! Hot Cross Buns! One, a pen - ny, Two, a pen - ny, Hot Cross Buns!

HOLY GOD, WE PRAISE THEY NAME

Words based on a translation by Clarence Walworth

Moderately
G G/B C G/D D7 G G/F# Em Em/D C G D
1. Ho - ly God, We Praise Thy Name, Lord of all, we bow be - fore Thee.
2. Hark the loud ce - les - tial hymn An - gel choirs a - bove are rais - ing,
3- 4. (See additional lyrics)
All on earth Thy scep - ter claim, All in Heav'n a - bove a dore Thee.
Cher - u - bim and Ser - a - phim In un - ceas - ing chor - us prais - ing,
D#dim7 Em C/E G C G/B Am7 G C6 G/D D7 G
In - fi - nite Thy vast do - main, ev - er - last - ing is Thy reign.
Fill the heav'ns with sweet ac - cord, Ho - ly, ho - ly, ho - ly, Lord.

Additional Lyrics

3. Lo, the apostolic train
Joins Thy sacred name to hallow.
Prophets swell the gald refrain
And the white-robed martyrs follow.
And from morn to set of sun
Thru the church the song goes on.

4. Holy Father, Holy Son,
Holy Spirit, Three we name Thee.
While in essence only one,
Undivided God we claim Thee.
And adoring bend the knee,
While we sing our praise to Thee.

HOME ON THE RANGE

Dr. Brewster Higley
Daniel E. Kelley

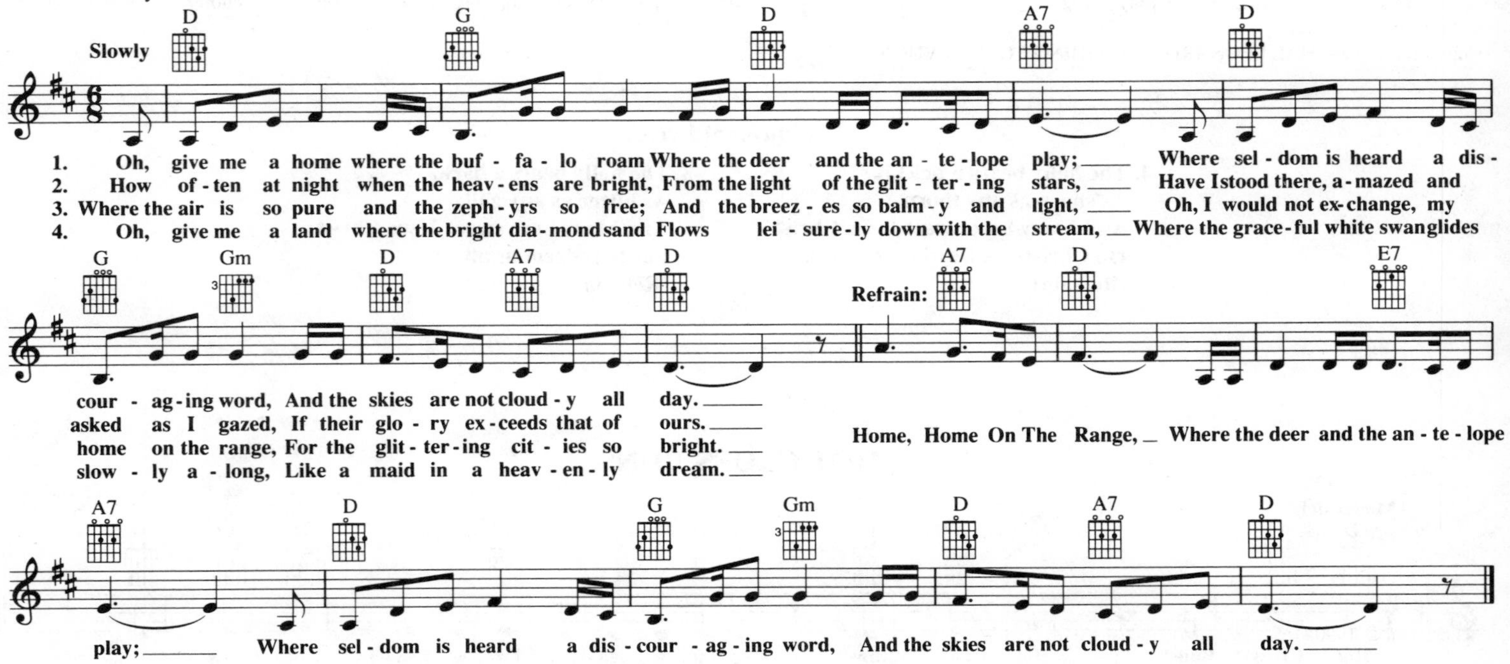
Slowly
D G D A7 D
1. Oh, give me a home where the buf - fa - lo roam Where the deer and the an - te - lope play; Where sel - dom is heard a dis -
2. How of - ten at night when the heav - ens are bright, From the light of the glit - ter - ing stars, Have I stood there, a - mazed and
3. Where the air is so pure and the zeph - yrs so free; And the breez - es so balm - y and light, Oh, I would not ex - change, my
4. Oh, give me a land where the bright dia - mond sand Flows lei - sure - ly down with the stream, Where the grace - ful white swan glides
G Gm D A7 D Refrain: A7 D E7
cour - ag - ing word, And the skies are not cloud - y all day.
asked as I gazed, If their glo - ry ex - ceeds that of ours.
home on the range, For the glit - ter - ing cit - ies so bright.
slow - ly a - long, Like a maid in a heav - en - ly dream.
Home, Home On The Range, Where the deer and the an - te - lope
A7 D G Gm D A7 D
play; Where sel - dom is heard a dis - cour - ag - ing word, And the skies are not cloud - y all day.

HOLY, HOLY, HOLY

Words by Reginald Heber
Music by John B. Dykes

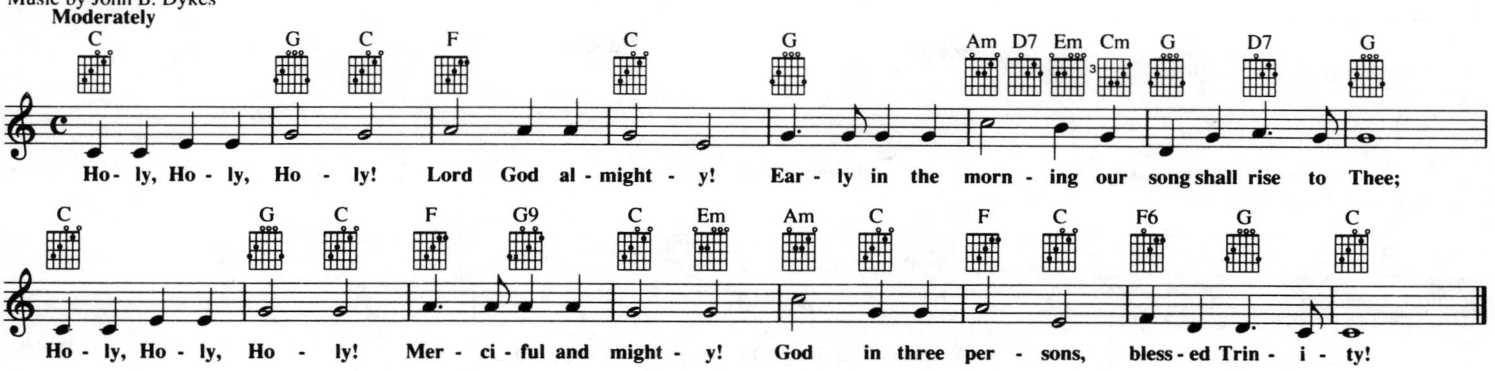
Moderately
C G C F C G Am D7 Em Cm G D7 G
Ho-ly, Ho-ly, Ho-ly! Lord God al-might-y! Ear-ly in the morn-ing our song shall rise to Thee;
C G C F G9 C Em Am C F C F6 G C
Ho-ly, Ho-ly, Ho-ly! Mer-ci-ful and might-y! God in three per-sons, bless-ed Trin-i-ty!

HONEY, WON'T YOU COME BACK TO ME?

Moderately
G A7
Hon-ey, Won't You Come Back To Me? I'm as lone-ly as a man can be.
Am D7 Am D7 G Em Am D7 D7#5
Since you went a-way I'm cry-ing ev-'ry day. Can't you hear me call-ing? Can't you hear me say? Oh,
G B7 E7
Hon-ey Won't You Come Back To Me? Hon-ey, won't you hear my plea? It's
Am7 D7 A7 D7 G6
break-ing my heart, hon-ey, since we're a-part. Hon-ey, Won't You Come Back To Me?

HOW DRY I AM!

Moderately
G D7 G
How Dry I Am! How Dry I Am! No-bod-y knows How Dry I Am.

HOME SWEET HOME

Lyrics by John Howard Payne
Music by Sir Henry Bishop

Slowly
D G D A7 D G D
1. 'Mid _ pleas - ures and pal - a - ces though __ we may roam, Be it ev - er so hum - ble, there's
2, 3. (See additional lyrics)
A7 D G D A7 D
no _____ place like home; A charm ___ from the sky seems to hal - low us there, Which,
G D A D G D
Chorus
seek _____ through the world, is ne'er met _____ with else - where. Home! Home! Sweet Home. ______ There's
A7 D G D A7 D
no _____ place like home. Home! Home! Sweet Home. ______ There's no _____ place like home.

Additional Lyrics

2. An exile from home, splendor dazzles in vain,
Oh, give me my lowly thatched cottage again;
The birds singing gaily, that come at my call;
Give me them, with that peace of mind, dearer than all.
Chorus

3. To thee, I'll return, overburdened with care,
The heart's dearest solace will smile on me there.
No more from that cottage again will I roam,
Be it ever so humble, there's no place like home.
Chorus

HOPAK

Modest Moussorgsky

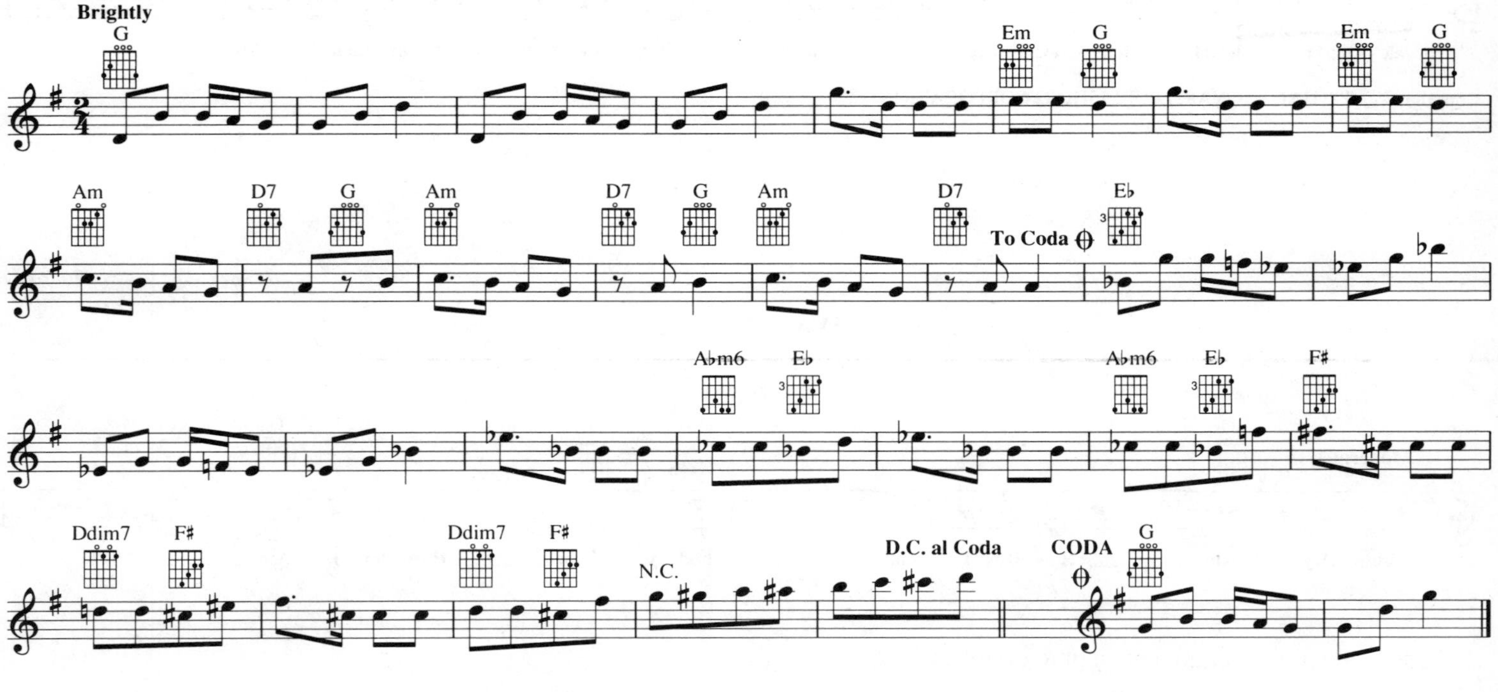
Brightly
G Em G Em G
Am D7 G Am D7 G Am D7 Eb
To Coda
Abm6 Eb Abm6 Eb F#
Ddim7 F# Ddim7 F#
N.C.
D.C. al Coda
CODA
G

A HOT TIME IN THE OLD TOWN TONIGHT

Words by Joe Hayden; Music by Theodore A. Metz

Brightly
G
When you hear them - a bells go ding ling ling, All join 'round And sweet - ly you must sing, And when the verse is through, In the cho - rus all join in, There'll Be A
D7
Hot Time In The Old Town To - night.
1 G Gdim Am7 D7
2 G
night.

HOUSE OF THE RISING SUN

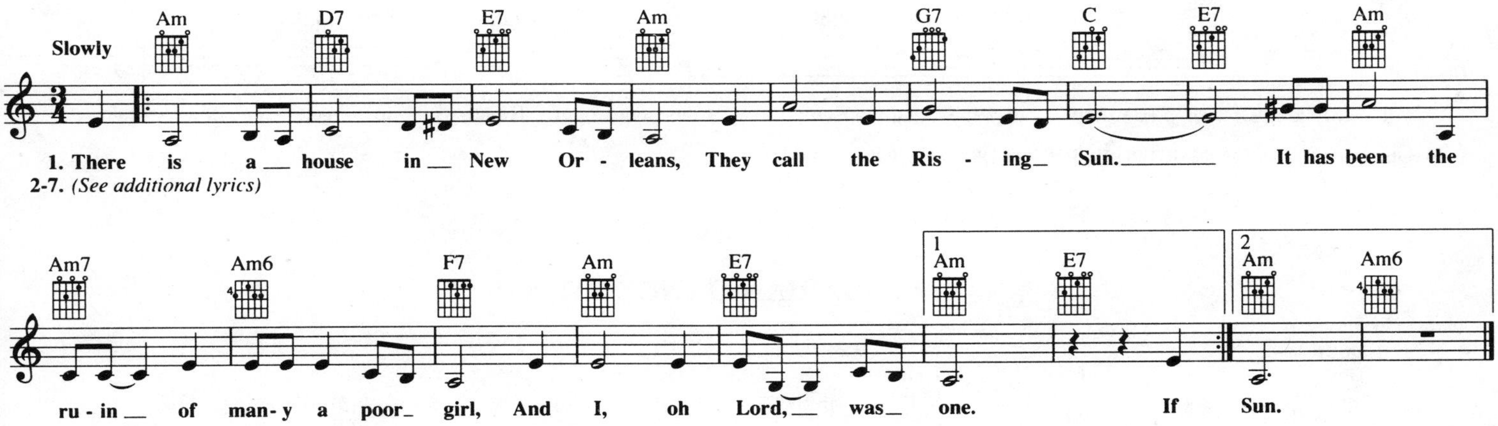
Slowly
Am D7 E7 Am G7 C E7 Am
1. There is a house in New Or - leans, They call the Ris - ing Sun. It has been the
2-7. (See additional lyrics)
Am7 Am6 F7 Am E7
ru - in of man - y a poor girl, And I, oh Lord, was one.
1 Am E7
If
2 Am Am6
Sun.

Additional Lyrics

2. If I had listened to what mama said,
I'd 'a' been at home today.
Being so young and foolish, poor girl,
Let a gambler lead me astray.

3. My mother, she's a tailor,
She sells those new blue jeans.
My sweetheart, he's a drunkard, Lord,
Drinks down in New Orleans.

4. The only thing a drunkard needs
Is a suitcase and a trunk.
The only time he's satisfied
Is when he's on a drunk.

5. Go tell my baby, sister,
Never do like I have done.
To shun that house in New Orleans,
They call the Rising Sun.

6. One foot is on the platform,
And the other one on the train.
I'm going back to New Orleans
To wear that ball and chain.

7. I'm going back to New Orleans,
My race is almost run.
Going back to end my life
Beneath the Rising Sun.

HUMORESQUE

Antonin Dvorák

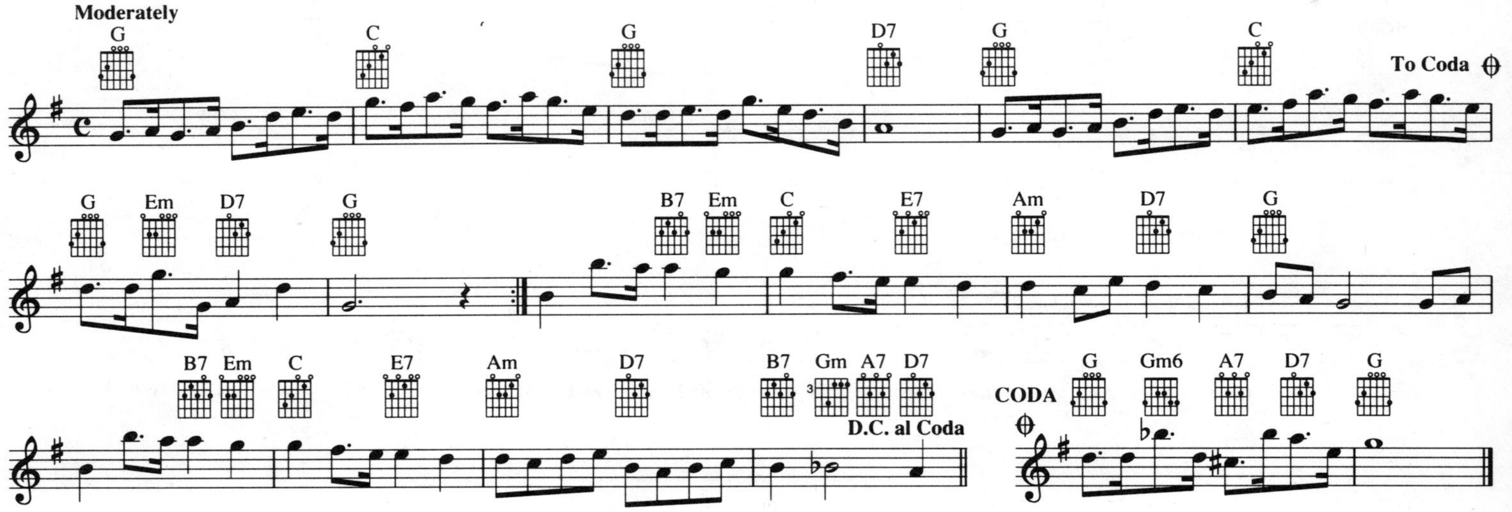

HUMPTY DUMPTY

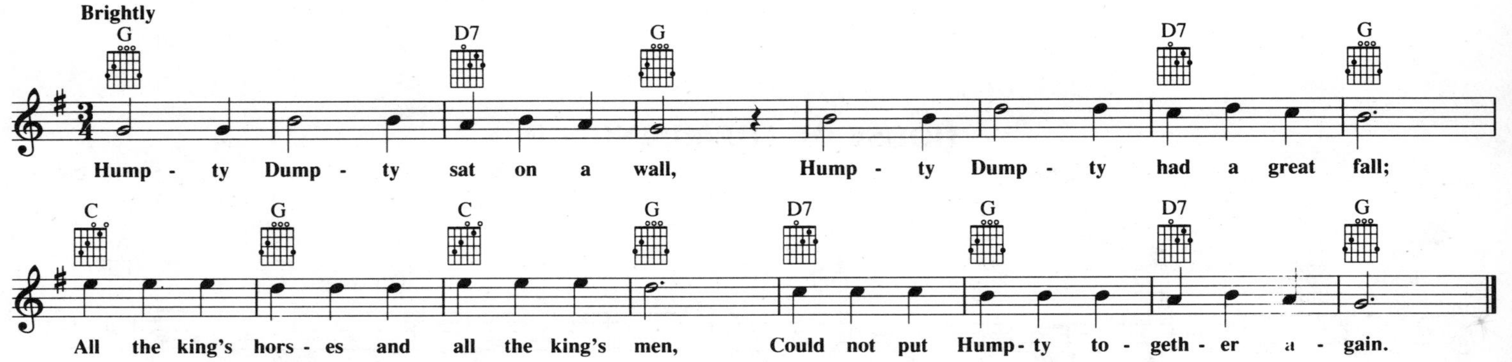

HUNGARIAN DANCE NO. 5

Johannes Brahms

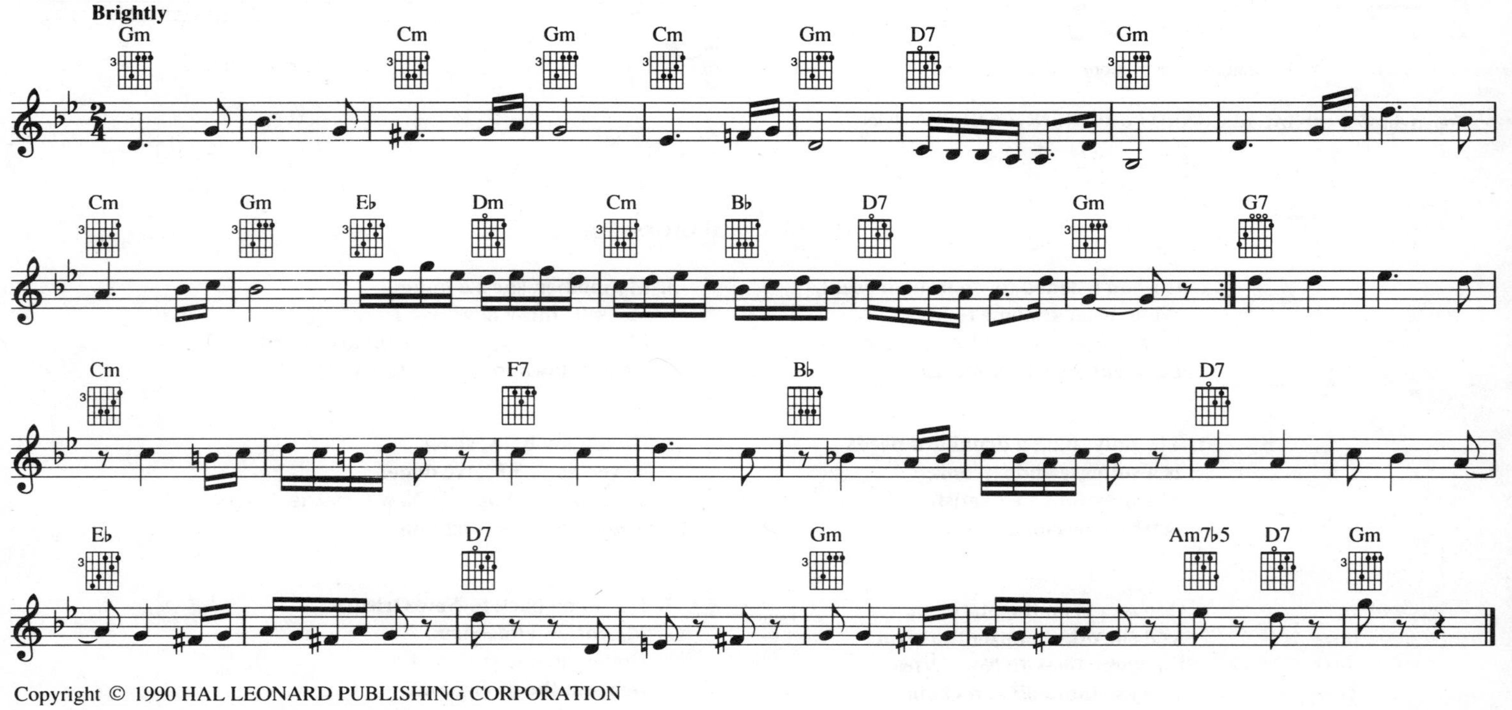

HUSH, LITTLE BABY

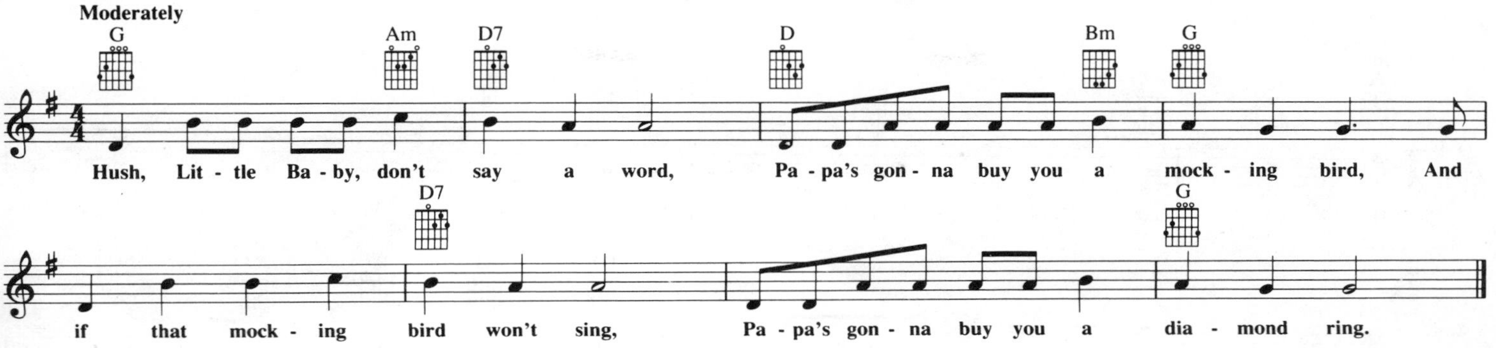
Moderately
G Am D7 D Bm G
Hush, Lit - tle Ba - by, don't say a word, Pa - pa's gon - na buy you a mock - ing bird, And
D7 G
if that mock - ing bird won't sing, Pa - pa's gon - na buy you a dia - mond ring.

I AM THE CAPTAIN OF THE PINAFORE

By W.S. Gilbert and Arthur Sullivan

Solo
Sprightly
G D G D G D G
I am the Cap-tain of the Pin - a - fore! And a right good cap - tain, too! You're
do my best to sat - is - fy you all! And with you we're quite con - tent. You're ex -
C G Gdim G A7 D A7 D
Chorus
ver - y, ver - y good, And be it un - der - stood I com - mand a right good crew. We're ver - y, ver - y good, And,
ceed - ing - ly po - lite, And I think it on - ly right To re - turn the com - pli - ment. We're ex - ceed - ing - ly po - lite, And he
A7 D A A7 D C Am B7
Solo
be it un - der - stood, He com - mands a right good crew. Though re - lat - ed to a peer, I can hand, reef and steer, Or
thinks it on - ly right To re - turn the com - pli - ment. Bad lan - guage or a - buse I never, nev - er use, What -
Em Em7 D/F# G A/G D/F# E/B D A
ship a sel va - gee; I am nev - er known to quail At the fu - ry of a gale, And I'm nev - er, nev - er sick at
ev - er the e - mer - gen - cy; Though "both - er it" I may Oc - ca - sion - al - ly say, I nev - er use a big, big
D A7/D D A7/Eb A7/E D7/F#
Chorus Solo Chorus Solo Chorus
N.C.
sea! What, never? No, never! What, never? Hard - ly ev - er! He's hard - ly ev - er sick at
D! What, never? No, never! What, never? Hard - ly ev - er! Hard - ly ev - er swears a big, big
Gdim G D G
sea! Then give three cheers, and one cheer more, For the har - dy Cap - tain of the Pin - a - fore! Then
D! Then give three cheers, and one cheer more, For the well - bred Cap - tain of the Pin - a - fore! Then
D7 1 G 2
give three cheers, and one cheer more, For the Cap - tain of the Pin - a - fore! I
give three cheers, and one cheer more, For the Cap - tain of the Pin - a - fore!

HARRIGAN

George M. Cohan

Bouncy
H - A - dou-ble R - I - G - A - N
Proud of all the I-rish blood that's
in me. "Di-vil" a man
dou-ble R - I -
G - A - N, you see, is a name tha
Har-ri-gan, that's
me!
Har-ri-gan, Mul-li-gan, Har-ri-ga
ul-li-gan, Har-ri-gan, that's me!

I WANT A GIRL

Words by William Dalton
Music by Harry Von Tilzer

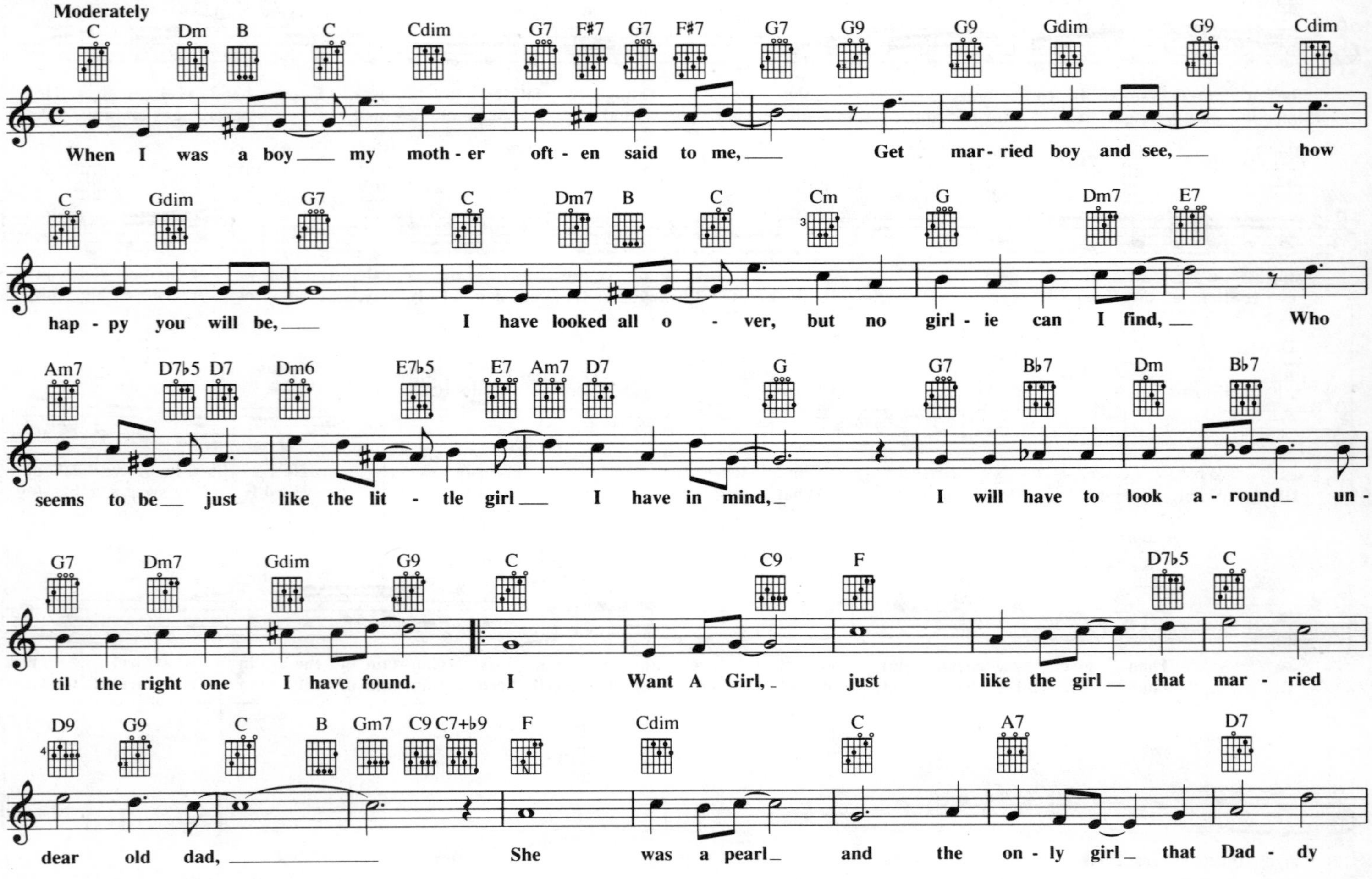
Moderately
When I was a boy my moth-er oft-en said to me, Get mar-ried boy and see, how
hap-py you will be, I have looked all o-ver, but no girl-ie can I find, Who
seems to be just like the lit-tle girl I have in mind, I will have to look a-round un-
til the right one I have found. I Want A Girl, just like the girl that mar-ried
dear old dad, She was a pearl and the on-ly girl that Dad-dy

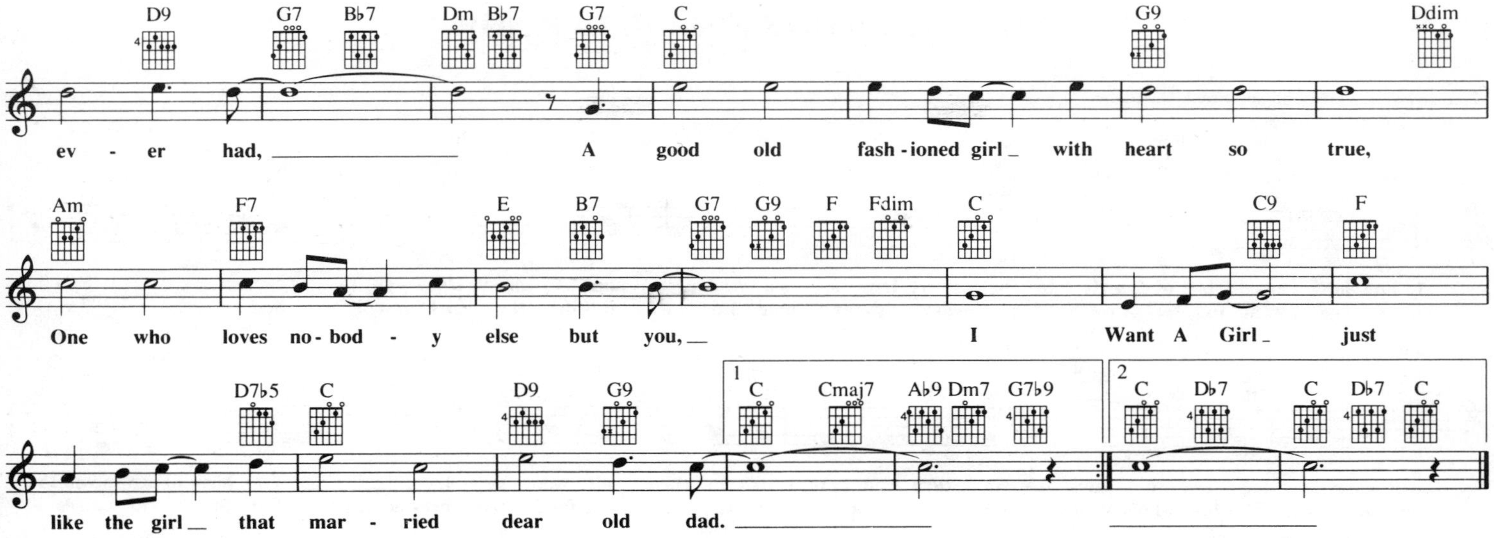
D9 G7 B♭7 Dm B♭7 G7 C G9 Ddim
ev - er had, A good old fash - ioned girl with heart so true,
Am F7 E B7 G7 G9 F Fdim C C9 F
One who loves no - bod - y else but you, I Want A Girl just
D7♭5 C D9 G9 1 C Cmaj7 A♭9 Dm7 G7♭9 2 C D♭7 C D♭7 C
like the girl that mar - ried dear old dad.

HELLO! MY BABY

Words by Ida Emerson
Music by Joseph E. Howard

Brightly
F G7 C7
Hel - lo My Ba - by, Hel - lo my hon - ey, Hel - lo my rag - time gal! Send me a kiss by wire;
F E E7 F Cdim7 C7 F G7
Ba - by my heart's on fire! If you re - fuse me, Hon - ey you'll lose me, Then you'll be left a - lone; Oh, ba - by,
C7 Cdim7 C7 G9 C7 1 F F6 Fdim7 C7 2 F
tel - e - phone, and tell me I'm your own. Hel - lo! Hel - lo! Hel - lo there! own.

I LOVE YOU TRULY

Carrie Jacobs Bond

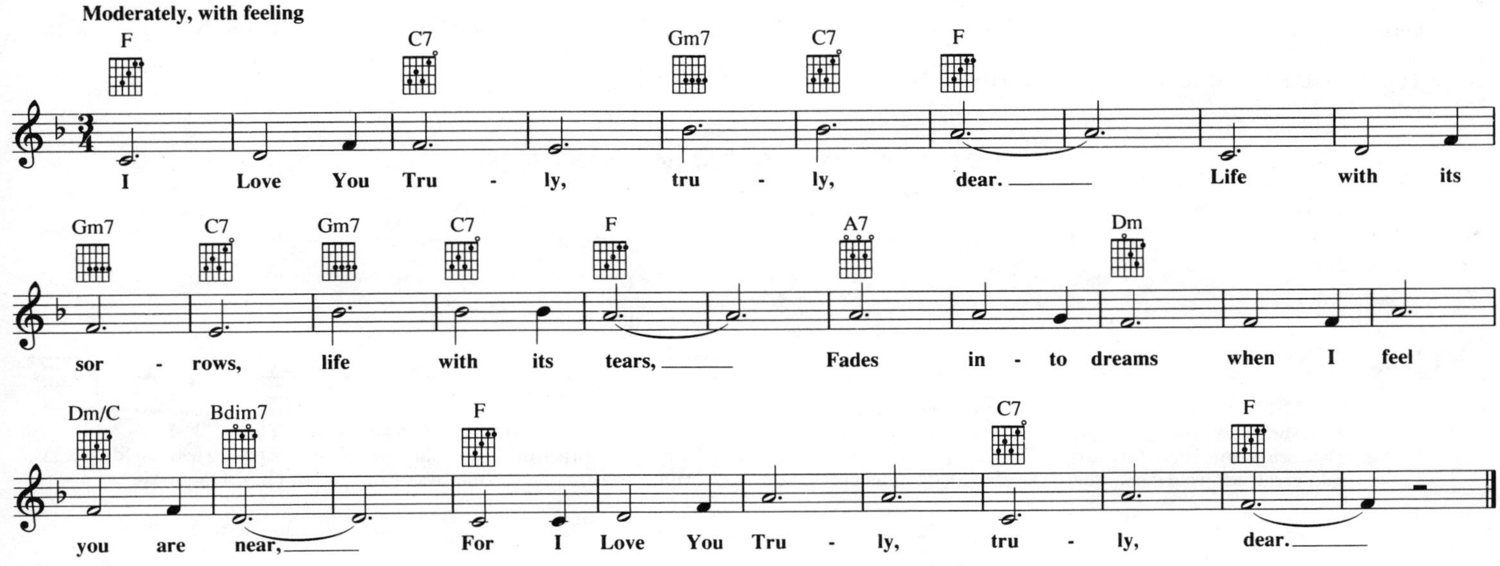
Moderately, with feeling
F C7 Gm7 C7 F
I Love You Tru - ly, tru - ly, dear. Life with its
Gm7 C7 Gm7 C7 F A7 Dm
sor - rows, life with its tears, Fades in - to dreams when I feel
Dm/C Bdim7 F C7 F
you are near, For I Love You Tru - ly, tru - ly, dear.

I WONDER WHO'S KISSING HER NOW

Words by Will M. Hough and Frank R. Adams
Music by Joseph E. Howard

Tempo di Valse
1. You have loved lots of girls in the sweet long a - go, And each one has meant Heav - en to you, You have
2. If you want to feel wretch - ed and lone - ly and blue, Just im - ag - ine the girl you love best In the
vow'd your af - fec - tion to each one in turn And have sworn to them all you'd be true; You have kissed 'neath the
arms of some fel - low who's steal - ing a kiss From the lips that you once fond - ly pressed; But the world moves a -
moon while the world seemed in tune, Then you've left her to hunt a new game, Does it ev - er oc -
pace and the loves of to - day Flit a - way with a smile and a tear, So you nev - er can
cur to you la - ter, my boy, That she's prob - ably do - ing the same?
tell who is kiss - ing her now, Or just whom you'll be kiss - ing next year.
I Wonder Who's Kiss - ing Her Now, Won - der who's teach - ing her how, Won - der who's look - ing in - to her eyes,
Breath - ing sighs, tell - ing lies; I won - der who's buy - ing the wine For lips that I used to call
mine, Won - der if she ev - er tells him of me, I Won - der Who's Kiss - ing Her Now.

I'VE GOT RINGS ON MY FINGERS

Words by Weston and Barnes
Music by Maurice Scott

Moderato
1. Jim O - 'Shea was cast a - way up - on an In - dian isle, The na - tives there they lik'd his hair They lik'd his I - rish
2. O'er the sea went Rose Mc Gee To see her na - bob grand, He sat with - in his pal - an - quin, And when she'd kissed his
3. Em - 'rald green he robed his queen, To share with him his throne, 'Mid east - ern charms and wav - ing palms, They'd sham - rocks, I - rish

smile, So made him chief Pan - jan - drum, The na - bob of them all, They call'd him Ji - ji - boo Jhai, And
hand, He led her to his ha - rem, Where he had wives ga - lore, She start - ed shed - ding a tear, Said
grown, Sent all the way from Dub - lin, To Na - bob J. O 'Shea, But in his pal - ace so fine, Should
rigg'd him out so gay, So he wrote to Dub - lin Bay To his sweet - heart just to say:
he, "Now have no fear! I'm keep - ing these wives here Just for or - na - ment my dear: } "Sure, I've Got
Rose for Ire - land pine, With smiles her face will shine, When he mur - mers, "Sweet - heart mine:
N.C.
Rings On My Fin - gers, bells on my toes, El - e - phants to ride up - on, my
lit - tle I - rish Rose, So come to your na - bob, and next Pat - rick's Day, Be
Mis - tress Mum - bo Jum - bo Jij - ji - boo J. O - 'Shea. Sure I've Got Shea."
N.C.
D.C.

IDA, SWEET AS APPLE CIDER

Words by Eddie Leonard; Music by Eddie Munson

Moderately
I - da, Sweet As Ap - ple Ci - der, Sweet - er than all I know.
Come out in the sil - v'ry moon - light, Of love we'll whis - per, so soft and low.
Seems I can't live with - out you, Lis - ten, oh hon - ey, do.
I - da, I i - do - lize you, I love you, I - da, 'deed I do.

IF I HAD MY WAY

Words by Lou Klein; Music by James Kendis

Moderate
C Cdim7 C C♯dim7 G G7 C G7
I'd like to make your gold - en dreams come true, dear, If I on - ly had my way, A
You'd nev - er know a care, a pain, or sor - row, If I on - ly had my way, I'd
C Cdim7 A7 G D7 E7 Am E7 Am D7 G G7
par - a - dise this world would seem to you, If I on - ly had my way.
fill your cup of hap - pi - ness to - mor - row, If I on - ly had my way.
If
C A7 D7 G7 G+ C Cdim7 C G7 C
I Had My Way, dear, for - ev - er there'd be a gar - den of ros - es for
E♭dim7 G7 C E7 F C D7
you and for me, A thou - sand and one things, dear, I would do, Just for you, just for
G7 C A7 D7 G7
you, just for you. If I Had My Way, we would nev - er grow old, And
C E7 F A7 Dm Cdim
sun - shine I'd bring ev - 'ry day. You would reign all a - lone Like a
C A7 D7 G7 1 C 2 C
queen on a throne, If I Had My Way. If Way.
D.C.

IN MY MERRY OLDSMOBILE

Vincent P. Bryan and Gus Edwards

Tempo di Valse
G D7 G
Young John - ny Steele has an Olds - mo - bile, He loves a dear lit - tle girl, She is the queen of his
They love to spark in the dark old park, As they go fly - ing a - long, She says she knows why the

D7 G A7 D
gas ma - chine; She has his heart in a whirl. Now, when they go for a spin, you know, She
mo - tor goes; The spark - er's aw - ful - ly strong. Each day they spoon to the en - gine's tune, Their
A D A D Ddim7 A
tries to learn the au - to, so He lets her steer while he gets her ear, And whis - pers soft and
hon - ey - moon will hap - pen soon, He'll win Lu - cile with his Olds - mo - bile And then he'll fond - ly
D D7 G G7 E7 A7 Gmaj9 A7 D7
low: croon: } Come a - way with me, Lu - cile, In My Mer - ry Olds - mo - bile, Down the road of
Cmaj9 D7 G D7 G G7 E7
life we'll fly Au - to - mo - bub - bling, you and I. To the church we'll swift - ly steal, Then our
A7 Gmaj9 A7 D7 G Em7 B7 Em A7 D7 G
wed - ding bells will peal, You can go as far as you like with me In My Mer - ry Olds - mo - bile.

IN THE GLOAMING

By A.F. Harrison and Meta Orred

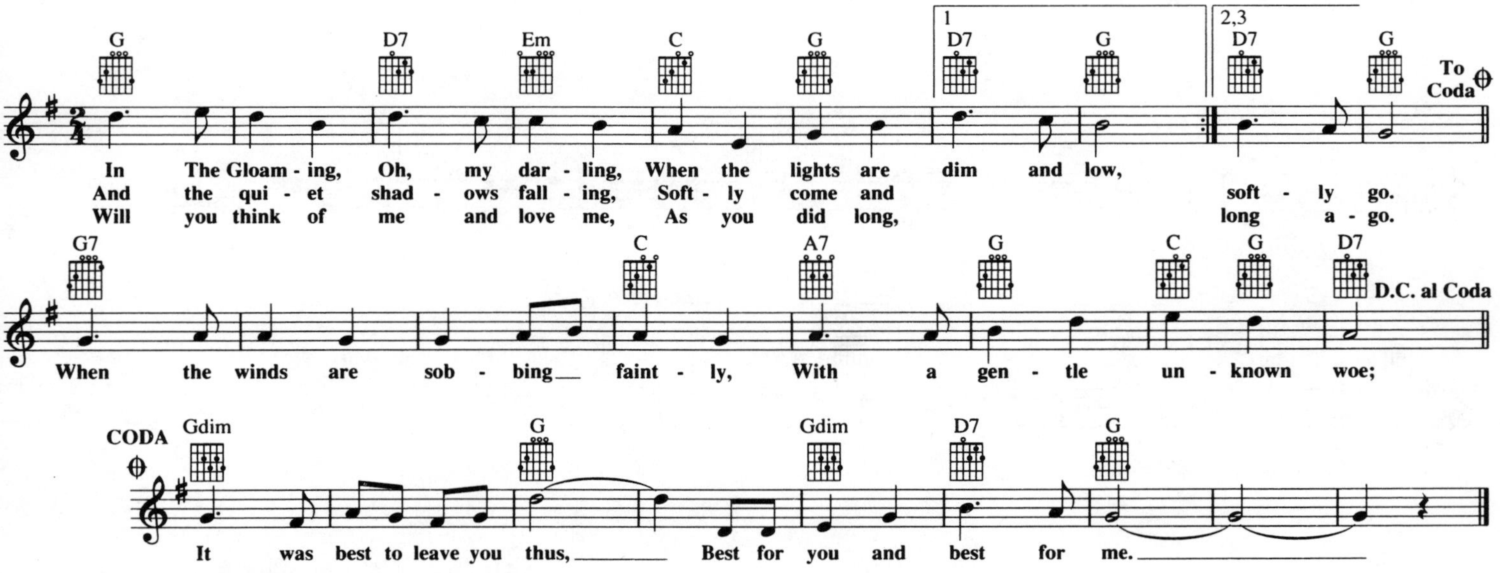
G D7 Em C G 1 D7 G 2,3 D7 G To Coda
In The Gloam - ing, Oh, my dar - ling, When the lights are dim and low,
And the qui - et shad - ows fall - ing, Soft - ly come and soft - ly go.
Will you think of me and love me, As you did long, long a - go.
G7 C A7 G C G D7 D.C. al Coda
When the winds are sob - bing faint - ly, With a gen - tle un - known woe;
CODA Gdim G Gdim D7 G
It was best to leave you thus, Best for you and best for me.

Additional Lyrics

In The Gloaming, oh my darling!
Think not bitterly of me!
Though I passed away in silence,
Left you lonely, set you free,
For my heart is crushed with longing,
What had been could never be.
It was best to leave you thus, dear,
Best for you and best for me.

IN THE SHADE OF THE OLD APPLE TREE

Words by Harry H. Williams
Music by Egbert Van Alstyne

Brightly
G Gdim G C G Gdim G D7 G
In The Shade Of The Old Ap - ple Tree, Where the love in your eyes I could see, When the
hear the dull buzz of the bee. In the blos - soms as you said to me, With a
D7 Am7 Ddim7 D7 G D7 Gdim G A7 E7 A7 D G
voice that I heard, Like the song of the bird, Seem'd to whis - per sweet mu - sic to me;
heart that is
D7 D7 G7 C Cm G E7 A7 D7 G G7 Cm6 G
I could true, I'll be wait - ing for you, In The Shade Of The Old Ap - ple Tree.

JOLLY COPPERSMITH

Carl Peter

Moderately
G D7 G
D A7
D A7 D D D7 G
D7 G D7 G
Gdim G D7 G D7 G D7

G D7 G D7
G Gdim G D7 G D7
G C G7 C G7 C
G7 C
D7 G
Am D7 G C G7
C G7
C G7 C G7
C
G7 C G7 C

I GAVE MY LOVE A CHERRY
(The Riddle Song)

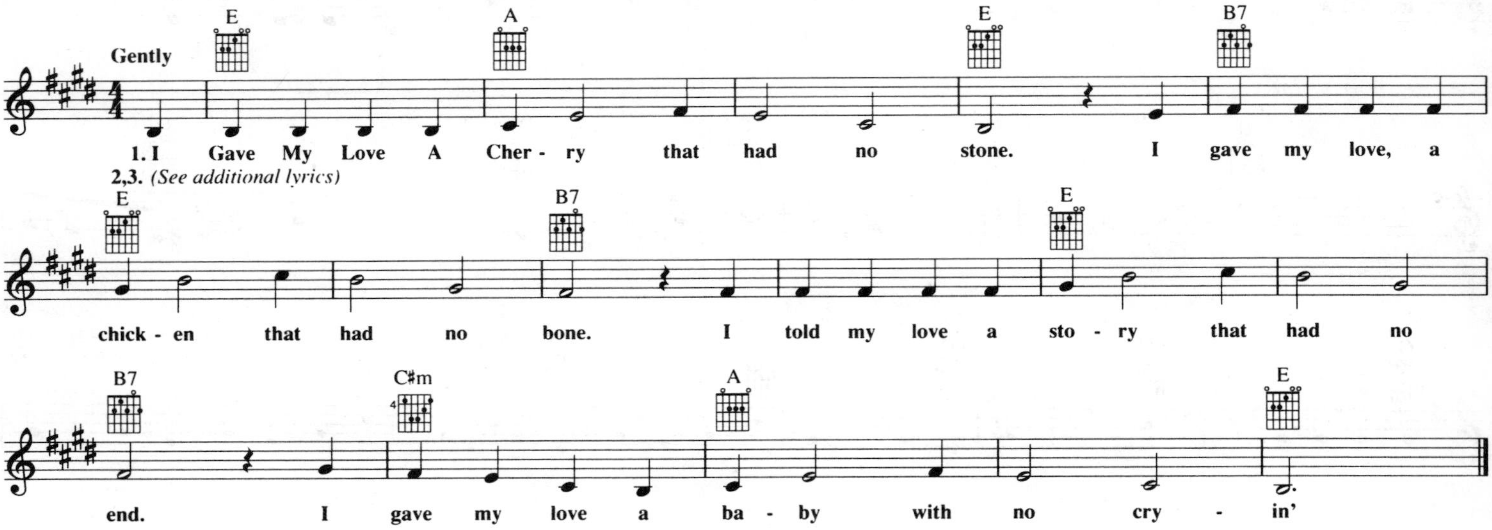
Gently
E A E B7
1. I Gave My Love A Cher - ry that had no stone. I gave my love, a
2,3. (See additional lyrics)
E B7 E
chick - en that had no bone. I told my love a sto - ry that had no
B7 C#m A E
end. I gave my love a ba - by with no cry - in'

Additional Lyrics

2. How can there be a cherry that has no stone?
How can there be a chicken that has no bone?
How can there be a story that has no end?
How can there be a baby with no cryin'?

3. A cherry, when it's blooming, it has no stone.
A chicken, when it's pipping, it has no bone.
The story that I love you, it has no end.
A baby, when it's sleeping, has no cryin'.

I HEARD THE BELLS ON CHRISTMAS DAY

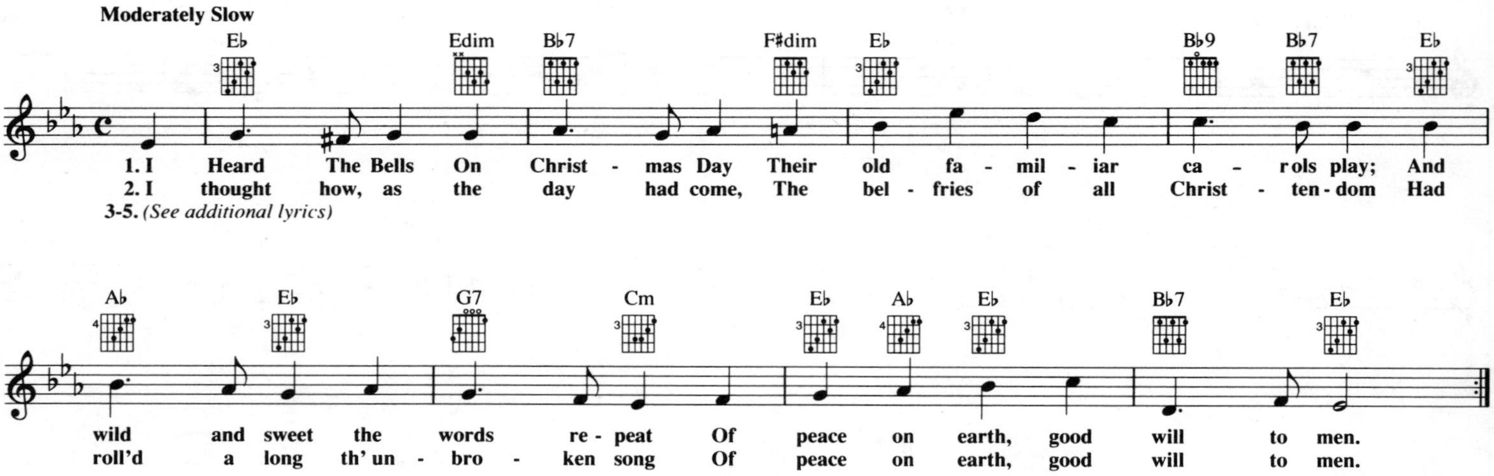
Moderately Slow
E♭ Edim B♭7 F#dim E♭ B♭9 B♭7 E♭
1. I Heard The Bells On Christ - mas Day Their old fa - mil - iar ca - rols play; And
2. I thought how, as the day had come, The bel - fries of all Christ - ten - dom Had
3-5. (See additional lyrics)
A♭ E♭ G7 Cm E♭ A♭ E♭ B♭7 E♭
wild and sweet the words re - peat Of peace on earth, good will to men.
roll'd a long th' un - bro - ken song Of peace on earth, good will to men.

Additional Lyrics

3. And in despair I bow'd my head:
"There is no peace on earth," I said,
"For hate is strong, and mocks the song
Of peace on earth, good will to men."

4. Then pealed the bells more loud and deep:
"God is not dead, nor doth He sleep;
The wrong shall fail, the right prevail,
With peace on earth, good will to men."

5. Till, ringing, singing on its way,
The world revolved from night to day,
A voice, a chime, a chant sublime,
Of peace on earth, good will to men!

I LOVE YOU WITH ALL MY HEART

Moderately
I Love You With All My Heart, I do. Yes, I do. I've loved you right from the start. Oh, you're my sweet dream come true. I'll love you till death do us part. My love, I cher - ish you. Yes, I Love You With All My Heart. I do, I do.

I SAW THREE SHIPS

Spirited
I Saw Three Ships come sail - ing in, On Christ - mas Day, on Christ - mas Day; I Saw Three Ships come sail - ing in, On Christ - mas Day in the morn - ing. And
what was in those ships all three, On Christ - mas Day, on Christ - mas Day; And what was in those ships all three, On Christ - mas Day in the morn - ing. The
Vir - gin Mar - y and Christ were there, On Christ - mas Day, on Christ - mas Day; The Vir - gin Mar - y and Christ were there, On Christ - mas Day in the morn - ing.

IF YOU'RE HAPPY
(And You Know It)

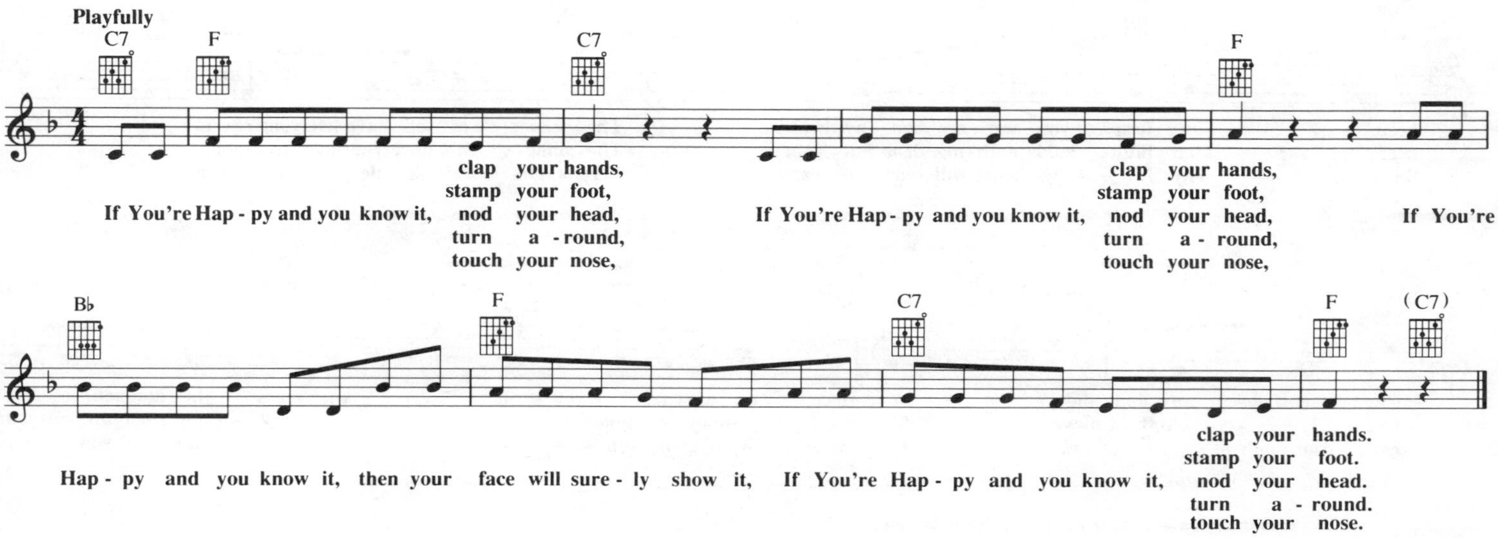
Playfully
If You're Hap - py and you know it, clap your hands, / stamp your foot, / nod your head, / turn a - round, / touch your nose,
If You're Hap - py and you know it, clap your hands, / stamp your foot, / nod your head, / turn a - round, / touch your nose,
If You're Hap - py and you know it, then your face will sure - ly show it, If You're Hap - py and you know it, clap your hands. / stamp your foot. / nod your head. / turn a - round. / touch your nose.

I WISH I WERE SINGLE AGAIN

By J.C. Beckel

Moderate Waltz
C F C D7 G7
I Wish I Were Sin - gle A - gain, I Wish I Were Sin - gle A - gain!
binged me, she banged me, oh then, She binged me, she banged me, oh then.
C C7 F Dm7 G7 C
Oh, when I was sin - gle my pock - ets would jin - gle, I Wish I Were Sin - gle A - gain!
She binged me, she banged me, she thought she would hang me, I Wish I Were Sin - gle A - gain!
C F C D7 G7
I mar - ried a wife, oh then, I mar - ried a wife oh then, I
She went for the rope oh then, She went for the rope oh then, She
C C7 F Dm7 G7 1 C 2 C
mar - ried a wife, she's ruin - ed my life, Oh I Wish I Were Sin - gle A - gain! She
went for the rope, but then it was broke, Oh I Wish I Were Sin - gle A - gain!

I'LL TAKE YOU HOME AGAIN, KATHLEEN

T.P. Westendorf

Slowly
F C7 Fdim F C7 F C7 Fdim
I'll Take You Home A - gain Kath - leen, A - cross the o - cean wild and wide, To where your heart has ev - er
I know you love me, Kath - leen dear, Your heart was ev - er fond and true; I al - ways feel when you are
To that dear home be - yond the sea, My Kath - leen shall a - gain re - turn, And when thy old friends wel - come
F C G7 C C7 F
been, Since first you were my bon - ny bride. The ros - es all have left your cheek, I've
near That life holds noth - ing dear but you. The smiles that once you gave to me, I
thee. Thy lov - ing heart will cease to yearn. Where laughs the lit - tle sil - ver stream, Be -
C7 F Dm B♭ Dm G7
watched them fade a - way and die; Your voice is sad when - e'er you speak And tears be - dim your lov - ing
scarce - ly ev - er see them now, Tho man - y, man - y times I see A dark - 'ning shad - ow on your
side your moth - er's hum - ble cot, And bright - est rays of sun - shine gleam, There all your grief will be for -

C F C7 Fdim F C7 F
eye.
brow.
got.
Oh, I will take you back Kath - leen, To where your heart will feel no pain. And
F7 B♭ Fdim F C7 F
when the fields are fresh and green, I'll take you to your home a - gain.

I'VE BEEN WORKING ON THE RAILROAD

With Vigor
F F7 B♭ F
I've Been Work - ing On The Rail - road, All the live - long day; I've Been Work - ing On The Rail - road, Just to
G7 C7 F B♭ A7
pass the time a - way. Can't you hear the whis - tle blow - in'? Rise up so ear - ly in the morn.
B♭ F C7 F B♭ G7
Can't you hear the cap- tain shout - in' "Di - nah, blow your horn!" Di - nah, won't you blow, Di - nah, won't you blow,
C7 F C7 F B♭ G7 C7
Di - nah won't you blow your horn? Di - nah, won't you blow, Di - nah, won't you blow, Di - nah won't you blow your
F C7 Gm C7
horn? Some - one's in the kitch - en with Di - nah, Some - one's in the kitch - en I know,
F B♭ Bdim7 F/C C7 F C7 F
Some - one's in the kitch - en with Di - nah, Strum - min' on the old ban - jo and sing - in', "Fee, fi, fid - dle - ee - i - o,
C7 Gm C7 F B♭ Bdim7 F/C C7 F
Fee, fi, fid - dle - ee - i - o, Fee, fi, fid - dle - ee - i - o," Strum - min' on the old ban - jo.

ICH LIEBE DICH
(I Love Thee)

Edvard Grieg

Moderately Slow
C G C#dim7 Dm A7 D9 Am7
Light of my life whose i - mage my heart hold - eth! Thou at whose feet I wor - ship and a - dore!
Du mein Ge - dan ke, du mein Sein und Wer - den! Du mei - nes Her - zens er - ste Se - lig - keit!
G7 C G C#dim7 Dm A7 D9
With wings of love my spir - it thee en - fold - eth, I love thee dear, I love thee dear, I
Ich lie - be dich wie nichts auf die - ser Er - den, ich lie - be dich, ich lie - be dich, ich
Dm7 Fm6 G C G7
love thee dear, now and for - ev - er - more! I love thee dear, now and for - ev - er - more!
lie - be dich in Zeit und E - wig - keit! Ich lie - be dich in Zeit und E - wig - keit!
C G C#dim7 Dm A7 D9 Am7 G7
I think of thee in dream - ing and in wak - ing, Thy per - fect bliss I set all else be - fore;
Ich den - ke dein, kann stets nur dei - ne den - ken, nur dei - nem Glück ist die - ses Herz ge - weiht;
C G C#dim7 Dm A7 D9 Dm9
Wher - ev - er fate my foot - steps may be tak - ing, I love thee dear, I love thee dear, I love thee dear, now and for -
wie Gott auch mag des Le - bens Schick - sal len - ken ich lie be dich, ich lie be dich, ich lie - be dich in Zeit und
Dm7 Fm6 G7 C G C#dim7 G7/D G7 C
ev - er - more. I love thee dear, now and for - ev - er - more!
E - wig - keit! Ich lie - be dich in Zeit und E - wig - keit!

IN OLD NEW YORK

Words by Henry Blossom; Music by Victor Herbert

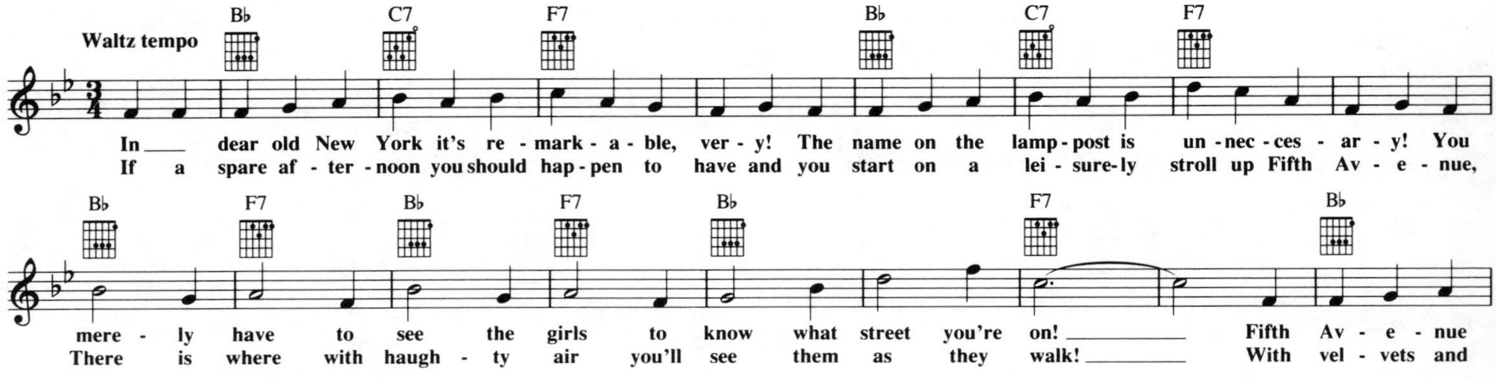
Waltz tempo
B♭ C7 F7 B♭ C7 F7
In ___ dear old New York it's re - mark - a - ble, ver - y! The name on the lamp - post is un - nec - ces - ar - y! You
If a spare af - ter - noon you should hap - pen to have and you start on a lei - sure - ly stroll up Fifth Av - e - nue,
B♭ F7 B♭ F7 B♭ F7 B♭
mere - ly have to see the girls to know what street you're on! ___ Fifth Av - e - nue
There is where with haugh - ty air you'll see them as they walk! ___ With vel - vets and

C7 F7 B♭ C7 F7 B♭
beau - ties and dear old Broad - way girls! The tail - or - made shop - pers, the Av - e - nue "A" girls, they're strict - ly all
la - ces and sa - bles en - fold - ing them, real - ly you'll near - ly fall dead on be - hold - ing them, luck - y's the
G7 Cm B♭ C7 F7
Chorus
B♭
right but they're dif - fer - ent quite in the dif - f'rent parts of town. In
earl that can mar - ry a girl from Fifth Av - e - nue, New York. In
Old New York, In
F7 B♭ F7 B♭ F Fdim
Old New York the peach crop's al - ways fine! They're sweet and fair and on the square! The
C7 F7 B♭ F7 B♭
maids of Man - hat - tan for mine! You can - not see in gay Pa - ree, in Lon - don
F7 B♭ B♭7 E♭ Edim B♭ F7 B♭
or in Cork! The queens you'll meet on an - y street In Old New York.

IL BACIO
(The Kiss)

Luigi Arditi

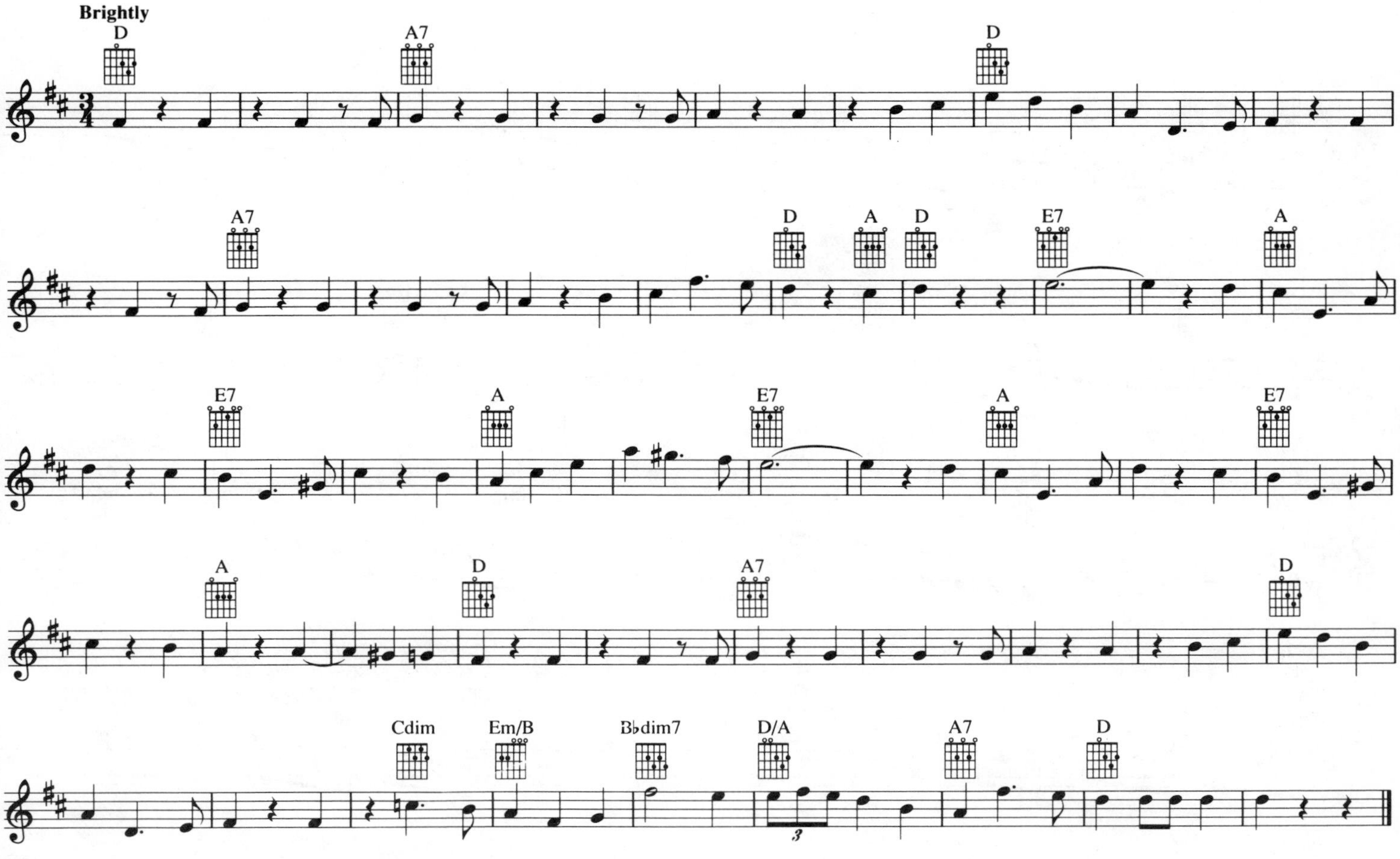
Brightly
D A7 D
A7 D A D E7 A
E7 A E7 A E7
A D A7 D
Cdim Em/B B♭dim7 D/A A7 D

IN THE EVENING BY THE MOONLIGHT

By James A. Bland

Moderately
F A7 Dm F7 B♭ B♭m F
In The Eve - ning By The Moon - light you could hear those young folks sing - in', In The
A7 Dm G7 C7 F Fmaj7
Eve - nin' By The Moon - light, you can hear those ban - joes ring - in', How the old folks would en -
F7 B♭ B♭m F D7 G7 C7 F
joy it, they would sit all night and lis - ten, As we sang In The Eve - ning By The Moon - light.

IN THE HALL OF THE MOUNTAIN KING

Edvard Grieg

Moderate March
Bm C#/B C/B Bm D Bm
C#/B C/B Bm D F# D+ F#
D+ F# D+ F# D+ F# Bm
C#/B C/B Bm D Bm C#/B C/B
Bm Bdim G Bm F#7 Bm

IN THE GOOD OLD SUMMERTIME

Words by Ren Shields; Music by George Evans

Moderate Waltz
B♭ C#dim7 F7
1. There's a time in each year that we al - ways hold dear, Good old sum - mer - time, With the
2. To swim in the pool you'd play "hook - ey" from school, Good old sum - mer - time, You'd
B♭ F C7 F7 B♭
birds and the trees and sweet scent - ed breez - es, Good old sum - mer - time, When your day's work is
play "ring a - ros - ie" with Jim, Kate and Jo - sie, Good old sum - mer - time, Those days full of
E♭ B♭ E♭
o - ver then you are in clo - ver, and life is one beau - ti - ful rhyme, No trou - ble an -
pleas - ure we now fond - ly treas - ure, when we nev - er thought it a crime To go steal - ing
B♭ E♭ C#dim7 B♭ G7♭5 F C7 F7 B♭
noy - ing, each one is en - joy - ing, The good old sum - mer - time.
cher - ries, with face brown as ber - ries, Good old sum - mer - time.
In The Good Old Sum - mer -
B♭7 E♭ B♭ G#dim7 F7 B♭ D7 Gm
time, In The Good Old Sum - mer - time, Stroll - ing thro' the shad - y lanes
C7 F7 B♭ B♭7 E♭
with your ba - by mine; You hold her hand and she holds yours, and that's a ver - y good
B♭ C#dim7 F7 B♭ D7 Gm B♭ C7 F7 B♭
sign That she's your toot - sey woot - sey In The Good Old Sum - mer - time.

IRISH WASHERWOMAN

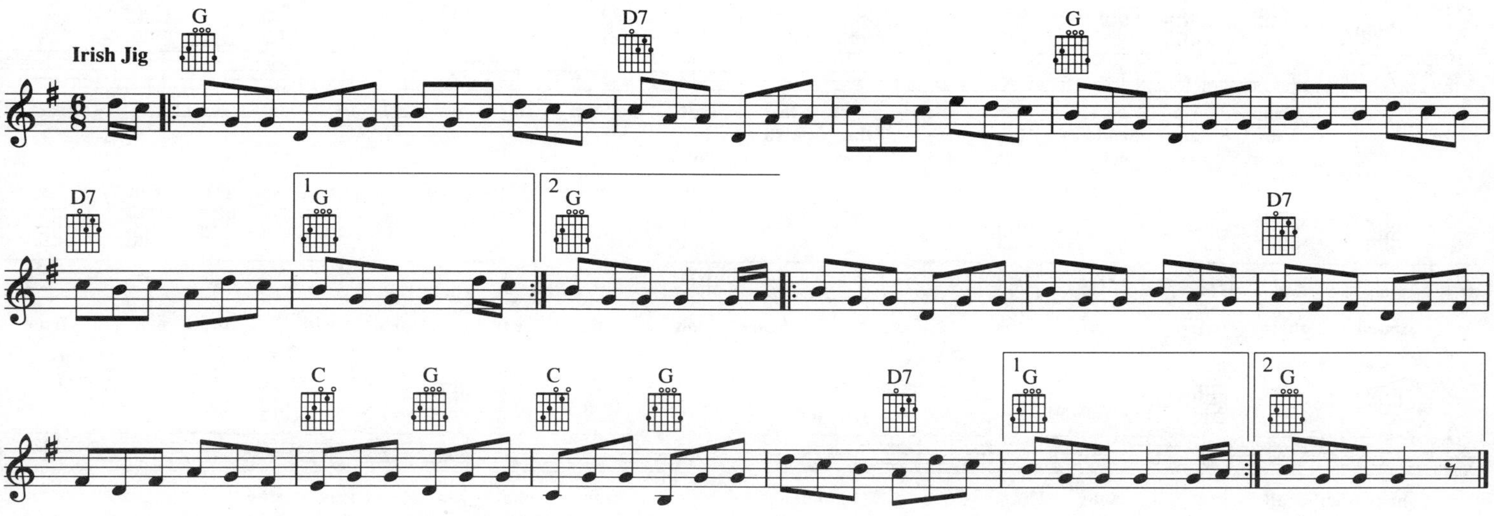
Irish Jig
G D7 G
D7 1 G 2 G D7
C G C G D7 1 G 2 G

IN THE SWEET BYE AND BYE

Words by S.F. Bennett; Music by J.P. Webster

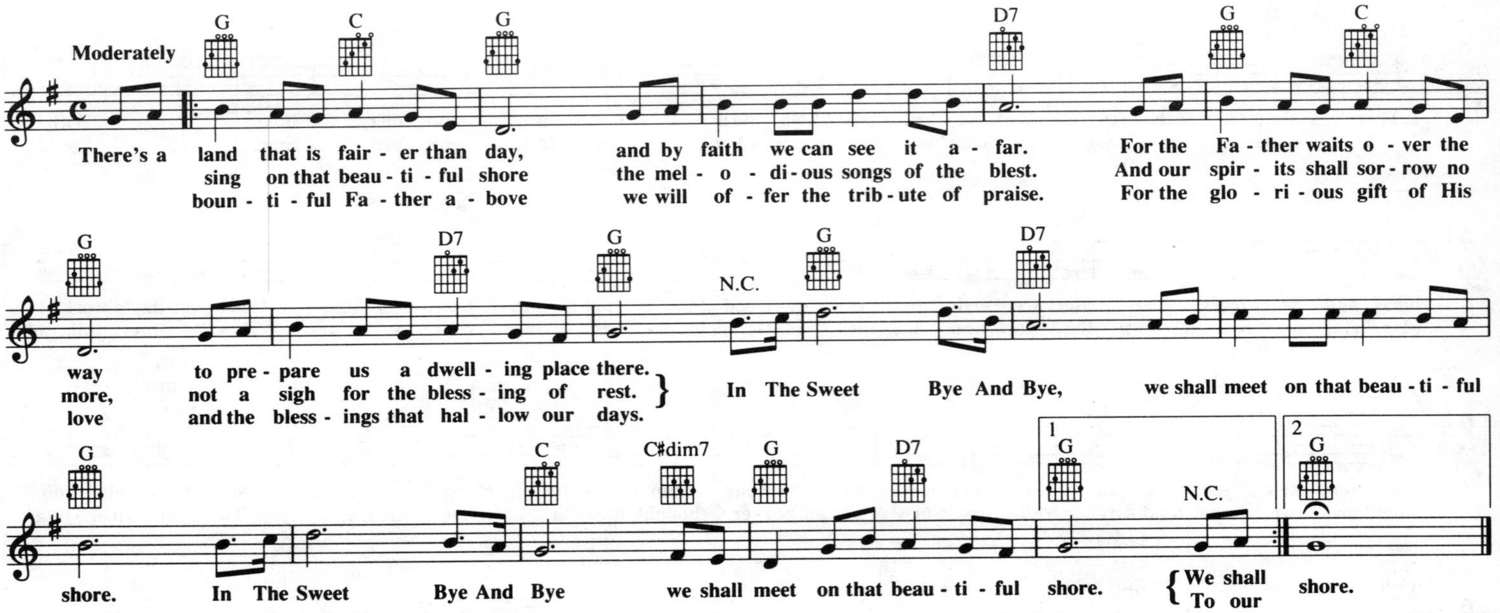
Moderately
G C G D7 G C
There's a land that is fair - er than day, and by faith we can see it a - far. For the Fa - ther waits o - ver the
sing on that beau - ti - ful shore the mel - o - di - ous songs of the blest. And our spir - its shall sor - row no
boun - ti - ful Fa - ther a - bove we will of - fer the trib - ute of praise. For the glo - ri - ous gift of His
G D7 G N.C. G D7
way to pre - pare us a dwell - ing place there.
more, not a sigh for the bless - ing of rest.
love and the bless - ings that hal - low our days.
In The Sweet Bye And Bye, we shall meet on that beau - ti - ful
G C C#dim7 G D7 1 G N.C. 2 G
shore. In The Sweet Bye And Bye we shall meet on that beau - ti - ful shore. We shall / To our shore.

IT AIN'T GONNA RAIN NO MO'

Bouncy
G D7
It Ain't Gon - na Rain No Mo', no mo' It Ain't Gon - na Rain No Mo'.
G
How in the heck will we wash the neck if It Ain't Gon - na Rain No Mo', no mo'?

IT CAME UPON THE MIDNIGHT CLEAR

E.H. Sears/R.S. Willis

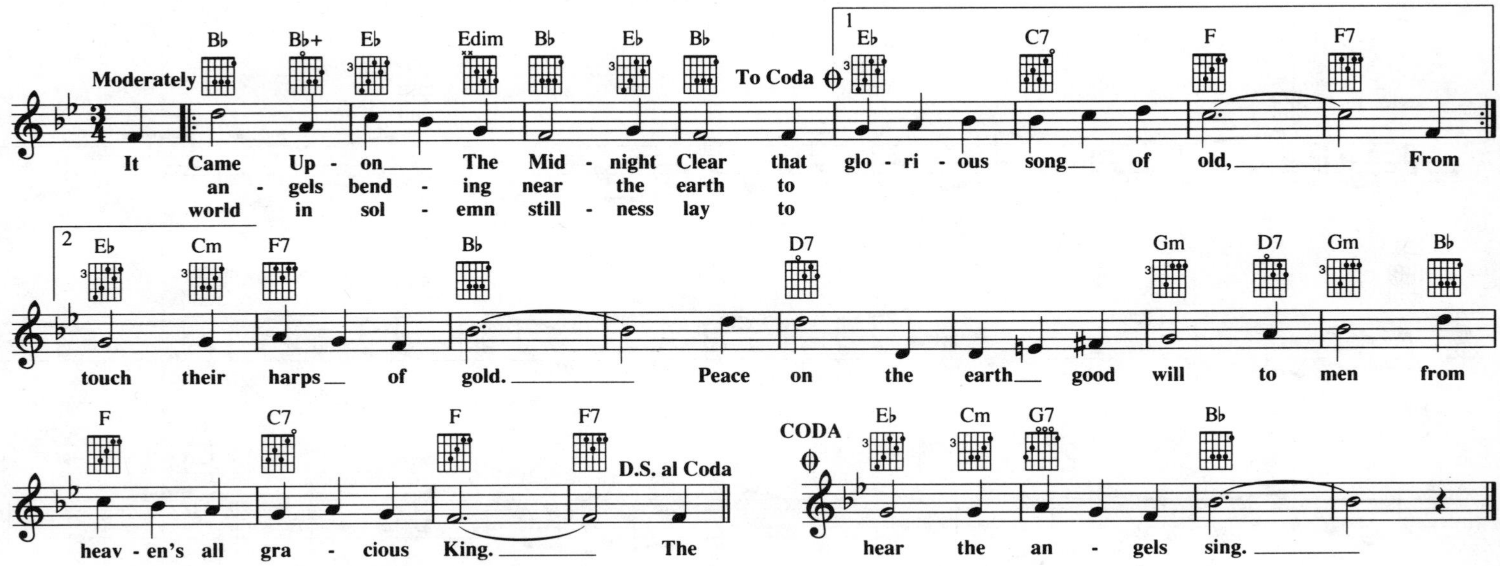
Moderately
B♭ B♭+ E♭ Edim B♭ E♭ B♭ To Coda 1 E♭ C7 F F7
It Came Up - on The Mid - night Clear that glo - ri - ous song of old, From
an - gels bend - ing near the earth to
world in sol - emn still - ness lay to
2 E♭ Cm F7 B♭ D7 Gm D7 Gm B♭
touch their harps of gold. Peace on the earth good will to men from
F C7 F F7 D.S. al Coda
heav - en's all gra - cious King. The
CODA E♭ Cm G7 B♭
hear the an - gels sing.

IT'S RAINING, IT'S POURING

Moderately
C
It's Rain - ing, It's Pour - ing, The old man is snor - ing. He
G7
C
went to bed and he bumped his head and he could not get up in the morn - ing.

ITALIAN STREET SONG

Lyric by Rida Johnson Young; Music by Victor Herbert

Moderate Waltz
D A D
Ah! my heart is back in Na - po - li, Dear Na - po - li, dear Na - po - li, and I seem to hear a -
A B7 E7 A E7 A
gain in dreams her re - vel - ry, her sweet re - vel - ry The man - do - li - nas play - ing sweet, the
D A Em7 A Em7 A7 Adim
pleas - ant fall of dan - cing feet, Oh! could I re - turn oh! joy com - plete! Na - po - li, Na - po - li,
A7
Moderately Fast
D
Na - po - li! Zing, zing, ziz-zy, ziz-zy, zing, zing, Boom, boom, aye. Zing, zing, ziz-zy, ziz-zy, zing, zing,
A7 Bm G Em Bm E
Man - do - lin - as gay. Zing, zing, ziz - zy, ziz - zy, zing, zing, Boom, boom, aye, La, la, la,
D E A D Em Bm E7 A7 D
Ha, ha, ha, Zing, boom aye. La, la, la, la, ha, ha, ha, zing, zing, aye.

INVITATION TO THE DANCE

By C.M. von Weber

C
G7
C
G7
C
F
E+
F
Cdim
To Coda
G
C
Am
D7
G
G7
Gdim
G7
C
C
Cm
G7
Cm
G7
D7
G
D7
G
D.S. al Coda
CODA
C
G7
C

IT'S A LONG, LONG WAY TO TIPPERARY

Words & Music by Jack Judge and Harry Williams

JESU, JOY OF MAN'S DESIRING

J.S. Bach

JACK AND JILL

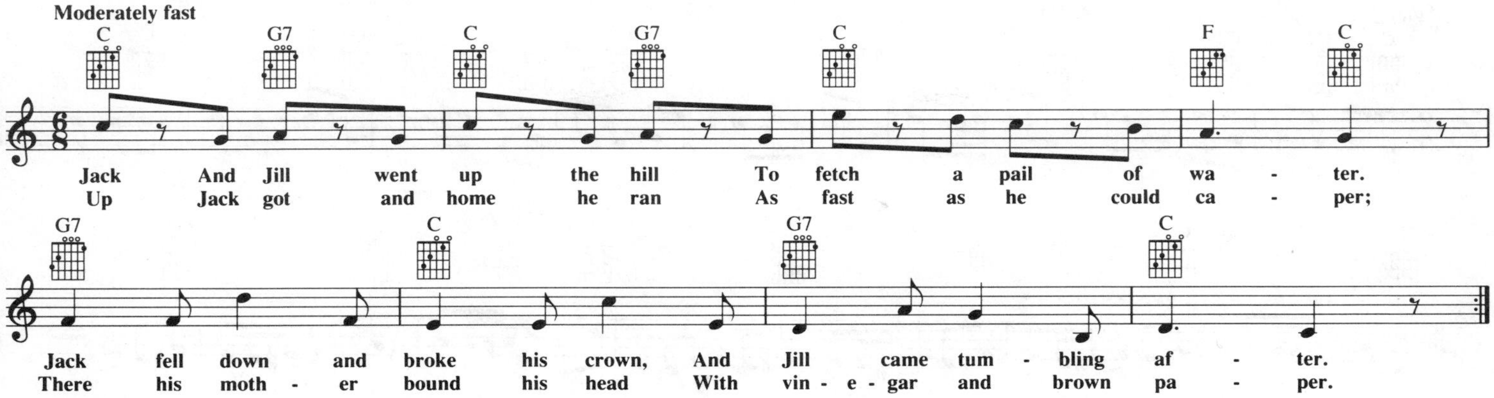
Moderately fast
C G7 C G7 C F C
Jack And Jill went up the hill To fetch a pail of wa - ter.
Up Jack got and home he ran As fast as he could ca - per;
G7 C G7 C
Jack fell down and broke his crown, And Jill came tum - bling af - ter.
There his moth - er bound his head With vin - e - gar and brown pa - per.

JEANIE WITH THE LIGHT BROWN HAIR

By Stephen C. Foster

Moderately
B♭ F Fdim F Dm B♭
1. I dream of Jean - ie With The Light Brown_ Hair, Borne, like a va - por
2. I sigh for Jean - ie, but her light form_ strayed far from the fond hearts
3. (See additional lyrics)
F G7 C7 B♭ F Fdim F
on the sum - mer air; I see her trip - ping where the bright streams_ play,
round her na - tive glade, Her smiles have van - ished and her sweet songs_ flown,
C F C G7 C C7
Hap - py as the dai - sies that dance on her way. Man - y were the wild notes her
Flit - ting like the dreams_ that have cheered us and gone. Now the nod - ding wild flow'rs may
F B♭ F A7 Dm G C B♭
mer - ry voice would pour, Man - y were the blithe birds that war - bled them o'er: I
with - er on the shore, While her gen - tle fin - gers will cull them no more; I
F Fdim Dm B♭ F B♭ F C7 F
dream of Jean - ie With The Light Brown_ Hair, Float - ing like a va - por on the soft, sum - mer air.
sigh for Jean - ie With The Light Brown_ Hair, Float - ing like a va - por on the soft, sum - mer air.

Additional Lyrics

2. I long for Jeanie with the day-dawn smile,
Radiant in gladness, warm with winning guile;
I hear her melodies, like joys gone by,
Sighing round my heart o'er the fond hopes that die;
Sighing like the night wind and sobbing like the rain,
Waiting for the lost one that comes not again;
Ah! I long for Jeanie and my heart bows low,
Never more to find her where the bright waters flow.

JENNY LIND POLKA

Polka
C G7 C G7 C G7 C G7 C
F C G7 C F C G7
8va
C G7 C G7 C G7 C G7 C
F C7 F C7 F
C Dm G7 C Dm G7 C
F C7 F C7 F

JESUS LOVES ME!

Moderately
F B♭ F B♭ F C7 F
Je - sus Loves Me! This I know, For the Bi - ble tells me so; Lit - tle ones to Him be - long, they are weak, but He is strong.
Je - sus from His throne on high, come in - to this world to die; That I might from sin be free, Bled and died up - on the tree.
B♭ F C7 F B♭ F C7 F
Yes, Je - sus Loves Me! Yes, Je - sus Loves Me! Yes, Je - sus Loves Me! The Bi - ble tells me so.

JOHN PEEL

J. Pierpont

Bright 2
G C Am D7
Dash - ing through the snow, in a one horse o - pen sleigh, O're the fields we go
day or two a - go I thought I'd take a ride; And soon Miss Fan - nie Bright was
Now the ground is white go it while you're young. Take the girls to - night And
G C
Laugh - ing all the way. Bells on bob - tail ring, Mak - ing spir - its bright, What
seat - ed by my side. The horse was lean and lank, Mis - for - tune seemed his lot, He
sing this sleigh - ing song. Just get a bob - tail bay, Two - for - ty for his speed, Then
Am G/D D7 G D7 G
fun it is to ride and sing a sleigh - ing song to - night! Oh!
got in - to a drift - ed bank and we, we got up - sot! Oh!
hitch him to an o - pen sleigh and crack! you'll take the lead! Oh!
Jin - gle Bells, Jin - gle Bells, jin - gle all the
G7 C G A7 D7 G
way. Oh what fun it is to ride in a one horse o - pen sleigh! Jin - gle Bells, Jin - gle Bells,
C G D7 G
Jin - gle all the way. Oh what fun it is to ride in a one horse o - pen sleigh! A

JOHN JACOB JINGLEHEIMER SCHMIDT

Brisk 4
F B♭ Gm7 C7 F
John Ja - cob Jin - gle - hei - mer Schmidt, His name is my name too. When - ev - er we go out And
B♭ C7 F N.C.
peo - ple al - ways shout, "John Ja - cob Jin - gle - hei - mer Schmidt." Dah dah dah dah, dah dah dah.
D.C.

JINGLE BELLS

Words by J.W. Graves

Moderately
Eb Bb7 Eb Ab Eb Fm7 Bb7 Eb
Do you know John Peel with his coat so gay, Do you know John Peel at the break of day, Do you know John Peel when he's far, far a - way, With his hounds and his horn in the morn - ing? } For the
Do you know John Peel with his coat so gay? He___ lived at Trout - beck ___ once on a day; But___ now he has gone far a - way, far a - way, We shall ne'er hear his voice in the morn - ing.
sound of his horn brought me from my bed, And the cry of the hounds which he oft - times led; For Peel's view hal - loo would___ awak - en the dead, or the fox from his lair in the morn - ing.

JOHN BROWN'S BODY

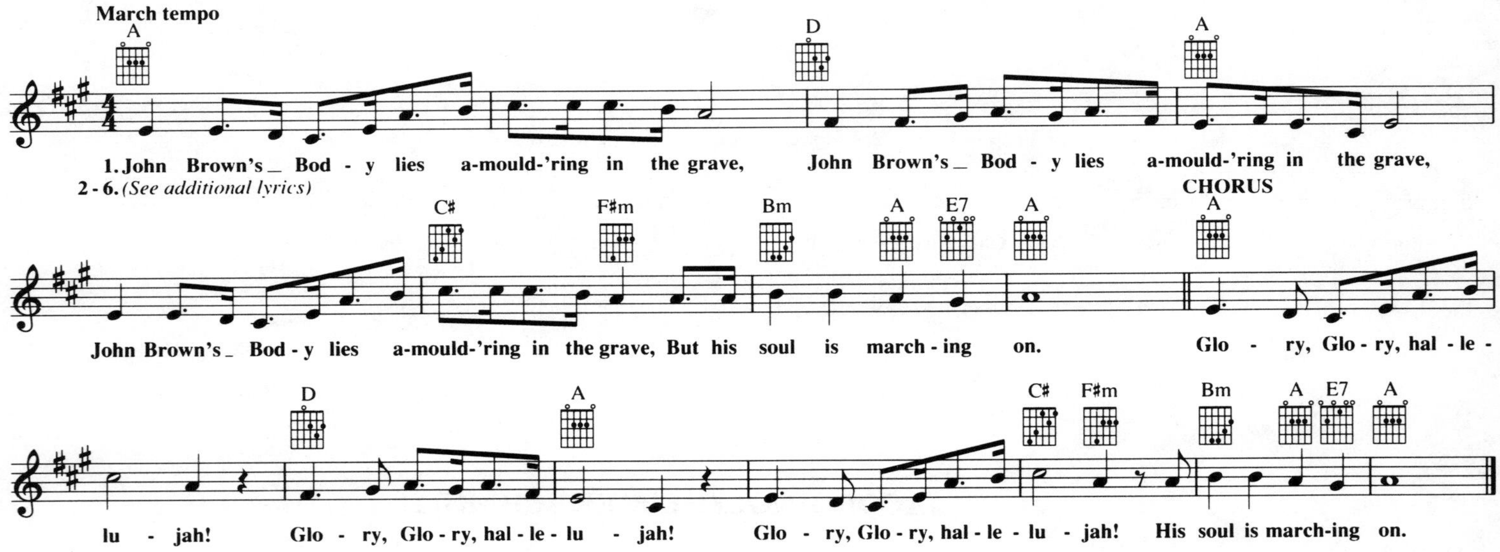
March tempo
A D A C# F#m Bm A E7 A
1. John Brown's_ Bod - y lies a-mould-'ring in the grave, John Brown's_ Bod - y lies a-mould-'ring in the grave,
2 - 6. (See additional lyrics)
John Brown's_ Bod - y lies a-mould-'ring in the grave, But his soul is march - ing on.
CHORUS
Glo - ry, Glo - ry, hal - le - lu - jah! Glo - ry, Glo - ry, hal - le - lu - jah! Glo - ry, Glo - ry, hal - le - lu - jah! His soul is march-ing on.

Additional Lyrics

**2. The stars of Heaven are looking kindly down, (etc.)
On the grave of old John Brown.**

**3. He's gone to be a soldier in the army of the Lord! (etc.)
His soul is marching on.**

**4. John Brown's knapsack is strapped upon his back, (etc.)
His soul is marching on.**

**5. His pet lambs will meet him on the way, (etc.)
And they'll go marching on.**

**6. They'll hang Jeff Davis to a sour-apple tree (etc.)
As they march along.**

JOHN HENRY

D
D7
A7
1. Well, ev - 'ry Mon - day morn - ing, When the blue - birds be - gin to sing,
2 - 7. (See additional lyrics)
D
G7
D
You can see John Hen - ry out on the line, You can hear John Hen - ry's ham - mer
1
2
ring, Lord, Lord, You can hear John Hen - ry's ham - mer ring. You can ring.

Additional Lyrics

2. When John Henry was a little baby,
A-sitting on his papa's knee,
He picked up a hammer and a little piece of steel,
Said, "Hammer's gonna be the death of me"...

3. Well, the captain said to John Henry,
"Gonna bring me a steam drill 'round,
Gonna bring me a steam drill out on the job,
Gonna whup that steel on down"...

4. John Henry said to his captain,
"A man ain't nothin' but a man,
And before I let that steam drill beat me down,
I'll die with a hammer in my hand"...

5. John Henry said to his shaker,
"Shaker, why don't you pray?
'Cause if I miss this little piece of steel,
Tomorrow be your buryin' day...

6. John Henry was driving on the mountain
And his hammer was flashing fire.
And the last words I heard that poor boy say,
"Gimme a cool drink of water 'fore I die"...

7. John Henry, he dorve fifteen feet,
The steam drill only made nine.
But he hammered so hard that he broke his poor heart,
And he laid down his hammer and he died...

8. The took John Henry to the graveyard
And they buried him in the sand.
And every locomotive comes a-roaring by says,
"There lies a steel-driving man"...

JOHNNY HAS GONE FOR A SOLDIER

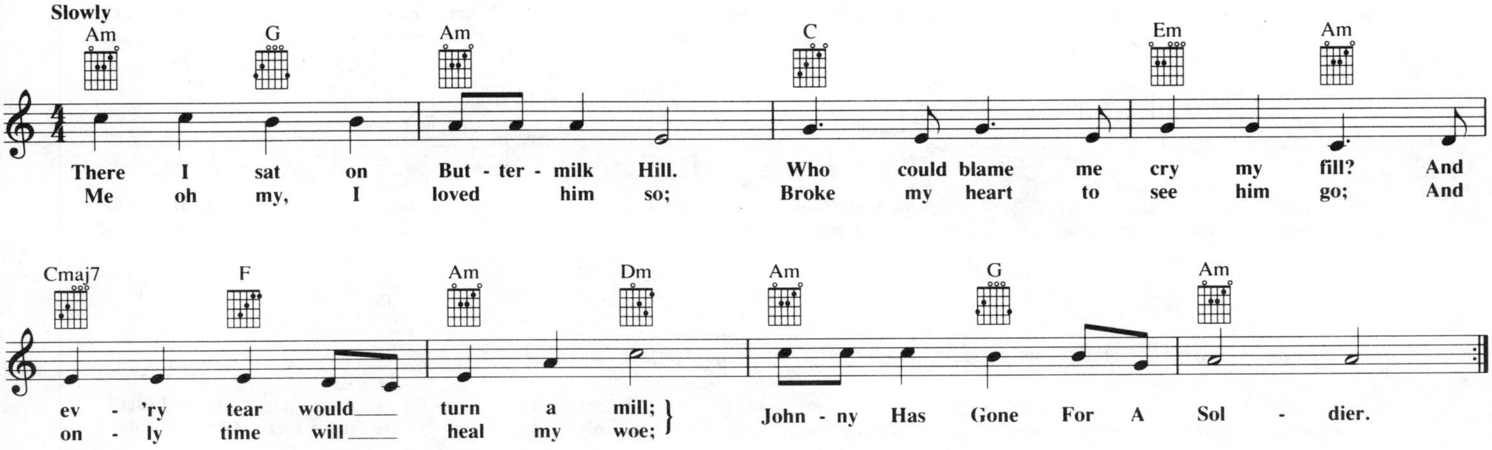
Slowly
Am
G
Am
C
Em
Am
There I sat on But - ter - milk Hill. Who could blame me cry my fill? And
Me oh my, I loved him so; Broke my heart to see him go; And
Cmaj7
F
Am
Dm
Am
G
Am
ev - 'ry tear would turn a mill;
on - ly time will heal my woe;
John - ny Has Gone For A Sol - dier.

JOY TO THE WORLD

G.F. Handel

Brightly
D G D Em D A7 D G A D
1. Joy To The World! The Lord is come; Let earth re - ceive her King;
2. Joy To The World! The Sav - ior reigns; Let men their songs em - ploy;
3 - 4. (See additional lyrics)
Let ev - 'ry heart pre - pare Him room. And heav'n and na - ture sing. And
while fields and floods, rocks, hills and plains, Re - peat the sound - ing joy. Re -
A A7 D G D Em D A7 D
heav'n and na - ture sing. And heav'n and heav'n and na - ture sing.
peat the sound - ing joy. Re - peat, re - peat the sound - ing joy.

Additional Lyrics

3. No more let sin and sorrow grow,
Nor thorns infest the ground,
He comes to make His blessings flow
Far as the curse is found,
Far as the curse is found,
Far as, far as the curse is found.

4. He rules the world with truth and grace,
And makes the nations prove
The glories of His righteousness,
And wonders of His love,
And wonders of His love,
And wonders, and wonders of His love.

JUANITA

Mrs. Norton

Moderately
D A D E7
Soft o'er the foun - tain, ling - 'ring falls the south - ern moon, Far o'er the moun - tain
When in thy dream - ing, moons like these shall shine a - gain, And day - light beam - ing
A D G A D
Breaks the day too soon! In thy dark eyes splen - dor Where the warm light loves to dwell,
Prove thy dreams are vain, Wilt thou not re - lent - ing, For thine ab - sent lov - er sigh,
G A D D#dim7 A7/E
Wear - y looks yet ten - der, Speak their fond fare - well. Ni - ta! Jua - ni - ta!
In thy heart con - sent - ing To a pray'r gone by? Ni - ta! Jua - ni - ta!
A7 D D#dim7 A7/E A7 D
Ask thy soul if we should part! Ni - ta! Jua - ni - ta! Lean thou on my heart.
Let me lin - ger by thy side! Ni - ta! Jua - ni - ta! Be my own fair bride.

JOLLY OLD ST. NICHOLAS

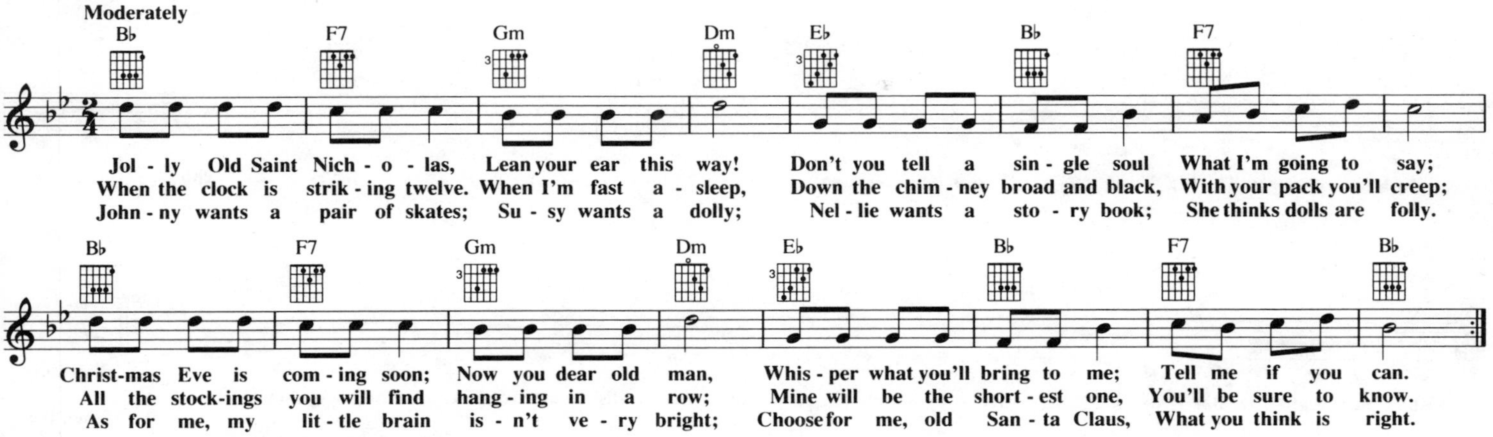
Moderately
B♭ F7 Gm Dm E♭ B♭ F7
Jol - ly Old Saint Nich - o - las, Lean your ear this way! Don't you tell a sin - gle soul What I'm going to say;
When the clock is strik - ing twelve. When I'm fast a - sleep, Down the chim - ney broad and black, With your pack you'll creep;
John - ny wants a pair of skates; Su - sy wants a dolly; Nel - lie wants a sto - ry book; She thinks dolls are folly.
B♭ F7 Gm Dm E♭ B♭ F7 B♭
Christ-mas Eve is com - ing soon; Now you dear old man, Whis - per what you'll bring to me; Tell me if you can.
All the stock-ings you will find hang - ing in a row; Mine will be the short - est one, You'll be sure to know.
As for me, my lit - tle brain is - n't ve - ry bright; Choose for me, old San - ta Claus, What you think is right.

JUST A CLOSER WALK WITH THEE

K. Morris

Slowly
C E♭dim7 Dm7 G7 Dm7 G7 C C7 F E♭dim7
I am weak, but thou art strong, Je - sus, keep me from all wrong, I'll be sat - is - fied as long As I
C G7 C E♭dim7 Dm7 G7 Dm7 G7 C
walk, let me walk close to Thee. Just A Clo - ser Walk With Thee, Grant it Je - sus is my plea,
C7 F F♯dim7 C G7 C E♭dim7 C G7 C
Dai - ly walk - ing close to Thee Let it be, dear Lord, let it be. Let it be, dear Lord, let it be.

KUM-BAH-YAH

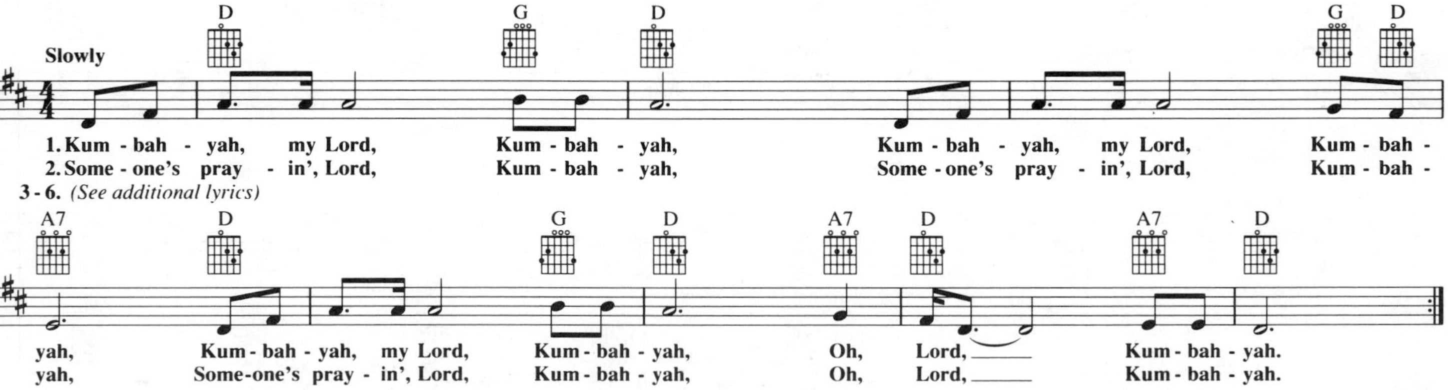
Slowly
D G D G D
1. Kum - bah - yah, my Lord, Kum - bah - yah, Kum - bah - yah, my Lord, Kum - bah -
2. Some - one's pray - in', Lord, Kum - bah - yah, Some - one's pray - in', Lord, Kum - bah -
3 - 6. (See additional lyrics)
A7 D G D A7 D A7 D
yah, Kum - bah - yah, my Lord, Kum - bah - yah, Oh, Lord, Kum - bah - yah.
yah, Some - one's pray - in', Lord, Kum - bah - yah, Oh, Lord, Kum - bah - yah.

Additional Lyrics

3. Someone's singin', Lord, Kum-bah-yah. . .
4. Someone's crying', Lord, Kum-bah-yah. . .
5. Someone's dancin', Lord, Kum-bah-yah. . .
6. Someone's shoutin', Lord, Kum-bah-yah. . .

JOSHUA FOUGHT THE BATTLE OF JERICHO

Spirited
Am
E7
Am
Josh - ua Fought The Bat - tle Of Jer - i - cho, Jer - i - cho, Jer - i - cho,
Josh - ua Fought The Bat - tle Of Jer - i - cho, And the walls came a - tum - blin' down.
Fine
You may talk a - bout your King of Gid - e - on, You may talk a - bout your men of Saul, But there's none like good old Josh - ua, At the bat - tle of Jer - i - cho.
Then the Up to the walls of Gid - e - on, They marched with spear in hand, "Go blow those ram horns," Joshua cried, "Cause the bat - tle is in my hand."
might - y horns be - gin to blow, The trum - pets be - gin to sound, Joshua commanded the children to shout, And the walls came a - tum - blin' down. Oh,
Oh,
1,2
3
D.C. al Fine

JULIDA POLKA

A. Grill

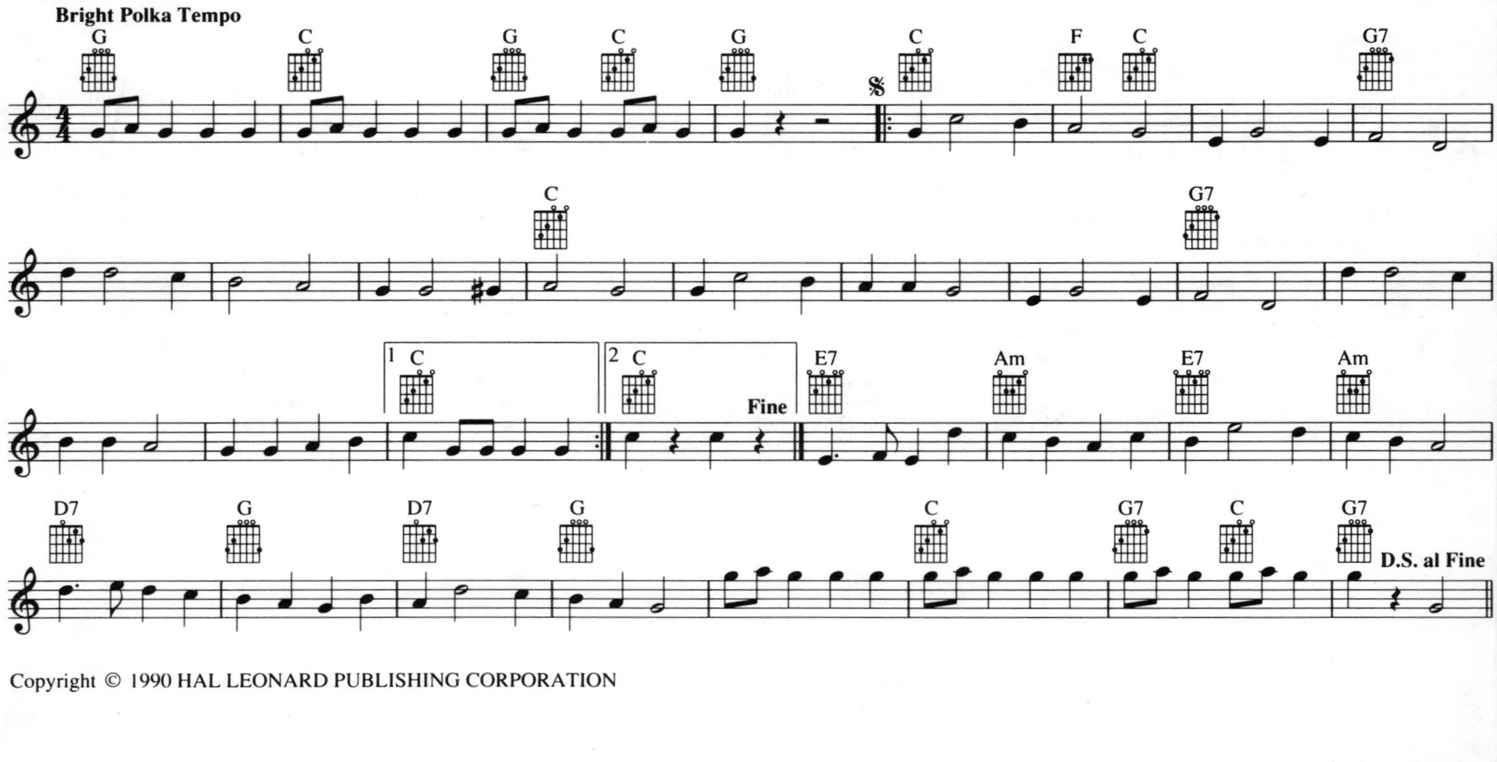
Bright Polka Tempo
G C G C G C F C G7
C G7
1 C
2 C
Fine
E7 Am E7 Am
D7 G D7 G C G7 C G7
D.S. al Fine

JUST A SONG AT TWILIGHT

Words by J. Clifton Bingham
Music by James L. Molloy

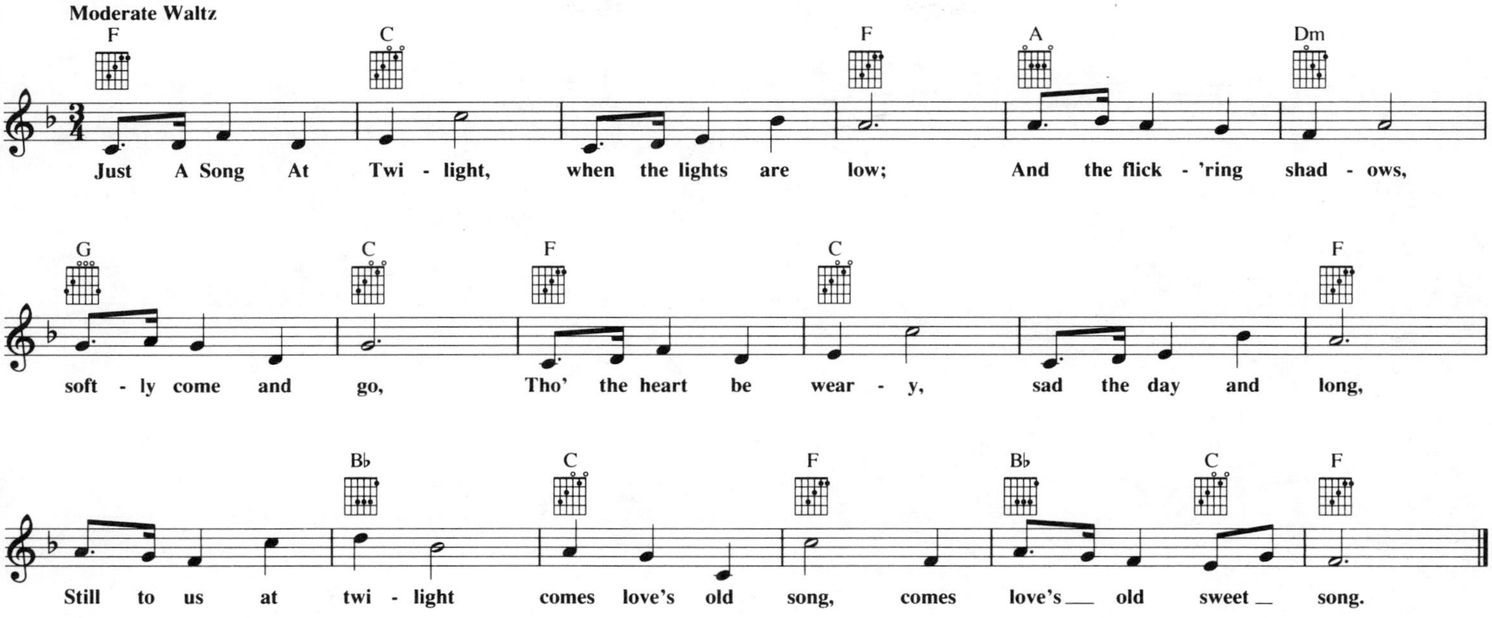
Moderate Waltz
F C F A Dm
Just A Song At Twi - light, when the lights are low; And the flick - 'ring shad - ows,
G C F C F
soft - ly come and go, Tho' the heart be wear - y, sad the day and long,
B♭ C F B♭ C F
Still to us at twi - light comes love's old song, comes love's old sweet song.

THE KERRY DANCE

J. L. Molloy

Brightly
F B♭ F G C7 F
O the days of the Ker - ry danc - ing, O the ring of the pi - per's tune! O for one of those
B♭ F C7 F C Am C Am
Fine
hours of glad - ness, Gone a - las! like our youth, too soon; When the boys be - gan to gath - er
C Am D7 G7 C C7 Cdim7 Fm6 C
in the glen, of a sum - mer night, And the Ker - ry pi - per's tun - ing made us long with
G7 C B♭ Am B♭ Gm7 C7
D.C. al Fine
wild de - light; O, to think of it, O to dream of it, Fills my heart with tears.

KING COTTON

John Philip Sousa

KOOKABURRA

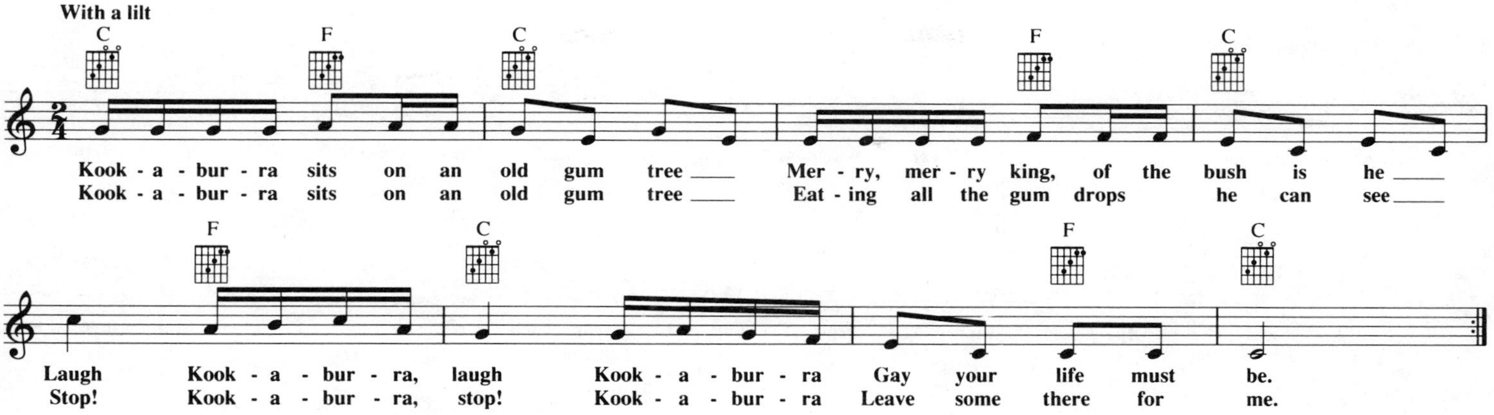
With a lilt
C F C F C
Kook - a - bur - ra sits on an old gum tree ___ Mer - ry, mer - ry king, of the bush is he ___
Kook - a - bur - ra sits on an old gum tree ___ Eat - ing all the gum drops he can see ___
F C F C
Laugh Kook - a - bur - ra, laugh Kook - a - bur - ra Gay your life must be.
Stop! Kook - a - bur - ra, stop! Kook - a - bur - ra Leave some there for me.

LA CUCARACHA

Bright Rhumba
Verse
G D7 G D7 G D7 G
Chorus

LA DONNA È MOBILE

Giuseppe Verdi

Brightly
Ab Eb Ab Eb
La Don - na è Mo - bi - le qual piu ma al ven - to mu - ta - d'ac - cen - to
ma - bi - le leg - gia - dro vi - so, in pian to o in ri - so
Eb7 Ab 1 2 Bb7 Eb C7
e di pen - sie - ro. Sem - pre un a -
è men - zo - gne - ro. La ___ don - na è mo - bil qual ___ piu - ma al
Fm Eb7 Ab Db6 Ab Eb7 Ab
ven - to mu - ta d'ac - cen - to e ___ di pen - sier.

LA GOLONDRINA

N. Serradell

Slow Waltz
A - cross the sky, A swal - low pass - es by. I hear a song. A love - ly tune.
A mel - o - dy of June. How I long to wear such wings. I too would love to
fly, Like those love - ly things. A - bove the clouds on high. The swal - low
knows of a nest in the branch of a tree, Where its mate is wait - ing,
Sing - ing a sweet mel - o - dy. A - cross the sky, They to - geth - er will fly,
While the song they sing Pours glad - ness in - to Spring.

LA MARSEILLAISE

Resolutely
A - rise, ye sons of France, to glo - ry! Your day of free - dom bids you rise! Your chil - dren,
fants de la Pa - tri - e! Le jour de gloire est ar - ri - vé! Con - tre
wives and grand - sires hoar - y, Be - hold their tears and hear their cries, Be - hold their tears and hear their
nous de la ty - ran - ni - e, L'é - ten - dard san - glant est le - vé! L'é - ten - dard san - glant est le -
cries! Shall hate - ful ty - rants mis - cheif breed - ing With hire - ling host, a ruf - flan band, Af -
vé! En - ten - dez - vous dans les cam - pagn - es Mu - gir ces fé - ro - ces sol - dats? Ils

Gm D D7 Gm D G
fright and des - o - late the land While peace and lib - er - ty lie bleed - ing? To arms, you sons of
vien - nent jus - que dans nos bras; E - gor - ger nos fils, nos com - pagn - es. Aux ar mes, ci - toy -
D G D G D G C G C#dim
France! To arms, your ranks ad - vance! March on! March on! all hearts re -
ens! For - mez vos ba - tail - lons! Mar - chons! Mar - chons! Qu'un Sang im -
D D9 G D7 1 G 2 G
solved On lib - er - ty or death! Al - lons, en -
pur, A - breu - ve nos sil - lons!

LA PALOMA

S. Yradier

Medium Tango
N.C.

LARGO
(From The "NEW WORLD SYMPHONY")

Anton Dvorak

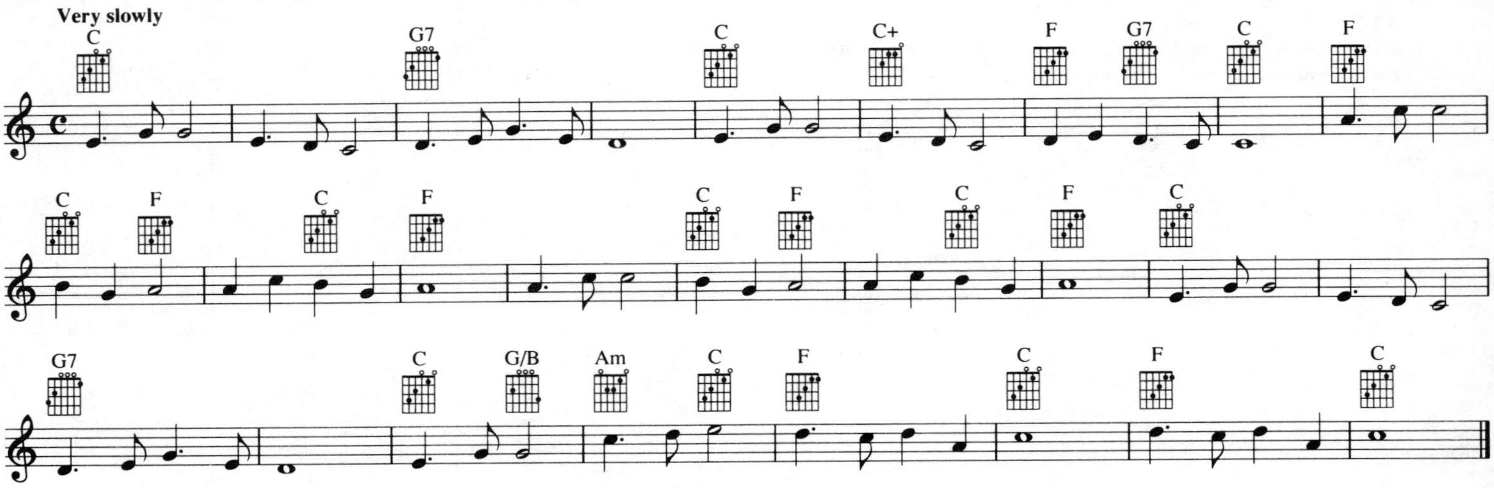
Very slowly
C G7 C C+ F G7 C F
C F C F C F C F C
G7 C G/B Am C F C F C

LAVENDER'S BLUE

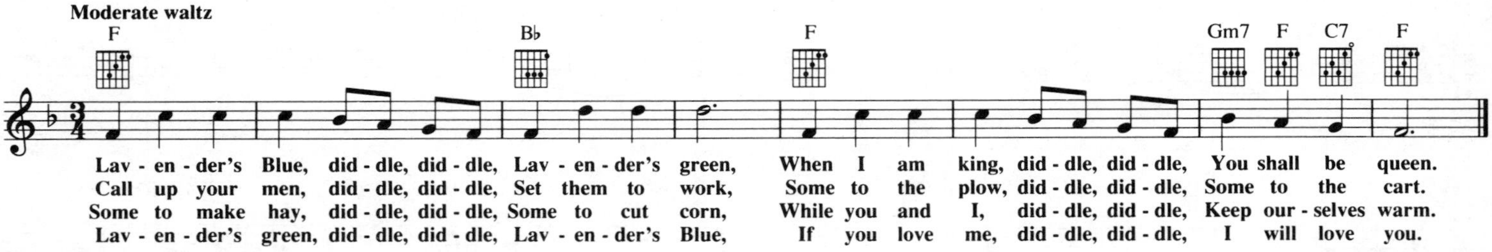
Moderate waltz
F Bb F Gm7 F C7 F
Lav - en - der's Blue, did - dle, did - dle, Lav - en - der's green, When I am king, did - dle, did - dle, You shall be queen.
Call up your men, did - dle, did - dle, Set them to work, Some to the plow, did - dle, did - dle, Some to the cart.
Some to make hay, did - dle, did - dle, Some to cut corn, While you and I, did - dle, did - dle, Keep our - selves warm.
Lav - en - der's green, did - dle, did - dle, Lav - en - der's Blue, If you love me, did - dle, did - dle, I will love you.

LET ME CALL YOU SWEETHEART

Words by Beth Slater Whitson
Music by Leo Friedman

Slowly
Bb Bbdim Bb Eb G7 C7 F7
Let Me Call You Sweet - heart, I'm in love with you
Let me hear you
Cm7 F7 Bb Bdim F7 Bb Bbdim Bb Eb
whis - per that you love me, too
Keep the love - light glow - ing in your eyes
G7 C7 Eb Edim Bb/F G7 C7 F7 Bb
so true
Let Me Call You Sweet - heart, I'm in love with you.

LAS MAÑANITAS

Moderato
B♭ F B♭ E♭ B♭ F
Es - tas son Las Ma - ña - ni - tas Que can - ta ba el rey Da - vid A las mu - cha - chas bo - ni - tas, Te las can -
B♭ E♭ F B♭ F B♭ E♭ B♭
ta - mos a ti. Es - tas son Las Ma - ña - ni - tas Que can - ta - ba el rey Da - vid, Qué can - ció - nes tan bo -
F B♭ E♭ F B♭ F7 B♭ F7
ni - tas, Las que can - ta - mos a - qui. Des - pier - ta, mi bien, des - pier - ta Por - que ya a - ma - ne -
B♭ E♭ B♭ F B♭
ció, Ya los pa - ja - ri - llos can - tan, La lu - na ya se me - tió.

LAZY MARY, WILL YOU GET UP?

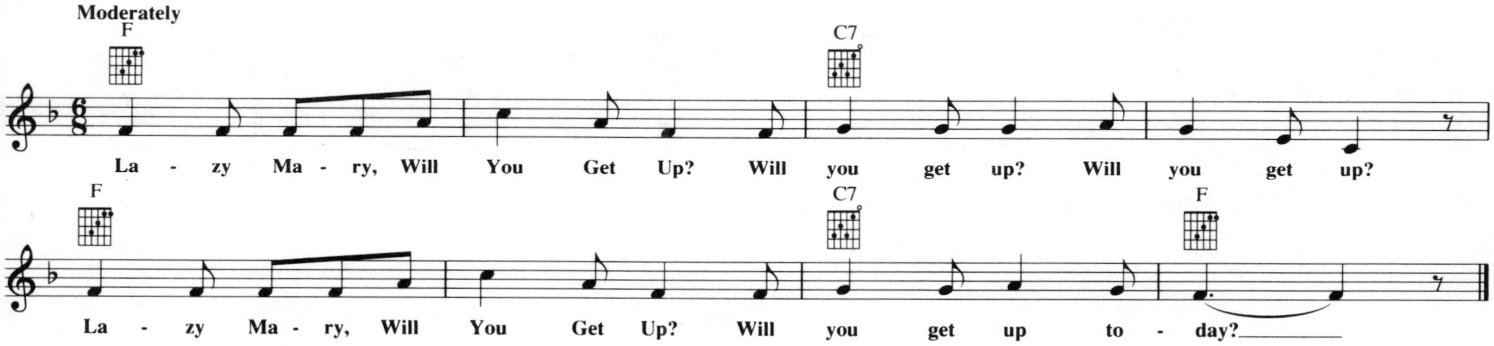
Moderately
F C7
La - zy Ma - ry, Will You Get Up? Will you get up? Will you get up?
F C7 F
La - zy Ma - ry, Will You Get Up? Will you get up to - day?

LET US BREAK BREAD TOGETHER

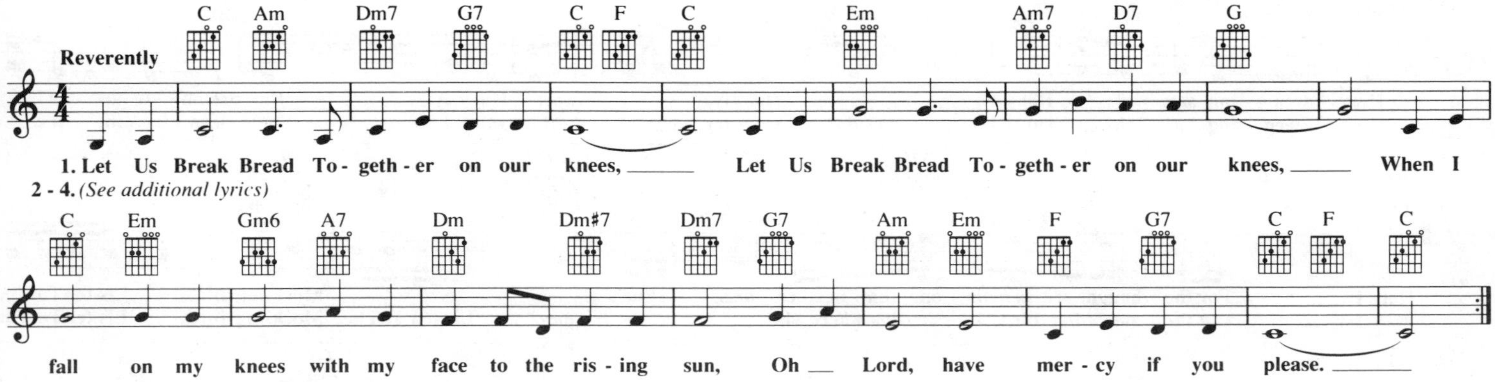
Reverently
C Am Dm7 G7 C F C Em Am7 D7 G
1. Let Us Break Bread To - geth - er on our knees, Let Us Break Bread To - geth - er on our knees, When I
2 - 4. (See additional lyrics)
C Em Gm6 A7 Dm Dm#7 Dm7 G7 Am Em F G7 C F C
fall on my knees with my face to the ris - ing sun, Oh Lord, have mer - cy if you please.

Additional Lyrics

2. Let us drink wine together. . .
3. Let us praise God together. . .
4. Let us all sing together. . .

THE LIBERTY BELL

John Philip Sousa

March tempo, in 2
F Bb F Bb Gm C7 F
C7 F
G7 C/G G
C G7 C G7 1 C 2 C N.C. F F/A Bb C7 F
C7 F Dm7b5 C/G G7 C Bb A A7 Dm Gm/Bb
A Gm/Bb F/C C7 1 F 2 F

LISTEN TO THE MOCKING BIRD

Alice Hawthorne

Moderately
I'm dream - ing now of Hal - ly, sweet Hal - ly, sweet Hal - ly, I'm dream - ing now of
sleep - ing in the val - ley, the val - ley, the val - ley, She's sleep - ing in the
Hal - ly, For the thought of her is one that nev - er dies. She's Mock-ing Bird, Lis-ten To The
val - ley, And the mock-ing bird is sing-ing where she lies. Lis-ten To The Mock-ing Bird, Lis-ten To The
Mock-ing Bird, The mock-ing bird still sing-ing o'er her grave: Lis-ten To The
Mock-ing Bird, Still sing - ing where the weep-ing wil - lows wave.

LIGHT CAVALRY OVERTURE

Franz von Suppe

LIEBESTRAUM

F. Liszt

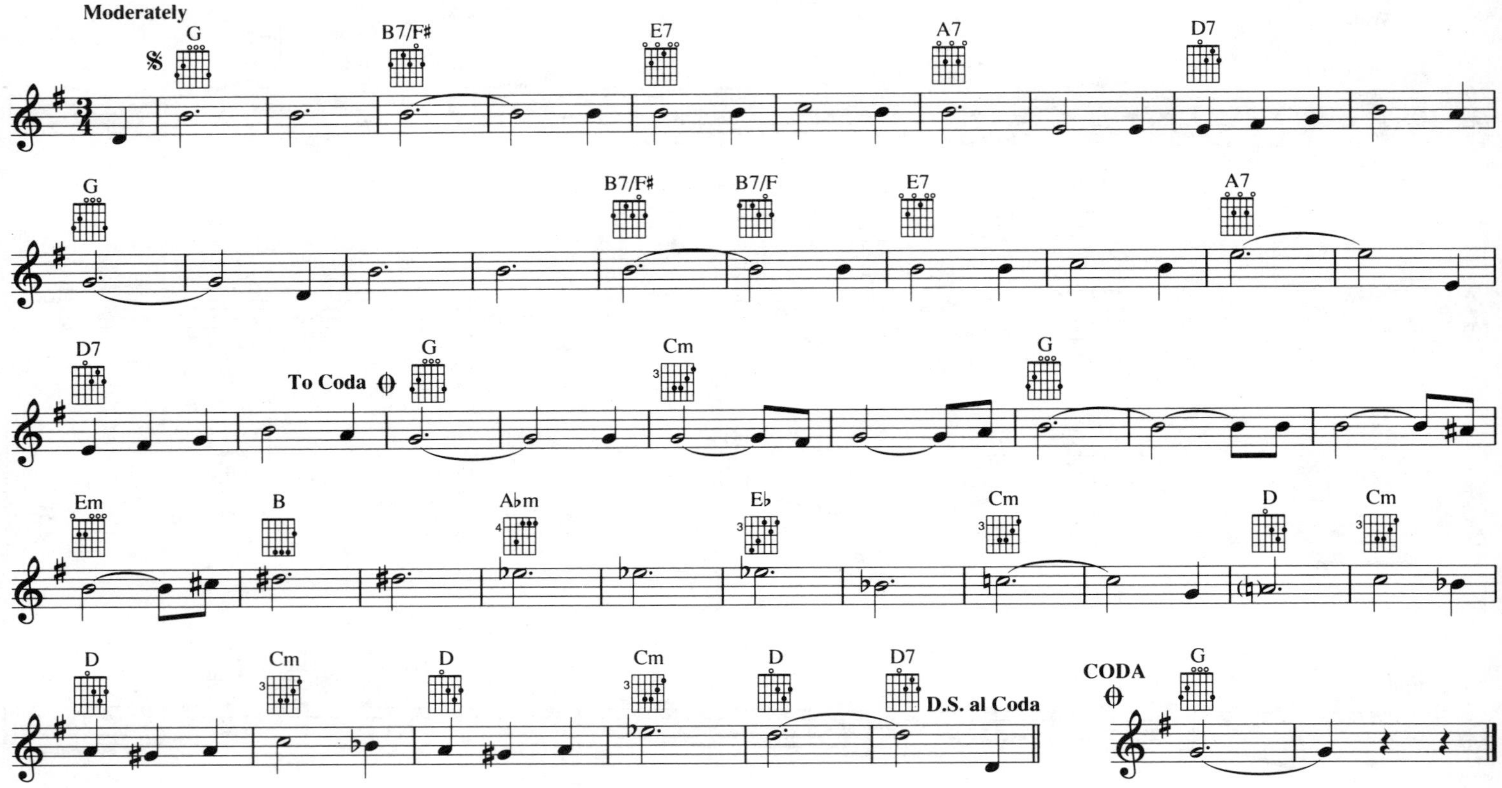
Moderately
G B7/F♯ E7 A7 D7
G B7/F♯ B7/F E7 A7
D7 To Coda G Cm G
Em B A♭m E♭ Cm D Cm
D Cm D Cm D D7 D.S. al Coda
CODA G

A LITTLE BIT OF HEAVEN

Words by Keirn Brennan
Music by Ernest R. Ball

Moderately
B♭7 E♭ G7 A♭ C7 Fm B♭7 Fm7 D7
Shure, A Lit - tle Bit Of Heav - en fell from out the sky one day, And ___ nes - tled on the o - cean in a
E♭maj7 Cm Gm C7 Fm C7 Fm Fm7
spot so far a - way; ___ And when the An - gels found it, Shure it looked so sweet and fair, They
D7 Gm Cm Gm B♭7 E♭ G7 A♭ C7 Fm Fm7
said sup - pose we leave it, for it looks so peace - ful there: So they sprink - led it with star dust just to make the sham - rocks grow: 'Tis the
B♭7 B♭+ E♭6 Gm E♭7
on - ly place you'll find them no mat - ter where you go; Then they dot - ted it with sil - ver, To
Fm C7 Fm C7 Fm E♭dim E♭ E♭dim E♭ A♭ A♭dim Cm A♭m6 E♭ Cm F7 B♭7 E♭
make it's lakes so grand, And ___ when they had it fin - ished shure they called it Ire - land.

LITTLE ANNIE ROONEY

Michael Nolan

Waltz time
E♭ A♭ E♭ A♭ E♭
She's my sweet - heart I'm her beau, She's my An - nie,
F7 B♭7 E♭
I'm her Joe Soon we'll mar - ry nev - er to
A♭ B♭7 E♭ A♭ E♭ B♭7 E♭
part, Lit - tle An - nie Roo - ney is my sweet - heart.

LITTLE BO PEEP

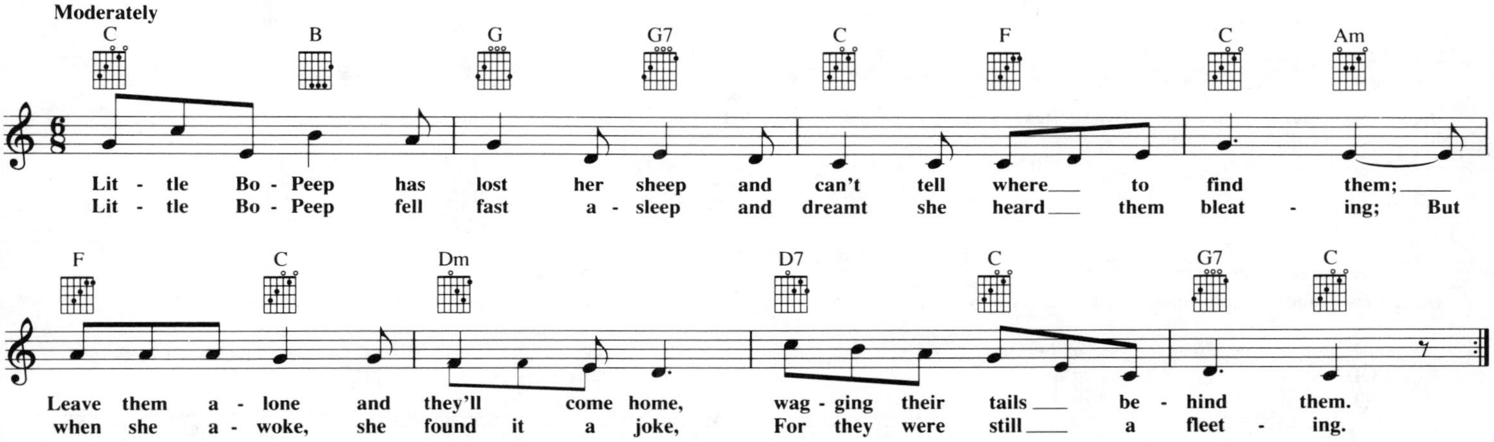
Moderately
C B G G7 C F C Am
Lit - tle Bo - Peep has lost her sheep and can't tell where to find them;
Lit - tle Bo - Peep fell fast a - sleep and dreamt she heard them bleat - ing; But
F C Dm D7 C G7 C
Leave them a - lone and they'll come home, wag - ging their tails be - hind them.
when she a - woke, she found it a joke, For they were still a fleet - ing.

LITTLE BOY BLUE

Moderately
F C7 F C7 F G7 C7
Lit - tle Boy Blue, come blow on your horn; There's sheep in the mead - ow and cows in the corn.
F B♭ C7 F B♭ Gm F C7 F
Where is the boy who looks af - ter the sheep? He lies in the hay - stack, fast a - sleep.

(I'm Called)

LITTLE BUTTERCUP

W. S. Gilbert and Arthur Sullivan

Moderate waltz tempo
I'm called Lit - tle But - ter - cup, Dear Lit - tle But - ter - cup, Though I could nev - er tell why; But
buy of your But - ter - cup, Dear Lit - tle But - ter - cup, Sail - ors should nev - er be shy; So
To Coda
still I'm called But - ter - cup, Poor Lit - tle But - ter - cup, Sweet Lit - tle But - ter - cup, I. I've
buy of your But - ter - cup,
snuff and to - bac - cy, and ex - cel - lent jack - y; I've scis - sors and watch - es and knives; I've
rib - bons and lac - es to set off the fac - es Of pret - ty young sweet - hearts and wives. I've
trea - cle and tof - fee, I've tea and I've cof - fee, Soft tom - my and suc - cu - lent chops; I've
chick - ens and co - nies, And pret - ty po - lo - nies, And ex - cel - lent pep - per - mint drops. Then
D.S. al Coda
CODA
Poor Lit - tle But - ter - cup; Come, of your But - ter - cup buy.

LITTLE JACK HORNER

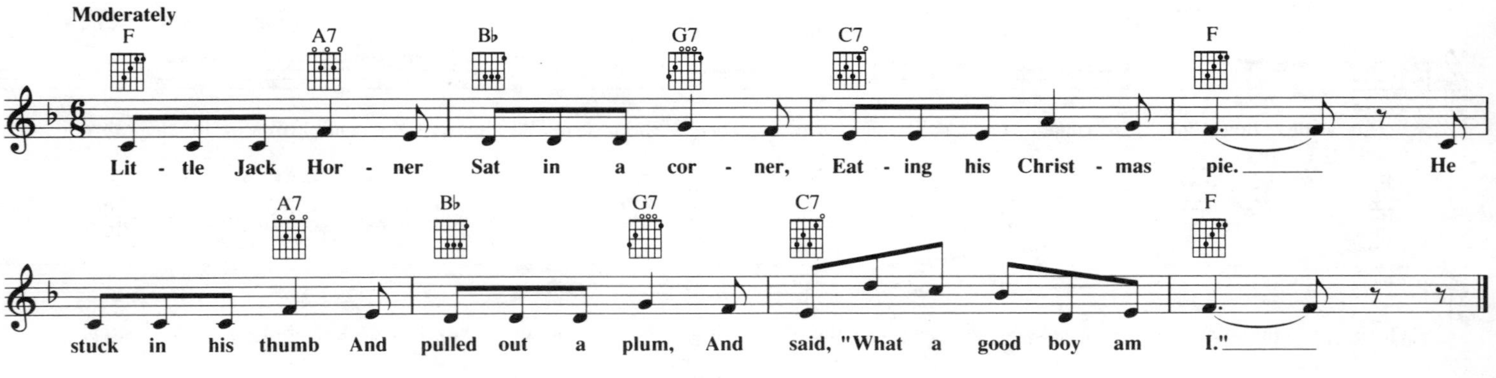
Moderately
Lit - tle Jack Hor - ner Sat in a cor - ner, Eat - ing his Christ - mas pie. He
stuck in his thumb And pulled out a plum, And said, "What a good boy am I."

LITTLE BROWN JUG

J.E. Winner

Gaily
C F G7 C F
My wife and I lived all a - lone in a lit - tle log hut we called our own, She loved gin and I loved rum, I
you who makes my friend my foes, 'Tis _ you _ who makes me wear old clothes, Here you are so near my nose, So
G7 C F G7 C G C
tell you what, we'd lots of fun!
tip her up and down she goes!
Ha, ha, ha, you and me, Lit - tle Brown Jug, don't I love thee! Ha, ha, ha,
1
F G7 C
you and me, Lit - tle Brown Jug don't I love thee! 'Tis
2
F G7 C
Ha, ha, ha, you and me, Lit - tle Brown Jug don't I love thee!

LITTLE MISS MUFFET

Moderately fast
C7 F C7 F
Lit - tle Miss Muf - fet Sat on a tuf - fet, Eat - ing some curds and whey. ___ There
C7 F C7 F
came a big spi - der And sat down be - side her, And fright - ened Miss Muf - fet a - way. ___

LITTLE TOMMY TUCKER

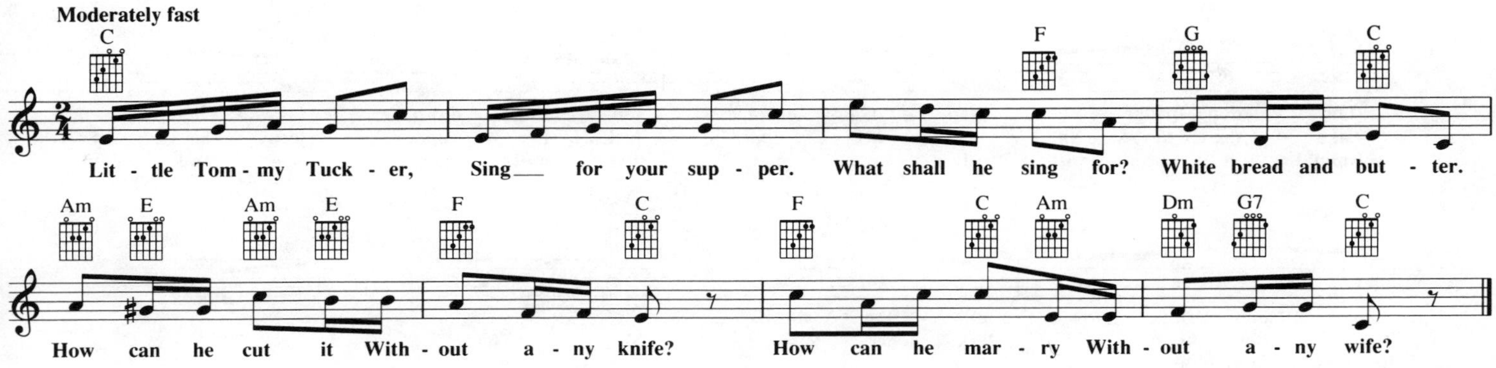
Moderately fast
C F G C
Lit - tle Tom - my Tuck - er, Sing ___ for your sup - per. What shall he sing for? White bread and but - ter.
Am E Am E F C F C Am Dm G7 C
How can he cut it With - out a - ny knife? How can he mar - ry With - out a - ny wife?

LO, HOW A ROSE E'RE BLOOMING

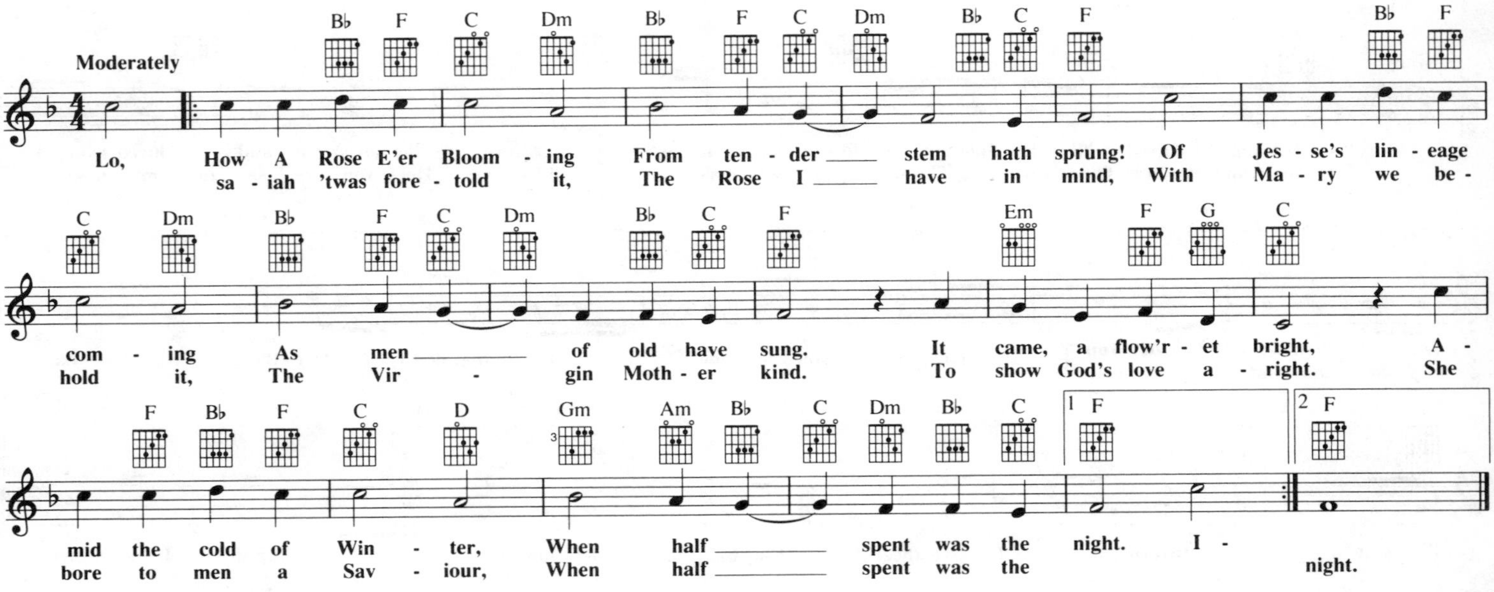
Moderately
B♭ F C Dm B♭ F C Dm B♭ C F B♭ F
Lo, How A Rose E'er Bloom - ing From ten - der ___ stem hath sprung! Of Jes - se's lin - eage
sa - iah 'twas fore - told it, The Rose I ___ have in mind, With Ma - ry we be -
C Dm B♭ F C Dm B♭ C F Em F G C
com - ing As men ___ of old have sung. It came, a flow'r - et bright, A -
hold it, The Vir - gin Moth - er kind. To show God's love a - right. She
F B♭ F C D Gm Am B♭ C Dm B♭ C 1 F 2 F
mid the cold of Win - ter, When half ___ spent was the night. I -
bore to men a Sav - iour, When half ___ spent was the night.

LOCH LOMOND

Moderately
F A B♭ Gm7 C7 F Gm7 F/A B♭ Am
Oh! ye'll take the high road, and I'll take the low road, And I'll be in Scot - land a - fore ye, But
Dm Am Gm7 Am B♭ C7 F B♭ F C7 F
me and my true love, Will nev - er meet a - gain, on the Bon - nie, Bon - nie banks of Loch Lo - mond.

LONDON BRIDGE

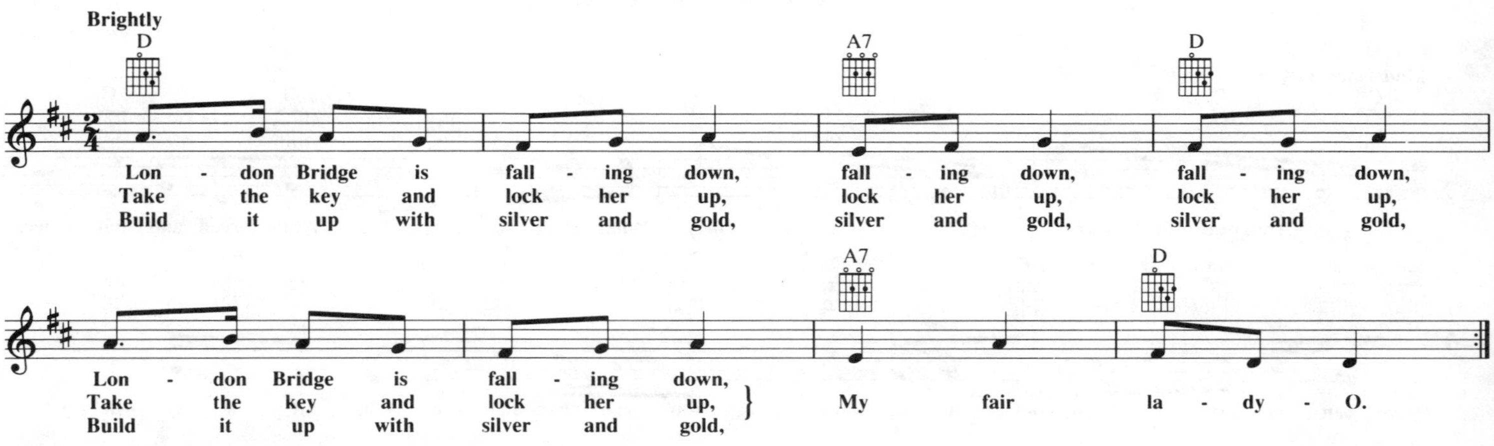
Brightly
D A7 D
Lon - don Bridge is fall - ing down, fall - ing down, fall - ing down,
Take the key and lock her up, lock her up, lock her up,
Build it up with silver and gold, silver and gold, silver and gold,
A7 D
Lon - don Bridge is fall - ing down,
Take the key and lock her up,
Build it up with silver and gold,
My fair la - dy - O.

LONESOME ROAD

Not too fast
D D7/C G/B Gm/B♭ D A7 D
Look down, look down, that Lone - some Road, Hang down your head and cry.
The best of friends must part some day, Then why not you and I?
True love, true love, what have I done, That you should treat me so?

LONESOME VALLEY

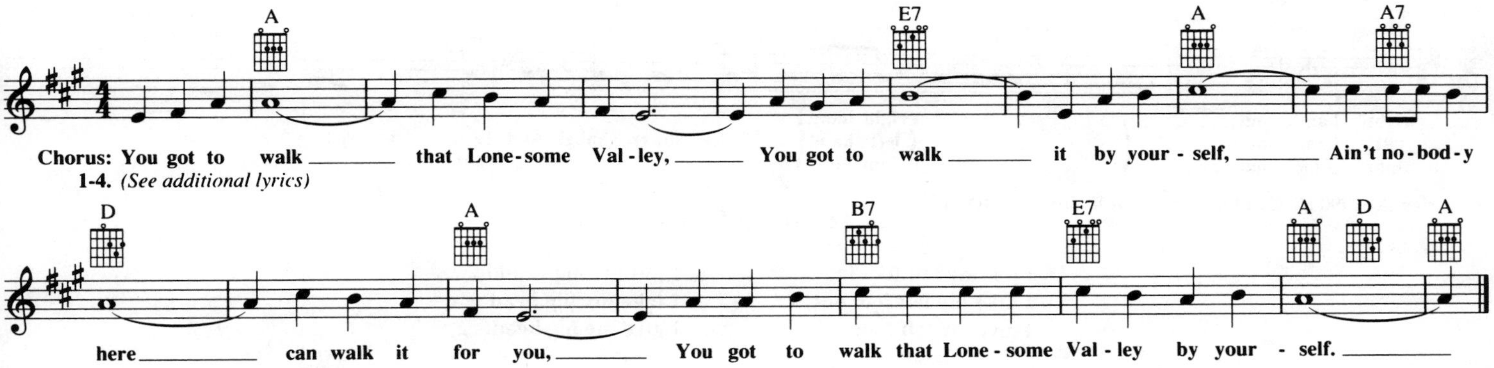
A E7 A A7
Chorus: You got to walk that Lone-some Val-ley, You got to walk it by your-self, Ain't no-bod-y
1-4. (See additional lyrics)
D A B7 E7 A D A
here can walk it for you, You got to walk that Lone-some Val-ley by your - self.

Additional Lyrics

1. Your mother's got to walk that Lonesome Valley. . .
2. Your father's got to walk that Lonesome Valley. . .
3. Your brother's got to walk that Lonesome Valley. . .
4. If you cannot preach like Peter,
   If you cannot pray like Paul
   You can tell the love of Jesus,
   You can say He died for all.

LONG, LONG AGO

Thomas Haynes Bayly

Moderately
F C7 F
Tell me the tales that to me were so dear, Long, Long A - go, Long, Long A - go, Sing me the songs I de -
Do you re - mem - ber the path where we met, Long, Long A - go, Long, Long A - go, Ah yes, you told me you
Tho' by your kind - ness my fond hopes were raised, Long, Long A - go, Long, Long A - go, You, by more el - o - quent
C7 F C7 F
light - ed to hear, Long, Long A - go, long a - go. Now you are come, all my grief is re - moved;
ne'er would for - get, Long, Long A - go, long a - go. Then to all oth - ers my smile you pre - ferred;
lips, have been praised Long, Long A - go, long a - go. But by long ab - cense your truth has been tried;
C7 F C F
Let me for - get that so long you have rov'd. Let me be - lieve that you love as you loved, Long, Long A - go, long a - go.
Love, when you spoke, gave a charm to each word. Still my heart treas - ures the prais - es I heard, Long, Long A - go, long a - go.
Still, to your ac - cents, I lis - ten with pride. Blest as I was when I sat by your side Long, Long A - go, long a - go.

LOOBY LOO

Brightly
Refrain
D
A7
D
Here we go Loo - by Loo,
Here we go loo - by light,
Here we go Loo - by
A7
D
Loo,
All on a Sat - ur - day night.
1. I put my right hand in,
I take my
2. I put my left hand in,
I take my
3. I put my right foot in,
I take my
4-6. (See additional lyrics)
A7
D
right hand out;
left hand out;
right foot out;
I give my
right hand
left hand
right foot
a shake, shake, shake! And turn my - self a - bout.

Additional Lyrics

4. I put my left foot in,
I take my left foot out;
I give my left foot. . .

5. I put my big head in,
I take my big head out;
I give my big head. . .

6. I put my whole self in,
I put my whole self out;
I give my whole self. . .

LOVE'S OLD SWEET SONG

Words by J. Clifton Bingham; Music by James L. Molloy

Slowly
F
C7
F
C7
Once in the dear dead days be - yond re - call,
When on the world the mists be - gan to fall,
Out of the dreams that
F
Dm7
G7
C
Gm
Dm
rose in hap - py throng,
Low to our hearts Love sung an old sweet song;
And in the dusk where fell the fire - light gleam,
G7
Am
Dm7
C
G7
C
C7
Chorus:
F
C7
Soft - ly it - self in - to our dream.
Just a song at twi - light, when the lights are
F
A7
Dm
G7
C7
F
C7
low,
And the flick - 'ring shad - ows soft - ly come and go,
Tho' the heart be wea - ry,
F
F7
B♭
Gm7
F
C7
F
B♭
C
F
sad the day and long,
Still to us at twi - light comes love's old song,
Comes Love's Old Sweet Song.

KEEP THE HOMEFIRES BURNING

Words by Lena G. Ford
Music by Ivor Novello

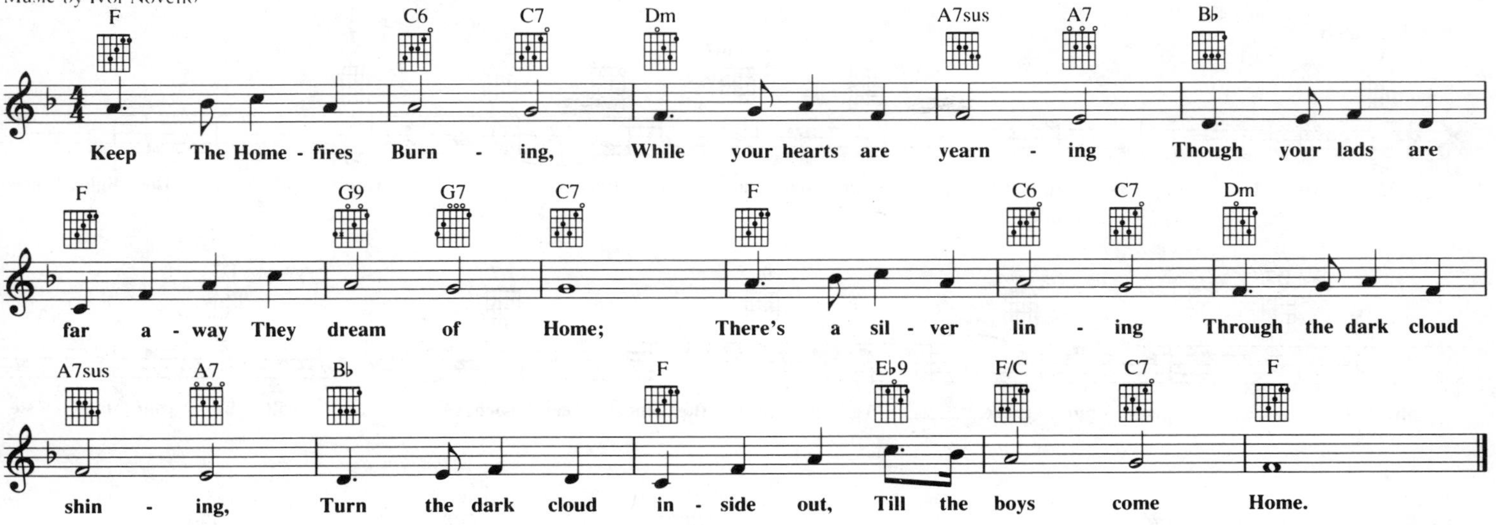
F C6 C7 Dm A7sus A7 B♭
Keep The Home - fires Burn - ing, While your hearts are yearn - ing Though your lads are
F G9 G7 C7 F C6 C7 Dm
far a - way They dream of Home; There's a sil - ver lin - ing Through the dark cloud
A7sus A7 B♭ F E♭9 F/C C7 F
shin - ing, Turn the dark cloud in - side out, Till the boys come Home.

MARY'S A GRAND OLD NAME

Words and Music by George M. Cohan

Moderately
G E7 A7 D7 G Edim D7 Am7 D7
For it is Ma - ry, Ma - ry, plain as an - y name can be; But with pro - pri - e - ty, so - ci - e - ty will
Ma - ry, Ma - ry, long be - fore the fash - ions
D7♯5 G G F7 E7 Am A7 D7 G
say Ma - rie. But it was came; And there is some - thing there that sounds so fair, it's a grand old name!

MATILDA

Brightly
Chorus
C F G7 Dm7 G7
Ma - til - da Ma - til - da Ma - til - da she took me mon - ey and
C G7 C C G7 C F
Verse
run Ven - e - zue - la! 1. That wo - man made a wreck of me, (broke me, oh) What she done to me you
2 - 4. (See additional lyrics)
G7 Dm7 G7 C G7 C
ought to see. Ma - til - da she take me mon - ey and gone Ven - e - zue - la!

Additional Lyrics

2. I save up, gonna make her my wife.
   But she wanta live another kind of life.
   Chorus

3. We were sleepin' in me bed,
   When she found the money me had hid.
   Chorus

4. What to do and where to go,
   Never trust a woman with your dough.
   Chorus

MEET ME IN ST. LOUIS, LOUIS

Words by Andrew B. Sterling; Music by Kerry Mills

Moderately
C F F#dim7 C G7 C
"Meet Me In St. Lou - is, Lou - is, Meet me at the fair, Don't tell me the lights are
D7 G7 E7 A7 D7
shin - ing an - y place but there, We will dance the Hooch - ee Kooch - ee I will be your toot - sie
G7 C D7 G7 1 C 2 C
woot - sie; Meet Me In St. Lou - is, Lou - is, Meet me at the fair." fair."

LA SORELLA

Ch. Borel-Clere

Moderately fast
F C7 F C7
1 F 2 F B♭ F7
B♭ B♭7 E♭ Edim
B♭ F7 1 B♭ 2 B♭ N.C. Cdim C7 F
C7 F C7 1 F 2 F

MINUET IN G

Ignace J. Paderewski

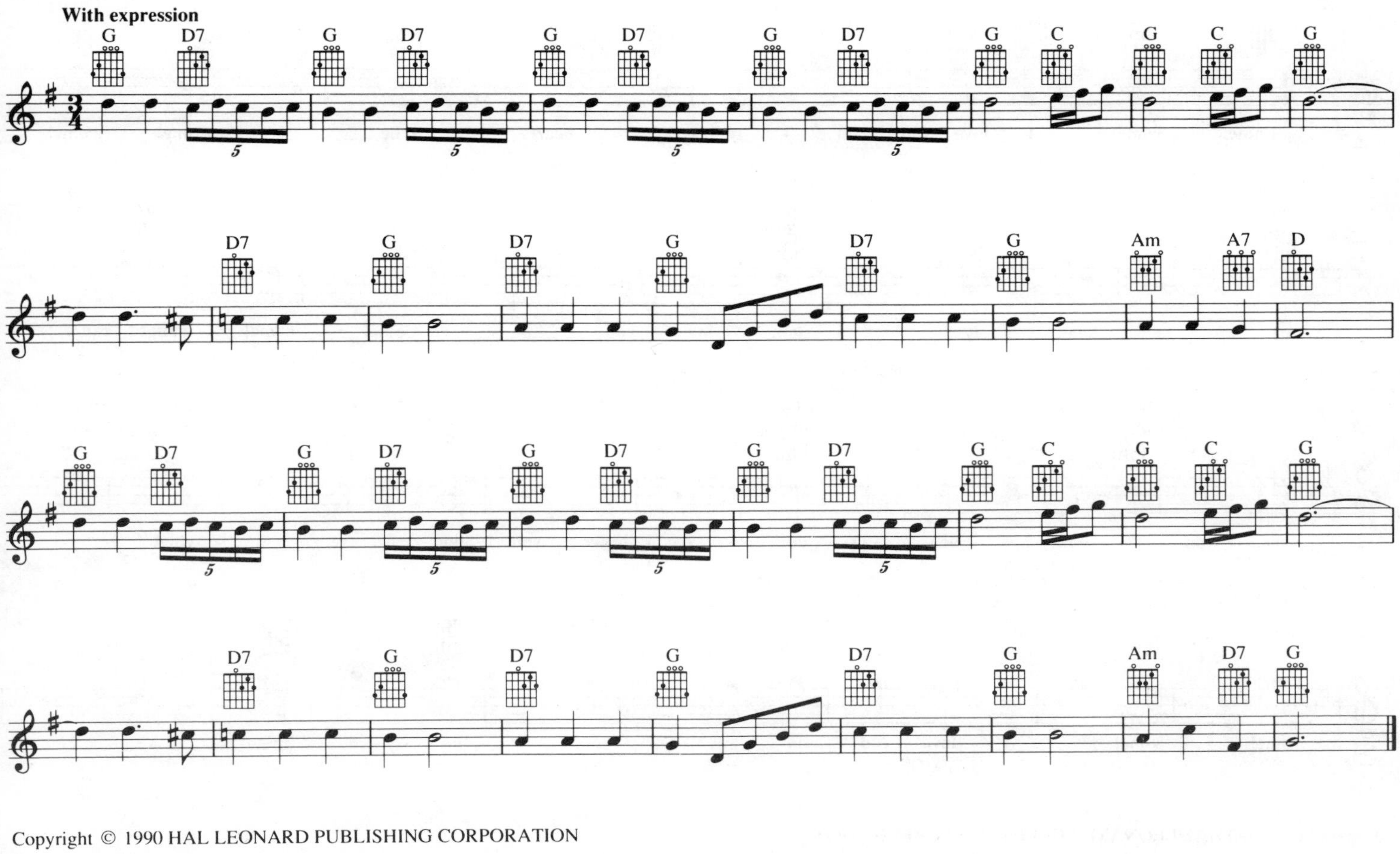

MERRY WIDOW WALTZ

F. Lehar

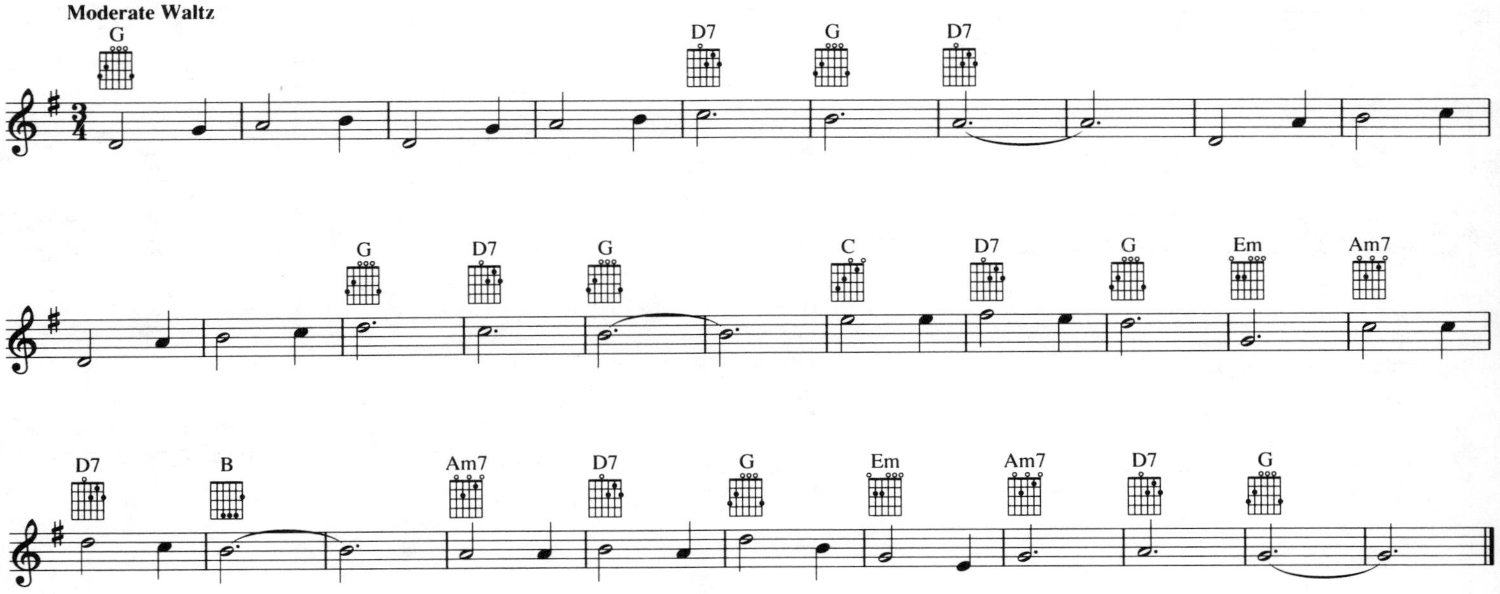
Moderate Waltz
G D7 G D7
G D7 G C D7 G Em Am7
D7 B Am7 D7 G Em Am7 D7 G

MY HERO

Oscar Straus

Slow Waltz tempo
E♭ Edim7 Fm7 B♭7 E♭ Edim7
Come! come! I love you on - ly my heart is true, Come! come!
Fm7 B♭7 E♭ Cm Fm7
my life is lone - ly I long for you; Come! come! naught can ef -
B♭7♯5 E♭ A♭ Gm Fm7 B♭7
face you, My arms are ach - ing now to em - brace you, Thou art di - vine!
E♭ C7 Fm A♭m B♭7 E♭
Come! come! I love you on - ly come, he - ro mine!

MOONLIGHT BAY

Words by Edward Madden; Music by Percy Wenrich

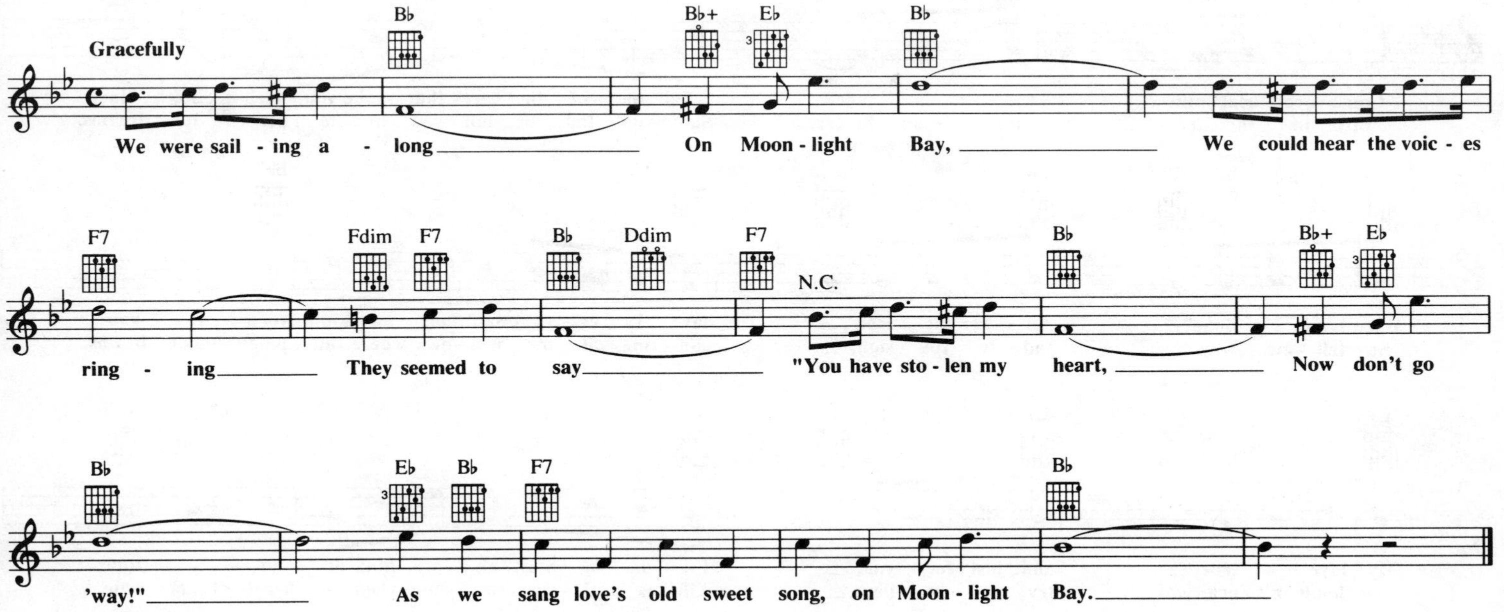
Gracefully
Bb Bb+ Eb Bb
We were sail - ing a - long On Moon - light Bay, We could hear the voic - es
F7 Fdim F7 Bb Ddim F7 N.C. Bb Bb+ Eb
ring - ing They seemed to say "You have sto - len my heart, Now don't go
Bb Eb Bb F7 Bb
'way!" As we sang love's old sweet song, on Moon - light Bay.

MY HEART AT THY SWEET VOICE

Camille Saint-Saens

Slowly
C Fm G7 C
Fm G7 E7 Am G7
C Am Dm G7 C

MY MELANCHOLY BABY

Words by George A. Norton; Music by Ernie Burnett

Moderately
E♭ B7 E♭ B7 E♭ G♭dim7 B♭7
Come sweet - heart mine, don't sit and pine. Tell me of the cares that make you feel so blue.
Birds in the trees, whis - per - ing breeze. Should not fail to lull you in - to peace - ful dreams.
Fm C7 Fm C7 F7 B♭7
What have I done? An - swer me Hon', have I ev - er said an un - kind word to you?
So tell me why sad - ly you sigh, Sit - ting at the win - dow where the pale moon beams.
E♭ B7 E♭ B7 E♭ G♭dim7 B♭7
My love is true, and just for you, I'd do al - most an - y - thing at an - y time.
You should - n't grieve, try and be - lieve. Life is al - ways sun - shine when the heart beats true.
F7 B♭ G7 C7 F7 Fm7 B♭7
Dear, when you sigh or when you cry, some - thing seems to grip this ver - y heart of mine.
Be of good cheer, smile thro' your tears, when your sad it makes me feel the same as you.
E♭ C7♯5 C7 Fm B♭7
Come to me, My Mel - an - chol - y Ba - by, cud - dle up and don't be blue; All your fears are fool - ish fan - cy,
F7 B♭7 E♭ Edim B♭7 E♭
may - be, you know, dear that I'm in love with you. Ev - 'ry cloud must have a sil - ver
C7♯5 C7 Fm A♭ Adim
lin - ing, wait un - til the sun shines through. Smile my hon - ey dear, while I
E♭ C7 Fm F7 B♭7 1 E♭ G♭dim7 B♭7 2 E♭
kiss a - way each tear, or else I shall be mel - an - chol - y too. Now won't you too.

THE MAN ON THE FLYING TRAPEZE

Lyrics by George Leybourne

Moderate Waltz tempo
G E7 A7 D7 G
1. Oh once I was hap-py, but now I'm for-lorn, Just like an old coat that is tat-tered and torn.
2-6. (See additional lyrics)
E7 A7 D7 G
Left in this wide world to fret and to mourn, Be-trayed by a maid in her teens. Now, this
Em B7 Em B7 Em
girl that I loved she was hand-some, And I tried all I knew her to please. But I
B7 Em B Em6 Bdim B7 D7
nev-er could please her one quar-ter so well As The Man On The Fly-ing Trap-eze. Oh! He'd
gliss.
G E7 A7 D7 G
float through the air with the great-est of ease, This dar-ing young man on the fly-ing trap-eze. His
E7 A7 D7 G
move-ments are grace-ful, all girls he does please, And my love he has pur-loined a-way.

Additional Lyrics

2. Now the young man by name was Señor Boni Slang,
Tall, big and handsome, as well made as Chang.
Where'er he appeared, how the hall loudly rang,
With ovations from all people there.
He'd smile from the bar on the people below
And one night he smiled on my love,
She winked back at him, and she shouted "Bravo!"
As he hung by his nose from above.

3. Her father and mother were both on my side
And tried very hard to make her my bride.
Her father, he sighed, and her mother, she cried
To see her throw herself away.
'Twas all no avail, she went there ev'ry right
And threw her bouquets on the stage,
Which caused him to meet her—how he ran me down,
To tell it would take a whole page.

4. One night I as usual went to her dear home,
And found there her mother and father alone.
I asked for my love, and soon 'twas made known,
To my horror, that she'd run away.
She packed up her boxes and eloped in the night,
With him with the greatest of ease.
From two stories high he had lowered her down
To the ground on his flying trapeze.

5. Some months after that I went into a hall;
To my suprise I found there on the wall
A bill in red letters which did my heart gall,
That she was appearing with him.
He'd taught her gymnastics, and dressed her in tights
To help him live at ease.
He'd made her assume a masculine name,
And now she goes on the trapeze.

Final Chorus:
She floats through the air with the greatest of ease;
You'd think her a man on the flying trapeze.
She does all the work while he takes his ease,
And that's what's become of my love.

MADEMOISELLE FROM ARMENTIERS

Moderately
G D7 G D7 G Ddim7 D7 G A7 D7 G Em A7 D7 G G
Ma - de - moi - selle From Ar - men - tières par - ley voo. Ma - de - moi - selle From Ar - men - tières, par - ley voo.
Ma - de - moi - selle From Ar - men - tières, she has - n't been hugged for for - ty years.
Hink - y dink - y par - ley voo. voo.

Additional Lyrics

1. **She might have been old for all we knew,**
   Parlez-voo, (*Sing 3 times*)
   When Napoleon flopped at Waterloo,
   Hinky Dinky Parlez-voo.

2. **You might forget the gas and the shell,**
   Parlez-voo, (*Sing 3 times*)
   But you'll never forget the mademoiselle.
   Hinky Dinky Parlez-voo.

3. **Oh, madam, have you a daughter fair?**
   Parlez-voo, (*Sing 3 times*)
   To wash a soldier's underwear?
   Hinky Dinky Parlez-voo.

4. **She got the palms and the Croiz-de-Guerre,**
   Parlez-voo, (*Sing 3 times*)
   For washing soldiers' underwear.
   Hinky Dinky Parlez-voo.

5. **The General got the Croix-de-Guerre,**
   Parlez-voo, (*Sing 3 times*)
   The son-of-a-bitch was never there.
   Hinky Dinky Parlez-voo.

6. **The officers get all the steak,**
   Parlez-voo, (*Sing 3 times*)
   And all we get is the belly-ache.
   Hinky Dinky Parlez-voo.

7. **The MPs say they won the war,**
   Parlez-voo, (*Sing 3 times*)
   Standing on guard at the cafe door.
   Hinky Dinky Parlez-voo.

8. **I didn't care what became of me,**
   Parlez-voo, (*Sing 3 times*)
   So I went and joined the infantry.
   Hinky Dinky Parlez-voo.

9. **They say they mechanized the war,**
   Parlez-voo, (*Sing 3 times*)
   So what the hell are we marching for?
   Hinky Dinky Parlez-voo.

A MAN WITHOUT A WOMAN

Words and Music by Alfred Williams

Slowly
G D7 G C G A7 D7 G D7 Am B E7 Am G D7 G
Oh, A Man With - out A Wom - an is like a ship with - out a sail; Is like a boat with - out a rud - der, Is like a
fish with - out a tail. Oh A Man With - out A Wom - an is like a wreck up - on the sand. There's on - ly
one thing worse in this whole darn u - ni - verse, And that's a wom - an I say a wom - an I mean a wom - an with - out a man.

MAPLE LEAF RAG

Scott Joplin

MARCH OF THE TOYS

By Victor Herbert

MARIANNE

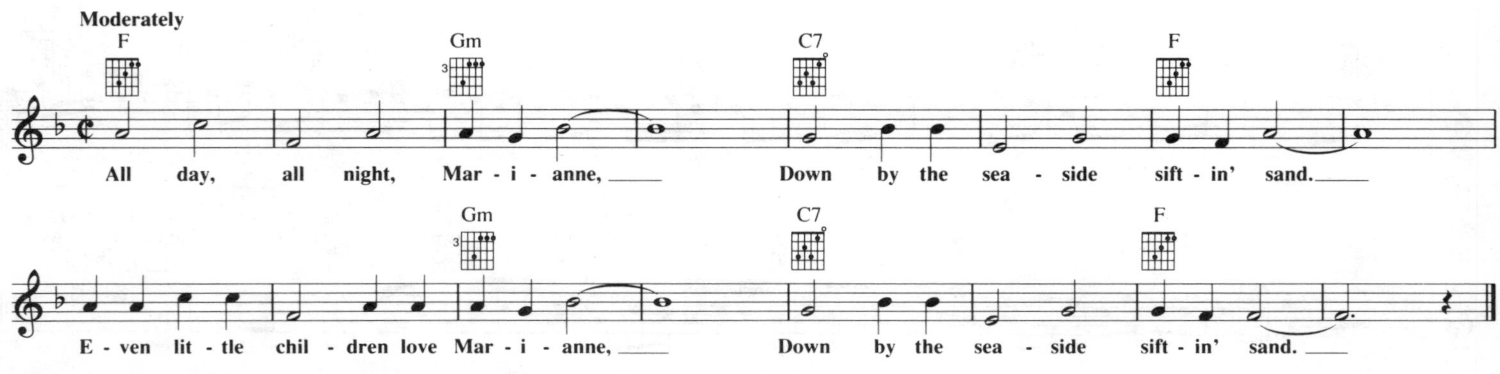

MARCH SLAV
(Tchaikovsky)

Peter Tchaikovsky

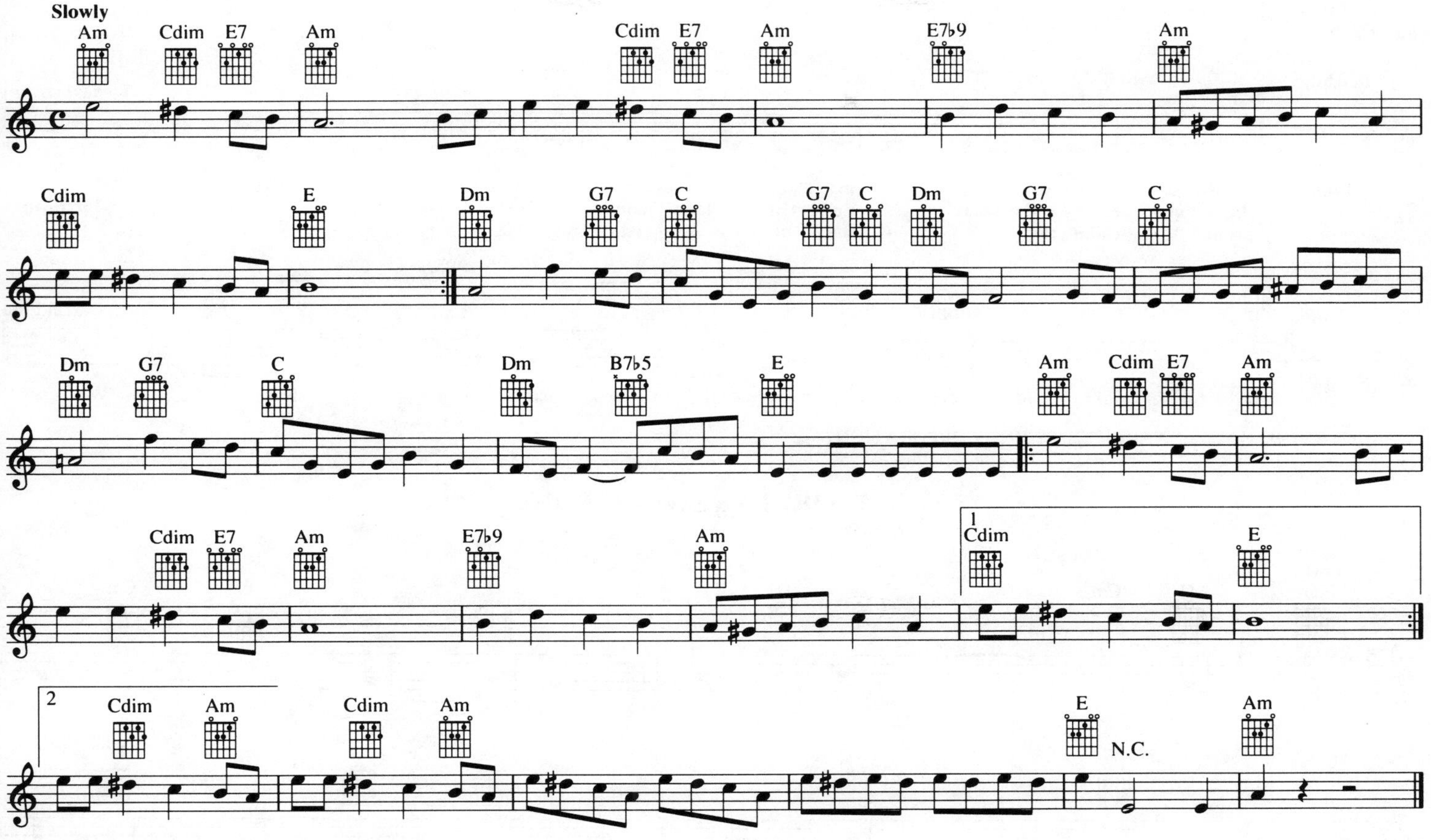

MARCH MILITAIRE

Franz Schubert

MARINE'S HYMN

MAORI FAREWELL SONG

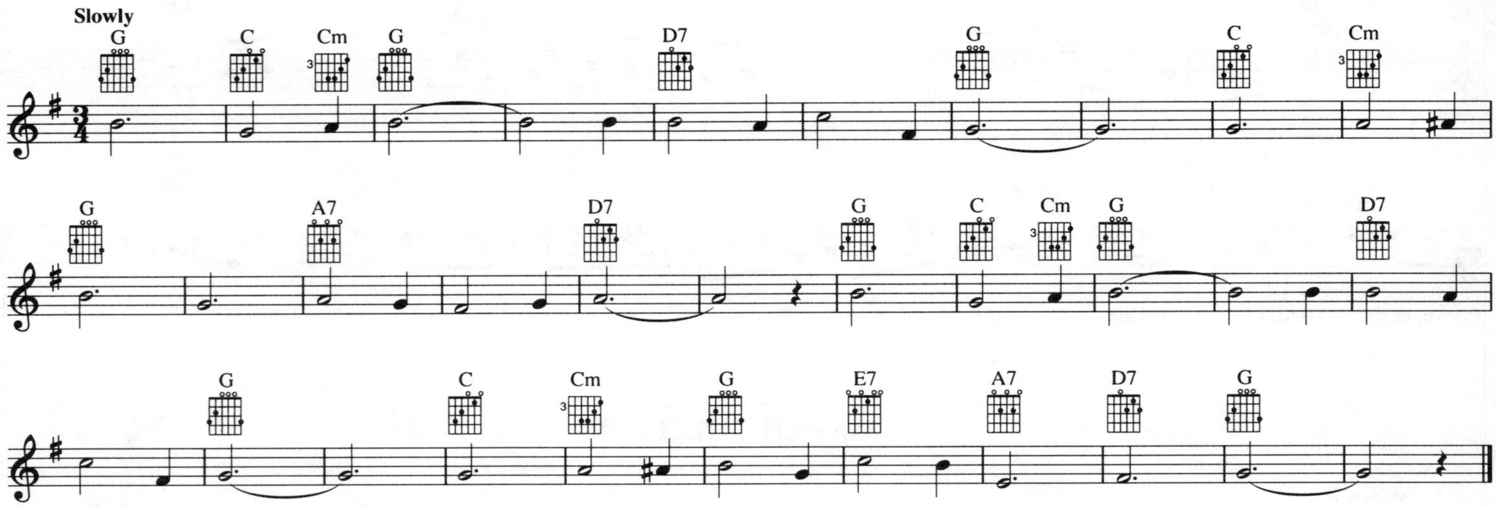

MATTINATA

Ruggiero Leoncavallo

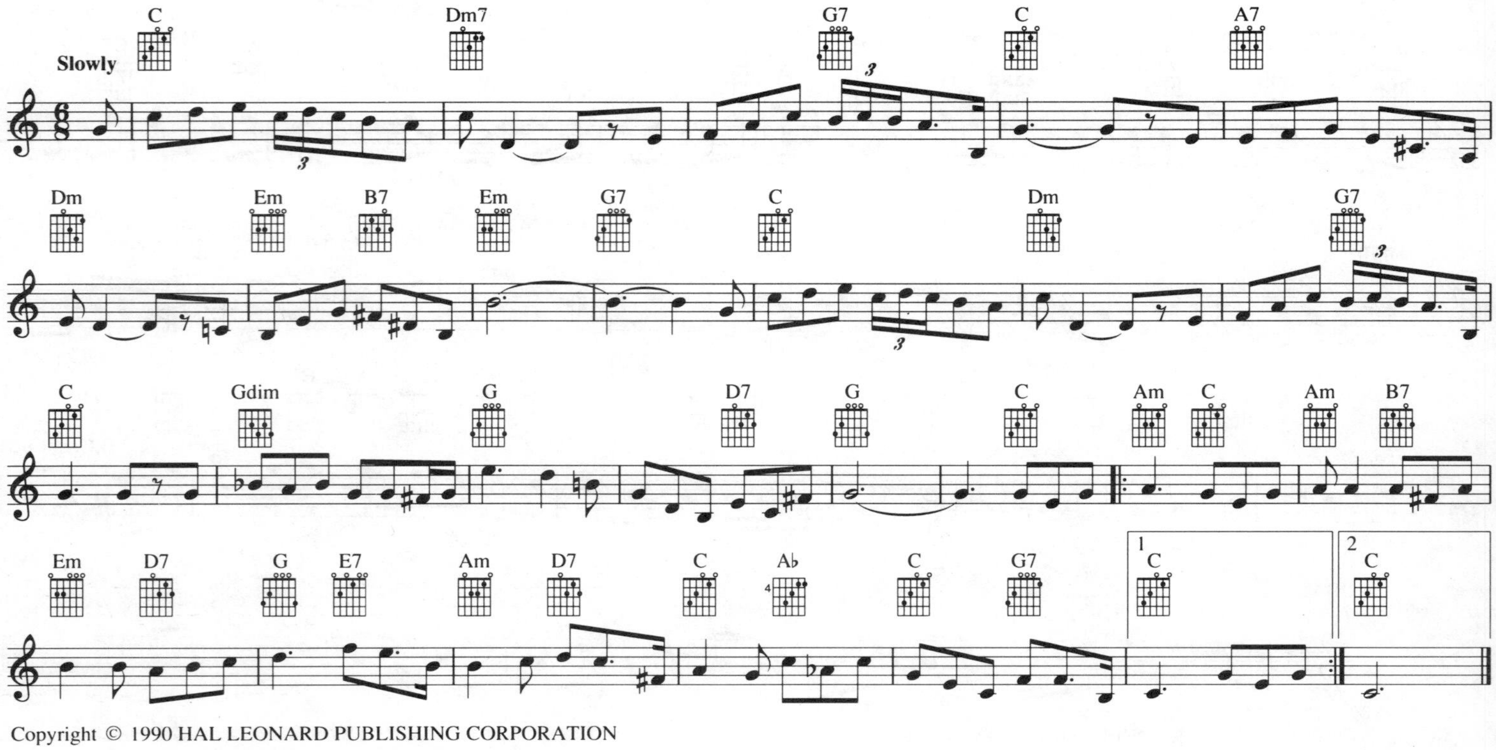

MIDNIGHT SPECIAL

Freely, but not too slow

G C G D G C G D G C G D G
1. Well you wake up in the morn - ing, hear the ding dong ring, You go march-ing to the ta - ble, see the same damn thing. Well, it's on - ly one ta - ble, knife and fork and a pan, And if you say a thing a - bout it, you're in trou - ble with the man.
2. If you ev - er go to Hous - ton, you'd bet - ter walk right, And you bet - ter not stag - ger, and you bet - ter not fight. 'Cause the sher - iff will ar - rest you, and he'll car - ry you down, And you can bet your bot - tom dol - lar, you're for Su - gar - land bound.
3. (See additional lyrics)
Chorus:
Let the Mid - night Spe - cial shine her light on me, Let the Mid - night Spe - cial shine her ev - er lov - in' light on me.

Additional Lyrics

3. Lord, Thelma said she loved me, but I believe she told a lie,
'Cause she hasn't been to see me since last July.
She brought me little coffee, she brought me little tea,
She brought me nearly everything but the jail house key.

A MIGHTY FORTRESS IS OUR GOD

Words by Frederick H. Hedge; Music by Martin Luther

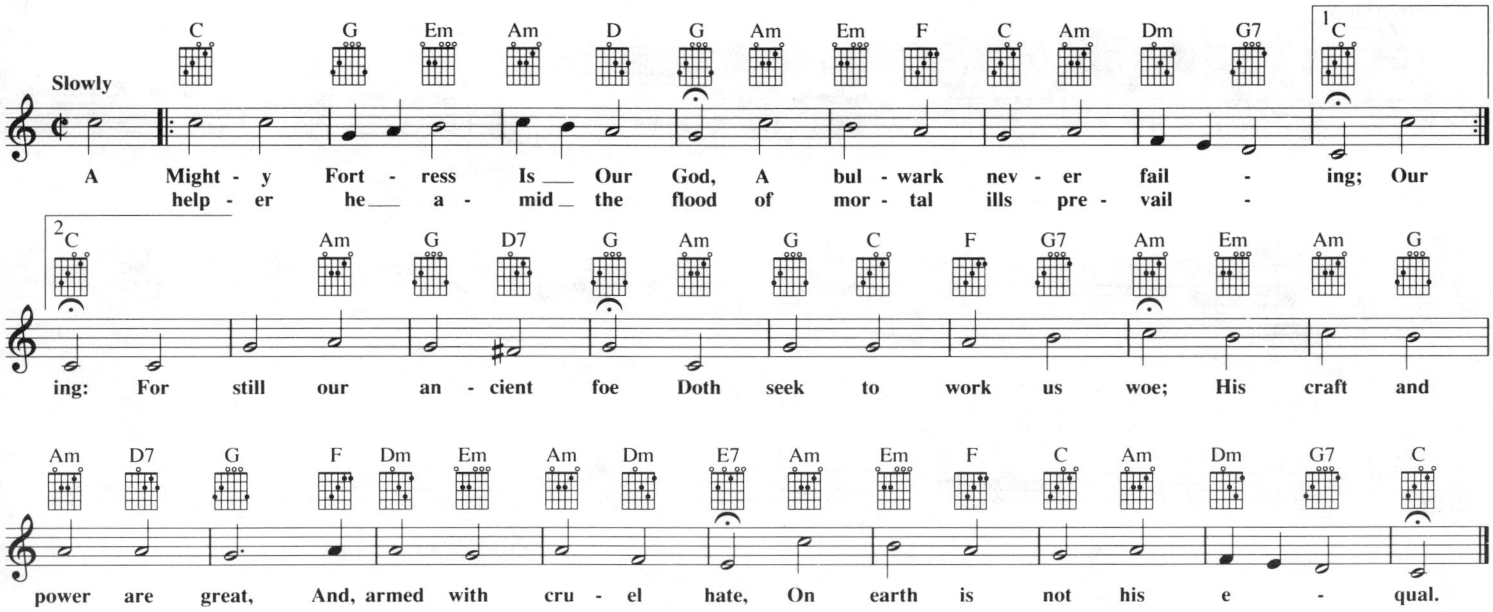
Slowly
C G Em Am D G Am Em F C Am Dm G7 C C Am G D7 G Am G C F G7 Am Em Am G Am D7 G F Dm Em Am Dm E7 Am Em F C Am Dm G7 C
A Might - y Fort - ress Is Our God, A bul - wark nev - er fail - ing; Our
help - er he a - mid the flood of mor - tal ills pre - vail - ing: For still our an - cient foe Doth seek to work us woe; His craft and power are great, And, armed with cru - el hate, On earth is not his e - qual.

MARTHA POLKA

MEDITATION
(From "THAIS")

Jules Massenet

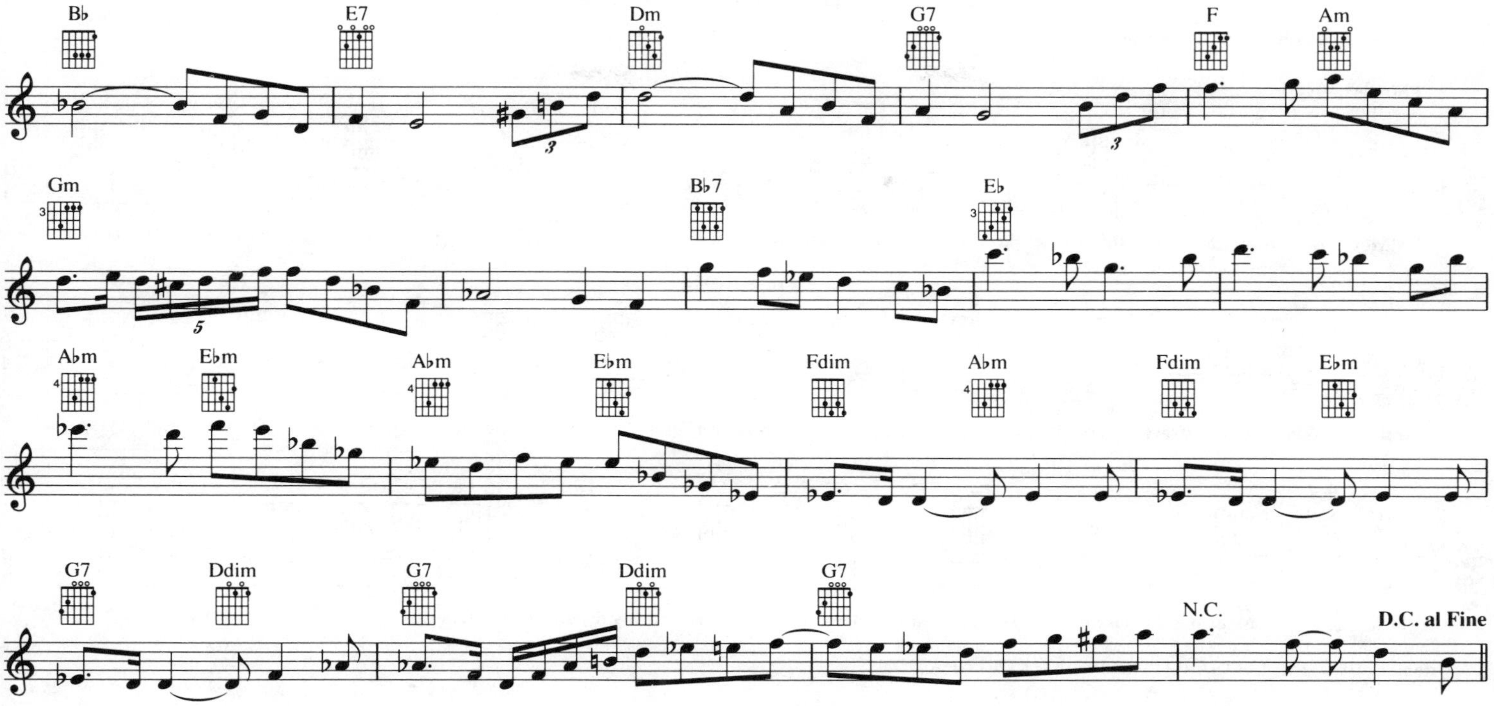
Bb E7 Dm G7 F Am
Gm Bb7 Eb
Abm Ebm Abm Ebm Fdim Abm Fdim Ebm
G7 Ddim G7 Ddim G7
N.C.
D.C. al Fine

MARY HAD A LITTLE LAMB

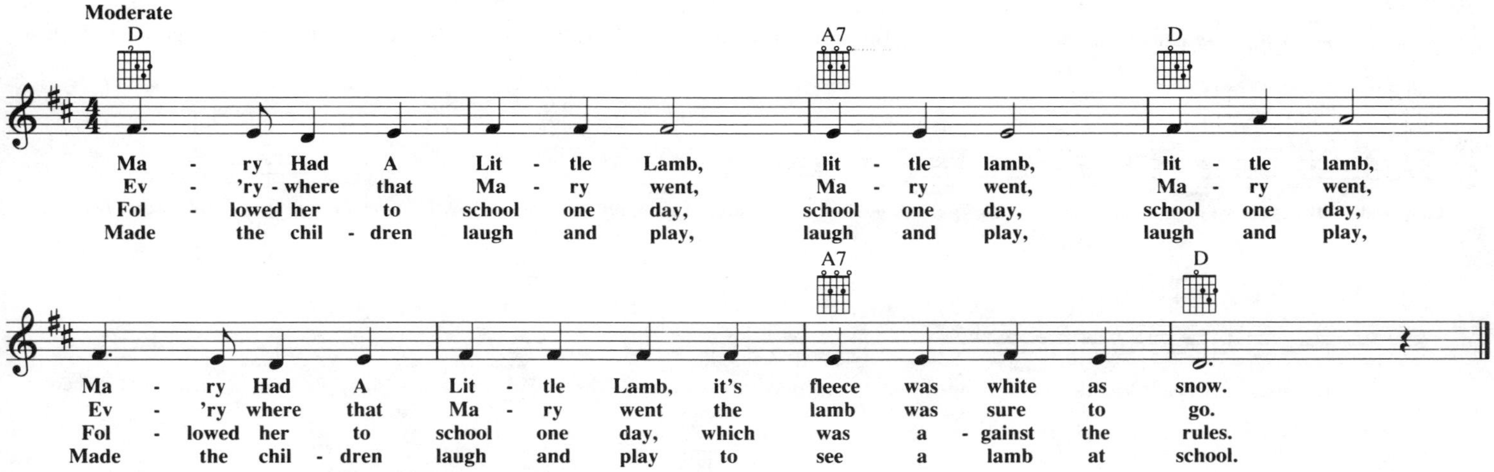
Moderate
D A7 D
Ma - ry Had A Lit - tle Lamb, lit - tle lamb, lit - tle lamb,
Ev - 'ry - where that Ma - ry went, Ma - ry went, Ma - ry went,
Fol - lowed her to school one day, school one day, school one day,
Made the chil - dren laugh and play, laugh and play, laugh and play,
A7 D
Ma - ry Had A Lit - tle Lamb, it's fleece was white as snow.
Ev - 'ry where that Ma - ry went the lamb was sure to go.
Fol - lowed her to school one day, which was a - gainst the rules.
Made the chil - dren laugh and play to see a lamb at school.

MAZEL TOV

Joyously
Em C#dim B
Em Am B7 Em

MEET ME TONIGHT IN DREAMLAND

Words by Beth Slater Whitson; Music by Leo Friedman

Moderately
Bb G+ G7 C7 F7 Bb G7 G+ G7 C7
Meet Me To-night In Dream-land Un-der the sil-v'ry moon Meet Me To-night In Dream-
Gm7 C7 F7 Bb G+ G7 C7 F7
land Where love's sweet ro-ses bloom Come with the love-light gleam-ing In your dear eyes of
Bb Bb7 Eb Edim Bb G7 C7 F7 1 Bb Gb7 Cm7 F7 2 Bb Bb7 Ebm Bb
blue Meet me in Dream-land sweet dream-y Dream-land There let my dreams come true. true.

MICHAEL FINNEGAN

Moderately, gradually increase tempo
C C/B C/A C/G Dm G7 C C/B C/A C/G
There was an old man named Mi-chael Fin-ne-gan. He had whisk-ers on his chin-ne-gan. He cut 'em off but they grew in a-gain.
Dm G C C C/B C/A C/G Dm
Poor old Mi-chael Fin-ne-gan. Be-gin a-gain. There was an old man named Mi-chael Fin-ne-gan. He went fish-ing
G C Dm G C A
with a pin a-gain. Caught a fish but it flopped back in a-gain. Poor old Mi-chael Fin-ne-gan. Be-gin a-gain. There
D D/C# D/B D/A Em A D
was an old man named Mi-chael Fin-ne-gan. Ran a race and tried to win a-gain. He fell down and bumped his shin a-gain.
Em A F#m B Em A D D/A D A D
Poor old Mi-chael, poor old Mi-chael, poor old Mi-chael Fin-ne-gan. Don't be-gin a-gain.

MERRILY WE ROLL ALONG

Brightly
Bb F Bb F7 Bb
Mer-ri-ly We Roll A-long, Roll a-long. Roll a-long. Mer-ri-ly We Roll A-long, O'er the deep blue sea.

MELODY IN A

Brig. Gen Charles G. Dawes

MELODY IN F

Anton G. Rubinstein

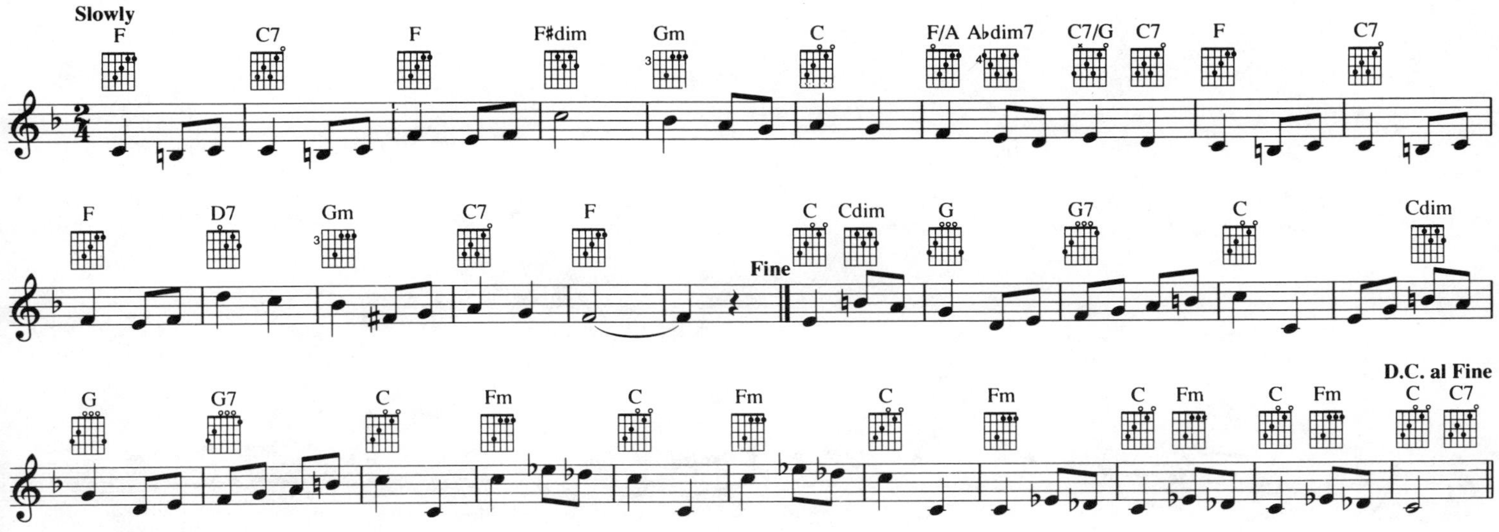

MELODY OF LOVE

H. Engelmann

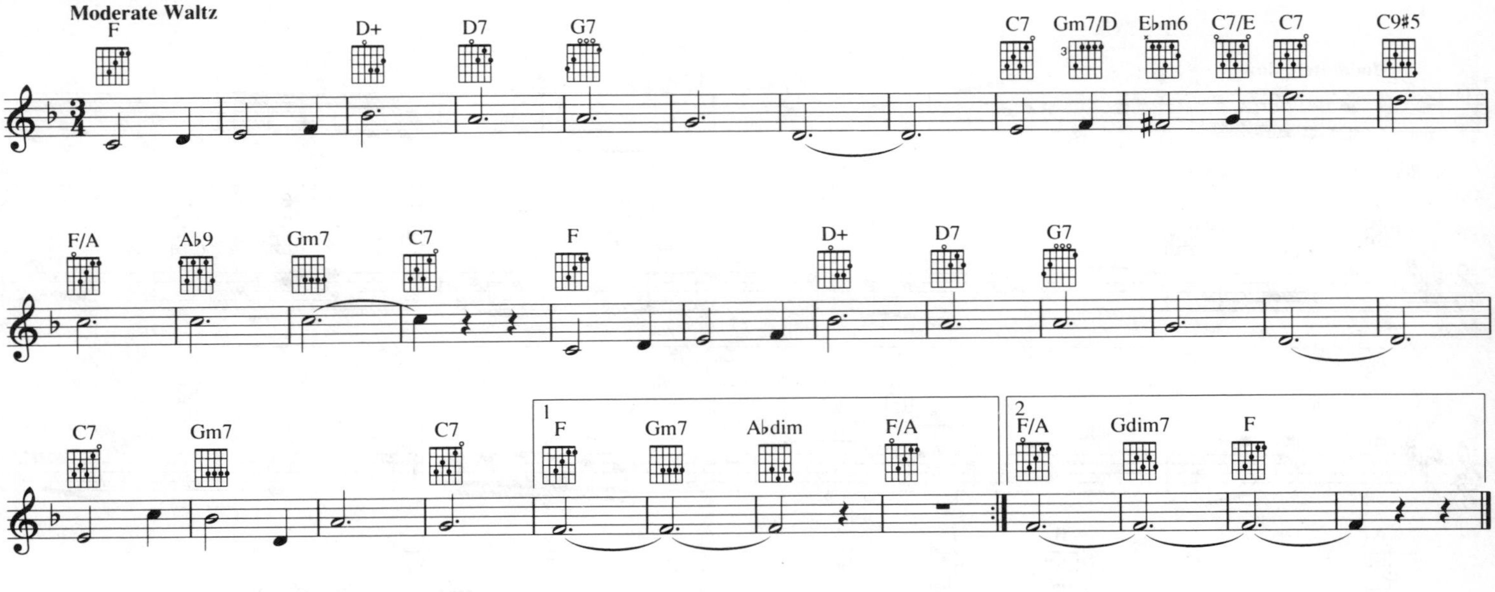

MEXICAN HAT DANCE

MICHAEL, ROW THE BOAT ASHORE

Moderately
C F C Em Dm C G7 C
1. Mi-chael, Row The Boat A-shore, Al-le-lu-ya, Mi-chael, Row The Boat A-shore, Al-le-lu-ya.
2 - 5. (See additional lyrics)

Additional Lyrics

2. Sister, help to trim the sail...

3. Michael's boat is a gospel boat...

4. Jordan's River is chilly and cold...
Chills the body but warms the soul...

5. Jordan's River is deep and wide...
Meet my mother on the other side...

MIGHTY LAK' A ROSE

Words by Frank L. Stanton; Music by Ethelbert Nevin

Slowly
E♭ B♭7#5 E♭ B♭7#5 E♭ Cm
Sweet-est lit-tle fel-low, Ev-'ry-bod-y knows, Don't know what to call him but he's
Look-ing at his mom-my With eyes so shin-y blue, Makes you think heav'n is
1 F7 B♭7 | 2 Fm B♭7 E♭ Fine
Might-y Lak A Rose! com-in' close to you!
Cm B♭7 E♭
When he's there a-sleep-in' in his ti-ny place,
B♭7 E♭ Cm Gm7
Think I see the an-gels look-in' thro' the lace. When the dark is fall-in',
Cm Gm Cm Gm7 Cm F7 B♭ B♭+ D.C. al Fine
When the shad-ows creep, Then they come on tip-toe to kiss him in his sleep.

M-I-N-E

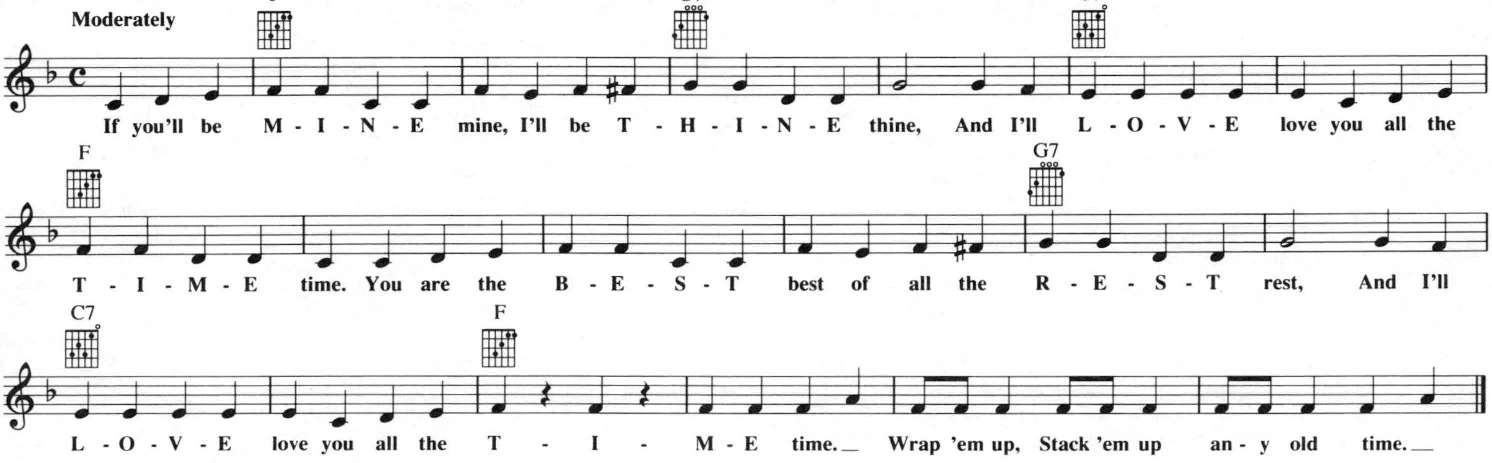
Moderately
F G7 C7
If you'll be M-I-N-E mine, I'll be T-H-I-N-E thine, And I'll L-O-V-E love you all the
F G7
T-I-M-E time. You are the B-E-S-T best of all the R-E-S-T rest, And I'll
C7 F
L-O-V-E love you all the T-I-M-E time. Wrap 'em up, Stack 'em up an-y old time.

THE MISSOURI WALTZ

Lyric by J.R. Shannon

Dreamily
Hush - a-bye, ma ba - by, slum - ber - time is com - in' soon; Rest yo' head up - on ma breast while
Mam - my hums a tune; The sand - man is call - in' where shad - ows are fall - in', While the
soft breez - es sigh as in days long gone by. 'Way down in Mis - sou - ri where I
heard this mel - o - dy, When I was a hap - py young - ster on ma Mam-my's knee; The
young folks were hum - min', Their ban - jos were strum - min' So sweet and
Fine
low. Strum, strum, strum, strum, strum, Seems I hear those ban - jos
play - in' once a - gain, Hum, hum, hum, hum, hum, That same old plain - tive
strain. Hear that mourn - ful mel - o - dy, It just haunts you the whole day
D.C. al Fine
long, And you wan - der in dreams back to Dix - ie, it seems, When you hear that old - time song.

MOONLIGHT SONATA
(1st Movement)

L thoven

Slow and Sustained

MOMENT MUSICALE
(Schubert)

Franz Schubert

Allegro Moderato

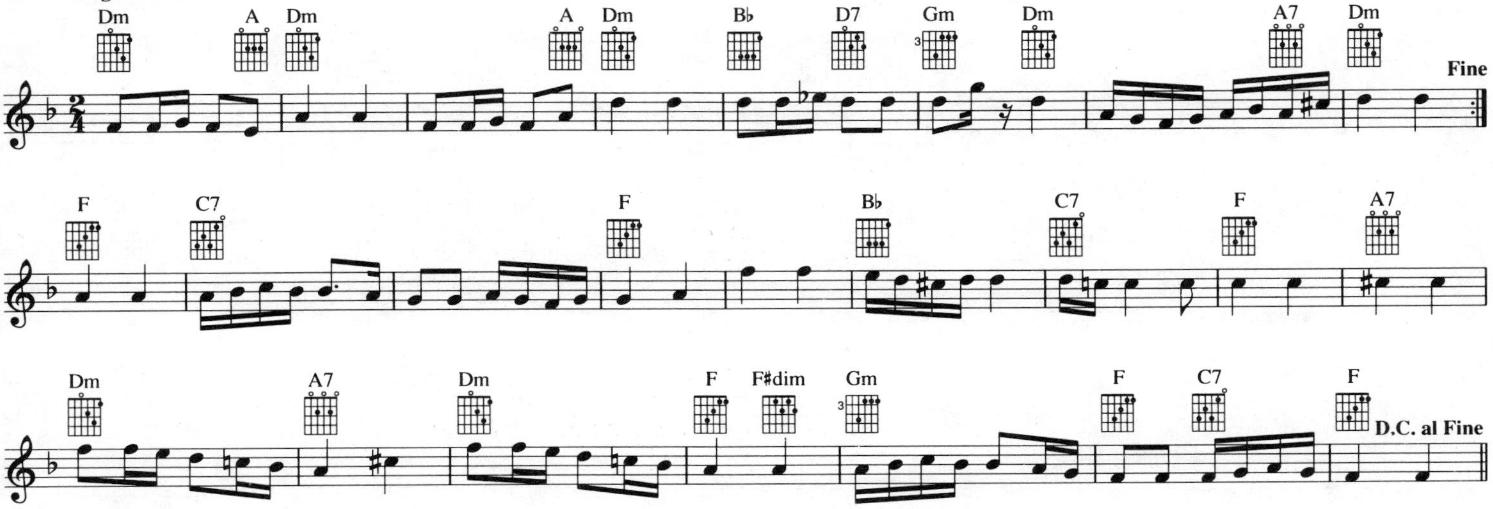

THE MULBERRY BUSH

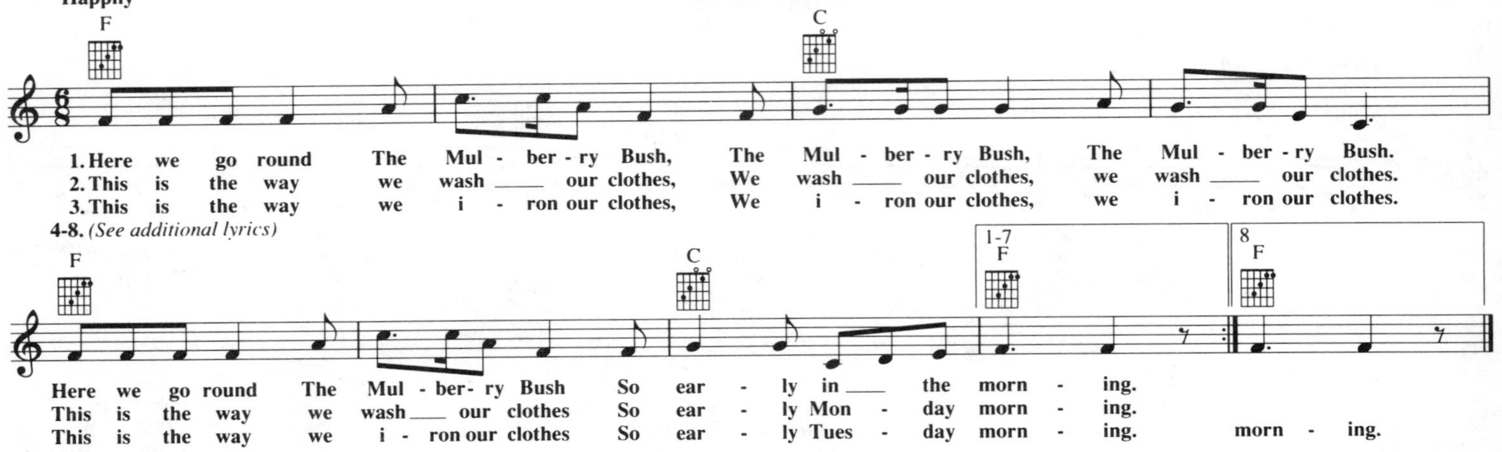
Happily
F
C
1. Here we go round The Mul - ber - ry Bush, The Mul - ber - ry Bush, The Mul - ber - ry Bush.
2. This is the way we wash ___ our clothes, We wash ___ our clothes, we wash ___ our clothes.
3. This is the way we i - ron our clothes, We i - ron our clothes, we i - ron our clothes.
4-8. (See additional lyrics)
1-7
8
Here we go round The Mul - ber - ry Bush So ear - ly in ___ the morn - ing.
This is the way we wash ___ our clothes So ear - ly Mon - day morn - ing.
This is the way we i - ron our clothes So ear - ly Tues - day morn - ing. morn - ing.

Additional Lyrics

4. This is the way we scrub the floor, etc.
So early Wednesday morning.

5. This is the way we mend our clothes, etc.
So early Thursday morning.

6. This is the way we sweep the house, etc.
So early Friday morning.

7. This is the way we bake our bread, etc.
So early Saturday morning.

8. This is the way we go to church, etc.
So early Sunday morning.

MORNING

Edvard Grieg

Slowly
Eb
Cm
Eb
Cm
G
G+
G
Cm
Bb
Bb7
Eb
Cm
Fm7
Fm6
Gm7
Eb
Abmaj7
Fm
G
Fm
G
Ab
G
Ab
G
Bb7
Eb
Cm
Eb
Cm
Eb
Cm
Eb
Cm
Eb
Cm
Eb

MUSETTA'S WALTZ

Giacomo Puccini

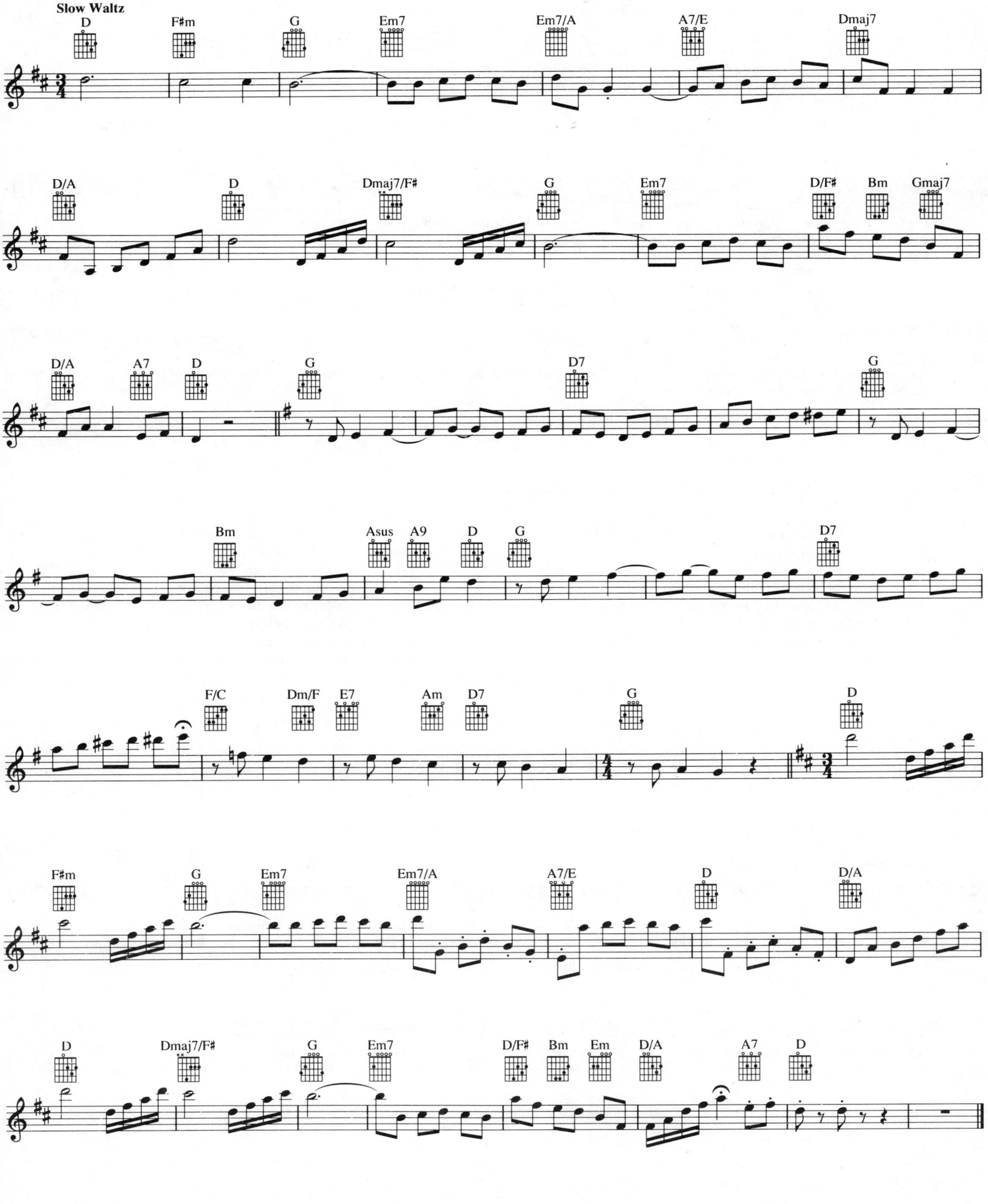

MY OLD KENTUCKY HOME

By Stephen Foster

Slowly
A A7 D A B7 E7
1. The sun shines bright on My Old Ken-tuck-y Home 'Tis sum-mer the work-ers are gay. The
young folks roll on the lit-tle cab-in floor, All mer-ry all hap-py and bright. By'n'
2-3. (See additional lyrics)
A A7 D A E7 A
corn top's ripe and the mead-ow's in bloom, While the birds make mu-sic all the day. The
bye hard times comes a knock-ing at the door, Then My
sing one song for My Old Ken-tuck-y Home, For My
2,3
B7 E7 A D A C#7 D A Dm
Fine
D.S. al Fine
Old Ken-tuck-y Home _ good-night. Weep no more, my la-dy, Oh! Weep no more to-day. We will
Old Ken-tuck-y Home far a-way.

Additional Lyrics

2. They hunt no more for the possum and the coon,
On meadow, the hill and the shore,
They sing no more by the glimmer of the moon,
On the bench by that old cabin door.
The day goes by like a shadow o'er the heart,
With sorrow where all was delight.
The time has come when the darkies have to part,
Then My Old Kentucky Home, good night.

3. The head must bow and the back will have to bend,
Wherever the poor folks may go.
A few more days and the trouble will end,
In the field where sugar-canes may grow.
A few more days for to tote the weary load,
No matter, 'twill never by light.
A few more days till we totter on the road,
The My Old Kentucky Home, good night.

MY WILD IRISH ROSE

Chauncey Olcott

Moderately
B♭ B♭+ E♭ B♭ C7 F7 Cm7 F7
If you lis-ten, I'll sing you a sweet lit-tle song Of a flow-er that's now drooped and dead, Yet
They may sing of their ros-es which, by oth-er names, Would smell just as sweet-ly they say, But I
B♭ B♭+ E♭ B♭ F7 E♭m F7 B♭ E♭6 B♭
dear-er to me, yes, than all of its mates, Tho' each holds a-loft its proud head. 'Twas
know that my Rose would nev-er con-sent To have that sweet name tak-en a-way. Her
F7 B♭ F7 B♭ D7 Gm C7 F7 Cm7 F7
giv-en to me by a girl that I know, Since we met, faith, I've known no re-pose, She is
glanc-es are shy when-e'er I pass by The bow-er where my true love grows; And my

Refrain:
With much expression
dear - er by far than the world's bright - est star, And I call her My Wild I - rish Rose.
one wish has been that some - day I may win The heart of My Wild I - rish Rose.
My
Wild I - rish Rose, The sweet - est flow'r that grows, You may
search ev - 'ry - where but none can com - pare with My Wild I - rish Rose. My
Wild I - rish Rose, The dear - est flow'r that grows And some
day for my sake, she may let me take The bloom from My Wild I - rish Rose.

NORWEGIAN DANCE

Edvard Grieg

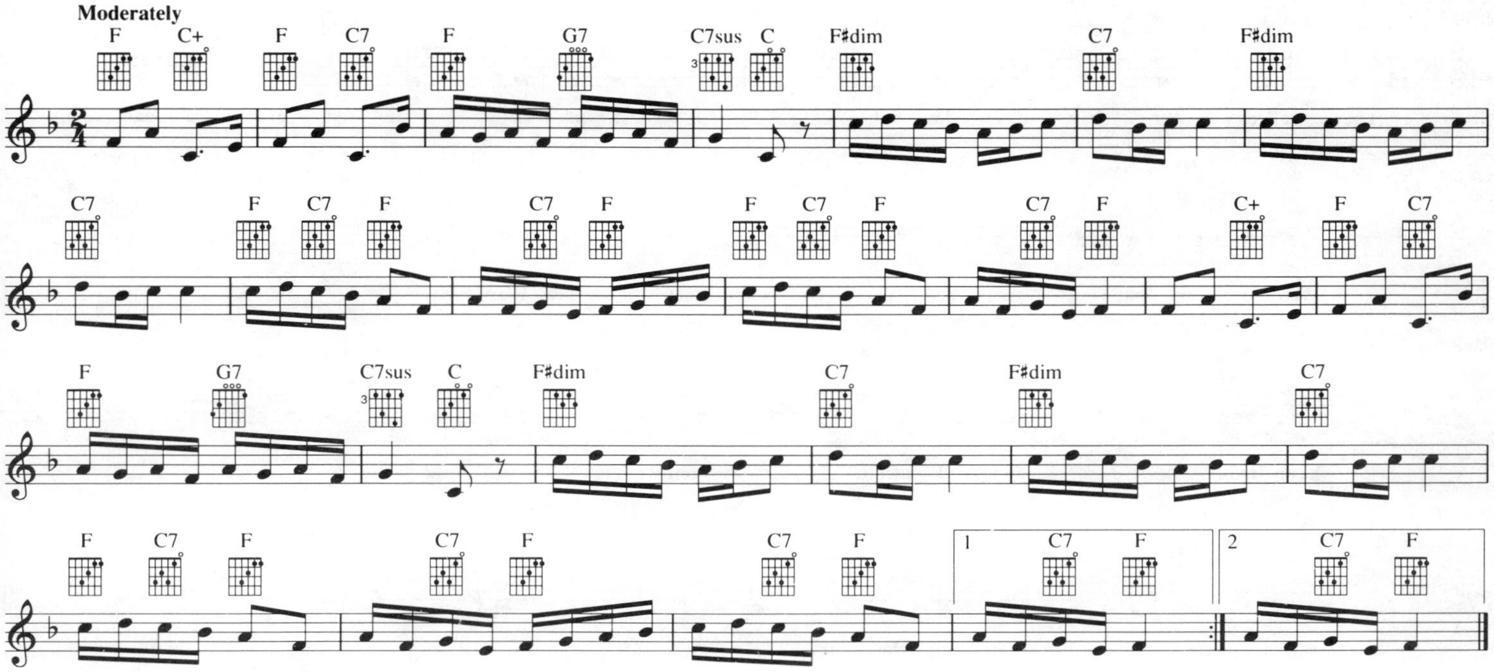
Moderately

MY BONNIE

Moderately
My Bon - nie lies o - ver the o - cean, My Bon - nie lies o - ver the sea.
My Bon - nie lies o - ver the o - cean, Oh bring back My Bon - nie to
me. Bring back, bring back, Bring back My Bon - nie to me, to
me, Bring back, bring back, Oh bring back My Bon - nie to me.

MY GAL SAL

Paul Dresser

Moderately
They called her friv - o - lous Sal, A pe - cu - liar sort of a gal,
With a heart that was mel - low, An all 'round good fel - low, Was my old pal.
Your trou - bles, sor - rows and care, She was al - ways will - ing to share. A
wild sort of dev - il, But dead on the lev - el, Was My Gal Sal.

NATIONAL EMBLEM

E.E. Bagley

NOEL! NOEL!

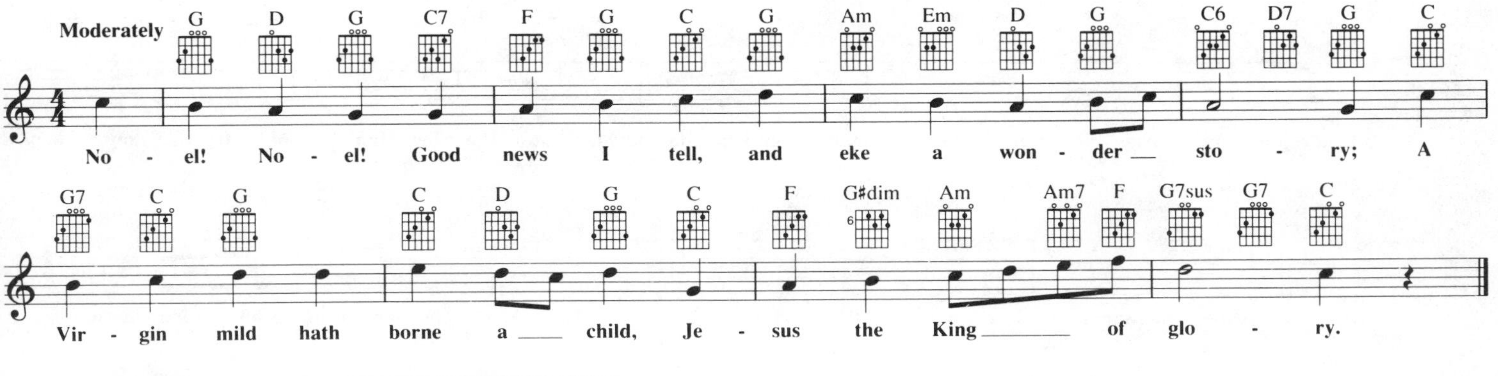

'NEATH THE OLD CHESTNUT TREE

Slowly
E E7 A E B B7 E E7
My way-far-ing ways took me a-way from the girl I loved so true. I kissed her on the cheek 'Neath The
A Am E/B B7 E E7 A E
Old Chest-nut Tree when I bid her a-dieu. The road I did ride was full of tears. I
B B7 E E7 A Am E/B B7
was so lone-some I could cry. Now I think of that girl 'Neath The Old Chest-nut Tree as I lay down to
E E7 A B7 G♯m7 C♯m F♯m7 B7 E E7 A B7
die. So bu-ry me 'Neath The Old Chest-nut Tree that we carved our names up-on. And this lone-some old cow-boy will
G♯m C♯m F♯m B7 E F♯m7 B7 E
fi-n'lly rest in peace. And that tree will still stand when I'm gone. I'll lie 'Neath The Old Chest-nut Tree.

NINE HUNDRED MILES

Moderately
Am
I am walk-ing down this track, I've got tears in my eyes, I'm try'n to read a let-ter from my home;
G Am
And if this train runs me right I'll be home Sat-ur-day night, 'Cause I'm Nine Hun-dred Miles from my home.
G Am G Am
And I hate to hear that lone-some whis-tle blow. That long lone-some train whis-tl-ing down.

NOBODY KNOWS THE TROUBLE I'VE SEEN

Prayerfully
E A E A B7 E A
No-bod-y Knows The Trou-ble I've Seen, no-bod-y knows but Je-sus; No-bod-y Knows The
E Fdim F#m7 B7 E A E E A E E G#m C#m
Trou-ble I've Seen, Glo-ry hal-le-lu-jah! Oh, lu-jah! 1. Some-times I'm up, some-times I'm down,
2. - 5. (See additional lyrics)
E A B7 E E7 A Am E B7 E
Oh, yes, Lord; Some-times I'm al-most to the groun', Oh, yes, Lord.
D.C.

Additional Lyrics

2. Now, you may think that I don't know, etc.
   But I've had my troubles here below, etc.

3. One day when I was walkin' along,
   The sky opened up and love came down.

4. What make old Satan hate me so?
   He had me once and had to let me go.

5. I never shall forget that day,
   When Jesus washed my sins away.

THE OLD GRAY MARE

Traditional

With Spirit
F C7 F C
Oh The Old Gray Mare, She ain't what she used to be, Ain't what she used to be,
F C7 F C7
Ain't what she used to be. The Old Gray Mare, She ain't what she used to be, man-y long years a-
D.S. al Fine
F F Bb F F Bb Bbm F C7
go. Fine Man-y long years a-go, Man-y long years a-go, Oh The

NOCTURNE
(Chopin)

Frederic Chopin

With expression
C Ddim C A A7 Gdim Dm G7
E7 Am F#dim Gsus G7 C Ddim
C A A7 Gdim Dm G7 E7 Am F#dim
Gsus G7 C G D7 F
Fm C C#dim A7 D7 Em Am D7 G G#7 C# A7 D7 G7
C G7 C A7
Gdim Dm G7 E7 Am F#dim G7 C

NOW THE DAY IS OVER

Sabine Baring-Gould
Joseph Barnby

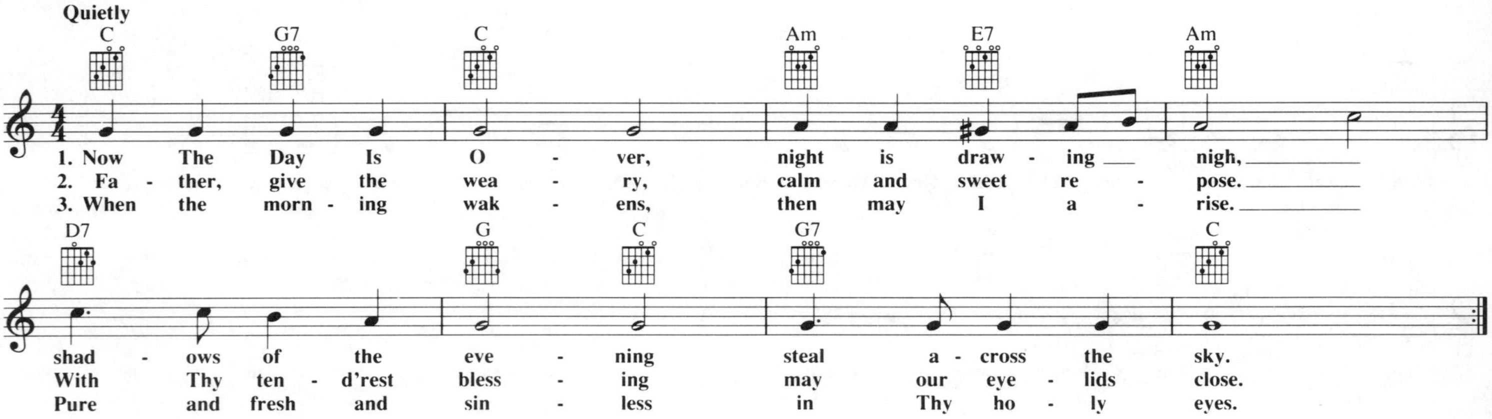
Quietly
C G7 C Am E7 Am
1. Now The Day Is O - ver, night is draw - ing nigh,
2. Fa - ther, give the wea - ry, calm and sweet re - pose.
3. When the morn - ing wak - ens, then may I a - rise.
D7 G C G7 C
shad - ows of the eve - ning steal a - cross the sky.
With Thy ten - d'rest bless - ing may our eye - lids close.
Pure and fresh and sin - less in Thy ho - ly eyes.

NOW THANK WE ALL OUR GOD

Johann Cruger

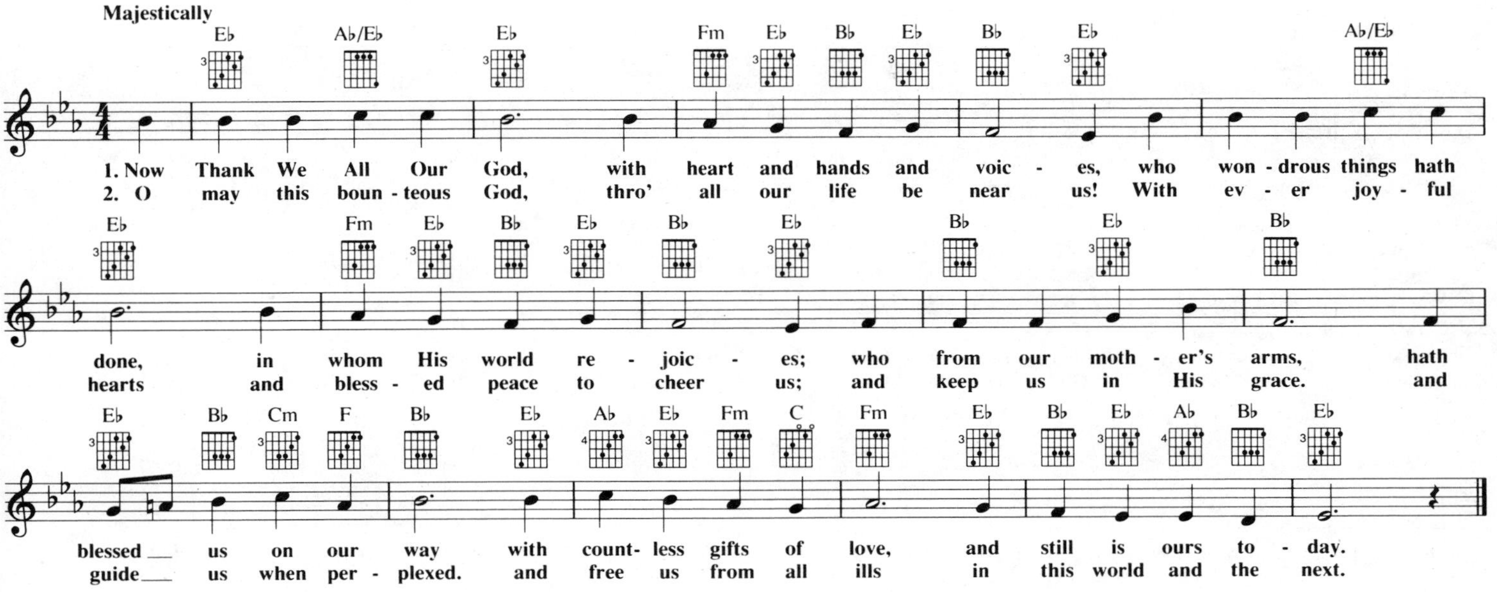
Majestically
Eb Ab/Eb Eb Fm Eb Bb Eb Bb Eb Ab/Eb
1. Now Thank We All Our God, with heart and hands and voic - es, who won - drous things hath
2. O may this boun - teous God, thro' all our life be near us! With ev - er joy - ful
Eb Fm Eb Bb Eb Bb Eb Bb Eb Bb
done, in whom His world re - joic - es; who from our moth - er's arms, hath
hearts and bless - ed peace to cheer us; and keep us in His grace. and
Eb Bb Cm F Bb Eb Ab Eb Fm C Fm Eb Bb Eb Ab Bb Eb
blessed us on our way with count- less gifts of love, and still is ours to - day.
guide us when per - plexed. and free us from all ills in this world and the next.

O CANADA!

Calixa Lavallee, l'Hon. Judge Routhier, and
Justice R.S. Weir

Maestoso
Eb Bb Cm Eb Bb Eb F Gm
1. O Can - a - da! Our home and na - tive land! True pa - triot love in
2. O Can - a - da! Where pines and ma - ples grow, Great prai - ries spread and
French: O Can - a - da! Ter - re de nos aï - eux, Ton front est cient de
Bb F Bb Fm Bb Eb Cm Ab
all thy sons com - mand, with glow - ing hearts we see thee rise, the true North strong and
lord - ly riv - ers flow, how dear to us thy vast do - main, from east to west - ern
fleu - rons glo - ri - eux! Car ton bras sait por - ter l'é - pé - e, Il sait por - ter la
Bb Fm Bb Eb Cm C Bb F7 Bb
free, and stand on guard, O Can - a - da, we stand on guard for thee.
sea, thou land of hope for all who toil! Thou true North strong and free.
croix! Ton his - toire est une é - po - pé - e Des plus bril - lants ex - ploits.
Refrain
Eb Bb/D Cm Fm Ab Bb Eb G7 Cm Fm C Fm
O Can - a - da, glo - rious and free, O Can - a - da, we stand on
Et ta va - leur, de foi trem - pée, Pro - té - ge - ra nos foy - ers
Ab Bb Eb Ab Eb/Bb Bb Eb
guard for thee. O Can - a - da, we stand on guard for thee.
et nos droits, Pro - té - ge ra nos foy - ers et nos droits.

O COME, ALL YE FAITHFUL

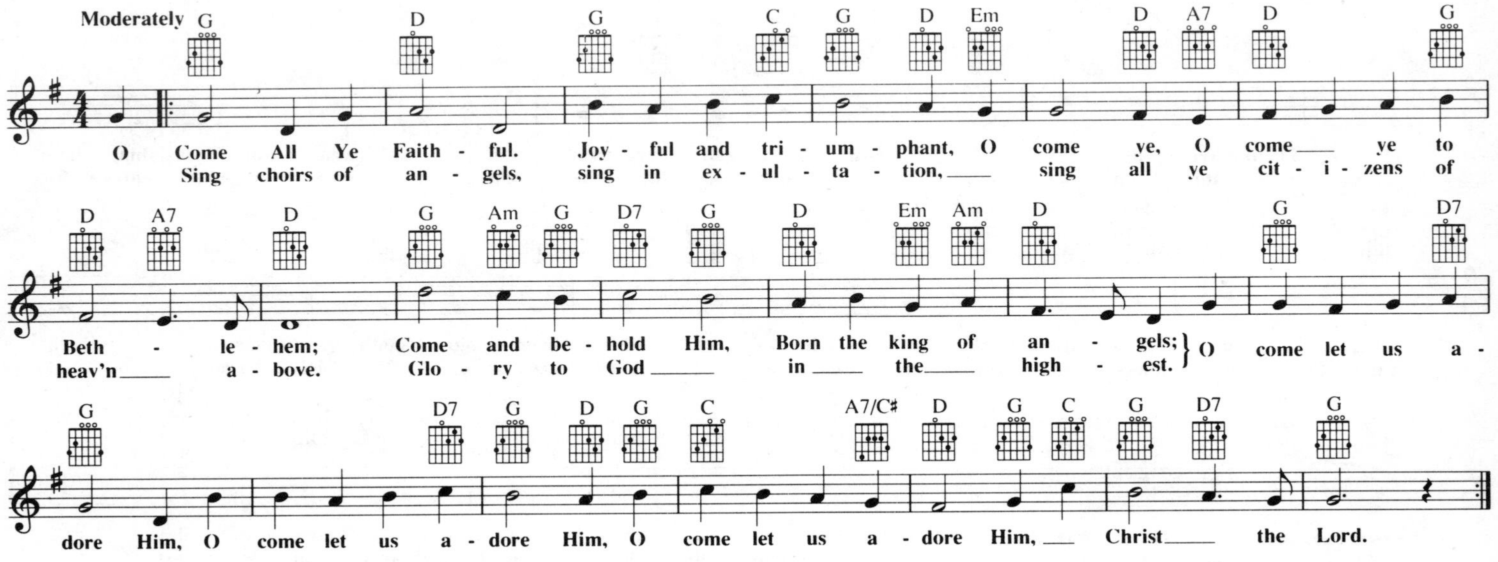
Moderately
G D G C G D Em D A7 D G
O Come All Ye Faith - ful. Joy - ful and tri - um - phant, O come ye, O come ye to
Sing choirs of an - gels, sing in ex - ul - ta - tion, sing all ye cit - i - zens of
D A7 D G Am G D7 G D Em Am D G D7
Beth - le - hem; Come and be - hold Him, Born the king of an - gels;
heav'n a - bove. Glo - ry to God in the high - est.
O come let us a -
G D7 G D G C A7/C♯ D G C G D7 G
dore Him, O come let us a - dore Him, O come let us a - dore Him, Christ the Lord.

O COME, LITTLE CHILDREN

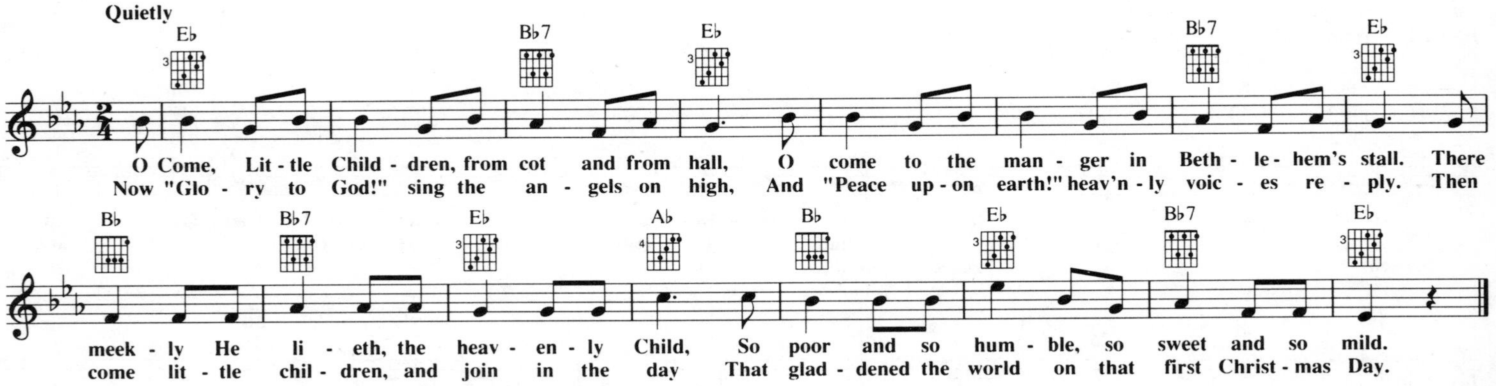
Quietly
E♭ B♭7 E♭ B♭7 E♭
O Come, Lit - tle Child - dren, from cot and from hall, O come to the man - ger in Beth - le - hem's stall. There
Now "Glo - ry to God!" sing the an - gels on high, And "Peace up - on earth!" heav'n - ly voic - es re - ply. Then
B♭ B♭7 E♭ A♭ B♭ E♭ B♭7 E♭
meek - ly He li - eth, the heav - en - ly Child, So poor and so hum - ble, so sweet and so mild.
come lit - tle chil - dren, and join in the day That glad - dened the world on that first Christ - mas Day.

O HOLY NIGHT

Words by J.S. Dwight
Music by Adolphe Adam

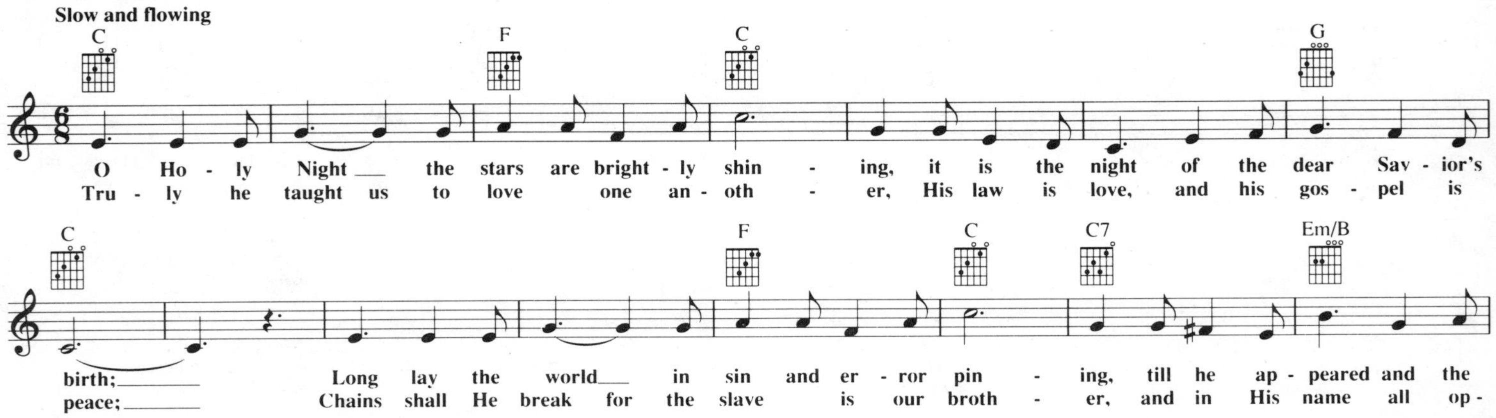
Slow and flowing
C F C G
O Ho - ly Night the stars are bright - ly shin - ing, it is the night of the dear Sav - ior's
Tru - ly he taught us to love one an - oth - er, His law is love, and his gos - pel is
C F C C7 Em/B
birth; Long lay the world in sin and er - ror pin - ing, till he ap - peared and the
peace; Chains shall He break for the slave is our broth - er, and in His name all op -

B7 Em G7 C G7
soul felt its worth. A thrill of hope the wea - ry soul re - joic - es, for yon - der
pres - sion shall cease. Sweet hymns of joy in grate - ful cho - rus raise we, let all with -
C Am Em Dm
breaks a new and glo - rious morn; Fall on your knees, oh, hear the an - gel
in us praise His ho - ly name; Christ is the Lord, oh, praise His name for -
Am C G7 C/E F C G7 C
voic - es! O night di - vine o night when Christ was born!
ev - er! His pow'r and glo - ry ev - er more pro - claim
1 G G7 C F C G7 C 2 G
O night O Ho - ly night O night di - vine!
His pow'r
G7 C/E F C G7 C
and glo - ry ev - er - more pro - claim!

O CHRISTMAS TREE

Moderately
G D7 G Am D7 G D7
O Christ - mas Tree! O Christ - mas Tree, You stand in ver - dant beau - ty! O Christ - mas Tree, O
Christ - mas Tree! O Christ - mas Tree, Much plea - sure doth thou bring me! O Christ - mas Tree, O
Christ - mas Tree! O Christ - mas Tree, Thy can - dles shine out bright - ly! O Christ - mas Tree, O
G Am D7 G C D7
Christ - mas Tree, You stand in ver - dant beau - ty! Your boughs are green in sum - mer's glow, And
Christ - mas Tree, Much plea - sure doth thou bring me! For ev' - ry year the Christ - mas Tree, Brings
Christ - mas Tree, Thy can - dles shine out bright - ly! Each bough doth hold its ti - ny light, That
G D7 G D7 G E7 Am D7 G
do not fade in win - ter's snow. O Christ - mas Tree, O Christ - mas Tree, You stand in ver - dant beau - ty! O
to us all both joy and glee. O Christ - mas Tree, O Christ - mas Tree, Much plea - sure doth thou bring me! O
makes each toy to spar - kle bright. O Christ - mas Tree, O Christ - mas Tree, Thy can - dles shine out bright - ly!

O COME, O COME EMMANUEL

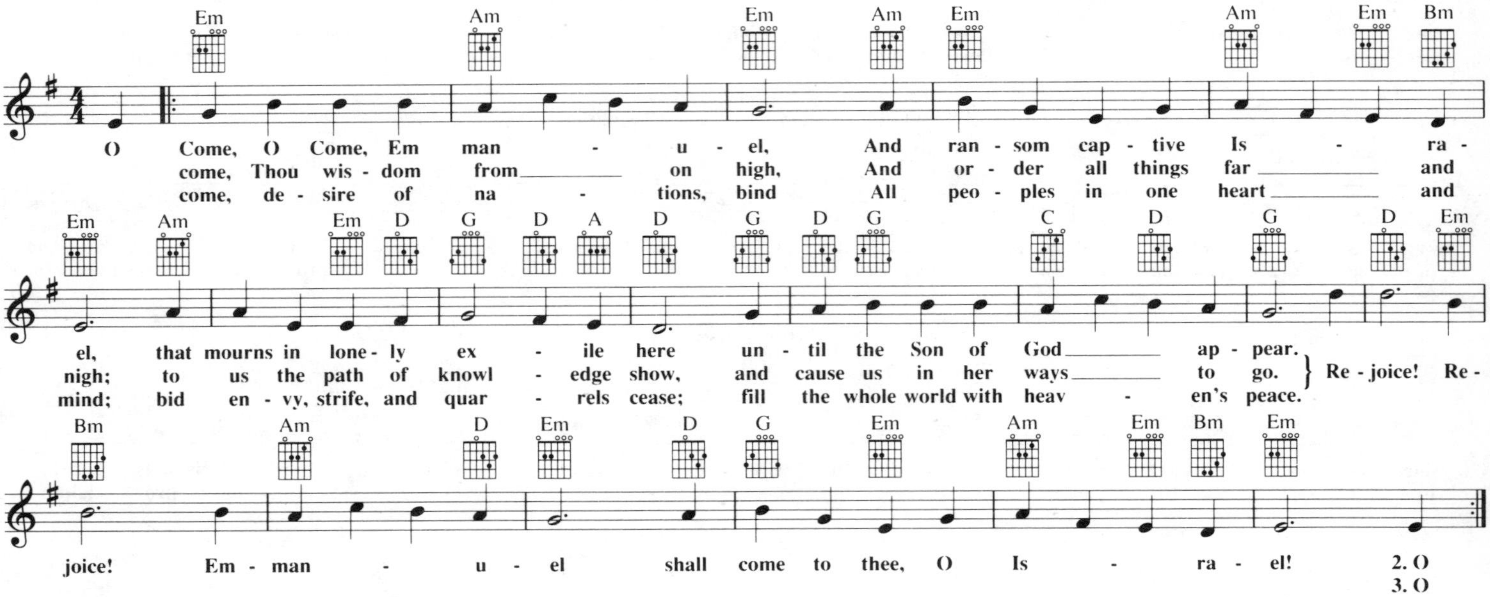
O Come, O Come, Em man - u - el, And ran - som cap - tive Is - ra - el, that mourns in lone - ly ex - ile here un - til the Son of God ap - pear.
come, Thou wis - dom from on high, And or - der all things far and nigh; to us the path of knowl - edge show, and cause us in her ways to go.
come, de - sire of na - tions, bind All peo - ples in one heart and mind; bid en - vy, strife, and quar - rels cease; fill the whole world with heav - en's peace.
Re - joice! Re - joice! Em - man - u - el shall come to thee, O Is - ra - el!
2. O
3. O

O LITTLE TOWN OF BETHLEHEM

Brooks/Redner

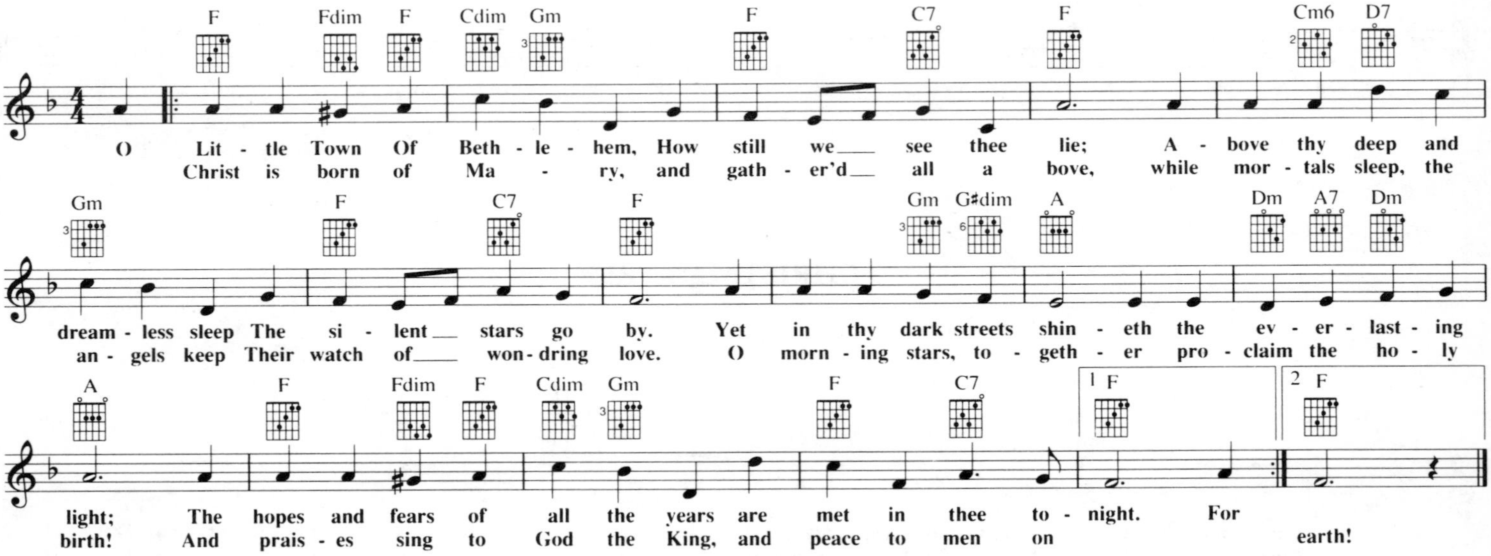
O Lit - tle Town Of Beth - le - hem, How still we see thee lie; A - bove thy deep and dream - less sleep The si - lent stars go by. Yet in thy dark streets shin - eth the ev - er - last - ing light; The hopes and fears of all the years are met in thee to - night. For
Christ is born of Ma - ry, and gath - er'd all a bove, while mor - tals sleep, the an - gels keep Their watch of won - dring love. O morn - ing stars, to - geth - er pro - claim the ho - ly birth! And prais - es sing to God the King, and peace to men on earth!

O SANCTISSIMA

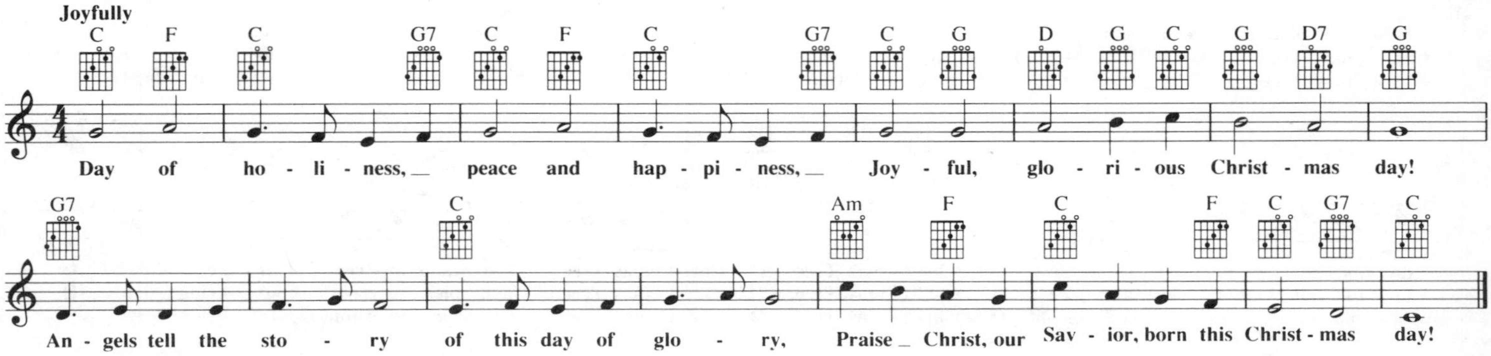
Joyfully
Day of ho - li - ness, peace and hap - pi - ness, Joy - ful, glo - ri - ous Christ - mas day!
An - gels tell the sto - ry of this day of glo - ry, Praise Christ, our Sav - ior, born this Christ - mas day!

O SOLE MIO

E. Di Capua

OBEREK

ODE TO JOY

Ludwig van Beethoven

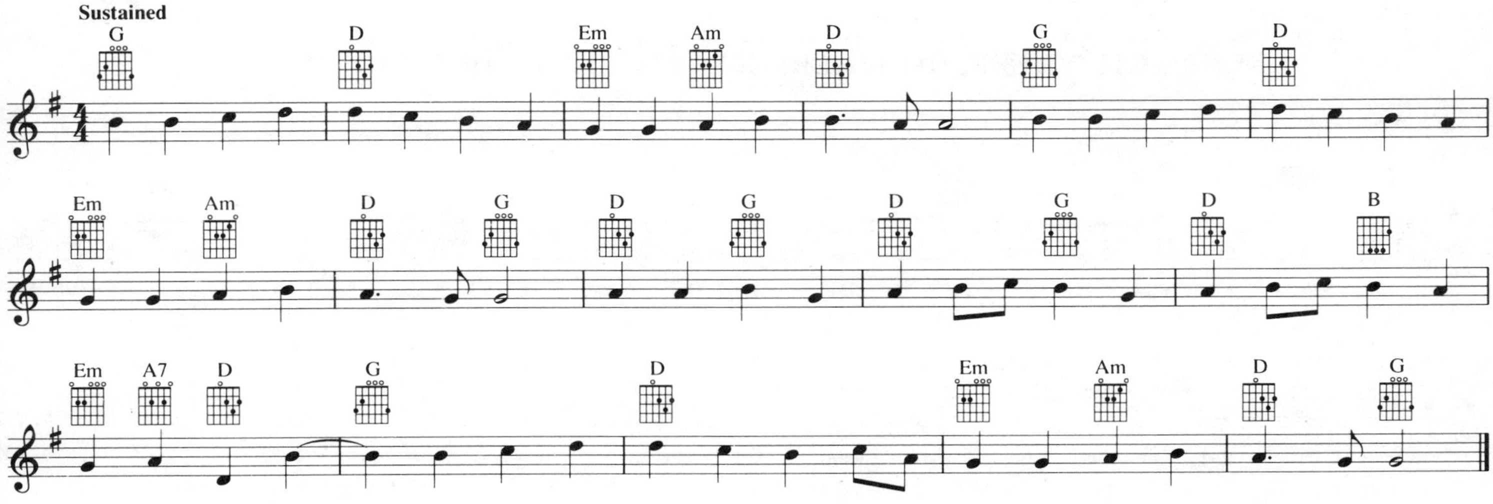

OATS, PEAS, BEANS AND BARLEY GROW

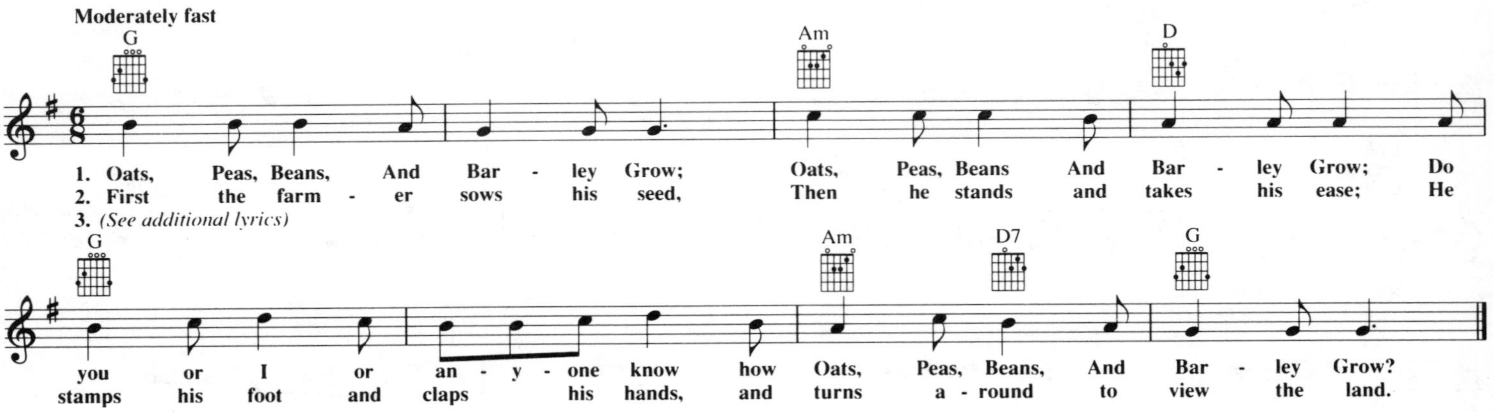
Moderately fast
G Am D G Am D7 G
1. Oats, Peas, Beans, And Bar - ley Grow; Oats, Peas, Beans And Bar - ley Grow; Do you or I or an - y - one know how Oats, Peas, Beans, And Bar - ley Grow?
2. First the farm - er sows his seed, Then he stands and takes his ease; He stamps his foot and claps his hands, and turns a - round to view the land.
3. (See additional lyrics)

Additional Lyrics

3. Waiting for a partner,
   Waiting for a partner,
   Open the ring and take one in
   While we all gaily dance and sing.

OH MARIE

E. Di Capua

Moderately
C G7 C A7 Dm Fm C/E E♭dim G7/D G7 C
Oh Ma - rie, Oh Ma - rie, there is no one but you, dear for me. My heart's re - peat - ing each word you can hear in it's beat - ing, Oh Ma - rie, Oh Ma - rie, fair - est flow - er in all It - al - y I beg of thee, hear my plea Oh Ma - rie.

OH WHERE, OH WHERE HAS MY LITTLE DOG GONE?

Moderately
F C7 F C7 F C7 F
Oh Where, Oh Where Has My Lit - tle Dog Gone? Oh where, oh where can he be? With his ears cut short and his tail cut long; Oh where, oh where can he be?

OH, SUSANNA

Stephen Foster

Moderately
C D7 G7 C
1. I come from Al - a - bam - a with a ban - jo on my knee. I'm goin' to Lou' - si
rained all night the day I left, the weath - er it was dry. The sun so hot I
2, 3. (See additional lyrics)
G7 1 C 2 C Chorus F
an - a my Su - san - na for to see. It Oh, Su - san - na, oh
froze to death, Su - san - na don't you cry.
C D7 G7 C G7 C
don't you cry for me, for I come from Al - a - bam - a with a ban - jo on my knee.

Additional Lyrics

2. I had a dream the other night
When everything was still.
I thought I saw Susanna
A-coming down the hill.

3. The buckwheat cake was in her mouth,
The tear was in her eye,
Say I, "I'm coming from the South,
Susanna, don't you cry."

OH, DEAR! WHAT CAN THE MATTER BE?

Merrily
F C7 F
Oh, Dear! What Can The Mat - ter Be? Dear, dear, what can the mat - ter be? Oh, Dear! What Can The Mat - ter Be?
Gm C7 F C7
John - ny's so long at the fair. He prom - ised to buy me a trin - ket to please me, and then for a smile, oh he
He prom - ised to bring me a bas - ket of po - sies, a gar - land of lil - ies, a
F Gm C7 F
vowed he would tease me, he prom - ised to bring me a bunch of blue rib - bons, to tie up my bon - nie brown hair.
gar - land of ros - es, a lit - tle straw hat to set off the blue rib - bons, that tie up my bon - nie brown hair.

OH, THEM GOLDEN SLIPPERS

James A. Bland

Moderately
A
E7
D
1. Oh, my gold - en slip - pers are laid a - way, 'Cause I don't 'spect to wear them till my wed - ding day, and my
2,3. (See additional lyrics)
long - tailed coat, that I loved so well, I will wear up in the char - iot in the morn. And my
long white robe that I bought last June, I'm goin' to get changed 'cause it fits too soon, and the
old gray horse that I used to drive, I will hitch him to the char - iot in the morn. Oh, Them
Gold - en Slip - pers Oh, Them Gold - en Slip - pers, gold - en slip - pers I'm goin' to wear, Be -
1
cause they look so neat.
2
goin' to wear to walk the gold - en street.

Additional Lyrics

2. Oh, my old banjo hangs on the wall,
'Cause it ain't been tuned since 'way last fall,
But the folks all say we'll have a good time,
When we ride up in the chariot in the morn,
There's old Brother Ben and his sister Luce,
They will telegraph the news to Uncle 'Bacco Juice,
What a great camp meeting there will be that day,
When we ride up in the chariot in the morning.

3. So, it's goodbye children, I will have to go,
Where the rain don't fall and the wind don't blow,
And your ulster coats, why, you will not need,
When you ride up in the chariot in the morn,
But your golden slippers must be nice and clean,
And your age must be just sweet sixteen,
And your white kid gloves you will have to wear,
When you ride up in the chariot in the morn.

OH, PROMISE ME

Words by Clement Scott
Music by R. de Koven

Slow
F
Gm7
B♭m
F
C7
Oh, Prom - ise Me that some - day you and I will take our love to - geth - er to some sky where

Gm Bb A6 C7
we can be a - lone, and faith re - new, and find the hol - lows where those flow - ers grew, ___ those
F Dm Am9 C Bb Gm7 D9 A7
first sweet vi - o - lets of ear - ly spring, which come in whis - pers, thrill us both, and sing O
Bb C7/Bb Dm7/A Gm7 C7#5 F C7 F Dm7 Gm7 C7
love un - speak - a - ble that is to be; Oh, Prom - ise Me! Oh, Prom - ise me! Oh,
F Gm7 Bbm F C7
Prom - ise Me that you will take my hand, the most un - wor - thy in this lone - ly land, and
Gm Bb A6 C7
let me sit be - side you, in your eyes see - ing the vi - sion of our par - a - dise,
F Dm Am9 C Gm7 D7 A7
hear - ing God's mes - sage while the or - gan rolls its might - y mu - sic to our ver - y souls; No
Bb C7/Bb Dm7/A Gm7 C7#5 F C7 F
love less per - fect than a life with thee; Oh Prom - ise Me! Oh Prom - ise me!

NEARER MY GOD TO THEE

Words by Sarah F. Adams
Music by Lowell Mason

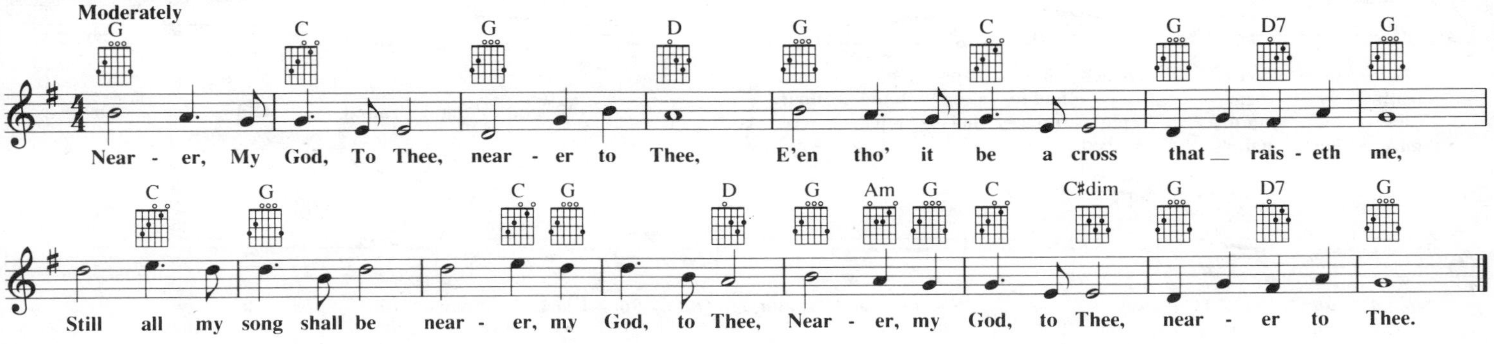
Moderately
G C G D G C G D7 G
Near - er, My God, To Thee, near - er to Thee, E'en tho' it be a cross that ___ rais - eth me,
C G C G D G Am G C C#dim G D7 G
Still all my song shall be near - er, my God, to Thee, Near - er, my God, to Thee, near - er to Thee.

THE OLD CHISHOLM TRAIL

Lively
E
Refrain
1. Well, come a - long, boys, and lis - ten to my tale I'll tell you all my trou - bles on The Old Chis - holm Trail. Come a
2-8. (See additional lyrics)
A B7 E B7 E
ti yi yip - py, yip - py yay, yip - py yay! Come a ti yi yip - py, yip - py yay!

Additional Lyrics

2. On a ten dollar horse and a forty dollar saddle
   I started out a-punchin' those long-horned cattle.
   Refrain

3. I'm up in the morning before daylight
   And before I gets to sleepin' the old moon's
   shining bright.
   Refrain

4. Oh, it's bacon and beans almost every single day
   And I'd sooner be a-eatin' prairie hay.
   Refrain

5. I went to the boss for to draw my roll,
   He had it figured out I was nine dollars in the hole.
   Refrain

6. So I went up to the boss and said I won't take that
   And I slapped him in the face with my old slouch hat.
   Refrain

7. I'll sell my outfit just as soon as I can,
   'Cause I ain't punchin' cattle for no mean boss man.
   Refrain

8. With my knees in the saddle and my seat in the sky,
   I'll quit punchin' cattle in the sweet by and by.
   Refrain

OLD JOE CLARK

Lively
D C D C D C
Old Joe Clark, he had a house, six - teen sto - ries high, Ev - 'ry sto - ry
I went up to Joe's new house, stepped right in the door, Joe was sleep - in' on a
Old Joe Clark, he had a dog, dumb as he could be, Barked a lad-y - bug
Old Joe Clark had a mean old cat, nev - er did sing or pray. Stuck her head in the
D C D
Refrain
in the house, smelled like ap - ple pie.
feath - er bed, I had to sleep on the floor.
up a stump, a pig up a hol - low tree.
milk - ing pail, washed her sins a - way!
'Round and 'round, Old Joe Clark,
C D C D
'round and 'round, I say; 'Round and 'round, Old Joe Clark, dance your cares a - way.

OLD DAN TUCKER

Quickly
A
E7
A
1. Went to town the oth - er night to hear a noise and see a fight, all the peo - ple were run - ning a - round, say - ing,
2. (See additional lyrics)
E7
A
A
D
E7
A
Old Dan Tuck - er's come to town. Get out the way, Old Dan Tuck - er, you're too late to come for sup - per,
D
E7
A
sup - per's o - ver and din - ner's cook - ing and Old Dan Tuck - er just stand - ing there look - ing.

Additional Lyrics

2. Old Dan Tucker's a fine old man,
Washed his face in a frying pan.
Combed his hair with a wagon wheel,
And died with a toothache in his heel.

3. Old Dan Tucker come to town,
Riding a billy goat, leading a hound.
Hound barked and the billygoat jumped,
Throwed old Dan right straddle of a stump.

4. Old Dan Tucker clumb a tree,
His Lord and Master for to see,
The limb it broke and Dan got a fall,
Never got to see his Lord at all.

5. Old Dan Tucker he got drunk,
Fell in the fire and he kicked up a chunk;
Red hot coal got in his shoe,
Lord Godamighty, how the ashed flew!

6. Old Dan Tucker he come to town,
Swinging the ladies 'round and 'round,
First to the right and then to the left,
And then to the one that you love the best.

OLD KING COLE

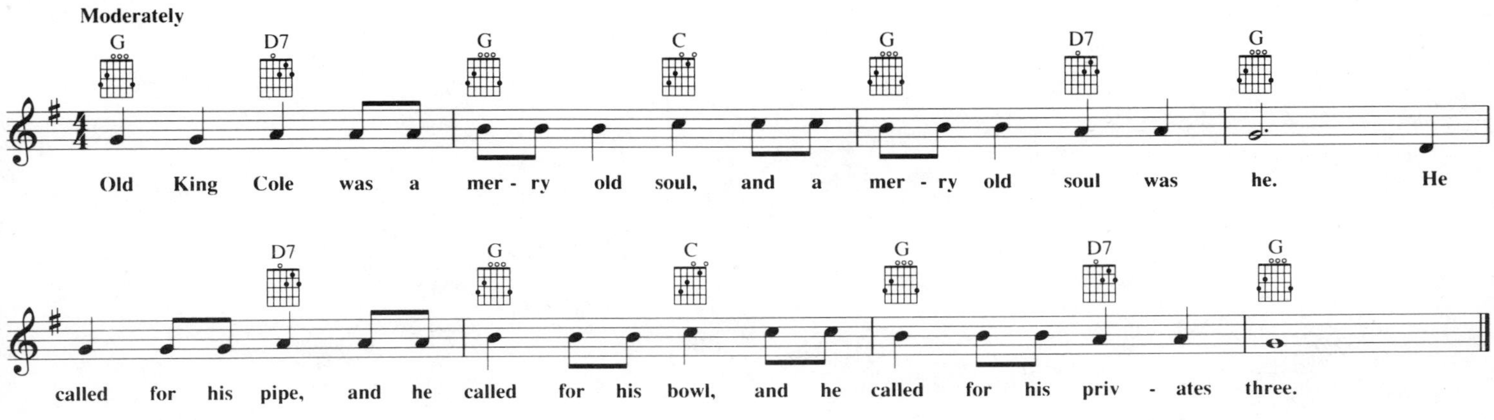
Moderately
G
D7
G
C
G
D7
G
Old King Cole was a mer - ry old soul, and a mer - ry old soul was he. He
D7
G
C
G
D7
G
called for his pipe, and he called for his bowl, and he called for his priv - ates three.

OLD FOLKS AT HOME

Stephen Foster

Moderately
D A7 D G D E7 A7
Way down up - on the Swan - ee riv - er, far, far a - way,
All 'round the lit - tle farm I wan - der'd, When I was young;
One lit - tle hut a - mong the bush - es, One that I love,
D A7 D G D A7 D A7
There's where my heart is turn - ing ev - er; There's where the old folks stay. All up and down the
Then man - y hap - py days I squan - der'd, Man - y the songs I sung. When I was play - ing
Still sad - ly to my mem - 'ry rush - es, No mat - ter where I rove. When shall I see the
D G D E7 A7 D A7 D G
whole cre - a - tion, Sad - ly I roam, still long - ing for the old plan - ta - tion,
with my broth - er, Hap - py was I, Oh, take me to my kind old moth - er,
bees a hum - ming, All 'round the comb? When shall I hear the ban - jo strum - ming,
D A7 D A7 D G
And for the Old Folks At Home.
There let me live and ___ die.
Down in my good old ___ home.
All the world is sad and drear - y Ev - 'ry - where I
D A7 D A7 D G D A7 D
roam, O how my heart is grow - ing wear - y, Far from the Old Folks At Home.

OLD MacDONALD HAD A FARM

Moderately
G C G D7 G C G
1. Old Mac - Don - ald Had A Farm E - I - E - I - O! And on this farm he had a duck,
2-10. (See additional lyrics)
D7 G
E - I - E - I - O! With a quack - quack here, and a quack - quack there, Here a quack, there a quack,
C G D7 G
Ev - 'ry where a quack, quack. Old Mac - Don - ald Had A Farm, E - I - E - I - O!

Additional Lyrics

2. Old MacDonald Had A Farm,
E - I - E - I - O!
And on this farm he had a chick,
E - I - E - I - O!
With a chick, chick here
And a chick, chick there,
Here a chick, there a chick,
Everywhere a chick, chick
Old MacDonald Had A Farm,
E - I - E - I - O!

3. Other verses:

3. Cow — moo, moo
4. Dogs — bow, bow
5. Pigs — oink, oink
6. Rooster — cock-a-doodle, cock-a-doodle
7. Turkey — gobble, gobble
8. Cat — meow, meow
9. Horse — neigh, neigh
10. Donkey — hee-haw, hee-haw

OLD OAKEN BUCKET

Words by Samuel Woodworth
Music by Edwin Krallmark

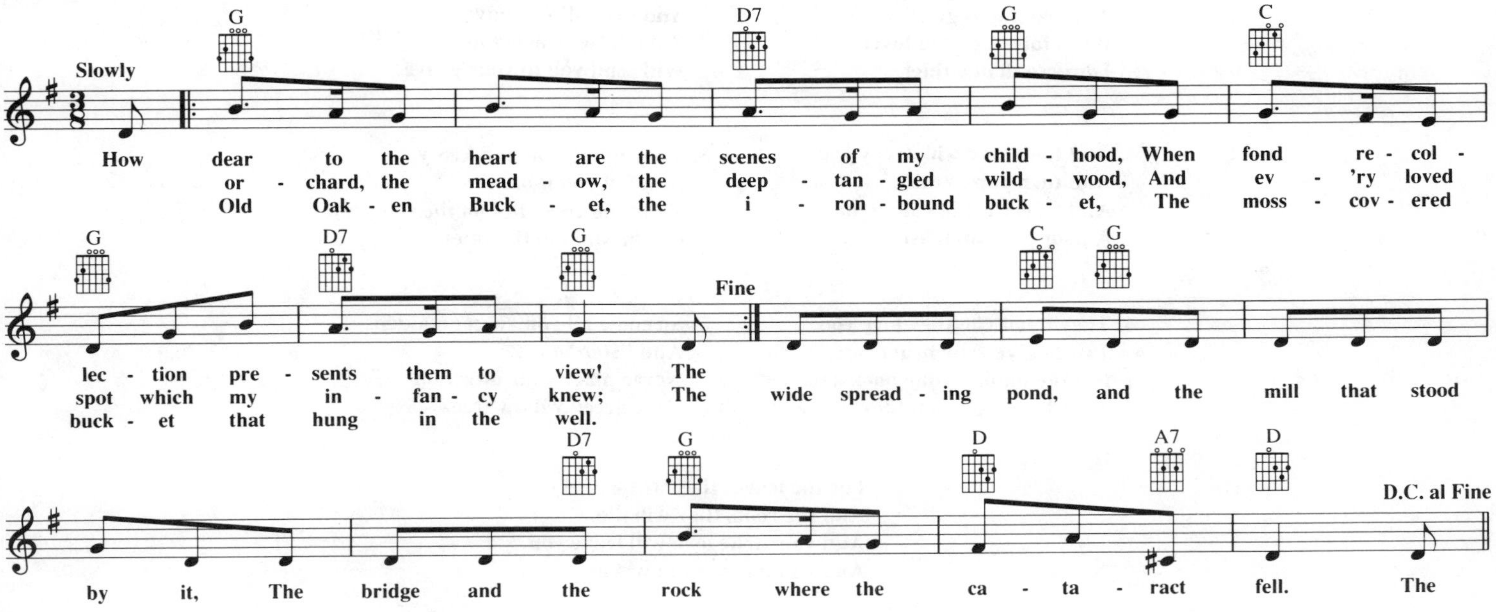
Slowly
G D7 G C
How dear to the heart are the scenes of my child - hood, When fond re - col -
or - chard, the mead - ow, the deep - tan - gled wild - wood, And ev - 'ry loved
Old Oak - en Buck - et, the i - ron - bound buck - et, The moss - cov - ered
G D7 G C G
Fine
lec - tion pre - sents them to view! The
spot which my in - fan - cy knew; The wide spread - ing pond, and the mill that stood
buck - et that hung in the well.
D7 G D A7 D
D.C. al Fine
by it, The bridge and the rock where the ca - ta - ract fell. The

ON THE BANKS OF THE WABASH

Paul Dresser

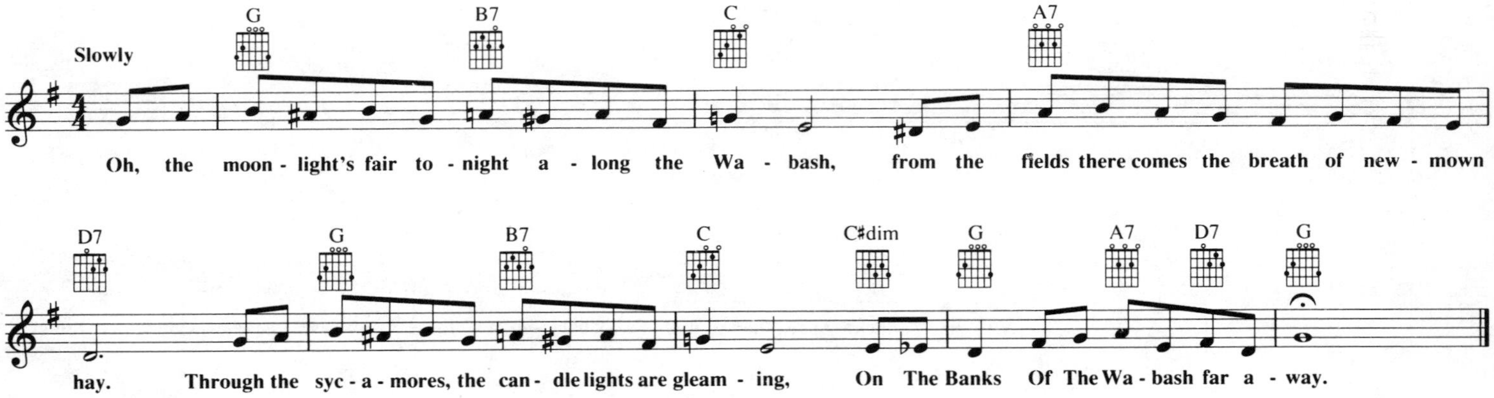
Slowly
G B7 C A7
Oh, the moon - light's fair to - night a - long the Wa - bash, from the fields there comes the breath of new - mown
D7 G B7 C C#dim G A7 D7 G
hay. Through the syc - a - mores, the can - dle lights are gleam - ing, On The Banks Of The Wa - bash far a - way.

ON TOP OF OLD SMOKY

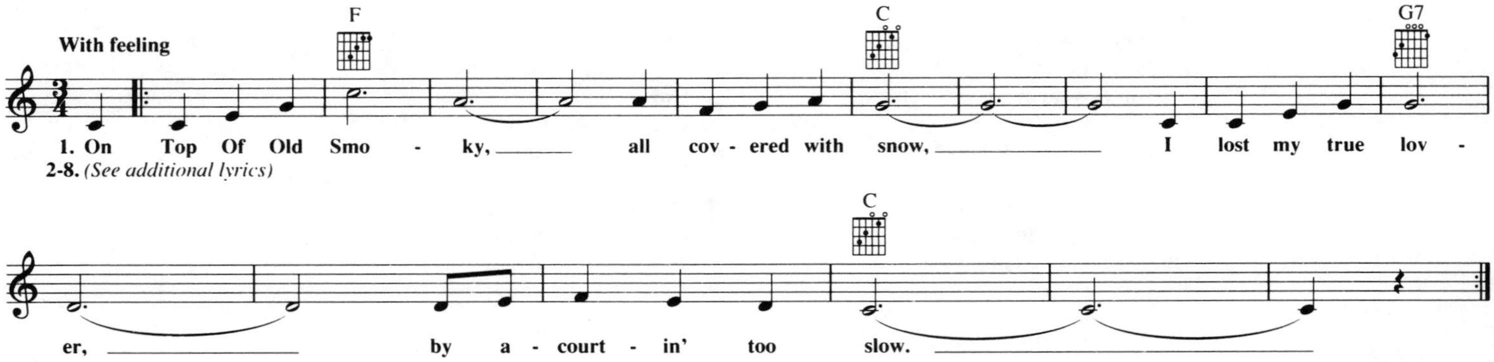
With feeling
F C G7
1. On Top Of Old Smo - ky, all cov - ered with snow, I lost my true lov -
2-8. (See additional lyrics)
C
er, by a - court - in' too slow.

Additional Lyrics

2. Well, a-courting's a pleasure,
   And parting is grief.
   But a false-hearted lover
   Is worse than a thief.

3. A thief he will rob you
   And take all you have,
   But a false-hearted lover
   Will send you to your grave.

4. And the grave will decay you
   And turn you to dust.
   And where is the young man
   A poor girl can trust.

5. They'll hug you and kiss you
   And tell you more lies
   Than the cross-ties on the railroad,
   Or the stars in the skies.

6. They'll tell you they love you,
   Just to give your heart ease.
   But the minute your back's turned,
   They'll court whom they please.

7. So come all you young maidens
   And listen to me.
   Never place your affection
   On a green willow tree.

8. For the leaves they will wither
   And the roots they will die,
   And your true love will leave you,
   And you'il never know why.

ON WISCONSIN!

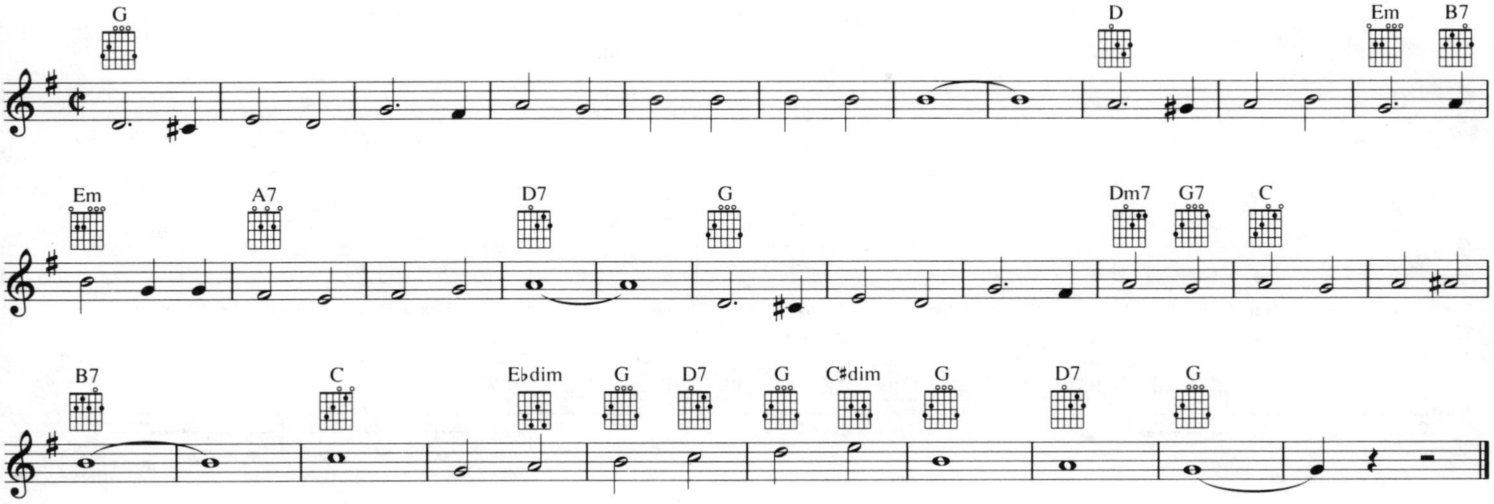

ONCE IN ROYAL DAVID'S CITY

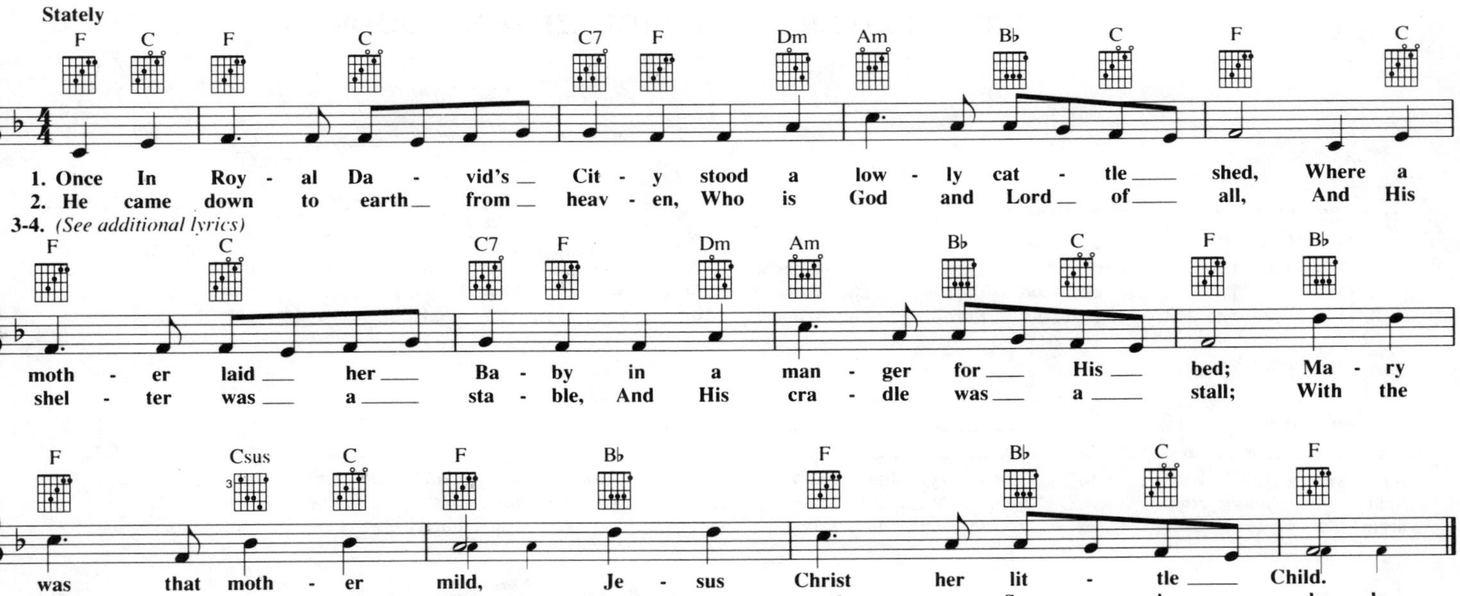
Stately
1. Once In Roy - al Da - vid's Cit - y stood a low - ly cat - tle shed, Where a
2. He came down to earth from heav - en, Who is God and Lord of all, And His
3-4. (See additional lyrics)
moth - er laid her Ba - by in a man - ger for His bed; Ma - ry
shel - ter was a sta - ble, And His cra - dle was a stall; With the
was that moth - er mild, Je - sus Christ her lit - tle Child.
poor, and mean, and low - ly, Lived on earth our Sav - iour ho - ly.

Additional Lyrics

3. Jesus is our childhood's pattern,
Day by day like us He grew;
He was little, weak and helpless,
Tears and smiles like us He knew;
And He feeleth for our sadness,
And He shareth in our gladness.

4. And our eyes at last shall see Him,
Through His own redeeming love;
For that Child so dear and gentle
Is our Lord in heav'n above:
And He leads His children on
To the place where He is gone.

ONWARD CHRISTIAN SOLDIERS

Words by Sabine Baring-Gould
Music by Sir Arthur Sullivan

Moderately
D A7 D Asus A
On - ward, Chris - tian Sol - diers, March - ing as to war. With the cross of Je - sus
E7 A D G
Go - ing on be - fore: Christ the roy - al mas - ter Leads a - gainst the foe;
D Em7 D G D Em7 D G D Em7 D A
For - ward in - to bat - tle, See His ban - ners go.
Chorus:
D A7
On - ward Chris - tian Sol - diers,
D G A7 Bm F♯m G D A D
March - ing as to war. With the cross of Je - sus, Go - ing on be - fore.

OVER THE RIVER AND THROUGH THE WOODS

C F C
1. O - ver The Riv - er And Thro' The Woods, To grand - fa - ther's house we go; The
2. O - ver The Riv - er And Thro' The Woods, To have a first rate play; Oh
3. O - ver The Riv - er And Thro' The Woods, And straight thro' the barn - yard gate, We
G7 C D7 G
horse knows the way to car - ry the sleigh, Thro' the white and drift - ed snow.
hear the bells ring, "Ting - a - ling - ling!" Hur - rah for Thanks giv - ing Day.
seem to go ex - treme - ly slow It is so hard to wait!
C F C
O - ver The Ri - ver And Thro' The Woods, Oh how the wind does blow! It
O - ver The Ri - ver And Thro' The Woods, Trot fast my dap - ple gray! Spring
O - ver The Ri - ver And Thro' The Woods, Now grand-moth - er's cap I spy! Hur -
F F♯dim7 C/G F Fm C G7 C
stings. the toes. And bites the nose, As o - ver the ground we go.
o - ver the ground, Like a hunt - ing hound! For this is Thanks - giv - ing Day.
rah for the fun! Is the pud - ding done? Hur - rah for the pump - kin pie!

OVER THE WAVES

By Juventino Rosas

Moderately
G
D7
G
Am
G
D7
G
Fine
D7
G
E7
Am
G
D7
G
D.C. al Fine

PAT-A-PAN

Bernard de la Monnoye

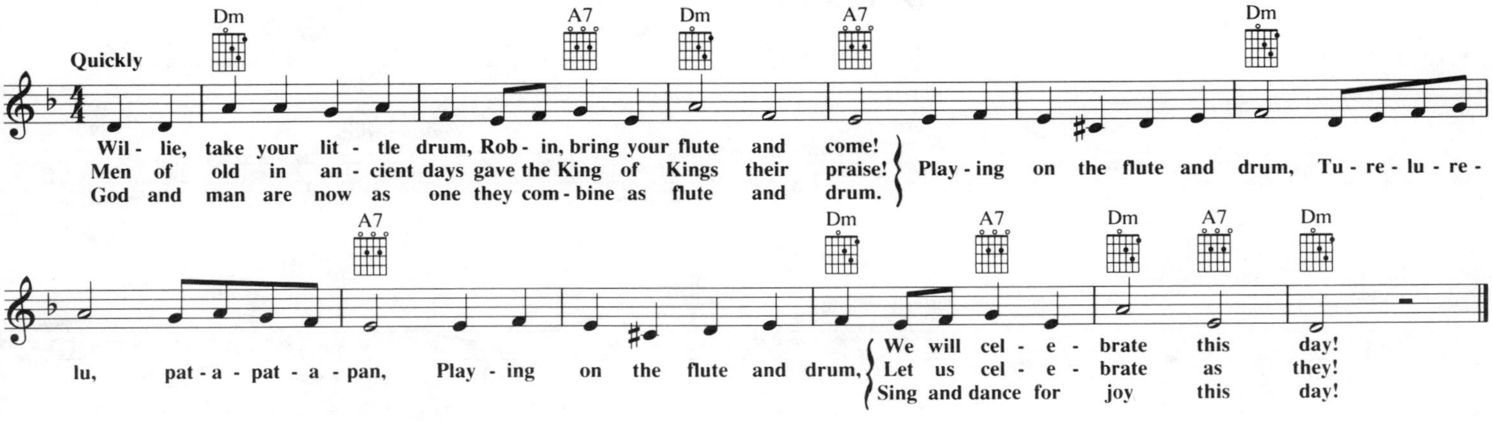
Quickly
Dm
A7
Dm
A7
Dm
Wil - lie, take your lit - tle drum, Rob - in, bring your flute and come!
Men of old in an - cient days gave the King of Kings their praise!
God and man are now as one they com - bine as flute and drum.
Play - ing on the flute and drum, Tu - re - lu - re -
A7
Dm
A7
Dm
A7
Dm
lu, pat - a - pat - a - pan, Play - ing on the flute and drum,
We will cel - e - brate this day!
Let us cel - e - brate as they!
Sing and dance for joy this day!

ORANGE MARMALADE RAG

OUR DIRECTOR MARCH

By F.E. Bigelow

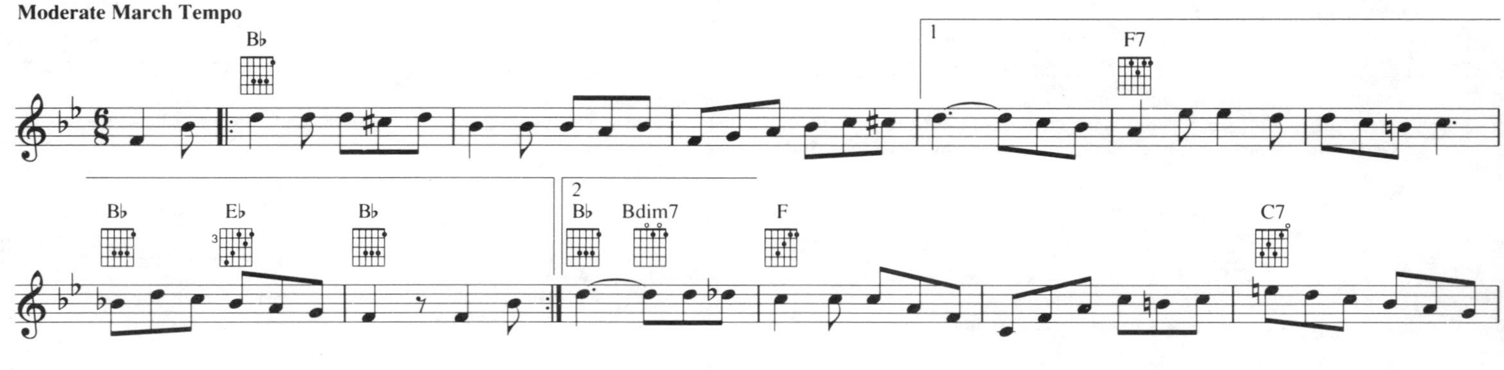

PIZZICATO POLKA

Johann and Josef Strauss

PEG O' MY HEART

Words by Alfred Bryan
Music by Fred Fisher

Slowly
B♭ C9 Cm7 F9 B♭ B♭maj7 D♭dim F7 F9 B♭
Peg O' My Heart, I love you, Don't let us part, I love you, I always knew, it woulld be you, Since I heard your lilt-ing laugh-ter, it's your I-rish heart I'm af-ter Come, make your home in my heart.
Peg O' My Heart, Your glanc-es make my heart say, "How's chanc-es", Come, be my own,
1
2

PLAY A SIMPLE MELODY

Irving Berlin

Medium rag tempo
E♭ B♭7 G♭dim B♭7+ Edim Fm7
Won't you Play A Sim-ple Mel-o-dy Like my moth-er sang to me One with good old fash-ioned har-mo-ny. Play A Sim-ple Mel-o-dy.
Mus-i-cal de-mon, set your hon-ey a dream-in', Won't you play me a rag Just change that clas-si-cal nag to some sweet beau-ti-ful drag If you will play from a cop-y of a tune that is chop-py, You'll get all my ap-plause And that is sim-ply be-cause I want to lis-ten to rag.

Duet
Eb Bb7 Eb Gdim Bb7
Mus-i-cal de-mon, set your hon-ey a-dream-in', Won't you play me some rag. Just change that
Won't you play a sim-ple mel-o-dy
Bb7+ Eb Edim Bb7 Fm7 Bb7
clas-si-cal nag. to some sweet beau-ti-ful drag. If you will
Like my moth-er sang to me.
Eb Bb7 Eb Gbdim Bb7
play from a cop-y of a tune that is chop-py, You'll get all my ap-plause And that is
One with good old fash-oined har-mo-ny.
Eb
sim-ply be-cause I want to lis-ten to rag.
Play A Sim-ple Mel-o-dy.

PUT YOUR ARMS AROUND ME, HONEY

Words by Junie McCree
Music by Albert von Tilzer

Moderately bright
Eb Bb7
Put Your Arms A-round Me, Hon-ey, hold me tight, hud-dle up and cud-dle up with
When they look at me, my heart be-gins to float, then it starts a-rock-in' like a
To Coda
Eb
all your might. Oh! Oh! Won't you roll those eyes eyes that
mo-tor boat. Oh! Oh!
D.C. al Coda
Bb7
CODA
Eb F7 Fm7 Bb7 Eb
I just i-dol-ize. I nev-er knew a-ny girl boy like you.

OH! YOU BEAUTIFUL DOLL

Words by A. Seymour Brown
Music by Nat D. Ayers

Moderately
F D7 G7 C7
Oh! You Beau - ti - ful Doll, _ you great big beau - ti - ful doll ___ Let ___ me put my arms a - bout you,
F C7 F Gm7 C7♭9 F D7 G7
I _______ could nev - er live with - out you. Oh! You Beau - ti - ful Doll, _ You great big beau - ti - ful doll! _
C7 F D♭
___ If you ev - er leave _ me, how my heart will ache, _ I want to hug _ you but I
F A7 Dm7 G7 C7 1 F 2 F
fear you'd break _ Oh! Oh! Oh! Oh! Oh! You Beau - ti - ful Doll! Doll!

ON A SUNDAY AFTERNOON

Words by Andrew B. Sterling
Music by Harry von Tilzer

Moderately
C Cdim C G7 C Cdim C
On A Sun - day Af - ter - noon, _______ in the mer - ry month of June, ______ Take a
G7 C
trip up the Hud - son or down the bay, Take a trol - ley to Co - ney or Rock - a - way. On A
Cdim C A7 Dm G7
Sun - day Af - ter - noon ______ You can see the lov - ers spoon; ______ They work hard on
C
Mon - day, But one day that's fun day is Sun - day af - ter - noon. ________

PETER AND THE WOLF

Serge Prokofiev

PUT ON YOUR OLD GREY BONNET

Words by Stanley Murphy
Music by Percy Wenrich

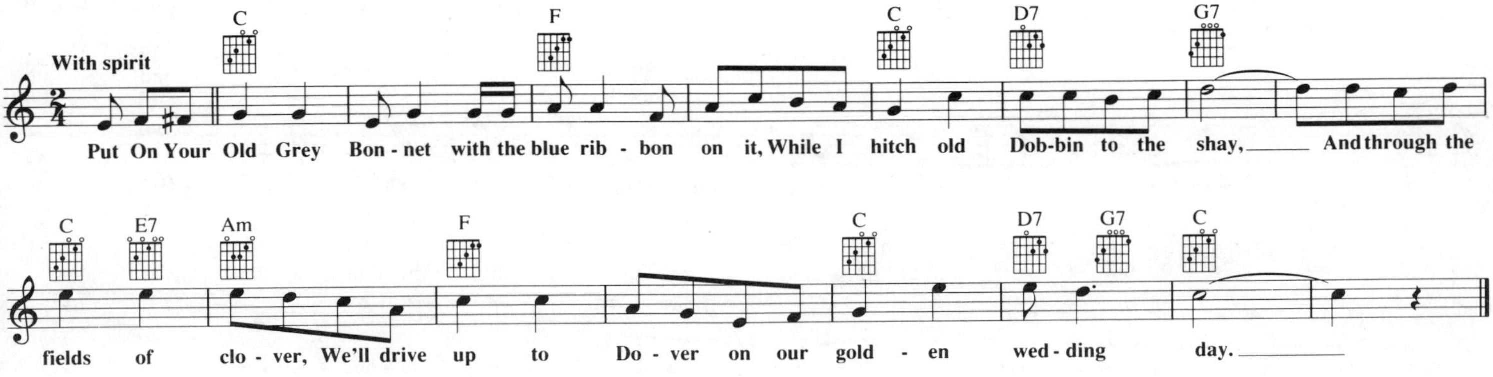

POLOVETZIAN DANCE

Alexander Borodin

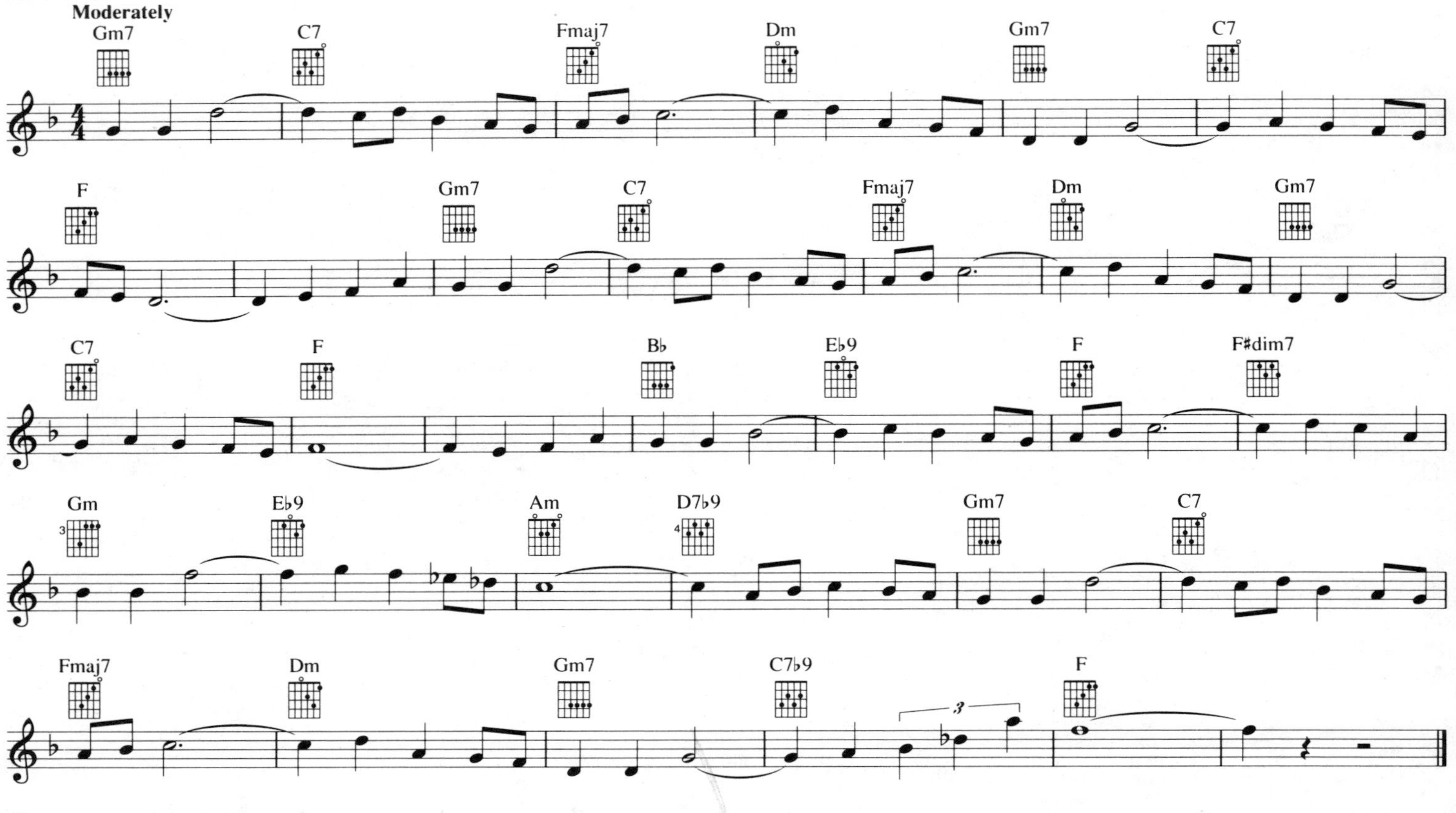
Moderately
Gm7 C7 Fmaj7 Dm Gm7 C7
F Gm7 C7 Fmaj7 Dm Gm7
C7 F B♭ E♭9 F F♯dim7
Gm E♭9 Am D7♭9 Gm7 C7
Fmaj7 Dm Gm7 C7♭9 F

RAGTIME COWBOY JOE

Words by Grant Clarke
Music by Lewis F. Muir and Maurice Abrahams

Moderately
C Am7 D7
He al - ways sings rag - gy mu - suc to the cat - tle, as he swings back and for - ward in the sad - dle, on a
G7 C C+ Am D7 G7
horse that is syn - co - pat - ed, gait - ed, and there's such a fun - ny me - ter to the sound of his re - peat - er. How they
C Am7 D7 Dm7 E7
run when they hear that fel - low's gun be-cause the West - ern folks all know, He's a
Am Dm Cdim Dm Am Dm Am D7♭5 C A7 D7 G7 C
high fa - lut - ing, scoot-ing, shoot - ing son - of - a gun from Ar - i - zo - na, Rag - time Cow - boy Joe.

POLLY WOLLY DOODLE

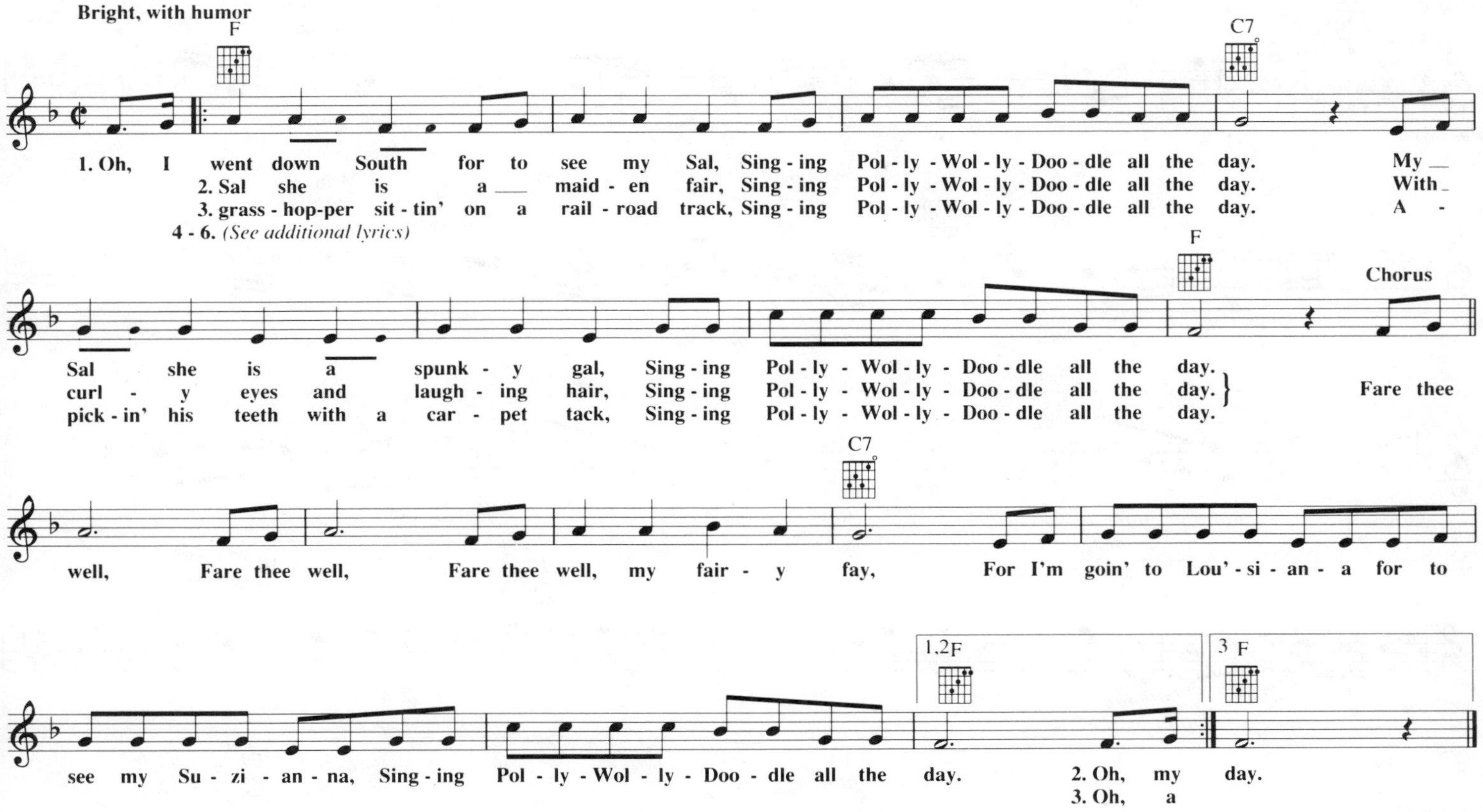
Bright, with humor
F
C7
1. Oh, I went down South for to see my Sal, Sing - ing Pol - ly - Wol - ly - Doo - dle all the day. My
2. Sal she is a maid - en fair, Sing - ing Pol - ly - Wol - ly - Doo - dle all the day. With
3. grass - hop-per sit - tin' on a rail - road track, Sing - ing Pol - ly - Wol - ly - Doo - dle all the day. A -
4 - 6. (See additional lyrics)
F
Chorus
Sal she is a spunk - y gal, Sing - ing Pol - ly - Wol - ly - Doo - dle all the day.
curl - y eyes and laugh - ing hair, Sing - ing Pol - ly - Wol - ly - Doo - dle all the day.
pick - in' his teeth with a car - pet tack, Sing - ing Pol - ly - Wol - ly - Doo - dle all the day.
Fare thee
C7
well, Fare thee well, Fare thee well, my fair - y fay, For I'm goin' to Lou' - si - an - a for to
1,2 F
3 F
see my Su - zi - an - na, Sing - ing Pol - ly - Wol - ly - Doo - dle all the day. 2. Oh, my day.
3. Oh, a

Additional Lyrics

4. Oh, I went to bed, but it wasn't no use,
Singing Polly-Wolly-Doodle all the day.
My feet stuck out like a chicken roost,
Singing Polly-Wolly-Doodle all the day.
Chorus

5. Behind the barn down on my knees,
Singing Polly-Wolly-Doodle all the day.
I thought I heard a chicken sneeze,
Singing Polly-Wolly-Doodle all the day.
Chorus

6. He sneezed so hard with the whooping cough,
Singing Polly-Wolly-Doodle all the day,
He sneezed his head and tail right off,
Singing Polly-Wolly-Doodle all the day.
Chorus

POMP AND CIRCUMSTANCE

Sir Edward Elgar

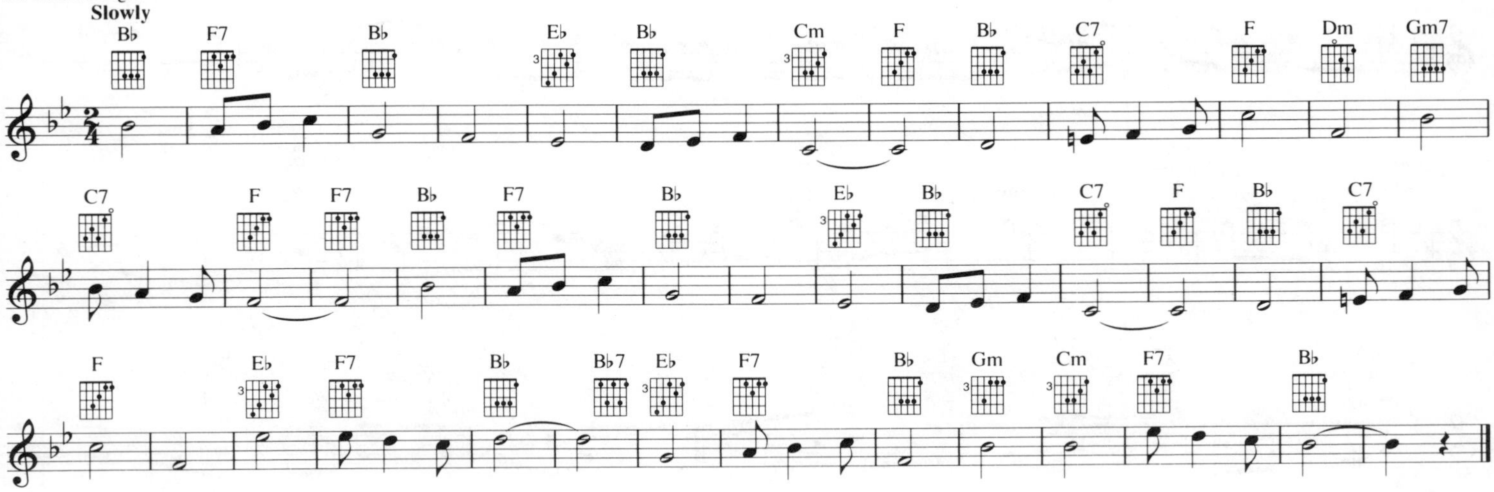
Slowly
B♭ F7 B♭ E♭ B♭ Cm F B♭ C7 F Dm Gm7
C7 F F7 B♭ F7 B♭ E♭ B♭ C7 F B♭ C7
F E♭ F7 B♭ B♭7 E♭ F7 B♭ Gm Cm F7 B♭

POET AND PEASANT OVERTURE

Franz von Suppe

POLONAISE, OPUS 53
(Chopin)

Frederic Chopin

PRAISE GOD FROM WHOM ALL BLESSINGS FLOW

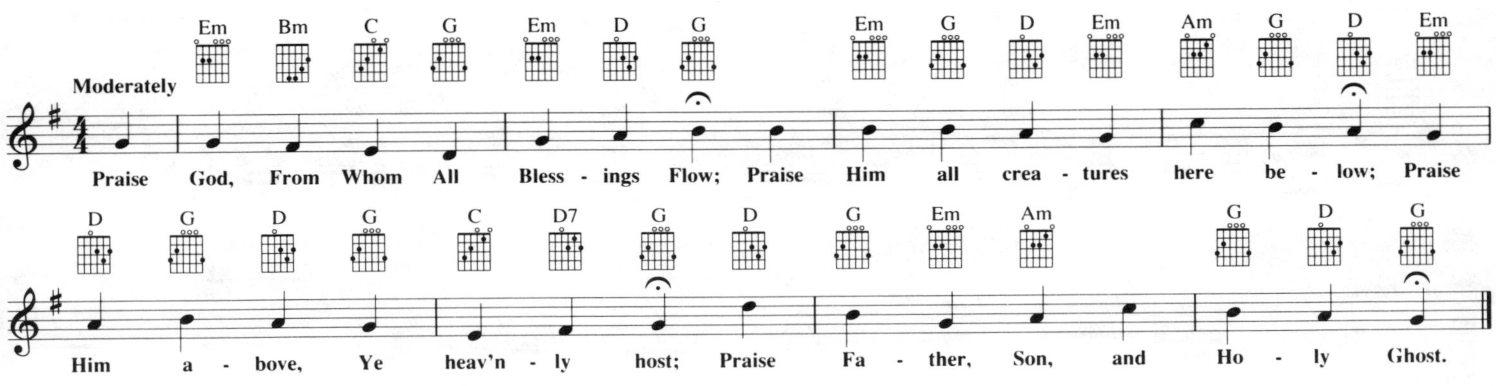

POP! GOES THE WEASEL

With spirit
D A7 D A7 D A7
D Bm Em7 A7 D Bm G A F#m Bm G
A F#m G Em7 A7 D
All a - round the cob - ler's bench, The mon - key chased the wea - sel. The mon - key thought 'twas all in fun,
Ru - fus has the whoop - ing cough, And Sal - ly has the meas - les, And that's the way the doc - tor goes,
Pop! Goes The Wea - sel. A pen - ney for a spool of thread, A pen - ney for a nee - dle. That's the way the mon - ey goes, Pop! Goes The Wea - sel.

PRELUDE
(From "CARMEN")

Georges Bizet

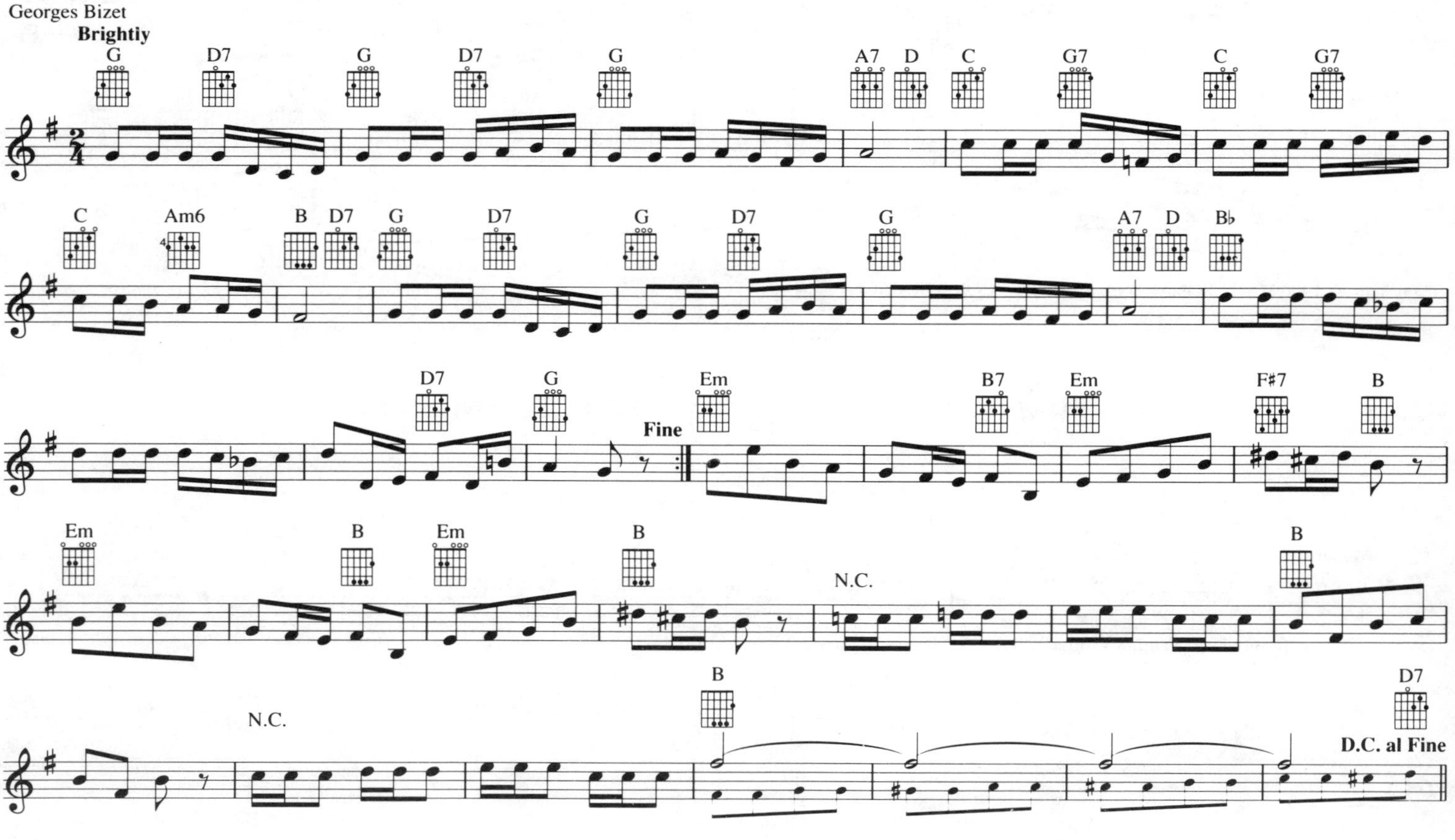
Brightiy
G D7 G D7 G A7 D C G7 C G7
C Am6 B D7 G D7 G D7 G A7 D Bb
D7 G Em B7 Em F#7 B
Fine
Em B Em B
N.C.
B
N.C.
B D7
D.C. al Fine

PRAYER OF THANKSGIVING

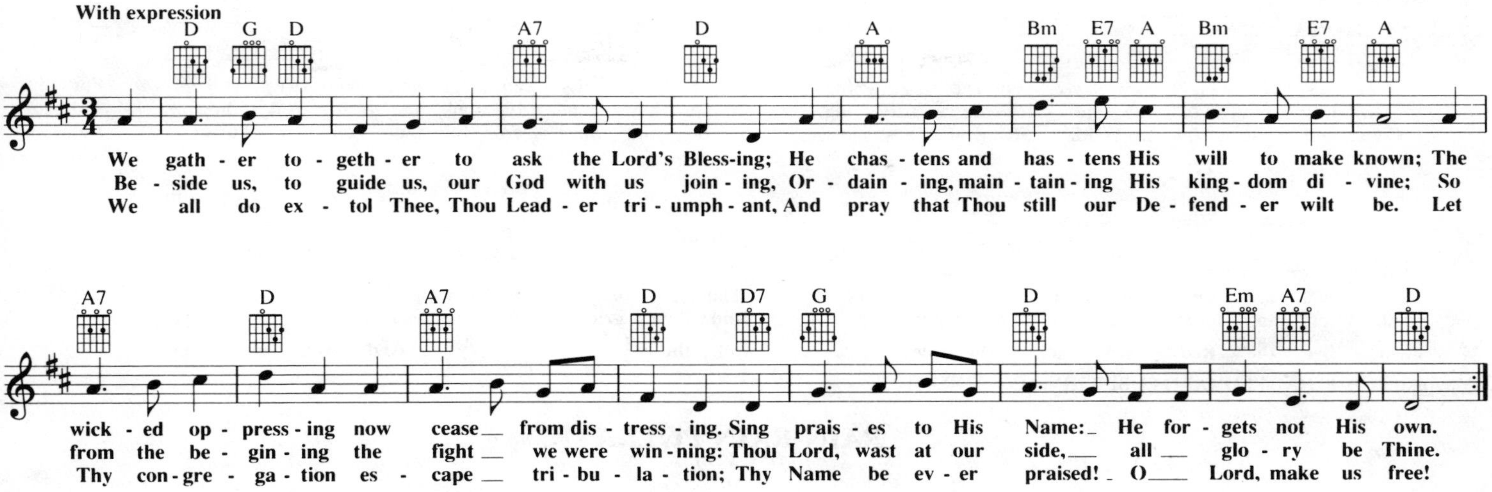
With expression
D G D A7 D A Bm E7 A Bm E7 A
A7 D A7 D D7 G D Em A7 D
We gath - er to - geth - er to ask the Lord's Bless-ing; He chas - tens and has - tens His will to make known; The
Be - side us, to guide us, our God with us join - ing, Or - dain - ing, main - tain - ing His king - dom di - vine; So
We all do ex - tol Thee, Thou Lead - er tri - umph - ant, And pray that Thou still our De - fend - er wilt be. Let
wick - ed op - press - ing now cease __ from dis - tress - ing. Sing prais - es to His Name: _ He for - gets not His own.
from the be - gin - ing the fight __ we were win - ning: Thou Lord, wast at our side, __ all __ glo - ry be Thine.
Thy con - gre - ga - tion es - cape __ tri - bu - la - tion; Thy Name be ev - er praised! _ O __ Lord, make us free!

RED RAVEN POLKA

Clayton E. Hopfensperger

With spirit
C G7 C
G7 1 C 2 C G
C G7 C G C
G7 1 C 2 C C7 F Trio F C7 F
C7 F
C7 F C7 F F7 B♭
Bdim F Gm C7 F 1 2

RED RIVER VALLEY

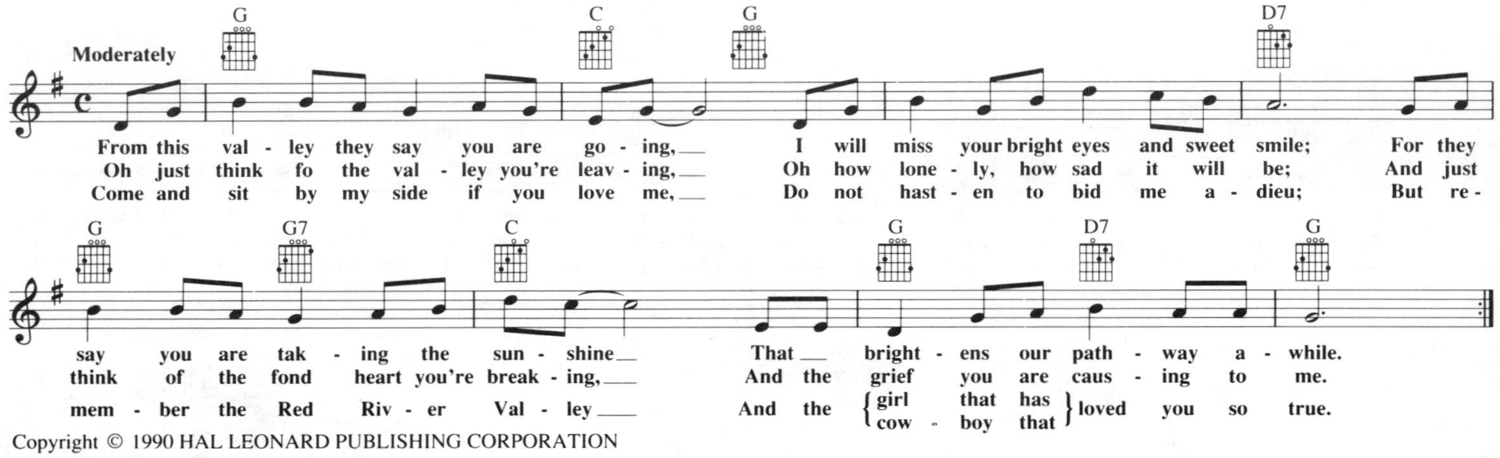
Moderately
From this val - ley they say you are go - ing, I will miss your bright eyes and sweet smile; For they
Oh just think fo the val - ley you're leav - ing, Oh how lone - ly, how sad it will be; And just
Come and sit by my side if you love me, Do not hast - en to bid me a - dieu; But re -
say you are tak - ing the sun - shine That bright - ens our path - way a - while.
think of the fond heart you're break - ing, And the grief you are caus - ing to me.
mem - ber the Red Riv - er Val - ley And the girl that has / cow - boy that loved you so true.

RAIN-RAIN POLKA
(Prsi-Prsi)

Fast
To Trio
D.C. al Trio
Trio

REUBEN AND RACHEL

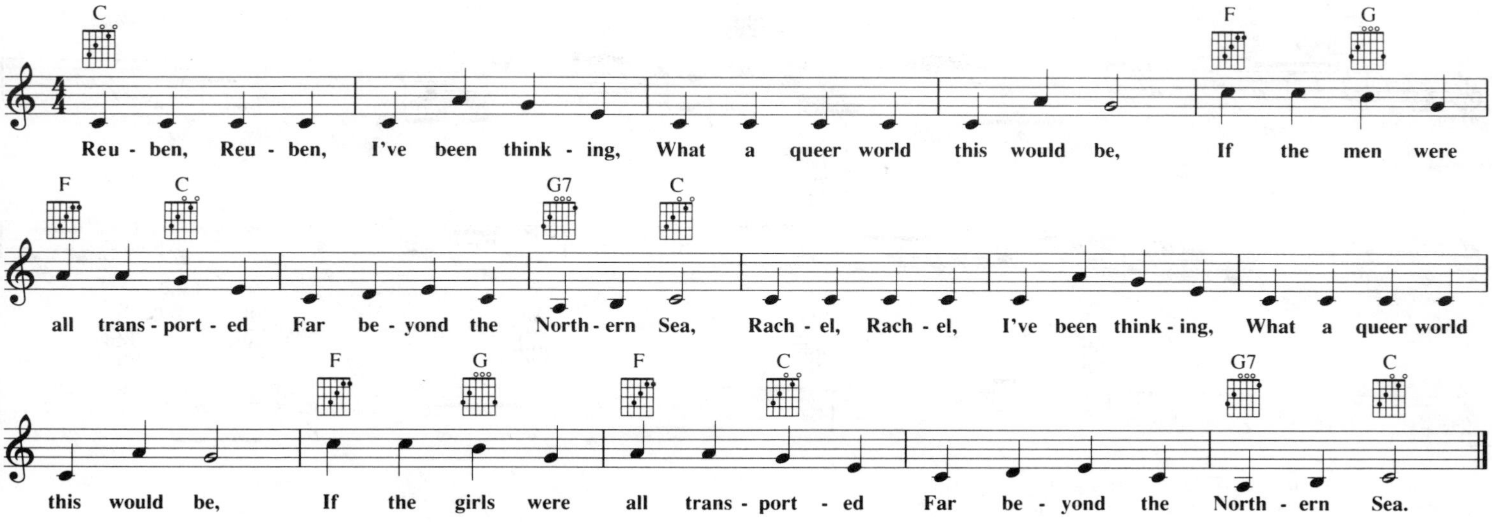

REVERIE

Claude Debussy

Slowly, with expression

RIDE OF THE VALKYRIES

R. Wagner

Moderately
Am C G C
Em E
G D G Am E Am E
Am F Am F E Am
C G C Dm Am Dm Am
B♭ E A

THE ROCK ISLAND LINE

Quickly
Chorus
G6
I say The Rock Is - land Line is a migh - ty good road, I say The Rock Is - land Line is the
D7 G6 G
road to ride, Oh, The Rock Is - land Line is a migh - ty good road, If you ev - er want to
C G D7 G
ride it, got to ride it like you're fly - in'. Buy your tic - ket at the sta - tion on The Rock Is - land Line.
Fine
D7 G
D.C. (Twice)
A, B, C, dou - ble X, Y, Z, Cat's in the cup - board, but he can't see me.
Now Je - sus died to save our sins, Glo - ry be to God, we're gon - na need Him a - gain.
I may be right and I may be wrong, I know you're gon - na miss me when I am gone.

RING THE BANJO

Stephen Foster

Moderately
F
C
F
Fdim7
1. The time is nev - er drear - y If a fel - low nev - er groans; The la - dies nev - er wea - ry With the
2. Oh! nev - er count the bub - bles While there's wa - ter in the spring: A fel - low has no trou - bles While he's
3 - 4. (See additional lyrics)
F C7 F C7
rat - tle of the bones: Then come a - gain Su - san - na By the gas - light of the moon; We'll
got this song to sing. The beau - ties of cre - a - tion Will nev - er lose their charm While I
F Bb F C7 F
play the old Pi - a - no When the ban - jo's out of tune.
roam the old plan - ta - tion With my true love on my arm.
Ring! Ring The Ban - jo! I
C7 F Bb F C7 F
like that good old song, Come a - gain my own true love! Oh, where you been so long.

Additional Lyrics

3. Once I was so lucky,
My master set me free,
I went to old Kentucky
To see what I could see:
I could not go no farther
I return to master's door,
I love him all the harder,
I'll go away no more.

4. Early in the morning
On a lovely summer day,
My master send me warning
He'd like to hear me play.
On the banjo tapping,
I come with dulcet strain;
Master fall a-napping,
He'll never wake again.

ROCK-A-BYE, BABY

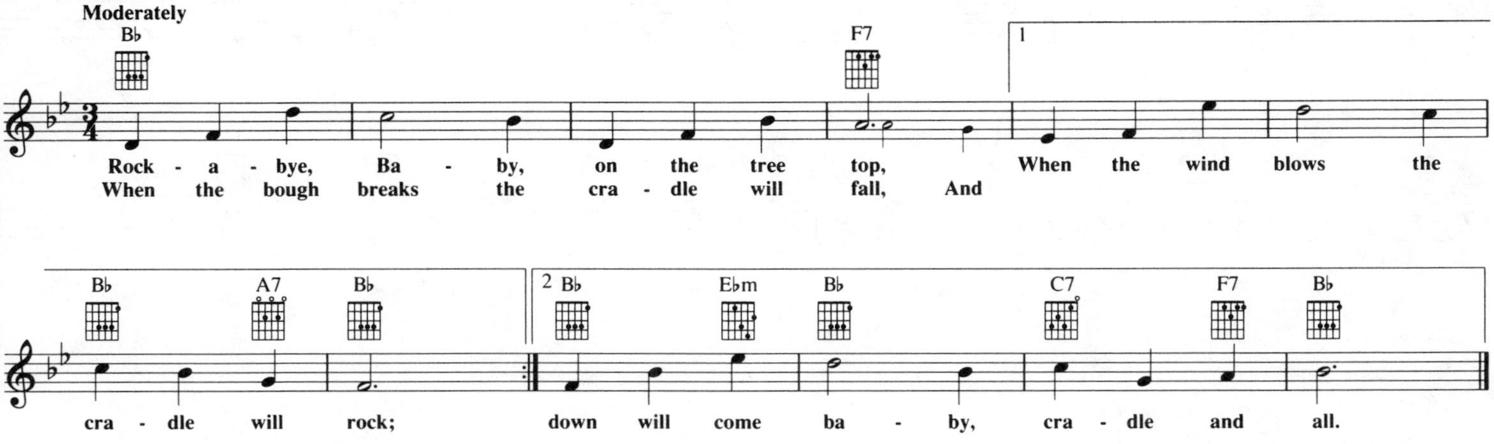
Moderately
Bb
F7
1
Rock - a - bye, Ba - by, on the tree top, When the wind blows the
When the bough breaks the cra - dle will fall, And
Bb A7 Bb
cra - dle will rock;
2 Bb Ebm Bb C7 F7 Bb
down will come ba - by, cra - dle and all.

ROCK OF AGES

Slowly
B♭ E♭ B♭ F7 B♭
Rock Of A - ges, cleft for me. Let me hide my - self in thee. Let the
tears for - ev - er flow Could my zeal no lan - gour know. These for
draw this fleet - ing breath, When my eye lids close in death. When I
F7 B♭ F7 B♭ E♭
wa - ter and the blood from Thy wound - ed side which flowed, be of sin, the dou - ble
sin could not a - tone, Thou must save, and Thou a - lone. In my hand, no price I
rise to worlds un - known, and be - hold Thee on Thy throne. Rock Of A - ges, cleft for
B♭ F7 1,2 B♭ 3 B♭ F7 B♭
cure, save from wrath and make me pure. Could my
bring, sim - ply to Thy cross I cling. While I
me, Let me hide my - self in Thee, Let me hide my - self in Thee.

ROMANCE
(Rubenstein)

A. Rubinstein

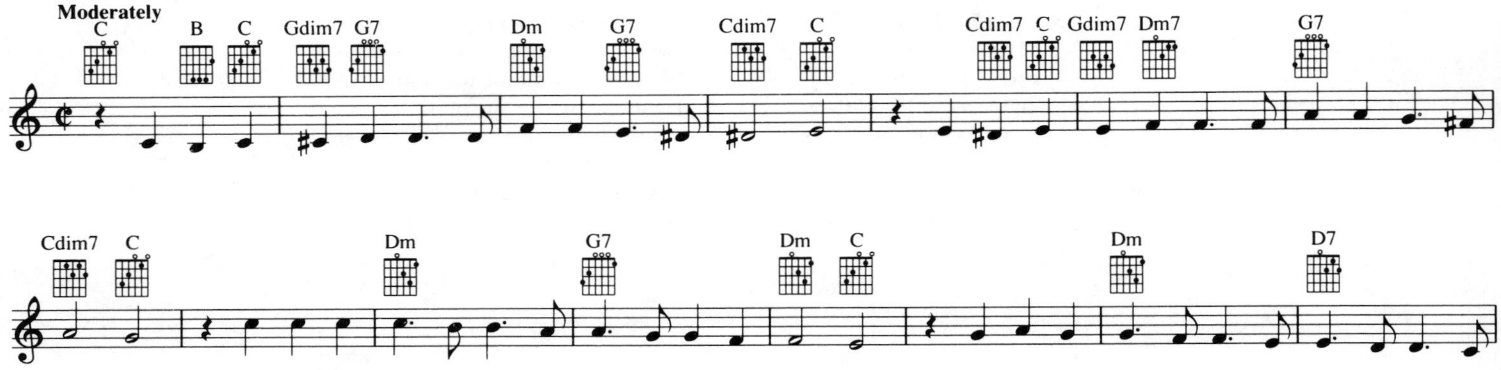
Moderately
C B C Gdim7 G7 Dm G7 Cdim7 C Cdim7 C Gdim7 Dm7 G7
Cdim7 C Dm G7 Dm C Dm D7
G7 C Dm7 G7 C Dm7 G7
C F E Am Dm7 G7 C

ROMEO AND JULIET

Peter Tschaikovsky

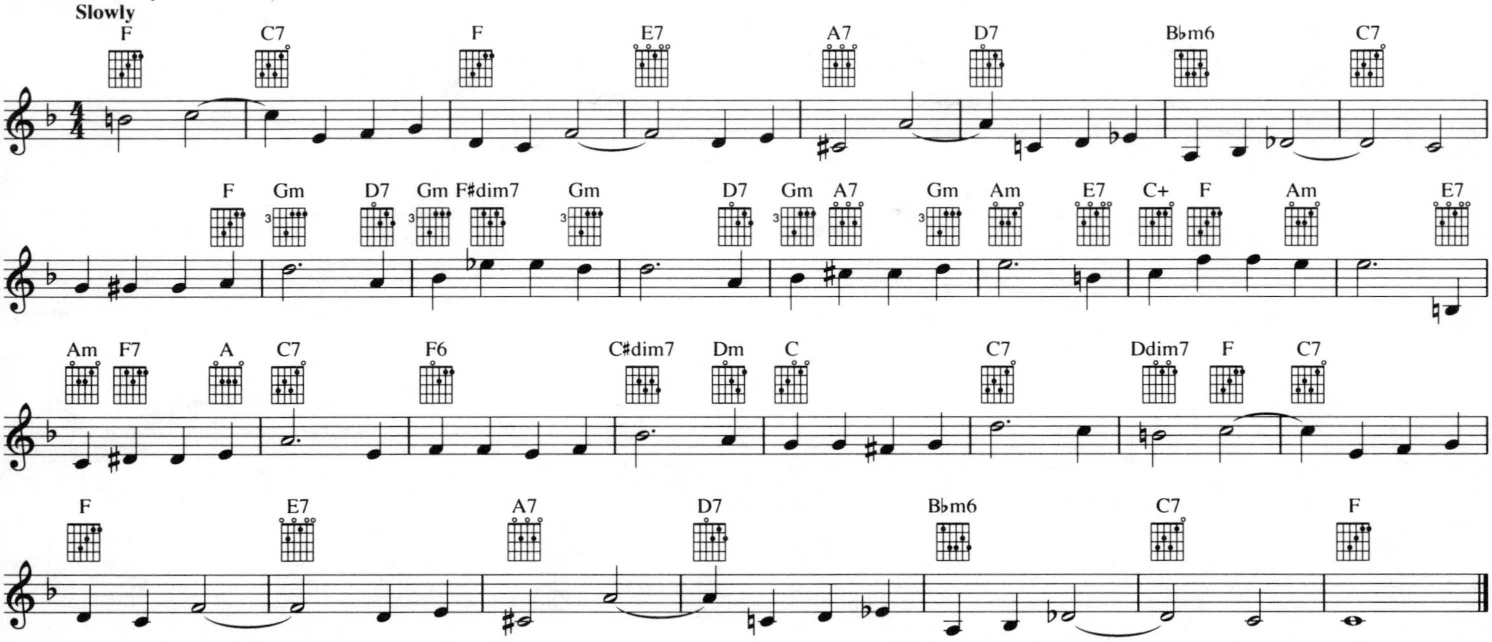
Slowly
F C7 F E7 A7 D7 B♭m6 C7
F Gm D7 Gm F♯dim7 Gm D7 Gm A7 Gm Am E7 C+ F Am E7
Am F7 A C7 F6 C♯dim7 Dm C C7 Ddim7 F C7
F E7 A7 D7 B♭m6 C7 F

THE ROSE OF TRALEE

Words by C. Mordaunt Spencer
Music by Charles W. Glover

Moderately
B♭ E♭ B♭ F7 B♭
The pale moon was ris - ing a - bove the green moun - tain, The sun was de - clin - ing be -
The cool shades of eve - ning their man - tle were spread - ing, And Ma - ry all smil - ing was
C7 F7 B♭ E♭ B♭
neath the blue sea, When I stray'd with my love to the pure crys - tal foun - tain That
list - 'ning to me, The moon thro' the val - ley, her pale rays was shed - ding, When
F7 B♭ B♭ E♭ B♭ Gm D Gm
stands in the beau - ti - ful vale of Tra - lee; She was love - ly and fair as the
I won the heart of The Rose Of Tra - lee; Though love - ly and fair as the
A7 D7 Gm Cm Gm D7 Gm F7 B♭
rose of the summer, Yet 'twas not her beau - ty a - lone that won me. Oh, no! 'Twas the
rose of the sum - mer, Yet 'twas not her beau - ty a - lone that won me. Oh, no! 'Twas the
E♭ B♭ F7 B♭ B♭/F F7 B♭
truth in her eye ev - er dawn - ing, That made me love Ma - ry, The Rose Of Tra - lee.
truth in her eye ev - er dawn - ing, That made me love Ma - ry, The Rose Of Tra - lee.

ROSES FROM THE SOUTH

Johann Strauss

ROW, ROW, ROW YOUR BOAT

RED WING

Words by Thurland Chattaway; Music by Kerry Mills

Moderately
Eb Eb7 Ab Eb Bb7
There once lived an In - dian maid, A shy lit - tle prai - rie maid, Who sang a lay, a
She watched for him day and night, She kept all the camp-fires bright, And un - der the sky, each
Eb Cm F7 Bb7 Eb
love song gay, As on the plain she'd while a - way the day. She loved a war - rior bold, this
night she would lie, And dream a - bout his com - ing by and by; But when all the braves re - turned, the
Ab Eb Bb7 Eb Cm F7 Bb7
shy lit - tle maid of old, But brave and gay, he rode one day to bat - tle far a -
heart of Red Wing yearned, For far, far a - way, her war - ri - or gay, fell brave - ly in the
Eb Ab Eb Edim7 Bb7
way.
fray.
Now, the moon shines to - night on pret - ty Red Wing, the breeze is sigh - ing,
Eb Ab Eb
the night bird's cry - ing, For a - far 'neath his star her brave is sleep - ing,
Edim7 Bb7 1 Eb 2 Eb
While Red Wing's weep - ing her heart a - way. Now, the way.

ROAMIN' IN THE GLOAMIN'

Words and Music by Harry Lauder

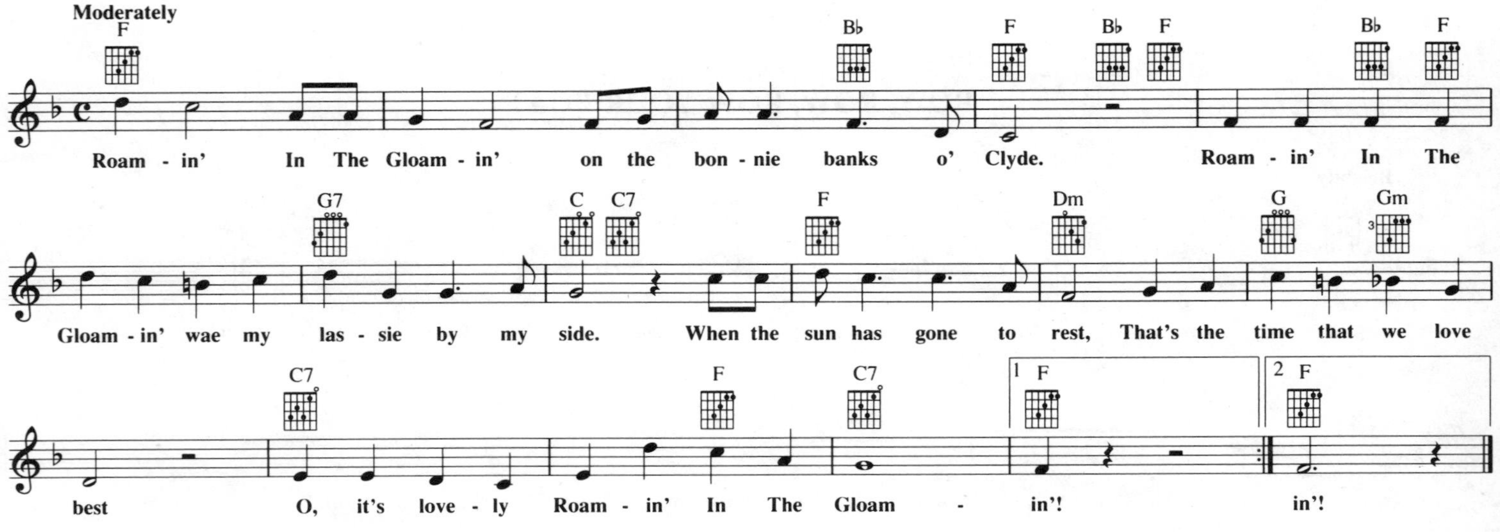
Moderately
F Bb F Bb F Bb F
Roam - in' In The Gloam - in' on the bon - nie banks o' Clyde. Roam - in' In The
G7 C C7 F Dm G Gm
Gloam - in' wae my las - sie by my side. When the sun has gone to rest, That's the time that we love
C7 F C7 1 F 2 F
best O, it's love - ly Roam - in' In The Gloam - in'! in'!

ROW, ROW, ROW

Words by William Jerome
Music by Jimmie V. Monaco

Brightly
G D7 G C E7 Am
And then he'd Row, Row, Row, Way up the riv - er he would Row, Row, Row, A hug he'd
A7 D7 G6 F#7
give her Then he'd kiss her now and then. She would tell him when He'd fool a - round and fool a - round and
G6 G#dim7 D7 N.C. G D7 G Am E7 Am
then they'd kiss a - gain. And then he'd Row, Row, Row, A lit - tle fur - ther he would row, oh, oh, oh, oh!
C Cm6 G A7 Am7 D7 G
Then he'd drop both his oars, take a few more en - cores, And then he'd Row, Row, Row.

SCARBOROUGH FAIR

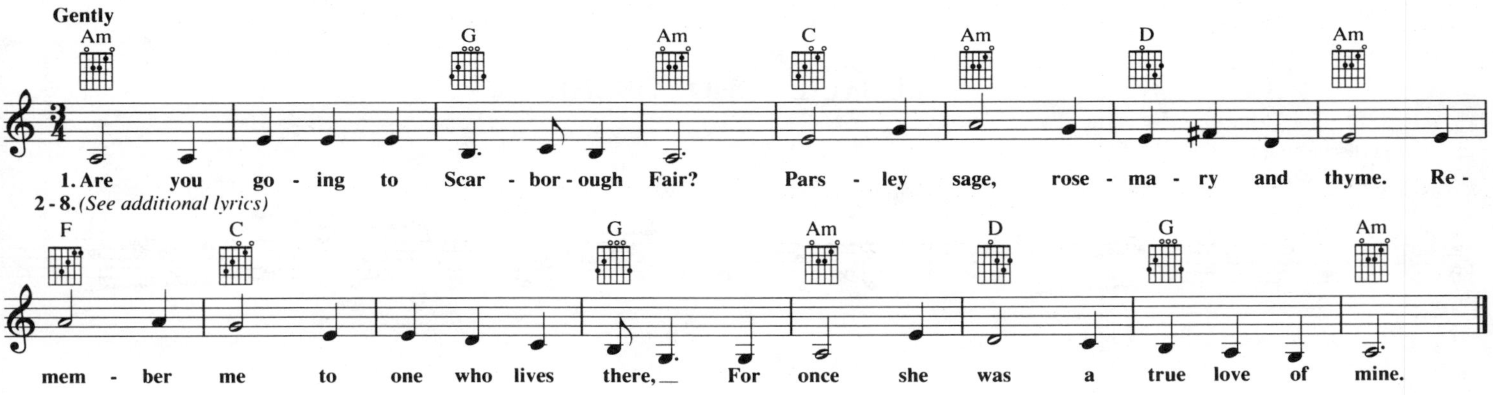
Gently
Am G Am C Am D Am
1. Are you go - ing to Scar - bor - ough Fair? Pars - ley sage, rose - ma - ry and thyme. Re -
2 - 8. (See additional lyrics)
F C G Am D G Am
mem - ber me to one who lives there, For once she was a true love of mine.

Additional Lyrics

2. Tell her to make me a cambric shirt...
Without any seam or fine needlework...

3. Tell her to wash it in younder dry well...
Where water ne'er spring, not drop of rain fell...

4. Tell her to dry it on yonder thorn...
Which never bore blossom since Adam was born...

5. Will you find me an acre of land...
Between the sea foam and the sea sand...

6. Will you plough it with a lamb's horn...
And sow it all over with one peppercorn...

7. Will you reap it with sickle of leather...
And tie it all up with a peacock's feather...

8. When you've done and finished your work...
Then come to me for your cambric shirt.
And you shall be a true love of mine.

RONDEAU
(Mouret)

Jean-Joseph Mouret

ROSALIE SCHOTTISCHE

Sep. Winner

SAILING, SAILING

Godfrey Marks

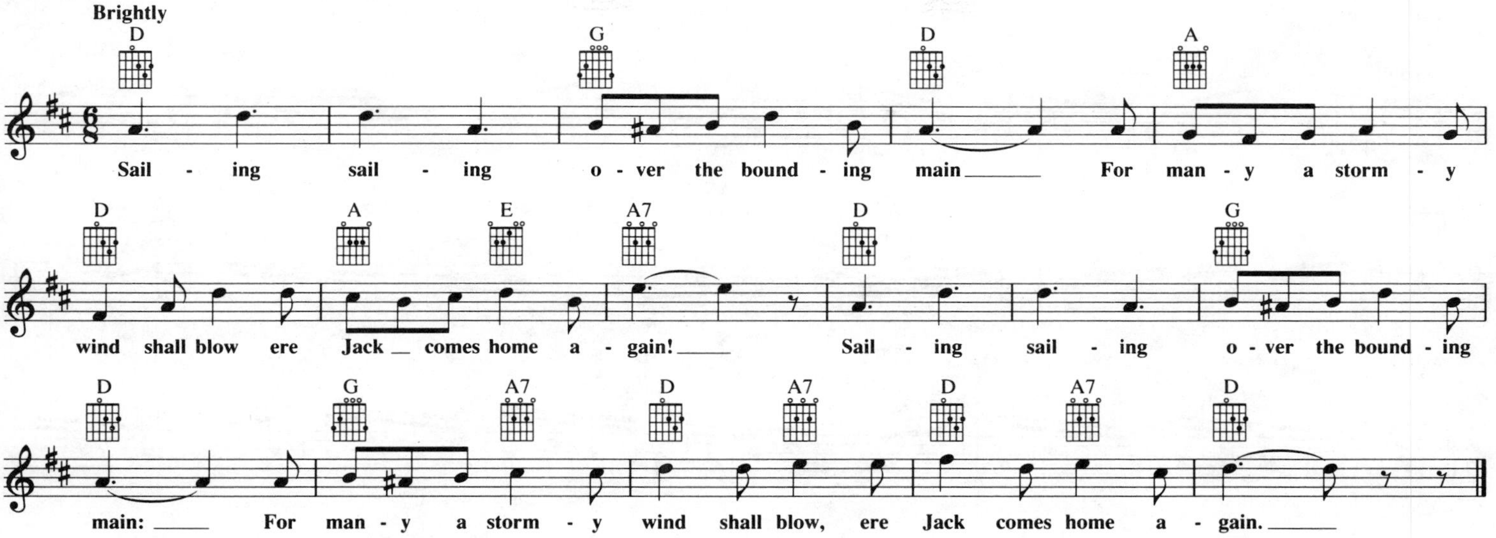
Brightly
D G D A
Sail - ing sail - ing o - ver the bound - ing main For man - y a storm - y
D A E A7 D G
wind shall blow ere Jack comes home a - gain! Sail - ing sail - ing o - ver the bound - ing
D G A7 D A7 D A7 D
main: For man - y a storm - y wind shall blow, ere Jack comes home a - gain.

SALTY DOG

In bright two
E A E A B7
Salt - y Dog, Salt - y Dog, I don't wa - na be your man at all, Hon - ey, let me
E A E A E
be your Salt - y Dog. Down in the wild - wood sit - ting on a log,
A B7 E A E
sing - ing a song a - bout a Salt - y Dog, Hon - ey, let me be your Salt - y Dog.

SCOTLAND THE BRAVE
(Tunes of Glory)

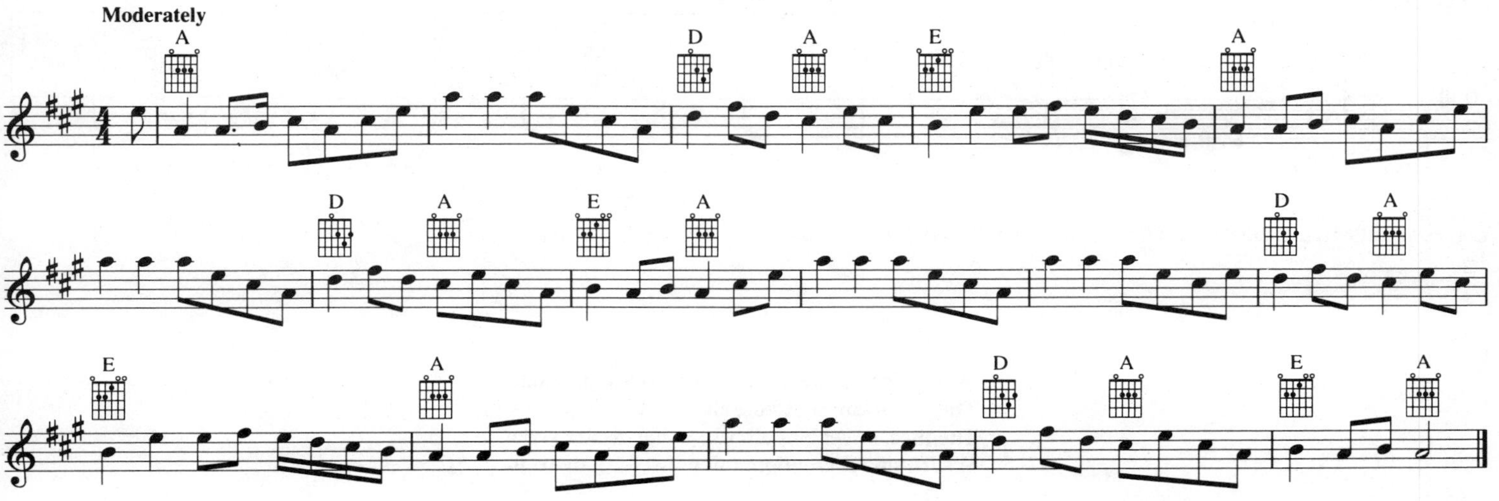
Moderately
A D A E A
D A E A D A
E A D A E A

SAILOR'S HORNPIPE

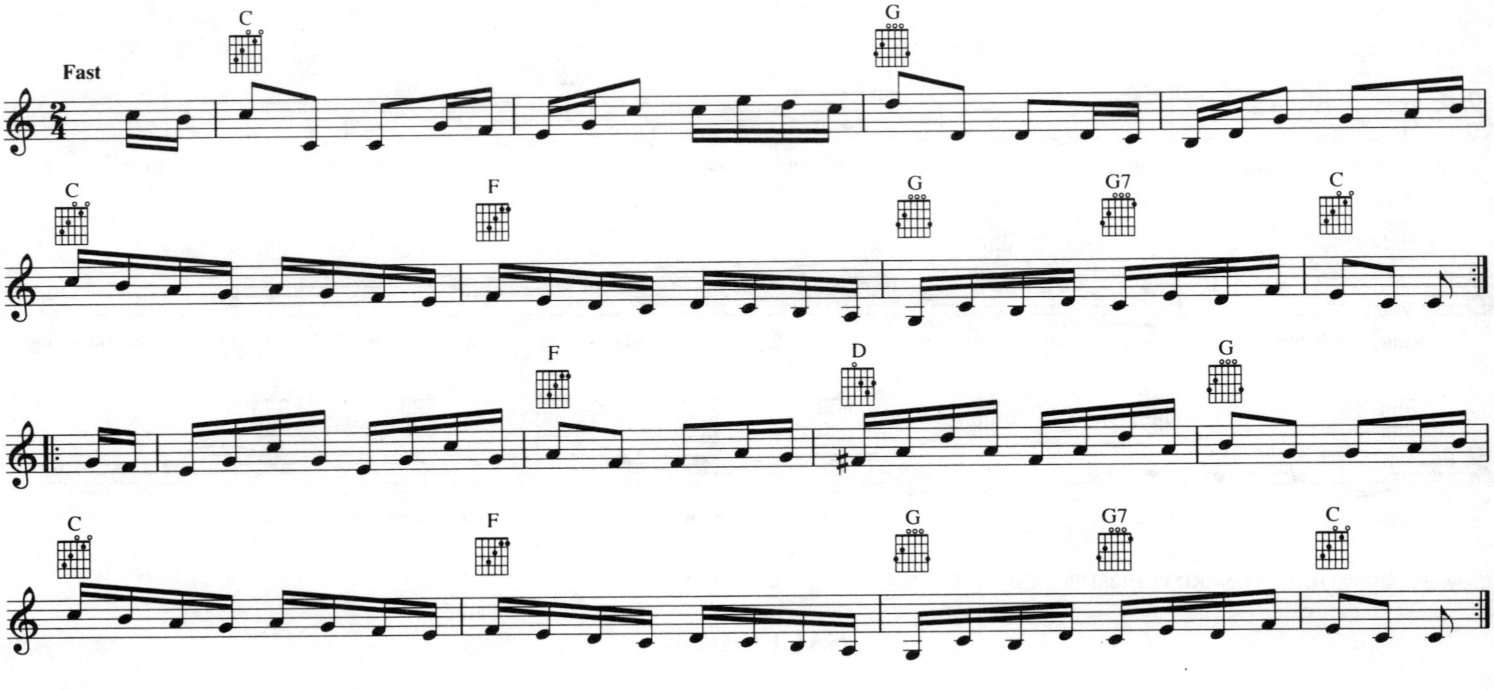
Fast
C
G
C
F
G
G7
C
F
D
G
C
F
G
G7
C

SANTA LUCIA

Moderate Waltz
G
D7
G
D7
1. Now 'neath the sil - ver moon o - cean is glow - ing o'er the calm bil - lows
Here balm - y breez - es blow pure joys in - vite ___ us and as we gent - ly row,
2. (See additional lyrics)
G
C
G
Chorus
soft winds are blow - ing.
all things de - light us.
Hark, how the sail - ors cry Joy - ous - ly ech - oes nigh
D7
1
G
2
G
San - ta ___ Lu - ci - a, San - ta Lu - ci - a. San - ta Lu - ci - a.

Additional Lyrics

2. When o'er the waters light winds are playing,
They spell can sooth us, all care allaying.
The thee, sweet Napoli, what charms are given,
Where smiles creation, toil blessed by Heaven.

SCHNITZELBANK

Moderately
C F C F C G7 C F C
1. Ei du schoe - ne ei du schoe - ne, ei du schoe - ne Schnit - zel - bank. Ist das nicht eine Schnit-zel-bank?
2 - 6. (See addtitional lyrics)
D.C. 1st time
G7 C F C G7 C G7 C
Ja, das ist eine Schnit-zel - bank. Ist das nicht eine kurz und lang? Ja, das ist eine kurz und lang. Kurz und lang un'er Schnit-zel - bank.
D.C. 2nd time
D.C. 3rd time
F C F C F C G7 C F C F C F C G7 C F C F C
D.C. 4th time
D.C. 5th time
F C G7 C F C F C F C G7 C F C F C F C G7 C

Additional Lyrics

2. Ei du schoene, ei du schoene,
Ei du schoene Schnitzelbank.
Is das nicht ein Hin und Her?
Ja, das ist ein Hin und Her.
Ist das nicht eine Lichtputzschere?
Ja, das ist eine Lichtputzschere.
Lichtputzschere, Hin und Her,
Kurz und lang un'er Schnitzelbank.

3. Ei du schoene, ie du schoene,
Ei du schoene Schnitzelbank.
Ist das nicht ein gold'ner Ring?
Ja das ist ein gold'ner Ring.
Ist das nicht ein schoenes Ding?
Ja, das ist ein schoenes Ding.
Schoenes Ding, gold'ner Ring, Lichtputzschere,
Hin und Her, kurz und lang un'er Schnitzelbank.

4. Ei du schoene, ei du schoene,
Ei du schoene Schnitzelbank.
Ist das nicht ein Krum und Grad?
Jas das ist ein Krum und Grad.
Ist das nicht ein Wagenrad?
Ja, das ist ein Wagenrad.
Wagenrad, Krum und Grad,
Schoenes Ding, gold'ner Ring,
Lichtputzschere, Hin und Her,
Kurz und lang un'er Schnitzelbank.

5. Ei du schoene, ei du schoene,
Ei du schoene Schnitzelbank.
Ist das nicht ein Geisenbock?
Ja das ist ein Geisenbock.
Ist das nicht ein Reifenrock?
Jas das ist ein Reifenrock.
Reifenrock, Geisenbock, Wagengrad,
Krum und Grad, Schoenes Ding,
Gold'ner Ring, Lichtputzschere, Hin und Her,
Kurz und lang un'er Schnitzelbank.

6. Ei du schoene, ei du schoene,
Ei du schoene Schnitzelbank.
Ist das nicht eine gute Wurst?
Ja das ist eine gute Wurst.
Ist das nicht ein grosser Durst?
Jas das ist ein grosser Durst.
Grosser Durst, Gute Wurst, Reifenrock,
Geisenbock, Wagengrad, Krum und Grad,
Schoenes Ding, gold'ner Ring,
Lichtputzschere, Hin und Her,
Kurz und lang un'er Schnitzelbank.

SERENADE
(Drigo)

Riccardo Drigo

Moderately

SERENADE
(Schubert)

Franz Schubert

With expression

SERENADE
(Toselli)

Toselli

Moderately
C G7 Dm7 G7 Dm7 G7 C
To Coda
G7 Dm7 G7 Dm7 G7
C G7 C Fmaj7 C
Em G7 C Fmaj7 F6 C Dm G7 C Am
N.C.
F6 C6 G7
D.C. al Coda
CODA
G7 C Dm7 C Dm7 C

SHALL WE GATHER AT THE RIVER

Words and Music by Robert Lowry

Moderate Country Gospel Tempo
C G7
Shall We Gath - er At The Riv - er Where bright an - gel feet have trod,
Ere we reach the shin - ing riv - er, Lay we ev - 'ry bur - den down;
Soon we'll reach the shin - ing riv - er; Soon our pil - grim-age will cease;
C G7 C C7
With its crys - tal tide for - ev - er Flow - ing by the throne of God?
Grace our spir - its will de - liv - er And pro - vide us a robe and a crown.
Soon our hap - py hearts will quiv - er With the mel - o - dy of peace.
Chorus
F C G7 C C7
Yes, we'll gath - er at the riv - er, The beau - ti - ful, the beau - ti - ful riv - er,
F C G7
1,2 C G7
3 C
Gath - er with the saints at the riv - er That flows by the throne of God.
God.

SEMPER FIDELIS

John Philip Sousa

SHE WORE A YELLOW RIBBON

Moderately
C D7 G7
'Round her neck She Wore A Yel - low Rib - bon, She wore it in the spring-time and in the month of May. And
C G7 C
if you asked her why the heck she wore it, She says, "It's for my lov - er who is far, far a - way." Far a -
F C G7 C
way, far a - way. She wore it for her lov - er far a - way. 'Round her
G7 C
neck She Wore A Yel - low Rib - bon, She wore it for her lov - er who is far, far a - way.

SHE IS MORE TO BE PITIED THAN CENSURED

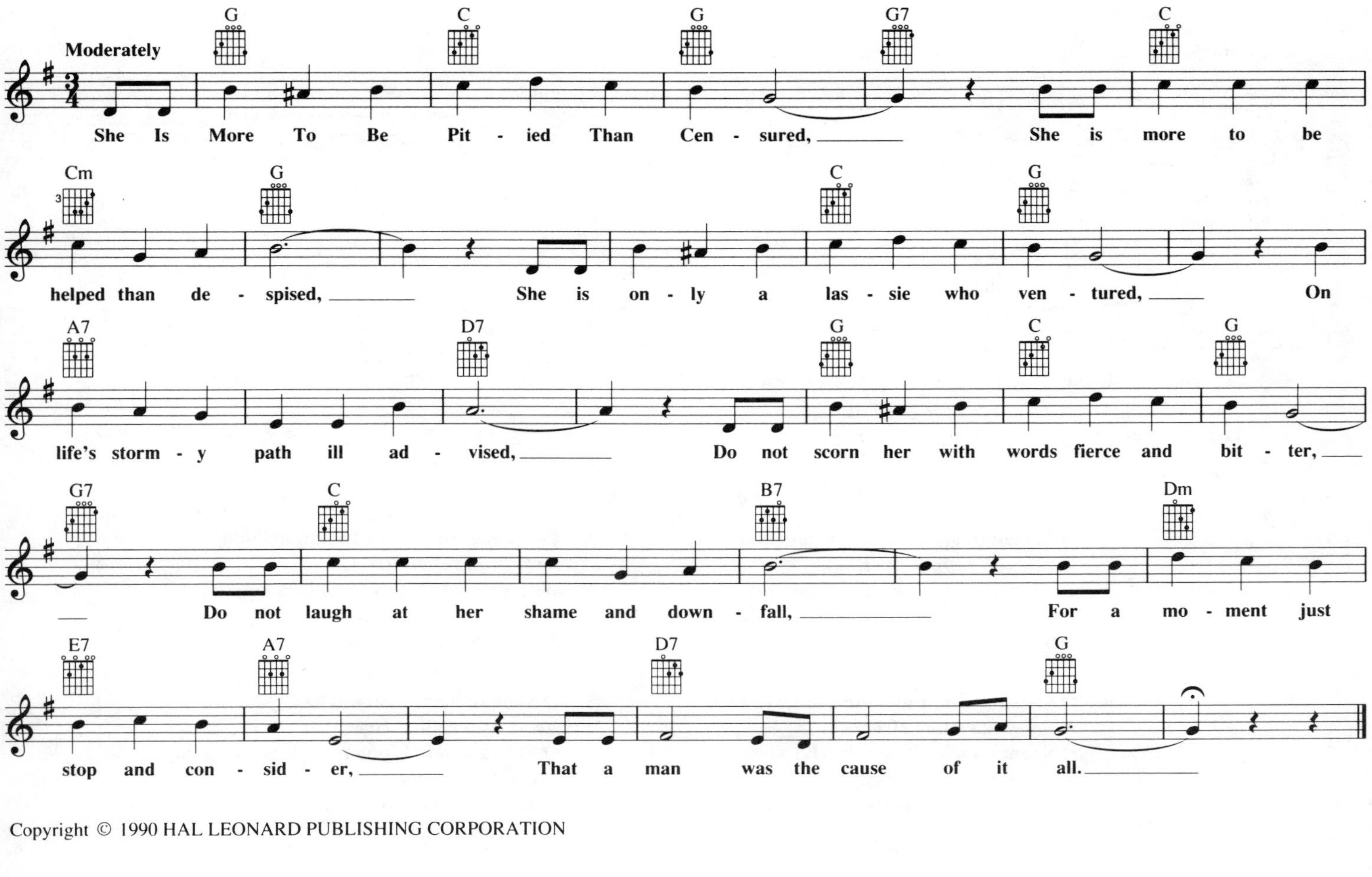
Moderately
G C G G7 C
She Is More To Be Pit - ied Than Cen - sured, She is more to be
Cm G C G
helped than de - spised, She is on - ly a las - sie who ven - tured, On
A7 D7 G C G
life's storm - y path ill ad - vised, Do not scorn her with words fierce and bit - ter,
G7 C B7 Dm
Do not laugh at her shame and down - fall, For a mo - ment just
E7 A7 D7 G
stop and con - sid - er, That a man was the cause of it all.

SHE'LL BE COMIN' 'ROUND THE MOUNTAIN

Fast
G
1. She'll Be Com - in' 'Round The Moun - tain when she comes, (when she comes.) She'll Be Com - in' 'Round The
2 - 4. (See additional lyrics)
D7 G G7
Moun - tain when she comes, (when she comes.) She'll Be Com - in' 'Round The Moun - tain, She'll Be
C G A7 D7 G
Com - in' 'Round The Moun - tain, She'll Be Com - in' 'Round The Moun - tain when she comes.

Additional Lyrics

2. She'll be drivin' six white horses when she comes,
She'll be drivin' six white horses when she comes,
She'll be drivin' six white horses,
She'll be drivin' six white horses,
She'll be drivin' six white horses when she comes.

3. Oh, we'll all go out to meet her when she comes,
Oh, we'll all go out to meet her when she comes,
Oh, we'll all go out to meet her,
Yes, we'll all go out to meet her,
Yes, we'll all go out to meet her when she comes.

4. She'll be wearin' a blue bonnet when she comes,
She'll be wearin' a blue bonnet when she comes,
She'll be wearin' a blue bonnet,
She'll be wearin' a blue bonnet,
She'll be wearin' a blue bonnet when she comes.

SHENANDOAH

Powerfully
D G D
1. O Shen - an - doah, I love to see you, A - way you roll - ing riv - er, Oh
2 - 4. (See additional lyrics)
G D Bm D G D Bm D A7 D
Shen-an - doah, I long to see you, A - way I'm bound a - way, A - cross the wide Mis - sour - i.

Additional Lyrics

2. O Shenandoah, I love your daughter,
Away, you rolling river,
For her I've crossed the rolling water,
Away, I'm bound away,
Across the wide Missouri.

3. The trader loved this Indian maiden,
Away, you rolling river,
With presents his canoe was laden,
Away, I'm bound away,
Across the wide Missouri.

4. O Shenandoah, I'm bound to leave you,
Away, you rolling river,
O Shenandoah, I'll not deceive you.
Away, I'm bound away,
Across the wide Missouri.

5. O Shenandoah, I long to hear you,
Away, you rolling river,
O Shenandoah, I long to hear you.
Away, I'm bound away,
Across the wide Missouri.

SHORTNIN' BREAD

Brightly
C G7 C
Put on the skil - let, put on the lid, Mam - my's gon - na make a lit - tle Short - nin' Bread.
G7 C
That ain't all she's gon - na do, Mam - my's gon - na make a lit - tle cof - fee too.
G7 C
Mam - my's lit - tle ba - by loves short - nin', short - nin', Mam - my's lit - tle ba - by loves Short - nin' Bread.
G7 C
Mam - my's lit - tle ba - by loves short - nin', short - nin', Mam - my's lit - tle ba - by loves Short - nin' Bread.

SILVER THREADS AMONG THE GOLD

H.P. Daniels

Slowly
B♭ F7 B♭ F7 B♭ F7 B♭
Dar - ling, I am grow - ing old, Sil - ver Threads A - mong The Gold, Shine up - on my brow to - day,
When your hair is sil - ver white, And your cheeks no lon - ger bright, With the ro - ses of the May,
Love can nev - er more grow old, Locks may lose their brown and gold, Cheeks may fade and hol - low grow,
Love is al - ways young and fair, What to us is sil - ver hair, Fad - ed cheeks or steps grown slow,
F7 B♭ F7 B♭ Bdim F C7 F7
Life is fast fad - ing a - way; But my dar - ling you will be, will be, Al - ways young and fair to me,
I will kiss your lips and say; Oh! my dar - ling mine a - lone, a - lone, You have nev - er old - er grown,
But the hearts that love will know; Nev - er, nev - er win - ter's frost and chill, Sum - mer warmth is in them still,
To the hearts thet beat be - low? Since I kissed you mine a - lone, a - lone, You have nev - er old - er grown,
Refrain
B♭ F7 B♭ F7 B♭ F7 B♭
Yea, my dar - ling you will be, Al - ways young and fair to me.
Yes, my dar - ling mine a - lone, You have nev - er old - er grown.
Nev - er win - ter's frost and chill, Sum - mer warmth is in them still.
Since I kissed you, mine a - lone, You have nev - er old - er grow.
Dar - ling, I am grow - ing, grow - ing old,
F C7 F7 B♭ F7 B♭ F7 B♭
Sil - ver Threads A - mong The Gold, Shine up - on my brow to - day, Life is fad - ing fast a - way.

SILENT NIGHT

Words by Joseph Mohr
English Tr. by John F. Young
Music by Franz Grüber

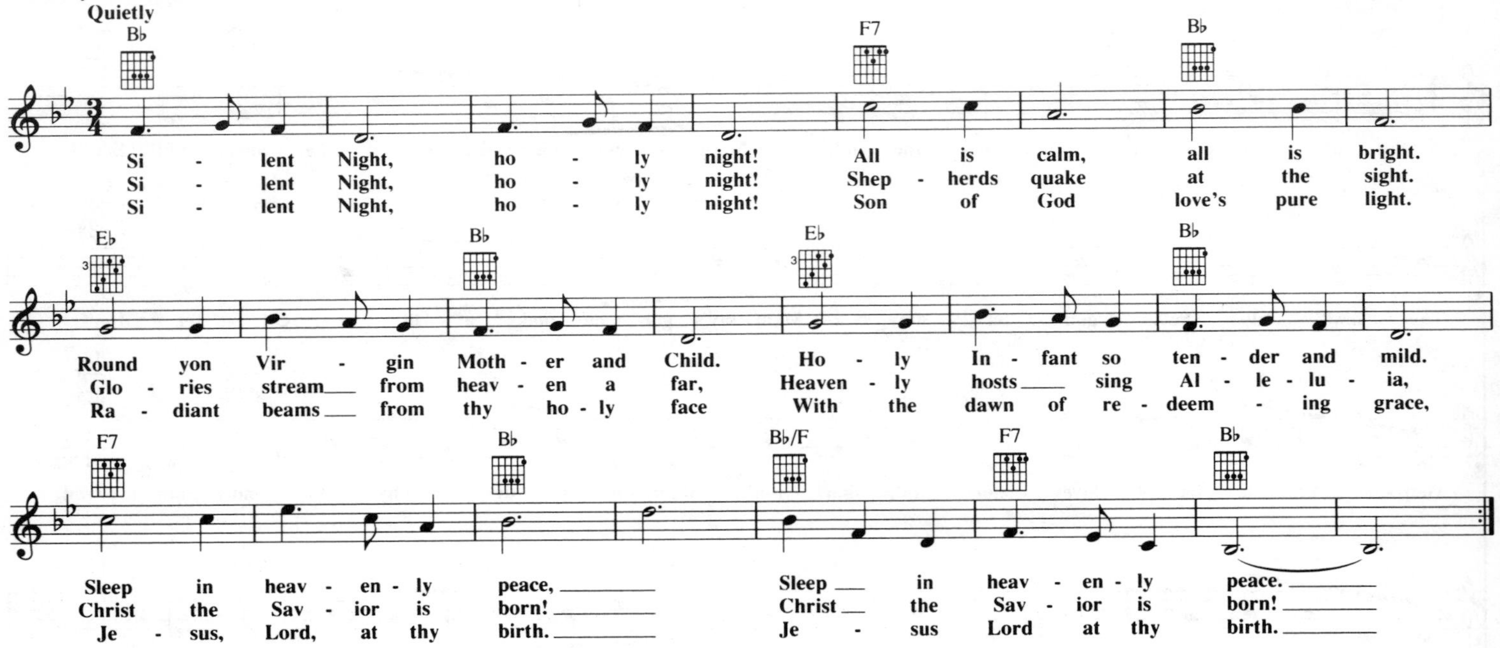
Quietly
B♭ F7 B♭
Si - lent Night, ho - ly night! All is calm, all is bright.
Si - lent Night, ho - ly night! Shep - herds quake at the sight.
Si - lent Night, ho - ly night! Son of God love's pure light.
E♭ B♭ E♭ B♭
Round yon Vir - gin Moth - er and Child. Ho - ly In - fant so ten - der and mild.
Glo - ries stream from heav - en a far, Heaven - ly hosts sing Al - le - lu - ia,
Ra - diant beams from thy ho - ly face With the dawn of re - deem - ing grace,
F7 B♭ B♭/F F7 B♭
Sleep in heav - en - ly peace, Sleep in heav - en - ly peace.
Christ the Sav - ior is born! Christ the Sav - ior is born!
Je - sus, Lord, at thy birth. Je - sus Lord at thy birth.

THE SIDEWALKS OF NEW YORK

Words by Charles B. Lawlor
Music by James W. Blake

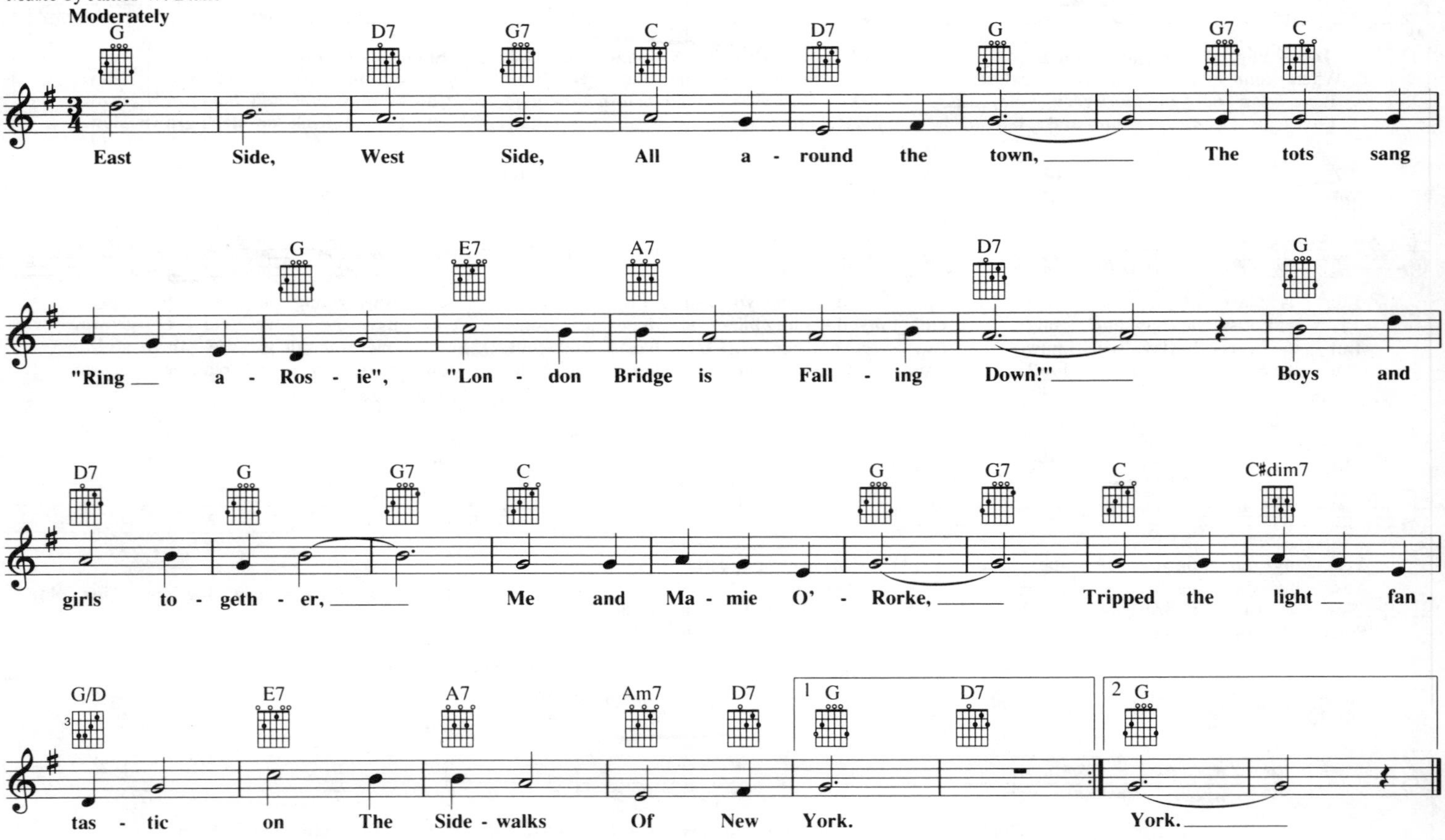
Moderately
G D7 G7 C D7 G G7 C
East Side, West Side, All a - round the town, The tots sang
G E7 A7 D7 G
"Ring a - Ros - ie", "Lon - don Bridge is Fall - ing Down!" Boys and
D7 G G7 C G G7 C C♯dim7
girls to - geth - er, Me and Ma - mie O' - Rorke, Tripped the light fan -
G/D E7 A7 Am7 D7 1 G D7 2 G
tas - tic on The Side - walks Of New York. York.

SIMPLE SIMON

With a steady beat

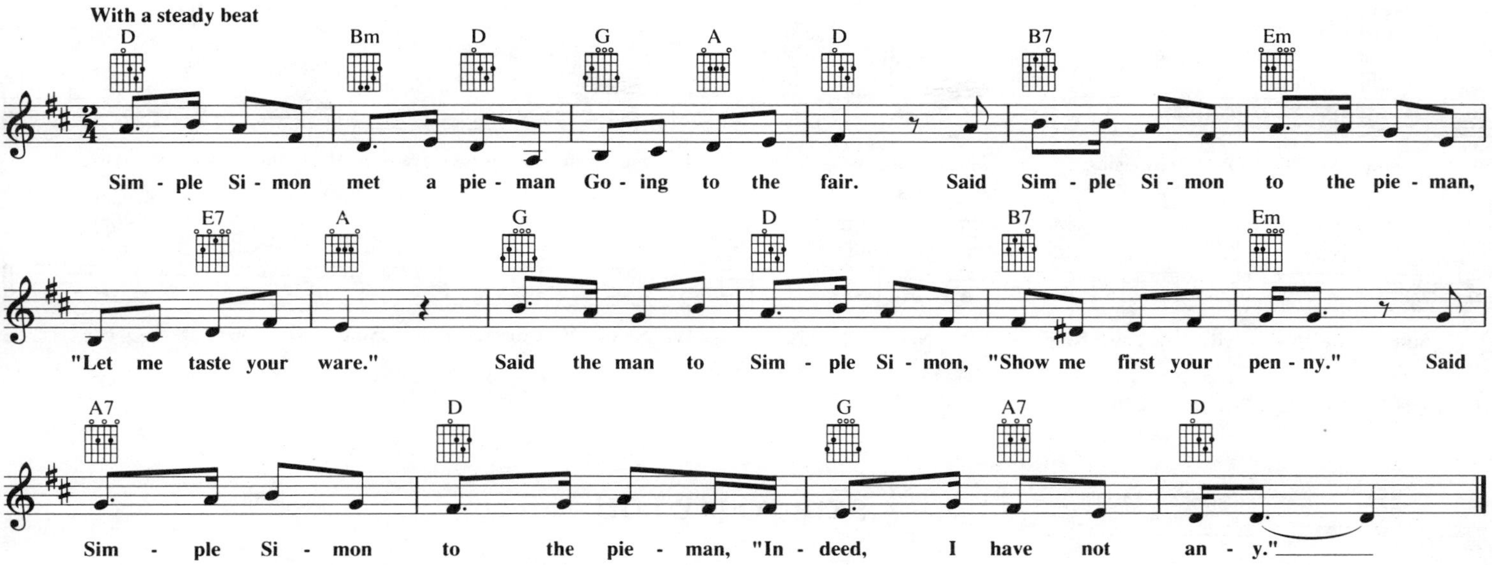
D Bm D G A D B7 Em
Sim - ple Si - mon met a pie - man Go - ing to the fair. Said Sim - ple Si - mon to the pie - man,
E7 A G D B7 Em
"Let me taste your ware." Said the man to Sim - ple Si - mon, "Show me first your pen - ny." Said
A7 D G A7 D
Sim - ple Si - mon to the pie - man, "In - deed, I have not an - y."

THE SKATERS

Emil Wauldteufel

Moderate Waltz

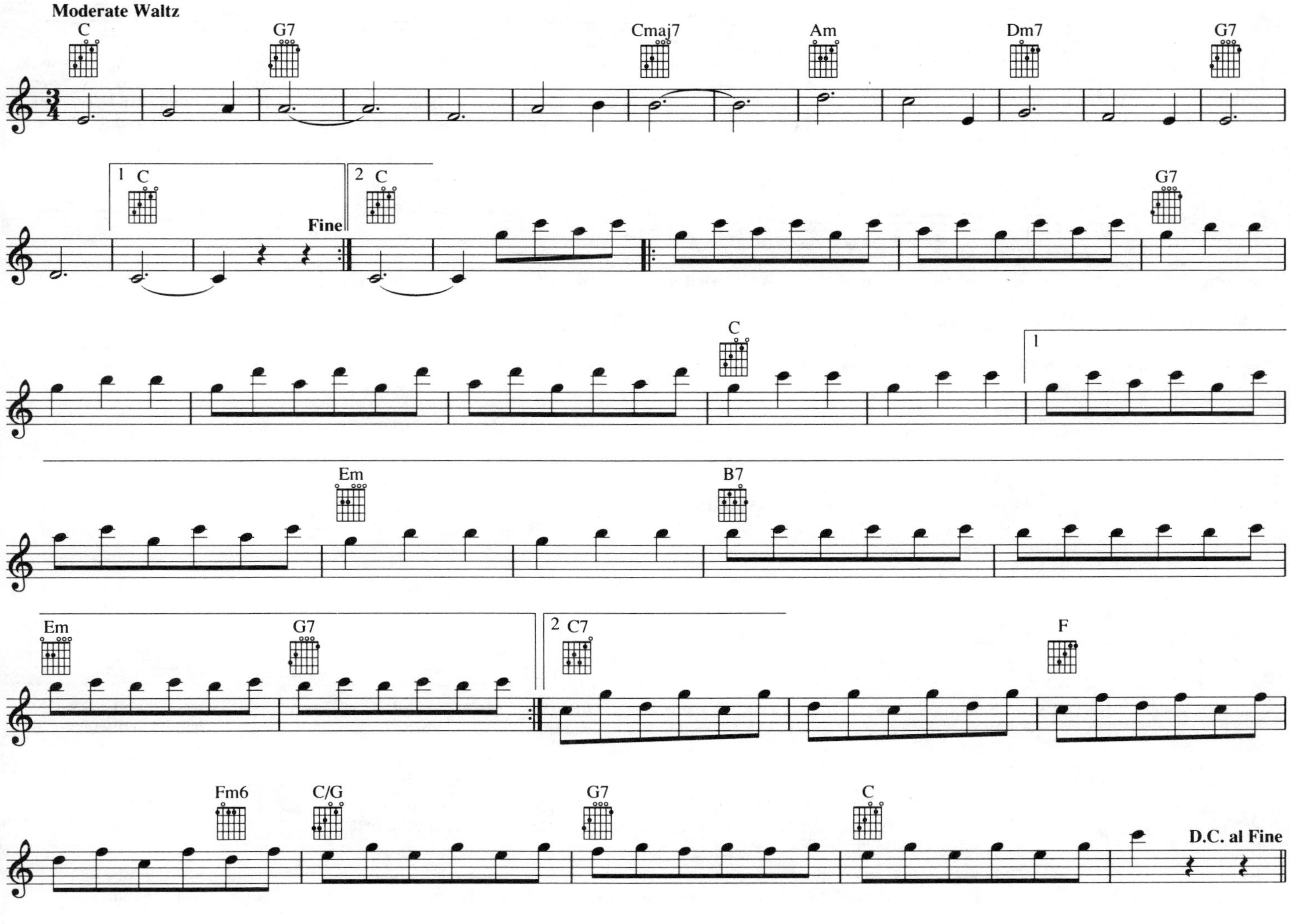
C G7 Cmaj7 Am Dm7 G7
1 C
Fine
2 C
G7
C
1
Em
B7
Em G7
2 C7
F
Fm6 C/G G7 C
D.C. al Fine

SING WE NOW OF CHRISTMAS

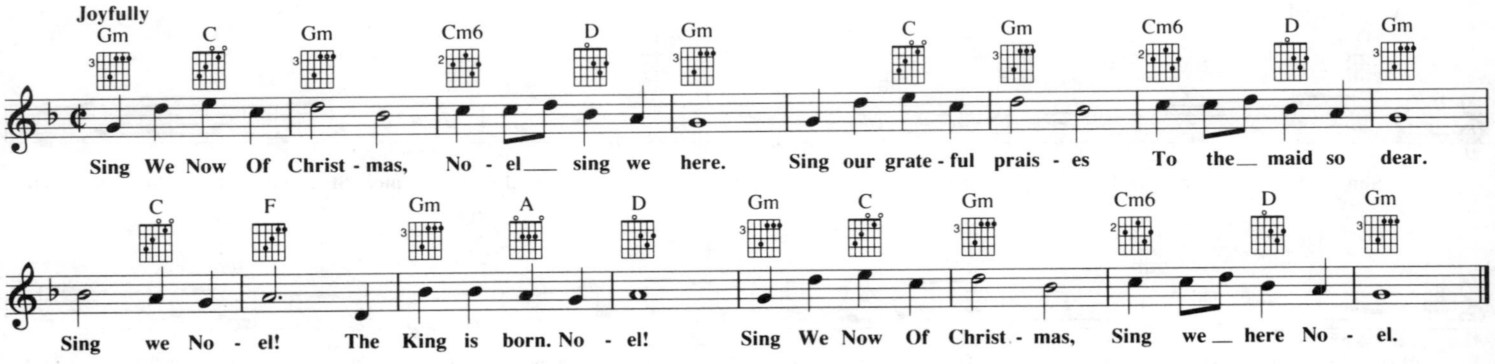
Joyfully
Gm C Gm Cm6 D Gm C Gm Cm6 D Gm
Sing We Now Of Christ - mas, No - el___ sing we here. Sing our grate - ful prais - es To the__ maid so dear.
C F Gm A D Gm C Gm Cm6 D Gm
Sing we No - el! The King is born. No - el! Sing We Now Of Christ - mas, Sing we__ here No - el.

SKIP TO MY LOU

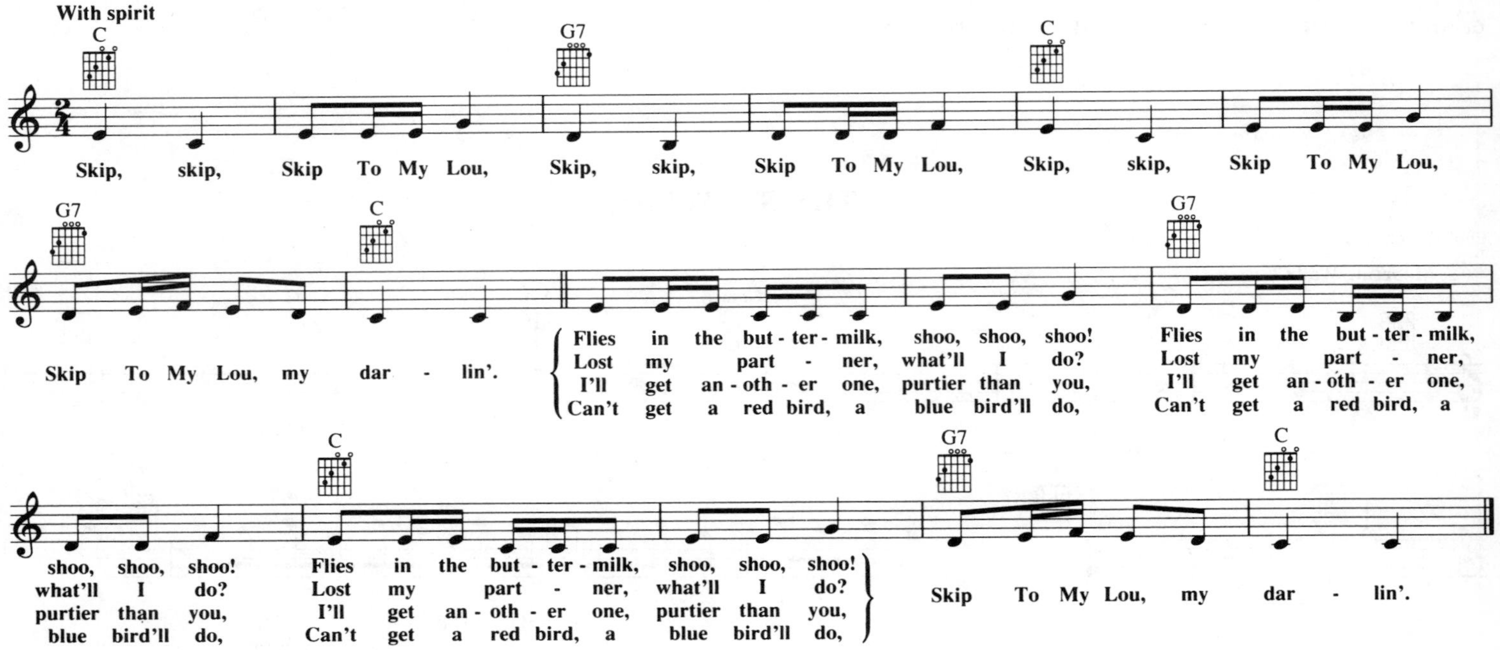
With spirit
C G7 C
Skip, skip, Skip To My Lou, Skip, skip, Skip To My Lou, Skip, skip, Skip To My Lou,
G7 C G7
Skip To My Lou, my dar - lin'.
Flies in the but - ter - milk, shoo, shoo, shoo! Flies in the but - ter - milk,
Lost my part - ner, what'll I do? Lost my part - ner,
I'll get an - oth - er one, purtier than you, I'll get an - oth - er one,
Can't get a red bird, a blue bird'll do, Can't get a red bird, a
C G7 C
shoo, shoo, shoo! Flies in the but - ter - milk, shoo, shoo, shoo!
what'll I do? Lost my part - ner, what'll I do?
purtier than you, I'll get an - oth - er one, purtier than you,
blue bird'll do, Can't get a red bird, a blue bird'll do,
Skip To My Lou, my dar - lin'.

SLEEP HOLY BABE

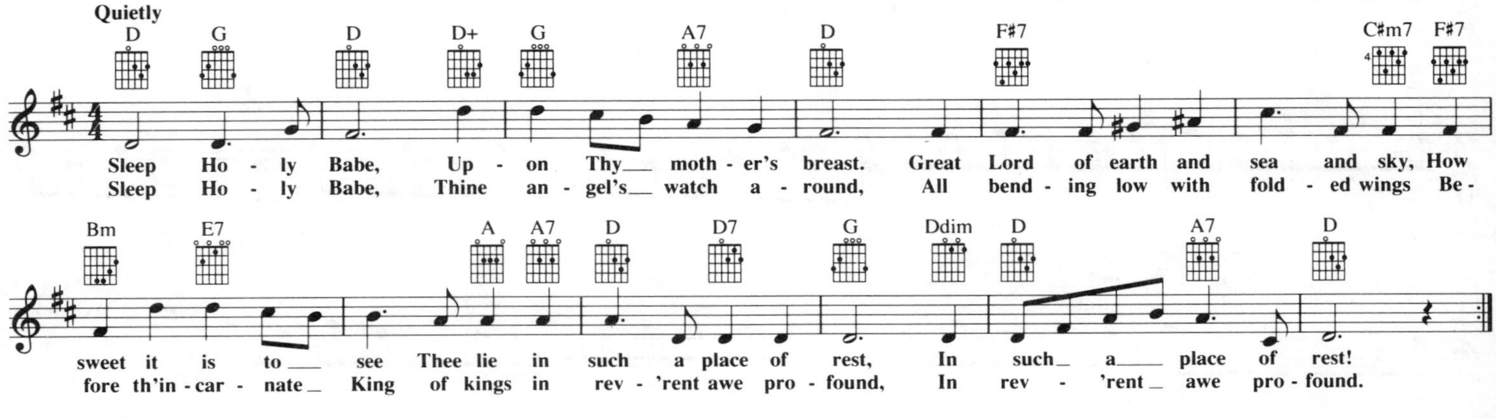
Quietly
D G D D+ G A7 D F#7 C#m7 F#7
Sleep Ho - ly Babe, Up - on Thy__ moth - er's breast. Great Lord of earth and sea and sky, How
Sleep Ho - ly Babe, Thine an - gel's__ watch a - round, All bend - ing low with fold - ed wings Be -
Bm E7 A A7 D D7 G Ddim D A7 D
sweet it is to___ see Thee lie in such a place of rest, In such_ a___ place of rest!
fore th'in - car - nate_ King of kings in rev - 'rent awe pro - found, In rev - 'rent_ awe pro - found.

SCHOOL DAYS

Words by Will D. Cobb
Music by Gus Edwards

Moderately
Noth-ing to do, Nel-lie Dar-ling Noth-ing to do you say, Let's take a
'Mem-ber the hill, Nel-lie Dar-ling And the oak tree that grew on its brow? They've built for-ty
trip on mem-or-y's ship, Back to the by-gone days. Sail to the old vil-lage
stor-ies up-on that old hill And the oak's an old chest-nut now. 'Mem-ber the mead-ows so
school house, An-chor out-side the school door, Look in and see, there's you and there's
green, dear, So fra-grant with clov-er and maize, In-to new ci-ty, lots and pre-ferred bus'-ness
me, A cou-ple of kids once more.
plots, They've cut them up since those days.
School Days, School Days, dear old gold-en rule
days, Read-in' and 'rit-in' and 'rith-me-tic, Taught to the tune of a hick-'ry stick.
You were my queen in cal-i-co. I was your bash-ful, bare-foot beau, And you wrote on my
slate, "I love you Joe," When we were a coup-le of kids. kids.

SLEEPING BEAUTY WALTZ
(Tchaikovsky)

Peter Ilyich Tchaikowsky

SONG OF INDIA

Nikolai Rimsky-Korsakov

SOMETIMES I FEEL LIKE A MOTHERLESS CHILD

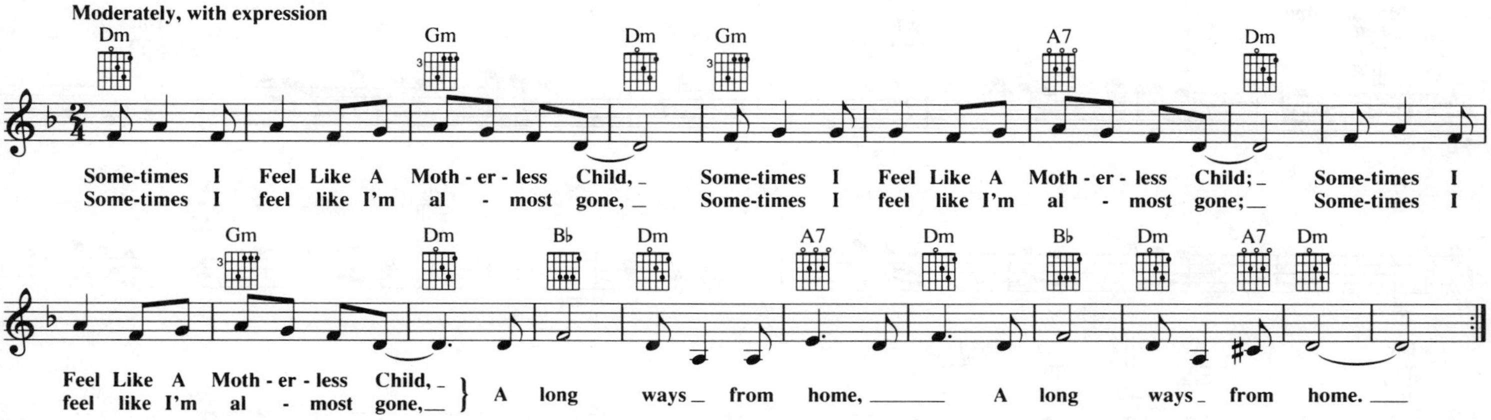

SONG OF THE VOLGA BOATMAN

SPRING SONG
(Mendelssohn)

Felix Mendelssohn

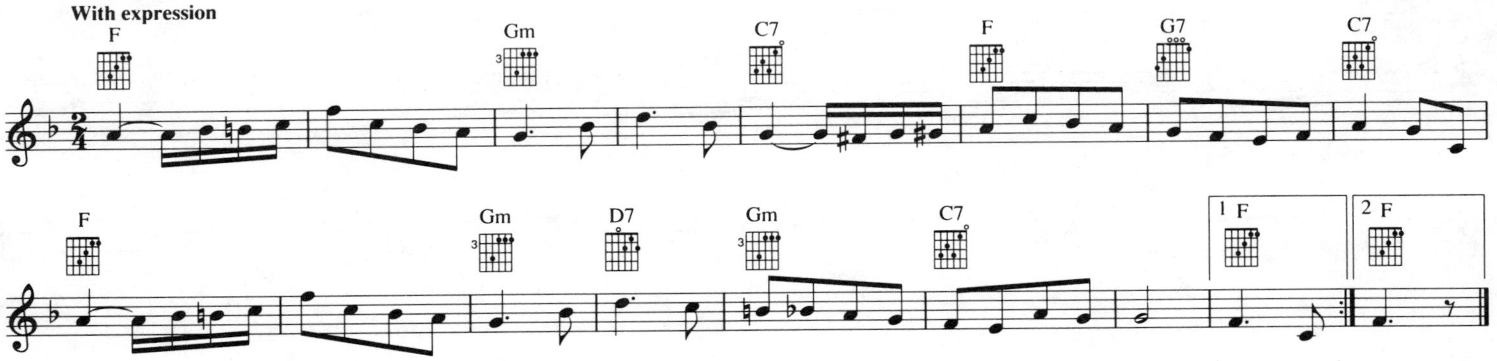

SOUND OFF

John Philip Sousa

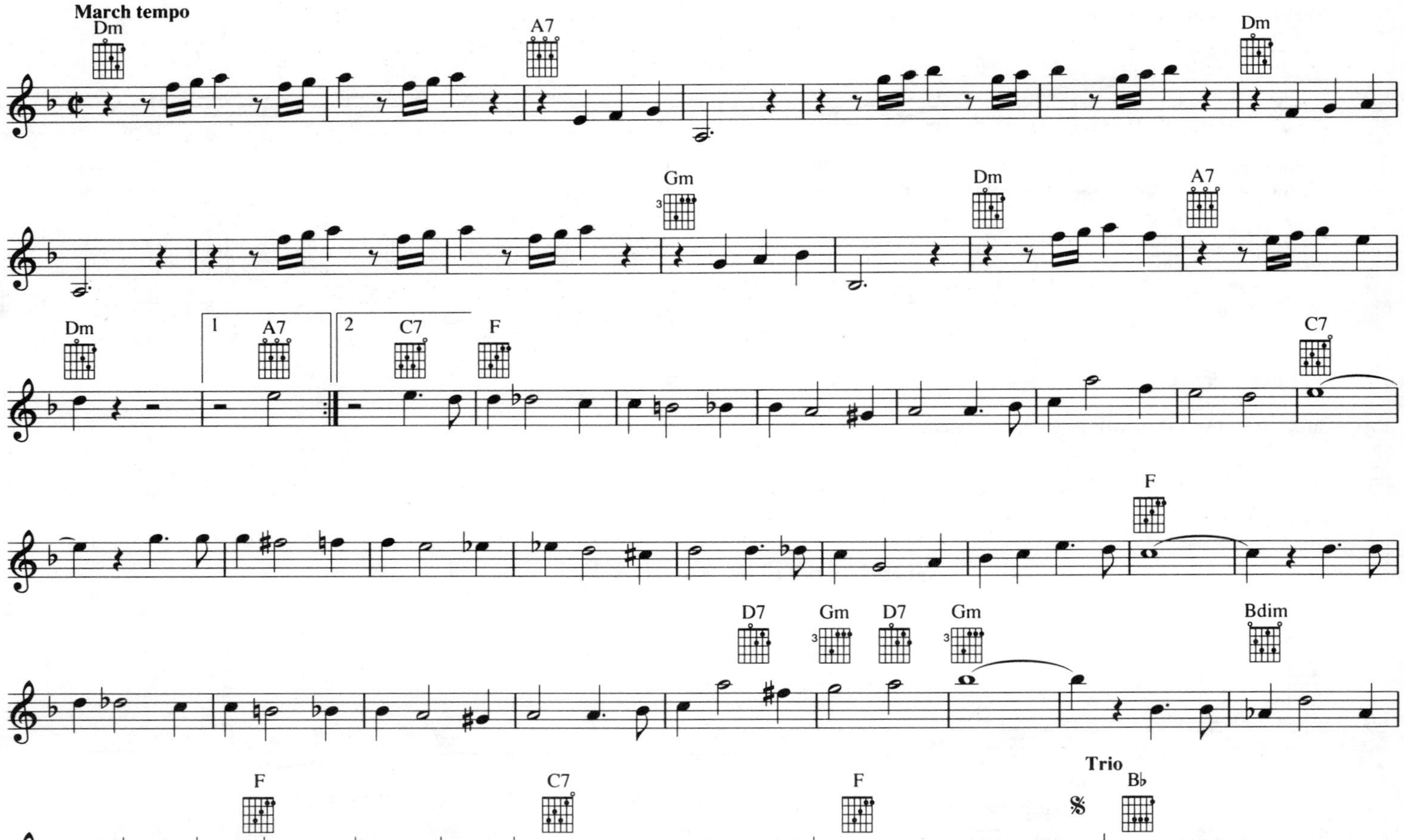

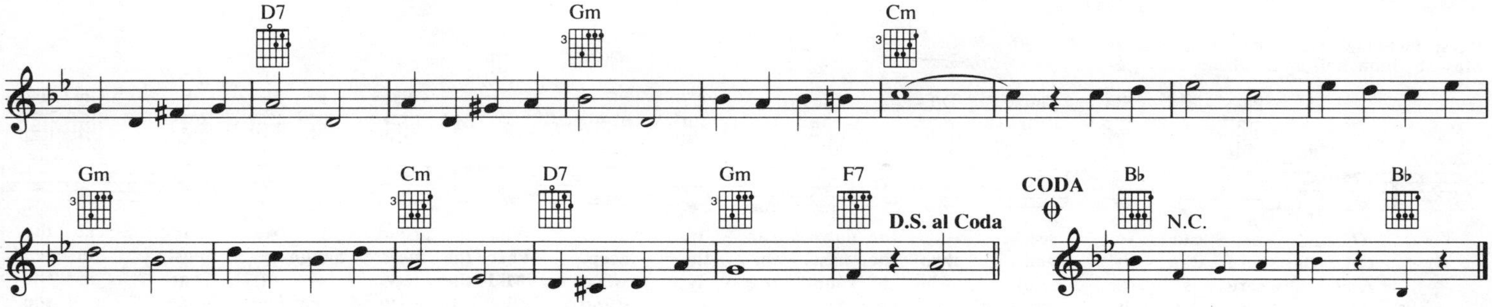
D7
Gm
Cm
Gm
Cm
D7
Gm
F7
D.S. al Coda
CODA
B♭
N.C.
B♭

ST. JAMES INFIRMARY

Slowly
Dm
A7
Dm
Gm
Dm
A7
1. I went down to the St. James In - firm - 'ry; To see my ba - by there. She was ly - in' on a long white
3 - 8. (See additional lyrics)
Dm
A7
Dm
A7
Dm
Gm
ta - ble, So __ sweet, so __ cool, _ so fair. 2. Went up to see the doc - tor, "She's ve - ry low," he
Dm
A7
Dm
A7
Dm
said; Went back to see my ba - by; Great _ God! She was ly - in' there dead.

Additional Lyrics

3. I went down to old Joe's barroom,
On the corner by the square;
They were servin' the drinks as usual,
And the usual crowd was there.

4. On my left stood Joe McKennedy,
his eyes bloodshot red;
He turned to the crowd around him,
These are the words he said:

5. Let her go, let her go, God bless her;
Wherever she may be;
She may search this wide world over
She'll never find a man like me.

6. Oh, when I die, please bury me
In my high-top Stetson hat;
Put a gold piece on my watch chain
So they'll know I died standin' pat.

7. Get six gamblers to carry my coffin,
Six chorus girls to sing my song,
Put a jazz band on my tail gate
To raise Hell as we go along.

8. Now that's the end of my story;
Let's have another round of booze;
And if anyone should ask you, just tell them
I've got The St. James Infirmary blues.

THE STAR SPANGLED BANNER

Words by Francis Scott Key
Music by John Stafford Smith

With spirit
O___ say, can you see, by the dawn's ear - ly light, What so proud - ly we hail'd at the
On the shore dim - ly seen thro' the mists of the deep, Where the foe's haugh - ty host in dread
And___ where is the band who so vaunt - ing - ly swore, 'Mid the hav - oc of war and the
O___ thus be it ev - er, when free men shall stand Be - tween their loved homes and the
twi - light's last gleam - ing? Whose broad stripes and bright stars, thro' the per - il - ous fight, O'er the ram - parts we
si - lence re - pos - es, What is that which the breeze, o'er the tow - er - ing steep. As it fit - ting - ly
bat - tle's con - fu - sion, A___ home and a coun - try they'd leave us no more? Their blood has wash'd
war's des - o - la - tion; Blest with vict' - ry and peace, may the heav'n res - cued land Praise the Power that hath
watch'd were so gal - lant - ly stream - ing? And the rock - et's red glare, the bombs burst - ing in air Gave
blows, half con - ceals, half dis clos - es? Now it catch - es the gleam of the morn - ing's first beam, In full
out their foul foot - step's pol - lu - tion. No ref - uge could save the___ hire - ling and slave From the
made and pre - served us a na - tion! Then con - quer we must, when our cause it is just, And
proof thro' the night that our flag was still there. O say, does that___ star - span - gled
glo - ry re - flect - ed now___ shines in the stream. 'Tis the star - span - gled___ ban - ner o
ter - ror of flight or the gloom of the grave; And the star - span - gled___ ban - ner in
this be our mot - to, "In God is our trust!" And the star - span - gled___ ban - ner in
ban - ner___ yet___ wave___ O'er the land___ of the free and the home of the brave.
long may___ it___ wave___ O'er the land___ of the free and the home of the brave.
tri - umph___ doth___ wave___ O'er the land___ of the free and the home of the brave.
tri - umph___ shall___ wave___ O'er the land___ of the free and the home of the brave.

STARS AND STRIPES FOREVER

John Philip Sousa

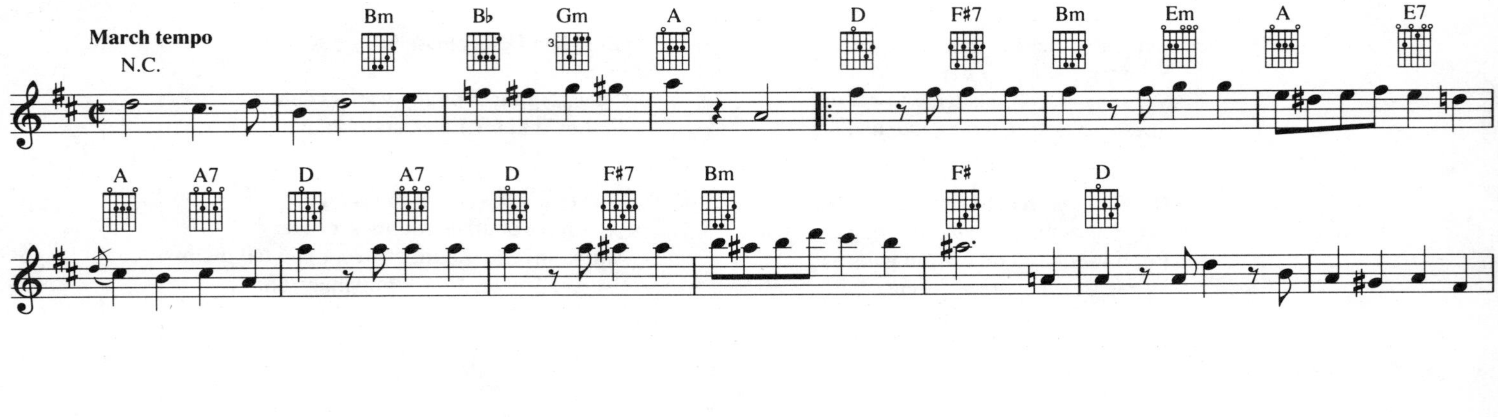
March tempo
N.C.

A7 D Dm E7 A
A D A7 D G E7 D A7
D A7 D D7 G Gm D A7 D
D G D7
G C D7 G
B7 Em Cm E♭
G D7 G Fine N.C.
Am B N.C. Cm D Cm6
N.C. Dm6 N.C.
Cm6 D7 N.C. D.S. al Fine

THE STREETS OF LAREDO

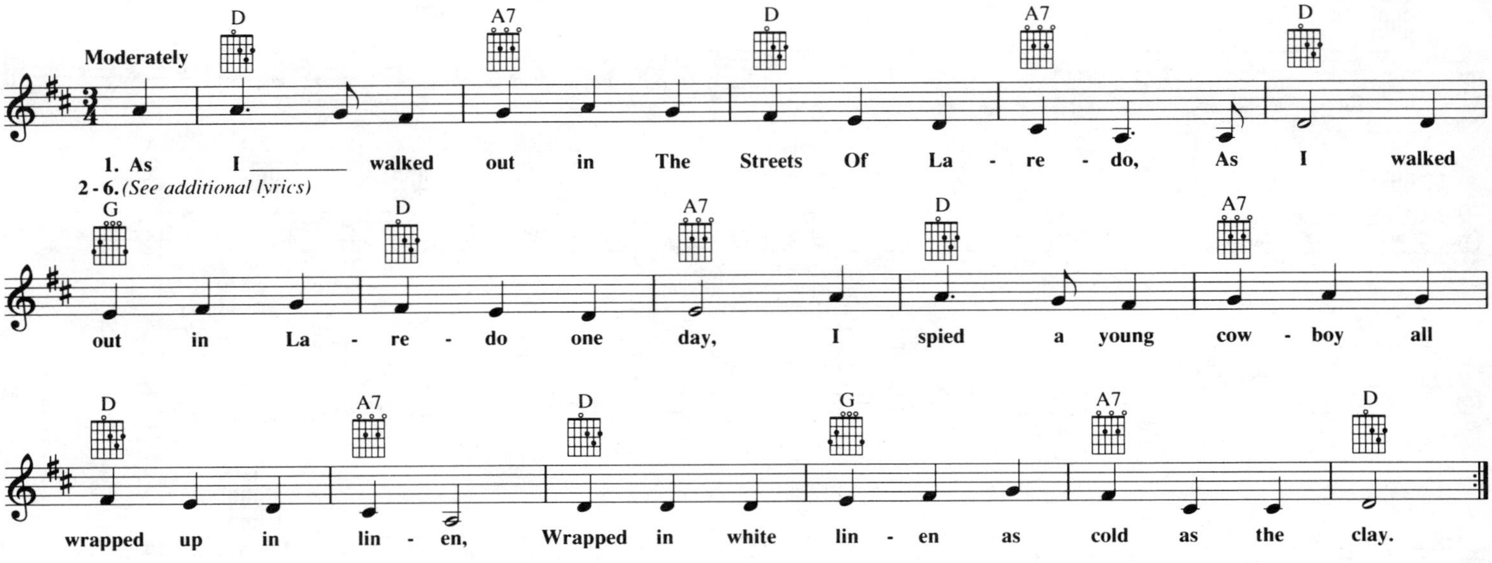
Moderately
D A7 D A7 D
1. As I ________ walked out in The Streets Of La - re - do, As I walked
2 - 6. (See additional lyrics)
G D A7 D A7
out in La - re - do one day, I spied a young cow - boy all
D A7 D G A7 D
wrapped up in lin - en, Wrapped in white lin - en as cold as the clay.

Additional Lyrics

2. I see by your outfit that you are a cowboy,"
These words he did say as I proudly stepped by,
"Come sit down beside me and hear my sad story,
Got shot in the breast and I know I must die.

3. "'Twas once in the saddle I used to go dashing,
'Twas once in the saddle I used to go gay;
'Twas first to drinkin', and then to card-playing,
Got shot in the breast and I'm dying today.

4. "Let six jolly cowboys come carry my coffin,
Let six pretty gals come carry my pall;
Throw bunches of roses all over my coffin,
Throw roses to deaden the clods as they fall.

5. "Oh, beat the drum slowly, and play the fife lowly,
And play the dead march as you carry me along,
Take me to the green valley and lay the earth o'er me,
For I'm a poor cowboy and I know I've done wrong."

6. Oh we beat the drum
slowly and we played the fife lowly,
And bitterly wept as we carried him along,
For we all loved our comrade, so brave, young and handsome,

SURPRISE SYMPHONY
(Theme)

Joseph Haydn

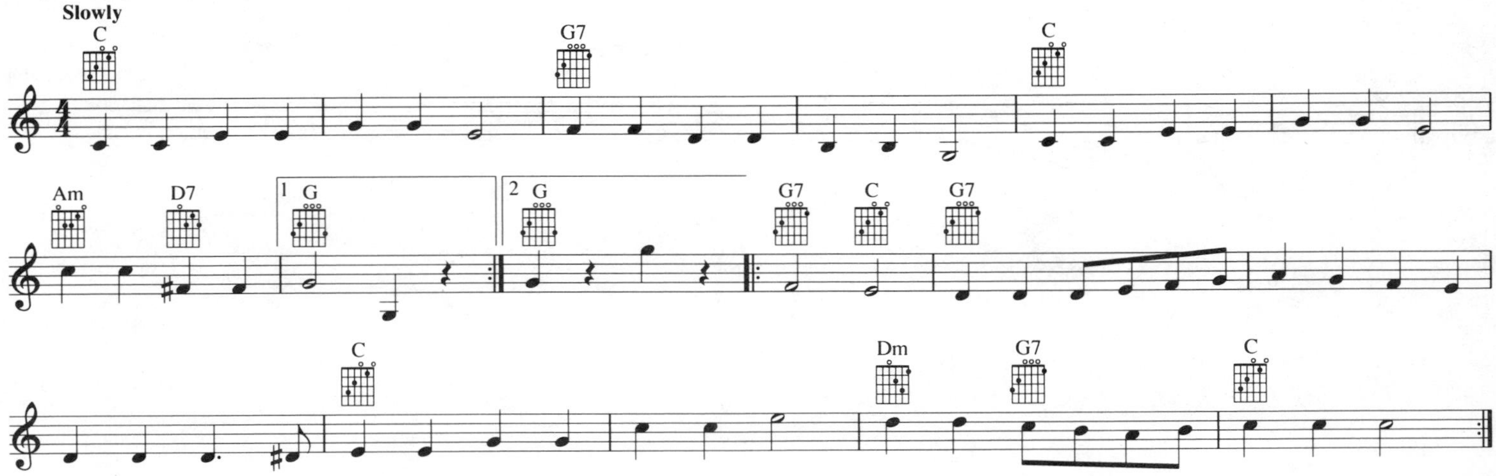
Slowly
C G7 C
Am D7 1 G 2 G G7 C G7
C Dm G7 C

SWAN LAKE
(Theme)

Peter Tschaikovsky

SWEET AND LOW

Poem by Alfred Tennyson
Music by Joseph Barnby

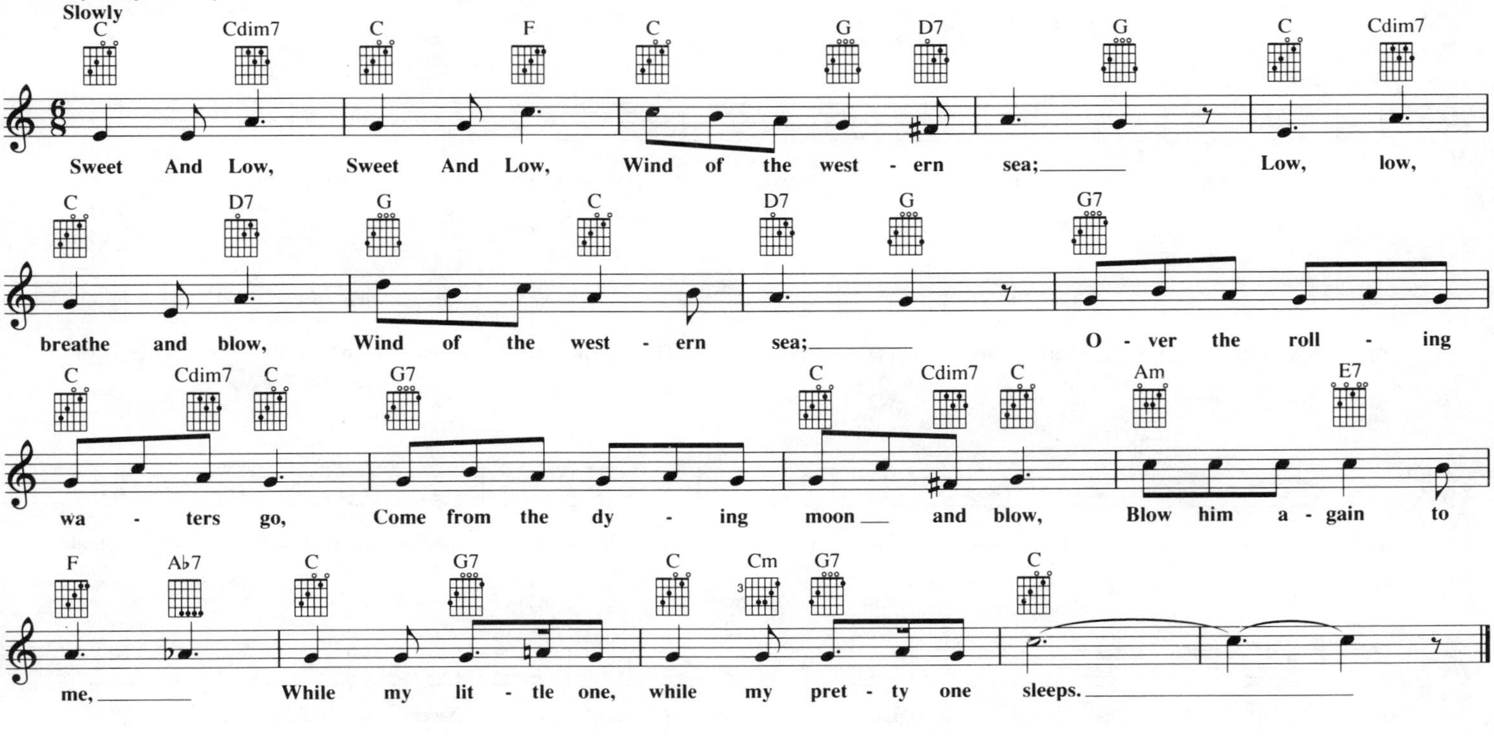

SWEET GENEVIEVE

Lyrics by George Cooper
Music by Henry Tucker

Moderately
G D7 G C Cm
O Gen - e - vieve, I'd give the world, to live a - gain the lone - ly past, The rose of youth was dew im - pearled; But
Fair Gen - e - vieve, My ear - ly love the years but make thee dear - er fair, My heart shall nev - er nev - er rove, Thou
G D7 G C G C Cm G
now it with - ers in the blast, I see thy face in ev - 'ry dream, My wak - ing thoughts are full of thee; Thy
art my on - ly guid - ing star, For me thy past has no re - gret, What - e'er the years may bring to thee; I
B7 Em Am B7 D7 G D7
glance is in the star - ry beam, That falls a - long the sum - mer sea!
bless the hour when we first met, The hour that gave me love and thee!
Oh! Gen - e - vieve, Sweet Gen - e - vieve, The
G C Cm G D7 G
days may come, the days may go, But still the hand of mem - 'ry weave, the bliss - ful dreams of long a - go.

SWEETHEARTS

Victor Herbert

Slow waltz
F7 B♭
Sweet - hearts make love their ver - y own, Sweet - hearts can live on love a - lone,
F7 B♭ Gm
For them the eyes where love - light lies O - pen the gates to Par - a - dise!
F7 B♭
All oth - er love is doomed to fade, It is like sun - shine veiled in shade,
G7 Cm D7/A Gm Edim7 F7 B♭
Such joys of life as love im - parts Are all of them yours, Sweet - hearts!

SING A SONG OF SIXPENCE

Moderately
D A7 D
Sing A Song Of Six - pence, a pock - et full of rye; Four and twen - ty black - birds Baked in a pie.
A7 G Em A7 D
When the pie was o - pened, The birds be - gan to sing. Was - n't that a dain - ty dish to set be - fore a king? The
A7 D
king was in the count - ing-house, Count-ing out his mon - ey. The queen was in the par - lor, Eat - ing bread and hon - ey. The
A7 G Em A7 D
maid was in the gar - den, Hang - ing out the clothes; A - long_ came a black - bird And pecked_ off her nose.

SWING LOW, SWEET CHARIOT

Moderately fast, steady tempo
F B♭ F Gm C7 F B♭ F
Swing Low Sweet Char - i - ot,_ Com - in' for to car - ry me home; Swing_ Low Sweet Char - i - ot,_
C7 F B♭ F C7
Com - in' for to car - ry me home;
I looked o - ver Jor - dan and what did I see?_ Com - in' for to car - ry me home, A
I'm on the_ up - ward heav - en - ly way,_ Com - in' for to car - ry me home, Since
If you get_ there_ be - fore_ I do,_ Com - in' for to car - ry me home, Tell
Some - times I'm_ up_ and some - times down,_ Com - in' for to car - ry me home, But
F B♭ F 1,2,3 C7 4 C7 B♭ F
band_ of an - gels com - in' af - ter me,_ Com - in' for to car - ry me home. Swing
Je - sus washed my sins_ a - way,_ Com - in' for to car - ry me home. Swing
all_ my friends I'm a com - in'_ too,_ Com - in' for to car - ry me home. Swing
still_ my soul feels heav'n - ly bound,_ Com - in' for to car - ry me home.

SWEET BETSY FROM PIKE

Moderately
D A7 D E7
1. Oh don't you re - mem - ber Sweet Bet - sy From Pike, Who crossed the big moun - tains with
2 - 8. (See additional lyrics)
A Bm F♯m G D A7
her lov - er Ike; With two yoke of cat - tle, a large yel - low dog, A ___ tall Shan - ghai roos - ter, and
D D A7 D
one spot - ted Hog, Say-ing good - bye, Pike Coun - ty, Fare - well for a - while,
We'll _ come back a - gain when we've panned out our pile.

Additional Lyrics

2. One evening quite early they camped on the Platte,
'Twas near by the road on a green shady flat,
Where Betsy, sore-footed, lay down to repose —
With wonder Ike gazed on that Pike County rose.

3. Their wagon broke down with a terrible crash,
And out on the prairie rolled all kinds of trash,
A few little baby clothes done up with care,
'Twas rather suspicious, but all on the square.

4. The Shanghai ran off, and their cattle all died;
That morning the last piece of bacon was fried;
Poor Ike was discouraged and Betsy got mad,
The dog drooped his tail and looked wondrously sad.

5. They soon reached the desert where Betsy gave out,
And down in the sand she lay rolling about;
While Ike, half distracted, looked on with surprise,
Saying, "Betsy, get up, you'll get sand in your eyes."

6. Sweet Betsy got up in a great deal of pain,
Declared she'd go back to Pike County again;
But Ike gave a sigh, and they fondly embraced,
And they travelled along with his arm round her waist.

7. They suddenly stopped on a very high hill,
With wonder looked down upon old Placerville;
Ike sighed when he said, and he cast his eyes down,
"Sweet Betsy, my darling, we've got to Hangtown."

8. Long Ike and sweet Betsy attended a dance;
Ike wore a pair of his Pike County pants;
Sweet Betsy was dressed up in ribbons and rings;
Says Ike, "You're an angel, but where are your wings?"

TAPS

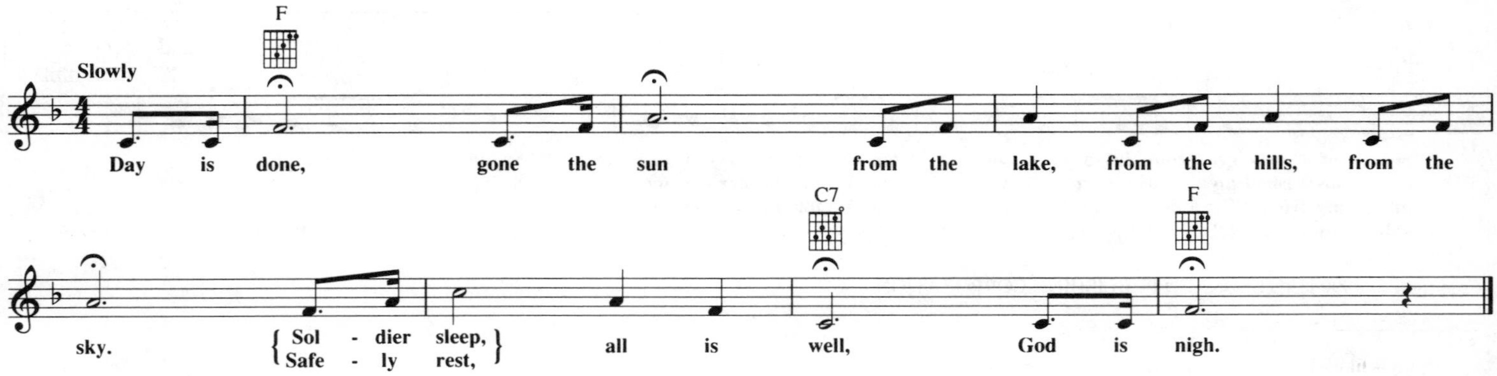
Slowly
F
Day is done, gone the sun from the lake, from the hills, from the
C7 F
sky. Sol - dier sleep, Safe - ly rest, all is well, God is nigh.

SHOO, FLY, DON'T BOTHER ME

With a strong beat
D A D A
Shoo, Fly, Don't Both - er Me, Shoo, Fly, Don't Both - er Me, Shoo, Fly, Don't Both - er Me, For
D
Fine
I be - long to some - bod - y.
I feel, I feel, I feel, I feel like a morn - in'
I hear, I hear, I hear, I hear all the an - gels
A7 D A7
D.C. (Twice) al Fine
star; I feel, I feel, I feel, I feel, I feel like a morn - in' star. Oh,
sing; I hear, I hear, I hear, I hear, I hear all the an - gels sing. Oh,

THAT'S WHY I DO LIKE I DO

F G7 C7
I took my girl out walk - ing, late one Sat - ur - day night; I took my girl out
F
walk - ing, the moon was mel - low and bright. I asked her if she'd mar - ry me and
G7 C7 F
what do you think she said? She said she would - n't mar - ry me if the whole darn world was dead.
Chorus
N.C. F G7 C7
That's Why I Do - Like - I - Do - like - I do - like - I do - like - I - do - like - I - do - do - do. Do - like - I - do - like - I -
F
do - like - I - do - like - I do - like - I - do - do - do. That's Why I Do - Like - I - Do - like - I do - like - I - do - like - I -
G7 C7 F B♭ F
do - like - I - do - do - do. Do - like - I - do - like - I do - like - I do - like - I do - like - I do - like - I do.

SHINE ON HARVEST MOON

Nora Bayes and Jack Norworth

Moderately slow
The night was might - y dark so you could hard - ly see, for the moon re - fused to shine.
I can't see why a boy should sigh, when by his side is the girl he loves so true.
Coup - le sit - ting un - der-neath a wil - low tree, for love they pine. Lit - tle maid was kind - a 'fraid of
All he has to say is, "Won't you be my bride, for I love you." Why should I be tell - ing you this
dark - ness so she said, "I guess I'll go." Boy be - gan to sigh, looked up at the sky,
se - cret when I know that you can guess har - vest moon will smile, shine on all the while,
told the moon his lit - tle tale of woe.
if the lit - tle girl should an - swer, "Yes."
N.C.
Oh, shine on, Shine On Har - vest Moon up in the
sky. I ain't had no lov - in' since Jan - u - ar - y, Feb - ru - ar - y, June or Ju - ly.
Snow time ain't no time to stay out-doors and spoon. So shine on,
Shine On Har - vest Moon, for me and my gal. Oh, Moon, for me and my gal.

ST. LOUIS BLUES

W.C. Handy

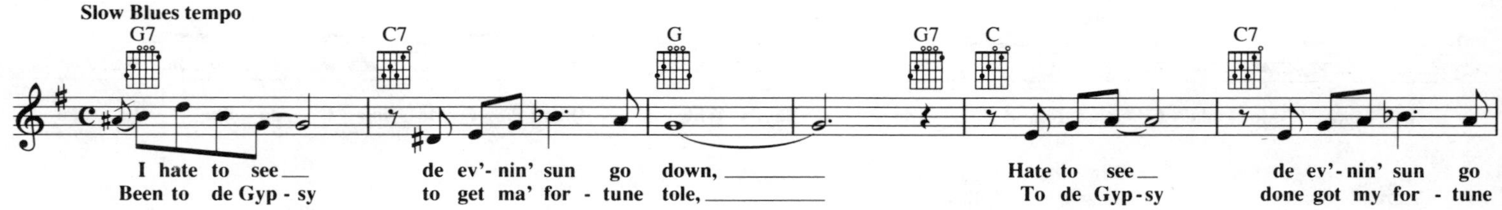
Slow Blues tempo
I hate to see de ev' - nin' sun go down, Hate to see de ev' - nin' sun go
Been to de Gyp - sy to get ma' for - tune tole, To de Gyp - sy done got my for - tune

G D7 G G7
down, 'Cause my ba - by, he done lef' dis town. Feel - in' to - mor - row
tole. 'Cause I'm most wile 'bout ma Jel - ly roll. Gyp - sy done tole me,
C7 G G7 C C7 G
lak I feel to - day, Feel to - mor - row lak I feel to - day.
"Don't you wear no black," Yes, she done tole me, "Don't you wear no black."
D7 G Gm Cm
I'll pack my trunk, make ma get a - way. St. Lou - is wom - an wid her di - a - mon'
Go to St. Lou - is, you can win him back. Help me to Cai - ro, make St. Louis by ma -
D7 G D7 Gm
rings Pulls dat man roun' by her a - pron strings. 'Twant for pow - der
self, Git to Cai - ro, find ma ole friend Jeff. Gwine to pin ma -
Cm C#dim7 D7 Gm A7 D7
an' for store bought hair De man I love would not gone no - where.
self close to his side, If ah flag his train, I sho' can ride.
Chorus
G C G C G C G7
Got de St. Lou - is Blues jes' as blue as ah can be, Dat
I loves dat man lak a school - boy loves his pie, Lak a
C6 C7 G C G C G C G
man got a heart lak a rock cast in the sea. Or else he wouldn't have gone
Ken - tuck - y Col - 'nel loves his mint an' rye. I'll love ma ba - by till
D D7 1 G 2 G
so far from me.
the day ah die.
(Spoken) Dog-gone it!

Additional Lyrics

3. You ought to see dat stove pipe brown of mine,
Lak he owns de Dimon' Joseph line.
He'd make a cross-eyed o' man go stone blind,
Blacker than midnight, teeth lak flags of truce,
Blackest man in de whole St. Louis.
Blacker de berry, sweeter is the juice.
About a crap game he knows a pow'ful lot,
But when work-time comes he's on de dot.
Gwine to ask him for a cold ten-spot.
What it takes to git it, he's certainly got.

Chorus

A black-headed gal make a freight train jump the track.
Said a black-headed gal make a freight train jump the track,
But a long tall gal makes a preacher ball the jack.

Extra Choruses

Lawd, a blonde-headed woman makes a good man leave the town,
I said a blonde-headed woman makes a good man leave the town,
But a red-head woman makes a boy slap his papa down.

O ashes to ashes and dust to dust,
I said ashes to ashes and dust to dust,
If my blues don't get you my jazzing must.

THE SWAN

Camille Saint-Saens

Slowly with expression
To Coda
D.C. al Coda
CODA
N.C.

SWEET ROSIE O'GRADY

Maud Nugent

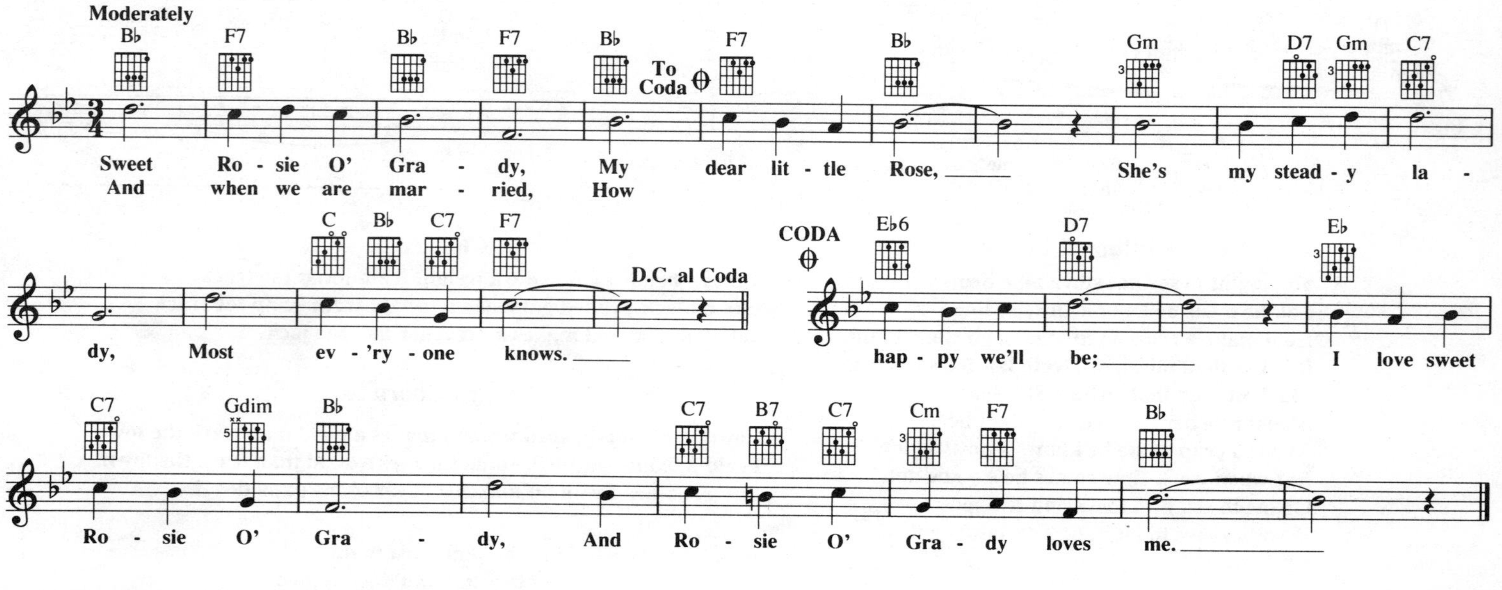
Moderately
To Coda
Sweet Ro - sie O' Gra - dy, My dear lit - tle Rose, She's my stead - y la - dy, Most ev - 'ry - one knows.
And when we are mar - ried, How hap - py we'll be;
D.C. al Coda
CODA
I love sweet Ro - sie O' Gra - dy, And Ro - sie O' Gra - dy loves me.

SWEET ADELINE

Words by Richard H. Gerard
Music by Harry Armstrong

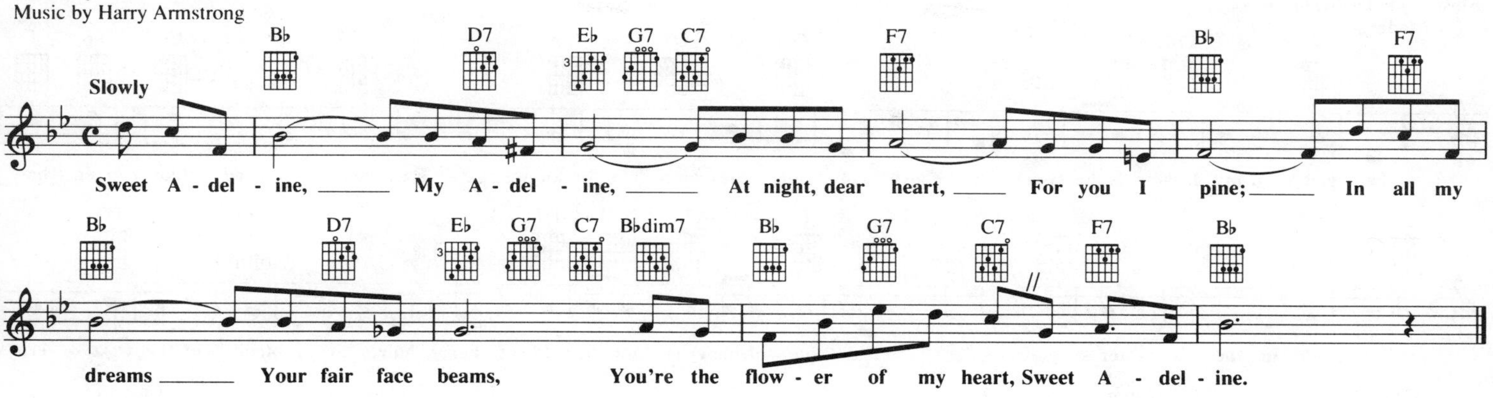

TANGO
(Albeniz)

Isaac Albeniz

THE SWEETHEART OF SIGMA CHI

Words by Byron D. Stokes
Music by F. Dudleigh Vernor

Moderately
F A7/E A7♭5/E♭ D7 Gm D7 Gm C7 C+ F6 F
The girl of my dreams is the sweet - est girl of all the girls I know. Each sweet co - ed, like a rain - bow
D7 G7 C7 F A7/E A7♭5/E♭ D7 Gm D7
trail, Fades in the af - ter glow. The blue of her eyes and the gold of her hair, are a blend of the west - ern
Gm D7 Gm Fdim E7 F F7 D7 G7 G7♯5 C7 F B♭m6 F6
sky; And the moon - light beams on the girl of my dreams She's The Sweet-heart Of Sig - ma Chi.

THAT'S A PLENTY

By Lew Pollack

Dixeland
Dm A7
Dm A7 Dm
A7 Dm A7
1 Dm 2 Dm C7 F
C7 F
C7 F Fdim7

F
D7
G7
C7
F
A7
Dm
A7
Dm
A7
F
G7
C7
Trio
B♭
G7
C7
F7
B♭
Cm7
F7
B♭
G7
C7
F7
B♭
1
To next strain
D
2
Fine
F
D.S. al Fine
F7

TAKE ME OUT TO THE BALL GAME

Lyrics by Jack Norworth
Music by Albert von Tilzer

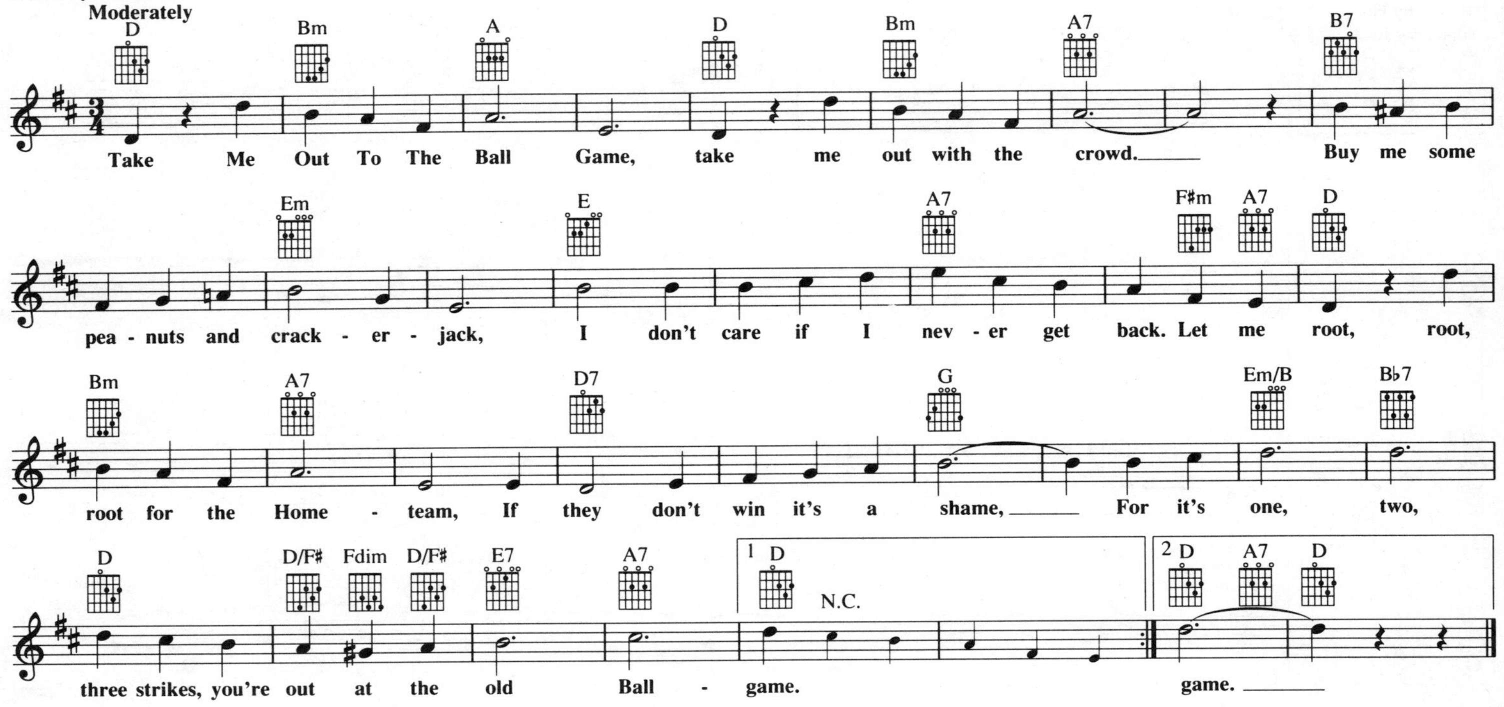
Moderately
D Bm A D Bm A7 B7
Take Me Out To The Ball Game, take me out with the crowd. Buy me some
Em E A7 F#m A7 D
pea - nuts and crack - er - jack, I don't care if I nev - er get back. Let me root, root,
Bm A7 D7 G Em/B B♭7
root for the Home - team, If they don't win it's a shame, For it's one, two,
D D/F# Fdim D/F# E7 A7 1 D N.C. 2 D A7 D
three strikes, you're out at the old Ball - game. game.

THERE'S A LONG, LONG TRAIL

Music by Zo Elliott
Words by Stoddard King

Moderately
G B7 Em C G D7 G
There's A Long, Long, Trail a wind - ing In - to the land of my dreams, Where the
C G E♭dim7 Em A7 D7
night - in - gales are sing - ing And a white moon beams: There's a
G C D7 G
long, long, night of wait - ing Un - til my dreams all come true; Till the
C G E♭dim7 Em A7 Am7 D7 1 G A7 D7 2 G
day when I'll be go - ing down That long, long, trail with you. There's A you.

THEY DIDN'T BELIEVE ME

Words by Herbert Reynolds
Music by Jerome Kern

Moderately
D7 G C6 Cm6
And when I told them how beau-ti-ful you are They Did-n't Be-lieve Me.
D7 G Em7 Am7 D7
They Did-n't Be-lieve Me! Your lips your eyes, your cheeks, your hair Are in a
Bm7 Em Bm F#7 Bm
class be-yond com-pare. You're the love-li-est girl that one could see!
E7 Am7 D7 G
And when I tell them, And I cert-n'ly am goin' to tell them, That I'm the
Am D7 G Em7 Am D7
man whose wife one day you'll be. They'll nev-er be-lieve me. They'll nev-er be-
G Dm6 E7 N.C. Am7 D7 D7-9 G
lieve me That from this great big world you've cho-sen me!

TOO-RA-LOO-RA-LOO-RAL
(That's An Irish Lullaby)

Words and Music by J.R. Shannon

Moderately, with expression
C F F#dim C F
Too-Ra-Loo-Ra-Loo-Ral, Too-ra-loo-ra-li, Too-Ra-Loo-Ra
C D7 G7 G7+5 C F
Loo-Ral, Hush now, don't you cry! Too-Ra-Loo-Ra-Loo-Ral, Too-ra-loo-ra
F#dim C F C D7 G7 C
li, Too-Ra-Loo-Ra-Loo-Ral, That's an I-rish lull-a-by.

12TH STREET RAG

By Euday L. Bowman

E♭ B♭7
E♭
G7 Cdim E♭ F9 B♭7 E♭
B♭7 E♭
B♭7
E♭
B♭7 F9
B♭7 E♭
B♭7
E♭ E♭7
A♭ B7 E♭ Cm7 F9 B♭7 E♭

THE TRAIL OF THE LONESOME PINE

Words by Ballard MacDonald
Music by Harry Carroll

Moderately slow
Bb F9 Bb Eb Bb Bbdim F7 Eb Ebm6 F7
On a moun - tain in Vir - gin - i - a. Stands a lone - some pine. Just be - low
Bb D7 Gm7 C7 F7 F9#5 Bb F9
is the ca - bin home of a lit - tle girl of mine her name is June and
Bb D7#5 Gm D7 Em7 A D A F7 Bb F7 Bb Cm7 Bb
ver - y, ver - y soon she'll be - long to me For I know she's wait - ing there for me
C7 Cm7b5 F7 F9 Bb Dm7b5 G7 C7
'Neath that lone pine tree: In the Blue Ridge Moun - tains of Vir - gin - ia On The
F7 Bb F7 Bb Dm7b5 G7 C7
Trail Of The Lone-some Pine In the pale moon-shine our hearts en - twine where she carved her name and
F C7 F7#5 Bb Eb6 Eb A7b5 D7 F9
I carved mine Oh! June Like the moun-tains I'm blue Like the pine I am lone-some for you In the
Bb Dm7b5 G7 C7 F7 1 Bb Bdim F9 2 Bb
Blue Ridge Moun-tains of Vir - gin - ia On The Trail Of The Lone-some Pine. In the Pine.

Henry J. Sayers

TA-RA-RA BOOM-DER-É

Brightly
Eb
Bb7
A sweet tux - e - do girl you see, Queen of swell so - ci - e - ty, Fond of fun as fond can be, When it's on the
blush - ing bud of in - no - cence, Pa - pa says at big ex - pence, Old maids say I have no sense, Boys de - clare I'm
strict Q. T. I'm not too young, I'm not too old, Not too tim - id, Not too bold, Just the kind you'd
just im - mence, Be - fore my song I do con - clude, I want it strict - ly un - der - stood, Tho' fond of fun, I'm
like to hold, Just the kind for sport I'm told.
nev - er rude, Tho' not too bad I'm not too good.
Ta - ra - ra Boom - der - é Ta - ra - ra Boom - der - é
Ta - ra - ra Boom - der - é Ta - ra - ra Boom - der - é Ta - ra - ra Boom - der - é Ta - ra - ra
Boom - der - é Ta - ra - ra Boom - der - é Ta - ra - ra Boom - der - é. I'm a Ta - ra - ra Boom - der - é.
1
2

TCHAIKOVSKY PIANO CONCERTO

(1st Movement)

Peter Ilyich Tchaikovsky

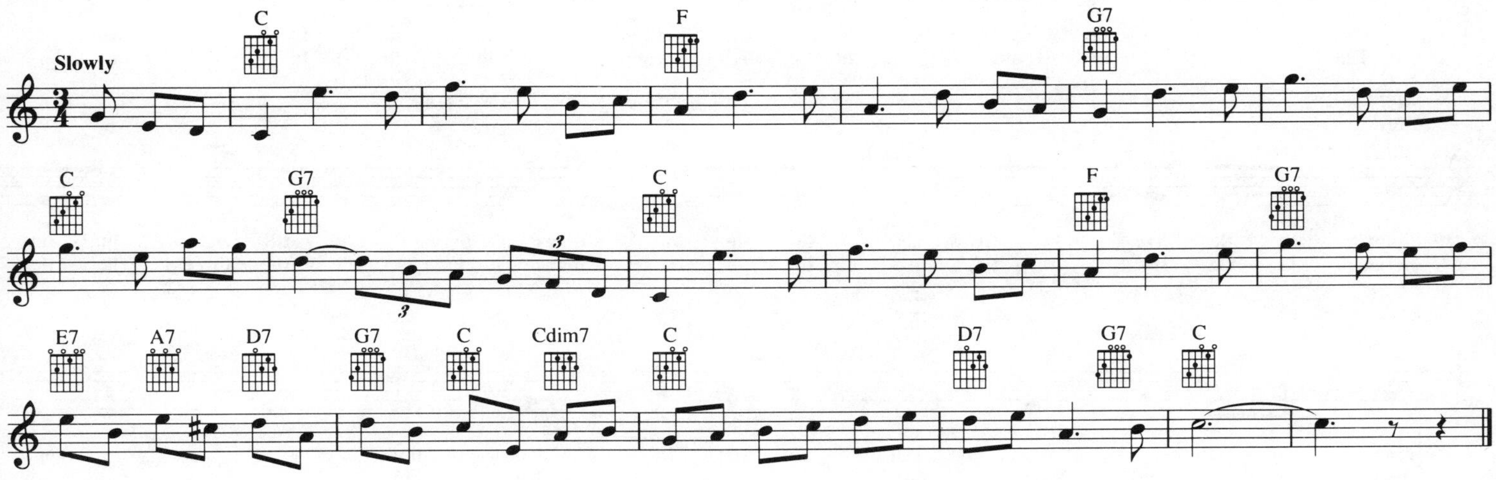
Slowly
C
F
G7
E7
A7
D7
Cdim7
3

TARANTELLA

Brightly
Gm Cm Gm D7 Gm
D7 Gm Gm Bb F7
Bb G7 Cm F7 Bb Bb Gm
Cm Gm Cm Gm D7 Gm Cm
Gm Cm Gm D7 Gm Gm F7 Bb
F7 Bb F7 Bb

TEN LITTLE INDIANS

Spirited
F
One lit - tle, two lit - tle, three lit - tle In - dians,
Ten lit - tle, nine lit - tle, eight lit - tle In - dians,
C7 F
Four lit - tle, five lit - tle, six lit - tle In - dians, Seven lit - tle, eight lit - tle,
Seven lit - tle, six lit - tle, five lit - tle In - dians, Four lit - tle, three lit - tle,
C7 F
nine lit - tle In - dians, Ten lit - tle In - dian boys.
two lit - tle In - dians, One lit - tle In - dian boy.

TCHAIKOVKSY SYMPHONY NO. 6
(1st Movement)

Peter Tchaikovsky

Slowly
Bb Gdim Bb F7 Bb Bdim
Eb Cdim Bb Gm6 Bb F7 Bb Bdim Eb Cdim
Bb Gm6 Bb F7 Bb Bb7 Eb6 Bb
Fine
C7 Cm Bb Eb6 Bb C7 Cdim
Bb Gb Bb Gb Bb
D.S. al Fine

TELL ME WHY

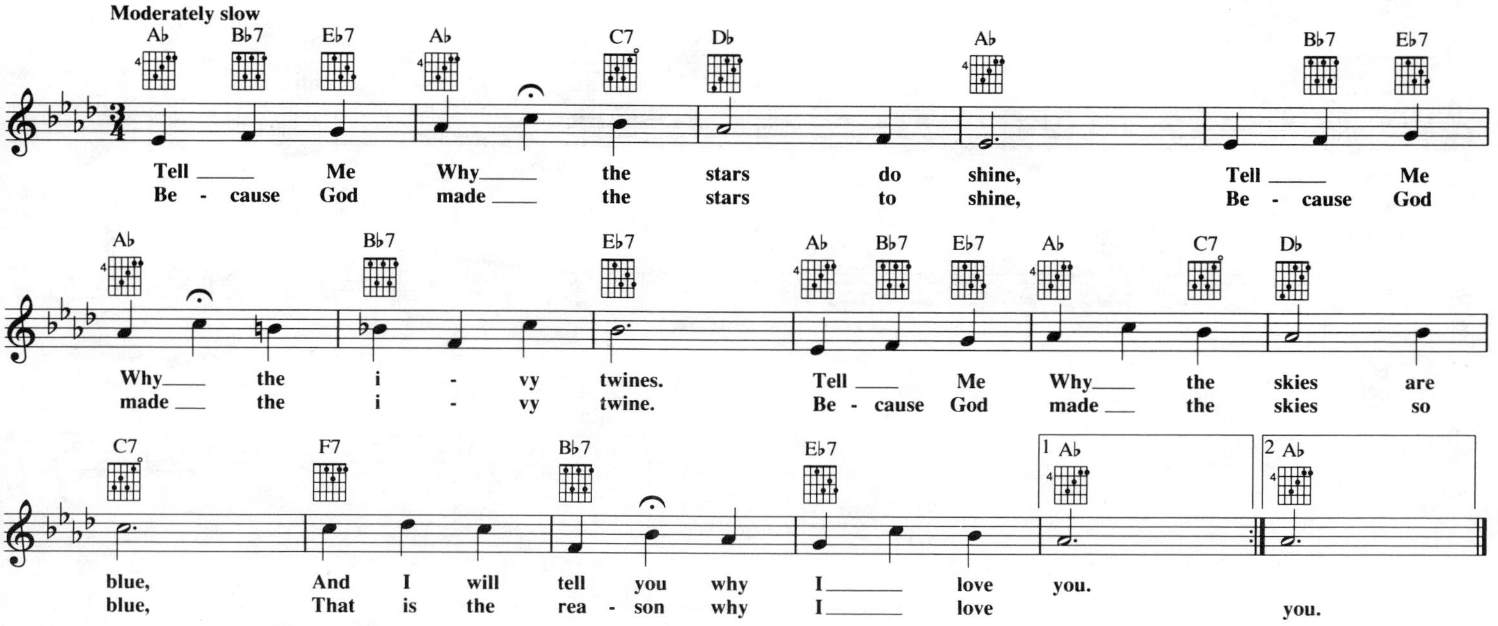
Moderately slow
Ab Bb7 Eb7 Ab C7 Db Ab Bb7 Eb7
Tell Me Why the stars do shine, Tell Me
Be - cause God made the stars to shine, Be - cause God
Ab Bb7 Eb7 Ab Bb7 Eb7 Ab C7 Db
Why the i - vy twines. Tell Me Why the skies are
made the i - vy twine. Be - cause God made the skies so
C7 F7 Bb7 Eb7 1 Ab 2 Ab
blue, And I will tell you why I love you.
blue, That is the rea - son why I love you.

TALES FROM THE VIENNA WOODS

Johann Strauss

Fm Eb Bb7 Eb 1 2 Bb
Cm F7 Bb
Cm D Gm D N.C. 1 2
Bb F7 Bb
G7 Cm Edim Bb F7 Bb

THERE WAS AN OLD WOMAN WHO LIVED IN A SHOE

Moderately
F Bb F C
There___ Was An Old Wom - an Who Lived In A Shoe; She had
G7 C G7 C F C
so man - y chil - dren, she did - n't know what to do. She___ gave them some broth with -
F C F Bb C7 F
out an - y bread; She___ whipped them all sound - ly and put them to bed.

THIS OLD MAN

Traditional

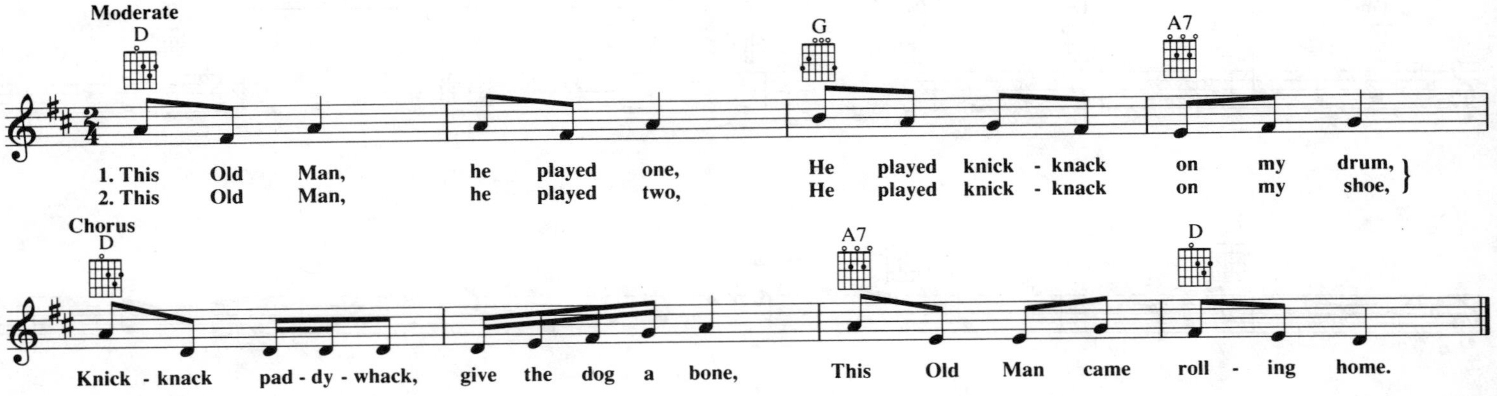
Moderate
D
G
A7
1. This Old Man, he played one, He played knick - knack on my drum,
2. This Old Man, he played two, He played knick - knack on my shoe,
Chorus
D
A7
D
Knick - knack pad - dy - whack, give the dog a bone, This Old Man came roll - ing home.

Additional Lyrics

3. This old man, he played three
He played knick-knack on my knee. (*Chorus*)

4. This old man, he played four,
He played knick-knack on my door. (*Chorus*)

5. This old man, he played five,
He played knick-knack on my hive. (*Chorus*)

6. This old man, he played six,
He played knick-knack on my sticks. (*Chorus*)

7. This old man, he played seven,
He played knick-knack up to heaven. (*Chorus*)

8. This old man, he played eight,
He played knick-knack at the gate. (*Chorus*)

9. This old man, he played nine,
He played knick-knack on my line. (*Chorus*)

10. This old man, he played ten,
He played knick-knack over again. (*Chorus*)

TENTING TONIGHT

Words and Music by Walter Kittredge

A
D
A
E7
1. We're Tent - ing To - night on the old camp - ground. Give us a song to
2-4. (See additional lyrics)
A
D
A
E7
cheer our wea - ry hearts, A song of home and friends we love so
A
D
dear. Man - y are the hearts that are wea - ry to - night
A
E7
A
Wish - ing for the war to cease. Man - y are the hearts that are

D A E7 A
Chorus
look - ing for the right to see the dawn of peace. Tent - ing To - night,
D E7 A
Tent - ing To - night, Tent - ing on the old camp - ground.

Additional Lyrics

2. We've been Tenting Tonight on the old camp-ground.
   Thinking of days gone by,
   Of the loved ones at home that gave us the hand,
   And the tear that said, "Goodbye."

3. We are tired of war on the old camp-ground,
   Many are dead and gone,
   Of the brave and true who've left their homes,
   Others been wounded long.

4. We've been fighting
   today on the old camp-ground,
   Many are lying near,
   Some are dead and some are dying,

THIS TRAIN

Moderately
E
1. This Train is bound for glo - ry, This Train,
2-6. (See additional lyrics)
This Train is bound for glo - ry,
B7 E E7 A
This Train,
This Train is bound for glo - ry, Don't ride noth- in' but the
E B7 E
right-eous and the ho - ly. This Train is bound for glo - ry, This Train.

Additional Lyrics

2. This Train don't carry no gamblers, (*3 times*)
   No hypocrites, no midnight ramblers,
   This Train is bound for glory, This Train.

3. This Train is built for speed now, (*3 times*)
   Fastest train you ever did see,
   This Train is bound for glory, This Train.

4. This Train don't carry no liars, (*3 times*)
   No hypocrites and no high flyers,
   This Train is bound for glory, This Train.

5. This Train you don't pay no transportation, (*3 times*)
   No Jim Crow and no discrimination,
   This Train is bound for glory, This Train.

6. This Train don't carry no rustlers, (*3 times*)
   Sidestreet walkers, two-bit hustlers,
   This Train is bound for glory, This Train.

THERE IS A TAVERN IN THE TOWN

Moderately
C
There Is A Tav - ern In The Town, in the town, And there my true love sits him
G7 C F G7
down, sits him down, _ and ___ drinks his wine as mer - ry as can be, And nev - er,
C G7 C
Chorus
nev - er thinks of me. ___ Fare thee well, for I must leave thee, Do not let this part - ing
G7 C F C
grieve thee, And re - mem - ber that the best of friends must part, must part. A - dieu, a - dieu, kind friends a -
G7 C
dieu, yes a - dieu, I can no long - er stay with you, stay with you ___ I'll ___ hang my
F G7 C
heart on the weep - ing wil - low tree, And may the world go well with thee. ___

Additional Lyrics

2. He left me for a damsel dark, damsel dark.
   Each Friday night they used to spark, used to spark.
   And now my love who once was true to me,
   Takes this dark damsel on his knee.

3. And now I see him nevermore, nevermore.
   He never knocks upon my door, on my door.
   Oh, woe is me, he pinned a little note,
   And these were all the words he wrote:

4. Oh, dig my grave both wide and deep, wide and deep.
   Put tombstones at my head and feet, head and feet.
   And on my breast you may carve a turtle dove,
   To signify I died for love.

THREE BLIND MICE

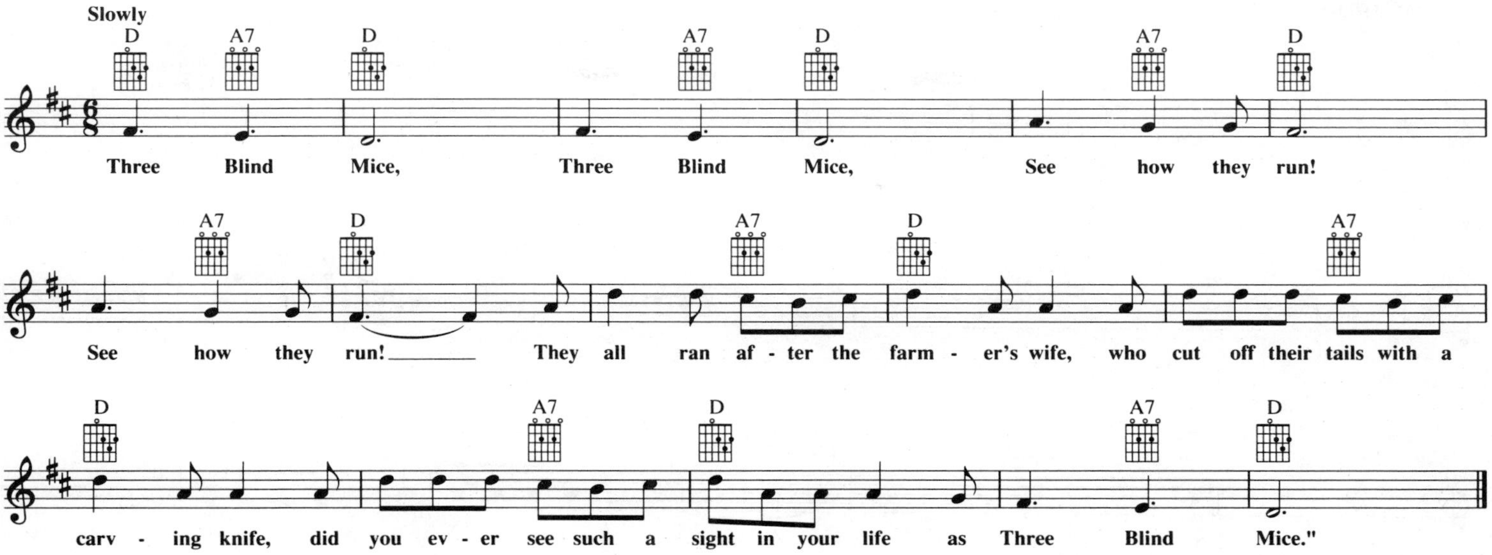
Slowly
D A7 D A7 D A7 D
Three Blind Mice, Three Blind Mice, See how they run!
A7 D A7 D A7
See how they run! They all ran af - ter the farm - er's wife, who cut off their tails with a
D A7 D A7 D
carv - ing knife, did you ev - er see such a sight in your life as Three Blind Mice."

Julius Fucik

THUNDER AND BLAZES

Brightly
C G7
C
B Em B
G7 D7 Eb7 G D7 G
C G7 C
Adim C G7 C

THUNDERER

John Philip Sousa

TOREADOR SONG
(Bizet)

Georges Bizet

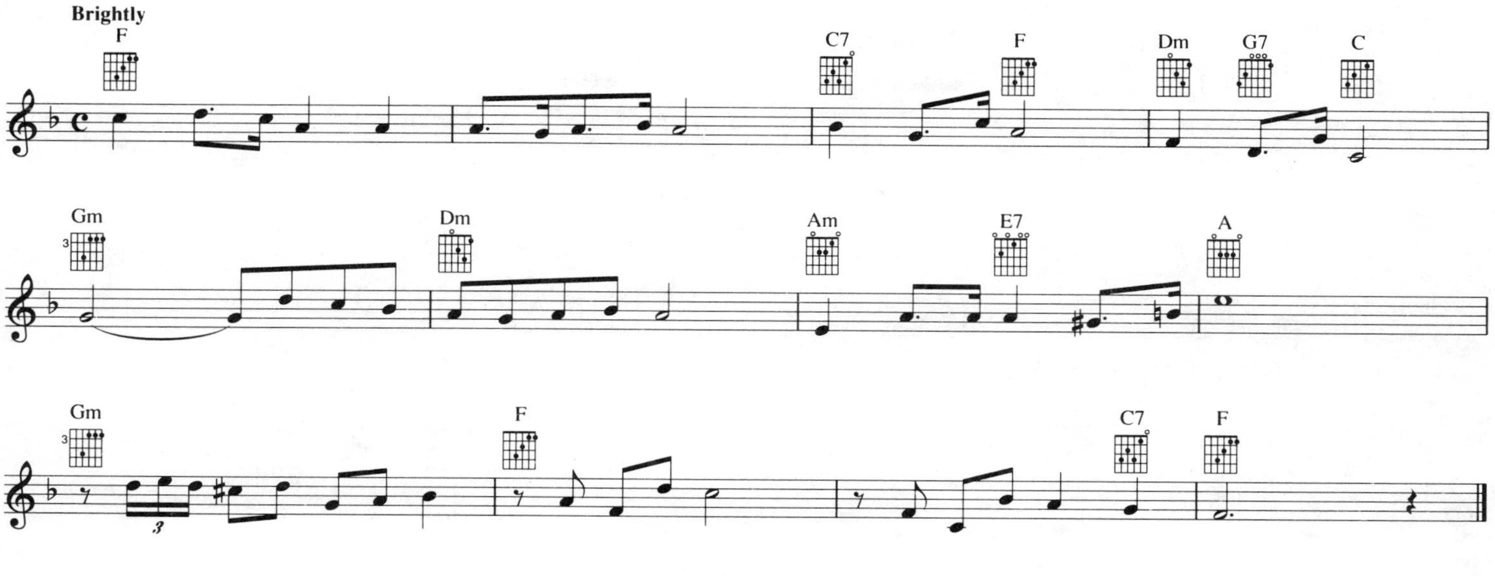
Brightly
F C7 F Dm G7 C
Gm Dm Am E7 A
Gm F C7 F

TRAMP! TRAMP! TRAMP!

George F. Root

Moderately
1. In the pris - on cell I sit, Think - ing, Moth - er dear of you, And our bright and hap - py home so far a - way; And the tears they fill my eyes, Spite of all that I can do, Though I try to cheer my com - rades and be gay.
2. In the bat - tle front we stood When their fierc - est charge they made, And they swept us off a hun - dred men or more; But be - fore we reached their lines, They were beat - en back, dis - mayed, And we heard the cry of vic - t'ry o'er and o'er.
3. So, with - in the pris - on cell, We are wait - ing for the day, That shall come to o - pen wide the i - ron door, And the hol - low eye grows bright, And the poor heart al - most gay, As we think of see - ing home and friends once more.
Chorus
Tramp! Tramp! Tramp! the boys are march - ing, Cheer up, com - rades, they will come, And be - neath the star - ry flag We shall breathe the air a - gain Of the free land in our own, be - lov - ed home.

TINKER POLKA

TIT-WILLOW

Gilbert and Sullivan

Wil-low!" And I said to him Dick - y bird, why do you sit Sing - ing
Wil-low!" And a cold pers - pi - ra - tion be - span - gled his brow, Oh
Wil-low, That 'twas blight - ed af - fec - tion that made him ex - claim, "Oh
wil - low, Tit - Wil-low, Tit - Wil-low?" "Is it weak - ness of in - tel - lect
wil - low, Tit - Wil-low, Tit - Wil-low! He sobb'd and he sigh'd, and a
wil - low, Tit - Wil-low, Tit - Wil-low!" And if you re - main cal - lous and
bird - ie?" I cried, "Or a rath - er tough worm in your lit - tle in - side?" With a
gar - gle he gave, Then he threw him - self in - to the bil - low - y wave, And a
ob - du - rate, I shall per - ish as he did, And you will know why, Tho' I
shake of his poor lit - tle head he re - plied, "Oh wil - low, Tit - Wil-low, Tit - Wil - low!"
e - cho a rose from the su - i - cide's grave, "Oh wil - low, Tit - Wil-low, Tit - Wil - low!"
pro - bab - ly shall not ex - claim as I die, "Oh wil - low, Tit - Wil-low, Tit - Wil - low!"

TO A WILD ROSE

Edward MacDowell

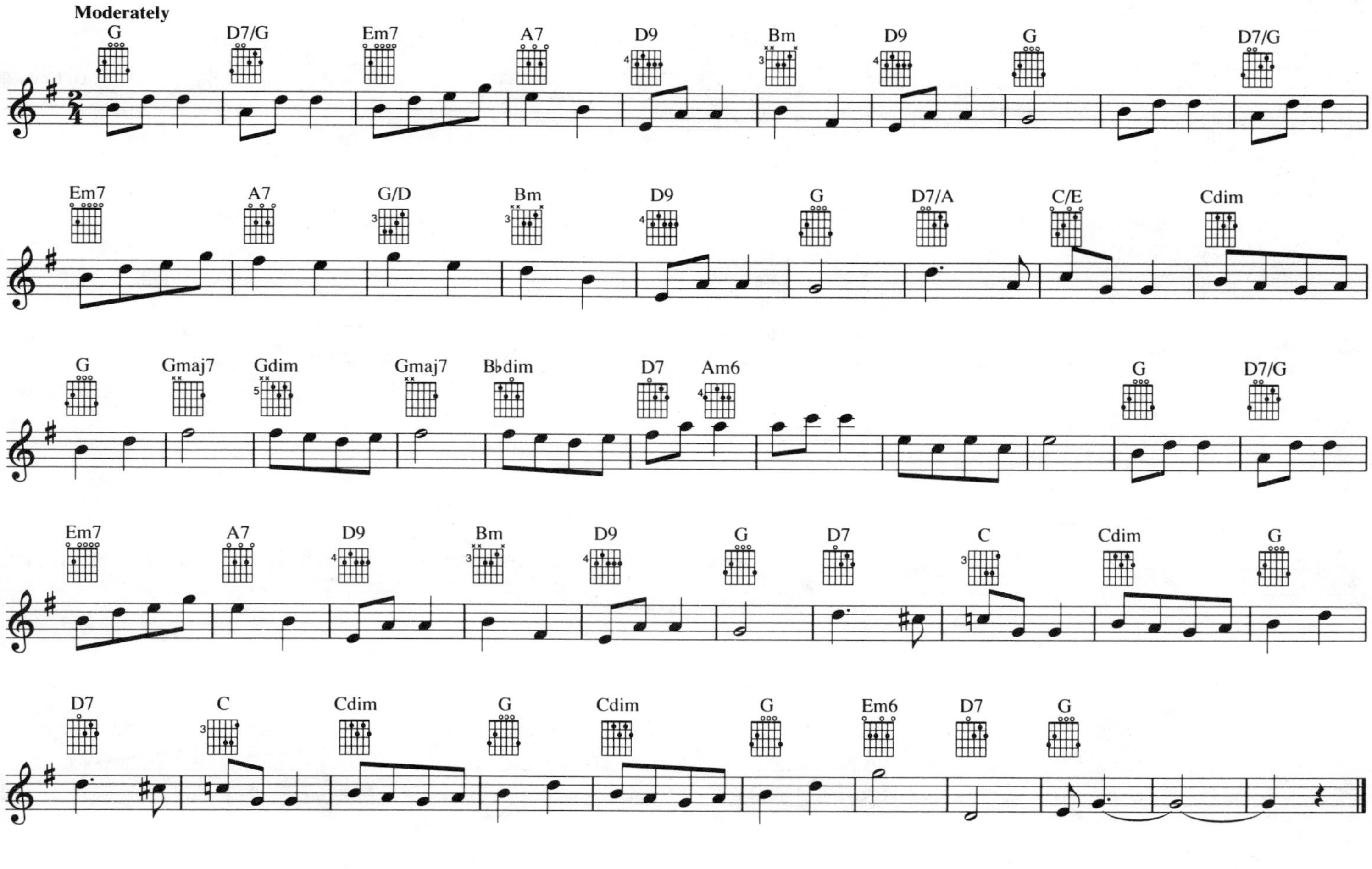
Moderately

TOYLAND

Music by Victor Herbert

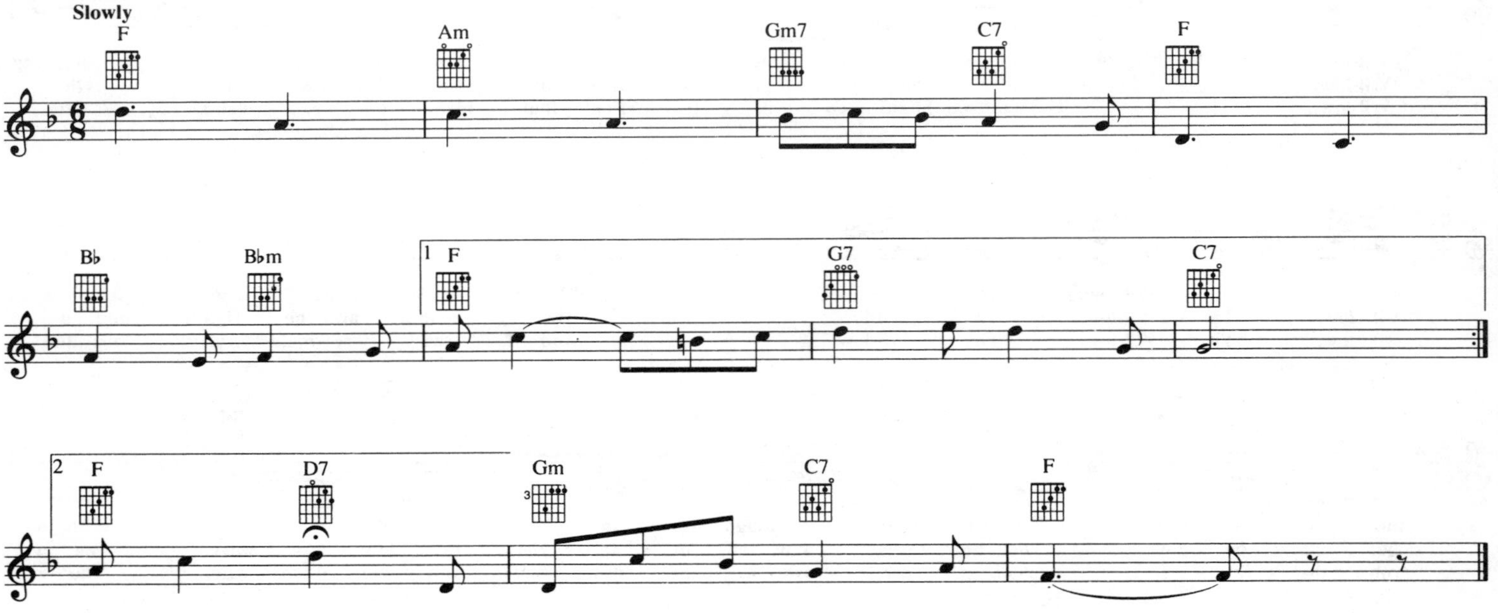

TRAUMEREI

Robert Schumann

TRUMPET TUNE

Jeremiah Clarke

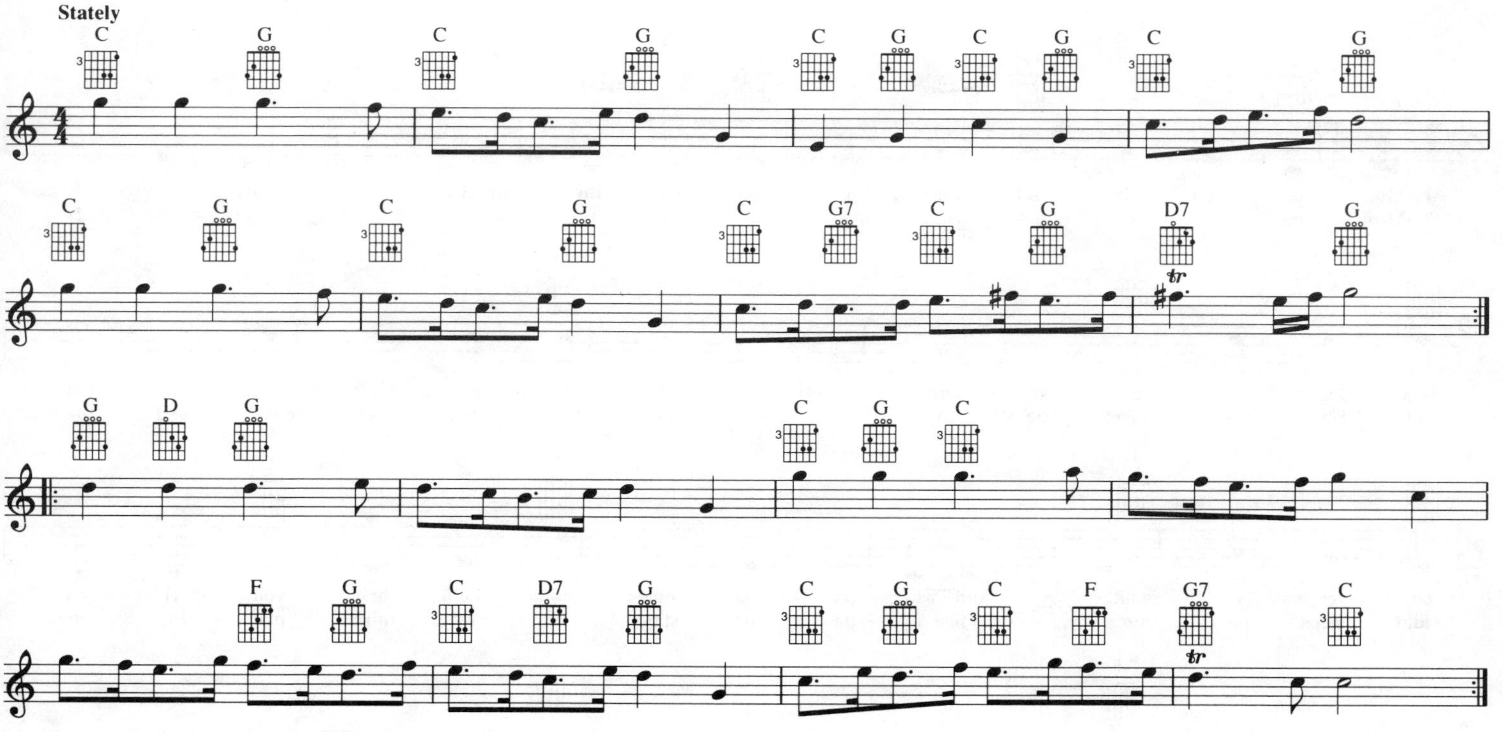
Stately

TURKEY IN THE STRAW

Rollicking
As I was a-go-ing on down the road, With a ti-red team and a heav-y load, I
cracked my whip and the lead-er sprung, I says day-day to the wa-gon tongue.
Chorus
Tur-key In The Straw, haw, haw, haw, Tur-key in the hay, hay, hay, hay,
Roll 'em up and twist 'em up a high tuck a-haw, And hit 'em up a tune called Tur-key In The Straw.

TOURELAY, TOURELAY

C G7 C
1. Oh, pa - pa is out break - ing rocks on the street, And ba - by is
2. When pa - pa has gum - drops and ba - by has none, If pa - pa is
D7 G C
sleep - ing so co - sy and sweet; O ba - by, don't cry now, but
fool - ish and gives ba - by one, When four o' - clock comes, and the
F C G7 C
be ver - y goot, And when pa - pa comes home he'll bring you ci - ga -
child sleeps no more, Then... pa - pa stays up all night pac - ing the
F C
root.
floor! Tou - re - lay, Tou - re - lay, With my
F N.C. F
fil - la - ga dee - sha, Skin - a - ma - roo - sha, bal - der - al - da boom ta - de - ay, Tou - re - lay,
C G7 C
Tou - re - lay, And the pride of the house is pa - pa's ba - bie.

TRIUMPHAL MARCH
(From "AIDA")

Giusseppe Verdi

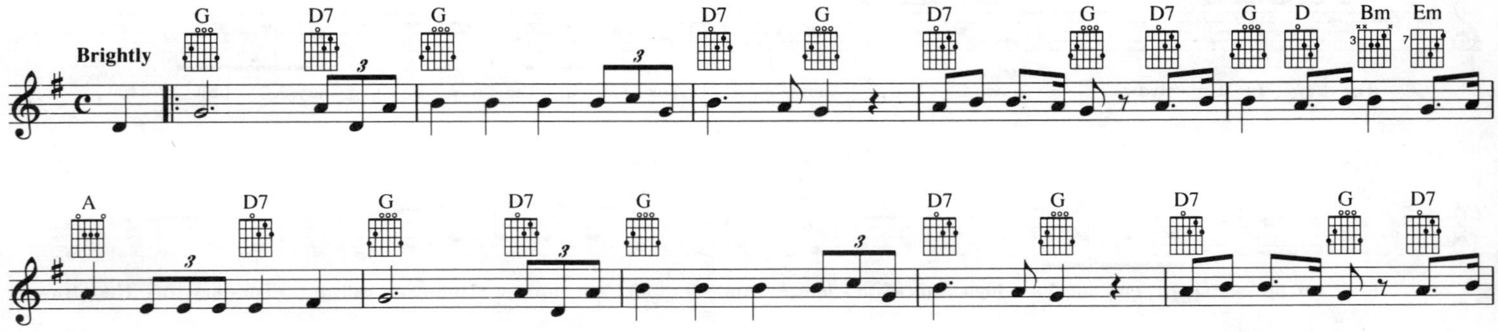
Brightly
G D7 G D7 G D7 G D7 G D Bm Em
A D7 G D7 G D7 G D7 G D7

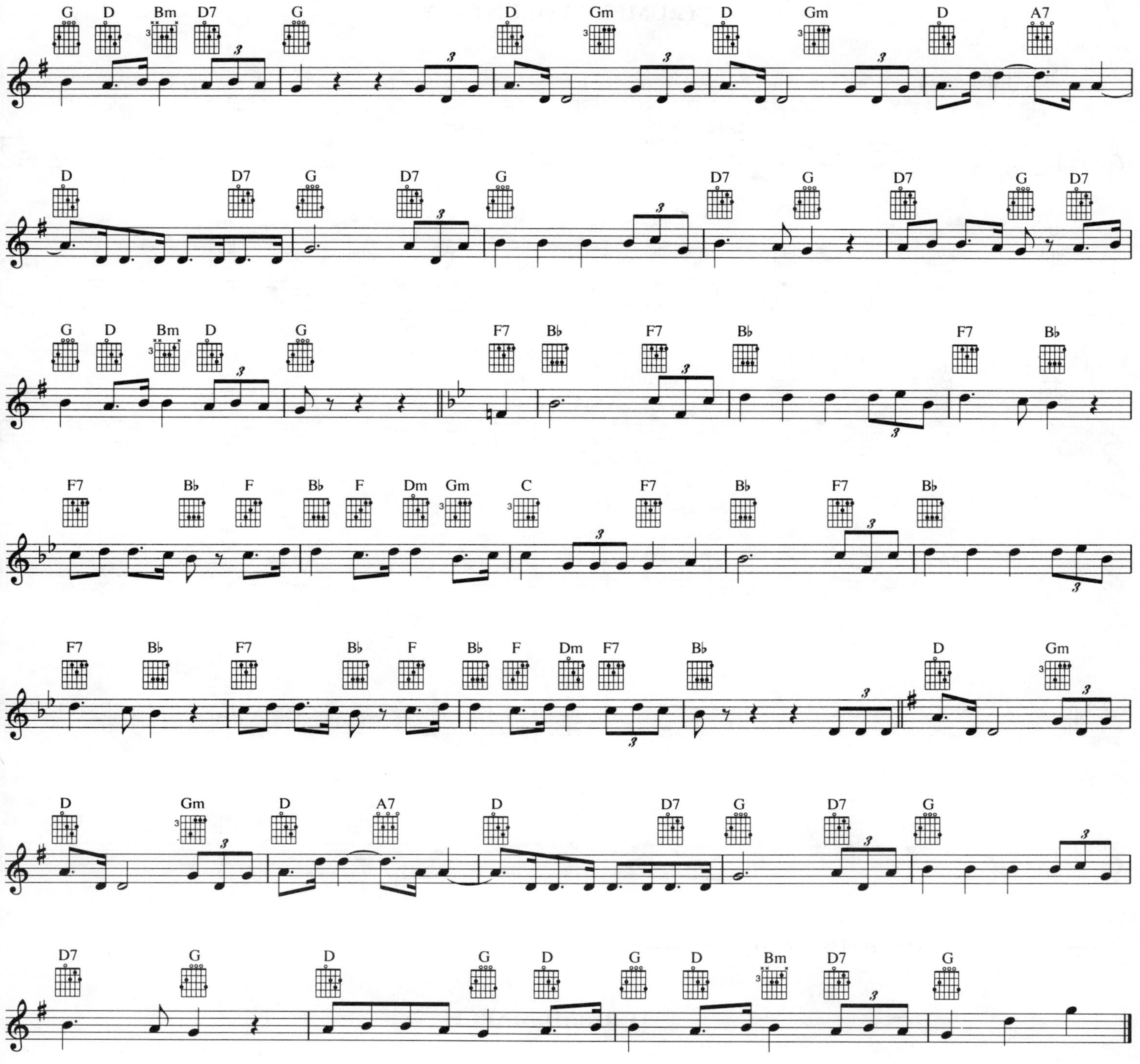

TWINKLE, TWINKLE, LITTLE STAR

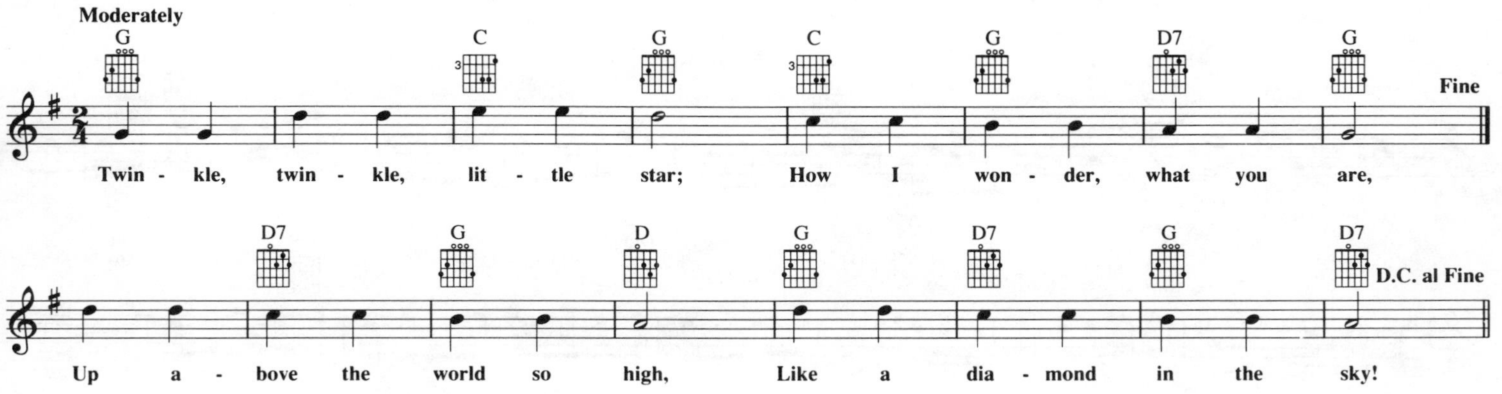

TRUMPET VOLUNTARY

Jeremiah Clarke

TURKISH MARCH

Ludwig Van Beethoven

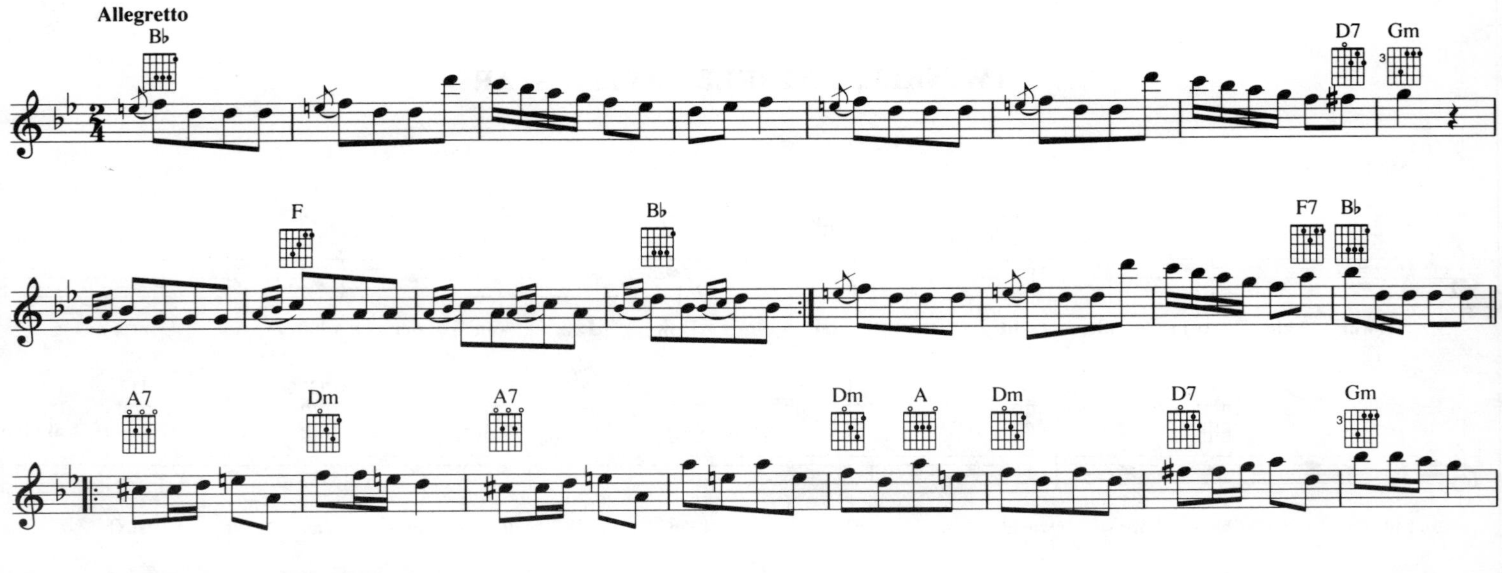

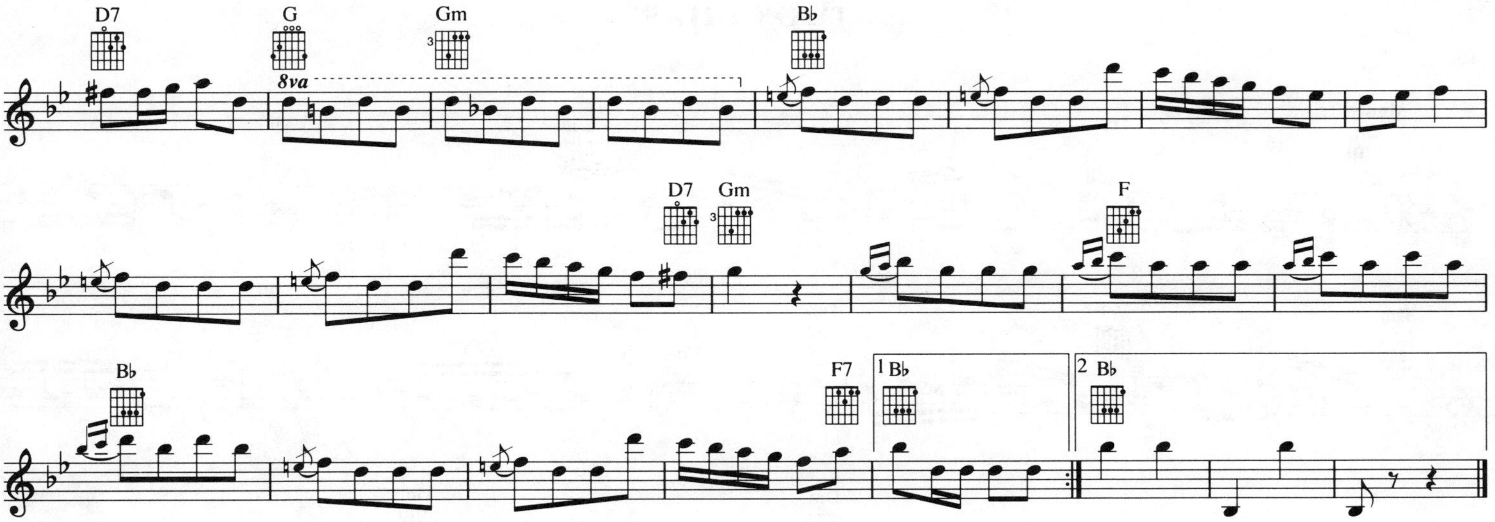
D7 G Gm Bb
8va
D7 Gm F
Bb F7 1 Bb 2 Bb

THE TWELVE DAYS OF CHRISTMAS

Traditional

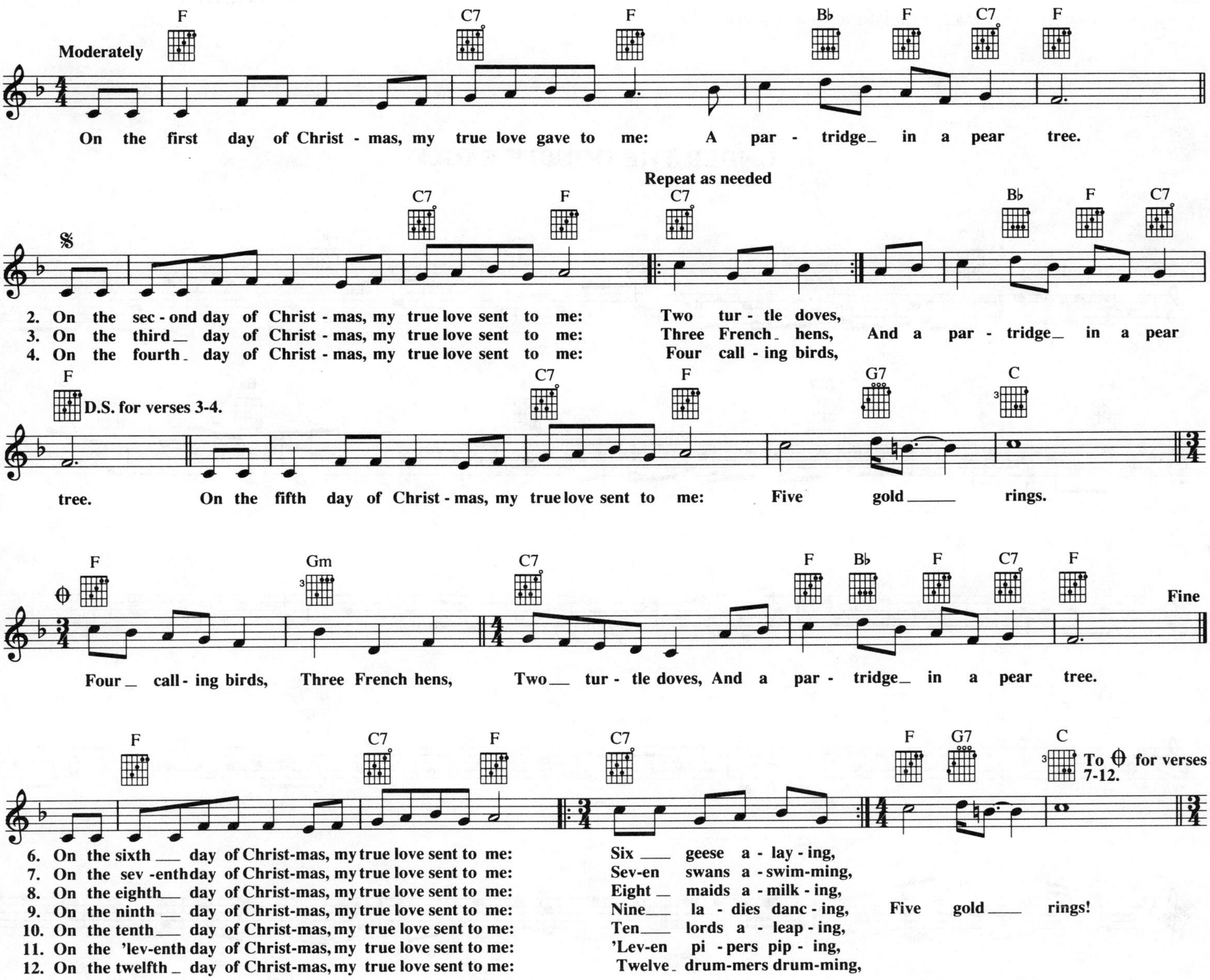
Moderately
F C7 F Bb F C7 F
On the first day of Christ - mas, my true love gave to me: A par - tridge_ in a pear tree.
Repeat as needed
C7 F C7 Bb F C7
2. On the sec - ond day of Christ - mas, my true love sent to me: Two tur - tle doves,
3. On the third_ day of Christ - mas, my true love sent to me: Three French_ hens, And a par - tridge_ in a pear
4. On the fourth_ day of Christ - mas, my true love sent to me: Four call - ing birds,
F D.S. for verses 3-4.
C7 F G7 C
tree. On the fifth day of Christ - mas, my true love sent to me: Five gold_____ rings.
F Gm C7 F Bb F C7 F
Fine
Four_ call - ing birds, Three French hens, Two_ tur - tle doves, And a par - tridge_ in a pear tree.
F C7 F C7 F G7 C
To ⊕ for verses 7-12.
6. On the sixth___ day of Christ-mas, my true love sent to me: Six___ geese a - lay - ing,
7. On the sev - enth day of Christ-mas, my true love sent to me: Sev-en swans a - swim-ming,
8. On the eighth___ day of Christ-mas, my true love sent to me: Eight__ maids a - milk - ing,
9. On the ninth___ day of Christ-mas, my true love sent to me: Nine___ la - dies danc - ing, Five gold___ rings!
10. On the tenth___ day of Christ-mas, my true love sent to me: Ten___ lords a - leap - ing,
11. On the 'lev-enth day of Christ-mas, my true love sent to me: 'Lev-en pi - pers pip - ing,
12. On the twelfth_ day of Christ-mas, my true love sent to me: Twelve_ drum-mers drum-ming,

TWO GUITARS

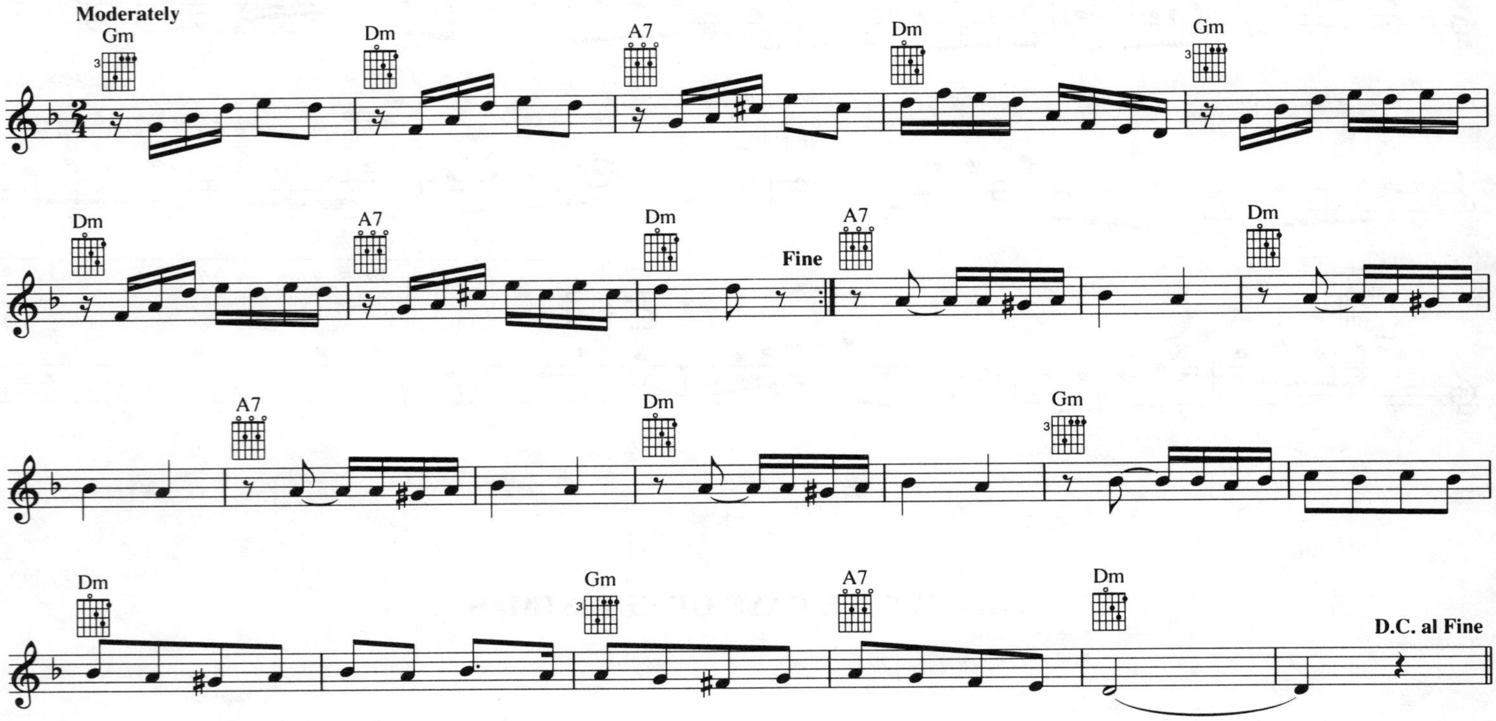

UNDER THE DOUBLE EAGLE

J. Wagner

E♭7
A♭
A♭7
D♭
B♭7
A♭
E♭7
1 A♭
2 A♭ E♭ A♭

UP ON THE HOUSETOP

Brightly
F B♭ F C7
Up On The House - top___ rein - deer pause, Out jumps good old San - ta Claus;
First comes the stock - ing of lit - tle Nell; Oh, dear San - ta, fill it well;
F B♭ F C7 F
Down thru the chim - ney with lots of toys, All for the lit - tle ones, Christ - mas joys.
Give her a dol - lie that laughs and cries, One that will o - pen and shut her eyes.
B♭ F C7 F
Ho, ho, ho! Who would-n't go! Ho, ho, ho! Who would - n't go! ______
B♭ F B♭ F C7 F
Up On The House - top, click, click, click, Down thru the chim - ney with good Saint Nick.

THE UNFINISHED SYMPHONY
(Theme)

Franz Schubert

VENETIAN BOAT SONG

Felix Mendelssohn

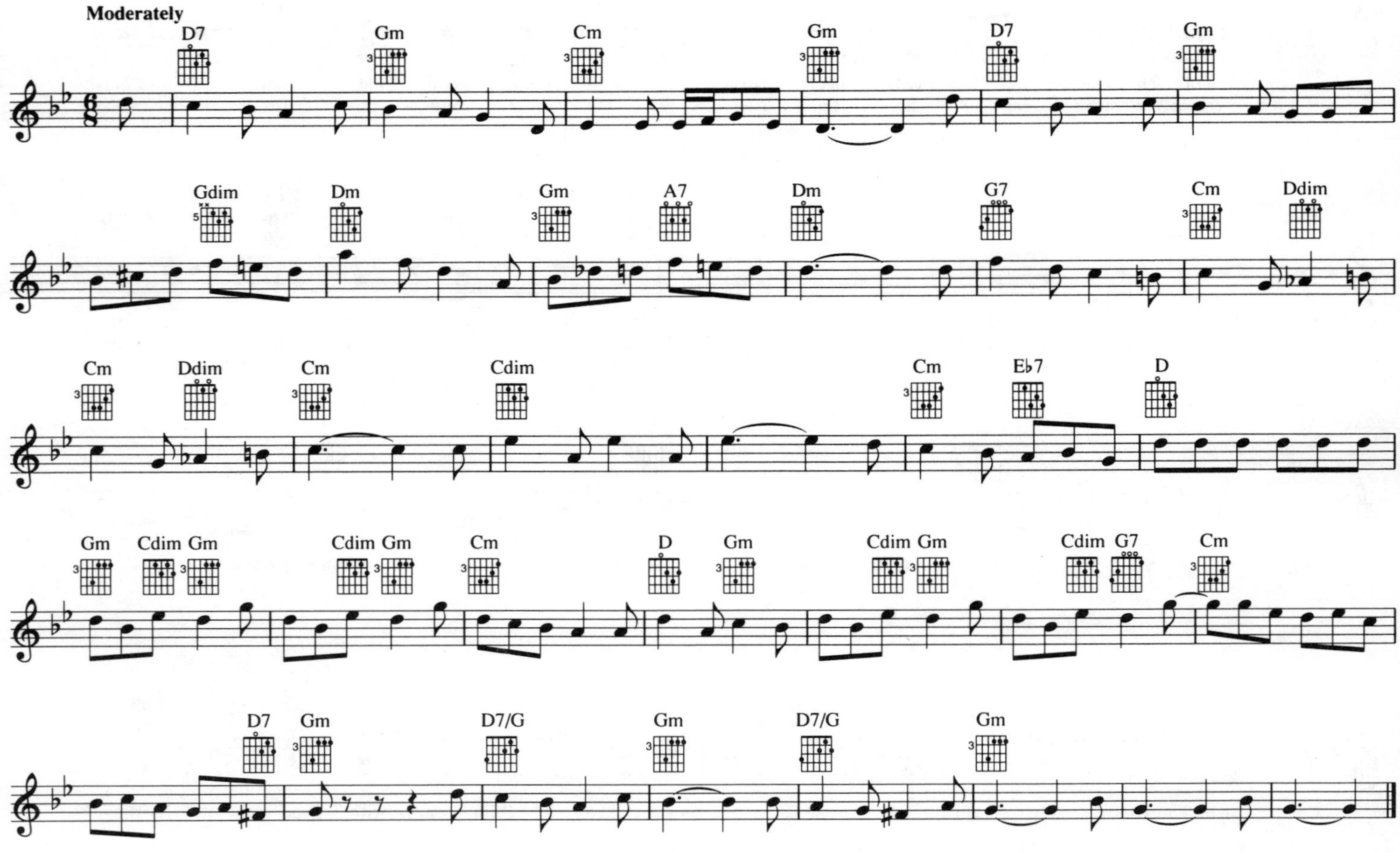

UNIVERSITY OF MICHIGAN SONG

Words and Music: Louis Elbert

VIENNA LIFE

Johann Strauss

VIVE L'AMOUR

Fast
B♭
F
B♭
1. Let ev - 'ry good fel - low now fill up his glass, Vi - ve la com - pag - nie, And
2. Let ev - er - y mar - ried man drink to his wife, Vi - ve la com - pag - nie, The
drink to the health of our glo - ri - ous class, Vi - ve la - com - pag - nie.
joy of his bo - som and plague of his life, Vi - ve la - com - pag - nie.
E♭
Vi - ve la, vi - ve la, Vi - ve L'a - mour, Vi - ve la, vi - ve la,
Gm
Cm
Vi - ve L'a - mour, Vi - ve L'a - mour, Vi - ve L'a - mour, vi - ve la com - pag - nie!

VALSE BLEUE

Alfred Margis

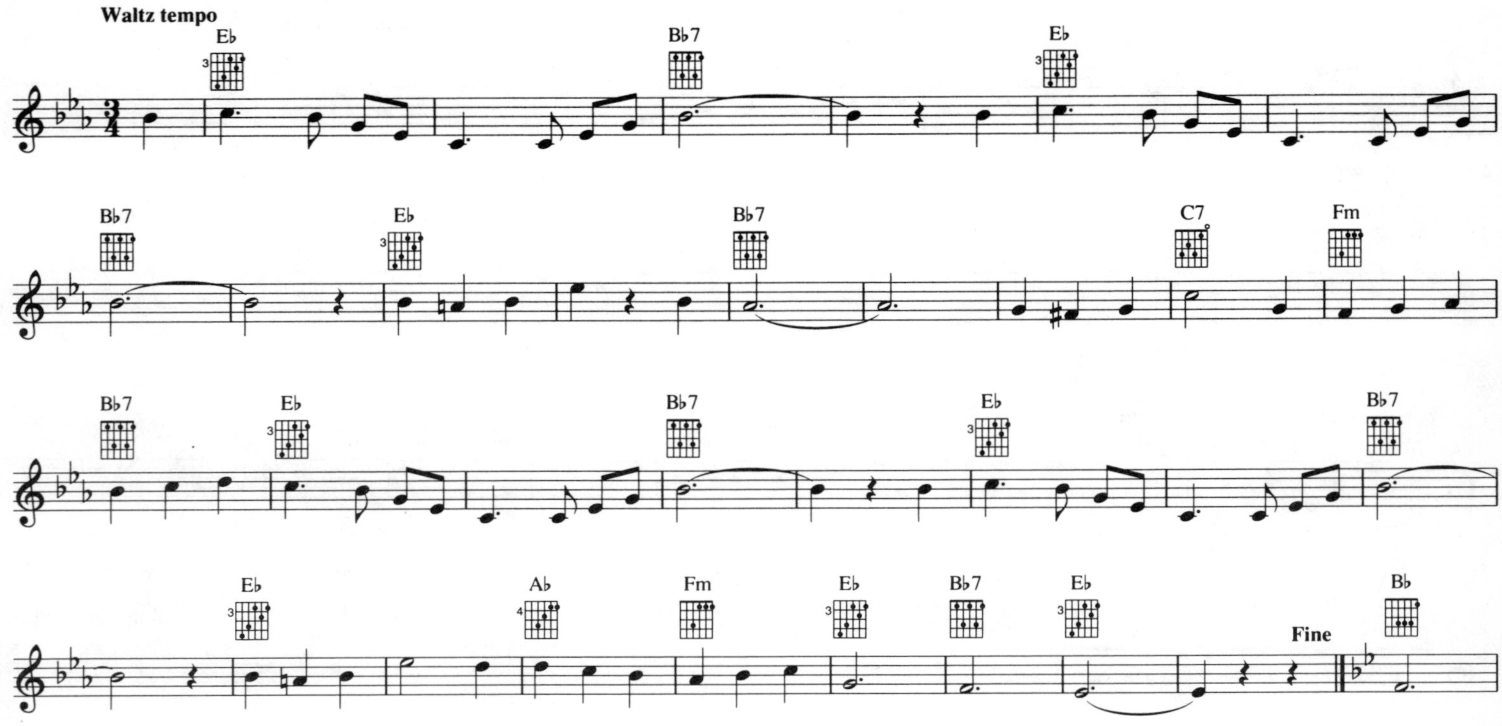
Waltz tempo
E♭
B♭7
C7
Fm
A♭
B♭
Fine

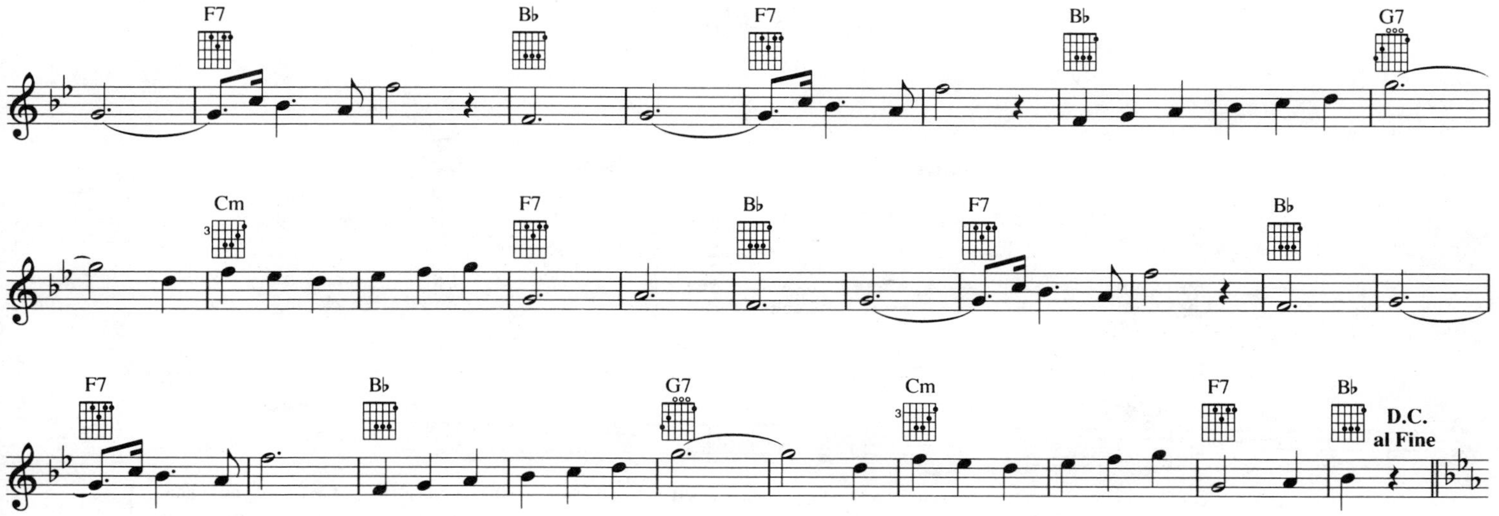
F7 B♭ F7 B♭ G7
Cm F7 B♭ F7 B♭
F7 B♭ G7 Cm F7 B♭
D.C. al Fine

THE WABASH CANNON BALL

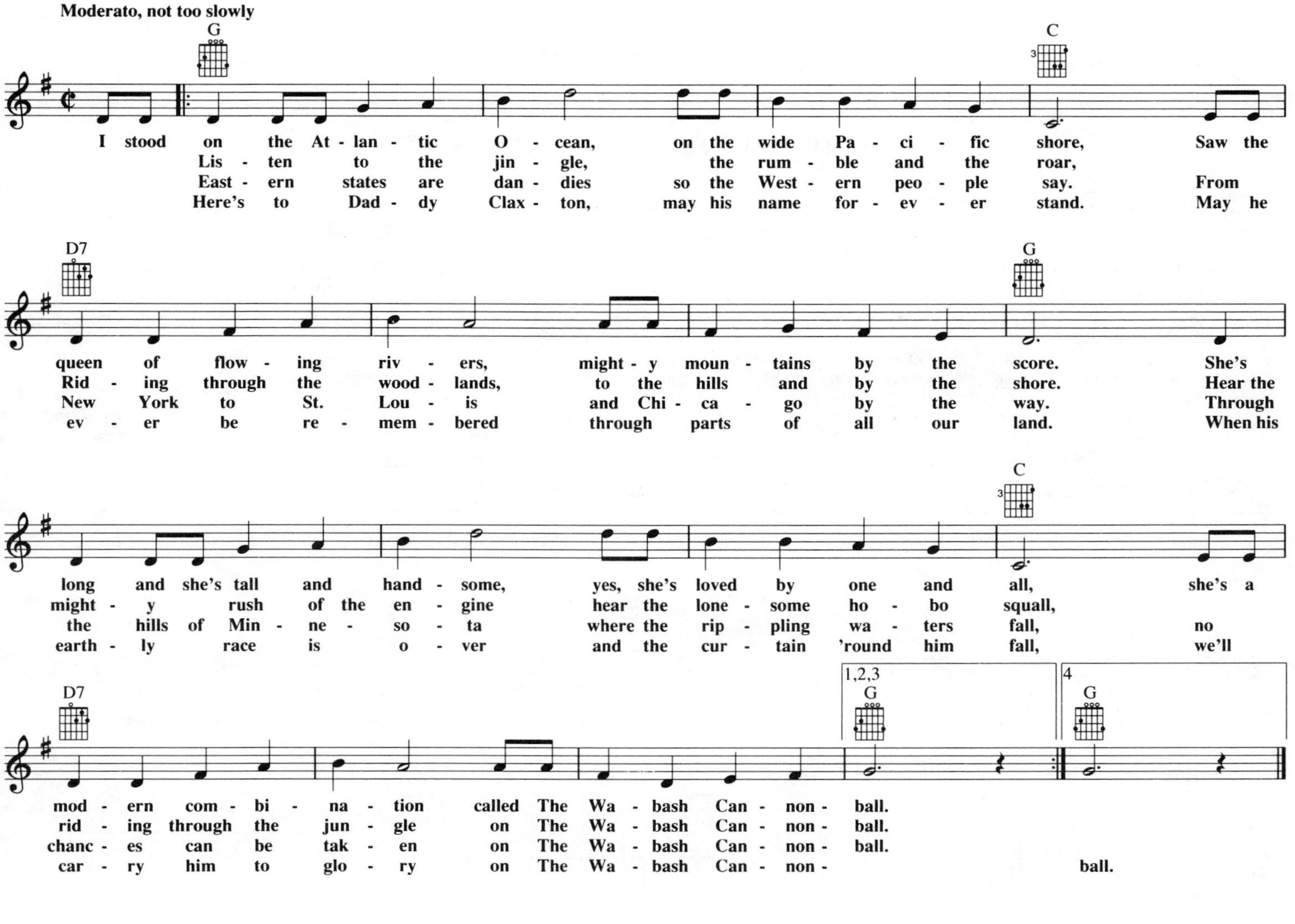
Moderato, not too slowly
G C D7 G C D7
1,2,3 G
4 G
I stood on the Atlantic Ocean, on the wide Pacific shore, Saw the queen of flowing rivers, mighty mountains by the score. She's long and she's tall and handsome, yes, she's loved by one and all, she's a modern combination called The Wabash Cannonball.
Listen to the jingle, the rumble and the roar, Riding through the woodlands, to the hills and by the shore. Hear the mighty rush of the engine hear the lonesome hobo squall, riding through the jungle on The Wabash Cannonball.
Eastern states are dandies so the Western people say. From New York to St. Louis and Chicago by the way. Through the hills of Minnesota where the rippling waters fall, no chances can be taken on The Wabash Cannonball.
Here's to Daddy Claxton, may his name forever stand. May he ever be remembered through parts of all our land. When his earthly race is over and the curtain 'round him fall, we'll carry him to glory on The Wabash Cannonball.

VILIA

Franz Lehar

Slowly
F C7 F C7 F Dm Am Cdim
Vil - ia, oh Vil - ia, oh where can you be? I'd come to you o - ver land, o - ver sea. Vil - ia, oh Vil - ia, oh where have you gone,
Vil - ia, oh Vil - ia, my heart calls to you, Come back, my love, to my love, ev - er true. Vil - ia, oh Vil - ia, I want you to know
1 C G7 C C7 Am C7
Leav - ing a love that lives on.
2 Gm C7
I love you, I love you
F Bb6 F Bb6 F
so, I love you so, love you so!

WAIT TILL THE SUN SHINES, NELLIE

Words by Andrew B. Sterling
Music by Harry Von Tilzer

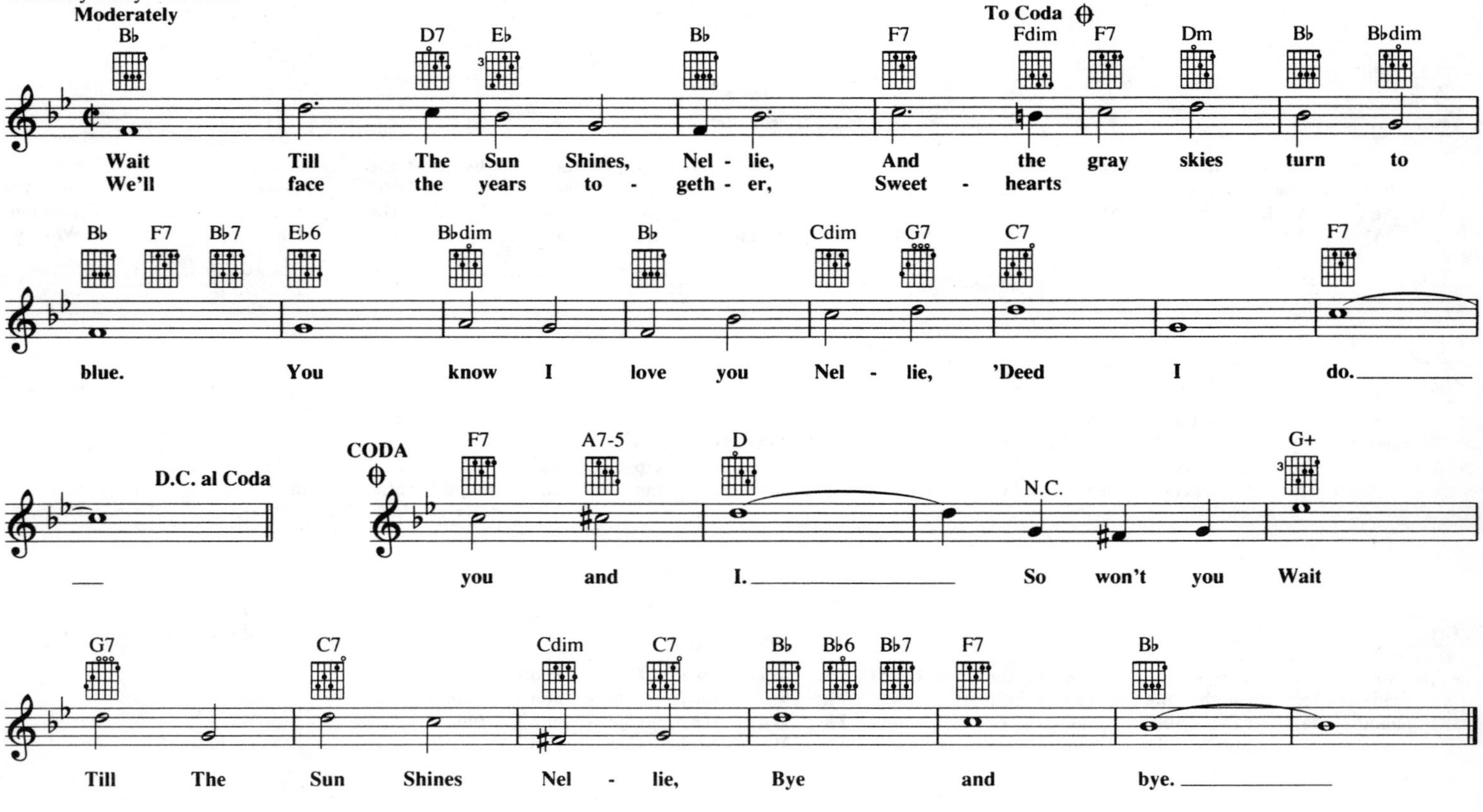
Moderately
Bb D7 Eb Bb F7 To Coda Fdim F7 Dm Bb Bbdim
Wait Till The Sun Shines, Nel - lie, And the gray skies turn to
We'll face the years to - geth - er, Sweet - hearts
Bb F7 Bb7 Eb6 Bbdim Bb Cdim G7 C7 F7
blue. You know I love you Nel - lie, 'Deed I do.
D.C. al Coda
CODA
F7 A7-5 D N.C. G+
you and I. So won't you Wait
G7 C7 Cdim C7 Bb Bb6 Bb7 F7 Bb
Till The Sun Shines Nel - lie, Bye and bye.

WAIT FOR THE WAGON

R. Bishop Buckley

Moderately
C G7 C
1. Will you come with me my Phil - lis, dear, To yon blue moun - tain free, Where the blos-soms smell the sweet - est, Come
ev - 'ry Sun - day morn - ing, when I am by your side, We'll jump in - to the wag - on, And
F G7 1 C 2 C Chorus C E7
rove a - long with me. It's
all take a ride. Wait For The Wag - on, Wait For The
F C F G7 C
Wag - on, Wait For The Wag - on and we'll all take a ride.

WALTZ
(Brahms)

Johannes Brahms

B♭ E♭ B♭ Gm B♭ Gm B♭
Dm A7 1 Dm 2 Dm F7 B♭ B♭7
E♭ C7 F7 B♭ E♭
B♭ Gm B♭ Gm B♭ F7 1 B♭ 2 B♭

WALTZ
(Chopin)

Chopin

WALTZ OF THE FLOWERS

Peter Tchaikovsky

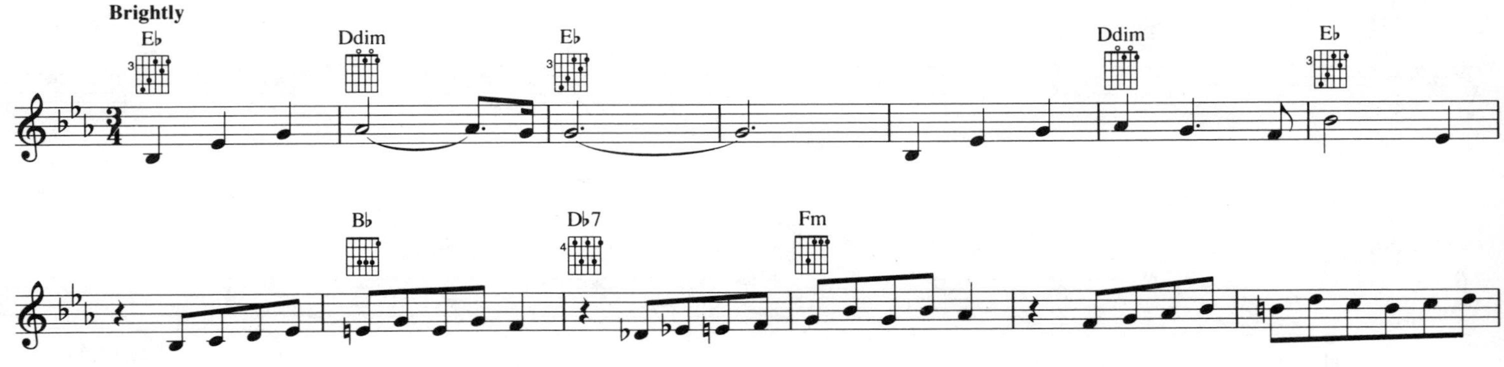

WE THREE KINGS OF ORIENT ARE

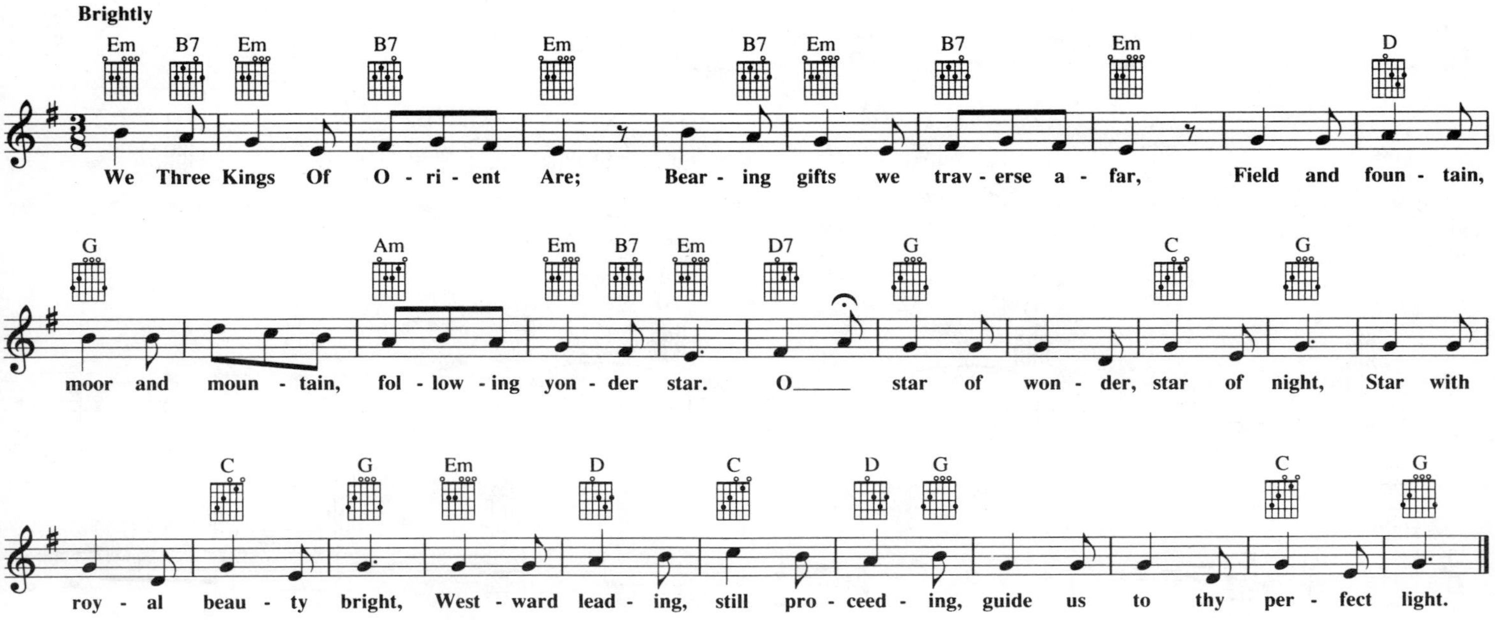
Brightly
We Three Kings Of O-ri-ent Are; Bear-ing gifts we trav-erse a-far, Field and foun-tain,
moor and moun-tain, fol-low-ing yon-der star. O___ star of won-der, star of night, Star with
roy-al beau-ty bright, West-ward lead-ing, still pro-ceed-ing, guide us to thy per-fect light.

WAYFARING STRANGER

WASHINGTON POST MARCH

John Phillip Sousa

WEDDING MARCH

Felix Mendelssohn

WE WISH YOU A MERRY CHRISTMAS

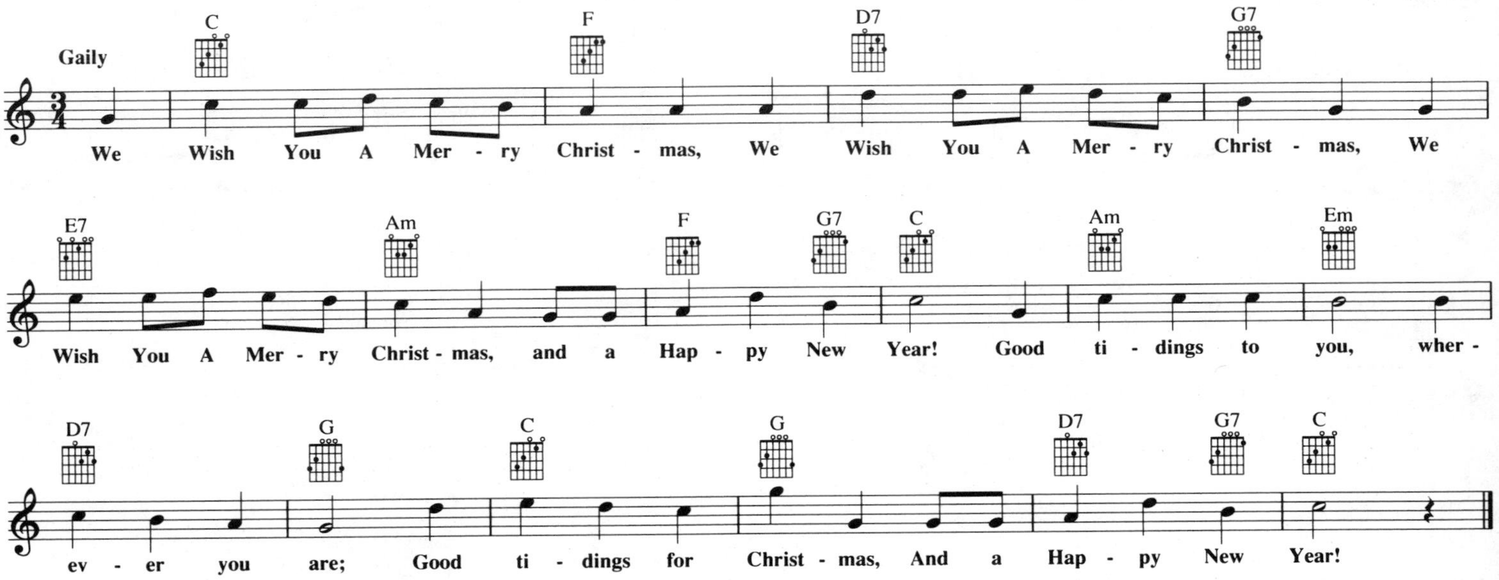
Gaily
C F D7 G7
We Wish You A Mer - ry Christ - mas, We Wish You A Mer - ry Christ - mas, We
E7 Am F G7 C Am Em
Wish You A Mer - ry Christ - mas, and a Hap - py New Year! Good ti - dings to you, wher -
D7 G C G D7 G7 C
ev - er you are; Good ti - dings for Christ - mas, And a Hap - py New Year!

THE WEARING OF THE GREEN

Moderately
E♭ B♭7 A♭
1. O ___ Pad - dy dear, and did you hear the news that's go - ing round, The Sham - rock is for -
2. Then ___ since the col - or we must wear, is Eng - land's cru - el red; Sure Ire - land's sons will
3. But ___ if at last our col - or should be torn from Ire - land's heart, Her sons, with shame and
E♭ A♭ E♭ Fm7 E♭
bid by law, to grow on I - rish ground; And Saint Pat - rick's day no more we'll keep, His
ne'er for - get the blood that they have shed; You may take the sham - rock from your hat, and
sor - row from the dear ould soil will part; I've heard whis - per of a coun - try, that lies
B♭7 A♭ E♭ A♭ E♭ Fm7 E♭
col - or can't be seen, For there's a blood - y law a - gainst the wear - ing of the green; I ___
cast it on the sod, But 'twill take root and flour - ish still, tho' un - der foot 'tis trod, When the
far be - yant the say, Where rich and poor stand e - qual in the light of free - dom's day. O ___
A♭ E♭ A♭ E♭
met the Nap - per Tan - dy and he took me by the hand, And he said "How's poor auld
law can stop the blades of grass from grow - ing as they grow, And ___ when the leaves in
E - rin, must we lave you, driv - en by the ty - rant's hand, Must we ask a moth - er's

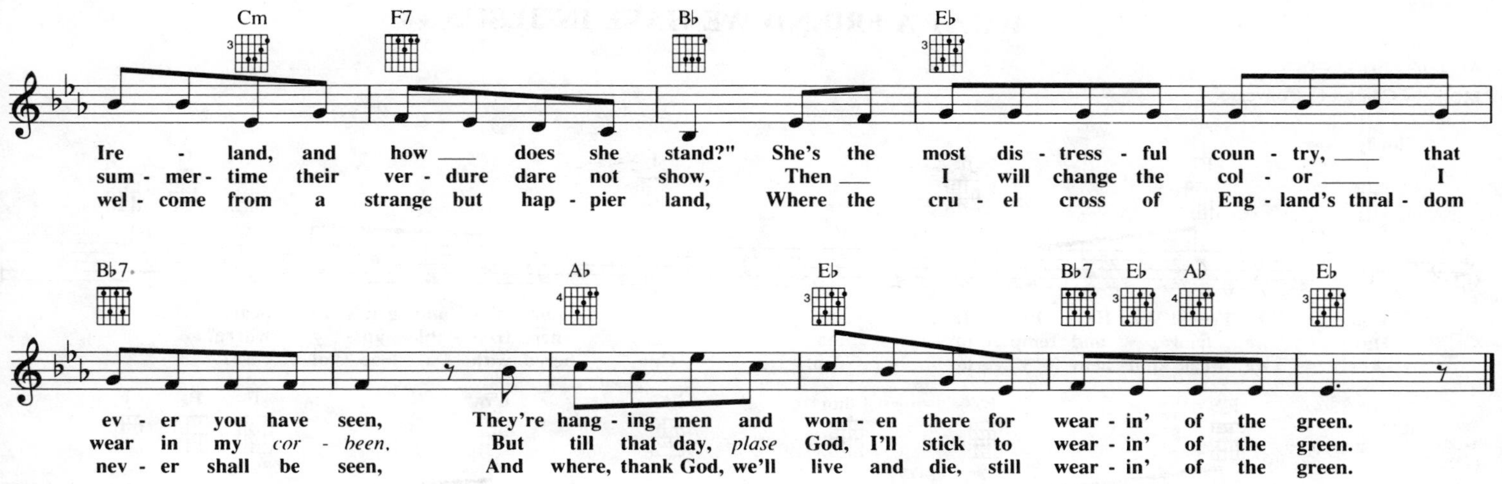
Cm F7 B♭ E♭
Ire - land, and how ___ does she stand?" She's the most dis - tress - ful coun - try, ____ that
sum - mer - time their ver - dure dare not show, Then ___ I will change the col - or _____ I
wel - come from a strange but hap - pier land, Where the cru - el cross of Eng - land's thral - dom
B♭7 A♭ E♭ B♭7 E♭ A♭ E♭
ev - er you have seen, They're hang - ing men and wom - en there for wear - in' of the green.
wear in my cor - been, But till that day, plase God, I'll stick to wear - in' of the green.
nev - er shall be seen, And where, thank God, we'll live and die, still wear - in' of the green.

WERE YOU THERE?

Slowly
E♭ B♭7 Cm B♭7 E♭ A♭ A♭m E♭
Were You There when they cru - ci - fied my Lord? ________ Were You There when they
There when they nailed Him to the tree? ________ Were You There when they
There when the sun re - fused to shine? ________ Were You There when the
There when they laid Him in the tomb? ________ Were You There when they
A♭ B♭7 E♭ F7 B♭ Fm Fdim B♭7 E♭
cru - ci - fied my Lord? ________
nailed him to the tree? ________
sun re - fused to shine? ________
laid Him in the tomb? ________
Oh! ________ Some - times _____ it
A♭ E♭ B♭ A♭ E♭ E♭6 Gm
caus - es me to trem - ble, ____ trem - ble, ____ trem - ble. ________
Were You There when they
Were You There when they
Were You There when the
Were You There when they
B♭7 Cm B♭7 1,2,3 E♭ A♭ A♭m E♭ B♭ 4 E♭ A♭ A♭m E♭
cru - ci - fied my Lord? ________ Were You
nailed Him to the tree? ________ Were You
sun re - fused to shine? ________ Were You
laid Him in the tomb? ________

WHAT A FRIEND WE HAVE IN JESUS

Words by Joseph Scriven
Music by Charles C. Converse

Slowly
F F7 Bb F C G C
What A Friend We Have In Je - sus, All our sins and griefs to bear,
Have we trials __ and temp - ta - tions, Is there trou - ble an - y - where?
Are we weak and heav - y la - den, Cum - bered with a load of care?
F F7 Bb Bdim F/C C7 F Bb F
What a priv - i - lege to car - ry Ev - 'ry - thing to God in pray'r.
We should nev - er be dis - cour - aged Take it to the Lord in pray'r.
Pre - cious Sav - ior still our ref - uge, Take it to the Lord in pray'r.
C F Bb F C G C F F7
O what peace we of - ten for - feit, O what need - less pain we bear, All be - cause we do not
Can we find a friend so faith - ful, Who will all our sor - rows share? Je - sus knows our ev - 'ry
Do thy friends de - spise, for - sake thee? Take it to the Lord in pray'r. In His arms He'll take and
Bb Bdim 1,2 F/C C7 F Bb F 3 F C7 Bb F
car - ry Ev - 'ry-thing to God in pray'r.
weak - ness, Take it to the Lord in pray'r.
shield thee Thou wilt find a sol - ace there.

WHEN JOHNNY COMES MARCHING HOME

Patrick S. Gilmore

Bright March
Gm Bb
When John - ny Comes March - ing Home a - gain, Hur - rah! Hur - rah! We'll
Gm Bb D
give him a heart - y wel - come then, Hur - rah! Hur rah! Oh the
Bb D7 Gm D7
men will cheer and the boys will shout. The la - dies they __ will all turn out, And we'll
Gm D7 Gm D Gm Cm D Gm
all feel gay, When John - ny Comes March - ing Home.

WHAT CHILD IS THIS?

Words by William Dix

Moderately Fast
Em G D Em Am B
1. What Child Is This ___ Who, laid to rest ___ On Ma - ry's lap, ___ is sleep - ing? Whom
2. Why lies He in ___ such mean es - tate, ___ Where ox and ass ___ are feed - ing? Good
3. So bring Him in - cense, gold, and myrrh ___ Come peas - ant, King ___ to own Him, The
Em G D Em B Em
an - gels greet ___ with an - thems sweet, ___ While shep - herds watch ___ are keep - ing?
Christ - tian, fear: ___ for sin - ners here ___ The si - lent Word ___ is plead - ing.
King of kings, ___ sal - va - tion brings, ___ let lov - ing hearts ___ en - throne Him.
Bm G D Em Am B
This, this ___ is Christ the King; ___ Whom shep - herds guard ___ and an - gels sing:
Nails, spear, ___ shall pierce Him through, ___ The Cross be borne, ___ for me, for you:
Raise, raise ___ the song on high, ___ The Vir - gin sings ___ her lull - a - by:
Bm G D Em B Em
Haste, haste ___ to bring Him laud, ___
Hail, hail, ___ the Word made flesh, ___
Joy, joy, ___ for Christ is born, ___
The Babe, ___ the Son ___ of Ma - ry!

WHEN IRISH EYES ARE SMILING

Music by Ernest R. Ball
Words by Chauncy Olcott & Geo. Graff Jr.

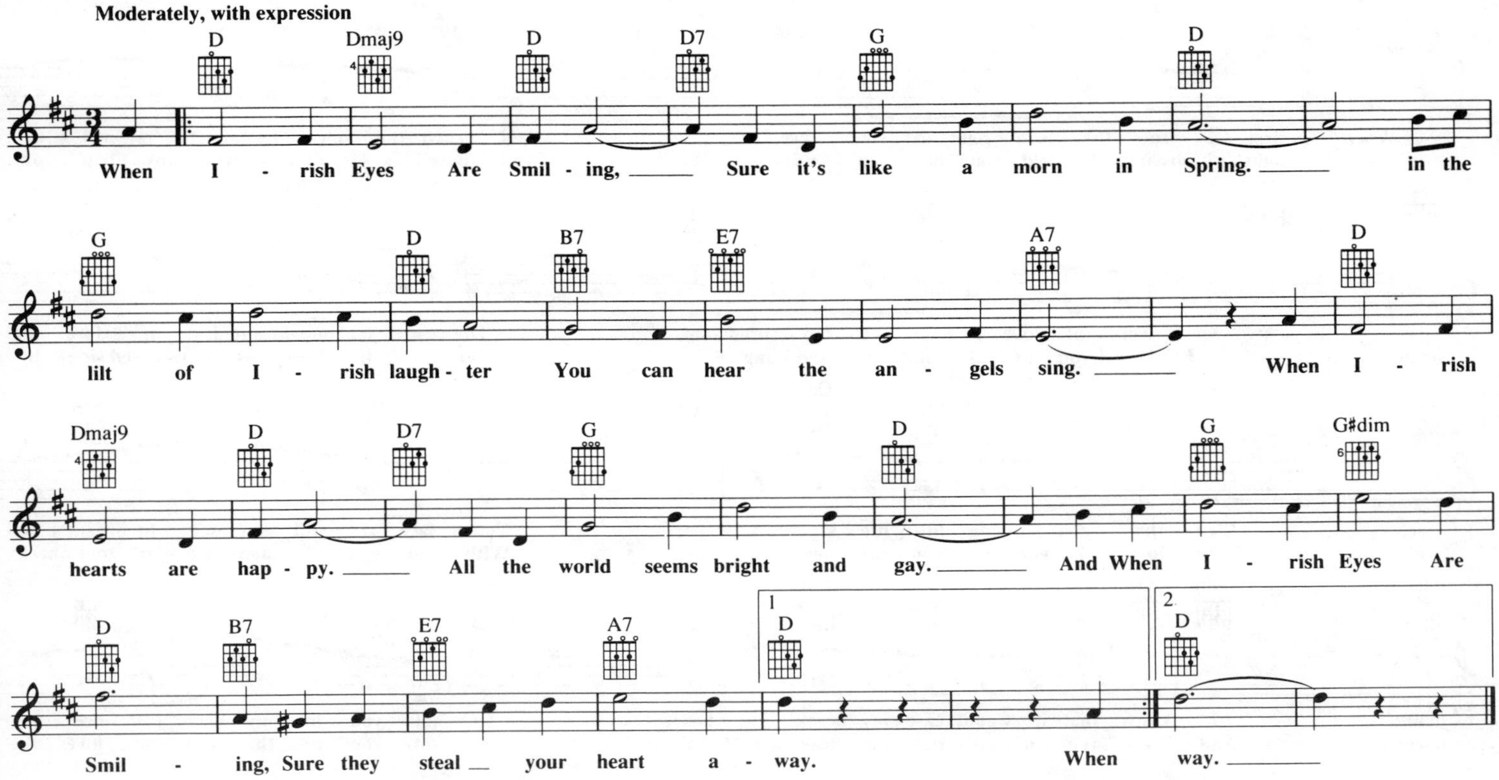
Moderately, with expression
D Dmaj9 D D7 G D
When I - rish Eyes Are Smil - ing, ___ Sure it's like a morn in Spring. ___ in the
G D B7 E7 A7 D
lilt of I - rish laugh - ter You can hear the an - gels sing. ___ When I - rish
Dmaj9 D D7 G D G G#dim
hearts are hap - py. ___ All the world seems bright and gay. ___ And When I - rish Eyes Are
D B7 E7 A7 1 D 2 D
Smil - ing, Sure they steal ___ your heart a - way. When way. ___

WHEN THE SAINTS GO MARCHING IN

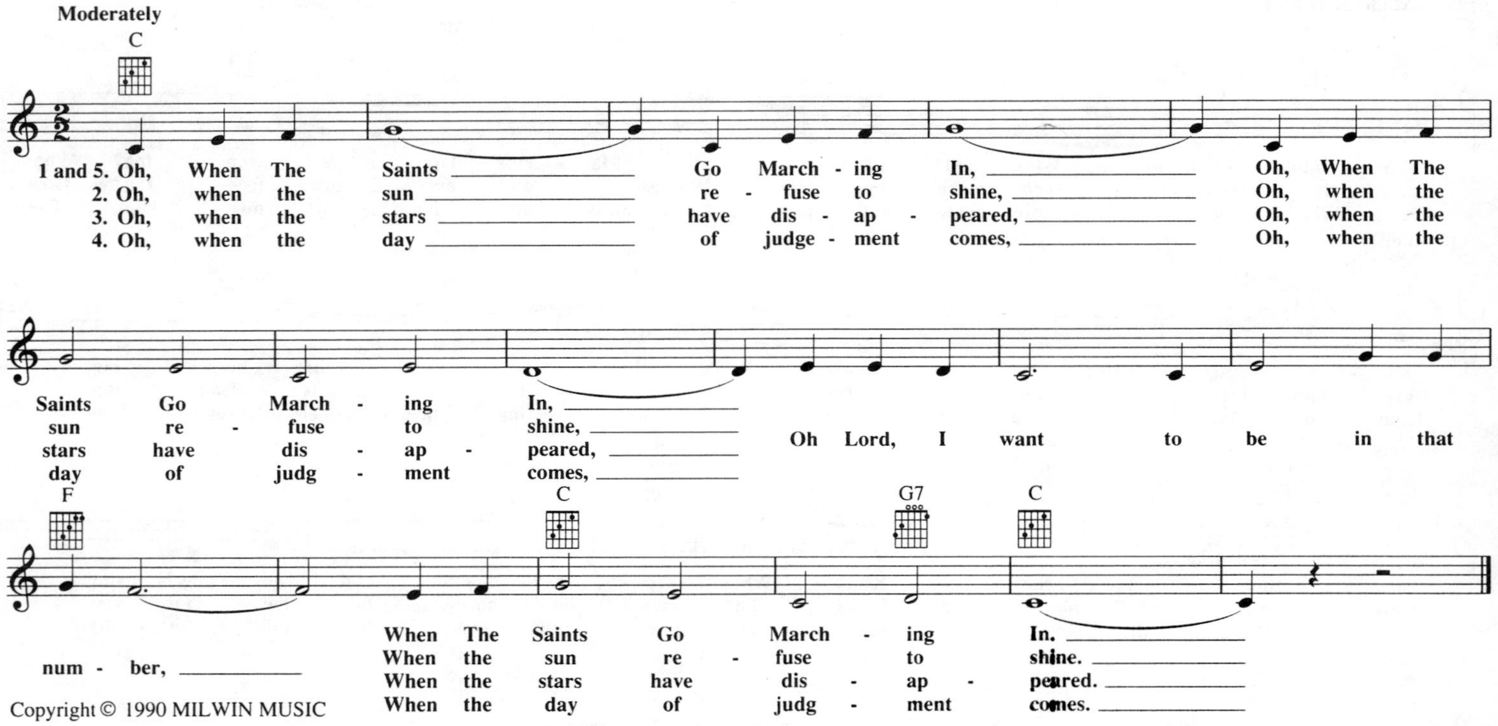
Moderately
C
1 and 5. Oh, When The Saints Go March - ing In, Oh, When The
2. Oh, when the sun re - fuse to shine, Oh, when the
3. Oh, when the stars have dis - ap - peared, Oh, when the
4. Oh, when the day of judge - ment comes, Oh, when the
Saints Go March - ing In,
sun re - fuse to shine,
stars have dis - ap - peared,
day of judg - ment comes,
Oh Lord, I want to be in that
F C G7 C
num - ber,
When The Saints Go March - ing In.
When the sun re - fuse to shine.
When the stars have dis - ap - peared.
When the day of judg - ment comes.

WHEN YOU WERE SWEET SIXTEEN

By James Thornton

Slowly
C C+ F G7
When first I saw the love - light in your eye, And heard the voice like sweet - est mel - o -
night I dreamt I held your hand in mine And once a - gain you were my hap - py
C G7 C C+ F Cdim C G7
dy Speak words of love to my en - rap - tured soul, The world had nought but joy in store for
bride. I kissed you as I did in Auld Lang Syne, As to the church we wan - dered side by
C G C Cm G C
me. E'en tho we're drift - ing down life's stream a - part, Your face I still can see in dream's do -
side. The love I bear for you can nev - er die; With out you I had rath - er not been
G Gdim G C Cm G D7
main; I know that it would ease my break - ing heart To hold you in my arms just once a -
born; And e - ven tho we nev - er meet a - gain, I love you as the sun - shine loves the

G D7 G7 C C+ F
gain. ___ morn. ___ I love you as I nev - er loved be - fore, Since
G7 C Gdim G7 C C+ F
first I met you on the vil - lage green. Come to me, or my dream of love is o'er, I
Cdim C Cdim C G7 C
D.S. Fine al Fine
love you as I loved you when you were sweet, When You Were Sweet Six - teen. Last

WHISPERING HOPE

Words and Music by Alice Hawthorne

Moderately slow, smoothly
C F C G7 C
Soft as the voice of an an - gel, Breath - ing a les - son un - heard, ___
If in the dusk of the twi - light, Dim be the re - gion a - far, ___
G C F F#dim C G7 C
Hope with a gen - tle per - sua - sion, Whis - pers her com - fort - ing word. ___ Wait till the
Will not the deep - en - ing dark - ness, Bright - en the glim - mer - ing star? ___ Then when the
G F#dim G7 C G D7 G C
dark - ness is o - ver, Wait till the tem - pest is done. ___ Hope for the
night is up - on us, why should the heart sink a - way? ___ When the dark
F C G7 C
sun - shine to - mor - row, Af - ter the show - er is gone. ___
mid - night is o - ver, Watch for the break - ing of day. ___
G7 C G7 C F
Whis - per - ing Hope, ___ Oh, how wel - come thy voice, ___ Mak - ing my
C G7 1. C 2. C F6 C
heart, ___ in its sor - row re - joice. ___ joice. ___

WHEN YOU AND I WERE YOUNG, MAGGIE

Words and Music by George W. Johnson and James A. Butterfield

Moderately
F Bb F C
I wan - dered to - day to the hill, Mag - gie, to watch the scene be - low; The
F Bb C F F7
creek and the old rus - ty mill Mag - gie, where we sat in the long, long a - go. The
Bb F C G C
green grove is gone from the hill, Mag - gie, where first the dai - sies sprung; The
F Bb F C 1 F 2 F
old rus - ty mill is still, Mag - gie, since you and I were young. I young.

WHEN YOU'RE AWAY

Music by Victor Herbert
Lyrics by Henry Blossum

Moderately Slow Waltz
F A Dm/F Am Gm Dm/F Gm Bb#5 Edim Bb#5
When You're A - way, dear, how wear - y the lone - some hours! Sun - shine seems gray, dear! The
C7 E7 F D/A D11 Gm A/E A11 Dm
frag - rance has left the flow'rs! Ev - er I hear you, in seem - ing, Whisp - 'ring soft love - words to me!
Bdim7 Db Dm/C G7/D F/C G7 C C7 F A Dm/F Am
Ah! If I knew 'twere but dream - ing! Ne'er to be! Then when you're near me, There's
Gm Dm/F Gm Bb#5 Edim Bb#5 C7 E7 F
naught that I strive to do, Save to en - dear me more fond - ly, my love, to you!
D/A D11 Gm A/E A11 Dm Bdim7
Nev - er a - gain let us part, dear! I die with - out you, mine own! Hold

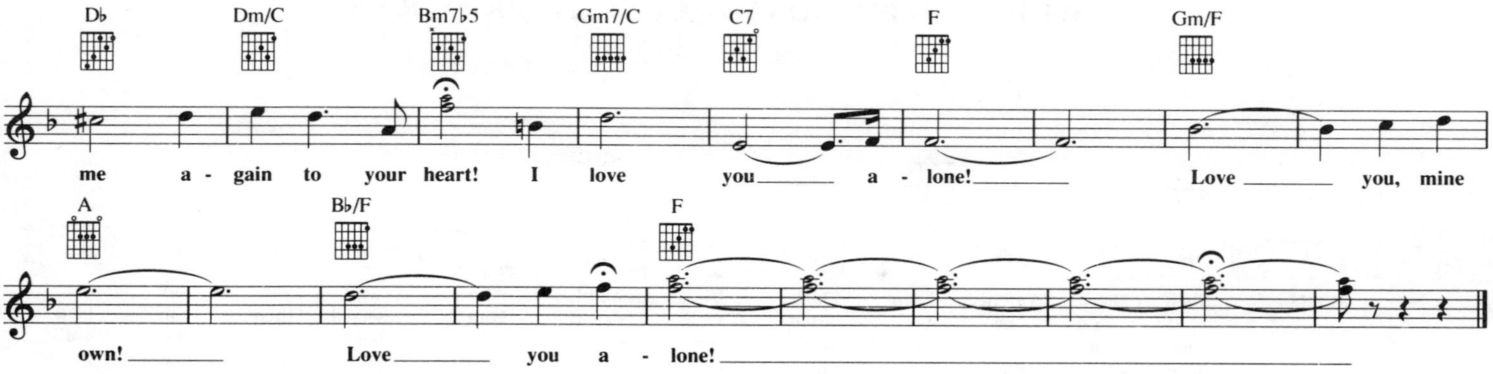

D♭ Dm/C Bm7♭5 Gm7/C C7 F Gm/F
me a - gain to your heart! I love you a - lone! Love you, mine
A B♭/F F
own! Love you a - lone!

WHILE STROLLING THROUGH THE PARK ONE DAY

By Ed Haley

Moderately
B♭ E♭ G7 C7 F7
While Strol - ling Thru The Park One Day, In the mer - ry month of May; I was
me - di - ate - ly rais'd my hat, And fi - nal - ly she re - mark'd: I
B♭ C7 F7
tak - en by sur - prise, by a pair of ro - guish eyes, In a mo - ment, my poor heart was stole a -
nev - er shall for - get that love - ly af - ter - noon, I met her at the foun - tain in the
B♭ D7 Gm D7 Gm D7 Gm D7 Gm
Fine
way. park. } A smile was all she gave to me. Of
C7 F C7 F C7 F F7
D.S. al Fine
course, we were as hap - py as can be, Ah! I im -

WHITE CORAL BELLS

Moderately
White cor - al bells up - on a slen - der stalk, Lil - ies of the val - ley deck my gar - den walk.
Oh, don't you wish That you could hear them ring? That will hap - pen on - ly when the fair - ies sing.

WHILE SHEPHERDS WATCHED THEIR FLOCKS

Moderately
D A G D Em
While Shep - herds Watched Their Flocks by night, All seat - ed on the
not!" said he for might - y dread Had seized their trou - bled
you, in Da - vid's town this day, Is born of Da - vid's
heav'n - ly Babe you there shall find To hu - man view dis -
D A A D7 Em A7 D
ground, The an - gel of the Lord came down, And
mind, "Glad tid - ings of great joy I bring, To
line, The Sav - ior who is Christ the Lord; And
played, All mean - ly wrapped in swath - ing bands, And
G D G D G D Em D G D A7 D
glo - ry shone a - round, And glo - ry shone a - round. "Fear
you and all man - kind, To you and all man - kind. "To
this shall be the sign, And this shall be the sign: "The
in a man - ger laid, And in a man - ger laid."

WILL THE CIRCLE BE UNBROKEN

Moderately fast
E E7
1. I was stand - ing by the win - dow On a
2. For I fol - lowed close be - hind her, Tried to
3. Went back home, Lord, and found it lone - some, 'Cause my
A E
cold and wind - y day, When I saw the hearse come
cheer up and be brave; But my sor - rows I could not
moth - er now was gone. All my broth - ers and sis - ters
A B7 E B7
roll - ing For to car - ry my moth - er a - way.
hide them When they laid her in the grave.
cry - ing What a home, so sad and lone.
Will The
Refrain:
E E7 A
Cir - cle Be Un - bro - ken bye and bye, Lord,

E B7 E
— bye and bye, There's a bet - ter home a -
A B7 E
wait - ing in the sky, Lord, in the sky.

WHO THREW THE OVERALLS IN MRS. MURPHY'S CHOWDER

Words and Music by George L. Giefer

Moderately
C
"Who Threw The O - ver - alls In Miss - es Mur - phy's Chow - der?" No - bod - y
D7 G7 C E7 Am
spoke so he shout - ed all the loud - er; "It's an I - rish trick that's true, I can
F C D7 G7 C
lick the mick that threw The o - ver - alls in Miss - es Mur - phy's chow - der."

WORRIED MAN BLUES

Moderately fast
G G7 C
1. It takes a wor - ried man to sing a wor - ried song. It takes a wor - ried
2. I went a - cross the river and I lay down to sleep. I went a - cross the
G B7
man to sing a wor - ried song. It takes a wor - ried man to sing a wor - ried
river and I lay down to sleep. I went a - cross the river and I lay down to
Em D7 G
song. I'm wor - ried now but I won't be wor - ried long.
sleep, when I woke up, had shack - les on my feet.

WILLIAM TELL OVERTURE

Gioacchino Rossini

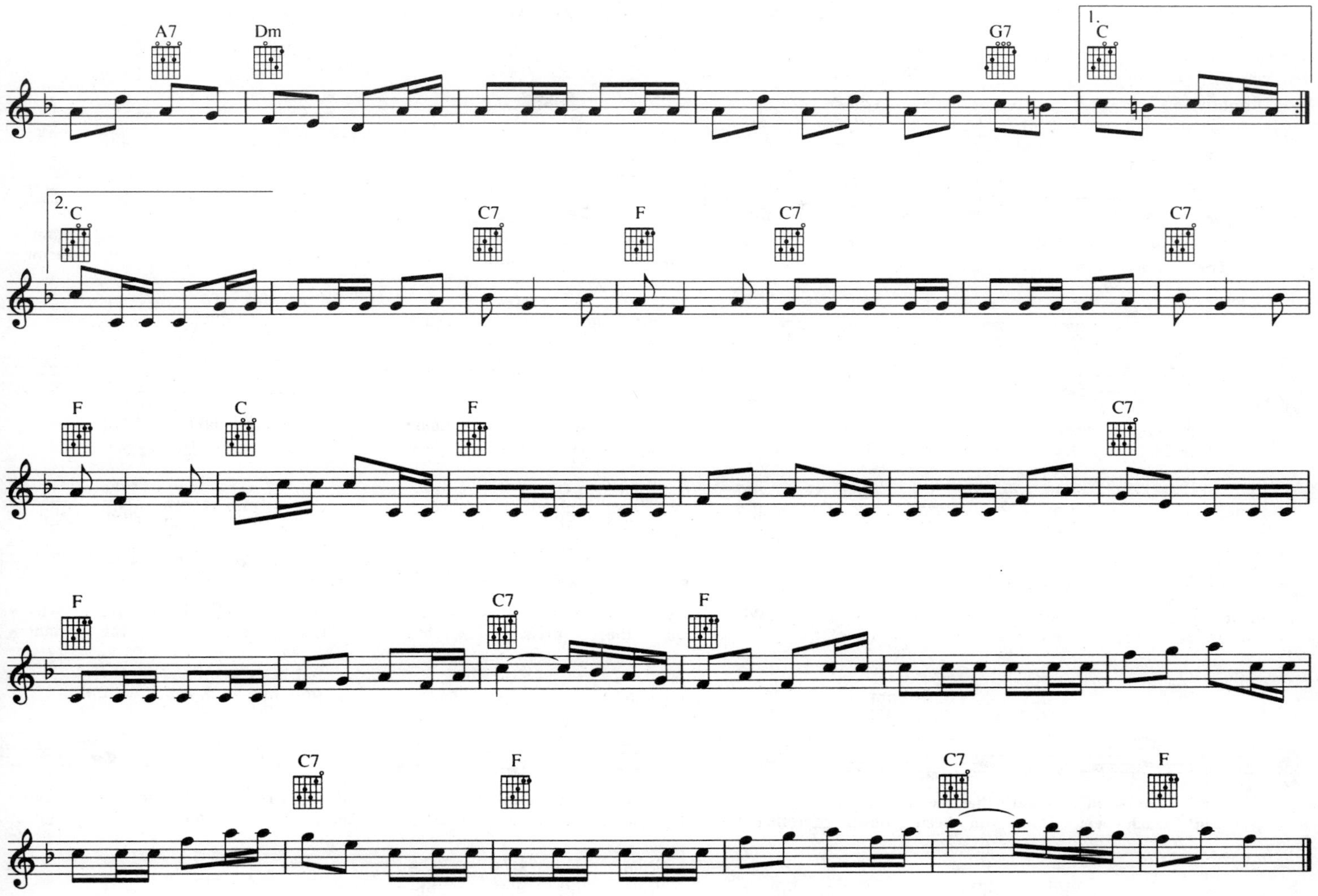
A7
Dm
G7
1. C
2. C
C7
F
C7
C7
F
C
F
C7
F
C7
F
C7
F
C7
F

YANKEE DOODLE

Brightly
F
C7
F
C7
F
F7
1. Fath'r and I went down to camp A - long with Cap - tain Good - win, And there we saw the
2. And there was Cap - tain Wash - ing - ton Up - on a slap - ping stal - lion, A - giv - ing or - ders
3. And then the feath - ers in his hat, They looked so ver - y fine, ah, I want - ed pes - ki -
B♭
C7
F
B♭
men and boys As thick as hast - y pud - din'.
to his men; I guess there was a mil - lion.
ly to get To give to my Je - mi - ma.
Yan - kee Doo - dle keep it up,
F
B♭
F
C7
F
Yan - kee Doo - dle dan - dy; Mind the mu - sic and the step, And with the girls be hand - y

WAITING FOR THE ROBERT E. LEE

Lyric by L. Wolfe Gilbert
Music by Lewis F. Muir

Brightly
'Way down on the lev - ee, In old Al - a - bam - y, There's dad - dy and mam -
The whis - tles are blow - in', The smoke - stacks are show - in', The ropes they are throw -
- my, There's E - phra'm and Sam - my; On a moon - light
- in'; Ex - cuse me, I'm go - in' To the place where
night you can find them all; While they are wait - in', The ban - jos are syn -
all is har - mo - ni - ous; E - ven the preach - er, They say, is the danc -
- co - pat - in'; What's that they're say - in'? Oh what's that they're say - in'? The while they keep play -
- in' teach - er; Have you been down there? Say, were you a - roun' there, If you ev - er go
- in', I'm hum - min' and sway - in'; It's the good ship
there, You'll al - ways be found there; Why, "dog - gone",
Rob - ert E. Lee That's come to car - ry the cot - ton a - way.
here comes my ba - by On the good old ship Rob - ert E. Lee.
Chorus
Watch them shuff - lin' a - long; See them shuff - lin' a -
long Go take your best gal, real pal, Go
down to the lev - ee, I said to the lev - ee! And then join that shuff -

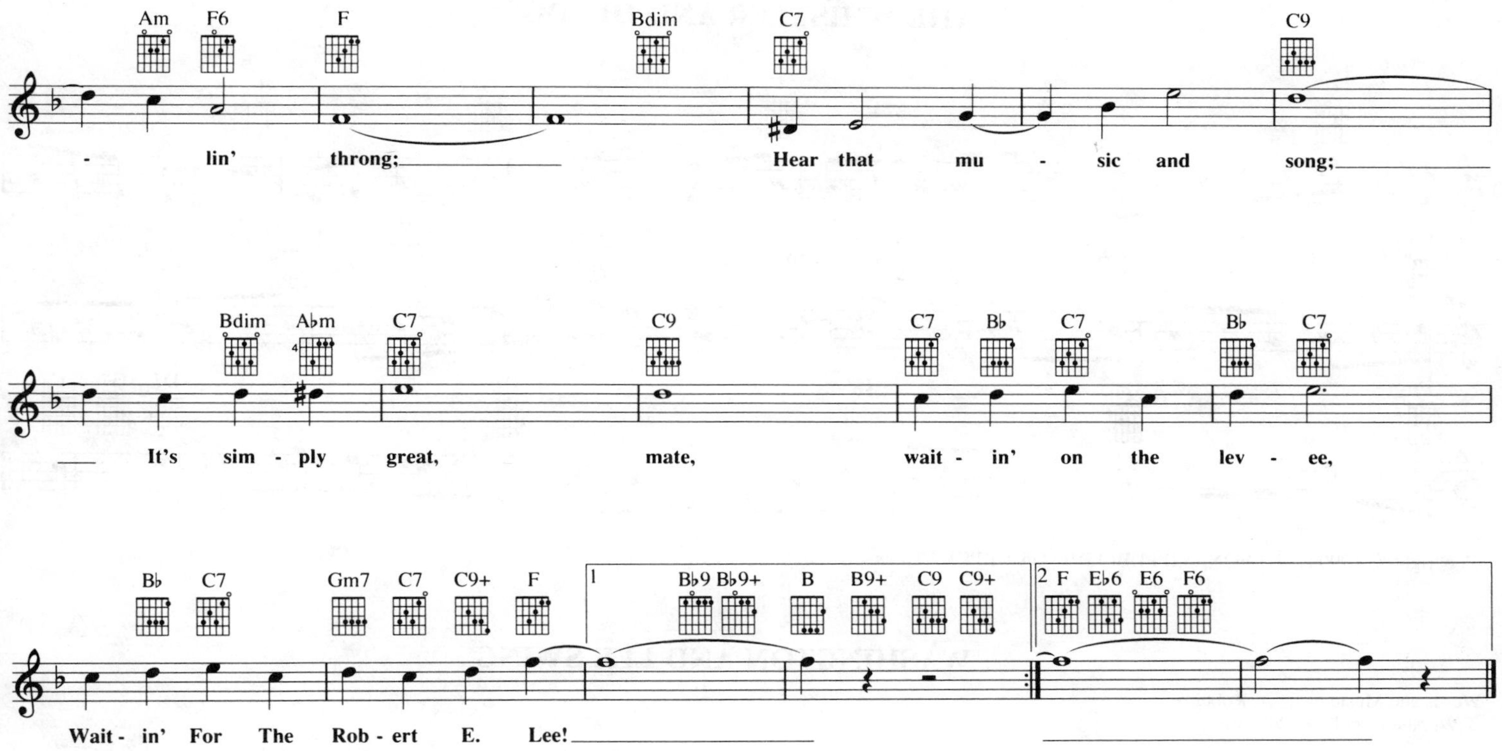
Am F6 F Bdim C7 C9
- lin' throng; Hear that mu - sic and song;
Bdim A♭m C7 C9 C7 B♭ C7 B♭ C7
It's sim - ply great, mate, wait - in' on the lev - ee,
B♭ C7 Gm7 C7 C9+ F 1 B♭9 B♭9+ B B9+ C9 C9+ 2 F E♭6 E6 F6
Wait - in' For The Rob - ert E. Lee!

WHEN YOU WORE A TULIP

Words by Jack Mahoney
Music by Percy Wenrich

Slowly
B♭ B♭9 E♭ E♭dim E♭ B♭ F7 B♭ B♭7
When You Wore A Tu - lip, a sweet yel - low tu - lip, and I wore a big red rose,
E♭ E♭m B♭ B♭dim B♭ G7 C7 F C7 F7
When you ca - ressed me, 'twas then Heav - en blessed me, what a bless - ing, no one knows.
B♭ B♭9 E♭ E♭dim E♭ Cm6 D7
You made life cheer - y when you called me dear - ie, 'twas down where the blue grass grows, Your lips were
G7 Gdim G7 C7 F7 B♭
sweet - er than ju - lep when you wore that tu - lip and I wore a big red rose.

THE WHISTLER AND HIS DOG

Arthur Pryor

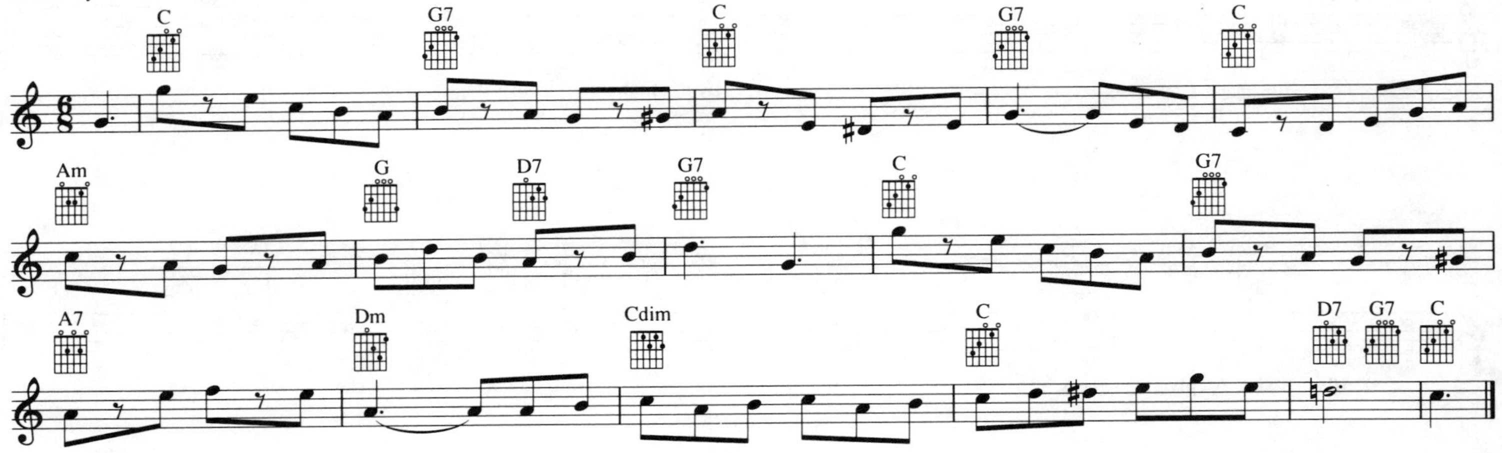

WASHINGTON AND LEE SWING

Words and Music by C.A. Robbins, T.W. Allen and M.W. Sheafe

March Tempo
Come cheer for Wash - ing - ton and Lee, We're going to win an -
oth - er vic - to - ry; The White and Blue we will ev - er wave in tri - umph,
For the U - ni - ver - si - ty. RAH! RAH! RAH! Fight to the
fin - ish we are with you, Break thru the line on ev - 'ry play;
Rush the ball on down the field and we will win this
game to - day. When Wash - ing - ton and Lee's men fall in line,
We're going to win a - gain an - oth - er time; For W. and L. I

yell, yell, yell, yell, yell, And for the u - ni - ver - si - ty I yell, I
yell like hell, So fight fight! fight! for ev - 'ry yard; Cir - cle the ends and
hit the line right hard! And roll the en - e - my up - on the sod!
RAH! RAH! RAH! When Wash - ing - RAH!

YOU MADE ME LOVE YOU

Words by Joseph McCarthy
Music by James V. Monaco

Slowly
You Made Me Love You, I did - n't wan - na do it, I did - n't wan - na do it, You made me want you
and all the time you knew it, I guess you al - ways knew it. You made me hap - py some - times,
you made me glad, But there were times, dear, you made me feel so bad. You made me
sigh for, I did - n't wan - na tell you, I did - n't wan - na tell you, I want some love that's
true, yes, I do, 'deed I do, you know I do. Gim - me, gim - me what I cry for, you
know you got the brand of kiss - es that I'd die for You know You Made Me Love You

THE YANKEE DOODLE BOY

Words and Music by George M. Cohan

Brightly
I'm a Yan - kee Doo - dle Dan - dy, a Yan - kee Doo - dle do or die; a
real live neph - ew of my Un - cle Sam's, Born on the Fourth of Ju - ly. I've
got a Yan - kee Doo - dle sweet - heart, She's my Yan - kee Doo - dle joy.
Yan - kee Doo - dle came to Lon - don just to ride the po - nies, I am a Yan - kee Doo - dle boy.

YOU'RE A GRAND OLD FLAG

George M. Cohan

Brightly
You're A Grand Old Flag, you're a high fly - ing flag; And for - ev - er in peace may you
wave; You're the em - blem of the land I love, The home of the
free and the brave. Ev - 'ry heart beats true un - der red, white and blue, where there's
nev - er a boast or brag; But, should auld ac - quain - tance be for -
got, Keep your eye on the grand old flag. You're A flag.

YOU TELL ME YOUR DREAM

Lyrics by Ceymour Rice and Albert H. Brown
Music by Charles N. Daniels

Slowly
G Gdim7 G E7 A7 D7
You had a dream, Well, I had one, too. I know mine's best,
G E♭7 D7 G Gdim7 G E7 A7
'Cause it was of you. Come, sweet - heart, tell me, Now is the
C C#dim G E7 A7 D7 G C#dim G
time. You Tell Me Your Dream, I'll tell you mine.

YOU ARE MY TRUE LOVE

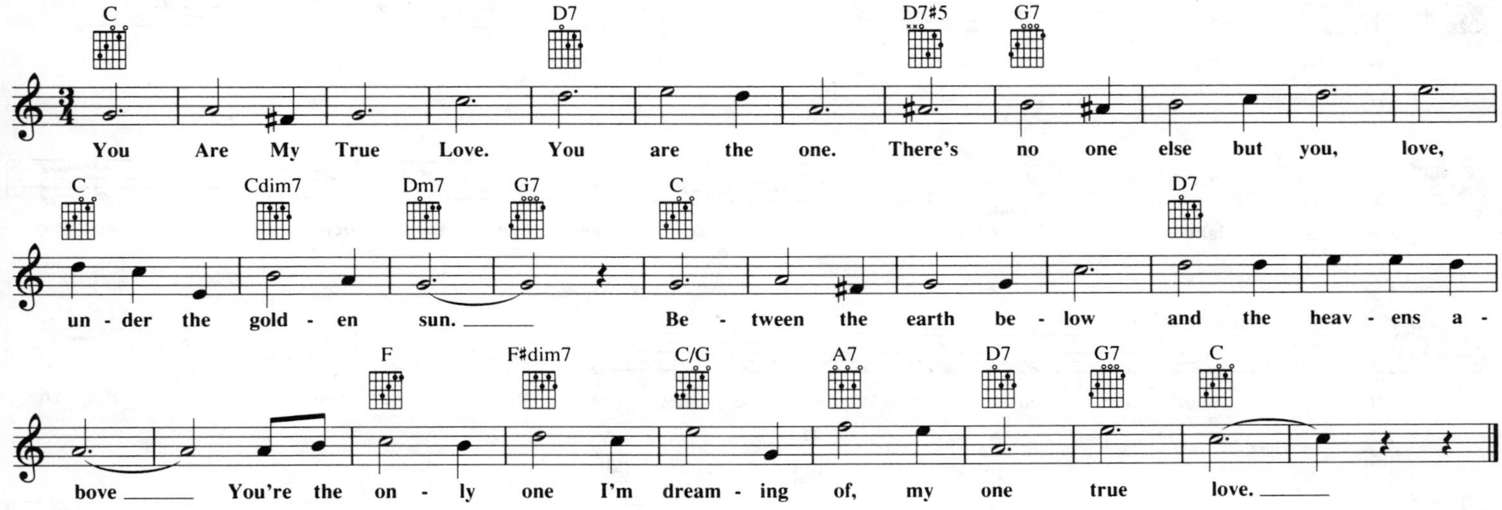
C D7 D7#5 G7
You Are My True Love. You are the one. There's no one else but you, love,
C Cdim7 Dm7 G7 C D7
un - der the gold - en sun. Be - tween the earth be - low and the heav - ens a -
F F#dim7 C/G A7 D7 G7 C
bove You're the on - ly one I'm dream - ing of, my one true love.

ZUM GALI GALI

Moderately
Dm Gm Dm Gm
Zum Ga - li Ga - li Ga - li, Zum Ga - li, Ga - li, Zum Ga - li Ga - li Ga - li, Zum Ga - li Ga - li.
Dm Gm Dm Gm Dm
He - cha - lutz le 'man a - vo - dah; A - vo - dah le 'man he - cha - lutz.
A - vo - dah le 'man he - cha - lutz; He - cha - lutz le 'man a - vo - dah.

Translation: "The Pioneer is meant for work. Work is meant for the pioneer."

THE YELLOW ROSE OF TEXAS

Lively, march tempo
A
1. There's a yel - low rose in Tex - as That I am goin' to see, No
2-3. (See additional lyrics)
E
oth - er fel - low loves her, No - bod - y, on - ly me. She
A
cried so when I left her, It like to broke my heart And
E7 A D A E7 A
if I ev - er find her, we nev - er - more will part. She's the
A
sweet - est rose of col - or This fel - low ev - er knew, Her
E7
eyes are bright as dia-monds They spar - kle like the dew. You may
A
talk a - bout your dear - est May, And sing of Ro - sa Lee But The
E7 A D A E7 A
Yel - low Rose Of Tex - as beats the belles of Ten - nes - see.

Additional Lyrics

2. Where the Rio Grande is flowing
And the starry skies are bright,
She walks along the river,
In the quiet summer night.
She thinks, if I remember,
When we parted long ago,
I promised to come back again,
And not to leave her so.

3. Oh, now I'm goin' to find her,
For my heart is full of woe,
And we'll sing the song together,
That we sang so long ago.
We'll play the banjo gaily
And we'll sing the songs of yore
And the Yellow Rose Of Texas
Shall be mine forevermore.